ATHENS AND SPARTA: Constructing Greek
Political and Social History from 478 BC

CROOM HELM
CLASSICAL STUDIES

ATHENS
— and —
SPARTA

Constructing Greek Political and
Social History from 478 BC

ANTON POWELL

ROUTLEDGE

First published in 1988 by
Routledge
a division of Routledge, Chapman and Hall
11 New Fetter Lane, London EC4P 4EE

Printed and bound in Great Britain by Mackays of Chatham Ltd, Kent

British Library Cataloguing in Publication Data

Powell, C.A.
  Athens and Sparta: constructing Greek
political and social history from 478 BC
  Greece — History — To 146 BC
  I. Title
  938   DF214

  ISBN 0-415-00337-7
       0-415-00338-5 pbk.

Published in North America in 1988 by
Areopagitica Press
9999 S.W. Wilshire
Portland, Oregon 97225, USA

ISBN 0-918400-09-0, hbk. only

Contents

Abbreviations

AE	R. Meiggs, *The Athenian empire*
ATL	B. D. Meritt, H. T. Wade-Gery, M. F. McGregor, *The Athenian tribute lists*
BCH	*Bulletin de correspondance hellénique*
CAH	*The Cambridge Ancient History*
CQ	*Classical Quarterly*
FGH	F. Jacoby, *Die Fragmente der griechischen Historiker*
HCT	A. W. Gomme, A. Andrewes and K. J. Dover, *A historical commentary on Thucydides* (vols 1–3 by Gomme; vol. 4 by Gomme, Andrewes and Dover; vol. 5 by Andrewes)
JHS	*Journal of Hellenic Studies*
JRS	*Journal of Roman Studies*
Meiggs-Lewis	R. Meiggs and D. M. Lewis, *A selection of Greek historical inscriptions to the end of the fifth century BC*
Origins	G. E. M. de Ste. Croix, *The origins of the Peloponnesian War*
P.Oxy.	*The Oxyrhynchus Papyri*
RE	Pauly-Wissowa-Kroll, *Real-Encyclopädie der classischen Altertumswissenschaft*
REG	*Revue des études grecques*
SIG	Dittenberger, *Sylloge Inscriptionum Graecarum*

These maps are adapted from maps in Talbert (ed.) *Atlas of Classical History*, (Croom Helm, London, 1985). Spellings of place names are in many cases romanised: so, for example, Boiotia, Iasos, Kerkyra, Korinth, Sollion appear in the maps as Boeotia, Iasus, Corcyra, Corinth and Sollium.

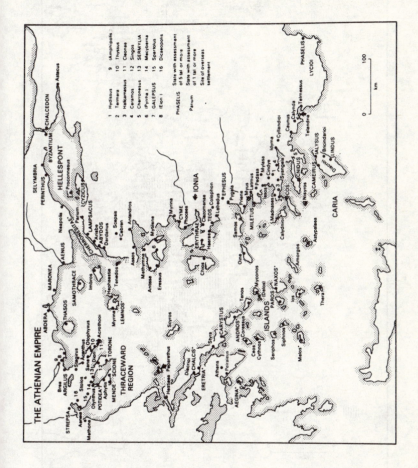

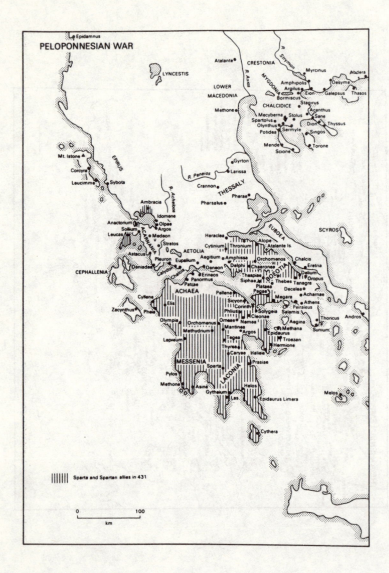

PELOPONNESIAN WAR

Epidamnus

LYNCESTIS

CRESTONIA

Atalante

Myrcinus

Amphipolis
Argilus
Bormiscus
Eion
Galepsus
Oesyme
Abdera
Thasos

LOWER
MACEDONIA

R. Strymon

R. Axios

MYGDONIA

CHALCIDICE

Stagirus
Acanthus

Methone

Mecyberna
Stolus
Spartolus
Olynthus
Potidea
Sermyle

Sane
Dion
Singos
Thyssus

Mende
Scione

Torone

Mt. Istone

Gyrton

Corcyra

EPIRUS

R. Peneios

Larissa

Leucimme
Sybota

Crannon

THESSALY

Pherae

SCYROS

Ambracia

R. Acheloos

Pharsalus

Idomene
Olpae
Argos

Anactorium
Solium
Leucas

Medeon

ACARNANIA

Heraclea

Alope
Atalante Is.

EUBOEA

Stratos

Cytinium

Thronium

Astacus

AETOLIA

Eupalium

Aegitium

Amphissa

Orchomenos

Chalcis
Eretria

Oeniadae

Calydon

Pleuron

Oeneon
Panormus
Petzae

Delphi

Chaeronea

Delium

CEPHALLENIA

Erineos

Thespiae

Siphae

Plataea

BOEOTIA

Thebes
Tanagra

Oropus

Decelea

Cyllene

ACHAEA

Pellene

Sicyon

Pegae

Megara

Acharnae

Zacynthus

Pheia

Elis

Phlius
Corinth

Cleonae

Solygeia
Nemea

Salamis

Athens
Peiraieus

Thoricus

Andros

Olympia

Orchomenus

Mantinea

Argos

Aegina

Methana

Sunium

Lepreum

Methydrium

Tegea
Thyrea
Caryae

Epidaurus
Troezen

Hermione

MESSENIA

Sparta

Halieis

Prasiae

Pylos

Methone

Asine

LACONIA

Gythaium
Las

Helos

Melos

Epidaurus Limera

Cythera

|||||| Sparta and Spartan allies in 431

0   100
         km

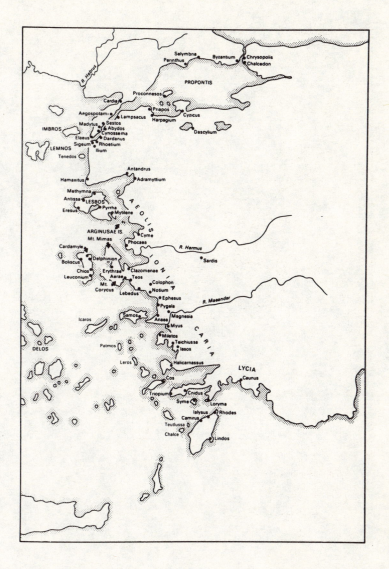

Selymbria
Byzantium
Perinthus
Chrysopolis
Chalcedon
R. Hebrus
PROPONTIS
Proconnesos
Cardia
Priapos
Aegospotami
Lampsacus
Cyzicus
Madytus
Sestos
Harpagium
Dascylium
IMBROS
Elaeus
Abydos
Cynossema
Dardanus
Sigeum
Rhoetium
LEMNOS
Ilium
Tenedos
Antandrus
Hamaxitus
Adramyttium
Methymna
Antissa
LESBOS
Eresus
Pyrrha
Mytilene
ARGINUSAE IS.
Cyme
Mt. Mimas
Phocaea
R. Hermus
Cardamyle
Delphinion
Sardis
Boliscus
Chios
Erythrae
Leuconium
Aerae
Teos
Clazomenae
Mt.
Colophon
Corycus
Lebedus
Notium
Ephesus
Pygela
Magnesia
Icaros
Samos
Anaea
R. Maeander
Myus
CARIA
DELOS
Miletos
Patmos
Teichiussa
Iasos
Leros
Halicarnassus
LYCIA
Caunus
Cos
Triopium
Cnidus
Syme
Loryma
Camirus
Ialysus
Rhodes
Teutlussa
Chalce
Lindos

AEOLIS

IONIA

Introduction

This work is intended as a handbook for the bright student beginning Greek history. It deals with method as well as with fact. It attempts to present an unusually large selection of the ancient evidence, and to provide clear analysis and narrative. We seek to highlight problems and to demonstrate explicitly some of the more important techniques of criticism and construction used by professional historians. It is hoped to suggest something of the contribution which Greek history can make to a liberal education, and to communicate the enjoyment to be had from careful exploitation of the Greek sources.

The shape of the book has been determined by the supply of good ancient literary evidence. Political history is studied in detail for the period 478–411 BC, for which we have the evidence of Thucydides; the last years of the Peloponnesian War, from 410 to 404 BC, are treated in outline. Our review of social history covers the fourth century as well as the fifth. Important inscriptional evidence is dealt with. But, since the book presumes no knowledge of Greek in the reader, there is no attempt to treat the reconstruction of epigraphic fragments.

The playwright Tom Stoppard has a character say that journalists do not write for the public; they write for other journalists. The warning implied in this useful overstatement is one which historians, too, should keep in mind when we write textbooks. In selecting and arranging material for the present work, the author has tried to apply his own experience of the needs of students new to the subject. For example, a teacher should probably begin a course of Greek history by stressing that in this subject the required (and enlightened) procedure is, not to repeat or synthesise the arguments of modern writers, but to look at what ancient sources say and to use independent judgement in constructing from that base. So, when a course begins with the Delian League, a student often turns, as instructed, to the Greek writers and, finding that Plutarch has far more to say on the subject than Thucydides, is tempted to draw on the former almost to the exclusion of the latter. Accordingly our first chapter, on the Delian League, tries to communicate the primacy of Thucydides as a source and to make clear some of the limitations of Plutarch. Although Thucydides is by far the most important source for the political section of this book, discussion of his characteristics is not confined to a single chapter. We have tried to apply the observation that great blocks of prolegomena are offputting to the student (and not only to the student). Discussion of Thucydides has been distributed, for the sake of digestibility. So has bibliography.

From the point of view of a liberal educator, one of the most valuable elements of Greek history, as normally studied, is the critical method applied to sources. Long after a student may have ceased to recall much detail of Greek matters, habits survive which were learned in the study of the Greeks: habits of scepticism, construction and imputation of motive. And once acquired, such habits are of course applicable far beyond Greek history. This is partly why we have laid much stress on method. For example, we introduce briefly but explicitly the standard logical device known as Occam's Razor; argument from silence is pointedly introduced; we also show how to test the significance of an explanation by asking whether in certain circumstances it might have served as a prediction.

Much of the book is concerned with psychology. Aristotle writes sensibly that the very young can excel at mathematics, as an exercise of pure logic, whereas the mastery of political theory requires experience. This raises the question of where the modern student is to acquire a knowledge of political and social psychology to apply to ancient Greece. Criticism of a Greek source requires not merely a study of its internal coherence and of its compatibility with other sources. In practice, successful study is informed by a knowledge of psychology derived in part from non-Greek cultures. The comparison of ancient and modern is dangerous, leading when wrongly performed to anachronism and conflation. This is precisely why the subject has to be addressed clearly and explicitly. In particular the last chapter of this book, on Athenian use of divination, is meant as a contribution to this subject.

We have tried often to make psychological principles explicit, in the hope of making them easier to evaluate and, where appropriate, to remember. Our emphasis on method and psychology may also serve as a small step towards increasing the attention paid to these matters by advanced students. In this area historians have usually proceeded intuitively, when greater explicitness and caution might have helped. How many scholars, for example, could readily present evidence on the power of long-term memory (memory of the kind on which our ancient sources often depended)? Are we always clearly aware whether the historical explanations which we daily advance should be taken as involving necessary cause, sufficient cause, or some other kind of cause? Occam's Razor dictates that entities should not be postulated beyond what is necessary: how clearly do we identify the differing nature of necessity in differing situations?

We have tried to inoculate our readers against a recurrent fault in the presentation of our subject, which consists in encouraging a patronising attitude towards the ancient Greeks. Considering the pedestal on which the general public assumes the Greeks to be placed by educators, it is remarkable how low an opinion of Greek practical intelligence has been communicated by many specialists, particularly in the twentieth century. In our view, it is a mistake to encourage derision even of such strange practices as the Spartan way of voting or the Athenian use of a painted rope to recruit assemblymen. The attitude of superiority is highly contagious among beginners. It appeals not merely to normal human vanity and to the easy presumption that modern is best, but also to the insecurity of the student in the face of a strange culture. An assumption that the motive for this or that Greek action may well be silly is likely to inhibit the search for rationality. And yet in the case of our two societies, Athens and Sparta, so high is the level of achievement — in their own terms — that rationality must have been the norm. This book may at times seem to go too far in ascribing reasonable motives to the Greeks. We have stressed the rational in the belief that the prior assumption of reasonableness is more conducive than its opposite to reflection and discovery in this field.

By tradition teachers of Greek history have encouraged their students to identify political enthusiasm and bias on the part of our ancient informants, and to make allowances accordingly. One anonymous Greek source has even been named after his bias — the Old Oligarch. But the constant (and desirable) attention to the bias of a source may in some circumstances have an unfortunate effect. If combined with the polite convention that we do not refer to political bias in modern scholars, it may suggest a belief that we, unlike the Greeks, have achieved objectivity. Such a belief would not only be wrong. By degrading the Greeks it might to some extent discourage students from seeking to discover rationality in Greek theory and behaviour. Occasionally, there-fore, when political enthusiasm seems to have affected the approach of a modern scholar, we have noted as much briefly but explicitly — as scholars anyway tend to do in private. This is not to censure. Political and moral enthusiasm has helped to produce some of the most important studies of the Greeks. We may think of George Grote, whose general history, still unsurpassed, was conceived in the early nineteenth century as a massive Utilitarian tract, hostile to traditional religion, warmly supportive of an extended franchise. An additional benefit of openness about modern bias might be to increase awareness in students of their *own* biases — one or two of which are also addressed explicitly in this book. Perhaps every author on a political subject should follow the example of George Orwell by warning the reader in advance of the writer's bias. The present writer therefore identifies certain personal convictions which he has tried not to indulge in this book — his belief in almost complete freedom of political information, in the wide and even spreading of wealth and of access to power.

As to style: I have tried to imitate two virtues of *oral* presentations at academic conferences — the short sentence and occasional humour. In syntax and vocabulary I have usually attempted to follow classicists' mandarin, but have sometimes used British demotic where that added to precision. The number of footnotes is very large, a necessity if the reader is to be given the fullest possible material for construction independent of the theories of others (including my own).

Finally, my acknowledgements. To Mr R. M. Lupton, my former teacher at Wyggeston Grammar School, Leicester, I owe my introduction to the criticism of Greek sources at the age of sixteen. With my early writing on Greek history I received generous personal help from Geoffrey de Ste. Croix. I have been able to watch the inspiring effect of his great study, *The origins of the Peloponnesian War*, on students of mine at the Working Men's College in London. Many of those students provided me with valuable ideas and criticism for my teaching, among them Kate Davies, Lesley Hannigan, Colin Harris, Ian Lambert, Ling Man Cheong, Ann Morris, Moira Ashcroft, Gill Ray and David Smith. Steve Hodkinson of the University of Manchester read my typescript and saved me from many faults. I am indebted to my editor, Richard Stoneman, without whose prompt and gratifying support this book very likely would not have been written.

The work is dedicated to my father and mother.

1

The Delian League:
Its Origins and Early History

Introduction

In 479 BC the city of Athens was in ruins. The invading forces of
the Persian king, Xerxes, had forced it to be abandoned in 480.
The greater part of its defensive wall and most of its houses were
subsequently destroyed.[1] The Athenian sailors who, with other
Greeks and under Spartan leadership, defeated Xerxes' fleet in
480 at nearby Salamis, were men without a city.[2] In 479 two
further Greek victories, at Plataia in Central Greece and at
Mykalē on the western coast of Asia Minor, spelled the end of the
Persian invasion. The Athenians could reoccupy the site of their
city, rebuild its perimeter wall and fortify the city's new port,
Peiraieus.[3] Allied with eastern Greeks who now rebelled from the
king of Persia, Athenian forces went onto the offensive.

Sparta's attempts to keep command of the naval alliance against
Persia were not wholehearted. Following up their success at
Mykalē, the Greeks sailed to assault the Persian force controlling
Sestos, on the northern shore of the Dardanelles. However, the
Spartan commander, King Leotykhidas, returned home: an
Athenian, Xanthippos, led the campaign.[4] Another Spartan, the
regent Pausanias, did lead the Greek fleet with some success
against Cyprus (defiantly close to the bases of Xerxes' best non-
Greek sailors, the Phoenicians) and Byzantion (strategically
placed to control the importing of corn from the Black Sea
territories to mainland Greece) — campaigns probably of 478.[5]
But Sparta acquiesced when, not long afterwards, the eastern
Greeks and the Athenians rejected the leadership of Pausanias
and his Spartan successors.[6] With the enthusiastic approval of the
eastern Greeks, command of the naval war against Persia was

1

formally given to Athens.[7]

The naval alliance under this changed leadership is called by scholars "the Delian League"; its treasury and meetings ("synods") were located on the symbolic mid-Aegean island of Delos.[8] By stages the League was transformed into an Athenian empire. The wealth it generated, and channelled to Athens, helped the spectacular rebuilding of the city: the construction, for example, of the Parthenon and of the gateway building of the Akropolis, the Propylaia, which to contemporary Greeks was perhaps even more remarkable.[9] In its later stages the Delian League seems to have promoted *dēmokratia*, the control of cities' internal affairs by and for their own (male) citizen poor;[10] the subsequent Athenian Empire certainly did.[11] But aristocratic and wealthy Athenians profited especially from the League and Empire.[12] The funding by rich Athenians of artistic activities, including the production of tragic and comic drama, was made possible or facilitated by the proceeds of Athenian domination. The Thracian goldmines, possession of which probably did much for the education and leisure of the historian Thucydides, may have been acquired through the activities of the Delian League and later were protected, at least indirectly, by the power of Athens' imperial navy.[13] Also, we may suspect that a fertile sense of their own importance arose in Athenian thinkers (even those opposed to *dēmokratia* and Athenian imperialism) from contemplating the extent of Athenian power and the understandable principles on which open *dēmokratia* proceeded. It is well known that the influence of these thinkers on later civilisations has been profound: in studying the origins of Athenian rule we are examining the material base of much of European culture.

*

Reconstructing the history of the Delian League should involve an exercise in self-restraint. We should not claim to have a satisfactory knowledge of the period; for one thing, it contains several years to which we cannot confidently assign a single recorded event. Our most important source of information, Thucydides, set out to describe a later episode, the war which began in 431 between the Athenians and the Peloponnesian alliance.[14] He was taking notes as an adult from that year,[15] had sufficient seniority to be a general of Athens in 424[16] and survived until at least 404.[17] His account of events before 432 is, with important exceptions, brief. At the start of his history he states that events of the pre-war period and earlier were "impossible to

2

discover with certainty because of the passage of so much time".[18] He adds that certain trustworthy inferences were, on the other hand, possible. The context of these remarks makes clear that Thucydides' concern here was particularly with the *scale* of events. But, as it stands, his statement about the obscurity of events embraces more than their scale. Also, it seems to apply to — among other periods — the time of the Delian League: that is, from 477 to *c*.450.

In his often-authoritative commentary on Thucydides, A. W. Gomme states that the historian's words on unknowable events "must mean, both in language and logic, 'Greek history before the Peloponnesian War', the whole of it": they must, that is, include the events of the Delian League.[19] Now this is a somewhat depressing conclusion for the professional historian, and Gomme is unwilling to accept that Thucydides himself did mean this. Gomme argues that the unknowable events for Thucydides belonged to an earlier period, before *c*.510. He implies that if Thucydides had meant that the period of the Delian League was obscure, he would have indicated as much when dealing in detail with the period between the Persian and Peloponnesian Wars.[20] Gomme, with other scholars, suggests that some of Thucydides' original words, which would have drastically changed the meaning of the text here, have been lost in the manuscript tradition.[21] But our manuscripts have no obvious sign of corruption at this point. Sound method requires that we work from the text which survives, failing strong evidence of corruption (such as the existence of conflicting versions of a text in different manuscripts, or of a text which yields absurdity or nonsense). Doing so in this case, we should conclude that Thucydides placed conspicuously at the start of his work a warning about the obscurity of events before the Peloponnesian War.

This conclusion is strengthened by a remark of Thucydides shortly afterwards (I 20 1): "Such I found the events of long ago to be, though it is difficult to depend on all the inferences made here about them." These "events of long ago", in the description of which imperfect inference rather than knowledge is involved, include some which belong to 480 and later, as the preceding chapters (18 and 19) show.[22] It seems, then, that Gomme is wrong to exclude events after *c*.510 from consideration here. That Thucydides did not repeat his caveat about the obscurity of events, when he dealt in detail with the decades from 479, should not trouble us. Having made the point conspicuously and repeatedly at the start of his work, he may have expected his readers to remember it.

Thucydides gives a detailed sketch of the precariously describable period 479–436, which includes the entire life of the Delian League, in Chapters 89 to 117 of Book I. What was his purpose in doing so? At I 89 1 he indicates an intention of showing how the Athenians "arrived at the situation in which they grew great".[23] He then describes the fortification of Athens and Peiraieus, the campaigns shortly preceding the founding of the Delian League, and the setting up of the League itself. Next, he makes it clear (I 97 1) that he is about to describe "what they [the Athenians] undertook in war and in the management of affairs between the Persian War and this one [the Peloponnesian], against the Persians, against their own allies who revolted, and against the Peloponnesians who came into contact with them on the various occasions". In justifying this digression from his main theme of the Peloponnesian War, he mentions that the inter-war period had been neglected by other writers, with the exception of Hellanikos, who dealt with it "briefly and with inaccurate chronology". He also states that the digression makes it clear how the Athenians' domination was established.

When using the writing of Thucydides, or of anyone else, as a historical source, it is important to investigate the author's purpose. For one thing, the writer's purpose controls our ability to make arguments from silence. Thus we could not argue, for example, that "there were no striking developments in the internal, constitutional, history of Athens or Sparta between 479 and 436, or Thucydides would have mentioned them", because it was apparently not his purpose to mention such events for their own sake. On the other hand, Thucydides did intend to describe Athenian undertakings against Persia. So the lack of clear reference in his work to a formal peace treaty between Athens and Persia in the early 440s should make us hesitate before accepting statements from elsewhere that there was something of the kind. (See below, Chapter 2.)

Origin and purposes of the League

Before we look at how the Delian League came to be formed, we should ask what the participant states intended the League to do.

As often for the historian of the fifth century, a very careful look is needed at the words of Thucydides, and in particular, in this case, at one Greek word, *proskhēma*. Thucydides explains very briefly, and seemingly in passing, why the Athenians instructed other members of the Delian League to supply funds or ships: he writes that "a *proskhēma* was to avenge what they (i.e. the League members) had suffered, by ravaging the territory of the king of Persia".[24] Until very recently even good scholars, and the authors of standard translations of Thucydides, seem to have given a slightly misleading translation of the word *proskhēma*. Thus P. A. Brunt takes it to mean 'the professed purpose' of the League;[25] Gomme writes of the 'announced intention',[26] while R. Meiggs in one passage renders Thucydides' expression simply as 'the purpose'.[27] However, G. E. M. de Ste. Croix has now pointed out that the word *proskhēma*, as used both by Thucydides and other Greek writers, carries an implication of unreliability or deceit.[28] It may best be translated as 'pretext'. De Ste. Croix also observes that the word here is not preceded in Greek by the definite article: it does not even mean 'the pretext', but rather 'a pretext'. This brief remark of Thucydides' is, then, very far from conveying what he saw as the real reasons for the Athenians' involvement in organising the League, but implies that some, at least, of those reasons could not easily have been admitted. The general and clearly stated theme of this part of Thucydides' work involves Athenian acquisition of power. De Ste. Croix plausibly states,

> I fancy that his choice of the word *proschema* would have left them [i.e. his readers] with the feeling that the talk of revenge through ravaging expeditions was at least partly a cover for ambitious Athenian designs for organising a large, active, powerful and rich alliance under their control.[29]

In testing this interpretation of Thucydides, we should look for any other passage in his work which refers to the Athenians' purpose in helping to form the Delian League. There is one such passage, VI 76 3, where Hermokrates the Syracusan is represented as saying that Athens became leader of willing allies in eastern Greece "as being a state which intended to punish the Persians". Now, even taken in isolation this expression does not mean that the desire to punish Persia was Athens' real reason for assuming the leadership.[30] And an examination of the context of the remark shows that Hermokrates is indeed alleging Athenian insincerity. He contrasts the fair words and, in his view, unfair intentions of the Athenians, stating that the Athenians resisted the Persians (through the Delian League, that is) "in order to enslave [the Greeks] to themselves".[31] Although not cited in this connection by de Ste. Croix, the speech attributed to Hermokrates does support his speculative reconstruction of Thucydides' own view of the Athenians' motives. Hermokrates speaks of Athenian insincerity, of the alleged desire to punish Persia and a real desire for the "enslavement" *(katadoulōsis)* of other Greeks to Athens. Thucydides in his own person, having written of a pretext concerning a desire to punish Persia, shortly afterwards uses a cognate, and similarly pejorative, word *(edoulōthē)* to describe Athens' "enslavement" of allies.[32] Hermokrates is an enemy of the Athenians, speaking to prejudice his audience against them, as Thucydides tells us.[33] His remark, then, would not be of great value on its own as evidence of Athens' purpose in forming the Delian League. Its importance lies in its showing that a pattern of thought involving an Athenian pretext of punishing Persia and a real desire for dominance over the eastern Greeks was indeed known to Thucydides.

We do not need to share any disapproval felt by Thucydides for Athenian motives. However, we may accept his implication, if such it was, that a desire for power and wealth did much to bring about the Athenians' vigorous participation in the Delian League. Apart from this, did the "pretext" to which Thucydides refers, a desire to ravage the Persian Empire to avenge sufferings caused by the Persians, reflect a real motive of any importance? A pretext would be chosen for its plausibility, in particular to Athens' eastern Greek allies. The sufferings referred to need not have been those of Athens alone, although she had suffered disproportionately in 480–479 with the destruction of her city. The eastern Greeks would remember misfortunes of their own, sustained during more than half a century of Persian rule: for example, the savage treatment of young people after the suppression by Persia of the Ionian Revolt of the 490s.[34] Also, though it might not often be mentioned, the eastern Greeks would have suffered much as a result of being forced to fight for Persia against the mainland Greeks in 480–479.

Scholars have sometimes believed that the ravaging of the Persian Empire was projected by the Delian League for the sake of loot.[35] The use of analogy with modern history may have misled here. Brunt comments that the members of the League "were to seek reparation for the damage they had sustained by ravaging the king's territory".[36] The word 'reparation' recalls, no doubt intentionally, the French and British policy of fining Germany for the damage caused by the First World War. (Demands for "reparations" produced, in the British general election campaign of 1918, the slogans 'Make Germany Pay' and 'Squeeze Germany till the Pips Squeak'.) Another scholar, A. H. Jackson, has shown, however, that Thucydides' words do not imply a policy of extracting plunder from Persian territory.[37] Jackson studied Thucydides' numerous uses of the word employed for 'ravaging' in this connection, *deioun*, and showed that it means destruction rather than looting. Brunt's suggestion about reparation may happen to reflect part of the allies' purpose in the early 470s; the biographer Plutarch has some interesting, though unreliable, details of lucrative plundering by League members,[38] and, much more importantly, Thucydides records the (profitable) enslavement, in the early years of the League, of people from the Persian's garrison-town of Eion.[39] But Thucydides' words on a *proskhēma* of the alliance do not themselves provide a basis for this view.

This last topic illustrates an important general principle about the drawing of analogies between modern and ancient history. Analogy of this kind can be very helpful in suggesting possible motives and patterns of thought in antiquity. But because ancient Greek cultures are in some ways deeply dissimilar from modern ones, great care is needed in checking that suggested modern analogues do indeed correspond with the evidence of our ancient sources. At all levels of study there may be a temptation to glance hastily at the latter, once a modern analogue is conceived of. A result is often an error of perception of a kind which modern psychology has carefully documented — the improper assimilation of the unfamiliar to the familiar.[40]

Greeks in the later fifth century, and historians today, are in a position to know that the great Persian invasion of 480–479 was not repeated in the following decades. Greeks in the early 470s were not. It is worth considering, briefly, whether their policy of attacking Persian territory by means of the Delian League was intended in part to prevent a recurrence of the great invasion. Persia had, of course, been heavily defeated in 480–479 but she retained most of her empire, including Egypt, the greater part of Asia Minor and, indeed, most of the Middle East. A repeated invasion might seem to outsiders, such as Athens and her naval allies, to be a political necessity for the Persians, if they were to prevent discontented subjects in their more remote provinces from drawing subversive conclusions about Persian weakness. This question can, however, elicit only a speculative answer, there being no direct fifth-century evidence on it.

A related motive for the founding of the Delian League is given in Thucydides III 10 2–3, as part of a speech attributed to ambassadors of Mytilēnē, a large town on the eastern Aegean island of Lesbos. The ambassadors say that when their state made an alliance with Athens, on the Spartans' departure from the anti-Persian campaigning, it did so "to free the Greeks from the Persians".[41] No additional reason is given. In assessing the value of a claim made in a speech, one should always look at the circumstances and desires of the speaker and his audience, to help to allow for omission, exaggeration and other distortion. This speech was made in 428, almost exactly 50 years after the formation of the Delian League, and to an audience of Peloponnesians, whose states had never taken any part in the League.[42] The audience's perception of the early history of the League was perhaps not much more than a partisan outline. The Peloponnesians at the time of the speech were at war with Athens. Mytilēnē had revolted from the Athenian Empire; her envoys were begging for Peloponnesian help and claiming that their previous decades of alliance with Athens did not disqualify them from sympathy.[43] It may seem that it would have suited the Mytilenean case very well to ascribe to their own state a blameless motive for joining the Delian League, a desire to liberate Greeks, even if the ascription had been untrue. But there is, perhaps, an important control on the Mytileneans' claim. Sparta, although never a member of the League, almost certainly had been well informed about the early motivation of its members, since, as we shall see, influential Spartan officials came into conflict with the states which were about to form the League, in circumstances which would have led to a careful enquiry at Sparta into what those states intended. Even after 50 years this might have checked any Mytilenean tendency to lie on the subject, especially since in 428 it was the Spartans above all others who, as leaders of the Peloponnesian alliance, needed persuasion by Mytilēnē.

A purpose of the original Delian League which the Mytileneans could *not* mention in this context was to get rid of Spartan control. Thucydides states that the Athenians took over the leadership of willing allies because of the hatred for Pausanias, the Spartan regent who had previously commanded them.[44] Pausanias, according to Thucydides, was unapproachable, behaved violently and gave — now or a little later — evidence of pro-Persian feelings.[45] Another probable grievance of the eastern Greeks against Sparta is suggested by Herodotos, though not by Thucydides. He writes that shortly after the battle of Mykalē [in 479] the Peloponnesian authorities (a phrase which must refer to the Spartans) proposed to evacuate the Ionian Greeks from western Asia Minor, where they were claimed to be indefensible against Persia, and to transfer them to territory elsewhere, which was to be seized from Greeks who had taken the Persian side (presumably in 480–479).[46] This proposal was defeated on Athenian insistence; the Athenians claimed, in accordance with a widely believed myth, that their city had founded the Ionian colonies and that colonists of theirs should not have their fate discussed by Peloponnesians.[47] Herodotos wrote as an eastern Greek himself,[48] and without seeming to have a strong bias against Sparta: if his story is true, the Ionians and other eastern Greeks may well have acquired at this point a lasting and influential suspicion that Sparta was unconcerned to defend them in the area where they most wished to be defended. Herodotos himself does not report the Ionians' reaction to the Peloponnesian proposal. In reconstructing it, Meiggs concentrates, in pleasantly English fashion, on the charm of the weather in Ionia, which the inhabitants might be reluctant to leave.[49] This may well have been important; Herodotos praises the Ionian climate very highly.[50] But one should look further.

In considering the reactions of a large community, or set of communities, such as "the Athenians" or "the Ionians", one should always reflect on the possibility of differences within the group. Our Greek sources are not, on the whole, sociologically sophisticated, but they frequently show us differences of reaction between rich and poor, and occasionally between old and young, city- and country-dwellers.[51] In Greek societies, as elsewhere, the influence of the wealthy and of the old tended to be very great.[52] Among the Ionians, we may guess that old people would be particularly reluctant to abandon their homes, as old men of Athens are reported to have been, when the evacuation of that city was proposed.[53] Also, wealthy Ionians, and especially landowners, would hesitate to exchange their established positions for promises of territory elsewhere, territory that was still occupied by Greeks who would probably resist expulsion.

Moreover, the expulsion of these other Greeks was to be punishment for siding with the Persians. But the Ionian communities themselves had done just that, and had joined Xerxes' invasion in great force.[54] They could claim plausibly that they had done so under compulsion. But so could the other Greeks, who were to be ejected in the Ionians' interest. Numerous influential Ionians must have seen the proposed evacuation as embarrassing and hazardous, both for their communities and for themselves. The proposal, if historical, will have added much to the attraction of Athenian, as against Spartan, leadership of the naval alliance.[55]

There were several other reasons for the replacement of Sparta by Athens. Offensive or defensive fighting against the Persians would require great sea-power, both for purely naval actions and for other campaigns which involved rapid travel along the coasts of Asia Minor. Athens had a far larger fleet than Sparta.[56] She had distinguished herself at Salamis, fighting with much the largest naval contingent on the Greek side.[57] At Mykalē, a battle fought on land by troops conveyed by sea, Athens had again been outstanding.[58] Similarities of dialect and customs between the Ionians and the Athenians would help understanding and reduce friction, as compared with Sparta, which was part of the different, Dorian, group of Greek states.[59] Also, the Persians had set up democracies in Ionia, when in control of the area in the 490s.[60] Athens had been governed by a form of democracy since 508/7.[61] Resulting similarities of procedure and temperament between the Ionians and the Athenians might have worked to the exclusion of Sparta, a state which was later to show much ineptitude in dealing with democratic politicians,[62] and which found it convenient to establish oligarchies in the states under its control.[63]

But, while the eastern Greeks had many reasons to reject Spartan leadership in favour of Athenian, the Delian League was not in its original purpose aggressively anti-Spartan. Thucydides states that the Spartans, at the time of the League's foundation, thought the Athenians suitable leaders of it from their own point of view — for the time being.[64] Since Pausanias was recalled to Sparta for investigation at the time of his rejection as commander by the eastern Greeks,[65] and since Dorkis and the others sent by Sparta to succeed him had themselves been rejected and had returned to Sparta,[66] the Spartan authorities at home would have been obliged to consider carefully the obvious question, whether the emergent Delian League was anti-Spartan in intention: Sparta's complaisant acceptance of Athenian leadership strongly suggests that it was not. And the League's subsequent record of anti-Persian, not anti-Spartan, campaigning in the first fifteen years of its existence confirms the Spartans' judgement.

When the Delian League was formed, the participant states swore "to have the same friends and enemies": that is, to have a common foreign policy.[67] In this connection, pieces of iron were dropped into the sea. So much we are told by the Aristotelian *Constitution of Athens* (abbreviated as *Ath. Pol.*), a work of the late fourth century BC.[68] The detail concerning the iron is made more plausible by Herodotos' account of a similar gesture performed on an earlier occasion by other eastern Greeks, the men of Phokaia.[69] Scholars who accept the Aristotelian account have in some cases believed that the dropping of the iron symbolised the intended permanence of the oaths: the members were not to leave the League until the iron floated.[70] The *Ath. Pol.* does not give this, or indeed any, interpretation of the action, but this is the explanation suggested by Herodotos of the earlier gesture of Phokaia.[71] Following this interpretation, it may be suggested that Athens was within her rights in refusing later to let certain states leave the League,[72] and that the purpose of an organisation thus intended to be permanent could not have been the predictably transient one of punishing Persia. However, H. Jacobson has called any such argument into doubt by adducing several oaths from other ancient societies around the Mediterranean in which the throwing down of objects symbolises not permanence but the destruction or casting out of anyone breaking the oath.[73] Jacobson notices that Plutarch describes the dropping of iron by the Delian League members as done in connection with the curse which accompanied the oath.[74] It may be, then, that Herodotos has misinterpreted the action of Phokaia, and that an idea of permanence was not involved in the oath of the Delian League either. With a restraint unusual in scholars who adduce interesting and important new information, Jacobson does not claim that his non-Greek analogues disprove the theory involving permanence, but merely — and realistically — that they call it seriously into question.[75]

Early organisation of the League

When was the Delian League founded? Thucydides gives no date, in contrast to the elaborate set of references which he employs to date the beginning of the Peloponnesian War, his main subject.[76] Scholars normally accept that the League was formed in the first half of 477; the Aristotelian *Ath. Pol.* assigns the first arrangement of *phoroi* (contributions to the Delian League in cash and, perhaps, in other forms[77]) to "the third year from the naval battle at Salamis, when Timosthenes was archon [i.e. at Athens]":[78] that is, to 478/7. Diodorus Siculus (on whose chronology, see below) puts the establishment of the League in the year when Marcus Fabius and Lucius Valerius were consuls at Rome: that is, in 477.[79] The former, Attic (Athenian), year and the latter, Roman, year coincide for the first half (approximately[80]) of 477. However, it should be acknowledged that the chronology of almost all events in Greek history between the Persian Wars and the late 430s is sadly insecure. Thucydides believed that he could correct his predecessor Hellanikos, who had written "with faulty chronology" on the period, but his own information need not have gone far beyond the *order* of the few events he mentions; in other respects he gives very few indications of chronology. For both ancient and modern minds it seems that chronology is an aspect of events especially easy to forget,[81] and it is no accident that chronology is the single feature of Hellanikos' work which Thucydides criticises as inaccurate. Chronological enquiry is less fruitful for the period 478–436 than for many other epochs; on the few occasions when we may feel confident about a date, investigation tends to be impoverished by a lack of other datable events which would have given the date significance. In accordance with the view given above, that the history of this inter-war period is generally obscure, even in aspects less vulnerable than chronology, little will be said on precise dating in the chapters which relate to the period. Complex studies of the question will be found in *The Athenian tribute lists (ATL)*, vol. III ch. 11, and in Gomme's *Historical commentary on Thucydides*, vol. I, pp. 389–413. On the tempting but profoundly erratic chronological indications given by Diodorus, with his year-by-year classification of events, see R. Meiggs, *Athenian empire*, pp. 11–12.

How large was the Delian League at its foundation? In the heyday of her power, from the 450s to 413, Athens seems to have had control over, or alliance with, most of the substantial communities on the islands of the Aegean and along its northern and eastern coasts. Athenian power at that period also extended through the Dardanelles and Propontis into the Black Sea, while in the south it embraced territories on the southern coast of Asia Minor.[82] As to the original extent of the League, our most important indication seems to be Thucydides' statement that the first assessment of *phoros*, the contribution to League resources which its members were required to make, was of 460 talents.[83] If this figure is accepted, it may appear that the League at the outset was not very much smaller than the Athenian Empire at its height. However, Thucydides' figure should be compared with the surviving "Athenian Tribute Lists" (ATLs). These are inscriptions on stone, made in the fifth century from 453 onwards: strictly, they record the one-sixtieth of the *phoros* which was given to the treasury of the goddess Athena, but since multiplication of each figure by 60 reveals the more interesting totals paid in cash to Athens by different subject states, the title 'Athenian Tribute Lists' has been assigned to the inscriptions by modern scholars.[84] Calculations based on these fragmentary but very helpful inscriptions suggest that even in the late 430s the total of cash *phoros* actually received by Athens was not much more than 400 talents a year.[85] If we assume that the original figure of 460 talents was meant as a regular annual payment, and that in the enthusiasm of the early League most of this required sum was actually paid, a problem appears — one which has greatly exercised scholars. We should expect the Athenian Empire in the late 430s to have been considerably larger than the Delian League in the early or mid-470s. States are known to have been added to the League after its foundation, Karystos and Aigina,[86] and there were probably numerous others.[87] And we cannot assume that these additions were offset by many successful defections from the League; as we shall see, Athens took vigorous and effective action to prevent even powerful states from falling away. To many smaller states, defection must have seemed quite impracticable. Why, then, if Athens' Empire in the late 430s was significantly larger than the early Delian League, is Thucydides' figure for the original *phoros* not considerably smaller than that for *phoros* received at the later period? The problem is compounded by the fact that all of Athens' allies by the late 430s seem to have been contributing in cash, with the exceptions of Khios and the towns of Lesbos.[88] We cannot assume that the figure for the late

430s would have been much larger if contributions in other forms had been expressed in cash terms.

One should not try to solve the problem by assuming that the rate of contribution required of Athens' allies had been, on average, much reduced since the foundation of the League. In the defences put forward for the Athenian domination of the Aegean area, Athens never claims credit for having made such a reduction.[89] Aristeides, the Athenian seemingly most responsible for fixing the original level of *phoros*,[90] became a byword for justice, not for demanding unusually high payments from other states.[91] Some scholars have, therefore, doubted or dismissed Thucydides' figure of 460 talents, as being too high for the League at its foundation.[92] Others, however, and most notably the editors of *The Athenian tribute lists*,[93] have defended the figure and argued that, unlike the calculation for the *phoros* of the late 430s, it reflects contributions made not only in cash but also in ships and men sent on League campaigns. Such contributions in kind could have been expressed, for convenience of accounting, in cash terms, and Thucydides makes clear that a scale of equivalences between contributions in cash and kind was constructed at some stage in the League's history.[94] This line of argument is promising, even though Thucydides' statement about the 460 talents is more easily interpreted in the Greek as referring only to payments in cash. But since Athens' large Empire in the late 430s still apparently produced less than this figure in cash from the *phoros*, Thucydides' 460 talents may need additional explanation.

One neglected hypothesis deserves consideration. The figures derived from the ATLs, including those from the late 430s, refer to contributions made only by Athens' subjects. Perhaps Thucydides' figure of 460 talents for the first assessment of the Delian League includes a substantial contribution from Athens herself. This assumption would greatly reduce the sum we have to suppose the allies were required to find, and would allow us to accept more comfortably the evidence that the League was indeed much smaller than the developed Empire. Obviously no precise measurement can be made of the Athenians' contribution to the early League, which was made in the form of ships and men[95] and, on this hypothesis, reflected in its cash equivalent by Thucydides' figure. It may perhaps have amounted to a third or more of the total.[96]

Has this hypothesis been neglected by scholars justifiably? It may have been assumed that Thucydides, if he had meant his figure of 460 talents to include an Athenian contribution, would have made the point much more clearly. After all, for his readers near the end of the fifth century *phoros* meant distinctively money paid to Athens by subjects.[97] But Thucydides strongly implies that in the early League Athens campaigned with her allies in a sense as equals[98] and was popular with them.[99] He may surely have expected his readers to assume that this equality and popularity required that when precisely measured contributions were laid upon the other allies, they were also laid upon the Athenians. The *phoros* was received, Thucydides tells us,[100] by a newly-created board of Athenian officials, called 'Hellenotamiai' ('Stewards of the Greeks'). The fact that they were Athenians did much for Athens' general control of the League's finances, and probably helped to produce its transition to an empire. But we should not assume that Athenian officials could only have collected *phoros* from non-Athenians. At Athens itself there were numerous fiscal officers collecting wealth from Athenian individuals. Also, we should beware of smuggling in by a mistranslation the assumption that Athens never paid *phoros*. In connection with the League several good scholars translate *phoros* as 'tribute',[101] a word with strong overtones of imperialism and subjection. Obviously the Athenian state would not pay imperial tribute, as a subject, to its own officials, the Hellenotamiai. But the word *phoros* in the early years of the League may have been largely or wholly free of these overtones, having been coined from the colourless verb *phero* ('I bring').[102] There is no logical difficulty in Athens' "bringing" contributions to the Hellenotamiai. Perhaps the most serious objection to the hypothesis here outlined is the one which applies also to the theory of the *ATL* editors: the fact that Thucydides' sentences about the first *phoros* seem to refer only to payments in cash, and thus to exclude Athens' contributions, which were in the form of ships and men. But to construe Thucydides in that way would leave us, as has been shown, in profound difficulty. It may seem better to assume that the League at its foundation was relatively small, and that Athens contributed much of its *phoros*.

Thucydides' narrative of the League's early warfare

At I 98 Thucydides begins his short account of the military

campaigning by Athens and other members of the Delian League:[103] "At first they captured by siege Eion, on the River Strymon, a town which the Persians held, and they enslaved its inhabitants: Kimon son of Miltiades was commander." At the mouth of a large river, Eion was well placed to hinder the passage westward of any future Persian invasion by land. Goldmines and timber (for shipbuilding) in the area may also have attracted the League to Eion.[104] Herodotos, more journalistic in style than Thucydides, adds colourful details about the Persian governor, Boges, who killed himself after arranging the deaths of his wife, concubines and slaves and throwing the town's gold and silver into the river — denying it to his king's enemies.[105]

Thucydides continues, "Then they enslaved the people of the Aegean island of Skyros, inhabited until then by Dolopians, and colonised the place themselves."[106] The Dolopians were Greeks who seem to have been accused of piracy,[107] an accusation which Meiggs firmly accepts.[108] This accusation may help to explain the severity of their treatment. But the winning side were obviously better placed than the Skyrians to establish their propaganda on the point in the historical tradition. Skyros was importantly situated on the route to the Black Sea, along which Athens imported large quantities of corn.[109] The island was the only anchorage between Euboia (near Athens) and the islands of Lemnos and Imbros (near the Hellespont). This too may have influenced the League's (or Athens') decision to attack. There are indications in later Greek writers that the attacks on both Eion and Skyros happened in the Attic year 476/5: it may be that the two campaigns belong respectively to the late summer of 476 and the early summer of 475.[110]

Next Thucydides records a war between Athens and Karystos, a town near the southern end of the long island of Euboia, and thus only a short distance by sea from Attikē.[111] It ended with a peace treaty.[112] The ATLs show Karystos paying *phoros* to Athens from 450.[113] Very likely Karystos by the terms of the peace treaty had been forced to join the Delian League. Thucydides says nothing about the reason(s) for the campaign against Karystos. But Karystos had, under pressure, helped the Persians against Athens both in 490 and 480,[114] something which would long be remembered. Meiggs, it is true, says of the campaign against Karystos, "It was too late merely for punishment and it seems most unlikely that Athens should, after the capture of Eion, have spoken of the danger from Carystus in the

16

event of another Persian invasion."[115] But for Athens now to have
mentioned Karystos' past involvement with Persia would have
had great political advantage. If other members of the Delian
League fought in this war against Karystos, reference to Persia
would have helped to meet any objection that the League's forces,
meant for use against Persia, were being employed far from
Persian territory for Athens' own purposes. Greek political
propaganda could invoke very remote events; for example, in the
late 430s the Spartans sought to damage Perikles by mention of an
episode from the seventh century.[116] At the time of the present
campaign against her, Karystos' siding with Persia was probably
an event within the previous ten years. Athenian desire to prevent
a recurrence, and to make an example of her dangerous
neighbour, could have been strong.

After his single sentence on Karystos, Thucydides continues
with a famous and important passage:

> The people of Naxos seceded [from the Delian League]: the
> Athenians went to war with them, and by means of a siege
> forced them to surrender. This was the first allied city to be
> enslaved contrary to established practice [or "contrary to the
> established terms of the League"[117]]: later it happened
> to others on separate occasions. Of the reasons for the
> defections [from the League] the most important were the
> failure to supply *phoros* and ships and occasionally desertion
> during campaigns. For the Athenians were strict organisers,
> and when they applied compulsion they irritated people
> who were not used to, and were not willing to undergo,
> hardships. In other ways too the Athenians were not as
> popular commanders as they had been; they did not take
> part in campaigns on an equal basis and it was easy for them
> to reduce to obedience those who seceded. The allies
> themselves were to blame for this; because of this shirking
> of campaigns the majority of them, so as not to be away
> from home, had themselves assessed to contribute money
> instead of the ships, at the appropriate rate. Athens' fleet
> grew as a result of the payments which the allies contrib-
> uted, while they themselves, at such times as they seceded,
> lacked resources and experience for war.[118]

Naxos was a large and formerly powerful island of the mid-
Aegean.[119] In what sense were its inhabitants, and those of other

communities within the League, "enslaved" by Athens? Thucydides' word for this "enslavement" (*edoulōthē*) seems inexact, rhetorical and hostile.[120] Elsewhere in his work almost all the uses of this word and its cognates, when applied to Athens, occur in speeches of her enemies attacking Athenian imperialism.[121] More generally in Thucydides, words from the same root (*doul-*) mean (1) chattel slavery, (2) political subjection of various degrees, (3) even more obviously metaphorical "enthralment" to some abstraction.[122] A close analysis of one passage, where the same verb is used for the "enslavement" of Athens' allies, suggests that these supposedly enslaved states had important votes at meetings of the Delian League *after their "enslavement"*:[123] on this and on League meetings in general, see Chapter 3. Words from the root *doul-* seem, then, to be used in Thucydides at times as terms of political abuse, applying the odium of chattel slavery to a condition of far less severe subjection. (We may compare the blurring of important distinctions in modern English political abuse, such as 'Fascist!' and 'The slave-states of Eastern Europe'.)

There is no indication, here or elsewhere, that the Naxians now were turned into chattel slaves. That "the Naxians" are recorded on ATLs as paying *phoros* to Athens from 447 onwards strongly suggests that they were not. Sensible modern suggestions as to what befell Naxos after its conquest by the Athenians include the imposition of a garrison or of a kleroukhy (a colony of Athenian citizens) to ensure obedience.[124] Another possibility is that an oligarchic form of government on Naxos was replaced by a *dēmokratia*, a regime more likely to produce loyalty to Athens.[125] We may suspect that Thucydides used the imprecise word *edoulōthē* partly for stylistic convenience, because its breadth of meaning would cover a variety of treatments imposed on the other states which he here goes on to describe as deprived of liberty. But the hostility he shows in this passage to the growth of Athens' dominance should be carefully noted, and recalled when we assess his remarks elsewhere on the developed Athenian Empire.[126]

Thucydides' dislike of Athenian imperialism is shared by several influential modern scholars. J. A. O. Larsen writes of "the decline of the League and its transformation into an empire"; his word 'decline' refers not to any diminution in power but to the League's moral standing, in his view.[127] Meiggs sees Athens' treatment of Thasos (on which see below) as an "unambiguous sign of tyranny".[128] Reasons for this common modern aversion will be briefly discussed in Chapter 3. But an important general principle may be considered now. All moralising in the study of antiquity is suspect. Even with hindsight, we know little of the reasons for the actions we wish to explain, compared with the people of antiquity who actually performed them. (For instance, in the case of the war against Naxos we cannot tell whether strict and exemplary action was made more attractive by the imminence of a large Persian invasion which, in the event, was headed off by warfare at the River Eurymedon; see below.) Also, our own advantage of hindsight may mislead us into supposing that what we know of events, looking back, reasonable people in antiquity should have predicted. This much is commonplace among the many scholars who are wary of moralising. It should be added, though, that in the study of highly successful states, such as Athens and Sparta, negative moralising may be more harmful than positive.[129] An admiration of Athens or Sparta may incline us to look for signs of rationality and ingenuity in their policies. And given the record of these states in gaining and keeping dominance over other Greeks who far outnumbered them, rationality and ingenuity there must have been. Moral revulsion, on the other hand, may obscure our vision in such cases.[130] There is considerable value in the French overstatement, 'To understand everything is to forgive everything.' Sensing something of the kind, if we take pleasure — self-consciously or not — in condemning, say, Athens or Sparta, we may be loth to look for rationality in their behaviour, because this, if discovered, would interfere with our pleasure. The successful practice of history may depend on the suspension or absence of disgust.

After his remarks on Naxos and the changes in the Delian League, Thucydides goes on:

> Following these events there occurred both a land battle by the River Eurymedon in Pamphylia and a sea battle between the Athenians and the allies on the one hand and the Persians on the other. The Athenians won on both elements on the same day, under the command of Kimon, son of Miltiades; they captured and destroyed all the Phoenician triremes to the number of 200.[131]

The River Eurymedon ran to the southern coast of Asia Minor and lay approximately half-way between Ionia and the Persians' naval bases in Phoenicia. This double victory of the Delian

League, usually dated to the early 460s, strengthened Athens' position as leader and contributed to the prolonged exclusion of the Persian navy from the Aegean. No properly Persian fleet operated there again in the fifth century. Even when Persia's ambitions revived, after the annihilation of a great Athenian fleet at Syracuse in 413, her intervention in the Aegean took the form for a time of financing the fleet of Sparta.[132] The gathering now of Persian ships at the Eurymedon, if meant to precede an invasion of the Aegean, would have given the League considerable warning. The Greek attack may have been pre-emptive. Again, the Persians themselves could have received warning of an impending attack and assembled defensively at the Eurymedon. Persia was lavish with money among the Greeks in pursuit of her diplomacy.[133] A self-appointed spy might have expected large rewards for taking to the Persians news of a coming Greek attack. Meiggs's argument, that Persia on this occasion intended the aggression, is not conclusive, even though, as he notes, when the possibility of Persian intervention in the Aegean was once more considered, in 411, Persia held a fleet at the Eurymedon.[134] On the course of the campaign, Diodorus adds nothing reliable to Thucydides, and garbles his account by including an episode belonging to Kimon's last campaign, more than 15 years later.[135] For a possible contribution by Plutarch, see below.

Next Thucydides records the revolt from the Delian League of Thasos, a large island of the northern Aegean with a goldmine and trading posts on the facing coasts of Thrace.[136] The mine and the trading posts, Thucydides states, were the subject of a dispute with the Athenians. He mentions a subsequent Athenian naval victory over the Thasians, and "at the same period" an ambitious attempt of Athens and her allies to found with 10,000 settlers a colony nearby on the River Strymon, on a site called 'Nine Ways' (*Ennea Hodoi*).[137] The colonists — all or most of them, Thucydides' narrative suggests — proceeded inland into Thrace and were "destroyed" by a force of (non-Greek) Thracians.[138] To plan, advertise and execute an interstate colonising expedition such as this would have been a long business. Since Thucydides, as we have seen, connects chronologically the first battle in Thasos' war of independence and the arrival nearby of the colonists sent by Athens, the *ATL* editors have sensibly suggested that news of the planned colony, which threatened the power and economy of Thasos, helped to provoke her revolt in the first place.[139] Thasos was besieged for between two and three years.[140]

After a promising but unsuccessful attempt to procure the armed intervention of Sparta against Athens, Thasos capitulated, giving up its ships, its mine and possessions on the mainland, and taking down its defensive wall.[141] Thasos also agreed to pay *phoros* and to make certain other payments which Thucydides does not describe precisely.[142]

Thasos was treated severely. If we wish to explain rather than to condemn this, we should explore the possibility of a link between Thasos and Persia which might have menaced the Delian League, once Thasos seceded. There was indeed such a link. In 491, shortly before a Persian attack on Athens, a prosperous Thasos had obediently disarmed and handed over its fleet to Persia.[143] When Thasos revolted from the League, seemingly in 465,[144] the Persians may still have seemed to threaten the northern Aegean. An Athenian inscription, probably from the period 465–463,[145] records casualties suffered at Thasos and also in the Hellespontine region, the latter, it may well be, in a campaign against Persian forces.[146] It is possible, also, that a Persian garrison remained at Doriskos on the River Hebros in eastern Thrace; Herodotos records the failure of Greek attempts to remove it.[147] Even after the victories at the Eurymedon, Greeks might reasonably have feared that Thasos, once out of the Delian League, might be dangerously compliant with Persia.

During their revolt, the Thasians were promised help by Sparta, which undertook to attack Athens by invading Attikē.[148] (Sparta's reasons for giving this promise, which was kept secret from the Athenians, will be explored in Chapter 4.) The promise could not be kept, however, because of a double disaster at Sparta: an earthquake and a revolt of Sparta's large subject population, the helots.[149] To crush this revolt, Sparta interestingly called for the help of Athens, still linked to her by the alliance made against Persia almost two decades before. Athens' skill in siegecraft, enhanced by her experience with the Delian League, was especially valued by the Spartans, who faced a strong helot position on Mount Ithōmē in Messenia, Sparta's subject territory of the south-western Peloponnese.[150] Urged, it seems, by her leading general, Kimon, Athens decided to help and sent a considerable force.[151]

Several modern scholars have believed that such a force would not have been sent, had Athens known of Sparta's hostility to her, expressed in the promise to Thasos made, perhaps, some three years previously.[152] In evaluating this idea, we should look, as usual, for possible analogies. Was there ever another occasion on which Athens, with reason to believe in latent Spartan hostility to herself, nevertheless agreed to help Sparta suppress a helot revolt? It happens that there was, in 421. Then, after ten years of inconclusive but full-scale war, Athens and Sparta made a treaty of alliance. In it Athens promised to send help to Sparta if the helots revolted.[153] The helots did not revolt during the life of this treaty, and Athens' word was not tested. But it was given at a time when a helot revolt must have seemed to the Athenians far from unlikely.[154] If they had no intention of keeping their promise, the Athenians in 421 were jeopardising at the start a treaty which they obviously valued. It may be that in the late 460s Athenians had indeed heard of Sparta's plan to invade Attikē, and were *prompted* by it into willingness to help Sparta, as they evidently were in 421, in the hope of heading off further Spartan aggression.

The Athenian force sent to Mount Ithōmē was, after a time, rejected by the Spartans and sent away under suspicion. The alien culture, boldness and revolutionary character of the Athenians repelled the Spartans, and led to fears that they would change sides and help the helots against Sparta.[155] The dismissal of the Athenians by Sparta had profound results for both powers, as we shall see. For Kimon it meant, in all probability, banishment from Athens by the process of ostrakism.[156] We do not know whether any Athenians had been killed at Mount Ithōmē; if, as is likely,[157] some had been, there would have been much bitterness at Athens over Kimon's role in promoting a costly expedition to help a state which responded with unfriendliness and, effectively, a public insult.

After the expedition to Mount Ithōmē, the only action of Kimon's which Thucydides mentions is his leadership of a great naval force to Cyprus (probably in or near the year 450[158]). Of the 200 triremes in the force, 60 were sent to Egypt to help a rebellious local ruler against his Persian overlords.[159] The main fleet won a battle against Persian forces off Cyprus, and there was an accompanying victory on land.[160] But before these victories occurred Kimon had died.[161] A few years before, in the mid-450s, Athens and her allies had suffered a terrible defeat in Egypt (on this see Chapter 2; Kimon almost certainly had not been involved). Amends had now been made for this defeat, at least in part: the Greek forces sailed home.[162]

Thucydides and Plutarch on the role of Kimon

The influence of Kimon on the history of the 470s and 460s may have been very great. De Ste. Croix states plausibly that he was in this period "by far the most important and influential figure in Athens".[163] Thucydides' evidence on Kimon is scanty and it may be tempting to give an account which draws most of its detail from the relatively full *Life of Kimon* written by Plutarch. However, since in general Thucydides is clearly much superior to Plutarch in political intelligence and access to material, his testimony should be carefully set apart and used as a basis against which the claims of Plutarch are tested.

Thucydides names Kimon in only five passages. At I 45 he shows that Kimon's son, who was an Athenian general in 433, had been named by his father 'Lakedaimonios', ('Spartan'). Chapters 98, 100 and 102 of Book I refer, as we have seen, to Kimon's leadership of campaigns to Eion, the Eurymedon and Mount Ithōmē. Book I 112 tells of his last expedition to Cyprus. These few references suggest both that Kimon was, in Thucydides' view, a person with great influence on events, and that he had a coherent policy. No other Athenian general is named by Thucydides in connection with the period from the foundation of the Delian League to the dismissal from Mount Ithōmē, whereas Kimon is so mentioned on three occasions. The apparent coherence of policy concerns Persia and Sparta: aggression towards the former, collaboration with the latter, in the hope of avoiding the appalling strain of a war on two fronts.[164] The naming of his son 'Lakedaimonios' suggests a deliberately indelible advertisement of Kimon's policy towards Sparta, made, at the very latest, in the mid-460s; an Athenian inscription shows that Lakedaimonios was old enough to be a commander of cavalry before 445.[165] Kimon's influence in directing Athenian expansionism against Persia may also be reflected by the apparent cessation of Athenian expeditions to the eastern Mediterranean from the year of his death. (On this, and the "Peace of Kallias" between Athens and Persia, see Chapter 2.)

On the quality of Kimon's generalship we have no precise indication from Thucydides. We cannot argue purely from the facts that he presided over successful campaigns against Persia and that he was repeatedly elected as general. An aristocratic commander may have little expertise and yet have a certain success against an enemy similarly led. (We hear, though not from reliable sources, that Persian forces both at Eion and at the Eurymedon were commanded by relatives of King Xerxes.[166]) At Athens a member of the nobility, such as Kimon, had great political advantages.[167] Also chance success in command could seem a sign of divine support and lead to repeated appointment.[168] In all probability Kimon would not have risen to command in the first place had he not been the son of an aristocrat and a general. But the career of his father Miltiades illustrates the drastic impatience of Athenians towards a general, albeit aristocratic, who failed. Miltiades, commander at the victory of Marathon in 490, was in the following year tried and sentenced to pay a crushing fine for a military failure elsewhere.[169] A similar rigour was applied to unsuccessful Athenian generals later in the fifth century.[170] Kimon's successes at Eion and Eurymedon make it highly probable that the Athenians used him as commander on campaigns of the 470s and 460s in addition to the three with which Thucydides connects him. If so, his survival as a much-tested commander until the affair of Mount Ithōmē, and his recall to a command of great importance around 450, should suggest that he gave evidence of considerable military skill.

Plutarch's *Life of Kimon* is too extensive to be treated in full here. No scholarly commentary devoted to it has been published in recent times, although on particular points one may conveniently consult the work of Gomme and especially of Meiggs. Some of the more important points of the *Life* will be considered now. In comparing Plutarch's account of Kimon's career with details given by Thucydides, we seek to apply techniques of criticism which are useful on the many occasions in Ancient History when an early, good, source and a later, inferior, one supply information on the same subject. Where two such sources correspond on a particular point, the later source is often discounted, as being itself possibly derived from the earlier source and so adding nothing in authority. Where the two sources vary somewhat, one should ask whether the difference may be explained merely as garbling of, or as inference from, the earlier source by the later. If there is a contradiction, the version of the earlier, in other respects better-informed, source is usually to be preferred, unless the version of the later source corresponds with seemingly independent information from elsewhere. More promising is the case in which information in the later source does not conflict with that of the first but seems not to have derived from it either; a very detailed ('circumstantial') account of this kind is particularly valued, as being very unlikely to have arisen from honest misunderstanding of the earlier source. Here we may suspect that the later writer has drawn on a different predecessor. (Research into the identity and value of the lost sources-of-our-sources has played a large, though often infertile, part in modern scholarship.) For the *Life of Kimon*, the possibility that Plutarch had a systematic and detailed fifth century source on political history apart from Thucydides seems to be almost ruled out by Thucydides' own comments, cited above (pp. 3f.), on the neglect of the relevant period by other writers. However, as we shall see below (Chapter 3), Plutarch may preserve valuable pieces of information from other early sources, now lost.

Plutarch's description of an episode in the conquest of Skyros, in which the body of Theseus, the legendary ruler and super-natural hero of Athens, was allegedly discovered on the island, should be taken seriously. It neither contradicts Thucydides nor is inferable from his history. Plutarch's statement that Kimon won great popularity at Athens by bringing back "Theseus'" body is in keeping with much that we hear elsewhere on the importance of religion in fifth century Athenian politics.[171]

Plutarch's account of the Eurymedon campaign also contains interesting material (on which in general see Meiggs, *The Athenian empire*, pp. 73–9). In this connection Plutarch states that Kimon altered the design of triremes to make them more suitable for numerous hoplites to fight from.[172] In the late fourth century the Aristotelian *Constitution of Athens (Ath. Pol.)*, in a plainly oversimplified context, represents Kimon as the champion of the wealthy class in Athenian politics,[173] a view echoed by Plutarch.[174] (In reality, because Kimon made a great contribution to the power of the Athenian navy, he also advanced the power of the often-radical Athenian poor who manned it.) Now hoplites, who were obliged to provide their own expensive arms and armour, were among the wealthier citizens of Athens. The view that Kimon championed the wealthy may perhaps have produced, by improper inference, the idea that he reshaped warships to accommodate the hoplites.

According to Plutarch, Kimon won the naval victory over Thasos and subsequently captured the town, acquiring the Thasians' goldmines for Athens.[175] All this may be true, but we cannot assume so. Plutarch, or a source of his, may very easily have inferred that Kimon *must* have commanded on such an important campaign, although Thucydides does not say so. Of the goldmine (singular), Thucydides says only that the Thasians gave it up, after mentioning that Thasos capitulated to the Athenians. Again, an inference derived, deliberately or carelessly, from Thucydides' text could have produced the idea that Athens acquired the goldmine for herself.

Plutarch represents Kimon as not requiring any state of the Delian League (other than Athens) to send men for service on campaigns, in contrast to "the other generals of the Athenians" who used lawsuits and punishments to extract personal service, making their rule offensive in the process.[176] According to Plutarch, Kimon allowed states to commute their contributions to the form of money and empty ships, while building Athens' naval power and imperial domination at the allies' expense.[177] If true, this would confirm our picture of Kimon as the most important of the politicians and generals who founded the Athenian Empire. Gomme disbelieves Plutarch here, and suggests that the distinction between the policy of Kimon and the practice of the other generals was invented to reconcile two traditions — that Kimon was popular with the allies and that Athenian leadership of the Delian League proved irritating (as Thucydides shows[178]).[179]

Gomme refers to Kimon as the "hero" of Plutarch's biography. This remark takes us to the heart of a profound defect in the *Life of Kimon*. The Athenian general is treated by Plutarch with extravagant and almost uncritical respect. Kimon's success at Eurymedon is said to surpass the victories of Salamis and Plataia.[180] Eurymedon so humbled the king of Persia that he made peace (the "Peace of Kallias") with Athens.[181] (In reality the "Peace of Kallias" was made, if at all, more than 15 years after the battle of Eurymedon.)[182] Significantly, in view of his bias, Plutarch concedes that Kimon was ostrakised after the campaign to Mount Ithōmē, but he claims that this was done "with little justification"[183] and that Athenian resentment against Kimon lasted "not long".[184] Kimon was specially recalled, according to Plutarch, after the battle of Tanagra (a battle which was fought, probably, in 458 or 457[185]); even Kimon's opponent, Perikles, saw his value and championed the recall.[186] Kimon's "gentleness" towards Athenians and allies is repetitively insisted upon.[187] And on his last campaign, to Cyprus, Kimon is said to win a naval battle over Phoenician and Cilician ships.[188] Plutarch adds that "after his [Kimon's] death, no outstanding exploit against the barbarians [i.e. the Persians] was ever again performed by a general of the Greeks".[189] Thucydides, too, mentions victorious warfare on sea (and on land) in this campaign, against Phoenicians, Cilicians and Cypriots. But in his account these victories were won some while after Kimon's death.[190] Outstanding exploits against the Persians were, in fact, achieved by Kimon's successor(s).

We should, then, be very suspicious when Plutarch's account diverges from that of Thucydides, in such a way as to glorify Kimon at the expense of other Greeks. It is all too probable that Kimon's alleged difference from other commanders in the matter of allied contributions to the League reflects a distortion by Plutarch, similar to the one concerning Kimon and the other generals on the campaign to Cyprus. On the subject of the contributions, Plutarch is in any case almost certainly going beyond his evidence. In this connection he says that Kimon as general did not apply compulsion to any of the Greeks.[191] In the study of Ancient History, and in many other areas, it is often illuminating to recast a negative generalisation, such as 'A never did x' or 'B never said y' into a more positive-seeming but equivalent form. Doing so in this case, we obtain the statement 'All Greeks at all times under Kimon's generalship were free from compulsion applied by him in this regard': our illumination may come in now seeing more clearly how wide a knowledge would have been needed to justify such a statement. It is highly probable that Plutarch did not have trustworthy information on Kimon's behaviour in this matter, to *all* League members, on *all* the relevant occasions in his generalship. There is a great intellectual gulf between Plutarch who, some five-and-a-half centuries after Kimon's death, believed that he should make so sweeping a claim, and Thucydides who, far closer to the events he described, insisted — although it made a difficulty for his own case — that occurrences of the period were strictly not knowable.

Notes

1. Thuc. I 89 3; Hdt. IX 13, compare VIII 53.
2. Compare Hdt. VIII 61.
3. Thuc. I 89 3 – 93 8.
4. Thuc. I 89 2; Hdt. IX 114–18.
5. Thuc. I 94 1–2.
6. Thuc. I 95. The expression 'the eastern Greeks' is used here to refer to inhabitants of the Aegean islands, of the coasts of the northern Aegean and Propontis, and of the coasts of western Asia Minor.

7. Thuc. I 96 1, cf. 99 2.

8. Thuc. I 96 2. Delos had long been a centre of worship and celebration for the neighbouring islanders, the Athenians and the Ionian Greeks of the eastern Aegean; Thuc. III 104. It thus symbolised unity.

9. Compare Thuc. II 13 3, where expenditure on "the Propylaia of the Akropolis and the other buildings" is mentioned. The Parthenon is not named by Thucydides, and counts here merely as one of "the other buildings". On the building of the Parthenon and Propylaia, see Chapter 3.

10. See Chapter 3; on *dēmokratia* and the poor, Arist. *Politics* 1279 B and Chapter 7.

11. See Chapter 3.

12. Thuc. VIII 48 6 and de Ste. Croix, *Origins*, 44. Compare Aristoph., *Wasps*, e.g. 656–712.

13. Thuc. IV 105 1, with A.W. Gomme, *HCT*, I, 300.

14. Thuc. I 1.

15. Thuc. I 1 1, V 26 5.

16. Thuc. IV 104 4.

17. Thuc. V 26 1–5.

18. Thuc. I 1 3.

19. Gomme, *HCT*, I, 91.

20. Ibid.

21. See Gomme, loc. cit., 92.

22. On the meaning of the Greek words here translated as 'the events of long ago' (*ta palaia*), compare de Ste. Croix, *Origins*, 205.

23. For a different interpretation, see Gomme, *HCT*, I, 256.

24. Thuc. I 96 1.

25. P.A. Brunt, *Historia*, II (1953–4), 150.

26. Gomme, *HCT*, I, 272.

27. Meiggs, *AE*, 463.

28. *Origins*, 302 with passages there cited. Compare Thucydides' use of the verb cognate with *proskhēma: proekhomai*.

29. Ibid.

30. The Greek word here rendered as 'as' (*hōs*) can be used by Thucydides, as by other writers, to introduce a feigned rather than a genuine purpose: compare VI 61 6, where Athenians facing serious criminal charges set sail *hōs* ('as if') for Athens, and then flee into exile.

31. Thuc. VI 76 4.

32. Thuc. I 98 4.

33. Thuc. VI 75 4.

34. Herodotos writes of the best-looking boys being castrated to serve as eunuchs, and the most beautiful unmarried girls being "snatched away to the King of Persia"; VI 32.

35. E.g. R. Sealey in *Ancient society and institutions: studies presented to Victor Ehrenberg* (ed. E. Badian), 237–42.

36. *Historia*, II (1953–4), 150.

37. *Historia*, XVIII (1969), 12–5.

38. Plut., *Life of Kimon* IX 2–3; compare XIII 2,6.

39. Thuc. I 98 1.

40. See, e.g., R.S. Woodworth and H. Schlosberg, *Experimental*

Psychology[3], 717; F.C. Bartlett, *Remembering*, 84, 93f.

41. Thuc. III 10 3.

42. Thuc. I 95 4; III 8, 15 1.

43. Thuc. III 9–14.

44. Thuc. I 95 1, 4; 96 1; 130 2.

45. Thuc. I 95 1, 3, 5; 128 5–130. On Pausanias' attitude towards Persia see also Chapter 4.

46. Hdt. IX 106.

47. Hdt., ibid. and I 147 2; Thuc. VII 57 4; Eur., *Ion*, 1581–8. On uses of this myth in propaganda of the Delian League, see J. P. Barron, *JHS*, LXXXIV (1964), 35–48.

48. He came from Halikarnassos, a town of south-western Asia Minor which was originally Dorian. His work, however, is written in Ionic, and not Dorian, Greek dialect. Not only was Ionic the dominant literary dialect of his time (the mid-fifth century); it was also used in official inscriptions of Halikarnassos.

49. Meiggs, *AE*, 34.

50. Hdt. I 142.

51. Plato states that a Greek city, when controlled by an oligarchy, consisted in reality of two cities, the poor and the rich, "always plotting against each other"; *Republic*, 551d, and see Chapters 3 and 7. On old and young, see below, n.52, and Thuc. VI 18 6. On city- and country-dwellers, Thuc. II 21 3; Aristoph. *Ekklēsiazousai*, 197–8 and *Akharnians*, *passim*.

52. Aristotle defined oligarchy, one of the commonest forms of Greek constitution in the classical period, as the rule of the rich; *Politics*, 1279b, 1290b. On the power of the rich in the Athenian *dēmokratia* see Chapter 7. On age: at Athens men under 30 were excluded from service as jurors or *bouleutai* (state councillors); see Chapter 7. It seems that at one period the right to speak in Athens' governing body, the general assembly (*ekklēsia*), was given according to age, the old speaking first, the young last; Aiskhines III 4, cf. I 23f., III 2. Thucydides states that the Athenian Alkibiades was, by the standards of other Greek cities, young to be eminent in politics (he was in his thirties); V 43 2 with Gomme-Andrewes-Dover, *HCT*, IV, 48–9; compare Thuc. VI 12 2, 17 1. The Greek words for 'ambassador' (*presbys*, *presbeutēs*) implied old age. The title of the Spartan senate, *gerousia*, meant literally (like the Latin *senatus*) 'body of old men'.

53. Hdt. VII 142.

54. See, e.g., Hdt. VII 94.

55. On Diodorus' very different account, see Meiggs, *AE*, pp. 413–4.

56. According to Herodotos, there were 180 Athenian and 16 Spartan triremes in the Greek fleet before Salamis; VIII 43–4.

57. Hdt. VIII 43–4, 93.

58. Hdt. IX 105.

59. Compare Thuc. I 95 1. On the importance of the distinction between Ionian and Dorian Greeks, cf. p. 44. Confusingly, Thucydides and other Greek writers seem on occasion to use the word 'Ionians' to include also Dorian and other Greek states of (or near) the western coast

The Delian League

of Asia Minor; Gomme, *HCT*, I, 257. This partly explains why we have preferred the term 'eastern Greeks'.

60. Hdt. VI 43 with A.R. Burn, *Persia and the Greeks*[2], 222. There is evidence of a democratic council on Khios in the sixth century; M. N. Tod, *A selection of Greek historical inscriptions*, no. 1.

61. C. Hignett, *A history of the Athenian constitution*, ch. VI.

62. Thuc. V 45; compare III 10 1 on the need for allies to be of similar character.

63. Thuc. I 19.

64. Thuc. I 95 7.

65. Thuc. I 95 4.

66. Thuc. I 95 6–7.

67. See de Ste. Croix, *Origins*, 298–307.

68. [Arist.] *Ath. Pol.* 23 5 (on which see below, Chapter 7); compare Plut., *Life of Aristeides* 25 1.

69. Hdt. I 165.

70. E.g. Meiggs, *AE*, 46.

71. See n. 69.

72. Compare J. A. O. Larsen, *Harvard Studies in Classical Philology*, 51 (1940), 187–8.

73. H. Jacobson, *Philologus*, 119 (1975), 256–8 and evidence there cited. In different ways, both Jacobson and de Ste. Croix (*Origins*, 298, n.1) compare the oath of the Delian League with oaths of the Hittites (a people of Asia Minor whose culture flourished in the second millennium BC).

74. Plut., *Life of Aristeides* 25 1.

75. Jacobson, op. cit., 258.

76. Thuc. II 2 1.

77. On the meaning of *phoroi* and its singular, *phoros*, see below.

78. *Ath. Pol.*, 23 5.

79. Diod. XI 44 6, 47 with Gomme, *HCT*, I, 272.

80. On the Athenian calendar, see B. D. Meritt, *The Athenian year*; J. D. Mikalson, *The sacred and civil calendar of the Athenian year*.

81. Chronology is often the most problematic aspect of Herodotos' work on the Persian wars, in some cases driving scholars to assume that a passage clearly located in time was in fact meant to be "timeless"; see, e.g., Burn, op. cit., 349, J. F. Lazenby, *Hermes*, XCII (1964), 265. For the gross chronological distortion, by later Athenians, of events of the mid-fifth century, see [Andokides] III, and, derived from that speech, Aiskhines II 172–3. From ordinary conversation of the present day we can often see that the chronology of an event has been quickly forgotten while other aspects of it are well remembered: "Let's see: was that last Thursday or last Friday? *(pause)* Anyway …".

82. See the maps of the various districts of the Athenian Empire in Meiggs, *AE*, following p. 621, and also the names of tribute payers, grouped by districts and reproduced by Meiggs on 540–59.

83. Thuc. I 96 2.

84. The standard work of reference on this subject is *The Athenian tribute lists* (*ATL*), by B. D. Meritt, H. T. Wade-Gery and M. F. McGregor (4 vols), which, in addition to reconstructing the lists,

contains important essays on several aspects of the Delian League and Athenian Empire.

85. Gomme, *HCT*, I, 273–4.

86. Thuc. I 98 3 (Karystos); I 105 2, 108 4 (Aigina). See also below and Chapter 2.

87. We happen to hear that Lampsakos (on the southern shore of the Dardanelles) and Myous (near Miletos in Ionia) remained for long in the power of Persia (probably until the 460s); Thuc. I 138 5. Later both places paid *phoros* to Athens: Lampsakos from 450 (or earlier; Meiggs, *AE*, 544), Myous from 451 (or earlier; Meiggs, *AE*, 540). Compare the unspecified conquests on the coasts of Thrace and the Hellespont referred to at Hdt. VII 106.

88. Thuc. I 19.

89. Defences of Athenian rule are found at Thuc. I 73–8, Isok., *Panegyrikos, passim.*

90. [Arist.], *Ath. Pol.* 23 5.

91. Plut., *Life of Aristeides, passim.* The famous anecdote of the Athenian who voted to ostrakise Aristeides because "tired of hearing him everywhere called 'the just'" (Plut., op. cit., VII 6) seems to relate to a period before the Delian League was formed, but fitted Aristeides' later image.

92. M. Chambers, *Classical Philology*, LIII (1958), 26–32.

93. *ATL*, III, 236–43.

94. Thuc. I 99 3.

95. Ibid.

96. Even before she became leader of the naval alliance, Athens contributed 30 ships (as against 20 of the Peloponnesians) to the campaigns against Cyprus and Byzantion; Thucydides is not precise about the number supplied now by other allies, saying only that these allies came in a great mass *(plēthos)*; I 94 1–2. Later, in her period of empire, Athens provided the majority of ships in the largest fleets of war; Thuc. I 19 and below, Chapter 3.

97. The term *phoros* was tactfully avoided when contributions were required in the fourth century for another Athenian-led alliance.

98. Thuc. I 99 2, III 10 4, 11 1, 4.

99. Thuc. I 99 2, III 10 4.

100. Thuc. I 96 2.

101. E.g. Meiggs, *AE*, 234.

102. O. Murray, *Historia*, XV (1966), 149–50.

103. Thucydides mentions only the Athenians, in several contexts. But I 100 1 shows that he can use 'the Athenians' as shorthand for 'the Athenians and their allies'.

104. On timber, Meiggs, *AE*, 195; on gold, e.g. Thuc. IV 105 1.

105. Hdt. VII 107.

106. Thuc. I 98 2.

107. Plut., *Life of Kimon* VIII 3–4.

108. Meiggs, *AE*, 69.

109. On the corn imports, see de Ste. Croix, *Origins*, 46–9, 265–6, with evidence there cited, and below, Chapter 7.

110. Scholiast (i.e. ancient commentator) on Aiskhines II 31 (Eion);

The Delian League

Plut., *Life of Theseus* 36 (Skyros).
111. Thuc. I 98 3.
112. Ibid.
113. Meiggs, *AE*, 558.
114. Hdt. VI 99, VIII 66.
115. Meiggs, *AE*, 70.
116. Thuc. I 126–7 with Gomme, *HCT*, I, 428–30.
117. On the ambiguity see Gomme, op.cit., I, 282; Brunt, op.cit., 152, n. 1.
118. Thuc. I 98 4 – 99 3.
119. Hdt. V 28; Plut., *Life of Nikias* III 4–6; Meiggs, *AE*, 43, 301.
120. Cf. VII 75 7.
121. *ATL*, III, 155–8 provides a convenient collection of references.
122. Ibid.
123. Thuc. III 10 5:.
124. *ATL*, III, 57; Naxos seems to have had a kleroukhy later. (On this and on kleroukhies in general, see Chapter 3.)
125. The first documented case of Athens' insistence on *dēmokratia* in a League member concerns Erythrai, probably in the late 450s: see Chapter 2.
126. Thucydides' complex and interesting personal position as regards the Athenian Empire will be examined in Chapters 3 and 5.
127. J. A. O. Larsen, *Harvard Studies in Classical Philology*, LI (1940), 200.
128. Meiggs, *AE*, 86.
129. The word 'successful' here is not used to imply that these two states, or either of them, should be approved of, but that each fulfilled ambitious desires.
130. Compare W. S. Ferguson's claim about the reaction of the Athenian assembly to a naval victory of 406: "the folly of the Athenians is explicable only on their own theory that those whom the Gods would destroy they first make mad" (*CAH*, vol. V, 359). Here a connection between disapproval and lack of understanding is all but admitted.
131. Thuc. I 100 1.
132. See Chapter 5.
133. See, e.g., Thuc. I 129 3, 109 2–3.
134. Meiggs, *AE*, 78 with references there given.
135. Diod. XI 60–2, with Gomme, *HCT*, I, 286 and n. 2, Meiggs, *AE*, 74–5.
136. Thuc. I 100 2.
137. Thuc. I 100 2–3. As Thucydides here says, this was the site later of Amphipolis, an important colony, on which see Chapters 3 and 5.
138. Thuc. I 100 3.
139. *ATL*, III, 258.
140. Thuc. I 101 3.
141. Thuc. I 101 1–3.
142. Thuc. I 101 3.
143. Hdt. VI 46 1 – 47 1.
144. See Gomme, *HCT*, I, 391.
145. For references, see Meiggs, *AE*, 80, n. 2.

146. Plut., *Life of Kimon* XIV 1; Meiggs, *AE*, 79–80.

147. Hdt. VII 106.

148. Thuc. I 101 1–2.

149. Ibid., 101 2. On the helots and their political importance, see Chapters 4, 5 and 6.

150. Ibid., 102 2–4.

151. Thuc. I 102 1; Aristoph. *Lysistratē*, 1137–44; Plut., *Life of Kimon* XVI 8, citing a fifth-century source, Ion of Khios.

152. E.g. Gomme, *HCT*, I, 298, de Ste. Croix, *Origins*, 179.

153. Thuc. V 23 3.

154. Compare Thuc. IV 41 3, 55 1, 80 2–4.

155. Thuc. I 102–3.

156. Plut., *Life of Kimon* XVII with Gomme, *HCT*, I, 326–7.

157. Thuc. I 102 3 implies that there was a period of unsuccessful attack on the helot position between the arrival and dismissal of the Athenians.

158. Thuc. I 112 1–4; Meiggs, *AE*, 124–5.

159. Thuc. I 112 2–3, compare 110 2.

160. Ibid. I 112 4.

161. Ibid.

162. Ibid.

163. op. cit., 172.

164. Compare de Ste. Croix, op. cit., 176.

165. *Inscriptiones Graecae*, I^2, no. 400. In the dating of inscriptions such as this, much help is gained from a study of the exact forms in which certain of the Greek letters, and particularly sigma, appear. The authoritative work on this point is R. Meiggs, *Journal of Hellenic Studies*, 86 (1966), 86–98.

166. Plut., *Life of Kimon* VII 1; Diod. XI 60 5, 61 3.

167. See Chapter 7.

168. Thuc. VI 17 1, with K. J. Dover, *HCT*, IV, 249.

169. Hdt. VI 110–1, 136.

170. See, e.g., Thuc. V 26 5, VII 48 3–4.

171. Plut., *Life of Kimon* VIII 5–6; on religion in the politics of Athens, see Chapter 9.

172. Plut., op. cit., XII 2.

173. [Arist.] *Ath.Pol.*, XXVIII 2.

174. Plut., *Life of Kimon* XV 1–2.

175. Ibid., XIV 2.

176. Ibid., XI.

177. Ibid., XI 2–3.

178. Thuc. I 99 1.

179. Gomme, *HCT*, I, 284–5. Plutarch lays much stress on the gentleness of Kimon (see below): it was perhaps this, rather than his popularity, that Plutarch was concerned to assert at this point.

180. Plut., op. cit., XIII 3.

181. Ibid., 4–6.

182. See Chapter 2.

183. Plut., op. cit., XVII 2.

184. Ibid., XVII 5.

185. See Chapter 2.
186. Plut., op. cit., XVII 6.
187. Ibid., III 1, V 4, VI 2, XVI 3.
188. Ibid., XVIII 5.
189. Ibid., XIX 2.
190. Thuc. I 112 4.
191. Plut., op. cit., XI 2.

2

From Delian League to
Athenian Empire

Developments on the Greek mainland and the
expedition to Egypt

In the latter part of the 460s several states, including Athens, sent military help to Sparta, to suppress the revolt of her subject population, the helots.[1] When the Spartans singled out and dismissed the Athenian force, they caused a sharp change in the politics of Greece. Thucydides says that this campaign (to Mount Ithōmē) led to the first open quarrel between Athens and Sparta (the first, that is, in the period after the Persian Wars).[2] He describes the Athenians as outraged by the dismissal; they

> judged that they were being sent away not for the more creditable reason [alleged by Sparta[3]] but because some suspicion had arisen; they considered it a great scandal, believing that they had not deserved such treatment from Spartans; immediately they got back [to Athens] they abandoned the alliance made with Sparta against the Persians and made an alliance with Argos, Sparta's enemy; an alliance with the same terms was made simultaneously by both states [Argos and Athens] with Thessaly.[4]

Not long before the helot revolt, the Spartans had issued a secret promise, to Thasos, that they would attack Athens (see Chapter 4). If the Athenians knew of this, Sparta's offensive action towards their men at Ithōmē may have confirmed their fears of eventual invasion. Or, if Sparta's promise was still unknown at Athens, the Athenians may instead have been shocked by their dismissal from Ithōmē, and have lost faith in their ability to predict Spartan action. In either case, military protection against Sparta's usually formidable land power must have seemed necessary. Alliance with Argos secured the support of one of the largest hoplite forces outside Sparta's control, while Thessaly was renowned for its cavalry.[5]

Modern scholars tend to explain political action as the result of motives which are ultimately economic, rather than to do with morality and status. Economic motives should always be looked for; in the case under review a desire to protect Athenian lives and property against Sparta was obviously important. But Thucydides suggests that moralising could also be a force in politics. Elsewhere, at III 36, he describes the Athenians as having second thoughts about a decision of their own because it was "cruel".[6] And his account here refers to moral indignation against Sparta, rather than to strategic concern. Athenians no doubt recalled that the helping of Sparta, so rudely requited, had involved considerable sacrifice by their own city. Thoughts of status and revenge may also have mattered now. The power of an insult usually depends on the reputation of the party uttering it, and the Spartans, who had effectively insulted Athens' citizen army, possessed the highest reputation in Greece as warriors.[7] For the sake of their own standing among the Greeks, many Athenians may have believed that a firm reply was needed to the degrading treatment received from this authoritative quarter. Vengeful Athenians would have the satisfaction of knowing that their new alliance with Argos posed a large problem for Sparta, at what for her was already a difficult time. In the recent past Argos had helped to organise a war against Sparta in the Peloponnese.[8] And Sparta's forces now were distracted by the continuing helot revolt.

Athens' shift away from Sparta, towards Argos and Thessaly, had interesting implications for the Delian League. At the foundation of the League, its members had not been aggressive towards Sparta, but had been strongly anti-Persian. Argos and Thessaly had a very different record. Argos had been outwardly neutral in the Persian Wars, and was said to have a friendly understanding with King Xerxes.[9] Thessaly, under severe pressure, had actively taken the Persian side.[10] There is no indication that Argos and Thessaly, on making their alliances with Athens in the late 460s, became members of the League. Indeed, none of the allies or subjects acquired by Athens in Central Greece and the Peloponnese from the 460s to the early 440s was represented on the tribute lists, when they began in 454/

36

3:[11] all may have been seen as separate from the Delian League. But, by her alliance with the tainted Argos and Thessaly, Athens probably aroused suspicions in members of the League that her anti-Persian enthusiasm had declined. It was also open to Delian League members to object that Athens was encouraging Persia by allying herself with the friends and former allies of the Great King against the loyalist Sparta. Such an objection would have been especially embarrassing to Athens if Athenians themselves had previously argued, as they may have,[12] that member states could not be allowed to leave the League for fear that the spectacle of the League's weakness would encourage Persia.

We should try to reconstruct some of the reactions within the League to Athens' new alliances. In doing so, it is worth applying a principle of psychology which historians sometimes overlook. When characters in history, political and domestic, evaluate the offensive acts of others, they commonly do not consider those acts as forming a series already completed. Instead, they are very often influenced mainly by a fear that similar actions may follow, from the previous agents or from others. Some of the best historians in antiquity have suggested as much. Thus, when Thucydides explains Sparta's recourse to war against Athens in 431, he does not say that the Spartans resented Athens' existing empire, but that they were *afraid* of Athens as her power grew.[13] Similarly the Roman historian Tacitus describes the revolt of a British tribe, the Iceni, as resulting from certain insults and "the fear of worse".[14] In remote retrospect, such concern with hypothetical developments is easily forgotten, especially when the developments in question were successfully prevented. Yet one should seek always to ask, when examining the motives of agents in the past, not only 'What did they remember?', but also 'What would they expect or fear?' In the present case, we may suspect that when other states of the Delian League heard of Athens' alliances with Argos and Thessaly, they were concerned not only with what had happened but with possible future reductions in Athens' hostility towards Persia, which might endanger their own positions on the fringe of the Persian empire.

Any alarm in the Delian League on this point would probably have been intensified by the manner in which Athens' political shift had been executed. Thucydides states that the Athenians made their alliance with Argos immediately on returning from the campaign against the helots. This indication of timing may be useful for reconstruction; it suggests that the alliance was made without consultation of a synod of the League. To bring together, at Delos, representatives of allied states which were scattered as far as Byzantion and Phaselis would have taken much time: if the Athenians had gone through that procedure, and taken that time, Thucydides could hardly have written of immediacy. Instead, we may guess that the first synod *after* the making of the Argive alliance was a lively affair.[15] The Athenians had to report not only an important change in their anti-Persian position, but one made without prior consultation with the League. The allies might reasonably wonder whether other and even more serious developments would be announced to them in future by Athens, developments which they would be given no chance either to prevent by dissuasion or even to predict. Also, about this time Athens' allies would have learnt that Kimon, previously at the head of successful anti-Persian campaigns, was discredited in his own city and therefore unlikely to reappear to lead against Persia, at least for some years. Much reassurance from Athenian spokesmen may have been needed. After revolting from the Great King in the 490s, eastern Greek cities had eventually been left to their fate by mainland Greeks, including the Athenians:[16] reconquest by Persia, and savage punishment, had followed. After the Battle of Mykalē, Sparta had suggested abandoning Ionia and moving its population. Many League members might now see, once more, a risk that they would be abandoned to a vengeful Persia, as Athens laid aside, or at least subordinated, her hostility to Persia in favour of warfare closer to home.

Thucydides proceeds (in I 103) to record developments which may have made it seem even likelier that Athens would shortly be preoccupied with a war against Sparta. The state of Megara, lying between the territories of Korinth and Athens, left Sparta's alliance because of a war with Korinth over boundaries, and joined Athens. The Athenians built walls from Megara to its eastern port of Nisaia, on the Saronic Gulf, to protect the city from siege, and installed a garrison of their own troops. "Chiefly from this," wrote Thucydides, "there originated the intense hatred of the Korinthians for the Athenians."[17] Resulting hostilities will be noted briefly below, and dealt with more fully in Chapter 4. For the moment, we should observe that Athens could now expect a prompt war with the Spartan alliance, especially if Sparta had already settled her war against the helots. And yet from the following chapter of Thucydides (I 104) we learn that around this time Athens and her allies from the Delian League mounted a very large campaign, with 200 triremes, to Cyprus, in an obvious challenge to the Persian empire. The Athenians would know that they were stretching their resources very thinly by pursuing this remote campaign while hostilities were likely at home, against the great hoplite army of Sparta and her allies. When, shortly afterwards, the Athenians clashed with the Korinthians, they were obliged to use inferior troops, "the oldest and the youngest men", in Thucydides' phrase.[18] There seems a good chance that the expedition to Cyprus at this pressing time was made partly to calm suspicions in the Delian League. Making war on two fronts, because of its very difficulty, would demonstrate emphatically that Athens would not let her quarrel with Sparta distract her from the defence of the eastern Greeks.

The great fleet of the League reached Cyprus, but turned aside to Egypt after receiving an invitation to intervene there. Thucydides explains that most of Egypt, a province of the Persian empire, had been seized by Inaros, king of the neighbouring parts of Libya, who issued the invitation to the Greeks.[19] Meiggs notes that members of the League must have recalled the lucrative trade of their states with Egypt in the sixth century, and that Egypt may also have appealed as a source of grain to Greeks.[20] Thucydides' account, on the other hand, helps us to understand the *opportunity* to intervene in Egypt, which the League now exploited. In Greek political and strategic thinking the notion of opportunity was highly important, and the word for it, *kairos*, occurs with great frequency. We shall see, in Chapters 4 and 5, that the military actions of Sparta may have been governed to a remarkable degree by a policy of waiting for special opportunity. The Greek dependence on opportunity has perhaps been insufficiently referred to by modern scholars. This may be due in part to a linguistic accident. The word in English which first comes to mind when we seek to refer to the systematic exploitation of opportunity, 'opportunism', generally means something rather different: the *unscrupulous* exploiting of opportunity.[21] Greek states, of course, could seize a chance unscrupulously, as Sparta did in capturing the city of Thebes, contrary to treaty, in 382.[22] But such action could provoke intense protest, even from those who normally supported the state concerned.[23] There is perhaps no convenient word in English for the far more common Greek practice of seizing an opportunity against an acknowledged enemy, of which Athens' intervention in Egypt is a good example.[24]

There are important doubts about the history of the League's

Egyptian campaign. We cannot even be sure of the name of the Greek commander, though a fourth century writer, Ktesias, states that it was Kharitimides.[25] Thucydides gives an outline of the campaign. At first the Greeks dominated Egypt, penning the Persians and some Egyptians who remained loyal to them in a part of the city of Memphis called White Castle. However, a large relief expedition was sent from elsewhere in the Persian empire; the Greeks were defeated in a battle, forced out of Memphis and were themselves besieged for 18 months on the island of Prosopitis. At the end of that period the Persians, by diverting water from a canal, stranded the Greek fleet and captured Prosopitis with a land force. The war had lasted for six years, and of the Greeks "the majority perished".[26] When a relief expedition from the League arrived belatedly, most of its 50 triremes were also destroyed.

Scholars have disputed whether more than a minority of the original 200 triremes were involved in the defeat at Prosopitis. The crew of a trireme was of about 200 men.[27] The loss of most of the two fleets (200 + 50 triremes) and their crews (about 40,000 + 10,000 men) would, it is sometimes argued, have had profound effects on Athenian power which Thucydides does not mention and which he, or other sources, would have been bound to reveal, *if* they had occurred. As Gomme says of the Athenians and their allies, "The disaster would have crippled them; yet no great change in their position relative either to Persia or to the rest of Greece occurred as a result of it."[28] Is it possible that a large section of the original 200 ships returned to Athens before the end of the campaign, thereby reducing the scale and importance of the defeat at Prosopitis? Thucydides mentions no such development. Did he perhaps make a serious error of omission?

Support for these suggestions has been found in a famous Athenian inscription of the early 450s. This commemorates those Athenians of the Erekhtheid "tribe"[29] who died on the campaigns of a particular year, almost certainly before the end of the Egyptian expedition:

These are the men of the Erekhtheid tribe who died in war, in Cyprus, in Egypt, in Phoenicia, at Halieis, on Aigina, at Megara, in the same year ...[30]

The order of "Cyprus, Egypt, Phoenicia" may be chronological. And yet it is very unlikely that after the defeat at Prosopitis the remnants of the Greek force ventured to Phoenicia, where

Persia's chief naval bases were. So, on the assumption that the order is chronological, it has been argued that a large section of the Delian League's fleet returned to Greece not long after the successful start of the campaign in Egypt, and raided Phoenicia *en route*.[31] Also, Ktesias records 40 (not *c*.200) Greek ships as involved in the Egyptian expedition, which suits the hypothesis that a large proportion of the fleet was withdrawn at an early stage. Ktesias worked at the Persian court and so may have had good access to information.[32] However, he makes demonstrable blunders on other subjects involving Persia; Meiggs has an interesting collection of them, which includes the reversing of the true order of the battles of Salamis and Plataia.[33] We cannot challenge the reliability of Thucydides with the assumption that the erratic Ktesias has correctly represented the size of the Greek fleet in Egypt.

If we assume that a very large fleet, perhaps half or more of all triremes possessed by the Delian League, was lost in Egypt, we have to meet the argument that such a loss would have had obvious and crippling consequences for Athenian power. In assessing this and other inferences in history, one should try where possible to avoid dependence on an intuitive feeling, derived from evidence one does not precisely recall, that *x* 'must have', or 'surely need not have', led to *y*. Instead, there should be a search for particular cases similar to the one under review, with which to test the inference made concerning it. In the case of the defeat in Egypt, perhaps the most useful event for comparison is the annihilation, at Syracuse in 413, of the great armada sent by Athens to conquer Sicily. Thucydides makes clear that the forces sent against Sicily comprised well over 40,000 men, nearly all of whom were eventually killed or captured.[34] Athenian and allied ships lost in the campaign probably amounted to just over 200.[35] An emphatic summary on the thoroughness of this defeat is given by Thucydides, in language interestingly similar to that used by him about the disaster in Egypt.[36] Did the defeat in Sicily "cripple" Athens?

After the Sicilian campaign, Athens remained head of an empire for some eight years. In that period her chief enemy, Sparta, more than once offered terms of peace which would have allowed her to retain the surviving Empire.[37] There were many serious revolts from the Empire in the aftermath of the Sicilian expedition, as factions in the subject states exploited their *kairos*.[38] (We can trace some, though less serious, revolts after

Athens' earlier defeat in Egypt.[39]) Also, Thucydides makes clear that the massive loss of men and ships in Sicily was very important for Athens' capacity to make war.[40] But he does not treat that loss as quite the greatest Athenian setback in the Peloponnesian War. Instead, he says of the plague, which affected Athens in 430–428 and 427/6, "nothing distressed the Athenians and damaged their power more than this",[41] and of the revolt of Euboia in 411, "neither the disaster in Sicily, though it had seemed of great importance at the time, nor anything else to date caused so much fear [i.e. to the Athenians]".[42] None of these three great disasters, the plague, the defeat in Sicily or the loss of Euboia, was followed promptly by Athenian ruin. Even in 411, when *all three* had occurred, Athens still had six years left as an imperial power. There were, of course, important differences between the circumstances of the 450s and those of 413 onwards.[43] But Athens' resilience after the Sicilian disaster seems to tell against the idea that the Egyptian episode of the 450s must have been crippling. Finally, if we were right to suggest that the Egyptian campaign was mounted to some extent as a result of pressure from Athens' allies in the Delian League, that in itself might have helped to restrain unrest within the League, and any challenge to Athenian power, when the campaign had ended in failure.

We may take Thucydides at face value, and assume that the League suffered a great catastrophe in Egypt in the mid-450s. Possible consequences of it will be considered shortly. First, however, attention should be given to events concerning the League which took place in or near mainland Greece while the Egyptian campaign was going on. There was much fighting now between Athens on the one hand and Sparta and allies of hers on the other. (On this see also below, Chapter 4.) In the course of this warfare (and perhaps in, or close to, 458) Athens went to war with Aigina, a large and prosperous island of the Saronic Gulf. With a large navy of its own and an extensive foreign trade, Aigina had long been a rival of Athens. It lay little more than ten miles south-west of the port of Athens, and was clearly visible from it. Aristotle states that the Athenian politician Perikles referred to Aigina as "the eyesore of the Peiraieus".[44] After a crushing naval defeat and a siege, Aigina was forced to join the Delian League and from 454/3 is found paying 30 talents a year in *phoros* (as Meiggs notes,[45] the largest known contribution of any state at the time).

Aigina is the first state recorded as having been forced into the League in spite of its having fought alongside Sparta and Athens against Persia in 480 and 479. In fact the men of Aigina were judged to have fought best of all the Greeks at Salamis.[46] Against Aigina, Athens appears to have used forces of the League. In the naval battle of Aigina, "the allies of both sides" were present to help the Athenians and Aiginetans.[47] The sailors of the Delian League are better candidates for identification here as Athens' allies than are the men of Argos and Thessaly, traditionally land powers. Allies from the League almost certainly fought alongside Athens shortly afterwards at Tanagra in Boiotia, against the Spartans and their allies who had invaded central Greece. Thucydides in this instance makes clear that Athens was attended not only by troops from Argos and Thessaly but also by "the other allies".[48] Confirmation that the League was involved at Tanagra comes from a Spartan dedication, at the shrine of Olympia, of spoils "from the Argives and Athenians and Ionians".[49]

Athens' use of the Delian League to fight Greeks who themselves had impressive records of opposition to Persia marks an important step in the development of the League into an empire. In the Peloponnesian War of 431 onwards, states of the Empire provided a large part of Athens' forces, used for whatever purposes the Athenians chose. These purposes could be remote from the expressed intentions of the League's founders, as when numerous states of the Empire took part in Athens' attempt to conquer Sicily in 415–413.[50] The Egyptian campaign helped to smooth the transition from League to Empire. Meiggs notes that, with the League making its great effort in Egypt against the Persians, war against Athens by the Peloponnesians could be represented as treachery.[51] We may add that such a charge would have been vivid and inevitable if the Athenians learnt now that the Great King had sent an agent to Sparta, to promote an attack on Athens by the Peloponnesians which would cause the Athenians to withdraw their troops from Egypt.[52] The King's agent Megabazos, a Persian sent with a considerable sum of money, may have been a conspicuous figure. Thucydides makes it clear that he arrived at Sparta at a fairly early stage in the Egyptian campaign: early enough, perhaps, for the Athenians to have known of his presence before they invoked the League's forces against Aigina. Megabazos returned to Asia when "his cause was making no progress and the money was being spent in vain": but Thucydides' language suggests that he was allowed to stay at Sparta for some little time,[53] and was not promptly dismissed in accordance with stern Greek patriotism. When they appealed for military aid from the League, the Athenians might express moral indignation concerning the actions, past and anticipated, of Sparta and her allies. They might add the warning that, if Athens did not receive help for her war in Greece, she might have to withdraw her forces from Egypt and leave the eastern Greeks exposed to retaliation from Persia.

Such arguments might be used with special effect concerning the great Spartan campaign to central Greece which culminated at Tanagra. That battle was precipitated by the Athenian construction of Long Walls for Athens itself, linking the city to Peiraieus and the sea (see Chapter 3). Without such walls, the city of Athens might be surrounded and cut off by a Spartan army and the Athenians prevented from sending help when needed to their allies. We know from an episode in 413 that many of Athens' subjects, after prolonged campaigning alongside Athenians, developed an almost suicidal loyalty to them.[54] The possession of a common enemy is often a profoundly cohesive force. The solidarity of the Delian League and later of the Athenian Empire may have owed much to the joint warfare at this period, not only against Persia but also against Greeks at the battles of Aigina, Tanagra and possibly Oinophyta (where, 62 days after Tanagra, Athens won control — for some ten years, as it turned out — of Boiotia[55]). This warfare between the Spartan alliance, mainly composed of Dorian Greeks, and the Delian League, consisting chiefly of Ionians, must have strengthened the feeling that there was a natural opposition between the two linguistic and cultural groups,[56] a feeling which would promote the coherence of the Athenian Empire later, during the Peloponnesian War.[57]

The Athenian Tribute Lists and the consolidation of Athenian power

The period from the mid-450s to the mid-440s contained several steps in the shift from League to Empire. As we shall see, it may have been within this period that the Athenians first officially described their allies (or some of them) as "the cities which the Athenians control". But the transition, even as the Athenians recognised it, cannot be tidily confined to this period of ten years or so. And modern notions of what constitutes an empire rather than a league are probably so various and imprecise that, even if we were fully informed on the history of the Greeks in this period (which we plainly are not), we could not agree on a point at which Empire succeeded League.

In the Athenian year 454/3 there began the series of inscriptions nowadays called the Athenian Tribute Lists (ATLs). Strictly speaking, these record, as we have seen, the fraction of the *phoros*, one sixtieth, which was paid to the góddess Athena at Athens. It is now widely assumed that 454/3 was also the year in which the accumulated treasure of the Delian League was moved from Delos to Athens.[58] That treasure certainly appears to have been at the Athenians' disposal by 447; inscriptions make clear that the building of the Parthenon began then,[59] and there is evidence (on which see Chapter 3) that the construction was financed from the League's treasure. Plutarch suggests that protection of the treasure from Persia was given by Athenians as a reason for its transfer.[60] After their victory in Egypt, the Persians might raid Delos, even if the treasury there was sited in a sacred precinct; they had notoriously looted Greek temples in 480.[61] Whenever it was made, the decision that the *phoros* should be taken to Athens, rather than to Delos, must have been widely seen as a symbol of Athens' growing domination. Thucydides notes, in connection with the revolt of Naxos (*c.*470), that the *phoros* was in effect strengthening the navy of Athens at the expense of the power of the allies.[62] Numerous allies were no doubt aware of this. But the new procedure of taking the *phoros* directly to Athens was probably viewed as more than a consolidation or acknowledgement of a well-established pattern. Like many political developments, it would be examined for its *predictive* significance. Further assertions of Athenian power might seem likely to follow. In fact, Athens before long seems to have claimed the right to spend the *phoros* on whatever she chose, provided that the allies were defended.[63]

Once we have the ATLs, we are in a far better position than before to estimate the number of states paying *phoros* at different periods and to identify those in revolt. Meiggs has shown how the evidence of the Lists may be exploited, with an ingenious argument that Miletos and Erythrai, two important states of Ionia, were in revolt soon after the defeat in Egypt.[64] He observes that in the first list, for 454/3, the name of Miletos does not occur in the place where it might be expected, next to the names of

Leros and Teikhioussa, two nearby communities which, when they appear in the ATLs, are normally linked with Miletos in payment of *phoros*. Erythrai, similarly, is missing from the list for 453/2. All ATLs are fragmentary, and it may be that the names of Miletos and Erythrai were recorded, on parts of the inscriptions now lost. Meiggs, however, has a more attractive explanation of their absence. He notes that, while the name of Erythrai is absent from the surviving list of 453/2, the associated nearby town of Boutheia is recorded under that year as having paid eighteen times as much in *phoros* as it normally did later, 3 talents instead of 1,000 *drakhmai*. Meiggs suggests that Erythraians loyal to Athens had gathered in Boutheia, while those who remained in Erythrai were in revolt. As we shall see (Chapter 3), many Greek communities later were profoundly divided by the question whether to secede from the Athenian Empire. And division within a *polis* often caused one faction to migrate into temporary exile nearby. (At Athens itself, during the troubles of 404–403, first a democratic faction migrated in this way, then an oligarchic one.[65]) A similar suggestion is made concerning Miletos. The communities of Leros and Teikhioussa, close to Miletos and normally linked with it politically, are only named occasionally on other ATLs. But in the list for 454/3, while Miletos itself is not named, payments are recorded from "Milesians in Leros" and "Milesians in Teikhioussa". The evidence again suggests a political split over loyalty to the Delian League, followed by temporary migration. Erythrai reappears in the list of 450/49 and Miletos rather earlier, in 452/1. In both cases military action by Athens may have been involved,[66] to restore the loyalists at the expense of their opponents.

Meiggs' theory is attractive partly because it conforms with an important rule of thumb, used in explanation in both the human and physical sciences, the rule known as Occam's Razor. In its classic formulation, by the medieval philosopher William of Occam, it is that 'The existence of things should not be assumed beyond what is necessary.' The rule requires that explanation be kept as economical as possible. In the present case one might assume that the temporary disappearances of Miletos and Erythrai from the ATLs resulted accidentally from the damage done over the years to the inscriptions. In that case, separate explanations would of course be presumed for the references to Boutheia, Leros and Teikhioussa. But Meiggs's account deals with these phenomena not with a plurality of separate explanations, but economically, with a unified hypothesis supportable by analogies from elsewhere in Greek history.

A lost Athenian inscription, known from an imperfect copy of the early nineteenth century, reflects upheavals at Erythrai.[67] It reveals that some citizens of Erythrai have taken refuge with the Persians; an Athenian garrison commander (*phrourarkhos*) has been installed; other Athenian officials (*episkopoi*, inspectors) are to ensure that a governing council (*boulē*) is chosen by lot; the council members are to swear to serve the interests of the general mass (*plēthos*) of citizens of Erythrai, of Athens and of the allies, and not to secede. The surviving text of this inscription (often referred to as 'the Erythrai Decree') does not contain a date. But the reference to loyalty to Athens *and* the allies has suggested the time of the Delian League rather than the period of the developed Empire, when Athens was less likely to refer to the allies as apparently on a par with herself. For that reason, and so as not to assume the existence of an additional episode of unrest at Erythrai in the time of the Delian League, in contravention of Occam's Razor,[68] we may wish, with Meiggs and others, to identify the circumstances of this decree with those of the late 450s.

The Erythrai Decree reflects forms of Athenian policy which were regular in the developed Empire. *Dēmokratia* is set up, or protected, in the states controlled by Athens. The choice of officials by lot, as mentioned in the Erythrai Decree, was a distinctively democratic device, favouring the appointment of ordinary, poor, citizens.[69] Aristotle noted that election in effect was oligarchic, favouring the rich.[70] The oath to serve the *plēthos* of Erythrai and the *plēthos* of Athens and of the allies also emphatically reflects democratic ideals; *plēthos* was a regular term for the great mass of poor citizens,[71] as distinct from the wealthy few (*oligoi*). The installation of political inspectors and of a garrison at Erythrai belongs to a pattern familiar from the later empire. Athenian officials serving in the Empire numbered, at one stage, some 700, according to the text of the Aristotelian *Ath. Pol.*[72] This figure should be compared with the number of states in the Empire, probably on average well under 250 in the decades before 413. Many of these communities were tiny. In the year 433/2, for which the ATL is unusually well preserved, at least 13 communities paid 500 *drakhmai* or less, while at least 56 others paid between 501 and 3,000 *drakhmai*.[73] A single labourer at Athens in the late fifth century might earn 300 *drakhmai* or more in a year.[74] If the total of 700 officials is approximately right,

several hundred at least were probably concentrated in the few
large states from which Athens received a big income and which
might contain dissidents with realistic ambitions to revolt. (In
433/2 at least 21 states paid five talents, i.e. 30,000 *drakhmai*, or
more. In the Peloponnesian War the sums at stake, and the
chances of revolt, increased.) We should, however, be somewhat
suspicious of the figure of 700. In the Greek text which contains
it, the same figure appears in a different connection shortly
before. There is an obvious chance that it has wrongly been
copied twice by an inattentive scribe at some stage in the
transmission of the text, by a process familiar to anyone who has
done extensive copying and known to textual critics as 'dittography'.

The use by Athens of garrisons,[75] political inspectors and also
of notably pro-Athenian politicians among the allies themselves[76]
reflects in part the great cost of capturing an allied town by siege,
once it had revolted. In 440–439 the war to conquer Samos after
its revolt cost over 1,200 talents.[77] The siege of Poteidaia, after its
secession in 432, cost 2,000 or more.[78] (Athens' public income
from the Empire, including *phoros*, may have amounted to some
600 talents per annum at this period.[79]) Siegecraft was unsophisti-
cated, and to prevent revolts was no doubt thought much cheaper
than to remedy them. Thucydides notes, in connection with the
year 427, that the cities of Ionia were unwalled.[80] The significance
of this is disputed; some have seen it as a concession made by
Athens to Persia.[81] However, it is also possible that the various
city walls had been removed as an Athenian precaution against
revolt.[82]

The probable revolts of Erythrai and Miletos in the late 450s
may have reflected a more widespread sense of Athenian
weakness in the aftermath of the Egyptian defeat.[83] If so, this was
no doubt countered to some extent by a new expedition against
the Persian empire, Kimon's last campaign — to Cyprus. The
reappearance of this veteran and successful opponent of the Great
King must in itself have encouraged the allies. The campaign to
Cyprus led, as we have seen (Chapter 1), to victories over Persian
forces on sea and land. The question of how the Athenians
reacted to these victories, and to Kimon's death shortly before
them, involves one of the most notorious problems of Greek
history. Did Athens (perhaps in 450–449) make a formal peace
with Persia, the so-called Peace of Kallias?

The Peace of Kallias

Our sources on this question are sadly defective and contradictory, and modern scholarly literature is voluminous in its attempts to account for them. Meiggs writes drily that "statistically an article on the Peace of Kallias can be expected every two years",[84] while himself adding a chapter and a long appendix on the subject. The controversy over whether there was a formal peace threatens to become self-sustaining, with so much modern work already in print that almost any classical scholar could find enough to criticise in it to form the basis of a further article. We can be fairly sure, from the silence of our sources, that large-scale hostilities between Athens and Persia ceased after Kimon's last expedition. Thucydides reports a speaker as referring (in 428) to the Athenians' having relaxed their enmity towards the Persians,[85] and there is good evidence of trade between Athens and the Persian empire in the 420s and later.[86] After 413 Persia used the Spartan fleet as a proxy for fighting Athens in the Aegean. But in spite of an occasional fear that the Persian fleet was about to intervene there,[87] after Kimon's last campaign the ships of Persia and Athens are never again recorded as having met in battle in the fifth century. The question whether this peace, in its early years, rested on a formal agreement is not a minor detail. If there was a peace treaty between these two powers, the various members of the Delian League must have learnt of it promptly. For one thing, the openness of proceedings in the Athenian assembly, which would have to approve the treaty, made secret agreements impossible.[88] League members, on learning of such a treaty, would have realised that part, at least, of the original basis of the League was being removed. Ravaging the Persian empire would no longer be permissible, and yet the need to equip the League to make such raids had provided a justification for the payment of *phoros*.[89] Athens' continuing to demand *phoros* after the Peace of Kallias would have been "a vital stage in the development out of Confederacy into Empire".[90]

The earliest surviving passage which is generally agreed to refer to the Peace is in a work of the Athenian speech-writer Isokrates, of 380.[91] He wrote of Athens' having by formal agreement limited the king of Persia's empire, and prevented him from sending ships into certain areas. Later Athenian orators, and other Greek writers, treated the Peace as historical, on occasion adding details on the matter of frontiers which conflict with those given by

49

Isokrates.[92] Diodorus Siculus (probably drawing his information from a fourth century writer, Ephoros) wrote of the Athenians *and their allies* making a peace treaty with Persia, whereby governors ('satraps') of Persian provinces were forbidden to come within three days' journey of the coast, Persian warships were excluded from specified areas, and the Athenians agreed not to campaign against the king's territory.[93] He records the treaty under the year 450/49, makes it swiftly follow the campaign to Cyprus, and names Kallias son of Hipponikos as the leading Athenian ambassador in the mission to Persia which concluded it.

Not only the orators but also Ephoros took in general a pro-Athenian line.[94] The Peace of Kallias was represented in the fourth-century as a glorious Athenian achievement, and contrasted with the Peace of Antalkidas of 387, whereby the Greeks under Spartan leadership allowed a revived Persia far greater influence over Greek actions.[95] A fourth-century writer who took a much less generous view of the Athenian democracy and its attainments was Theopompos of Khios.[96] Two brief excerpts from his work make clear that he condemned as a forgery the text of a treaty between the Athenians and the Persians.[97] We have evidence from elsewhere that the text of official Athenian documents could be forged or tampered with,[98] and Theopompos' opinion has long been taken as a very serious objection to the reality of the Peace of Kallias. However, one of the excerpts from Theopompos does not make clear which treaty between Athens and Persia he had in mind, while the other refers to the treaty made "with King Darius". Now, King Darius II came to the throne in 424–423. There is some evidence, again involving tangled questions, that Athens made, or renewed, a treaty of peace with him.[99] But the Peace of Kallias, if historical, belonged to the reign of his predecessor, Artaxerxes. We cannot, then, assume that Theopompos was referring to the Peace of Kallias. Some scholars have suggested that the reference to Darius was not made by Theopompos but was added by some mistaken copier of his work, Theopompos himself having meant to refer to the time of Artaxerxes.[100] The text of his work, as excerpted by another writer, is certainly not fully trustworthy, but here, as usually elsewhere, we should work from the text that survives. Theopompos objected that the text of the peace treaty was inscribed in Ionic, and not in Attic, lettering. Presumably he argued from the fact that Ionic script only became normal for Athenian documents in the last decade of the fifth century, contending that the inscription was thus made much later than the treaty allegedly was, and that the treaty in consequence should be regarded as a fiction. We cannot tell whether this was Theopompos' only argument against the reality of whatever treaty he had in mind. But it has often been found unconvincing. Several inscriptions in Ionic letters are known from earlier parts of the fifth century than its last decade,[101] and since a treaty with Persia particularly concerned the Ionians, the Athenians might have had good reason for recording it in that script rather than their own.[102]

The strongest argument against the historicity of the Peace of Kallias is that Thucydides does not mention it. Even D. S. Stockton, who assembles perhaps the most effective modern case against the Peace,[103] does not convey the full significance of this; the formal ending of warfare with Persia would have fallen within Thucydides' scope, because at I 97 1 he commits himself to giving an outline of that warfare. We know that Thucydides occasionally omits important information, even within his main topic, the Peloponnesian War; best known, perhaps, is his failure to mention the very large increase in *phoros* which Athens demanded from 425 onwards.[104] But such demonstrable omissions by Thucydides are rare. On the other hand, it is also uncommon for several ancient writers to agree on the reality of a conspicuous public event within the historical period which demonstrably did not occur. Weighing the silence of Thucydides against the positive testimony of the fourth-century politicians and Ephoros leaves us, perhaps, in an impasse. We should, however, examine a positive fifth-century reference to Kallias which may tilt the balance in favour of the Peace.

Herodotos gives an account, which he personally neither accepts nor rejects, of an embassy from Argos to the court of Persia.[105] The Argive representatives asked King Artaxerxes whether the friendship which their city had made with King Xerxes was still accepted by him, or whether he now regarded the Argives as enemies. Artaxerxes replied that the friendship was still very much in existence, and that he regarded no city as more friendly than Argos. By chance, an embassy from Athens, consisting of Kallias son of Hipponikos and others, was at the Persian court at the same time "on other business", in Herodotos' tantalisingly vague phrase. Was this business the making of the Peace of Kallias? Establishing a date is crucial. Scholars have commonly believed that the likeliest time for these embassies to have occurred is near the start of Artaxerxes' reign, when the validity of pre-existing relations was bound to come under review.[106] Artaxerxes began to rule in 465–464,[107] some 15 years before the period to which the Peace would belong. However, H. W. Wade-Gery argued that the two embassies belonged to that later period, and that Kallias' embassy could have made the Peace:[108] his argument deserves to be restated, and may perhaps be reinforced.

Wade-Gery was impressed by the reported question whether the Argives were regarded as enemies by the King. He suggested that it was more likely to be asked at the end of the 450s than 15 years earlier. By the end of the 450s the Argives could reasonably wonder whether their alliance with Athens had angered Persia. The Persians, as we saw, had been trying to persuade Sparta to attack Athens, while Argos had in effect obstructed this by defending the Athenians. In the mid-460s, on the other hand, Argos would have no reason for fearing that Persia was hostile, so far as we know. Rather, Argos' hostility to Sparta at that earlier period might seem welcome to Persia, as a distraction to the former leader of anti-Persian resistance. Probably in 451 or 450, Argos abandoned the alliance with Athens, and made a peace treaty for 30 years with Sparta.[109] Argos' evident anxiety about her relations with Sparta might well lead her to explore then the possibility of Persian support. And her break with Athens would explain why Artaxerxes gave the Argives so friendly a reply. A date at the end of the 450s may indeed seem best, for the Argive embassy and so for that of Kallias.

Stockton properly asks why, if Kallias was in Persia to make peace, the account reported by Herodotos should have referred to his mission as concerned with "other business".[110] For in that case the Argives' business would have been very similar. An answer may be available, if we look at the *context* of the remark about "other business". The account of the Argive embassy, which Herodotos reports, seeks to illustrate Argos' failure to oppose the Persians in 480–479. Its tone is plainly anti-Argive, and Kallias' embassy seems to have been mentioned only to explain how other Greeks learnt of Argos' friendship with the Persians. It would have seriously interfered with the purpose of the account, to vilify Argos for not resisting Persia, if there had been a clear reference in this context to Athens' seeking peace with the Great King, albeit at a much later date.

It may seem, then, that there is fifth-century evidence for

Kallias' negotiating with the King of Persia at the period to which, on other evidence, the Peace may seem to belong. The case for the Peace may be rather stronger than the case against. And even if there was no formal peace in, or near, 450–449, there is a chance that something occurred which for practical purposes was rather similar — an understanding within the Delian League that there would be no further aggression against Persia.

Plutarch records an Athenian decree, passed on the motion of Perikles, inviting other Greek states to take part in a congress at Athens. This was to discuss "the Greek shrines which the barbarians burnt, the sacrifices vowed to the gods during the war against the barbarians and now owed [by the Greeks] on behalf of Greece, and the sea — how all may sail in security and keep the peace".[111] We hear of this decree from no other source, and Plutarch gives no clear indication of its precise date. However, if peace with Persia was made in, or close to, 450–449, the terms of this decree would fit remarkably well with Athens' needs immediately thereafter.[112] In inviting "all the Greeks, wherever they lived, in Europe or Asia" to the congress, Athens could advertise a new justification for continuing to demand *phoros*: the need to fund a large Athenian fleet to police the seas, perhaps to suppress piracy and to guard against a surprise attack from Persia.[113] Also, religious building on a large scale recommenced in Athens at this period, seemingly from funds accumulated over the years by the Delian League. The Athenians might wish to propagate a defence of this. A plausible defence was certainly at hand; Athens had suffered more than most states from the Persian destruction of temples. Plutarch reports that twenty men, "over fifty years old",[114] were sent from Athens to tour Greece with invitations. His precise and lengthy details of the areas assigned to the various envoys suggest that he or his source had read the text of the decree,[115] which would be bound to go into such detail, in the way that most literary accounts would not. In the event, the congress did not take place; the Spartans, it was said, opposed it. But the Athenians surely anticipated this. We may suspect that from the first they had no great hopes that the congress would become a reality.[116] Greeks were familiar with the idea that a diplomatic proposal could be made with the expectation, or even the hope, that it would be rejected — leaving the proposer in a good light, and the rejecter in a bad one.[117] (Such proposals are commonplace in modern diplomacy and in bargaining over wages.) Whatever was to become of the congress at Athens, invitations to it would create interested audiences around Greece, to which the Athenian envoys could put their city's arguments for her continuing domination of the allies and their *phoros*.

Assuming that the Congress Decree existed, as Plutarch reports, and that it belongs in 450 or 449, we may be able to explain why there may have been a year's pause in the collection of *phoros*, in 449/8. If the Athenians indeed proposed a congress to discuss the continuation of *phoros*, tact may have required that they appeared not to prejudge its outcome, by insisting meanwhile upon payments. Since some notice of any moratorium would have been needed, we might expect that a proposal for a congress in 450/49 would give rise to a lack of *phoros* payments in the following year.[118] However, the argument that there was such a moratorium is somewhat insecure; it derives from there being, apparently, too little space available in the ATLs inscribed over the period 449/8 – 447/6 to have accommodated the lists of three years.[119] Considering the doubt over the existence of the Peace of Kallias, over the timing, at least, of the Congress Decree, and over the existence and timing of this pause in *phoros* collection, we should be reluctant to advance a theory which requires the existence and dating of all three. It may be more profitable to turn to the analysis of a process which undoubtedly occurred, and perhaps gave rise to a more colourful controversy than is usually realised — the building of the Parthenon.

Notes

1. Thuc. I 102; II 27 2; IV 56 2; III 54 5; cf. Xen. *Hell.* V 2 3, Gomme, *HCT*, I, 300.
2. Thuc. I 102 3.
3. The Spartans had claimed that the Athenians were no longer needed; Thuc., ibid.
4. Thuc. I 102 4.
5. For references, see de Ste. Croix, *Origins*, 182–3, nn. 53–4.
6. It may perhaps be suspected that the Athenians were mainly concerned with how this "cruel" decision might appear to other Greeks. If so, that would relocate the influential moralising.
7. When, in 425, a group of Spartans chose to surrender rather than to die fighting against overwhelming opposition, more surprise was caused in Greece than by any other event of the Peloponnesian War, according to Thuc. IV 40 1. The story of Spartan heroism at Thermopylai, in 480, had no doubt created expectations of extreme

valour.

8. See Chapter 4.

9. Hdt. VII 148–52.

10. Ibid., IX 31, cf. VII 132.

11. These allies and subjects included Argos, Thessaly, Megara, Akhaia, Troizen, Phokis and Opuntian Locrians.

12. Compare the argument attributed by Thucydides to an Athenian speaker in 416: the Aegean island of Melos could not be allowed to stay independent of Athens, because that would signal Athenian weakness; Thuc. V 95.

13. Thuc. I 23 6.

14. *Annals* XIV 31.

15. Thuc. I 102 4 suggests that the alliance with Argos preceded that with Thessaly, though perhaps only by a short time.

16. Hdt. V 103.

17. Thucydides begins I 103 by describing the end of the helot revolt and Athens' accommodation, "from hatred of the Spartans", of the helots who survived. There is, however, much doubt as to when these events took place; see Chapter 4.

18. Thuc. I 105 4. By this time other Athenian troops were engaged at Aigina; Thuc., ibid.

19. Thuc. I 104 1.

20. Meiggs, *AE*, 95.

21. Compare the similarly loaded expression, 'kicking a man when he's down'.

22. Xen. *Hell.* V 2 25–36, 4 1.

23. Ibid., V 4 1; Xenophon himself, a good friend of Sparta, expresses strong disapproval.

24. The nineteenth-century Irish nationalist Daniel O'Connell is said to have used the phrase 'England's difficulty is Ireland's opportunity'.

25. Ktesias 63f.

26. Thuc. I 104, 109–10.

27. Hdt. VII 184, VIII 17; Thuc. VI 8 1 with 31 3; J. S. Morrison and R. T. Williams, *Greek oared ships*, 128ff. On possible changes introduced by Kimon, see Chapter 1.

28. Gomme, *HCT*, I, 322.

29. Athenian citizens were classified for certain administrative purposes into ten *phylai* (traditionally translated as 'tribes'), membership of each tribe being hereditary.

30. The Greek text may be found in Meiggs-Lewis, no. 33.

31. *ATL*, III, 174–5.

32. Diod. II 32 4.

33. Meiggs, *AE*, 106–7, 475.

34. Thuc. VII 75 5 for the total of "not less than 40,000" at the end of the campaign. Many others had already died at earlier stages of the expedition. For the thoroughness of the Athenian defeat in Sicily, see especially Thuc. VII 87 and compare II 65 12.

35. 160 of these were Athenian ships; Thuc. VI 43, VII 20 1f, 42 1.

36. Thuc. VII 87 6; Meiggs, *AE*, 105.

37. Diod. XIII 52 (410 BC); Aristotle cited by scholiast on Aristoph.

Frogs, 1532 (406 BC).

38. Among the most important were the revolts of Khios, Lesbos, Knidos, Rhodes, Byzantion and Euboia; Thuc. VIII 5, 35, 44, 80, 95. A majority of all the allies revolted at this period, according to Thuc. II 65 12.

39. See below.

40. Thuc. II 65 12, VIII 1.

41. Thuc. III 87 2.

42. Thuc. VIII 96 1; compare 95 1 on the importance of Euboia at the time.

43. There was no doubt some difference in the proportion of Athenian warships lost in the 450s, as compared with 413. (More than half of Athens' ships were involved in the Sicilian disaster; Thuc. II 65 12. We have no comparable statement for the 450s.) Also, the widespread social conflict within Greek cities during the Peloponnesian War created a pressure upon wealthy individuals to lead revolts from Athens, which had not, so far as we know, existed in the 450s.

44. Arist., *Rhet.* III 10 7, cf. Plut. *Life of Perikles*, VIII. Grote commented, "we may be sure that Peiraeus, grown into a vast fortified port within the existing generation, was in a much stronger degree the eyesore of Aegina" (*A history of Greece*, V, Ch. 45). Perikles' remark, if historical, need not have belonged to the 450s, however. There were circumstances in 431 which could have elicited it; see Chapter 5.

45. Meiggs, *AE*, 98.

46. Hdt. VIII 93, 122. Earlier, in the 490s, Aigina had submitted to Persia (ibid., VI 49), but hostile reference to this fact would have little force by the 450s, in the light of Aigina's performance at Salamis.

47. Thuc. I 105 2.

48. Thuc. I 107 5.

49. Pausan. V 10 4, Meiggs-Lewis, no. 36.

50. Thuc. VII 57. On Athens' use of mercenary sailors from abroad, see M. Amit, *Athens and the sea*, 30–49, Meiggs, *AE*, 439–41.

51. Meiggs, *AE*, 98.

52. Thuc. I 109 2f.

53. Ibid.

54. In the obviously desperate circumstances of the end of the Sicilian expedition, it seems that a majority of Athens' allies refused advantageous terms of surrender which would have involved abandoning the Athenians; Thuc. VII 82 1 and Gomme-Andrewes-Dover, *HCT*, IV, 396; G. E. M. de Ste. Croix, *Historia*, III (1954–5), 11.

55. Thucydides does not say that Athens' allies were at Oinophyta, but he mentions their presence at Tanagra shortly before, and we have seen (in Chapter 1, n. 103) that having once mentioned the Athenians and their allies he can refer to both together simply as 'the Athenians'; he may have done so in the case of Oinophyta. On Athens' domination of Boiotia, see Gomme, *HCT*, I, 318, Meiggs, *AE*, 99–100, 176–7.

56. See Chapter 1, n. 59. The Boiotians, however, belonged culturally to the Aiolian group, which also included several communities within the Delian League — those of Lesbos and the neighbouring mainland.

57. Compare, for example, Thuc. VI 82, Gomme-Andrewes-Dover, *HCT*, IV, 220, 433.

58. Though contrast W. K. Pritchett, *Historia*, XVIII (1969), 19.

59. For the texts of these inscriptions, see *IG*, I², nos. 339–53.

60. Plut. *Life of Perikles*, XII.

61. E.g. Hdt. VIII 33–53, Aiskhylos, *Persians*, 809–10. Compare Hdt. VI 101 for an earlier episode.

62. Thuc. I 99.

63. Plut. *Life of Perikles*, XII.

64. Meiggs, *AE*, 112–18.

65. Aristotle (*Politics* 1300a) tells of a case at Megara in which to have participated in a particular migration became a formal qualification for office.

66. Meiggs, *JHS*, LXIII (1943), 25–7; J. P. Barron, *JHS*, LXXXII (1962), 1–6 (on Miletos).

67. Meiggs-Lewis, no. 40. For bibliography on this decree, Meiggs, *AE*, 113, n. 1.

68. See, however, Meiggs, *AE*, 421–2. Erythrai did revolt again, many years after the end of the Delian League, in 412; Thuc. VIII 14 2.

69. Arist. *Pol.* 1273a, 1274a, 1294b, 1317b. The poor were everywhere in the majority; ibid. 1279b.

70. Ibid., 1294b, and see below, Chapter 7.

71. The term was used regularly in addressing a group which represented the *dēmokratia* of Athens; *to plēthos to hymeteron*, 'the general body of your citizens' (e.g., Plat. *Apology* 31c). For the *plēthos* contrasted with "the few", see, e.g., Thuc. V 84 3.

72. [Arist.] *Ath. Pol.* ch. 24.

73. That is, if we accept the restorations in Meiggs' tabulation of *phoros* payments (Meiggs, *AE*, 540–59).

74. See the accounts of wages paid to workers on the temple known as the Erekhtheion; *IG* I ², 374. Sailors with the Sicilian expedition were each paid one *drakhmē* or more per day, which may perhaps have been an unusually high rate; Thuc. VI 8 1, 31 and Gomme-Andrewes-Dover, *HCT*, IV, 293–5.

75. On this see A. S. Nease, *Phoenix*, III (1949), 102–11.

76. See Chapter 3.

77. Gomme, *HCT*, I, 355–6 and references there given.

78. Thuc. II 70 2.

79. Thuc. II 13 3, with Gomme, *HCT*, II, 17–18.

80. Thuc. III 33 2.

81. See H. T. Wade-Gery, *Essays in Greek history*, 219.

82. Meiggs, *AE*, 150. Athens ordered the removal of walls after suppressing the revolts of Thasos (in the late 460s) and Samos (in 439); Thuc. I 101 3, 117 3. Compare Potidaia; Thuc. I 56 2.

83. Meiggs, *AE*, 118–24.

84. Ibid., 598. See now E. Badian, *JHS*, CVII (1987), 1–39.

85. Thuc. III 10 4.

86. Thuc. II 69, VIII 1 35; Old Oligarch II 7; Meiggs, *AE*, 267–9.

87. Thuc. I 116 3, VIII 87–8.

88. G. E. M. de Ste. Croix, *CQ*, n.s., XIII (1963), 110–19.

89. Thuc. I 96 1.
90. The phrase quoted is from D. Stockton, *Historia*, VIII (1959), 65.
91. Isok. IV 118, 120.
92. On this conflict of information, and on the general question of the Peace, see Wade-Gery, *Essays in Greek history*, 201–32; Meiggs, *AE*, Ch. 8 and app. 8; de Ste. Croix, *Origins*, app. 7.
93. Diod. XII 4.
94. On Ephoros' bias, see G. L. Barber, *The historian Ephoros*, 90ff. and app. 9.
95. Isok. IV 120; compare Dem. XV 29.
96. Gomme, *HCT*, I, 46–9.
97. These excerpts, in Greek, are quoted in Meiggs, *AE*, 488–9.
98. See especially Lysias XXX 3 and D. M. Lewis, *CQ*, n.s., XI (1961), 61; C. Habicht, *Hermes*, LXXXIX (1961), 1–35; Meiggs, *AE*, app. 10.
99. On this see especially Wade-Gery, op.cit., 207–11; Gomme, *HCT*, I, 333–4; Stockton, art. cit., 72–9.
100. E.g., Stockton, art. cit., 62.
101. Wade-Gery, op. cit., 206; B. D. Meritt, *Hesperia*, XIII (1944), 215.
102. Grote, *A history of Greece*, V, 45. See Meiggs, *AE*, 137–8, for the use in the mid-fifth century of Ionic script, on Athenian inscriptions of particular concern to the allies of Athens.
103. Stockton, art. cit., 61–79.
104. See below, Chapter 5.
105. Hdt. VII 151–2.
106. For example, E. M. Walker in *CAH*, V, 470. Meiggs, too, dissociates this embassy from the making of the Peace of Kallias; *AE*, 93.
107. R. A. Parker and W. H. Dubberstein, *Babylonian chronology*, 17f.
108. *Essays in Greek history*, 228–9.
109. Thucydides states that in 421 a 30–year peace treaty between Argos and Sparta was about to expire; V 14 4, 28.
110. Stockton, art. cit., 69 n. 20; Meiggs, *AE*, 93, has a similar objection.
111. Plut. *Life of Perikles*, XVII.
112. Wade-Gery, *Hesperia*, XIV (1945), 216ff.
113. On piracy, see below, Chapter 3. On surviving fears of Persian attack, above n. 87.
114. This precise and unusual specification as to age would make remarkably good sense if the decree was indeed issued in 450 or soon afterwards. For in that case every envoy would have been of at least the minimum age (*c.* 20) to fight the Persians in 480–79.
115. A collection of Athenian decrees was published by Krateros; Plutarch refers to it at *Life of Aristeides* XXVI, *Life of Kimon, XIII*.
116. H. Nesselhauf, *Klio*, Beiheft XXX (1933), 33.
117. Hdt. VII 150.
118. Against any moratorium, see de Ste. Croix, *Origins*, 312.
119. Meiggs-Lewis, 133ff. Compare A. W. Gomme, *Classical Review*, LIV (1940), 66.

3
The Athenian Empire

The building of the Parthenon

In the early years of their Empire, Athenians created a building
which to modern tastes is perhaps the most satisfying work of art
of Antiquity, the temple of Athena known as the Parthenon.
When we look for evidence of how contemporary Athenians
viewed the building, there is a special need to guard against
wishful thinking. Very little is heard about the Parthenon from
ancient writers:[1] we should like to be able to believe what we do
hear, rather than admit ignorance on so alluring a topic. There are
some surviving building accounts concerning the Parthenon,
inscribed on stone at Athens.[2] These make clear that the building
began in 447, and reveal something of the bureaucracy which
controlled the work, but do not help us much in reconstructing
any special ideals or enthusiasms connected with the new temple.[3]
Some stray remarks by a literary commentator of the second
century AD may indicate that it was in 450/49 that the Athenians
prepared to use accumulated funds from the Delian League for
the building.[4] But the only account of contemporary attitudes to
the building project, a highly colourful account, is contained in
Plutarch's *Life of Perikles*.[5] Plutarch depicts Perikles as cham-
pioning the policy of funding Athenian buildings from the
treasure of the Delian League, and as meeting lively opposition
from other Athenians, seemingly led by Thucydides son of
Melesias (a politician perhaps related to Thucydides the historian[6]).

It is argued by A. Andrewes that Plutarch's account of this
conflict is "worthless", that in the main it is not based on
contemporary records or memories, but reflects rhetorical reconstruction of a later age, with anachronism from the Roman

59

period.[7] Now we know that Plutarch was not able to draw on any contemporary and systematic history of the period, other than that of Thucydides, who makes no mention of controversy over Athenian building. And there are points which give some plausibility to Andrewes' view. For example, Plutarch represents Perikles as arguing that Athens could reasonably decide for herself what to do with money from the League, so long as Athenians succeeded in keeping the Persians away, while the allies contributed "not a horse, not a ship, not a hoplite but only money".[8] In reality, we know that some states were still contributing ships and men rather than money: Khios, Lesbos and Samos.[9] However, Andrewes seems to overstate his case. He shows that Thucydides son of Melesias may well have had a creditable military record, and implies that Plutarch misrepresents him as a civilian, with "no record in the field".[10] But Plutarch does not do this; he states that Thucydides son of Melesias was "less of a warrior than Kimon, but more of a civilian politician", which is very different. There were probably many Athenian politicians with good military records which fell short of Kimon's.[11] The misrepresentations in Plutarch's account seem insufficient to require us to reject it in its entirety. Even the exaggeration about horses, ships and hoplites may faithfully reflect fifth-century rhetoric. Thucydides himself reports a speech with a distortion which would have been hardly less obvious to a contemporary audience. He shows an Athenian speaker claiming that Athens fought alone against the Persians at Marathon,[12] although it was well known that she was supported in the battle by allies from Plataia.[13]

On the other hand, there are signs, normally overlooked, that Plutarch's account reflects ideas of the classical period and may indeed derive from that time. Enemies of Perikles stated, according to Plutarch, that

> Greece seems to be wilfully degraded with a terrible degrading arrogance and to be the victim of blatant tyranny, as she sees us [Athenians] using what she contributed under necessity for the war to gild our city and to give her a pretty face, like an *alazōn* woman, decked out with expensive stones and statues and thousand-talent temples.[14]

This passage, with its famous comparison of Athens to a woman, has traditionally been misunderstood. The word *alazōn*, left untranslated in the above version, is translated variously by modern scholars. A. R. Burn takes it to mean a *vain* woman; Meiggs translates '*wanton* woman'.[15] In other contexts, however, the meaning of this word is not in dispute; it means 'pretentious', 'falsely boastful'.[16] Why has it not been given its normal meaning, in translations of this passage? As we have seen elsewhere (Chapter 1), there is a common error of perception which involves assimilating the unfamiliar to the familiar. Such an error may have occurred in the present case. The picture of a woman deceitfully putting on a pretty face may have suggested the modern cliché 'tarting up'; this would explain why Meiggs has imported the idea of wantonness, which is not present in Plutarch's Greek. Until the re-appearance of feminism around 1970, few scholars were concerned to gain a detailed knowledge of the history of Greek women.[17] One effect of such knowledge may be to shed renewed light on how Greek ideas of feminine behaviour were applied to the great building programme at Athens.

Xenophon, an Athenian who wrote in the first half of the fourth century, told of a wife who tried to make herself more attractive to her husband. This woman is described as having come from a sheltered background, and as married to a man of some standing.[18] Far from behaving as a whore, she is of almost exemplary virtue.[19] The cosmetic techniques which she uses, until admonished by a philosophic husband, are the application of white lead to suggest fair skin, of red dye from the plant alkanet (perhaps for the cheeks), and the wearing of built-up shoes.[20] The white and red make-up is also mentioned by the comic poet Aristophanes, in connection with Athenian women of a less respected class.[21] The effect of her cosmetics on Xenophon's lady corresponds interestingly with the effect which the Parthenon might have on the view of Athens. In the first place, the new temple made the Akropolis slightly taller, as elevated shoes would do to a woman. The sculpture of the Parthenon was brightly painted, in red and other colours,[22] and so might recall a woman's colourful make-up. But the main visual effect of the temple would probably come from the glittering newly-cut marble of its columns; one Greek word for marble, *marmaros*, was derived from the verb *marmairein*, 'to glitter'. The main body of make-up on a woman's face would be, correspondingly, white.

Plutarch uses the phrase 'like a deceitful woman' to amplify the reference to "putting on a pretty face".[23] It is noteworthy that, of all the fine Athenian buildings of the mid-fifth century, the Parthenon, because of its scale and position, would be the likeliest to be seen as Athens' new "face".[24] If Plutarch, or rather his ultimate source, had the Parthenon particularly in mind, that would fit well with the implication that the party of Thucydides son of Melesias was responsible for this colourful rhetoric. There was another exceptionally impressive and expensive Athenian building of the mid-century, the Propylaia, begun in 437/6, but by that date Thucydides son of Melesias had been ostracised for some seven years. It was probably the Parthenon to which he and his supporters directed their critical attention.

The reported simile for the Parthenon seems to have point as a reference to deceit, rather than to vanity, wantonness or whoredom. If it could be shown that Greeks in the classical period did, in any case, regard the Athenian building programme as somehow deceitful, that would give confirmation to this theory. It would also suggest that the simile of the deceitful woman was not merely a bright piece of satire, but was a brilliantly memorable part of a serious argument.

Thucydides nowhere singles out the Parthenon for reference, but he does make one remark about the impression left by Athens' sacred buildings. He writes that if Athens were to become deserted, with only its religious buildings and the bottom of other structures remaining, what met the eye would make people of much later times assume that the military power of Athens had been twice as great as it had been in reality.[25] Thucydides does not say that these temples were built with any intention of deceit. But his words prove that the idea of inferring the power of a state from the grandeur of its buildings was alive in the classical period. He also suggests that, in relation to the power of Athens, the scale of the city's temples and other buildings was unusually great. It seems, then, that some Athenians could indeed have viewed the building programme of the 440s as being deceptive, as intended to suggest the argument that a state with so much to spend on religious and decorative structures must have a vast fund available for war. Thucydides makes it clear, in another connection, that the principle of using expenditure on religious show to make a military point to contemporaries was known in his time. In 415 Perikles' nephew, Alkibiades, is shown as defending his own lavish expenditure on the chariot race at the Olympic games, a festival in honour of Zeus. Thucydides represents him as arguing thus, in a speech to the Athenian assembly:

The things for which I am being loudly criticised bring ...
benefit to my native city. For, whereas the Greeks
previously had expected our city to have been exhausted by
war, they have come to believe that she is even more
powerful than in reality she is, because of my brilliant show
at the Olympic festival, as a result of my having entered
seven chariots, a number never before entered by a private
individual, and come first and second and fourth and in all
other respects laid on a show to match my victory. It is a
convention that this sort of thing brings prestige, but from
what one does people also get an impression of what one
could do, of one's power. Moreover, whatever I do inside
Athens which brings me distinction, paying for [religious]
choruses and whatever else, naturally produces envy in my
fellow citizens, but to visitors from other cities this too
suggests strength.[26]

Scholars have already noticed that other sections of this speech of
Alkibiades are reminiscent of Periklean ideas.[27] It is interesting
that the ideas of this section would have applied with few changes
to a defence by Perikles of the building programme of the 440s,
and that, if they were expressed then, they could easily have
brought forward the charge of deceit which Plutarch records.
Why opponents of Perikles should have been concerned to make
that charge will be examined shortly.

The sentence of Plutarch which refers to "putting a pretty
face" on a "deceitful woman" also includes an emphatic claim
that Athens is behaving like a tyrant towards the Greeks with
wilful, degrading, arrogance (*hybris*: the word is stressed in the
Greek by repetition.[28]) Before assuming that these remarks about
tyranny and *hybris* are coarse and mechanical rhetoric, we should
compare Greek ideas on the subjects. Aristotle makes a neglected
but possibly relevant remark about tyranny — the pre-classical
system of autocratic government, originally resting on popular
support but, after its disappearance, widely regarded with hatred.
Many tyrannies, he states, had fallen because of degrading and
arrogant acts (*hybreis*) by women.[29] Correct or not, if this idea was
commonplace in the classical period, it would have given precise
point to the connection now of tyranny, *hybris* and the "deceitful
woman". It would have invoked an unpleasant set of memories,
and suggested that Athens' behaviour might lead to her downfall.[30] The Greek tyrants were also remembered for grandiose

building projects, which were intended, Aristotle suggests, to keep the tyrants' subjects poor and dependent.[31] Here again was an uncomfortably close analogy to Athens' behaviour towards her former allies of the Delian League.[32]

If this analysis of the criticism reported by Plutarch is in large measure correct, it is worth asking how much of the "deceitful woman" passage he is likely to have understood. None of the above reconstruction is, of course, made by him. We have no reason to think that by his day (the late first and early second centuries AD) there was still a lively tradition that arrogant women had caused the downfall of Greek tyrannies (some six centuries or more earlier). And in Plutarch's time grand building schemes seem to have been regarded as a means of distributing wealth among an autocrat's subjects rather than of impoverishing them.[33] It may seem that the rhetoric in Plutarch's account would have appealed in an exact, concentrated and forceful way to Greek ideas and prejudices of the classical period. The suggestion that it was composed by an ill-informed writer in an exercise of rhetorical imagination centuries later is not an attractive one. Instead, we may suspect that Plutarch has preserved an important and authentic tradition,[34] largely stripped of explanatory detail, not because he understood it but because it contained emphatic and paradoxical remarks on some buildings and a politician of perennial interest.

Why should this policy of creating public buildings have provoked opposition from Thucydides son of Melesias, and his associates? These men seem to have represented the interests of wealthy and conservative Athenians.[35] Before we look briefly at their possible attitude towards the building projects of the 440s, it is worth considering the impact on Athenian domestic politics of the previous great building project, the creation of the Long Walls in the early 450s. These walls, by creating a fortified and secure passage from Athens to the sea, greatly reduced the threat to Athens from a besieging land army of Peloponnesians. The Athenians could look to their overseas allies and trading partners for supplies, and would have no compelling need to challenge an invading Peloponnesian army in the field. The likelihood thus grew that the Peloponnesians would be left free to ravage the estates of Attikē. Precisely this strategy was later adopted, under the leadership of Perikles and after his death, when Sparta and her allies made almost annual invasions of Attikē from 431. The wealth of rich and aristocratic Greeks by tradition consisted largely of landed estates. Some rich Athenians in the early 450s reacted to the new building project, which threatened their estates, by trying to betray the city to the Spartans. They hoped, in Thucydides' words, "both to abolish the democracy and to stop the building of the Long Walls".[36]

We cannot assume that Thucydides son of Melesias and his supporters were involved in the unsuccessful plot against the Long Walls. But, if indeed they represented rich and conservative interests, they may well have seen themselves as similarly threatened by the building schemes of the 440s. These schemes would cause the wealth of the Delian League to be widely distributed among the population of Athens,[37] and thus would cement the enthusiasm of the Athenian masses for the policy of dominating the eastern Greeks. This policy will probably have been seen as promoting *dēmokratia*, rule for the poor, as encouraging the defence of overseas possessions rather than the estates of Attikē, and as likely to frighten and offend Sparta — thus increasing the risk that Attikē would be invaded. Also, impressive public buildings created in Athens during the 470s and 460s may have been seen in the main as derived from aristocratic patronage.[38] Now, however, the *dēmos* of Athens was arranging its own sources of finance for such things, and this independence may itself have worried some of the rich. It is not hard to see why the great building schemes of the early Empire may have encountered dogged opposition and forceful rhetoric.

An interesting re-interpretation of the purpose of the Parthenon has been put forward by J. Boardman.[39] He suggests that the building and its sculpture were meant to commemorate the battle of Marathon. His case, as he admits,[40] is purely circumstantial; no ancient writer tells us that the building referred especially to that battle. But, as we have seen, ancient references to the Parthenon are in any case scanty. Commemoration of Marathon may have well suited Athens' propaganda in the early Empire. At Marathon in 490 a Persian army had been beaten by a force of Athenians who, apart from a small contingent from Plataia, fought alone without help from allies. In particular, the absence of effective help from Spartans or other Peloponnesians would be remembered. Athens' performance at the battle helped in later years to provide moral justification for Athenian leadership, again without Peloponnesian involvement, of the eastern Greeks. Thucydides shows Marathon being cited to this effect by Athenian speakers at Sparta in 432.[41]

The Parthenon, as Boardman notes,[42] was built over the ruined foundations of a temple begun soon after, and perhaps meant to celebrate, the battle of Marathon. The art of the Parthenon has without doubt a military flavour. The sculpture of the metopes[43] shows a battle between Lapiths and Centaurs. The great gold and ivory statue of Athena, which stood inside the temple to a height of some forty feet, held in its hand a statue representing victory. Amazons fought Greeks on the shield of Athena, and possibly also on the metopes. Boardman suggests that the struggles against the barbarous Centaurs and Amazons were meant as mythological counterparts of the Athenians' struggle against the barbarism of the Persian Empire.[44] His main argument, however, concerns the long frieze which ran along the outside of the *cella* (the inner section of the temple) and the porticos at each end of the *cella*. It is widely agreed that the frieze shows a procession of worshippers at the Great Panathenaia, a four-yearly festival at Athens in honour of Athena. Crucial for this interpretation is a section of the fourth (eastern) side of the frieze, which shows a young person with a folded garment. This almost certainly represents the famous *peplos*, the robe which clothed the most sacred, olive wood, statue of Athena and which was changed at the Great Panathenaia.[45] Boardman suggests that figures in the frieze represent the Athenians killed at Marathon, and that they are here shown as heroes worshipping Athena. By far his strongest argument is drawn from the Athenian belief that these victims of Marathon totalled 192.[46] For, according to one method of reconstructing and interpreting the incomplete remains of the frieze, the most important figures on the three sides of the *cella* also numbered 192.[47]

There are, however, important points against this theory. The depiction on Greek religious buildings of figures from the recent past is scarcely known in other contexts.[48] The total of 192 for the important figures in the (chariot-borne) procession is reached by rejecting many of the participants as insignificant. The charioteers are not considered to count; this is in accordance with (for example) the *Iliad*, in which charioteers are portrayed as far less important than the warriors they escort. But other questionable figures, the young dismounted grooms, are adjudged to count.[49] This may seem to be unfair manipulation of the evidence to suit a desired conclusion. However, if by *any* regulated system of counting a total of 192 were reached, the coincidence would still be impressive. More seriously perhaps, the number 192 is arrived at by inference about the total of important figures on the lost section of the frieze, and scholars disagree as to how many these were.[50]

An alternative explanation of the frieze might be that it represents the first ever Panathenaic procession.[51] This would fit with the interest in origins certainly reflected in other art of the Parthenon. The most prominent sculptures of all, in the gables ('pediments') at the east and west ends of the temple, showed, respectively, the birth of Athena and the establishment of the goddess as patron divinity of Athens. The wars of Amazons and Greeks, Centaurs and Lapiths, could similarly reflect the origin of civilisation, protected from the threat of overwhelming barbarism.[52] If this explanation of the frieze were correct, part of its purpose may again have been to impress foreign visitors, for imperial purposes. Athenians were certainly concerned with the impression made in their city on such visitors, as the speech of Alkibiades cited above reminds us.[53] And the work of Isokrates in the fourth century shows that Athens' mythical contribution to the founding of civilisation could be used to argue that she deserved her continuing eminence.[54]

Finally, we should not forget that the Parthenon was meant to honour, and perhaps to thank, Athena. As we have seen, the temple was begun soon after the point at which hostilities against the Persians came to an end. At the worst crisis of that warfare, in 480 when the city of Athens was about to be abandoned to the Persians, Athena and a sacred snake associated with her were believed to have given the Athenians guidance which helped to produce their eventual victory.[55] When Athena was portrayed in the Parthenon by the gold and ivory statue, beside her was shown the sacred snake.[56] As well as reflecting imperial economics and propaganda, the great temple expressed ideas which may seem more remote from modern experience.[57]

Cementing the Empire

At this period Athens made further moves which reflect her increasing, or increasingly frank, domination over the allies. Seemingly in or close to 450, the Athenians sent out groups of their own citizens to settle on land of certain allied states. These settlements are known as 'kleroukhies' (a *klēroukhos*, literally, was an allotment holder): the settlers remained Athenian citizens, the kleroukhy not being a *polis* in its own right.[58] Our information on when and where the kleroukhies were established is in general not good.[59] Diodorus and another late writer, Pausanias, mention that settlements were founded on the islands of Euboia and Naxos by the Athenian general Tolmides.[60] Diodorus does give a date for this, 453/2, but it cannot be relied on. More important is the information that Tolmides died at the battle of Koroneia, a defeat which caused Athens to lose control of Boiotia, and which occurred in 447 or 446.[61] This suggests that, for the founding of these two kleroukhies, the period 447/6 is — in the historians' phrase — a *terminus ante quem* (a chronological limit before which an event must have occurred[62]). Plutarch also gives the names of certain kleroukhies, and connects their foundation with the struggle for power between Perikles and Thucydides son of Melesias, after the death of Kimon.[63] The establishment of one kleroukhy mentioned by Plutarch, that on the isle of Andros, may be reflected in the records of payment by Andros in the ATLs.[64] Andros' *phoros* is halved; from 12 talents in 451/0 to 6 in 450/49. This reduction could easily be understood if the Athenians now took much of the Andrians' land. That the payment of *phoros* and the accommodation of a kleroukhy might be seen as interchange-able burdens is shown by Thucydides. He writes that the Athenians, after the great revolt (on Lesbos) in 428–427, "did not impose *phoros* on the people of Lesbos, but rather formed 3,000 *klēroi* (allotments) on their land ... and sent out *klēroukhoi*, chosen by lot, from their own citizens".[65] Both Plutarch and Diodorus state that a kleroukhy was sent to the Khersonese (the land to the north of the Dardanelles): in this case, too, a reduction in *phoros* can be traced on the ATLs after 450/49.[66]

These kleroukhies of the mid-century were perhaps meant in part as informal garrisons, in reaction to unrest among the allies after the defeat in Egypt and around the time of the ending of war with Persia. As we have seen, the later kleroukhy on Lesbos was certainly set up in the aftermath of a long and serious revolt there. Plutarch states that the earlier kleroukhies did have a defensive military purpose: he also claims that they were created to relieve Athens of "an idle and interfering mob".[67] Now, Plutarch in general provides a useful though coarse guide to external, public, events of the historical period. In the present case, his evidence that kleroukhies were established in the mid-fifth century coheres with the information given by the ATLs and Diodorus. Plutarch's *reconstruction of motives*, however, is very frequently unsuccessful. His reference here to the desire to be rid of a mob seems indeed to be an anachronistic reflection of Roman politics close to his own time. Rome notoriously contained a land-hungry mass of poor, to which oligarchic and autocratic politicians made offers of allotments for manipulative purposes of their own. In any case we should ask, 'How could Plutarch know, as he claims, that Perikles sought to be rid of an idle and interfering mob?' Some of Perikles' private remarks may have been recorded by a contemporary collector of gossip,[68] but even a private reference to an idle and interfering mob would have been exceptionally indiscreet in so successful a politician. Perikles could hardly have revealed such a motive in public. The decision to create kleroukhies was formally not his to take; it had to be taken by the general assembly of Athens' male citizens. If, as is likely, Perikles promoted the plan for kleroukhies, he is not likely to have commended it to the assembly by informing his fellow citizens that thousands of them were an idle and interfering mob, which needed to be got rid of. The pejorative word used by Plutarch and here translated as 'interfering' is, in Greek, *polypragmōn*: by chance we have a strong suggestion in a passage of Thucydides that Perikles in fact refused to use that word as a pejorative.[69] Plutarch here seems out of touch with the spirit of classical *dēmokratia*. When assessing his evidence in general, we should remember the difference in quality between the record of external events and the description of motives.

The kleroukhies were probably formed as a means of improving the fortunes of the Athenian poor, for their own sake, as well perhaps as meeting a military need. The use of the lot to choose the members of the kleroukhy for Lesbos in the 420s strongly suggests that there was great demand to take part. (On Lesbos local people were allowed to work the land, leaving the Athenian *klēroukhoi* as landlords to draw rents.[70]) The great interest of the Athenian poor in overseas settlements is reflected in an Athenian inscription, which records the arrangements for a colony at Brea (a site in the Thraceward region[71]). The assembly ruled that only the two poorer classes of Athenian citizens could take part.[72] Two Athenian writers hostile to the aspirations of the poor, the orator Antiphon and the comedian Aristophanes, refer to profits from the Empire. Antiphon refers to a possible desire to give all landless citizens enough wealth to become hoplites.[73] Aristophanes, in a satirical exaggeration of democratic dreams, imagines the formerly poor *dēmos* of Athens, having extended its rule over the

Middle East, sitting triumphantly at the heart of the Persian Empire and licking sweets.[74] It should also be noted that some of the Athenian rich profited from land-holdings abroad.[75] Athenian acquisition of land in allied states seems to have been widely resented. In 377, some 28 years after the collapse of the Athenian Empire, many eastern Greeks were once more willing to accept Athens as the leader of an alliance. But they insisted that certain features of the Empire should not be repeated: a feature most emphatically prohibited was the Athenian ownership of land in other states.[76]

Another imperial act, probably belonging to the mid-fifth century, was the passing of an Athenian decree which ordered the allies to use only Athenian weights, measures and silver coinage.[77] It is now commonly believed that the Coinage Decree belongs before 445, because a fragment of one copy of it, found on the isle of Kos and inscribed in Attic script, uses the form of sigma with three bars. The three-bar sigma seems to have gone out of use by 445.[78] We cannot be sure why this decree was passed, no ancient explanation of it being available. It would, however, obviously help Athenian exporters by freeing them from the expensive services of money-changers, and raise the value of the silver mined in Attikē by giving Athens a monopoly in the production of silver coin. Coins were a durable, perhaps even a glamorous, form of political and economic propaganda. Athenians might feel some pride that the *drakhmai* which symbolised their power, coins with Athena's helmeted head on one side and the goddess's owl on the other, would now circulate even more commonly in the Aegean and beyond. It seems that at least one state, Samos, continued for some years to issue her own silver coinage, in probable breach of the decree.[79] This defiance may be connected with a spirit of resistance which in 440 led the oligarchs of Samos to revolt from Athens.

Meiggs associates with the early 440s two further developments in Athenian control of the allies. He notes that on two decrees made before 445 (dated again by three-bar sigmas) Athens refers to her associates not as "the alliance" or "the allies" but as "the cities which the Athenians control".[80] In the Erythrai Decree, probably of the late 450s, we saw that the less presumptuous expression, 'the alliance', was used. However, we cannot assume a neat transition from the one expression to the other; Athenian usage may have been inconsistent. As J. K. Davies has pointed out, we do not know when Athens first used the phrase 'the cities which the Athenians control' in an official document. It may even have been before the Erythrai Decree. In an inscription of 439/8 the expression 'the allies' was used once more: obviously the Athenians were capable of reversion.[81]

Meiggs also suggests that after the early 440s there were no further synods of the Delian League.[82] He notes the authoritarian tone of Athenian decrees concerning the allies from this period onwards, and the lack of any reference in them to synods of the League. He is probably right to argue that the synods had ceased to exist by 432; Thucydides describes at considerable length the diplomatic preliminaries to war which occurred then: if hostilities had been discussed at a synod, we should expect him to have mentioned it. But A. H. M. Jones has argued that there was a synod as late as 440. Spokesmen from Mytilene, seeking Peloponnesian support in 428 for their revolt from Athens, are represented by Thucydides as claiming that "the allies, isolated by the multiple voting system (*polypsēphia*) and so unable to resist, were enslaved with the exception of ourselves [the Mytileneans] and the Khians."[83] 'The multiple voting system' refers to synods of the League. Jones held that since Samos (a large and conspicuous state) is not mentioned with Lesbos and Khios as an exception to the alleged enslavement of the allies, it was understood as one of the places which were so treated, as a result of voting at a synod. Samos was "enslaved" in 440–439, when Athens imposed *dēmokratia* on the island, then (after a revolt) deprived Samos of its fleet and walls: Jones therefore concludes that a synod was held at that time. There is a chance that here, as occasionally elsewhere,[84] Thucydides has deliberately allowed a speech to contain inaccuracy. He undertook when recording speeches to keep close to what had actually been said,[85] and speeches in the period of Greek rhetoric which we know best, the fourth century, contain numberless inaccuracies. But we cannot assume that this claim attributed to the Mytileneans is wrong. It may be that synods died out in the early 430s, a period of which relatively little is known.

To conclude on the synods, for which this short reference is probably our most important piece of evidence:[86] the Mytileneans do not say explicitly that votes were taken at the synods on how to treat revolts from the League.[87] But it is obviously implied that the synods had not become perfunctory; they were serious enough to create the presumption that such votes might be taken. The reference to a multiple voting system is again not entirely clear. However, the rare word *polypsēphia* has been interpreted as meaning that the Delian League, like the Peloponnesian alliance, gave every state a single vote, and that the resulting mass of votes controlled by tiny states gave (as the Mytileneans imply) effective power to Athens, because the minor states would be afraid to offend her.[88]

In 447 or 446 an Athenian force was defeated, at Koroneia in Boiotia, by an army consisting of men exiled from the Athenian-dominated cities of Boiotia and Euboia and also of Lokrians.[89] As a result, control of Boiotia was lost to Athens, who had herself been aided in the battle by "the allies in their various contingents".[90] The battle of Koroneia must have greatly increased the prestige and influence of the Euboian exiles in their native cities. Seizing their opportunity, Euboians and other opponents of Athens made a set of (probably concerted) moves.[91] The cities of Euboia revolted from Athens. When an Athenian army, commanded by Perikles, had crossed to the island to tackle the revolt, it was reported that Megara had abandoned its alliance with Athens and rejoined the Peloponnesians. With the Megarid now passable, the Spartans invaded Attikē. Megara, as it turned out, was lost to Athens for good. But the Spartan army turned for home without attacking the city of Athens itself, perhaps because its commander had been bribed.[92] Athens was free to reconquer Euboia, which she did. Under the terms of the resulting settlement, the inhabitants of the northern Euboian city of Hestiaia were forced to evacuate their territory, which Athenians then proceeded to occupy.[93] (Plutarch states that the Hestiaians had massacred the captured crew of an Athenian ship.[94])

The surviving text of an Athenian decree records the rules which Athens now laid down for the Euboian city of Khalkis.[95] Khalkis was required to be loyal to Athens (not to Athens and the allies, as Erythrai had been in the late 450s).[96] Certain legal cases arising at Khalkis were ordered to be transferred to Athens[97] — the cases in which the penalties were death, exile or loss of citizen rights. Later in the Athenian Empire it seems that no state could enforce a death sentence without reference to Athens.[98] The most systematic study of judicial procedure under the Empire has been made by de Ste. Croix.[99] He suggests that by controlling the application of these serious penalties Athens could hope to prevent her supporters in the allied states from being persecuted with legal charges for political reasons.[100] We can still read fragments of decrees in which the Athenians issued special protection from murder or other mistreatment for their supporters in the Empire.[101] These decrees seem closely connected in spirit with the control of serious legal sentences in the allied states. Violence and judicial persecution were associated as extreme political devices.[102] In Kerkyra, a state allied to Athens at the time but outside the Athenian Empire, both were used against a single person. Peithias, a prominent democrat and supporter of Athens, was put on trial in 427 for promoting Athens' interests: when the prosecution failed, he was murdered.[103]

After Sparta had withdrawn her forces from Attikē, and Athens had overcome her difficulties in Euboia, the two great powers made a treaty of peace in 446/5: it was designed to last for 30 years.[104] The terms of the Thirty Years' Peace are not fully established.[105] It is evident, however, that each side swore not to attack the other if the other was willing to accept arbitration.[106] Athens gave up her control of Nisaia and Pegai, the ports of Megara; she also relinquished two territories in the Peloponnese, Akhaia and Troizen, which she had acquired, probably in the 450s.[107] Sparta conceded in effect that the Athenians might retain their Empire, although Athens may have been induced to promise a special restraint in the treatment of Aigina, Sparta's lost ally.[108]

The Thirty Years' Peace lasted, in the event, until 432–431. In the intervening period Athens had to deal, as we have seen, with the revolt of Samos, in 440–439. Samos had gone to war with another member of the Athenian Empire, the nearby state of Miletos. Athens imposed *dēmokratia* on the Samians, some of whom then began the revolt in collaboration with Persians on the mainland, and restored oligarchic government.[109] Thucydides goes into considerable military detail: the Samians, with a large fleet, gained a temporary naval ascendancy over the Athenians but were eventually overcome (at enormous financial cost[110]) by forces under the command of Perikles.

There are many references, by writers other than Thucydides, to the Athenians' setting up and protecting democratic constitutions in the states of the Empire. An anonymous writer, usually labelled 'the Old Oligarch' gives evidence to that effect, probably in the late fifth century.[111] So do fourth-century writers, most importantly Aristotle.[112] The comments of these writers are, however, tantalisingly vague and general. This passage concerning Samos is the only one in which Thucydides, our best literary source, recounts with precise reference to time and place the establishment of *dēmokratia*, by Athens, in a state of the

Empire.[113] That there were many states in the Empire with that form of constitution is strongly implied by Thucydides.[114] We may suspect that under Athenian rule *dēmokratia* was almost universal,[115] but the amount of information given by Thucydides on the subject is rather disappointing.

The main recorded events in imperial history from the period 438–404 will be dealt with in narrative order in later chapters, and in some cases will be mentioned in an analytic connection in the last pages of this one. But, for clarity, a brief anticipatory survey is needed here. In 437/6 the Athenians began to build, with the help of income from the *phoros*, the spectacular Propylaia, the gateway building for the Akropolis which to contemporaries may have been more impressive than the Parthenon.[116] At the same period Athens established a large colony, Amphipolis, on the strategically important River Strymon, which dominated an area productive of timber and gold. In the nearby area of Khalkidikē, from 432 a set of revolts threatened the Athenian Empire perhaps more seriously than scholars have usually realised; by bringing Athens and Korinth into conflict, the revolt of Poteidaia precipitated the outbreak of the great Peloponnesian War. This conflict, in reality a succession of wars between the Athenian and Spartan alliances, lasted until 404. In 427, after crushing the revolt of Mytilēnē, Athens executed the oligarchs who had led the uprising. In 425, after a famous victory over a Spartan force, Athens sharply increased the amount of *phoros* demanded of the allies. Further revolts in the north, in 424–423, included that of Amphipolis, a treasured colony which Athens was never to recover. Nearby Skionē, however, was regained in 421, and its male citizen population executed.

In 415 Athens sought to extend her Empire far to the westward, invading Sicily with massive and loyal support from her allies. In 413 the *phoros* was replaced by a 5 per cent duty on seaborne goods. In the autumn of that year the expeditionary force in Sicily was annihilated; oligarchic factions in many allied states seized their chance and launched revolts, encouraged by Sparta. Sparta herself built a fleet of triremes and, funded in part by Persia, challenged the Athenians in the Aegean. This Ionian War (412–405), after successes for both sides, ended with a freak naval victory for Sparta at Aigospotamoi, in the Hellespont. With the loss of her navy, Athens could not protect ships bringing the grain she needed from the Black Sea. The Athenians were starved into surrender, and lost their Empire to Sparta, in 404.

Costs and benefits of the Empire.
The question of its popularity

How was the Athenian Empire viewed by citizens of the subject states? Before we examine some of the intriguingly complex evidence on this point, it may be well to say a little more on general costs and benefits of the Empire. How heavy in practical terms was the *phoros*? No fully satisfactory answer can be made, because so little is known of the wealth of the subject states, or of how they distributed the burden of *phoros* among individuals.[117] We may suspect that normally the *phoros* was not oppressive. In the mid-420s the Athenians probably increased the amount demanded annually to more than 1460 talents, about three times the level of earlier decades[118] — a rise which probably outstripped the level of inflation over the period of the Delian League and Athenian Empire.[119] The Athenians evidently considered that the earlier payments had been far less than the maximum which the allies' economies could sustain, at least over a short period. We have already seen that many small communities of the Empire paid an annual *phoros* which amounted to little more than the yearly income of a single Athenian labourer.[120] When, in 413, the Athenians replaced the *phoros* with a tax of 5 per cent on sea-borne exports, they considered that the new levy would bring in more than the *phoros*.[121] A tax of 5 per cent on a single aspect of economic activity may again seem unlikely to have proved a great burden:[122] it is interesting that the *phoros* received in the preceding period was expected to amount to even less.

In return for payments to Athens,[123] her subjects gained an effective defence against Persia. For long periods, membership of the Athenian Empire involved being at war with the Peloponnesian alliance: while that had obvious costs, it did provide opportunities for mercenary service which were welcomed by many of the poor, in subject states as in Athens itself.[124] By providing funds for Athens' navy, members of the Empire probably helped to secure a reduction in the activities of pirates. Little is heard of piracy in the period of Athenian domination, although a character in a comedy of 414 speaks of the need to avoid pirates when sailing between the Aegean islands.[125] In a strongly pro-Athenian work of 380, Isokrates claims that there was a great contrast between the security of the seas under the old Athenian Empire and the situation of his time in which "drowners [i.e. pirates] control the sea".[126]

Reduction in piracy might help greatly in the promotion of trade. Athenians used their navy to control trade, and prices, to the advantage of their own city. We happen to learn, from an Athenian decree of 426, that the community of Methōnē on the coast of Macedonia was allowed to import a specified amount of corn each year from Byzantion, as a privilege.[127] Other states were no doubt excluded from the important grain markets on the Black Sea coasts; the reduction in competition would allow Athenian traders to buy more cheaply, and perhaps even to form a cartel to impose prices on the producers.[128] The Peiraieus, to which corn and many other commodities would come,[129] became an attractive market for traders from many states. Favourable conditions of domicile were given by Athens to the metics (*metoikoi*, resident aliens) by whom much of the city's commerce was carried on.[130] Some members of the Empire, including traders and those who could afford to travel for leisure, would also enjoy the spectacular entertainment, some of it intellectual, at the numerous and lavishly endowed Athenian festivals.[131]

Greek reactions to the Empire of Athens varied greatly, as we shall see, from one period to another. They also differed as between democrats and oligarchs, since Athens tended to promote *dēmokratia*. Modern scholars may themselves have been influenced by their own political preferences when analysing and presenting evidence on this topic. When we try to assess the popularity, or otherwise, of the Athenian Empire, considerable effort may be needed, not merely to compensate for the bias of other modern analysts, but also to identify and restrain our own. Political opinions and tastes derived from the twentieth century may produce serious anachronisms when applied to classical Greece.

Two scholars who have made outstanding contributions to the study of Greek history, Grote and de Ste. Croix, have been — by the standards of their colleagues — on the left politically.[132] Both have shown an unusual sympathy with the Athenian *dēmos*, and have frequently succeeded in demonstrating rationality and sophistication in its behaviour. But there is a danger, for less skilled historians, in sympathising warmly with the poor of Athens and their leaders. It may be tempting to play down evidence that many Greeks, and not merely oligarchs, found aspects of Athenian rule repellent.

De Ste. Croix has sought to show a similarity, in one respect, between Athenian and Soviet notions of democracy.[133] However, classical scholars are very often of conservative disposition, and it seems possible that concern with the Russian Revolution has tended to affect analyses of the Athenian Empire with results very different from the work of de Ste. Croix. Several scholars have disapproved emphatically of Athens' use of her power, as was noted in connection with the Delian League (Chapter 1). Such disapproval was particularly frequent in the decades after 1917. In the original *Cambridge Ancient History*, a work of the 1920s and 1930s, W. S. Ferguson referred to the *dēmos* of Athens as a "citizen pack", and suggested that on occasion it was mad.[134] In the same work, H. Last wrote that Athenian imperial government constituted a "warning which gives some slight value to even the worst of failures".[135] The Athenian politician Isokrates, while praising his native city, claimed that her subjects paid *phoros* "not to preserve Athens, but to preserve their *dēmokratiai* and their freedom and to avoid the great evils of oligarchy".[136] In the 1940s, the *ATL* editors commented: "this ridiculous statement, which equates democracy with a sort of Utopia, has little relation to the historical situation of the Empire".[137] Now, Isokrates here makes a partisan claim about oligarchy, and his remark about freedom is a vague commonplace of rhetoric. But, far from being ridiculous, his statement interestingly resembles Thucydides' picture of democratic partisans seeking Athenian intervention in their states, to counter their local oligarchic opponents (III 82). Also, Isokrates' words contain nothing to suggest that *dēmokratia* had utopian qualities. One may suspect that when the heated comment in the *ATL* was written, its authors had in mind not so much the Athenian Empire as another regime for which, in the 1930s and 1940s, utopian claims *were* still being made. Scholars hostile to the Athenian Empire emphasise, correctly, that many Greeks resented it. The corresponding fault of this approach is not to attend sufficiently to the evidence suggesting that numerous other Greeks welcomed it.

The Athenians' stress on freedom of speech (*parrhēsia*) and on political gentleness in their own city[138] should show immediately that any general assimilation of Athenian to Russian politics would be profoundly inappropriate.[139] Nowadays, with the Russian analogy fading in its influence, another opinion derived from modern politics is likely to distort perceptions of the Athenian Empire, especially among younger students. This is the view, dominant at the United Nations, that all imperialism is wrong.[140] Imperialism, in the sense of the violent acquisition of territory, is a much more dangerous process today than in past ages, because of the nature of modern weapons and the interdependence of modern economies. The existence of empire was for long widely approved of; in the nineteenth century, for example, the British Raj in India was regarded as beneficent, for varying reasons, by capitalist merchants and manufacturers, Christian philanthropists, Karl Marx and very large numbers of Indians. This may be noted not as a comment on the morality of empire, but as weakening any assumption derived from modern history that Greeks generally, or the more intelligent ones, must have regarded Athenian imperialism as unjustified interference with local liberties.

Our main evidence on the contemporary standing of the Athenian Empire comes from Thucydides. His account contains much generalisation and detail, posing intricate problems, some of which relate to his own position as moralist. He writes that, at the start of the Peloponnesian War, "Public favour [in Greece] inclined very largely towards the Spartans, especially because they announced that they would free Greece. Every individual and every city was eager to help them in any way possible in word and deed".[141] In a famous study, *The character of the Athenian Empire*, de Ste. Croix has collected a mass of evidence from Thucydides' own history to the effect that numerous Greeks, in the Empire and elsewhere, acquiesced in or desired Athenian rule.[142] Most of this evidence arises from the period after 431; while not formally contradicting the large generalisation about "every individual" quoted above, the main body of evidence does obviously pose a problem in relation to it. However, as de Ste. Croix observed, there is one section of the history which seems to be in formal contradiction with the picture of "every individual" supporting Sparta at the start of the war.[143] Thucydides describes the passage through Thessaly of a Spartan army, on its way to campaign against Athenian interests, in 424. He states that if Thessaly had been governed by a constitutional regime, rather than by an arbitrary form of oligarchy,[144] the Spartans would not have been able to make their passage, because the great mass (*plēthos*) of the Thessalians had always favoured Athens.[145] The notion 'always' is emphasised in the Greek,[146] and the term used for 'favour' is the same as in the earlier passage which stated that the Greeks generally favoured Sparta.[147] Thessaly was not part of the Athenian Empire, but the division between poor citizens who supported, or tolerated, Athenian hegemony and a wealthy minority who supported Sparta is one noted repeatedly by Thucydides elsewhere, of states belonging to the Empire and of others.[148] We may also see below that the contradiction, between the historian's generalisation on the one hand and his narrative on the other, falls into a comprehensible pattern within his work.

Thucydides represents the politicians Perikles (for whom he had much respect[149]) and Kleon (for whom he did not[150]) as telling the Athenians that their Empire was like a tyranny.[151] This evidence of unpopularity is important, but its significance can be exaggerated. As we have seen, Thucydides sometimes attributes exaggerations and other distortions to his speakers;[152] in a speech answering Kleon's, another Athenian politician, Diodotos, is made to state, "At present the *dēmos* in every city is favourably disposed (*eunous*) to you [Athenians]."[153] Kleon's remark is cast in the form of a complaint, that the Athenians do not reflect on the fact that their Empire is a tyranny. And Perikles' claim is made in an emphatic way which suggests that it may have been a novelty to his audience at Athens. Athenians are, of course, likely to have indulged in wishful thinking about the acceptability of their Empire, but we should beware of treating the remarks about tyranny as if they reflected a generally held view.

The speeches of Kleon and Diodotos were made in 427, after the revolt on Lesbos had been suppressed. As that revolt had neared its end, the oligarchs of Mytilene, who had led it,[154] distributed hoplite equipment to the *dēmos* of the city. On receiving these weapons, the members of the *dēmos* ceased to obey their rulers, informing them that if they did not distribute hidden stocks of food they would surrender the city to Athens.[155] The oligarchs took this threat seriously: rather than be excluded from terms of surrender, they themselves handed over Mytilēnē to the besieging Athenians.

Similar divisions between "the few" and "the many", oligarchs and *dēmos*, commonly affected attitudes towards Athenian rule. A famous, moralising, passage of Thucydides describes the civil conflict (*stasis*) along those lines which broke out in 427 on the isle of Kerkyra and later became general in Greece:

> With such cruelty did the conflict progress, and it made a greater impression because this was the first case of it, whereas later virtually the whole of the Greek world was affected by it, with divisions in each state between the champions of the *dēmos* trying to bring in the Athenians and

the oligarchs trying to bring in the Spartans. In peacetime they would not have had an excuse to invite them in, nor would they even have been willing to, but in wartime with an alliance available to each faction for damaging its opponents and promoting its own interests, those wanting revolution had good opportunities for bringing in help from foreign powers.[156]

In this context, Thucydides mentions "those citizens who were in the middle", and who, he says, were destroyed by both factions, either because they took no part in the struggle or because people begrudged their survival.[157] With this in mind, there may be a temptation, when reconstructing the attitudes of different groups to the Athenian Empire, to apply one of the most influential clichés of Indo-European thought, the three-part model.[158] However, Greek states were not divided simply into pro-Athenian democrats, pro-Spartan oligarchs and neutrals. Thucydides says that in peacetime the different factions would have lacked an excuse to bring in a foreign power. Now, an excuse implies a person or group to be persuaded or placated by the excuse. In the present case who would that be? Certainly not the rival faction, and almost certainly not Thucydides' neutrals; the rival faction would be intransigent, and Thucydides' neutrals were later set upon and destroyed by both sides, rather than being thought worthy to receive excuses. We should probably assume the existence in peacetime of two further groups, luke-warm democrats and luke-warm supporters of oligarchy, including some who might shift from one group to the other. These were the people at whom the excuses might have been aimed. The unavailability of the excuses in peacetime could have been important, Thucydides suggests, in restraining the chief partisans from bringing in the Athenians or Spartans: the influence of these groups which needed to receive the excuses was evidently considerable. Within the five-fold model proposed here (extreme partisans on each side, luke-warm supporters of each and neutrals) the luke-warm democrats may have been the largest group. Thucydides several times refers to the aggregate of democrats in a state as "the many" and "the great mass",[159] yet even in the large state of Samos the extreme partisans of *dēmokratia* numbered at one stage only some 300.[160] The assumption that such extreme partisans were greatly outnumbered by luke-warm democrats would explain why "the champions of the *dēmos*", in Thucydides' phrase, were so dependent on others' accepting their excuse for bringing in the Athenians. According to our interpretation of Thucydides, a majority of citizens in the states not controlled by Athens was, in peacetime, unwilling to excuse the introduction of Athenian rule. And that, of course, must reflect on feelings within the Empire.

In the Peloponnesian War, as Thucydides shows, the prospect of being under Athenian or Spartan control was acceptable to great numbers of those who favoured, respectively, *dēmokratia* and oligarchy. In general, the champions of the *dēmos* sought to bring in the Athenians to their various states, and by implication, members of the *dēmos* accepted their excuses for so doing. This drastic change from the attitudes of peacetime probably reflected a fear in the champions and supporters of *dēmokratia* that their domestic opponents would anyway bring in the Spartans, to impose a new or more severe oligarchy.[161] Those who favoured oligarchy were no doubt influenced by corresponding fears about Athenian intervention and the imposition of *dēmokratia*. Within the Athenian Empire, patterns of loyalty to, or revolt from, Athens corresponded to some extent with the fluctuating military fortunes of the Athenians. The appearance of a Spartan army, led by Brasidas, in the Thraceward area in 424 led to a series of local revolts from Athens. After Athens' great defeat in Sicily in 413, numerous oligarchic factions sought to exploit their opportunity by revolt. J. de Romilly has suggested that there was an exact correspondence between Athens' military position at each stage and the positions of the democratic and oligarchic factions in the Empire: "the strength and audacity of each of these two parties were in proportion with their practical hopes"; "if we try to write a history of opinion in the cities according to their practical behaviour, we shall finally be writing a history of the war, and of the Athenian success at war."[162] However, there was no general outbreak of revolts at the start of the Peloponnesian War when, according to Thucydides,[163] some Greeks expected the Athenians to hold out for one year, others for two years, but none thought they could resist for more than three years if the Peloponnesians invaded Attikē — which they did.[164]

According to Thucydides, some revolts arose from wishful thinking: "the subjects of the Athenians had a willingness to revolt which exceeded their capacity, because they judged affairs under the influence of passion and would not even hear of the Athenians being able to survive the following summer [412]."[165]

(In fact the Athenian Empire survived until 405–404.) This is not the only connection in which Thucydides records the power of wishful thinking in politics.[166] We may guess that both oligarchs and democrats were influenced by it when they assessed the military prospects of Athens and Sparta. In the aftermath of the Sicilian disaster the picture of revolt from Athens is not uniform. Democrats on Samos and others in the Carian state of Iasos moved politically closer to Athens, against the general trend.[167]

Thucydides has not given a case-by-case comparison of the social struggles which had so much effect on attitudes towards the Athenian Empire. We should, however, consider briefly some of the behaviour and attitudes likeliest to have been involved. Thucydides describes the social conflict on Kerkyra as the earliest of the Peloponnesian War, but not the worst; social warriors in other states learnt from their predecessors elsewhere and perpetrated greater excesses.[168] Informal violence and unjust condemnation in court were of general occurrence, he implies.[169] On Kerkyra, after oligarchs had failed in their prosecution of the pro-Athenian Peithias, he in turn prosecuted the five richest of his opponents, and succeeded. When, in addition, Peithias was thought to be about to persuade the general mass (*plēthos*) of citizens to share the foreign policies of Athens, his enemies entered the council meeting with daggers, killing him and some 60 others. General violence followed between oligarchs and democrats, during which private quarrels were also settled, some debtors killing their creditors.[170] Thucydides seems to have meant his fairly long account of the social strife on Kerkyra to stand as the chief illustration of internal conflicts in the states of the Athenian Empire and elsewhere, conflicts which he believed human nature would continually produce.[171] From other periods of Greek history we hear of demands by the poor for the general abolition of debts and redistribution of land.[172] Athens' support of democratic factions in her Empire must have aroused such demands from many, who would be anxious to avoid being (or continuing) on the poorer side of the social gulf, the "two cities" of rich and poor, which Plato later described as characteristic of states governed by oligarchy.[173] Depending on the resources of their community, the poor might hope for redistribution of wealth in various forms, including payment for military or civil service and largesse at festivals, as occurred on a grand scale at Athens, the richest and one of the most developed of the *dēmokratiai*.[174]

Closely connected with economic ambition in the poor would be a concern with social status. At Athens, as we have seen, the local freedom of speech was often praised: this suggests that, according to the Athenians, such freedom was far from universal. Greek myth, in the form of the *Iliad*, recalled how Thersites, an agitator using anti-aristocratic rhetoric, was simply beaten and humiliated by the princely Odysseus.[175] *Isonomia*, equality before the law, was a slogan of the democrats in the social conflicts of the Peloponnesian War;[176] this evidently reflects a claim, detectable as early as the eighth century, that courts were often biased against the poor.[177] The poor might also wish to be rid of arrogant behaviour by some of the rich; Aristotle later noted regretfully that the rich did not always behave as gentlemen.[178] *Hybris*, the arrogance which degraded another, was treated as a serious crime by the Athenian *dēmokratia* and thought especially likely to be committed by the rich.[179]

Wealthy men in the subject states of the Empire had much to fear from Athenian rule and the *dēmokratia* it promoted. The rich seem to have been threatened not only by their local democrats but also by freelance prosecutors from Athens. The latter, known to their enemies as "sykophants", were subsequently blamed by some Athenians for precipitating the collapse of the Empire;[180] no doubt they were accused of provoking oligarchic revolts.[181] Wealthy men at Athens complained that *dēmokratia* had reduced their status; they could not hit other men's slaves in public, because slaves and poor citizens dressed indistinguishably (and a citizen assaulted in mistake for a slave would bring a lawsuit).[182] The rich were obliged anxiously to seek the favour of the poor, and to give way to them in the street.[183] They also had to sit next to poor and unwashed people in the assembly.[184] No doubt rich men in the states of the Empire had similar grievances, while the poor made corresponding complaints. The pre-classical poet, Semonides of Amorgos, wrote of women with aristocratic manners who, according to him, would not sit by the oven for fear of getting dirty, would not remove excrement from the home, grind grain or do other "slave's work". Instead, such women used perfume, kept their hair combed and wore flowers in it, and washed two or three times a day. A woman of this kind, writes Semonides, is fine to look at, but a bad thing for her husband, unless he is a ruler.[185] The repulsion between a sweaty small-holder and a washed, scented, aristocrat may have done much to preserve social distances. (We may recall that George Orwell in the 1930s suggested that many did not become socialists because the poor smelled.[186]) No doubt there were other differences of appearance and manner between rich and poor which, at this distance in time, may seem trivial, but which for Greeks of the classical period intensified the rancour that occasionally erupted into social war.[187]

How are we to treat Thucydides' statement, that at the start of the Peloponnesian War "every individual and every city" was eager to help Sparta against Athens, in the light of his further statements that the mass of citizens in Thessaly always favoured Athens, and that democratic leaders generally sought Athenian intervention in their communities from the time of the troubles in Kerkyra?[188] If we suspect that the remark about "every individual and every city" is an overstatement, it may be useful to compare some of the few statements of Thucydides on other topics which have come under this suspicion. Full analysis of these statements involves complex and often disputed exposition, some of which will be touched on in later chapters. But if we were to find, in several of the remarks suspected of being overstatements, hints of a shared and (for Thucydides) unusual psychology, that might strengthen our suspicion that the historian has in these various cases deviated from his usual accuracy.

Normally Thucydides does not show signs of passion, or seem to moralise. This has done much to persuade scholars that his work is largely free of bias. But occasionally there are indications of strong feeling on the historian's part, and these correspond to an interesting degree with the areas in which overstatement is, for other reasons, suspected. Thucydides plainly disapproved of the politician Kleon.[189] He states that sensible men at Athens considered it would be a good thing if Kleon were got rid of.[190] He also has been thought to exaggerate Kleon's failings. He describes as "mad" a promise which Kleon made in 425, to overcome a group of Spartan soldiers within 20 days.[191] Yet this promise was fulfilled, as Thucydides admits,[192] and with a victory which brought great benefit to Athens. In addition, Thucydides may have seriously underestimated Kleon's military attainments in the campaign against Brasidas in the Thraceward area.[193]

Thucydides seems to have disapproved of the use of divination in politics and warfare.[194] He describes the Athenian politician Nikias as "somewhat excessively attached to divination and that kind of thing", and says, of a prophecy that the Peloponnesian War would last for 27 years, "for those who asserted anything on the basis of oracles, *only* this was reliably confirmed by events".[195] The word here italicised, 'only', is stressed in the Greek by the emphatic particle *dē*. Thucydides knew that large numbers of oracles were uttered during the Peloponnesian War:[196] his forthright claim that all but one had failed to be confirmed probably implies general disapproval of this form of prediction. However, his statement about the almost complete failure of trust in oracles is contradicted by a passage of his own work, in which he describes the fulfilment of a prophecy about a section of Athenian land.[197]

It may now seem that Thucydides' questionable statement about the unpopularity of Athens in 431 falls into a pattern within his work, a pattern of underestimating people or practices judged by him to be at fault. It has already been seen that he implies disapproval of the Athenian Empire when describing Athens as "enslaving" other Greeks.[198] He also disapproved of *dēmokratia*, the form of government which characterised Athenian rule. He writes unfavourably of the workings of *dēmokratia* at Athens; the Athenians act "as a crowd is accustomed to",[199] "as a mob is accustomed to"[200] and Athens' sailors (a group with great political influence) are referred to as a "naval mob".[201] When, after the death of Perikles, the *dēmos* of Athens acted without firm restraint, numerous mistakes resulted, according to Thucydides.[202] These in his view included the conduct of the Sicilian expedition. He notes acidly that *after* the Sicilian disaster the Athenians were willing to meet the immediate danger in a disciplined fashion, "as a *dēmos* is accustomed to".[203] It should be noted that the criticism implied here, that *dēmokratia* is normally undisciplined, is conveyed in terms which apply not merely to Athens but to *dēmokratia* in general. In 411 the poorest and most numerous section of the Athenian *dēmos* was, briefly and exceptionally, excluded from formal power: Thucydides describes the constitution at one stage in that year as "obviously better administered than in any previous part of my lifetime", because "it combined in a moderate way the interests of the many and the few".[204] This passage may suggest that pure oligarchy was not Thucydides' ideal, and elsewhere he criticises certain oligarchs adversely.[205] But his disapproving remarks about *dēmokratia* are both more frequent and more general than the criticisms of oligarchy. That, of the two, he preferred oligarchy is also suggested by a passage in which he refers to oligarchy by the pretentious title employed by oligarchic partisans — *sōphrosynē*, 'sensible self-restraint'.[206]

Elsewhere, after mentioning the domestic prosperity of the state of Khios, Thucydides writes that, so far as his own information went, only Khios and Sparta had combined prosperity and sensible self-restraint (*sōphrosynē*, again).[207] In assessing this praise, as evidence of Thucydides' own values, we should recall that Sparta, which behaved as the patron of oligarchies in other states,[208] had a constitution markedly aristocratic in tone.[209]

It seems reasonable to suspect that Thucydides' apparent exaggeration of the dislike for the Athenian Empire, and of its failure to win support, arose from his own disapproval of the Empire and of the *dēmokratia* which it promoted. He himself fought for the Athenian Empire as a general against Brasidas' Spartan force in 424.[210] But after the fall of Amphipolis to Brasidas, Thucydides was dismissed and forced into exile for some 20 years.[211] His own misfortune, and his wealth, may have prompted anti-democratic feelings in him. Also, once in exile he was probably exposed above all to the opinions of Athens' enemies.[212] Thucydides had an intellect of rare power, and we could not infer simply from our small knowledge of his personal history that circumstances would have made him oppose *dēmokratia*. But there remains the possibility that they did, and in any case his disapproval of *dēmokratia* and the Empire seems to be established. In an earlier chapter it was suggested that negative enthusiasm may interfere with the judgement of modern scholars. It now seems that we should also guard against its effects when dealing with the best of our ancient informants.

Notes

1. See, however, two writers of the Roman period: Pausanias I 24 and Pliny the Elder, *Natural History*, XXXVI 18–19. Modern bibliography on the Parthenon is enormous. For an introduction see *Parthenos and Parthenon*, supplement to *Greece and Rome* X (1963); M. Robertson, *A history of Greek art*, I, 292–322 with notes thereto. Other references are given below.
2. *IG*, I², nos. 339–53.
3. On the supervision of the building work and on the role of the sculptor Pheidias, see now N. Himmelmann, 'Phidias und die Parthenon-Skulpturen' in *Bonner Festgabe Johannes Straub*, 67–90.
4. R. Meiggs, *AE*, 515–18.
5. Chs XII, XIV.
6. See J. K. Davies, *Athenian propertied families*, 600–300 BC, 233–6.
7. A. Andrewes, *JHS*, XCVIII (1978), 1–5.

8. Plut., op. cit. XII.

9. Thuc. I 19, 116 2, 117 2; III 10; VI 85 2; VII 20 2 (Khios and Lesbos). Compare [Arist.] *Ath. Pol.*, 24 2.

10. Andrewes, art. cit., 1. See Plat., *Lakhes* 179c and Plut., *Life of Demosthenes*, XIII.

11. Andrewes also objects (art. cit., 4–5) that Plutarch is unrealistic in attributing to Perikles' Athenian opponents an objection in principle to imperialism. He cites Thuc. VIII 48 6 where wealthy and conservative Athenians, the successors of Thucydides son of Melesias, are mentioned as leading exploiters of Athens' subjects in the late Empire. That passage, however, is consciously paradoxical; the "so-called" fine gentlemen are in fact (in spite of their pretensions) exploiters of the Empire. Andrewes himself notes evidence that conservative Athenians did pose as champions of certain allies (art. cit., 4). The paradoxical nature of Thuc. VIII 48 6 is confirmed by the description there of the Athenian *dēmos* as a chastener (*sōphronistēs*) of the fine gentlemen; normally it was the fine gentlemen who claimed that they chastened the *dēmos* — Thuc. III 82 8, VIII 64 5.

12. Thuc. I 73 4; cf. III 54 3 with Gomme, *HCT*, ad loc.

13. Hdt. VI 108, 111, 113.

14. Plut. *Life of Perikles* XII.

15. A. R. Burn, *A traveller's history of Greece*, 185; Meiggs, *AE* 132. The translation 'wanton' is also found in B. Perrin's version of Plutarch (Loeb edition).

16. See especially Aristotle, *Nikomakhean ethics 1127a–b;* Theophrastos *Characters* 23.

17. One important exception was A. W. Gomme; see his 'The position of women in Athens in the fifth and fourth centuries BC'. in *Essays in Greek history and literature*, 89–115. See also below, Chapter 8.

18. Xen. *Oikonomikos* VII 5; VI 12, 16–17.

19. Ibid. X 1; XI 1.

20. Ibid. X 2.

21. Aristoph. *Ekklēsiazousai*, 878, 929, 1072; *Ploutos* 1063–5. The comedian Alexis referred to the use of built-up shoes, white lead and rouge by whores; J. M. Edmonds, *The fragments of Attic comedy*, II, 416.

22. F. Brommer, *The sculptures of the Parthenon*, 17.

23. Meiggs (*AE*, 132) translates the word *kallōpizontas*, ('putting on a pretty face') as 'decking', which obscures the metaphor and seems to miss the point.

24. Cf. the reference to Athens' "high heads" in Hdt. VII 140.

25. Thuc. I 10 2.

26. Thuc. VI 16 1–3. Compare Isok. XV 234.

27. For references see Gomme-Andrewes-Dover, *HCT*, IV, 246; Thuc. VI 16 6.

28. On this concept in general see N. R. E. Fisher, *Hybris*.

29. Arist. *Pol.* 1314b .

30. See Aristotle, ibid., on the resentment caused when tyrants lavished money taken from poor subjects on "courtesans, foreigners and craftsmen".

31. Arist., *Pol.* 1313b.

32. The Old Oligarch, *Constitution of Athens*, 15, claims that it was the policy of Athenian democrats to keep the allies on a subsistence income, too poor and busy to plot. Plato, *Republic* 567a, suggests that tyrants used wars for a similar purpose.

33. See, for example, Suetonius' *Life of the Divine Vespasian* XVIII.

34. He may have drawn on one of the fifth-century gossip collectors mentioned below (n. 68).

35. [Arist.] *Ath. Pol.* XXVIII; Plut. *Life of Perikles* XI.

36. Thuc. I 107 4.

37. Plutarch, op. cit., XII with A. Burford in *Parthenos and Parthenon*, supplement to *Greece and Rome* X (1963), 23–35.

38. R. Meiggs in *Parthenos and Parthenon*, 43–4.

39. J. Boardman, 'The parthenon frieze — another view' in *Festschrift für F. Brommer*, ed. U. Höckmann and A. Krug, 39–49.

40. Boardman, ibid., 48.

41. Thuc. I 73.

42. Boardman, art. cit., 39.

43. Metopes — sculptured blocks placed in the spaces between the ends of the roof-beams. See F. Brommer, *Die Metopen des Parthenon* and *The sculptures of the Parthenon* (with illustrations).

44. Boardman, art. cit., 39.

45. Boardman, art. cit., 41; M. Robertson, *The Parthenon frieze*, 11.

46. Hdt. VI 117.

47. Boardman cites the estimate of W.-H. Schuchhardt, *Jahrbuch des Deutschen Archäologischen Instituts*, XLV (1930), 274–8.

48. Compare A. W. Lawrence, *Greek and Roman sculpture*, 144. But see also E. B. Harrison in *American Journal of Archaeology*, LXXVI (1972), 353–78.

49. Boardman, art. cit., 48–9.

50. Robertson writes of the frieze, "Some forty five feet out of the original five hundred and twenty odd are lost without record"; *A history of Greek art*, I, 307.

51. Cf. Boardman, art. cit., 43.

52. The legendary ruler Theseus, who was believed to have established the Athenian state by uniting the petty states of Attikē (Thuc. II 15 1f.), was also said to have fought against Amazons (Aiskhylos, *Eumenides* 685–7) and, in later times at least, was thought to have helped the Lapiths fight the Centaurs (Plut., *Life of Theseus* XXX).

53. Compare Aristoph. *Akharnians* 502–3.

54. Isok. IV 22–33.

55. Hdt. VIII 41. See also below, Chapter 9.

56. Pausan. I 24. The small surviving statue known as the Varvakeion Athena, which is thought to represent approximately the design of the great gold and ivory statue by Pheidias, reflects a pronounced interest in snakes. Between the goddess's left leg and her shield is a large snake, corresponding with the snake mentioned by Pausanias. Also, there are two snakes meeting around her midriff to form a girdle, and a further snake around each wrist. Compare M. Robertson, *A history of Greek art*, I, 301, for the possibility that a snake was shown in the pedimental sculpture of the Parthenon.

57. For some little-known areas of resemblance between ancient and modern divination, see below, Chapter 9.

58. Contrast the colony, *apoikia*, which was a separate state, though with obligations to its *mētropolis* (mother city); A. J. Graham, *Colony and mother city in ancient Greece*, *passim*.

59. See Gomme, *HCT*, I, 344–7, 373–80; Meiggs, *AE*, 121ff.

60. Diod. XI 88; Pausan. I 27 5.

61. Diod. XII 6; Thuc. I 113.

62. The corresponding piece of useful jargon is *terminus post quem* — a point *after* which an event must have occurred.

63. Plut. *Life of Perikles* XI.

64. Gomme, *HCT*, I, 380; Meiggs, *AE*, 121.

65. Thuc. III 50 2.

66. Plut., op. cit., XI; Diod. XI 88; Meiggs, *AE*, 160.

67. Plut., op. cit., XI.

68. See Plutarch's references to Ion of Khios (op. cit., V, XXVIII) and to Stesimbrotos of Thasos (op. cit., VIII, XIII, XXVI, XXXVI), both contemporary with Perikles.

69. In Thuc. II 40 2, Perikles is represented as refusing to apply the opposite term, *apragmōn*, as a compliment to those who abstained from politics. See also Thuc. II 63 2. Gomme's note on Thuc. II 40 2 (*HCT*, ad loc.) seems to oversimplify Athenian attitudes towards "activism". Better are his remarks in *Essays in Greek history and literature*, 101.

70. Thuc. III 50 2.

71. Meiggs-Lewis, no. 49, lines 13–17; on Brea see Graham, op. cit., *passim*; Meiggs, *AE*, 158–9.

72. Brea decree (see preceding note), lines 39–42.

73. Antiphon's surviving work is most easily available in *Minor Attic orators*, vol. I (Loeb edition); the fragment cited here is on p. 301.

74. Aristoph. *Knights* 1088–9.

75. Meiggs, *AE*, 262; compare Thuc. VIII 48 6.

76. For the Greek text, M. N. Tod, *A selection of Greek historical inscriptions*, II, no. 123, lines 25–31, 35–46. See also Meiggs, *AE*, 262, 402.

77. Meiggs-Lewis no. 45; Meiggs, *AE*, 167–72, 599–601, Gomme *HCT*, I, 383–4.

78. See R. Meiggs, 'The dating of fifth-century Attic inscriptions', *JHS*, LXXXVI (1966), 86–98 and esp. 92f. For coinage as a political symbol, Aristoph. *Frogs* 718ff.

79. J. P. Barron, *The silver coins of Samos*, 59–67, 80–93; Meiggs, *AE*, 170–1.

80. Meiggs, *AE*, 171.

81. J. K. Davies, *Democracy and classical Greece*, 94; Meiggs-Lewis, no. 56, line 19.

82. Meiggs, *AE*, 173.

83. A. H. M. Jones in *Proceedings of the Cambridge Philological Society*, n.s., II (1952–3), 45; Thuc. III 10 5.

84. Above, n. 12 and especially Thuc. IV 108 5.

85. Thuc. I 22 1. For an introduction to the modern controversy about Thucydides' method in composing the speeches, G. E. M. de Ste.

Croix, *Origins*, 7–16.

86. See also Thuc. I 96 2–97 1, III 11; *ATL*, III, 138–41.

87. *Polypsēphia* could, for example, have been used to prevent the taking of votes on proposals for action.

88. *ATL*, loc. cit.; de Ste. Croix, *Origins*, 303. Compare A. H. M. Jones, art. cit. For conflicting modern views on the formal position of Athens in votes of the Delian League, see the arguments and references collected by de Ste. Croix, *Origins*, 303–7.

89. Thuc. I 113. Athens had previously taken 100 wealthy men as hostages from the Opuntian Locrians, a people to the north of Boiotia; Thuc. I 108 3.

90. Thuc. I 113 1.

91. Thuc. I 114. On the timing of these attacks see Chapter 4.

92. Thuc. II 21 1, V 16; Gomme, *HCT*, I, 341 and below, Chapter 4.

93. Thuc. I 114 3.

94. Plut. *Life of Perikles* XXIII.

95. Meiggs-Lewis, no. 52.

96. Lines 21–4; Meiggs, *AE*, 179.

97. Lines 71–6. Compare Gomme, *HCT*, I, 342, n. 2; Meiggs, *AE*, 224–5; G. E. M. de Ste. Croix, *CQ*, n.s., XI (1961), 271–2.

98. Antiphon V 47.

99. G. E. M. de Ste. Croix, 'Notes on jurisdiction in the Athenian empire' in *CQ*, n.s., XI (1961), 94–112, 268–80.

100. De Ste. Croix, *art. cit.*, 95, 270, 272 .

101. See Davies, *Democracy and classical Greece*, 81–2, 85, referring to S. E. G. (*Supplementum Epigraphicum Graecum*), X 23, 76.

102. Thuc. III 82 8.

103. Thuc. III 70.

104. Thuc. I 115 1.

105. For a reconstruction, de Ste. Croix, *Origins*, 293–4.

106. Thuc. I 140 2, VII 18 2.

107. For the alliance with Akhaia, Thuc. I 111 3.

108. Thuc. I 67 2, 139 1, 140 3; de Ste. Croix, *Origins*, 293–4.

109. Thuc. I 115 2–5.

110. Over 1,200 talents; Gomme, *HCT*, I, 355–6 and references there given.

111. Old Oligarch I 14, III 10–11. On this writer see A. W. Gomme, *More essays in Greek history and literature*, 38–69; de Ste. Croix, *Origins*, 307–10; W. G. Forrest, *Klio*, 52 (1970), 107–16 and below, Chapter 7.

112. Arist. *Pol.* 1307b. Compare Xen., *Hell.* III 4 7; Isok. IV 104–6, VIII 79, XII 54, 68. Most of the inscriptions cited in *ATL*, III, 150 as evidence of Athenian promotion of *dēmokratia* in the subject states are, in their fragmentary condition, disappointingly inconclusive.

113. See Thuc. VIII 21 for help given by Athenians, who chanced to be present, to democratic revolutionaries against an oligarchic government, again at Samos, in 412.

114. Thuc. VIII 64 5.

115. The Erythrai Decree required that Erythraians act justly towards the *plēthos* of Athens and the *plēthos* of the allies. On the democratic associations of the term *plēthos*, see Chapter 2 above.

116. Chapter 1, n. 10.

117. A fragment of a speech by Antiphon suggests that on the isle of Samothrace, in the northern Aegean, local rich men were chosen to collect the *phoros*; see *Minor Attic orators* (Loeb edn), I, 293. If embezzlement were suspected, a rich man had wealth to distrain upon.

118. Meiggs, *AE*, ch. 18.

119. A. French, *The growth of the Athenian economy* 95, 129, 168.

120. See above, p. 47.

121. Thuc. VII 28 4.

122. One should remember, however, that the margin between the income received by traders and producers and the income needed for their subsistence would not match the margins familiar in modern industrialised countries. A reduction of 5 per cent in a poor man's receipts may be disastrous.

123. The Empire provided the Athenian state with income in addition to the *phoros* reflected in the ATLs. Perikles is reported to have mentioned the figure of 600 talents as an approximate average of annual income to Athens from the Empire; Thuc. II 13 3. For a discussion of this problematic passage, Gomme, *HCT*, II, 17–20.

124. Meiggs, *AE*, 439–41. On the widespread enthusiasm for military service among the Athenian poor, Thuc. VI 24; Aristoph. *Ekkl.* 197–8; cf. Arist. *Pol.* 1297b.

125. Aristoph. *Birds* 1427; compare Thuc. I 5 3 on the survival of piracy in north-western Greece. On piracy in the Aegean after the end of the Athenian Empire, G. L. Cawkwell, *JHS*, CI (1981), 48 n.32.

126. Isok. IV 115. Isokrates is given to large exaggeration; for example, he says at section 106 of this speech that the member states of the Delian League and Athenian Empire lived for 70 years without social conflict — contrast Thuc. III 82. But at the time of this speech, 380, he and his audience might know more of contemporary piracy than they did of tensions in the long-departed Athenian Empire.

127. Meiggs-Lewis, no. 65, lines 34–6.

128. The decree concerning Methone (see preceding note) refers to an Athenian patrol guarding the Hellespont; lines 36–40. On the Athenian corn trade see de Ste. Croix, *Origins*, 45–9; P. D. A. Garnsey, 'Grain for Athens' in *Crux: Essays presented to G. E. M. de Ste. Croix* (P. A. Cartledge and F. D. Harvey (eds)), 62–75. Compare the attempt of Athens in the fourth century to corner the market in the valuable ruddle (red dye) produced on the isle of Keos; Todd, op. cit. (above, n. 76), vol. II, no. 162.

129. A picturesque account of products imported by Athens survives in a fragment of the late fifth-century comedian Hermippos (quoted by Athenaeus I 27e–28a and partially translated by Meiggs, *AE*, 264). See also Thuc. II 38 2; Old Oligarch II 7.

130. On metics see Chapter 7.

131. For foreigners at Athenian festivals, Aristoph. *Akharnians* 502–3.

132. Grote was a Utilitarian and a banker who, as a Member of Parliament in Britain, advocated the widening of the franchise; see M. L. Clarke, *George Grote. A biography*. In de Ste. Croix's work *The class struggle in the ancient Greek world* social conflicts are considered partly in

the light of ideas of Karl Marx; see, e.g., 19–30, 79.

133. *Historia*, III (1954/5) 23.

134. W. S. Ferguson, *CAH*, V, 286, 348, 359.

135. H. Last, *CAH*, XI, 435.

136. Isok. XII 67–8.

137. *ATL*, III, 152.

138. On freedom of speech see, e.g., Eur. *Hippolytos* 421–3; on political gentleness, Dem. XXIV 51; [Arist.] *Ath. Pol.* 16, 22, 40; below, Chapter 7.

139. There are, of course, innumerable other points of difference between the two cultures. Attitudes towards the private ownership of land, chattel slavery, frank imperialism and the position of women come immediately to mind.

140. Meiggs' work *The Athenian Empire* may encourage this currently widespread view, with remarks hostile to imperialism of various kinds. So (*AE*, 363): "the moderates went into exile at Atarneus. They were still there after the war, defying the puppets of Sparta in Chios and out of sympathy with the other Ionian cities who were not prepared to fight for their liberties." The somewhat loaded language ("moderates", "puppets", "fight for liberties") seems to express an enthusiasm for local autonomy. Compare p. 373 on the Spartan commander Kallikratidas, who "had little sympathy with a policy that depended on Persian support"; he "preferred to fight a Greek war in a Greek way but his decent instincts needed success to nourish them".

141. Thuc. II 8 4.

142. *Historia*, III (1954/5), 1–41. The evidence collected by de Ste. Croix is too extensive to be treated in full here. In addition to the selected passages dealt with in the main text below, see, e.g., Thuc. IV 84, 130, VIII 9 3, 14 2.

143. De Ste. Croix, art. cit., 4.

144. A *dynasteia* (Thuc. IV 78 3): on this form of government, Thuc. III 62 3, Arist. *Pol.* 1292b.

145. Thuc. IV 78 2f.

146. With the words *aiei pote*; Liddell-Scott-Jones, *Greek-English Lexicon*, under *pote* III 3.

147. *eunoun* here, *eunoia* at II 8.

148. See below, and especially de Ste. Croix, art. cit., *passim*.

149. Thuc. II 65.

150. See below.

151. Thuc. II 63 2, III 37 2.

152. Above, n. 12 and Thuc. IV 108 5.

153. Thuc. III 47 2; the word *eunous* is used once more.

154. Gomme, *HCT*, II, 290.

155. Thuc. III 27.

156. Thuc. III 82 1.

157. Thuc. III 82 8.

158. Among the innumerable results of triadic thinking are the rewarding of three competitors in athletic and other contests; the division of university class lists into three groups; the classification of computers (mainframe, mini- and micro-); social classification (upper, middle and

working class); the perception of historical epochs (ancient, medieval and modern). Historians of the English language now distinguish between Old English, Middle English and Modern English, and again between Early Modern English, Modern English and Late Modern English. Triadic thinking seems especially common in folklore, religion and archaeology. Welsh folk wisdom, for example, was traditionally expressed in triads; R. Bromwich, *Trioedd Ynys Prydein* ('Triads of the Island of Britain'). Triads are prominent in the reporting of the Passion of Christ in the gospels; Judas betrays Christ for 30 pieces of silver; St. Peter denies Him thrice; Christ prophesies that He will rise on the third day; Pilate asks the crowd three times about the treatment of Christ; Christ is crucified with two others, and at the third hour; "and when the sixth hour was come, there was darkness over the whole land until the ninth hour" (Mark 15:33). Diviners of Classical Greece showed a special interest in the expression 'thrice nine'; Thuc. V 26, VII 50 and *Bulletin of the Institute of Classical Studies*, 26 (1979), 47–8. More generally, G. Dumézil, *L'Idéologie tripartie des Indo-Européens, Collection Latomus*, XXXI, 1958). Archaeologists divide the Greek Bronze Age into Early, Middle and Late Helladic; Late Helladic (LH) is itself divided into LHI, II, III, and LHIII is in turn divided into LHIIIa, b and c. Such formulaic thinking is likely to impose distinctions which should not exist and to neglect others which should.

159. E.g. Thuc. IV 66, VIII 9 3.

160. Thuc. VIII 21 with 73.

161. The Spartan Brasidas seems to have found it necessary to counter such a fear; Thuc. IV 86, 114.

162. J. de Romilly, *Bulletin of the Institute of Classical Studies*, 13 (1966), 3, 5.

163. Thuc. VII 28 3.

164. De Ste. Croix, *Origins*, 207.

165. Thuc. VIII 2 2.

166. Compare III 3 1, IV 108 4.

167. Thuc. VIII 21, Xen. *Hell*. II 3 6, Meiggs, *AE*, 357 (Samos); Thuc. VIII 28 2 with Diod. XIII 104 (Iasos).

168. Thuc. III 82 3.

169. Thuc. III 82 8.

170. Thuc. III 70–82.

171. Thuc. III 82 2.

172. G. E. M. de Ste. Croix, *The class struggle in the ancient Greek world* 298, 608, n. 55.

173. Plato, *Republic* 551d; compare 422e–423a.

174. On the reluctance of oligarchs to provide adequate finance for warfare, Plato, *Republic* 551e. (Contrast Thuc. VIII 63 4.) On festivals see below, Chapter 7.

175. *Iliad* II 212–69.

176. Thuc. III 82 8.

177. Hesiod, *Works and days* 219, 248ff. Even in democratic Athens the power of bribery might tell against the poor litigant; below, Chapter 7.

178. Arist., *Pol.* 1297b.

179. Below, Chapter 7.

180. Below, Chapter 7.

181. Compare Old Oligarch I 14 and Aristophanes' satirical picture of a sykophant living off Athens' subjects: *Birds*, 1422ff.

182. Old Oligarch I 10; Plat. *Rep.* 563b.

183. Xen. *Symp.* IV 30f.; Plato, *Republic* 563c, complains that horses and asses in a *dēmokratia* share their masters' independent manners, refusing to make way for people in the streets.

184. Theophrastos *Characters* XXVI.

185. Lines 57–70 in H. Lloyd-Jones, *Female of the species: Semonides on women*; cf. Aristoph. *Clouds* 49ff. In France, in the highly political atmosphere of summer 1968, the present writer observed people being teased as "*aristos*" for seeking not to eat successive courses off a single plate.

186. *The road to Wigan Pier* Ch. 8. Compare the Latin word *lautus*, 'washed', which came to mean 'elegant'.

187. The use of the word *pakhys* ('stout') as a synonym for 'wealthy', as by Aristophanes (*Knights*, 1139; *Peace*, 639), was probably more than metaphorical; see Plato, *Republic* 556d, who refers to wealthy men as frequently overweight and pale, in contrast to lean, sunburnt, poor men.

188. De Ste. Croix suggests that when Thucydides wrote of "every individual" he was thinking mainly of his own social group, the wealthy; *Historia*, III (1954–5), 31. For a modern analogue, compare the following letter to *The Times* of 6 July 1940: "Sir, Honour is satisfied. *The Times* emerges yet again as the champion of the fighting spirit. All are delighted: the Company Commander, the Eton boy, and Your obedient servant, (Lord) Mottistone."

189. See G. Grote, *A history of Greece*, VI, ch.52 and VII, ch. 54; A. W. Gomme, *More essays in Greek history and literature*, 112–21.

190. Thuc. IV 28 5.

191. Thuc. IV 39 3.

192. Ibid.

193. See A. G. Woodhead, 'Thucydides' portrait of Cleon' in *Mnemosyne*, Series IV, vol. XIII (1960), 289–318.

194. See C. A. Powell, 'Thucydides and divination' in *Bulletin of the Institute of Classical Studies*, 26 (1979), 45–50, and (for different views) S. I. Oost, *Classical Philology*, LXX (1975) 186–96; N. Marinatos, *Thucydides and religion*.

195. Thuc. VII 50 4, V 26 3f.

196. Thuc. II 21 3; compare II 8 2.

197. Thuc. II 17 1f. with Powell, art. cit., 45–6.

198. See above, Chapter 1.

199. Thuc. II 65 4.

200. Thuc. IV 28 3, cf. VI 63 2.

201. Thuc. VIII 72 2, compare 48 3. At III 87 3 part of Athens' land army is referred to by Thucydides as a "mob".

202. Thuc. II 65 11.

203. Thuc. VIII 1 4.

204. Thuc. VIII 97 2, referring to the constitution of the Five Thousand. In his generally sensible article, 'The politics of the historian

Thucydides' (*Phoenix*, 10 (1956), 93–102), M. F. McGregor mistranslates part of this passage as "the Athenians appear to have had": Thucydides was more emphatic. Also, McGregor seems not to detect the *general* criticism of *dēmokratia* at VIII 1 4. On Thucydides' politics see also P. A. Brunt, *Classical Review*, 69 (1955), 251 ("Thucydides ... did not believe in democratic ideals."); K. J. Dover, *Thucydides*; Andrewes, *HCT*, V, 332f., 335–9.

205. Thuc. III 82 8, VIII 89 3.
206. Thuc. VIII 64 5; compare 64 4.
207. Thuc. VIII 24 4.
208. Thuc. I 19, compare III 82 I and below, Chapter 5. On Khios, de Ste. Croix, *Historia*, III (1954–5), 6, n. 10.
209. For example, Sparta's chief military commanders on foreign expeditions were her kings, hereditary dyarchs; see Chapter 4.
210. Thuc. IV 104–6, V 26.
211. Thuc. V 26 5.
212. Ibid.

4

Sparta: Her Problems and Her Ingenuity, 478–431

Sparta's alleged lack of intelligence

The history of Sparta through most of the classical period is largely one of success, in her own terms. Having dominated the Peloponnese since the mid-sixth century,[1] in 480–479 she was recognised as the leader of the Greek states which resisted the Persians.[2] As eastern Greeks defected from the Persian Empire, Sparta's authority extended — although briefly — across the Aegean. Severe setbacks followed; these, and some of the techniques with which Sparta overcame them, are the subjects of this chapter. By 404 Sparta had conquered the Athenian Empire, and thus added dominion by sea to her traditional land-based hegemony. She remained by far the greatest single Greek power, until deprived of her position abruptly and for ever in 371.

Since ancient times the Spartan way of life has attracted much moralising.[3] Some have admired the physical courage, military discipline and the general subordination at Sparta of the individual to the group. Others, especially in recent times, have been repelled by the Spartans' treatment of their subject population, the helots. Neither group has been much concerned to investigate, or admit, the intelligence with which the Spartans pursued their ends. Instead it is often suggested that the Spartans were fools. In important modern textbooks Sparta is accused of "folly",[4] "arrogant stupidity",[5] disastrous ineptitude[6] and "characteristic selfishness and lack of foresight".[7] The view that Spartans in general were not very bright may have been encouraged by words of Thucydides. He writes that Brasidas, the eminent soldier and politician of the 420s, was "an able speaker — for a Spartan".[8] Elsewhere he states emphatically that, with

96

their slowness and lack of (strategic) daring, the Spartans "proved ..., as on so many other occasions, the most convenient people in the world for the Athenians to oppose in war".[9]

Spartans themselves may deliberately have encouraged the view that they were simple, obedient, soldiers; Thucydides represents the Spartan king Arkhidamos as boasting of the way in which ignorance in certain areas promoted the sound judgement of his people.[10] The occasion of this remark was a private one,[11] for Spartans only, but if Thucydides reconstructed this section of Arkhidamos' speech in the knowledge that Spartans made such boasts to a wider audience, our suspicions should perhaps be aroused. The Spartans had a lively sense of what it suited non-Spartans to know. Thucydides comments on the secrecy which characterised Sparta's political arrangements; his remark must always be borne in mind when we ask how much can now be known about the Spartans.[12] The idea of Spartan simplicity may have been a convenient one for the Spartans themselves to propagate.[13] Sparta's enemies might be demoralised by the thought that her military ascendancy was due to the sheer discipline and physical hardness of her men, since in those respects few non-Spartans could expect their cities to make the sacrifice of comfort or of peaceful economic activity needed to match Sparta. Strategic skill, on the other hand, might be thought capable of being assimilated and countered more easily.[14] Spartans may have been eager for their enemies not to understand how much they depended on such skill.

The idea of Spartan stupidity is, in any case, difficult to maintain if we consider the scale and duration of Sparta's ascendancy and the smallness of the citizen population with which the ascendancy was achieved. Personal errors, corruption and ingrained constitutional defects did affect Sparta's performance, as we shall see. But the more shortcomings we identify, the more obvious should be the need to discover the positive qualities which allowed the Spartans to gain and keep their power. The prowess of Sparta's hoplites is not enough to explain her ascendancy. At the start of the Peloponnesian War, the 13,000 hoplites of Athens probably outnumbered those of Sparta by more than 3 to 1;[15] Sparta kept her empire until 371, by which time her hoplites seem to have numbered scarcely more than 1,000.[16] In looking for signs of strategic acumen in the Spartans, it may prove interesting to check Thucydides' generalisation on the subject against the details of his own narrative.

The helots: their impact on Sparta and her foreign policy

The Spartans in their homeland had a perennial problem. Their conquests of Lakonia and Messenia in earlier centuries had left them with a subject population which, unlike the slaves of other Greek communities, had not been imported piecemeal from a variety of foreign lands. Sparta's helots were Greeks, conscious of their community and of their lost freedom, as de Ste. Croix has stressed in perhaps the most profound and successful treatment of Spartan history so far published.[17] Helots, and especially those of Messenia, watched for a chance to revolt; as Aristotle put it, "they continually lie in wait, as it were, to take advantage of the Spartans' misfortunes".[18] As farmers and craftworkers, helots produced most of the wealth on which Sparta's citizens, the Spartiates, lived.[19] The degree of the Spartiates' dependence on their subject population was unusually great, even by the standards of classical Greece.[20] Their vulnerability is suggested by certain round (and therefore at best approximate) numbers given by Herodotos in connection with the battle of Plataia, in 479. He writes that Sparta fought with 5,000 of her own citizen hoplites, 5,000 of the *perioikoi* (free men, but not citizens of Sparta, who lived within Spartan territory),[21] while for every Spartiate on the campaign there were also present seven helots.[22] Thucydides, without giving figures, suggests in a passing reference that Sparta had more slaves than any other Greek state.[23]

A modern ruling group, if similarly dependent on a large and hostile population, might protect its position by the use of informers, of terror and of superior technology. We hear of informers among the helots,[24] and of the use of terror by the state,[25] but even the most sophisticated armaments of the day would not have been proof against makeshift weapons in the hands of numerically far superior helots. So the Spartiates turned their own bodies into weapons of the highest order. In a striking passage, de Ste. Croix compares the Spartans with a monster of Germanic myth:

> Like Fafner, who after appropriating the Rhinemaidens' treasure was obliged to turn himself into a dragon and live a nasty life in a cave, the Spartans could never again relax ... Aristotle, of all surviving ancient writers, expresses this most clearly: the Spartans, he says, by imposing on their

young men exercises designed solely to impart courage, have made them 'beast-like'.[26]

Details of daily existence at Sparta will be examined in a later chapter, but a word of caution may be needed here. We should beware of thinking the Spartan way of life so horrible that we are obliged to see the Spartans as irrational in maintaining it. For one thing, the hardships involved in the Spartan discipline would of course be less daunting to habitués than to people from less rigorous cultures. Also, the happiness of individuals often depends on whether they think they are good at what they think really matters. (We may notice in our own time that people, by a species of wishful thinking, commonly construct schemes of value which give prominence to whatever they themselves happen to excel in; the scholar respects learning, the undergraduate values sharp wits, the footballer reveres athleticism, and so on.) Spartan culture possessed, to a most unusual extent, a harmony between values and self-image.

As Aristotle suggests, Spartan ideals mainly concerned military prowess.[27] And in that sphere, while Greeks were thought (by themselves) to be superior to non-Greeks, an opinion reinforced by the Persian Wars, Spartans seemed superior to other Greeks. Thus Spartans could believe that they were the best in the world at the thing they most respected.[28] This no doubt gave them an immense satisfaction, making bearable the physical nastiness of their lives. When Aristotle states, "... it is clear that they [the Spartans] are not a happy people and that their legislator was not a good one", he is thinking, as he himself stresses, of the period after 371 – "now that the Spartans no longer rule over others".[29] At that period, the values of the defeated Spartans conflicted to some extent with their current achievement, though even then they might persuade themselves that *man for man* they were the finest soldiers in the world, who had been defeated in 371 by sheer force of numbers.[30]

The corporate pride of the Spartans may have intensified as their numbers dwindled in the fifth and early fourth centuries; the fewer they were, the more impressive was their military feat in dominating Greece. Scholars have often puzzled over why Sparta tolerated the decline in her own population, which led, as Aristotle puts it, to Sparta's perishing through shortage of people;[31] it is this which elicited the unhelpful modern comment about "characteristic selfishness and lack of foresight" at Sparta.

We should not suggest that the Spartans planned, or were complacent about, their own decline in numbers.[32] But pride may have reduced the eagerness to rebuild the population. Since the decline in Spartan numbers reflected more and more glowingly on the military skills of the survivors, the obvious reform — to widen the franchise — would have meant not only that some lands might have been taken from existing citizens,[33] but that the cherished military prestige of those citizens would have been diluted.

The need to keep the helots obediently at work imposed several aspects of Sparta's foreign policy. Foreign invaders, who might protect or encourage disaffected helots, had to be kept out. As de Ste. Croix observes, "It is a striking fact that the very first time a large hostile army of good hoplites penetrated deeply into the Peloponnese, in 370/69 under Epaminondas, Sparta lost Messenia."[34] To keep Sparta's northern neighbour, Tegea, as a buffer state was of obvious value. A friendly Tegeate government would also refuse to harbour helots, who might otherwise think of escaping over the long, mountainous and unpoliceable frontier which Sparta and Tegea shared.[35] An unfriendly neighbour, by encouraging desertions, might subvert the Spartan economy, as Sparta herself damaged Athens from 413 by sheltering *her* runaway slaves.[36]

Foreign expeditions had a profound disadvantage for Sparta in drawing off troops who might be needed to deter or defeat a rising of helots at home. As Thucydides states,[37] Sparta was not quick to embark on foreign wars unless compelled (the qualification is important[38]); for this the helots provide much of the explanation. But Sparta's system of foreign alliances, while providing the potential for numerous distracting wars, compensated by supplying allies against helot revolts .[39] The support of foreign states may well have been crucial in containing the great revolt which began in the mid-460s.[40] Sparta's eagerness for such support was so great that even Athens, in the immediate aftermath of a long, inconclusive war with Sparta, was asked for a promise to provide it.[41]

The distribution of power within Sparta

In the states under her control Sparta sought to establish oligarchies friendly to herself; so Thucydides makes clear.[42] This in itself might cause us to infer that Sparta's own constitution was oligarchic, since in the ancient world, as today, great powers tend to promote in their satellite states political and economic arrangements which resemble their own.[43] Some aspects of Spartan life superficially resembled *dēmokratia*.[44] All male citizens had an equal vote in the general assembly which decided great issues, such as whether to go to war,[45] and poor men were often chosen as ephors[46] — the officials who, in annually-changing panels of five, theoretically dominated the Spartan state. But the power of the wealthy was profound. Aristotle notes that the ephors, when poor, were easily and successfully bribed,[47] and bribery of course tends to favour those with the largest inducements to offer. Two wealthy royal families, the Agiads and Eurypontids, each supplied one member at a time for the dual kingship, an appointment for life which usually brought command over certain foreign expeditions,[48] as well as great power at home. A king had the ability to promote or obstruct over an indefinite period, and so might have much influence over an ephor whose tenure of office was not repeatable and would expire within the year.[49] Other families, in addition to royalty, enjoyed special influence, partly as a result of inherited wealth and of prestige derived from eminent ancestors.[50]

In our records of fifth-century Sparta, the names of kings occur far more often than those of ephors.[51] This may slightly under-represent the real power of the ephorate.[52] In analysing Spartan history we should be aware that our information almost always comes from, or at least via, non-Spartan sources. Non-Spartans would hear disproportionately much about kings and little about ephors, because of the special prominence of a king who led an expedition outside Spartan territory and because kings held office for longer. The name of a long-lived king, such as Arkhidamos in the fifth century or Agesilaos in the fourth, would be mentioned abroad year after year. And, as modern experiment has con-firmed,[53] repetition powerfully aids memory. So does simplifi-cation,[54] which will have occurred as one king was found easier to refer to by name than a plurality of ephors. However, the preponderance of royal names in our sources must reflect the possession of considerable power by the kings.

Thus influence at Sparta was possessed in oligarchic fashion by a wealthy few. But in another sense we may see the whole Spartan community as an oligarchy in relation to the helots, the more numerous, disfranchised, Greek poor who in other circumstances might have been recognised as the *dēmos* of Lakonia and

Messenia.[55] It has not been normal among scholars to regard the helots in this way, because the helots, unlike the Greek poor under other oligarchies, were not acknowledged as citizens who were allowed to own land and were protected from certain abuses. But on close examination the Spartans may appear in this respect to have differed from the typical oligarchy chiefly in point of efficiency, in oligarchic terms. We may compare the way in which, according to Plato, oligarchs elsewhere were commonly fat, unhealthy men, whose feebleness on the battlefield gave subversive ideas to soldiers present from their own *dēmos*.[56] The Spartans, far more efficient from an oligarchic viewpoint, made themselves into models of fitness and disarmed their subjects.

Fifth-century Sparta may, then, be seen as an oligarchy within an oligarchy.[57] A few thousand citizens dominated the masses of helot poor, and within the few thousand citizens a few wealthy families had special power.[58] Plato observes that oligarchies in general were beset by jealousy, that is, by rivalry and resentment among the leading men over status and wealth.[59] Correspondingly we find at Sparta rancour between the two royal families.[60] Thucydides records a case in which the Spartans refused to reinforce a successful army of their own, "to some extent through jealousy on the part of the leading men" towards its commander, Brasidas.[61] Later the victorious Lysandros encountered similar jealousy .[62] Difficulties arose repeatedly for Sparta as her most powerful men sought by illicit means to promote themselves over, or to protect themselves from, rivals and enemies within the ruling circle.[63]

The fall of Leotykhidas and Pausanias

At the start of our period, in 478, the two royal families, the Eurypontids and the Agiads, were represented respectively by King Leotykhidas and by Pausanias, regent for the young son of the late King Leonidas. Both men had presided over a great victory, Leotykhidas at Mykalē and Pausanias at Plataia. Both, like Brasidas and Lysandros later, would have incurred a certain jealousy at Sparta, where military success was so valued. Some time after the withdrawal of the defeated Persians from Greece, probably in the 470s, Leotykhidas led a force to attack the Thessalians, who under pressure had joined the Persian side. An incident on this campaign seems to have conduced to the Spartan king's downfall. Herodotos writes:

> He [Leotykhidas] commanded a Spartan campaign against
> Thessaly, and when he had it in his power to get total
> control he accepted a large bribe of silver. Caught red-
> handed there in the camp, sitting on a glove full of silver, he
> was exiled from Sparta by the sentence of a court and his
> property was demolished. He fled to Tegea where he died.[64]

It is implied that the bribe diverted the king from fulfilling
Sparta's purpose of conquest. But we should always beware of
assuming that a bribe when accepted corrupts the will of the
accepter, or that, even where the accepter is corrupted, he
manages to achieve what the briber wishes. We hear from
Thucydides of a Persian envoy who came to Sparta in the early
450s to promote, by distribution of money, a policy of attacking
Athens:[65] in this case it was eventually perceived that "the money
was being spent in vain". What went on in Leotykhidas' tent
would be known to very few, even at the time; even fewer would
know how far he was influenced by any bribe. We cannot judge
whether this was a case of royal malpractice or of the king's
enemies and rivals conspiring against him. The bare details which
were verifiable outside Sparta are more secure: a Spartan
expedition against Thessaly was not a complete success, and
Leotykhidas became an exile in Tegea.

In another area of war, the abrasive behaviour of the regent
Pausanias had been largely responsible for Sparta's loss of control
over her eastern Greek allies (see Chapter 1). Thucydides states
that the Spartans were glad to be rid of the Persian war, and
thought the new leaders, the Athenians, to be suitable for the role
and to be friendly towards Sparta, at the time.[66] He also makes it
clear that the Spartans feared that other commanders of theirs, if
sent to the war, might degenerate as Pausanias had done. The fear
of bribed or unruly generals may have inhibited Sparta for as long
as her hegemony lasted.[67].

Thucydides gives much colourful detail on the fall of Pausanias.
The Spartan regent had treasonable correspondence with the
King of Persia, proposing to marry his daughter[68] and to bring
the Greeks under Persian rule. He gave himself a bodyguard of
men from the Persian Empire, again while commander of the
Greeks against Persia. He was recalled to Sparta, acquitted of a
charge of medism but censured on another matter. After a further

spell at the Hellespont, this time as a freelance, he was again recalled to Sparta and imprisoned. When freed he continued to correspond with King Xerxes, and invited the helots to join him in a revolution at Sparta, promising them freedom and citizenship. Helots informed the Spartan authorities; so did a man whom Pausanias was sending as messenger to Persia and who had discovered that the secret message from Pausanias contained an instruction to put him, the messenger, to death. By arrangement with this man, ephors were hidden in a hut and listened to Pausanias talking treasonably to him. When the ephors came to arrest Pausanias, he fled to religious sanctuary where, imprisoned and exposed, he reached the point of death. The authorities broke sanctuary to remove him, whereupon he died.[69]

Much of this story has been doubted.[70] It is not in the normal manner of Thucydides. Elsewhere he remarks on the absence of story-telling from his own work[71] and notes the impossibility of discovering exactly what went on at this period.[72] Yet in this connection he tells a lively tale (in more detail than can be given here), and claims to have precise detail even of secret material, such as the wording of letters between Pausanias and King Xerxes. Several aspects of the story have been found implausible, such as the offer to marry Xerxes' daughter and the use, by one commanding a force against Persia, of Persian bodyguards and other trappings. With testimony ancient and modern, it is often rewarding to ask, "For this to be accurate, what must its ultimate source have been?" Elements of the present story, the conversation in the hut, the wording of the correspondence with Xerxes and the testimony of the helot informers, presumably derived — if accurate — from the Spartan authorities. But the latter, after causing Pausanias' death, had a strong interest in demonstrating that he had been deeply guilty. Ugly questions might otherwise have arisen concerning the ungrateful treatment of a once-victorious commander. Has Thucydides mistakenly accepted official propaganda?

It is interesting that three members of Spartan royalty, whose careers come to unhappy ends in this period, go out in colourful style. Leotykhidas sits on a gloveful of silver, Pausanias talks treasonably in the presence of lurking ephors, while King Kleomenes, another source of trouble for the authorities at Sparta, killed himself in the 480s by slitting his own flesh into rags.[73] Such details — shocking, simple, graphic and memorable — recall modern journalism. Also, like journalism, they tend to damn the individual and to deflect criticism from abstractions, such as the constitution of Sparta. Are these details fictitious? Thucydides does not take responsibility for, or indeed mention, the stories concerning Leotykhidas and Kleomenes. Twice in the tale of Pausanias he suspends judgement on a detail or set of details, with the qualifying phrase, 'it is said'.[74] But he gives emphatic personal endorsement to the report that Pausanias was "up to something" with the helots.[75] In Thucydides' defence, we should note that his general remark at the very beginning of his work, on the unreliability of information about this pre-war period, may have been meant as a warning about the status of this account among others. On the positive side, the historian states that he spent much time with the Peloponnesians during his exile of twenty years (from 424/3).[76] Also, some elements of his account of Pausanias would have external witnesses: the details of Pausanias' haughty behaviour as commander of the Greeks against Persia, and the text of a boastful epigram which Thucydides records Pausanias as having published at Delphoi.[77]

Pausanias' position was indeed dangerous, psychologically and politically. By commanding victoriously at the hoplite battle of Plataia he had attained, fairly young, almost the highest success conceivable according to Spartan values. He was thus exposed to grandiose pride; his inscription at Delphoi referred to himself in the singular as having "destroyed the Persian army".[78] Large ambition is likely enough in such a person, as other Spartans, perhaps anyway jealous of his widespread reputation,[79] would no doubt be aware. Thucydides refers to personal enemies of Pausanias at Sparta, and to the requirement that he be "on a level with the existing constitution".[80] While enemies would seek to reduce his status, Pausanias' desire to promote himself would be intensified by the thought that, as regent, his position was borrowed. We do not know at what age a king of Sparta was reckoned to reach his majority.[81] But the young King Pleistarkhos, to whose minority Pausanias owed his formal position, would be twenty at the latest in 460–459, since his father, Leonidas, had died in mid-480. The constitution of Sparta thus offered the youngish victor of Plataia a long and premature twilight to his career, unless he took unusual measures. There should be no certainty that Thucydides has seriously misrepresented the measures he did take.

Resistance to Sparta within the Peloponnese: the helot revolt

The date of Pausanias' death has not been established, but probably belongs in the period around 470.[82] Also in that period, and perhaps partly as a result of her domestic difficulties, Sparta lost control of allies in the central and northern Peloponnese. Our information on this is skeletal, and tends to be neglected by students approaching the subject for the first time. But on these troubles, now reflected in dry outline, depended Sparta's survival as a great power. Without her Peloponnesian allies, Sparta could not hope to continue sending large hoplite armies abroad and would face far greater problems with the control of the helots, on whom her economy depended.

Difficulties with the Peloponnesian allies had existed for some years. Herodotos notes in passing that at a point before the battle of Plataia, Sparta was not on friendly terms with Tegea, a state whose importance we have already observed.[83] At Plataia Tegea did fight alongside Sparta, but two other Peloponnesian states, Elis and Mantineia, arrived late in circumstances which suggest that they had reservations about Spartan leadership.[84] Afterwards, Elis was given public credit for taking part in the battle but Mantineia was not — "rather unfairly", as one historian notes.[85] Looking, as usual, to understand rather than to moralise, we may see this discrimination as an attempt by Sparta to split the two states by creating resentment between them. Sparta in the late sixth century succeeded in creating a perennial quarrel between Athens and Boiotia;[86] in 431 she can be seen trying to create dissension within Athens.[87] Spartans evidently understood the principle which at Rome was to be formulated as 'divide and rule' (*divide et impera*)[88].

The chief evidence of similar trouble in the Peloponnese after 479 comes in two sentences of Herodotos.[89] He is describing the career of a soothsayer, Tisamenos, who "took part with the Spartans in five very great and victorious contests":

> The five contests were these: the first was ... at Plataia, then came the one at Tegea against the Tegeates and Argives, after that the one at Dipaieis against all the Arkadians except the Mantineians, then the one against the Messenians at Ithōmē, and finally the one at Tanagra against the Athenians and the Argives.[90]

Twice, that is, Sparta fought a major battle against Tegea, with the Tegeates on the first occasion allied to Argos and on the second to fellow Arkadians. These battles, at Tegea and Dipaieis, come second and third in Herodotos' chronologically arranged list. The first battle mentioned, at Plataia, took place in 479; the war against the helots at Ithōmē belongs to the years from 465 (see below); the battle of Tanagra occurred in the early 450s, probably 458 or 457. The wars against Tegea and her allies should be assigned, then, to the period 479–465, but precision seems unattainable. Writing about a century later, the Athenian Isokrates urged the Spartans, "Remember the men who fought at Dipaia [sic] against the Arkadians; they are said to have won against many tens of thousands although themselves drawn up only one rank deep".[91] This is almost certainly an exaggeration. While acknowledging as much, Andrewes has suggested that a reliable tradition is reflected here, to the effect that the Spartans were spectacularly outnumbered; he believes that this probably occurred at a time when Sparta was most seriously distracted. Accordingly he synchronises the battle of Dipaieis with Sparta's worst known crisis of the period, which arose from the earthquake of 465 and the subsequent helot revolt.[92] But we can hardly be sure that the exaggeration of Isokrates has respected a particular limit, and that in consequence the Spartan army was indeed almost desperately thin at Dipaieis. The synchronism is not compelling.

Difficulties for Sparta seem to be reflected also by an event recorded by Diodorus under the year 471/0, concerning the territory of Elis in the north-western Peloponnese. "The Eleians," he writes, "who inhabited several small cities, now came together into one city which was named Elis."[93] Such a process, known as synoikism, was very likely connected with the establishment of *dēmokratia*.[94] A concentrated population would more easily communicate and perceive its own strength, and would be less readily controlled — divided and ruled — by rural landlords. Sparta generally opposed *dēmokratia*, and the Eleians may well have chosen a time of Spartan weakness to make their change. But Diodorus is not a good source, and, like better historians, he has special difficulties with chronology.[95] We cannot use his date for the synoikism of Elis as a precise indication of when Sparta was distracted by war with the Tegeates and their allies.

Peloponnesian movements against Sparta may have been helped by the Athenian Themistokles, when ostracised from his own city. In a brief but fertile reference Thucydides says that, after his ostracism, Themistokles had residence at Argos but was "making frequent visits to the rest of the Peloponnese".[96] Themistokles' willingness to resist Sparta was shown in 479–478, when he first misled then defied the Spartans over the rebuilding of Athens' defensive wall.[97] Argos, the new base of his choice, was Sparta's steadiest enemy, and was represented with Tegea in a large battle against Sparta in the period 479–465, as we have seen. After the fall of Pausanias, Sparta pressed Athens to persecute Themistokles, which she did, causing him to flee to the Persian Empire.[98] This pressure, and the Argive connection, strongly suggest that on his "frequent visits to the rest of the Peloponnese" Themistokles had been acting against the Spartans' interests. That he did so to some effect, we might guess both from Sparta's reaction and from our general knowledge of his political acumen. Thucydides gives him rare and lavish praise for this quality.[99] Themistokles in earlier times had contrived the building of the fleet with which Athens resisted Persia in 480; he had conceived, and managed to impose, the victorious strategy at Salamis, and by fortifying the Peiraieus had prepared the way for Athens' naval empire. His intellect and force of personality may have made his machinations in the Peloponnese a grave threat to Sparta.

The date of Themistokles' stay at Argos is notoriously a problem.[100] Thucydides represents him as fleeing across the Aegean, after being driven from Argos, and as encountering on the way the Athenian fleet which was besieging Naxos. Now, the siege of Naxos is usually dated in or near 470, and certainly not later than 467. Yet Thucydides suggests that, having eluded the Athenians at Naxos, Themistokles quickly reached Persian territory, early in the reign of King Artaxerxes — who is known to have come to the throne in 465–4.[101] A precise chronology may never be attainable; for our present purpose it may be enough that Themistokles was probably at Argos early in the 460s. This may have been a time when Peloponnesian states were at war with Sparta. It was also a time when there was pending for Sparta a serious problem of a different kind.

Probably in 465, the island state of Thasos revolted from the Delian League and, interestingly, thought it worthwhile to ask Sparta for help against Athens in the form of an invasion of Attikē.[102] The Spartans, Thucydides writes, "gave a promise, kept hidden from the Athenians, that they would help thus and were on the point of doing so, but were prevented by the earthquake which occurred, at which the helots ... revolted against them and took to Mount Ithōmē".[103] Sparta's attitude towards Athens will be examined in detail below. The scale of the earthquake, which prevented the invasion of Attikē, was evidently considerable. Thucydides elsewhere refers to it as "the great earthquake".[104] Details from later writers cannot be trusted,[105] but we may guess that the Spartans lived in more substantial structures than the helots, and so suffered disproportionately when roofs and walls fell in. In seizing this chance to revolt, the helots were exploiting Sparta's misfortunes, as Aristotle later put it.

Trouble seems to have been building up for some time. Pausanias, as we have seen, may have incited revolution among the helots. In another connection Thucydides refers to the killing by the Spartans of helots who had taken religious sanctuary,[106] "action which they [the Spartans] actually think caused the great earthquake at Sparta". The earthquake, that is, seemed to be a divine punishment,[107] which suggests that the relevant offence, killing the helots, had happened not long before. That killing was probably itself both a cause and an effect of wider trouble. In addition, the hand of Themistokles may again be seen. Scholars have perhaps not exploited fully Thucydides' phrase about Themistokles' "making frequent visits to the rest of the Peloponnese". There is no reason to assume that Thucydides meant by this to exclude Lakonia and Messenia, which together made up most of the southern Peloponnese and where helots were in a majority. Did the perceptive Themistokles promote a helot revolt as an economical way of paralysing Sparta?

The revolt, when it came, was deeply menacing. Even some of the *perioikoi*, normally trusted by the Spartans,[108] joined in. Herodotos makes a passing reference to the annihilation, at a place named Stenyklaros, of a Spartan-led army of 300;[109] he describes this as part of "a war against all the Messenians", an indication of the scale of the revolt. 'Messenians' could be used to refer to helots in general, most helots being descended from a conquered population of Messenia, as Thucydides says.[110] As the war against the helots lengthened, Sparta called in outsiders as allies. We learn from scattered references that contingents came from Mantineia ,[111] Aigina ,[112] Plataia[113] and Athens .[114] But nowhere do we have a list of allies which purports to be complete; it may be that Sparta succeeded in procuring even more help than we hear of. The Athenians were invited mainly because of their reputation for siegecraft .[115] The Spartans' own military education probably did not develop the versatile spirit of which Athens boasted[116] and which would inspire the conduct of a siege.[117] But at the present siege of Mount Ithōmē, Athens did not make sufficient progress; her force was sent away by the Spartans, "fearing their [the Athenians'] bold and revolutionary character; thinking them aliens and afraid that ... they would, under the influence of [the helots], attempt a revolution" .[118] We have considered elsewhere the severe impact of this dismissal on the relations between Athens and Sparta; Athens promptly made alliances with Argos and Thessaly, two powers hostile to Sparta.[119] Sparta, amid her difficulties, could ill afford to convert a powerful friend into a powerful enemy. But still less could she afford to have Athens change sides in what was already a difficult war for the highest stakes. In order to convict the Spartans of stupidity in their dismissal of the Athenian force we should have to show that they were foolish in their suspicions about Athens, and that we cannot do. The Athenians, Thucydides states, thought their dismissal unfair, which suggests that they had not planned to change sides. But the history of modern warfare contains many examples of soldiers fighting loyally for a cause which verbally they condemn.[120] What had the Spartans heard?

It is an unresolved question whether the helot revolt lasted between nine and ten years, as stated in the surviving text of Thucydides, or for about half that time, as suggested by the order of events in his narrative .[121] Those helots who resisted to the end were allowed by the Spartans to leave the Peloponnese under truce. Thucydides implies that Sparta was influenced by a Delphic oracle, urging her to "let go the suppliant of Zeus of Ithōmē" .[122] He suggests elsewhere that fear of divine punishment could greatly inhibit Spartan aggression .[123] We have already noticed the belief at Sparta that mistreatment of helot suppliants had brought on the great earthquake. A statement from Delphoi on the same subject might well be taken seriously, in the aftermath of the earthquake and of the helot revolt.[124] Helots who now left the Peloponnese were received by the Athenians, "in keeping with their [the Athenians'] new hatred of the Spartans", and were settled by them at Naupaktos, a port on the northern side of the Korinthian Gulf.[125]

Athenian pressure on the Spartan alliance

The occupation of Naupaktos, conveniently situated for attacks on Korinth's naval traffic, was one of a series of Athenian actions belonging in or near the 450s and tending to erode Sparta's sphere of influence. These are described in outline by Thucydides, and can only be briefly noted here. The state of Megara, well placed to interrupt Spartan communications with central Greece, left Sparta's alliance — perhaps in 460 — as a result of a war with Korinth, and joined Athens.[126] By building long walls, Athens created a fortified corridor between the city of Megara and the Aegean sea, to prevent a Peloponnesian siege of the city and to give access to Athenian sea-borne traffic. "Chiefly from this," Thucydides goes on, "there first arose the excessive hatred of Korinth for Athens."[127] After a naval victory over ships of the Spartan alliance, near Kekryphaleia off the north-eastern Peloponnese, Athens attacked the island state of Aigina, from which troops had gone to help Sparta against the helots — troops which may still have been with the Spartans if the helot war lasted for 9–10 years.[128] Korinth and allies, seeking now to exploit the absence of Athenian troops in Egypt and at Aigina, invaded the Megarid and were memorably humiliated by an army of Athenian reservists.[129] It was probably at this period, in the very early 450s, that the Persian Megabazos was received at Sparta, but spent money in vain trying to procure a swift invasion of Attikē.[130]

Athens now built for herself, as she had at Megara, long walls to the sea. The city was thus joined to Peiraieus, and was protected against Sparta's anyway defective siegecraft.[131] During the building, probably in 458 or 457, an army led by Sparta entered central Greece, nominally at least to protect the embattled statelet of Doris, which Spartans regarded as their mother city.[132] Oligarchic Athenians, seeing their chance, treasonably incited the Spartans to move against Athens; encouraged by this, and reluctant to march home through the Megarid which the Athenians seemed likely to block, Sparta's army joined battle with that of Athens at Tanagra in Boiotia.[133] Using round and probably approximate numbers, Thucydides states that in Sparta's force 1,500 hoplites were from her own territory and 10,000 from her allies'.[134] By whatever means, Sparta had evidently restored her Peloponnesian league to reasonable shape. If, as is possible, the helot revolt had not yet ended, the campaign to Tanagra would be a remarkable tribute to the Spartans' energy and organisation. The battle of Tanagra was won by Sparta, but the heavy losses on both sides would have acted as a warning to her, with her own relatively small population. The Spartans went home and, so far as we know, stayed there for several years. Athens was thus able, two months after Tanagra, to re-emerge and win control both of Boiotia and of the neighbouring Phokis.[135] Aigina surrendered to Athens.[136] Later in the 450s Athenian forces burnt Sparta's dockyard in the southern Peloponnese,[137] and twice defeated the forces of Sikyon, to the west of Korinth.[138] Further along the northern coast of the Peloponnese, the Akhaians became allies of Athens.[139] The Athenians also won the adhesion of Troizen, a state of the north-eastern Peloponnese.[140] During a five-year truce with Athens, which probably ran from 451 to 446, a Spartan army, perhaps unaccompanied by allies, went to Delphoi to restore local people to control and no doubt to gain for Sparta privileged access to the oracle for the future.[141] When the Spartans had left, the Athenians appeared, as with Boiotia some years before, and reversed Sparta's arrangements.[142] Thus until 447 the Athenians dominated central Greece, held Megara and Aigina, and had more than a toe-hold in the northern Peloponnese. But events were soon to move in Sparta's favour.

In 447 (or possibly 446) the resistance of Boiotians and others, culminating at the battle of Koroneia, deprived Athens of control of central Greece.[143] Shortly afterwards, in 446, with the five-year truce having probably expired, there comes an interesting cluster of events. Encouraged, no doubt, by the example of Boiotia, the cities of Euboia revolted from Athens. When an Athenian army had crossed to the island to face the insurgents, it heard that Megara had also seceded and that a Peloponnesian army was about to invade Attikē.[144] Back the Athenians came, but the Peloponnesians, led by the young Spartan king, Pleistoanax (son of Pausanias), went only a short distance into Attikē then turned for home.[145] Spartans afterwards claimed that Pleistoanax had been bribed by Athens, and exiled him.[146] Perhaps he was bribed,[147] but the son of Pausanias would hardly have gone back to Sparta snug with a bribe, if he had thought his campaign sure to be interpreted as a corrupt fiasco. Instead he no doubt hoped to persuade Spartans generally that his policy made sense; he had supported, and temporarily relieved the pressure on, Euboia, and consolidated the revolt of Megara without risking Spartan lives in a full-scale battle with Athens. His army had also given Athens a nasty fright. Such a policy could have appealed to him on its own merits; any bribe may have been incidental.

The Thirty Years Peace and its breakdown

The striking synchronism, with Sparta on hand with a large army to exploit a pair of revolts, may suggest skilful planning. It fits, as we shall see, into a pattern of opportunistic Spartan strategy. But once the army had returned to the Peloponnese, with an ugly charge against its commander, there was little chance of its being remobilised within the year, whatever the domestic authorities at Sparta wished. When Sparta attempted the like in 428, her Peloponnesian allies proved too slow, even though (in contrast to 446) the integrity of her command was then not in doubt.[148] The opportunity of 446 had gone; Athens regained Euboia, and Sparta thereupon agreed to a formal peace treaty with Athens, to apply for thirty years.[149] Athens was to give up the areas she controlled in the northern Peloponnese and two surviving bases in the Megarid;[150] otherwise each state was to hold what it had.[151] Sparta thus recognised the Athenian Empire, including Aigina, Sparta' recent helper now humiliatingly abandoned.[152] To guard against breakdown of the Thirty Years Peace, Sparta and Athens agreed that neither should bear arms against the other if the other wished to go to arbitration.[153]

When the pious Spartans swore to the peace treaty, they must have been sincere in their religious oaths. But, rather like penitents at confessional, they underestimated the strength of future temptation. In a speech of 433, as reported by Thucydides, the Korinthians state that during the revolt of Samos from Athens (440–439) the Peloponnesians were "divided in their vote" on whether they should defend the Samians — that is, break the peace and fight Athens.[154] The Korinthians in their speech also talked of "the fact that, because of us, the Peloponnesians did not help them [the Samians]".[155] We know of nothing which tells against the Korinthians' claim. If Sparta had not favoured the idea of war, it seems unlikely that she would have allowed the matter to come to a vote. It is still less likely that pressure from her allies could have forced her to fight against her wishes.[156] We recall that those allies included oligarchies protected by, and friendly to, Sparta. Thucydides' detailed description of the preliminaries to the Peloponnesian War suggests that Sparta would first decide privately whether war was desirable, and then consult her allies. If the Spartans desired war in 440–439, it is probable that they were deterred by the reluctance of Korinth; helping Samos directly would require a fleet, and Korinth controlled much the largest fleet on the Peloponnesian side.

In 431 Sparta actually did go to war with Athens. Korinth had veered from opposing the idea to fervently canvassing it. This, as we may see below, released a brake on Sparta's aggression. Hostilities proceeded from Sparta's side. On the diplomatic level, the Spartans invited complaints against Athens from their allies;[157] Sparta's own assembly then judged that the Thirty Years Peace treaty had been broken and that the Athenians were in the wrong.[158] After gaining a promise of support from Delphic Apollo, Sparta called a further conference of allies which, in 432, formally decided to make war.[159] After an interval in which promises and implied threats were delivered to Athens — that she could have peace if she repealed a decree against the Megarians, that she could have peace if she "allowed the Greeks to have autonomy"[160] — physical hostilities began in the spring of 431 when Thebes, an ally of Sparta, attacked Plataia, an ally of Athens.[161] Shortly afterwards, Sparta led an invasion of Attikē.[162] Looking back almost twenty years later, the Spartans themselves conceded that their side had been chiefly to blame for the breach of the Thirty Years Peace, with the attack on Plataia and with Sparta's refusal beforehand to accept the Athenian offer of arbitration.[163] The refusal of this offer was an act for which the Spartans later believed they were divinely punished.[164]

In a famous summary on the causation of the war, Thucydides states:

> the truest explanation (*prophasis*), least uttered, was — I think — that the Athenians growing great and frightening the Spartans made war inevitable. On the other hand, the accusations (*aitiai*) made openly on both sides, on the basis of which they dissolved the peace treaty and went to war, were as follows ...[165]

There follows a long narrative of two episodes which involved conflict between Athenian and Korinthian forces — the campaigns for Kerkyra and Poteidaia. The passage quoted above has caused much dispute among scholars, its difficulty arising in part from the fact that the word translated as 'explanation' (*prophasis*) means, in some other contexts, 'false excuse',[166] while the word rendered here as 'accusations' (*aitiai*) can at times mean 'valid explanation'. But his use of 'truest' makes it certain that in some sense Thucydides understood the growing power of Athens to be more important than the matters cited in accusations about Kerkyra and Poteidaia. Did he give such great attention to the episodes involving these two states merely because of their prominence in the mutual accusations which preceded the Peloponnesian War? This question may not be finally answerable. If we answer "yes", we are faced with a further question, as to why Thucydides in contrast gave so little space to the relations of Athens and Megara. For these too featured prominently in the pre-war propaganda and, unlike the affairs of Kerkyra and Poteidaia (so far as we know), were actually the subject of a conditional peace offer from Sparta to Athens — even if that offer was hollow. By basing ourselves largely on Thucydides, while diverging somewhat from him in interpretation, we shall argue below that the episode involving Poteidaia importantly affected Sparta's willingness to go to war when she did.

In explaining how, in his view, Athens made it inevitable that Sparta would fight, Thucydides gives his account of the growth in Athenian power from the aftermath of the Persian invasion to the Samian war of 440–439. He also records an influential speech made to the Athenians on the eve of the Peloponnesian War by Perikles, who argued against the principle of appeasement, claiming that a concession by Athens over the treatment of Megara would bring not a secure peace but merely another demand from Sparta.[167] But it is Sparta which, during the preliminaries of war, claims more attention from Thucydides. Thus he does not give a detailed account of the arguments which were voiced at Athens against Perikles' policy of firm resistance to Sparta.[168] In contrast the historian reports at length both sides of a corresponding clash of arguments at Sparta. Perhaps Thucydides, like many modern scholars, believed that it was relatively simple to understand why a state in Athens' position chose the risk of being attacked rather than to give way. Empires normally do not make one-sided concessions to menacing rivals. Nor do dominant states commonly submit without a fight to making sacrifices such as would have been involved in the Athenians' "letting the Greeks be autonomous". On the other hand, Sparta chose war without being faced with any immediate physical threat, or diplomatic demand, from Athens: it is the Spartans' decision to fight which over the years has attracted the main interest of historians.

To summarise Thucydides' narrative of events concerning Kerkyra and Poteidaia: Korinth and her colony Kerkyra, adversaries of old, went to war in 435 after a quarrel concerning the town of Epidamnos. Kerkyra won a naval victory, at Leukimmē in 435, and proceeded to raid the territory of states which had supported Korinth. The fleets involved were, after that of Athens, the most important in Greece; Korinth campaigned in 433 with 90 of her own ships and 60 of her allies' while Kerkyra deployed 110.[169] Each side in 433 sought the co-operation of Athens. The Athenians hesitantly accepted Kerkyra into alliance, wishing to prevent her great navy from falling into Korinthian hands, believing that war between Athens and the Peloponnesian powers (including Korinth) was inevitable, and looking to exploit the convenient geographical position of Kerkyra for ships travelling to Italy and Sicily.[170] In the ensuing battle of Sybota (433), Athenian ships, defending Kerkyra, clashed with ships of Korinth.[171] Thucydides states, "This for the Korinthians constituted the first grounds (*aitia*) for war against the Athenians — that the latter during a time of treaty [the Thirty Years Peace] were fighting against them at sea alongside the men of Kerkyra."[172] In reality, Athens had been careful diplomatically and in battle to defend Kerkyra without taking the offensive against Korinth, so as to preserve at least the letter of the Peace.[173]

"Immediately afterwards," writes Thucydides, "there arose also the following differences, prompting war, between the Athenians and the Peloponnesians."[174] He goes on to state that, as Korinth looked for revenge against Athens, the Athenians moved to prevent revolt in Poteidaia, a state within their Empire but over which Korinth retained some influence. The Poteidaians applied to Sparta for help, and received a remarkable promise from the Spartan authorities; Sparta would invade Attikē, which would mean starting a war with Athens, if the Athenians attacked Poteidaia.[175] The importance of this early indication of Sparta's belligerence is sometimes missed; we shall consider below the nature of Sparta's interest in the affair of Poteidaia. A force of volunteers to aid Poteidaia was organised at Korinth.[176] It may have lacked formal government sanction,[177] as a device for avoiding a blatant breach of the Thirty Years Peace; the states on each side had sworn not to aid the allies of the other in revolt.[178] But the force of Korinthian and other volunteers could not have been organised at Korinth without the connivance of the government there.

After its arrival in the region of Poteidaia, the force from Korinth was involved in a defeat at the hands of the Athenians.[179] Korinth was now able to approach Sparta with a complaint that her citizens were being besieged at Poteidaia by Athens.[180] The Korinthians threatened that, unless Sparta fought Athens, Korinth would look for an alliance elsewhere, meaning with Argos or perhaps even with Athens.[181] In another connection, Thucydides states that during the period of growth in Athenian power — between the Persian Wars and the 430s — Sparta mostly remained inactive towards Athens, but moved (in the late 430s) when Athens effectively threatened the integrity of her (Sparta's) system of alliances.[182] In stating this, Thucydides may well have had in mind the threat delivered now by Korinth. As de Ste. Croix has pointed out,[183] if Korinth defected, Megara might be hard to retain as an ally of Sparta's, and the Spartans' ability to lead armies from the Peloponnese might be seriously impaired. But we shall see that there is much evidence in Thucydides' own account which tells against the view of a fundamentally peaceful Sparta reacting only to the direct threat. Korinth's pressure may have been superfluous from the point of view of causing war. All that was needed, perhaps, was her willingness to fight; Sparta's own belligerence might see to the rest.

On the eve of war, the Spartans conducted a diplomatic offensive against Athens, aiming "to give themselves the best excuse for going to war, if the Athenians paid no heed".[184] Stress was laid on the decree by which the Athenians had excluded citizens of Megara from the market place of Athens and the harbours of the Empire. To judge by the small space which he gives to this matter, Thucydides considered as empty the Spartan promise to keep the peace if Athens repealed the decree. The decree had been passed to punish or restrain the Megarians who, so the Athenians said, had cultivated land on the border with Athens in defiance of religious and other prohibitions, and had sheltered slaves on the run from Athens.[185] It seems that the decree was not meant, and was not likely, to force Megara to leave her alliance with Sparta and to join Athens. Perikles thought it necessary to argue in the Athenian assembly that the decree was not a small matter. Such argument would hardly have been needed if the decree was thought likely to govern the strategically important question of Megara's allegiance.[186]

In the final debate before the Spartan assembly formally judged that the Peace had been broken, King Arkhidamos is shown as giving an intelligent appraisal, free of wishful thinking, of Athens' strategic advantages over Sparta. The Athenians were superior in money and ships, and had an empire scarcely accessible to Sparta's armies of infantry; accordingly, Arkhidamos urged delay at least, and an acceptance of the Athenian offer of arbitration.[187] The ephor Sthenelaïdas spoke in opposition, calling for war with a speech which, as Thucydides represents it, was both brief and crude beside that of Arkhidamos.[188] After administering the vote once, Sthenelaïdas called for those for and against to stand in separate places. This may have had the effect of increasing the majority for war.[189] In a culture which revered military courage above other virtues, many may have lacked the moral courage to advertise their wish to avoid a war. Thucydides shows elsewhere that Spartans, like other Greeks, believed Athens could be quickly defeated; invasion of Attikē would draw the Athenians out to battle, to defend their rural property, and Sparta's hoplite army would then come into its own.[190] But why go to war in the late 430s? Sparta's timing may be shown to have depended on calculations more subtle than anything attributed by Thucydides to Sthenelaïdas.[191]

The theory of Spartan opportunism

Thucydides explained the outbreak of hostilities "so that no one should ever enquire how the Greeks became involved in such a great war".[192] However, there has been much enquiry and much disagreement, with scholars in recent years tending to belong to one of two schools. Some have seen the clash of 431 as one instance of a deep and long-lasting aggression towards Athens on the part of Sparta.[193] Others have viewed the war as having resulted from a special expansion of Athenian power in the 430s.[194] Those who believe in a profoundly aggressive Sparta can point to invasions of Attikē, executed or merely proposed, stretching back to the late sixth century[195] and forward to 446 and 440–439. The chief difficulty for this view has been how to account for the long periods, including most of the 430s, when Sparta was *not* actively aggressive towards Athens. Conversely, those scholars who believe in a peaceful Sparta, goaded reluctantly into war by events of the 430s, point to the long spells of peace but have trouble dealing with the numerous cases of Spartan hostility towards Athens. We shall outline here a theory which may allow us to face squarely both the instances of hostility and those of restraint. It will be argued that Sparta's aggression towards Athens was both more profound and more intelligently applied than has usually been realised.[196]

It has sometimes been observed that Sparta tried to exploit certain Athenian crises of the mid-fifth century.[197] However, there are two questions — related but distinct — which seem not to have been explored systematically. 'Did the Spartans, from 465 to 405, usually or always wish to attack Athenian interests when some weakness of Athens gave them a good opportunity for doing so?' And, 'Did Sparta consistently refrain from new aggression except when there existed a special Athenian weakness?' If the answer to both questions could be shown to be 'yes', it would appear that Sparta in 431 probably would not have gone to war, save for the special Athenian difficulty then.

Below are listed in adjacent columns occasions of two kinds, coming when there had been at least three years without aggression by Sparta against Athenian interests outside the Peloponnese. Column I contains those occasions which the Spartans may have identified as their best opportunities to damage severely the power of Athens. Such occasions, coming when the Spartans thought themselves free, or possibly free, to act, included the revolts or imminent revolts of allies important to Athens, revolution and treachery (actual or threatened) within Athens, and the withdrawal from Attikē of very large numbers of troops in such a way that they could not quickly return to help Athens. Column II contains the instances of Sparta's having hoped or decided to open hostilities with Athens outside the Peloponnese.

I	II
465. Revolt of Thasos.[198]	465–464. The Spartans promised the Thasians to invade Attikē, and "were likely to do so".[199]
c.460–455. Athenian expedition to Cyprus and Egypt;[200] c.459–457, Athens' war with Aigina;[201] 458–457, threat of treachery at Athens.[202]	458–457. Spartan campaign to Tanagra.[203]

446. Defections of Euboia and Megara.[204]	446. Spartans invaded Attikē.[205]
440–439. Revolts of Samos and Byzantion.[206]	440–439. Conference of Peloponnesian league voted on whether to aid the Samians.[207]
445–435(?). Proposed revolt of Lesbos.[208]	
432. Revolts of Poteidaia, the Bottiaians and Khalkidians.[209]	432. Spartan decision in favour of war.[210]
415–413. Sicilian expedition.	415/4. Sparta arranged help for Syracuse, and planned to garrison Dekeleia.[211]

The correspondence between the two tables is impressive. On six occasions special Athenian weakness coincided with a decision or wish by Sparta to attack Athenian interests. The proposed revolt of Lesbos, to be dealt with below, appears as the sole exception. But before we conclude that we have found a key to Spartan foreign policy, several tests must be applied. Is there any evidence of the Spartans' acting in the way suggested in any other sphere? Is the deliberate exploitation of opportunity *explicitly* noted by a source of the classical period? Have the lists above been compiled correctly? There is a cynical but useful statement current among researchers: "if you look for evidence you will find it. When we seek to demonstrate an ambitious general thesis, we have to beware of wishfully contriving evidence to sustain it and of overlooking counter-evidence. Aristotle observed sharply of an implausible idea that no one would adopt it "unless he were defending a thesis".[212] For the present thesis, like others, we must try to anticipate criticism.

First, then, did the Spartans on any other set of occasions act aggressively in a way which synchronised with the times of an opponent's weakness? The answer appears to be 'yes'. During the Peloponnesian War, the occasions on which Sparta opened hostilities in a new district correspond remarkably, in an even longer set, with the times of special Athenian difficulty. The full list is given in the next chapter.[213] As examples for the present we may note:

I	II
428–427. Revolt of Lesbos.[214]	427. Spartan-led fleet sent to E. Aegean to help Lesbos.[215]
427. Revolution at Kerkyra.[216]	427. Sparta sent fleet to Kerkyra.[217]
425/4. Allies and former allies of Athens appealed for Spartan aid to Thraceward region.[218]	424. Expedition under Brasidas sent to Thraceward region.[219]
413–412. Aftermath of Sicilian disaster: revolts (proposed or consummated) of Khios, Erythrai, Lesbos, Euboia, Knidos, Rhodes.[220]	412. Sparta assembled large fleet in E. Aegean; aided revolts of Khios, Erythrai, Lesbos, Knidos, Rhodes.[221]
412–411. Athenian siege of Khios.[222] 411, spring. Rule of the Four Hundred at Athens imminent or actual.[223]	411, spring. First Spartan incursion into Hellespontine area.[224]

With a state as secretive as Sparta, external actions — which were perceptible by other Greeks and so are knowable by us — are perhaps the most promising basis for reconstructing motives. Sparta's warlike initiatives, and the diplomatic preliminaries for them, fall into this class. The timing of them, in our two sets, puts virtually beyond doubt that Sparta depended consciously on opportunity.[225]

Thucydides shows Sparta and Argos carefully guarding against such opportunism in each other.[226] In 420 the two states agreed a scheme whereby each could challenge the other to decide by battle the ownership of a disputed piece of land. There was, however, a proviso: the challenge should be issued "when neither Sparta nor Argos had a plague or a war on her hands".[227] The treaty which contained this reflection of opportunistic thinking was, of course, an external matter, and Thucydides' knowledge of it need not have depended on the word of the Spartans. In other contexts he is explicit on Sparta's conscious exploitation of Athens' difficulties. The Athenians, he records, perceived that

Sparta's hostile preparations against them (in 428) were made "because of contempt for their weakness".[228] In 413 the Spartans recommenced attacks on Attikē: Thucydides writes that they were encouraged to do so chiefly by two considerations, one of which was that the Athenians would be weakened by their war in Sicily.[229] When the Sicilian war had ended in disaster for Athens, the Spartans intensified their efforts with an optimism which Thucydides describes as deriving partly from that disaster and from the thought that Athens' allies might revolt.[230] In 411 Athens was distracted by an internal revolution: Thucydides writes that the Spartan king, Agis, with his army,

> descended to the very walls of Athens, hoping either that civil disturbances might help to subdue the Athenians to his terms, or that, in the confusion to be expected within and without the city, they might even surrender without a blow being struck; at all events he thought he would succeed in seizing the Long Walls, bared of their defenders.[231]

Using an enemy's time of weakness was in fact a widely practised Greek strategem. In 428 speakers from Lesbos, urging Sparta and her allies to make a special effort against Athens, argue:

> You have an opportunity such as you never had before. Disease and expenditure have wasted the Athenians: their ships are either cruising round your coasts or engaged in blockading us; and it is not probable that they will have any to spare, if you invade them a second time this summer by land and sea[232]

Notice again the reference to attacking an enemy afflicted by disease.[233] We are a long way from the genteel English ideal of "not hitting a man when he's down". Two further cases of opportunism have already been noted in other connections. When the Korinthians attacked the Megarid, *c.*459, they did so "thinking that the Athenians would be unable to come to the help of the Megarians, since they had large armies away in Egypt and Aigina".[234] And we recall Aristotle on the helots, who "lie in wait, as it were, to take advantage of the Spartans' misfortunes". Helot and master evidently shared more than the Greek language.

Finally, before we seek to interpret what seems to be Sparta's unusually thorough exploitation of opportunity, we should ask whether the tables which suggest this thoroughness have been compiled in a systematic way. In identifying and listing Sparta's best opportunities for aggression, allowance has been made for the varying circumstances of Athens. For example, we do not count the period 410–406 as one of special opportunity for Sparta, whereas the years 432–431 are counted as such. Yet Athens was far weaker in 410–406 than she had been in 432–431. Does this point to inconsistency in the way in which the tables have been compiled? Probably not. *By the standards of the time* Sparta did not have an unusually good chance to begin fruitful aggression in 410–406, whereas she did in 432–431.[235] As Athens declined, Sparta's estimate of a good opportunity is likely to have changed. She did not wish to attack when Athens was merely weak, but when Athens was as weak as possible.

Even allowing for some shift in Sparta's standards, it would still be possible for us to have wrongly omitted some episodes from our tables, and to have wrongly included others. Either mistake might cause a distorted picture of Spartan psychology. Examination of every episode chosen for omission or inclusion is a long business, and hardly suitable for print. Instead, it is perhaps enough to look briefly at three points which may raise most doubts. We have not counted as a good opportunity for Sparta the aftermath of Athens' Egyptian disaster of the mid-450s, when Athenian morale and resources were damaged and when Miletos, Erythrai and other places probably defected from the Delian League.[236] Nor have we included Kimon's expedition a few years later, which took 200 ships away to distant Cyprus and involved a siege (of Kition).[237] Is it right to exclude these episodes? On the other hand, Poteidaia is not normally considered one of Athens' more important allies; is it right to include the revolt of Poteidaia among Sparta's best opportunities?

The revolts of Miletos and Erythrai in the 450s were probably far from wholehearted, as we have argued elsewhere.[238] In any case, no Athenian military campaign from that period, against a former member of the Delian League, was long or difficult enough to have left any clear trace in our literary sources.[239] We cannot identify any good opportunity for Spartan aggression. If the Spartans had thought of invading Attikē in the wake of Athens' defeat in Egypt, they could have expected to meet a hoplite army not less strong than the one which had resisted them forcefully in 458–457, at Tanagra.[240] In addition, the Athenians now controlled Boiotia, a country of formidable infantrymen. Even more importantly, after Egypt and during Kimon's campaign to Cyprus the Athenians controlled the Megarid. The importance of this, as a block to Spartan armies,[241] is now widely accepted.[242] Before Tanagra the Spartans had flinched at the thought of seeking to pass the Athenian positions near Megara.[243]

Sparta's opportunity in 432–431 makes a striking contrast. The Megarid then was controlled by her allies; the road to Attikē lay open. And a special incentive arose from Athens' problems with the Poteidaians and their neighbours. The number of Athenian hoplites engaged against Poteidaia was apparently never less than 3,000;[244] for much of the time the number was to approach 4,600 and at one point almost 7,000 hoplites were employed, more than half of Athens' total.[245] Poteidaia's companions in revolt, the nearby Khalkidian and Bottiaian associations, were a formidable enemy, as Meiggs has emphasised.[246] He points out that towns in the area which were apparently in revolt in 431 had been assessed collectively to pay some 40 talents a year in tribute to Athens, a large sum.[247] Athens never succeeded in crushing militarily the associations of Khalkidians and Bottiaians, and was to suffer serious defeats at their hands in 429 and 425.[248] When, in 432, Sparta made her formal decision that Athens had broken the Thirty Years Peace, the revolts of Poteidaia and her associates were already in progress.[249] The Spartans could trust in a twofold possibility; they could hope for a cheap victory in Attikē if Athens were to keep a large proportion of her hoplites at Poteidaia, and if those hoplites were brought back, the revolters of the northern Aegean would be greatly fortified: other subjects of Athens might follow their example. The opportunity for Spartan intervention against Athens at this period was better than has usually been realised.

The proposed revolt of Lesbos appears as the only case of a possible opportunity for the Spartans which did not in the event arouse their hopes of attacking Athens. The significance of Sparta's refusal to help the Lesbians cannot, however, be firmly assessed because of the uncertainty as to when it occurred. Thucydides shows that it happened before the Ten Years War and in peacetime; a date between 445 and 435 is likeliest.[250] If the proposal to revolt was made between 445 and 441, Spartan aggression at times of great and exploitable Athenian difficulty would have to be seen not as invariable, but merely as normal.

However, a date between 439 and 435 would not have this effect, because a Spartan refusal then could have been caused by a belief that there was in reality no good opportunity for aggression. The conference to discuss the Samian revolt of 440–439, at which the Peloponnesians had been "divided in their vote", would have made clear Sparta's probable inability either to collect the naval help which Lesbos required or to mount a land invasion of Attikē on the scale which the close-fought battle of Tanagra had shown to be necessary. While this case must be acknowledged as a possible exception to the pattern of Spartan aggression, the regularity of that aggression at other times may well suggest that Lesbos' proposal was indeed made in the unpromising period 439–435, rather than earlier. In any event, the affair of Lesbos does not affect one of our two main contentions: that Sparta appears never to be willing to begin a war against Athenian interests without some special opportunity.

How should we interpret the patterns of correspondence traced above, between opportunity and aggression? Two possible theories may be dealt with briefly. It might be enquired whether Sparta took the initiative in creating most of the Athenian difficulties which she proceeded to exploit. If Sparta took the first step in setting off the revolts of Athens' allies, the timing of those revolts might indicate little more than that Sparta had decided to fight then *for other reasons*. However, when an important Athenian ally is known to have negotiated with Sparta as a preliminary to revolt, the negotiation was probably or certainly begun by the ally, not by Sparta.[251] We hear of Spartan interest following the revolts of Thasos (in 465), of Samos (in 440) and after the initial impulse of Poteidaia to secede, but Thucydides does not indicate that any of these events sprang from reliance on special help from the Spartans.[252] It seems that movements to revolt precipitated Spartan action, rather than the other way round.

When Athens had an army away, invading foreign lands or combating a revolt, she was temporarily weakened, but was also threatening to increase her power by an eventual conquest. Was it that threat, rather than the passing weakness, which tended to impel Sparta to act? That would harmonise with Thucydides' words on the growing power of Athens forcing Sparta into the Peloponnesian War. But there is much that tells against such an idea. The Spartans had reasons for keeping foreign expeditions to a minimum, as we have seen. If their aggression against Athens had been precipitated only by threats of Athenian aggrandisement, we should expect them to have reacted to promising revolts, such as those of Megara and Euboia in 446 and Samos in 440, by waiting to see whether the revolts would succeed, and thus whether the aggrandisement would indeed take place. The case of the Sicilian expedition is especially enlightening. The expedition threatened vast Athenian aggrandisement, and also presented a good opportunity of attacking Attikē. Sparta did duly attack. Later, when the Athenian forces in Sicily had been annihilated, and numerous allied states were willing to revolt from Athens, the threat to Sparta became far less and her chances of crushing Athens considerably better. But Spartan aggression did not then decline with the threat; it grew with the opportunity.

So far we may have understood the *timing* of Sparta's aggression. But why attack Athens at all? An awareness of Sparta's timing may show us where to look for an answer. Many scholars have directed their attention to signs of Athenian expansion in the late 440s and the 430s, which may have alarmed the Spartans. The colonisation of Thouria,[253] the conquest of Samos, the founding of Amphipolis,[254] the decree excluding Megarians, the alliance with Kerkyra and the campaign against Poteidaia have all been thought relevant. But it may now appear that, even without these events, Sparta would have retained her wish in principle to reduce the power of Athens.

As often in the writing of ancient history, it is worth making an effort to apply a process of analysis such as we would use in our daily lives. Let us imagine that our neighbour, in other respects a rational person, has on seven consecutive occasions emerged to say harsh things to us as we have passed his house. His invective, however, has not been sufficiently precise for us to make clear why he is annoyed with us. If asked to identify his motives in addressing us yesterday, the time of the seventh confrontation, we should probably not concentrate immediately on events which occurred between the sixth and seventh such occasions. More likely, and more promisingly, we should ask what led to the *first* confrontation or what *lasting* behaviour or characteristics of ours have annoyed the man. So with the case of Sparta: the steadiness of her aggression for more than half a century from the mid-460s suggests some permanent source of fear or resentment, already existing by the mid-460s. Here, Thucydides' "truest explanation" can be applied. Given the extent of Athens' naval power by the mid-460s, little subsequent expansion was perhaps needed to keep the Spartans chronically ready for war. But Athens' power did expand, most importantly with the consolidation of the Delian League into an Athenian empire. So, for explaining Sparta's recourse to war in 431, Athenian expansion after 446 may well be, in a sense,[255] superfluous. Thucydides does not make it sufficiently clear what in particular the Spartans feared that the Athenians would do. But he does stress Sparta's concern in the late 430s over Athenian pressure on her own alliance. We may surmise that above all Sparta was afraid of intervention by Athens in the Peloponnese. Diplomatically Athens might seek to detach allies from Sparta. Militarily she might use swift descents with her navy to encourage risings against the Spartans, whose own fleet was almost trivial beside that of Athens.

We may introduce here a logical device useful for evaluating all explanations, scholarly and informal alike. To an everyday question such as 'Why did that woman do that?', we may be offered an explanation 'Because she is an x sort of person and because she thought y and z.' If we invert this, or any other explanation, we can test its value. We ask, 'If we had known her to be an x sort of person, who was thinking y and z, and if we had borne in mind everything else about human nature and particular circumstances which the explanation takes for granted, could we on that basis alone have inferred that she would act as she did?' If the answer is 'no', the explanation cannot be depended on as complete. This technique in effect makes us confront the question, 'Am I aware of any rule that, where x, y and z are the case, such-and-such will ensue?' If we know of no such rule, we cannot reasonably be sure that the presence of x, y and z in a particular case was sufficient to cause the event under review.

The above procedure should be applied to the question, 'Why did Sparta go to war in 431?' Many have explained Sparta's action purely by reference to Athenian aggrandisement and the threat it posed to the Spartans. But given the existence of that aggrandise-ment and that threat, and a set of normal assumptions about human nature, could we on that basis have predicted Sparta's action in 431? The answer is almost certainly 'no'. We know of no rule, whether a general law of human nature or even a pattern within this period, to sustain such a prediction based only on those premises. On the other hand, by using the tables constructed earlier in this chapter we could infer with great confidence that the *opportunity* offered by the revolts of 432–431 would precipitate the outbreak of war then, and with even greater confidence that without such an opportunity Sparta would not begin war against Athens at that time.

We began this chapter by claiming that the Spartans must have conducted their imperialism with more intelligence than they are often given credit for. We may end by observing the wisdom, from the Spartans' viewpoint, of their method of making war against Athens. To confine aggressive initiatives to times of Athenian weakness was a policy well adapted to the needs of Sparta, with her chronic shortage of manpower. Spartan troops were not expendable. In another respect, policy towards Athens was not perfectly consistent, as we saw from Sparta's willingness to make and break the Thirty Years Peace. But the Spartans avoided the wishful thinking which, as Thucydides emphasises, influenced the making of important decisions by other Greek states.[256] In spite of the Spartans' strong and long-lasting desire to crush Athens, wishful thinking never in the fifth century produced a decision to attack without the existence first of an unusually good opportunity. Other Greeks, as we have seen, practised military opportunism. But it might be difficult to find in any period of history another state which for so long and so systematically began, extended, and refrained from aggression against another.

Notes

1. Hdt. I 68.
2. E.g., Hdt. VIII 2f.
3. E. Rawson, *The Spartan tradition in European thought*.
4. W. G. Forrest, *A history of Sparta*, 105, 139, cf. 100.
5. Ibid. 138.
6. A. H. M. Jones, *Sparta*, 59.
7. H. Michell, *Sparta*, 39f., cf. 335 and P. A. Brunt, *Historia*, II (1953–4), 141; Meiggs, *AE*, 355.
8. Thuc. IV 84 2; cf. a remark made some two centuries earlier by the poet Alkaios of Lesbos, frag. 360 in D. A. Campbell (ed.), *Greek Lyric* (Loeb edition), vol. I, and the distinction made at Plat. *Rep.* 548e.
9. Thuc. VIII 96 5.
10. Thuc. I 84 3, cf. II 40 3.
11. Thuc. I 79 1.
12. Thuc. V 68 2, cf. II 39 1.
13. Hdt. III 46 1f. Here it is stated that the Spartan authorities, after hearing a long speech from a Samian embassy, replied that they had forgotten the start of it and did not understand the remainder; cf. Thuc. I 86 1, Plat. *Protag.* 342.

14. Cf. Thuc. I 121 4.

15. II 13 6, 31 1f. (Athens); on Sparta, Thuc. V 68 with Forrest, op. cit., 131–7, Gomme-Andrewes-Dover, *HCT*, IV, 110–7, de Ste. Croix, *Origins*, 331f.

16. For references see de Ste. Croix, *Origins*, 332.

17. Ibid., 89ff.

18. Arist. *Pol*. 1269a.

19. Below, Chapter 6.

20. Cf. Plat. *Rep*. 565a for the claim that in *dēmokratiai* most citizens supported themselves by their own labour.

21. Little is now known of this important group; see de Ste. Croix, *Origins*, 93 and below, Chapter 6. Where ancient writers refer, in military contexts, to the numbers of Spartans (*Lakedaimonioi*) the *perioikoi* are often included in the total, as very clearly at Hdt. IX 28. The term for Spartan citizens, as distinct from *perioikoi*, is *Spartiatai*; see, e.g., Hdt., ibid.

22. Hdt. IX 10f, 28f.

23. Thuc. VIII 40 2.

24. Thuc. I 132 5.

25. Thuc. IV 80 and below, Chapter 6.

26. De Ste. Croix, *Origins*, 91 with references there given; cf. Michell, *Sparta*, 74.

27. Arist. *Pol*. 1271b, 1338b.

28. Cf. Plat. *Laws* 638a.

29. Arist. *Pol*. 1333b; de Ste. Croix's translation.

30. Compare the feeling in the German army after the defeat of 1918; E. M. Remarque, *All quiet on the Western Front*, ch. XI.

31. Arist. *Pol*. 1270a; cf. Xen. *Const. Spart*. I 1; P. Cartledge, *Sparta and Lakonia*, ch. 14.

32. See Arist. *Pol*. 1270b for measures to keep up the population.

33. Citizenship at Sparta depended on the possession of a certain wealth, presumably in the form of land; ibid., 1271a.

34. De Ste. Croix, *Origins*, 93.

35. For an agreement on this subject between Tegea and Sparta, see Plut., *Moralia* 292b with de Ste. Croix, *Origins*, 97.

36. Thuc. VII 27 5.

37. Thuc. I 118 2.

38. See de Ste. Croix, *Origins*, 94f.

39. Ibid. 98.

40. See below, pp. 109–10.

41. Thuc. V 23 3 (relating to 421 BC).

42. Thuc. I 19; cf. IV 126 2.

43. So, in the ancient world, Athens promoted *dēmokratia* (above, Chapter 3) and Rome oligarchy (see de Ste. Croix, *The class struggle in the ancient Greek world*, 307ff.). In recent times Russia and the United States have done likewise. One thinks also of the attempts of British governments, when decolonising, to set up in African countries two-chamber parliaments on the Westminster model.

44. For ancient discussion of the nature of Sparta's constitution, Plat. *Laws* 712d-e; Arist. *Pol*. 1294b with de Ste. Croix, *Origins*, 128.

45. By far the best surviving account of the Spartan assembly at work is given by Thucydides, I 79–88. Notice (Ch. 87) the manipulation of the vote, performed by the ephor Sthenelaïdas. On the limits to the assembly's power, de Ste. Croix, op. cit., 128ff.

46. Arist. *Pol*. 1270b.

47. Ibid; cf. 1271a, Thuc. I 131 2.

48. Arist. *Pol*. 1285b.

49. See especially de Ste. Croix, op. cit., 148f.

50. Arist. *Pol*. 1306a; for further references, de Ste. Croix, op.cit. 137f, 353f; D. M. Lewis, *Sparta and Persia*, 35. Note, for example, the eminence in successive generations of Kleandridas (Plut. *Life of Perikles* 22 etc.) and Gylippos, his son (Thuc. VI 93 2 etc.); of Sthenelaïdas (Thuc. I 85 3) and his son Alkamenes (VIII 5 1).

51. De Ste. Croix, op. cit., 138–49.

52. On the power of ephors, de Ste. Croix, op. cit., 149; Lewis, *Sparta and Persia*, 40ff.; S. Hodkinson, *Chiron*, 13 (1983), 260–5.

53. R.S. Woodworth and H. Schlosberg, *Experimental Psychology*[3], 729, 731.

54. Ibid., 696, 704.

55. Cf. Old Oligarch III 11.

56. Plat. *Rep*. 556d.

57. Cf. Thuc. V 66 4.

58. Compare Arist. *Pol*. 1306a–b for the idea of an oligarchy within an oligarchy, with reference to Sparta — which for him was an aristocracy, an oligarchy in a special sense.

59. *Republic* 550e; cf. Thuc. VIII 89 3.

60. See especially Arist. *Pol*. 1271a and de Ste. Croix, *Origins*, 140, with references there given.

61. IV 108 7.

62. Xen. *Hell*. II 4 29; cf. III 5 25.

63. See Thuc. I 132 1f. for the personal enemies at Sparta of the regent Pausanias, and for pressure on him not to become too powerful for the existing (oligarchic) constitution. Compare the later attempts of the Roman oligarch Catulus to limit the power of any one commander; Cassius Dio, XXXVI 31ff. On rivalry within Sparta, Hodkinson, art. cit., 278–80.

64. Hdt. VI 72.

65. Thuc. I 109 2f.

66. Thuc. I 95 7.

67. Ibid.; cf. VIII 50 3, Xen. *Hell*. I 6 10, V 2 25ff., V 4 20ff., and the references collected by F. D. Harvey in *Crux: Essays presented to G. E. M. de Ste. Croix*, 90, n. 54 (eds: P. A. Cartledge and F. D. Harvey).

68. Contrast Hdt. V 32.

69. Thuc. I 95, 128–34.

70. For an introduction to modern bibliography, de Ste. Croix, *Origins*, 173 and (e.g.) M. L. Lang, *Classical Journal*, LXIII (1967/8) 79–85; P. J. Rhodes, *Historia*, XIX (1970), 387–400.

71. Thuc. I 22 4.

72. Thuc. I 1 3.

73. Hdt. VI 75.

74. Thuc. I 132 5, 134 1.
75. Thuc. I 132 4.
76. Thuc. V 26 5.
77. Thuc. I 132 2f.
78. On Pausanias' relative youth, M. E. White, *JHS*, LXXXIV (1964), 149.
79. Thuc. I 130 1, 132 1; Arist. *Pol.* 1304a.
80. Thuc. I 132 2.
81. White, art. cit., 140–52.
82. Note the suggestion conveyed by Thucydides (I 135 2) that the downfall of Pausanias came not long before that of Themistokles, on which see below, and White, art. cit.
83. Hdt. IX 37.
84. Hdt. IX 26, 77; A. Andrewes, *Phoenix*, VI (1952), 2.
85. Andrewes, loc. cit.
86. Hdt. VI 108.
87. Thuc. I 127 2.
88. Cf. Xen. *Hell.* V 1 36.
89. Cf. Thuc. I 18 3, 80 1; 118 2.
90. Hdt. IX 35. The manuscript reading is 'Isthmos', not 'Ithōmē'. See Cartledge, *Sparta and Lakonia*, 219.
91. Isok. VI 99.
92. Andrewes, art. cit., 5.
93. Diod. XI 54 1.
94. When, in the early fourth century, Mantineia was forcibly converted by Sparta from *dēmokratia* to oligarchy, the reverse process occurred — dispersal into villages; Xen. *Hell.* V 2 7.
95. De Ste. Croix, *Origins*, 171; Gomme, *HCT*, I 52. On Diodorus and Peloponnesian history of this period, D. M. Lewis, *Historia*, II (1953–4), 413–5.
96. Thuc. I 135 3. See now J. L. O'Neil in *CQ*, 31 (1981), 335–46.
97. Thuc. I 89 3–92.
98. Thuc. I 135 2–138. On the fall of Themistokles see especially de Ste. Croix, *Origins*, 173–8, 378f.
99. Thuc. I 138 3 with de Ste. Croix, *Origins*, 176–8.
100. See especially Gomme, *HCT*, I, 397–401.
101. Thuc. I 137 2f., and above, Chapter 2, n. 107.
102. Thuc. I 100 2–101 3.
103. Thuc. I 101 2.
104. Thuc. I 128 1.
105. For references, Gomme, *HCT*, I, 298.
106. Thuc. I 128 1.
107. For other instances of Spartan religiosity, Hdt. VI 106, 120, IX 33–5; Thuc. V 54 2, VII 18 2, and R. C. T. Parker, 'Spartan religion', in A. Powell (ed.), *Classical Sparta*.
108. Thuc. I 101 2; de Ste. Croix, *Origins*, 93.
109. Hdt. IX 64.
110. Thuc. I 101 2.
111. Xen. *Hell.* V 2 3.
112. Thuc. II 27 2, IV 56 2.

113. Thuc. III 54 5.
114. Thuc. I 102 and see below.
115. Thuc. I 101 2.
116. Thuc. II 41 1.
117. See Hdt. IX 70 and Gomme, *HCT*, I, 301.
118. Thuc. I 102 3.
119. Thuc. I 102 4, and see above, Chapter 2.
120. Compare the songs of British infantry in the First World War, such as 'Hanging on the Old Barbed Wire'. More literary, but no less damning, were the poems of certain officers, as 'Anthem for Doomed Youth' and 'Dulce et Decorum Est' by Wilfred Owen, MC. From the German side in the same war, see especially Chs I and XI of E. M. Remarque, *All quiet on the Western Front*.
121. Thuc. I 103 1 with Gomme, *HCT*, I, 302f., 401–11.
122. Thuc. I 103 1f.
123. Thuc. VII 18 2f.
124. Indeed, this oracle may perhaps have helped to produce the idea that the earthquake was a divine punishment.
125. Thuc. I 103 3.
126. Thuc. I 103 4.
127. Ibid.
128. Thuc. I 105 1–3. For differing views on the dating of these and associated military events, *ATL*, III, 174, n. 53. For an Athenian and Argive victory over Sparta at Oinoē (in the north-eastern Peloponnese), perhaps belonging to this period but not mentioned by Thucydides, Meiggs, *AE*, 469–72.
129. Thuc. I 105 3–106 2.
130. Thuc. I 109 2f.
131. Thuc. I 107 1, 4.
132. Thuc. I 107 2.
133. Thuc. I 107 3–108 1. On the motives of these oligarchic Athenians see above, Chapter 3.
134. Thuc. I 107 2.
135. Thuc. I 108 2f.
136. Thuc. I 108 4.
137. Thuc. I 108 5.
138. Thuc. I 108 5, 111 2.
139. Thuc. I 111 3, cf. 115 1.
140. Thuc. I 115 1.
141. Thuc. I 112 5 and below, Chapter 9.
142. Thuc. I 112 5.
143. Thuc. I 113.
144. Thuc. I 114 1.
145. Thuc. I 114 2.
146. Thuc. II 2 1, V 16 3.
147. Plut. *Life of Perikles* 22f., cf. Aristoph. *Clouds* 859 with scholion on the passage.
148. Thuc. III 15 1f., 16 2.
149. Thuc. I 115 1 etc. For full references, and discussion of the terms of the Thirty Years Peace, de Ste. Croix, *Origins*, 293f.

150. Troizen and Akhaia; Nisaia and Pegai.
151. Thuc. I 140 2.
152. Was Aigina given special status by the Treaty? See de Ste. Croix, *Origins*, 293.
153. Thuc. I 140 2, VII 18 2, cf. I 85 2.
154. Thuc. I 40 5.
155. Thuc. I 41 2.
156. De Ste. Croix, *Origins*, 200–3.
157. Thuc. I 67.
158. Thuc. I 79 1–88.
159. Thuc. I 118 3, 119–125 1.
160. Thuc. I 139 1, 3.
161. Thuc. II 2.
162. Thuc. II 10ff.
163. Thuc. VII 18 2.
164. Ibid.
165. Thuc. I 23 6.
166. See de Ste. Croix, *Origins*, ch. II *passim* and esp. p. 54.
167. Thuc. I 139 4–145, esp. 140 4–5.
168. Thuc. I 139 4.
169. Thuc. I 46 1, 47 1 with Gomme, *HCT*, I 190–4.
170. Thuc. I 44.
171. Thuc. I 49 7.
172. Thuc. I 55 2.
173. Thuc. I 44 1, 45 3, 49 4.
174. Thuc. I 56 1.
175. Thuc. I 58 1.
176. Thuc. I 60.
177. De Ste. Croix, *Origins*, 82–5 with references there given; Gomme-Andrewes-Dover, *HCT*, IV, 26.
178. Thuc. I 140 2.
179. Thuc. I 62–4.
180. Thuc. I 66 – 67 1.
181. Thuc. I 71 4–6; de Ste. Croix, *Origins*, 59–60.
182. Thuc. I 118 2.
183. De Ste. Croix, op. cit. 60.
184. Thuc. I 126 1.
185. Thuc. I 139 1f.
186. Thuc. I 140 4f.; an almost exhaustive account of this decree and the evidence concerning its context is given by de Ste. Croix, *Origins*, ch. VII.
187. Thuc. I 80 – 85 2.
188. Thuc. I 86.
189. Thuc. I 87 2f.
190. Thuc. II 11 6–8, IV 85 2, V 14 3, VII 28 3; de Ste. Croix, *Origins*, 207.
191. Plato suggests that the Spartans tended to choose as officials men who were hearty, disposed to war, and rather simple-minded — a description which matches remarkably Thucydides' sketch of Sthenelaïdas. But in the same passage of Plato (*Rep.* 547e–548a) we read of Spartan

respect for tricks and contrivances of war.

192. Thuc.I 23 5.

193. E.g. de Ste. Croix, *Origins*, 3, 50, 180; cf. A. H. M. Jones, *Proceedings of the Cambridge Philological Society*, n.s., II (1952–3), 43f.

194. E.g. D. Kagan, *The outbreak of the Peloponnesian War*, 346, cf. 300; cf. Meiggs, *AE*, 203f.

195. De Ste. Croix, *Origins*, 167.

196. What follows is an abridgement of a paper entitled 'Athens' difficulty, Sparta's opportunity: causation and the Peloponnesian War', which appeared in *L'Antiquité classique*, XLIX (1980), 87–114.

197. Thus E. Meyer noted Sparta's hostile reaction at the time of Thasos' revolt, in the 460s; *Forschungen zur alten Geschichte*, II, 311; cf. Meyer, *Geschichte des Altertums*, IV, 1, 713, on Sparta's "incomparable opportunity ... to make a sudden attack on Athens while her naval power was seriously engaged", during the Samian revolt of 440–439; cf. D. MacDowell, *JHS*, 80 (1960), 121; A. Andrewes, *CQ*, n.s., IX (1959), 235; A. H. M. Jones, loc. cit.; P. A. Brunt, *Phoenix*, XIX (1965), 258; Meiggs, *AE*, 99.

198. Thuc. I 100 2. References to events included in the following lists will in most cases involve only the first notice of them by Thucydides.

199. Thuc. I 101 2.

200. Thuc. I 104 1f.

201. Thuc. I 105 2–4.

202. Thuc. I 107 4, 6.

203. Thuc. I 107 2–4; 108 1.

204. Thuc. I 114 1.

205. Thuc. I 114 1f.

206. Thuc. I 115 2ff.

207. Thuc. I 40 5; 41 2.

208. Thuc. III 2 1; 13 1.

209. Thuc. I 58 1.

210. Thuc. I 87 3, 88.

211. Thuc. VI 93 2f.

212. Arist. *Nik. Eth.* 1096a.

213. p. 148.

214. Thuc. III 2 1.

215. Thuc. III 16 3, 26 1.

216. Thuc. III 69 2, 70 1ff.

217. Thuc. III 69 2, 76.

218. Thuc. IV 79 2.

219. Thuc. IV 70 1, 78.

220. Thuc. VIII 5 4 (Khios and Erythrai); 5 1 (Euboia); 5 2 (Lesbos); 35 1 (Knidos); 44 (Rhodes).

221. Thuc. VIII 12 3; 23 1 5; 26 1; 35 1; 39 1 (assembly of large fleet); VIII 14; 22–23 4; 24 6; 35 1f; 44 1f. (aid to revolts).

222. Thuc. VIII 24.

223. Thuc. VIII 63 3.

224. Thuc. VIII 62 1.

225. Cf. the remark attributed to the ephor Khilon on the importance of opportunity: Kritias frag. no. 7 at H. Diels – W. Kranz, *Die Fragmente*

der Vorsokratiker, II 380. See also Thuc. V 9 4; Xen. *Hell*. III 5 5, *Agesilaos* I 31 and below.

226. The word 'opportunism' is used here and below without any moral content.

227. Thuc. V 41 2.

228. Thuc. III 16 1.

229. Thuc. VII 18 2.

230. Thuc. VIII 2 1–4.

231. Thuc. VIII 71 1 (Crawley's translation).

232. Thuc. III 13 3f. (Crawley's translation).

233. Xen. *Ages*. X 1.

234. Thuc. I 105 3.

235. Compare the speculator who buys stock at 1 dollar when expecting it to rise in price, but delays a further purchase of the same stock when later it stands at 50 cents — because expecting a further fall.

236. Above, Chapter 2.

237. Thuc. I 112 2–4.

238. Above, pp. 45–6.

239. *L'Antiquité classique*, XLIX (1980), 97, n. 69.

240. Ibid. 97.

241. Ibid. 99 n. 77 on the circumstances of Sparta's intervention at Delphoi, shortly after 450.

242. Brunt, *Phoenix*, XIX (1965), 258; Meiggs, *AE*, 111, and esp. de Ste. Croix, *Origins*, 190–5.

243. Thuc. I 107 3f.

244. Thuc. I 61 1f., II 31 2, III 17 4.

245. Thuc. I 64 2f., III 17 4; II 58 1 with 56 2 (cf. 58 2 on Phormion's force of 1,600); II 13 6, 31 1f.

246. Meiggs, *AE*, 210f., 309f., cf. Gomme, *HCT*, I, 210f.

247. Meiggs, *AE*, 310.

248. Thuc. II 79, cf. VI 10 5.

249. Thuc. I 58 1, 61 1, 87f.

250. III 2 1, 13 1; cf. de Ste. Croix, *Origins*, 204f., Meiggs, *AE*, 194.

251. Thuc. III 2 1, 13 1; III 4 4ff.; VIII 5 2, 32 1 (Lesbos, on three separate occasions); I 58 1 (Poteidaia); VIII 5 4 (Khios and Erythrai); VIII 5 1 (Euboia); cf. VIII 44 1 (Rhodes); VIII 80 2f. (Byzantion).

252. For fragmentary evidence of a possible appeal by Samos for Peloponnesian help in 440–439, see Meiggs-Lewis, no. 56 1.12 and cf. Meiggs, *AE*, 190.

253. On which see especially Diod. XII 9ff. with V. Ehrenberg, *American Journal of Philology*, LXIX (1948), 150ff.; A. Andrewes, *JHS*, XCVIII (1978), 5–8.

254. In 437/6. See above, Chapter 3.

255. On overdetermination or "redundant" causes, *L'Antiquité classique*, XLIX (1980), 106–10.

256. Thuc. III 3 1, IV 108 4, VIII 2 2.

5

The Peloponnesian War, 431–404

The character of Thucydides' account

It is a reflection on Thucydides that, over the years, the study of the Peloponnesian War has been carried on with such interest. As a source for the hostilities down to 411 (where his account breaks off), Thucydides' history is more important than all other sources combined; it is also, at times, challengingly elusive. Even our notion of *the* Peloponnesian War, 431–404, may well be due to Thucydides. He defines as a unity the warfare over that period between the alliances of Athens and Sparta. Otherwise we might have wished to have a broader conception of the war, as involving the clashes from c.460 to 404. Alternatively, different stages of fighting within the period 431–404 might have been regarded as separate wars: that view was evidently in the air in Thucydides' time, since he combats it with (for him) unusual pugnacity ("Anyone who thinks that the intervening period of truce did not amount to war is wrong"[1]). The question what to count as one war is not a sterile matter of classification. Incautiously accepted, Thucydides' idea of the war might cause us to overlook continuity with the earlier period, as, for example, in the matter of Sparta's consistent aggression towards Athens before and after 431. It might also cause us to underestimate differences in character between periods within "the" war: 431–422, in which Sparta and Athens campaigned against each other vigorously; 421–414, in which clashes were less frequent and no Spartan army entered Attikē; and 413–404, during which Sparta had a permanent fortified post in Attikē and for the first time made a serious challenge for naval supremacy in the Aegean. For the sake of convenience we shall use the term 'Peloponnesian War' in its traditional sense, but for the sake of accuracy we must beware of its monolithic implication.

Scholars often call attention to defects perceived in Thucydides' work. We shall have to do likewise in a moment. The frequency of this criticism might cause a newcomer to the subject to underestimate the lasting reputation of Thucydides. But it is in part *because* he is so respected that so much criticism goes on. To fault him with novel and convincing argument may perhaps be valued as a feat of the intellect; in any case, it is performed seldom enough for us not to feel that our general grip on events is threatened by it. (Compare Plutarch: few, perhaps too few, try to identify his patterns of error; to do so might be expected to be all too easy and to yield a depressing spectacle of unreliability.) In beginning a critical review of Thucydides' account of the war, we should consider — inevitably in brief — what are its main merits as a source for the period.

In the first place there is Thucydides' contemporary access to information. He was elected general at Athens for 424/3,[2] from which we infer that he had a good practical understanding of politics in his own city and conversed with other astute and successful men with good information of their own. To this he added a knowledge of the Peloponnesians, gained during his 20 years of exile following what was deemed his military failure in 424.[3] Then there is the fact that Thucydides' picture of human nature corresponds reassuringly with the picture we draw from sources close to, or within, our own time. In this respect, students of Thucydides vary as to the generalisations of his from which they derive most satisfaction. Many, for instance, have felt a pleasure of recognition at Thucydides' account of a mass meeting (the Athenian assembly) vindictively forcing a speaker to live up to an apparently rash undertaking: "as a crowd tends to do, the more Kleon tried to avoid sailing, and to back out of what he had said, the more they ... shouted at him to sail".[4] The present writer feels particular admiration for Thucydides' concept of popular recourse to divination in time of crisis,[5] and for his description of wishful thinking: "people are accustomed to apply careless hope to what they yearn for, but to reject with sovereign reason what they do not find attractive".[6] Both ideas apply remarkably to modern political experience.[7]

Thucydides' details on particular aspects of the war, as — for example — on the identity of military and political leaders, on statistical matters and on the development of campaigns, are for the most part taken on trust by scholars. It is worth asking why this should be so, given that we have so little independent detail from contemporary sources to use as a general check on his accuracy. A crude but important argument is drawn from our view of Thucydides' intelligence in generalising about human nature and in (usually) managing to avoid inconsistency in spite of the mass of his material. Basing ourselves again on modern experience, we may feel that a person with such a grasp of psychology and logic is unlikely to commit many blunders of fact, particularly in a work likely to be exposed to the criticism of people contemporary with the events described. Occasionally modern archaeology gives striking confirmation of detail in Thucydides, as in the case of the sculpture which he records as used in the urgent construction of an Athenian defensive wall.[8] But, as with arguments drawn from biblical archaeology, it should be remembered that long-surviving physical fabric would be unusually easy for an ancient writer and his readers to remember, because it might be seen repeatedly and checked at will. A bygone word or deed normally presented very different problems for our ancient informants.

The hypothesis of an unreliable Thucydides would be a very depressing one for the student of antiquity. One reason, therefore, for treating this subject with great care is the danger of wishful thinking in ourselves. There is one class of event in the late fifth century which Thucydides judged relevant to his history, to which he had access and which we can reconstruct with certainty on independent evidence as a check on his accuracy: eclipses. He wrote that eclipses of the sun were more frequent during the Peloponnesian War than in what was remembered of earlier times. Astronomy now records that there were six solar eclipses visible at Athens in the period of hostilities 431–404. The reports of particular eclipses, two solar and one lunar, which Thucydides makes are all confirmed in their dating by modern astronomy.[9] (Contrast Plutarch, who carries the report of an eclipse in a setting which in reality contained none.[10]) Thucydides' record of particular eclipses is, then, correct as far as it goes, but incomplete. Now the outline notice of an eclipse is far simpler for a contemporary observer to achieve than the analysis of a political or military movement. Thucydides' treatment of eclipses is not sufficient basis on which to infer his general level of accuracy. But his performance with eclipses interestingly resembles his achievement, as scholars on other grounds judge it to have been, in many other areas. His positive word on all contemporary matters is taken very seriously indeed, but the argument from his silence has much less force. In his unfinished work he is capable of serious omissions even in the areas which interested him.

In certain areas which were not of great concern to him Thucydides has intentionally omitted much. He evidently did not set out to write constitutional or social history; his work contains far less than we might like on the regular processes of Athenian *dēmokratia* and of Sparta's government, on women, slaves and the mass of poor male citizens. His references to the latter may at times seem casual as compared with his treatment of wealthier men. He gives figures for those Athenians of the upper classes who died from plague early in the war: not less than 300 cavalrymen and not less than 4,400 hoplites. But "of the remaining crowd" there died, Thucydides writes, "an undiscovered number".[11] Given that the deaths of poorer men might well make a conspicuous impression on the numbers available to crew Athens' fleet, among which the poor (the "naval crowd"[12]) predominated, we may ask whether Thucydides could have been more helpful.[13]

There may be a pattern in the cases where Thucydides suggests that he personally deplored sufferings. The general Nikias deserved a wretched end, "definitely least of all the Greeks of my time".[14] The 120 or so Athenian hoplites killed by Aitolians in 426 were "definitely the best men from Athens to be killed in the war".[15] Thucydides indicates his disapproval of the persecution, at Athens in 415, of supposedly anti-democratic plotters; among those imprisoned were "many men of note",[16] as the Athenians acted on the information of "rogues".[17] In contrast, Thucydides rarely seems to show personal concern over unfortunates who were poor.[18] Even the 2,000 helots, rewarded for their services by being deceived and murdered,[19] evoke no special comment.

Is Thucydides biased in favour of Athens and against Sparta, as regards the moral standing of the two sides in the war or their skill in war-making? A preliminary answer might be 'Not in any simple or obvious way'. A fuller treatment of the question leads us into one of the busiest areas of modern Thucydidean scholarship. As we have seen, Thucydides' broad statements about human nature are among the features of his work which have done most to establish his credit. But he does make other wide-ranging statements, about the late fifth century, which have created intriguing problems because they seem to be at odds with, or at least unsupported by, detail elsewhere in his own work. One such case we looked at in Chapter 3: Thucydides' apparent exaggeration of the unpopularity of the Athenian Empire.[20] Other broad and problematic claims will be considered below, and are far from flattering to Athens or Sparta. Among them are, that the Athenians after the death of Perikles mistakenly reversed his strategy; that Kleon, for a period the most influential politician in Athens, was evilly motivated; that the Spartans were in many matters definitely the most convenient enemies that Athens could have had. There are passages in which Thucydides has seemed to write with pride about Athens, stressing her resilience after the failure of the Sicilian expedition and the boldness and initiative of her warfaring generally.[21] But a look at context should reveal that in neither passage was Thucydides' main aim to praise Athens; in one case it was to show the wisdom of Perikles' high estimate of Athenian strength and the folly of the Athenians in departing from the strategy he laid down, and in the other it was to decry the general slowness and lack of daring which Thucydides attributed to Spartan warfare. It may be, then, that we have to reckon with a bias against both Athens and Sparta in respect of their competence as states at war. Such a bias is likely to be of great importance if we are concerned to uncover the ingenuity and rationale of the two states.

Thucydides' history contains many speeches. The exact status of them is disputed. Thucydides himself warns the reader that probably not everything in the speeches was actually said by the speakers indicated; "to recall accurately what was said was difficult, both for me in the case of the things I heard myself and for my informants from elsewhere".[22] This candid admission matches the results of modern experiments on memory, which suggest that its capacities are far more modest than historians have often assumed.[23] Thucydides' cautious claim for his own memory, as well as for that of others, means that he did not always take notes on the spot. (However, his statement at I 1 1, that he began writing his history as the war began, places an important limit on his capacity for mis-remembering.) Having mentioned the difficulty of accurate recall, Thucydides goes on to state, in a passage which has been variously interpreted, that in reporting speeches he kept as closely as possible to the actual main thesis of the speaker or to the general sense of what was really said.[24] This, too, effectively suggests some deviation from the speeches as originally uttered. The style and content of some of the speeches, with their abstract expressions and psychological generalisations, have on occasion been thought more likely to be the products of Thucydides' own brain than of the speakers he names. However, we lack the amount of contemporary material which would be needed to decide on this point. It may just be that speeches in this manner were the fashion in the early and mid Peloponnesian War, and that we have been barred from knowledge of this through the fact that most of them have perished. A better-established instance of Thucydidean intervention concerns speeches reported from the eve of war, in one of which Perikles is shown answering at Athens arguments which Thucydides records as made at Sparta. It has been observed that the point-by-point answering here of one speech by another suggests that a single editor (Thucydides) has been influential, rather than that Perikles and his audience knew of, and tenaciously followed, arguments made in the enemy camp.[25]

While at times elements of the speeches seem to reflect the mind of Thucydides, there is also much which corresponds interestingly with the various characters of the speakers, in so far as those characters are known from other parts of the historian's work. Nikias, whom Thucydides describes as much given to divination, is shown employing religious prophecy when speaking at the end of the Sicilian expedition.[26] Alkibiades, who — to judge by his political success first at Athens, then at Sparta, then with Persian nobility — was evidently a moral chameleon, is shown by Thucydides speaking at Athens in a way which echoed the charismatic democrat Perikles (Alkibiades' uncle), and subsequently dismissing *dēmokratia* before a Spartan audience with a phrase of terse, Lakonic confidence ("admitted folly").[27] It will be argued below that the words of the Athenian side in the Melian Debate of 416, which many have thought out of character for the speakers and likely to reflect Thucydides' own ideas, may in fact be realistic and well attuned to the circumstances of the debate. And the Spartan Brasidas is represented by Thucydides as lying[28] to an audience of non-Spartans, consistently with the picture of Spartan mendacity which we derive from other contexts.[29] The whole topic of misrepresentation in the speeches is an important and somewhat neglected one. Not only is public lying very common in modern experience of war; more significantly, we have abundant evidence of it as carried on both by Spartans and (in law-court speeches of the fourth century) by

Athenians.[30] The speeches reported by Thucydides contain much that is slanted.[31] But the lie of Brasidas, identified as a falsehood by Thucydides, is unusual.[32] The evident scarcity of outright untruth in the speeches may be seen as evidence of editorial intervention by Thucydides. We may guess that, with his love of the didactic general truth and a desire to use the speeches in part as accurate scene-setting, he feared that the thorough reporting of lies would mislead his readers.[33] To summarise: the speeches should not be regarded as an accurate record of what the various speakers said; on the other hand, they are likely to contain much that was said, or which closely resembles what was said, and they are valuable besides as evidence of the very existence of certain ideas at our period.

Principles of warfare

Two related themes run through the strategic history of the Peloponnesian War, prominent in Thucydides' account but not always sufficiently emphasised by modern scholars: that of exploiting an enemy's weakness and that of *stasis* (conflict or treachery within a state). In the previous chapter we looked at evidence of a Spartan policy of opening war against Athens at times of special Athenian vulnerability. Below will be assembled detail suggesting that Sparta applied a similar policy during the Peloponnesian War towards the spreading of hostilities to new geographic areas. Other states pursued the policy, though less thoroughly. To add just a few instances to those cited elsewhere: a Boiotian leader in 424 is shown suggesting that it was both commendable and customary for a threatened state to begin a war "if opportunity (*kairos*) presents";[34] a few years later Argos attacked her neighbour Epidauros, "hoping to take the place by force when empty of men, away because of the war",[35] and Epidauros retaliated by moving against Argive territory when it in turn was "empty of men" because of war elsewhere.[36] The process can be picturesque; we recall Aristotle on the helots waiting to exploit Spartan weakness, while the Spartans, as we know, similarly watched Athens.[37] The Greek states had an experience of war far greater than our own; they evidently learnt to wait and watch for a vulnerable posture with something of the intentness of cats in confrontation. In addition to the obvious secular advantage in attacking under such circumstances, there was for the Greeks on occasion a religious reason. A run of good luck for oneself or of bad luck for an opponent was often thought to result from divine intervention and thus to be more likely to continue than if it had been the result of pure chance.[38] Thucydides describes the Athenians, pressing their advantage after the victory on Sphakteria: "exploiting their current good fortune, they expected nothing to stand in their way".[39]

During the Peloponnesian War both great powers played to their own strengths with a degree of self-discipline greater than Thucydides gives credit for, in his generalisations. Athens, with (until 413) far superior naval resources, put most of her efforts into sea-borne campaigning, and consistently refused to commit the bulk of her hoplites against the superior forces of the Peloponnesians, even when the latter provocatively invaded Attikē itself. Sparta, correspondingly, concentrated on her land army, attempting little at sea — except on occasions of special Athenian weakness — until Athens' catastrophic naval loss at Syracuse. Thucydides comments on the striking spectacle presented by Athens during the last stages of the Sicilian expedition: with the Peloponnesians besieging their city from a fortified base in Attikē, the Athenians refused to withdraw their forces from Sicily, but persisted in the attempt to capture a city (Syracuse) no less great than their own. He seems to have meant in this passage that Athens was being excessively ambitious in the use of her great resources.[40] But, given that Athens had come very close to conquering Syracuse, Thucydides might instead have commended the Athenian government for its cool resolution in refusing to abort the sea-borne venture, and for following the Periklean policy of not meeting the main Peloponnesian army in the field.

The policy of opportunism and of playing to one's strengths interacted with *stasis*. Again and again a Greek state saw, or thought it saw, a chance of capturing, defeating or neutralising an enemy cheaply, by exploiting a faction or merely a few treacherous citizens within the enemy state. The Peloponnesian War began with such a case, as we shall shortly see; Thebes sought to capture Plataia with the help of insiders. Much later (in 382) Thebes herself was to be the victim of perhaps the most famous such stroke in Greek history. Some Theban dissidents offered control of the city to the commander of a passing Spartan army who, with his city's tradition of opportunism, found the offer irresistible: Sparta seized Thebes, though the two cities were not even at war[41]. While opportunist strategists exploited *stasis, stasis* itself flourished as opportunity presented in the form of armed might belonging to another state. In the aftermath of the Sicilian expedition, as Sparta seemed likely to take over control of the Aegean from Athens, oligarchic factions emerged and prospered in previously democratic states of the Athenian Empire. Such factions could be deliberately fostered by an outside power. Thucydides shows King Arkhidamos of Sparta, on the eve of war, considering the prospect of doing this against the Athenian Empire.[42] The *stasis* which afflicted Kerkyra, and which Thucydides took as his illustrative model,[43] was begun by oligarchic agents implanted in the city by Korinth with the aim of bringing over the place to the Korinthian side.[44] We recall the action of the German authorities in 1917 in conveying Lenin to Russia, in the hope that he would promote revolution there and thus distract Russia from her war against Germany.

Collaborating with an outside power against many of one's own citizens would be less heinous when that power was Greek rather than foreign;[45] community of language and culture would facilitate the practical arrangements. With Athens tending to promote *dēmokratia* and Sparta oligarchy, partisans in other cities might collaborate with one or the other for reasons which were, and which seemed, not wholly selfish. But much self-interest there was. At Samos a faction mounted a coup against the local oligarchs in the name of *dēmokratia*, won, and later itself became oligarchic.[46] Oligarchic plotters at Athens in 411 were willing, in the last resort, to hand over their city to Sparta, giving up its empire, walls and ships, and to let it be governed anyhow — provided that their own lives were safe.[47] In all probability one of these was Antiphon, a man whom Thucydides describes as "second to none of his Athenian contemporaries, in virtue".[48] It may seem that Thucydides himself was far from thinking that it was always gravely wrong to hand over a city to an outside power even when (as in 411) there was a choice. Collaboration with an enemy was often made temptingly easy by the dependence of city states on defensive walls with gates which a few men could open. Greek siegecraft being primitive, a small number of defenders behind a strong wall could keep off a far larger army, but once a gate was opened the defenders lost most of their positional advantage. The movement at Athens which overthrew Antiphon and his colleagues began as a protest against their building of a new fortification with entrances which were correctly suspected of being designed to let in the Spartans.[49]

The war begins: Spartan and Athenian strategy

The attack on Plataia by Thebes began the war by virtue of the fact that Plataia was an ally of Athens, and Thebes an ally of Sparta. Thucydides writes:

> It was Plataians who brought them [the Thebans] in and opened the gates, Naukleides and his associates, who — for the sake of personal power — wanted to kill fellow citizens who opposed them and to hand over the city to the Thebans.[50]

Until the moment of the attack Thebes and Plataia, opponents of old, had been formally at peace.[51] Later in the war, when the Spartans had come to believe that they were being divinely punished by misfortune, they were to remember guiltily that it was their side which had first taken up arms and broken the treaty of peace.[52] As it happened, the Plataians managed to beat off this attack from Thebes, after both sides, as Thucydides briefly records, had received some feminine assistance.[53] The historian states that the mass of the Plataians did not want to secede from Athens,[54] a detail difficult to square with his claim a few chapters later that, at the start of the war, every city and individual energetically sought to help the Spartan cause, unless perhaps Thucydides made the latter generalisation with the wealthy rather than the masses in mind.[55]

On learning of the attack on Plataia, Athens arrested all Boiotians in her territory;[56] she and Sparta prepared for war. Sparta's first direct move against Athens was to send an army of her own and allied infantry against Attikē, under the command of King Arkhidamos, in 431. (This and subsequent such invasions have given rise to the title 'Arkhidamian War' for the period of hostilities which Thucydides calls less misleadingly the 'Ten Years War'.[57]) The invasions inflicted serious damage on the property, morale and health of many Athenians. As the smoke rose from burning farms, only recently restored from the destruction caused by Persian invaders half a century before,[58] intense frustration was felt by the countrymen of Attikē, who demanded in vain that an army be sent out to give battle.[59] King

Arkhidamos hoped that the large and influential rural community of Akharnai might resist the strategy of fellow Athenians, which was to abandon the countryside, and might create *stasis* within the city:[60] so Thucydides reports, cautiously but plausibly, given Sparta's use of divide-and-rule on other occasions.[61] And if the Athenians were to come out to fight, Arkhidamos could expect to benefit from the absence of many Athenian hoplites, away at Poteidaia. Most Athenians were country people;[62] now they became evacuees, uncomfortable in a crowded city, where they probably facilitated the spread of plague.[63] After the outbreak of the plague, in 430, the Athenians offered terms of peace to Sparta, contrary to the policy of Perikles.[64] Thucydides does not specify them. In any case, Sparta refused, holding out for more.

The Spartans had enjoyed some success with their war policy, but they overestimated its potential. Like the majority of other Greeks (according to Thucydides), the Spartans expected that the invasion of Attikē would bring down Athens within a few years at most.[65] In this they may have committed an error of strategic thinking still prevalent today — the excessive assimilation of a future war to a previous one. In 446 Spartan-led forces had invaded Attikē but had gone no further than Eleusis and the road to Thria. Rather than fight, the Athenians had bribed the Spartan commander, King Pleistoanax, or so Spartans believed. In any case, after the Spartan withdrawal of 446 the Athenians had made a treaty with Sparta involving large concessions. Similar Athenian capitulation may have been expected in 431. Even Arkhidamos, whom Thucydides shows arguing earlier against the belief in a short war,[66] delayed when just inside the border of Attikē in the hope (it was said) that the Athenians then would make terms; that is, that history would come close to repeating itself.[67] The Athenians in turn hoped that Arkhidamos would imitate Pleistoanax in turning for home, though this time there is no suggestion of their having offered a bribe.[68] We may think of French preparation for the Second World War by creating the Maginot Line on the strategic principles of the First; or of the way British and American hegemonic thinking has been governed in more recent times by fear respectively of "another Suez" and "another Vietnam". Faced with a shortage of analogues from which to make predictions, it may be a general human failing to place too much confidence in the one or two available models, at the expense of a needed degree of agnosticism.

Under the guidance of Perikles, the Athenians neither capitulated nor sent out their hoplite army to challenge the Peloponnesians. The latter, after a short season of ravaging,[69] withdrew. They perhaps had little choice; the Spartans had helots to police at home, and probably lacked the reserves of cash needed to fund a large army abroad for long. Sparta's allies, unlike most of Athens', did not pay tribute.[70] However, Sparta did lead a brief invasion of Attikē every year from 431 to 425, with the exceptions of 429 (when fear of the plague may have deterred) and 426 (when the occurrence of numerous earthquakes was taken as an omen).[71] In 428, after the regular invasion, a second was projected by Sparta, to exploit Athens' special weakness at the time.[72] Sparta's allies, however, successfully dragged their feet.[73] They too had estates to look after at home, and they were weary of campaigning.[74]

At the start of the war, Sparta demanded that states friendly to her in Sicily and Italy prepare ships to create a fleet of 500 (if our manuscripts have preserved the number correctly[75]). This would have far exceeded even the fleet of Athens, where Perikles boasted of 300 seaworthy triremes.[76] Perhaps Sparta's demand was made more in hope than expectation, in the spirit of the modern saying 'If you don't ask, you don't get.' However, no large fleet materialised from the west; even after Athens' great Sicilian expedition, when western Greeks had been taught unforgettably the relevance to themselves of politics on the Greek mainland, it may be that only some 23 ships came from the west to help Sparta.[77]

Sea-borne troops could usually be moved from one coastal area to another with far more speed and directness than an army on foot. And the Peloponnesian War was, for the most part, to be fought in areas near coasts where Greek communities, shunning the mountainous interior of the country, mainly were. Recognising Athens' great superiority in naval resources, Sparta proceeded abroad with much caution. Although it involves anticipating our main account, it may be helpful to give now (column II below) a list of those occasions in the Peloponnesian War on which Sparta sent forces outside the Peloponnese to begin warfare against Athenian interests, in a new area.[78] Alongside (column I) is a list of the occasions which Sparta may have identified as presenting the best opportunities for damaging those interests. As argued in the previous chapter, Sparta rigorously restricted her warlike initiatives to times of great opportunity, and (which is not the same thing) she always or almost always made such an initiative when there was a good opportunity. To be successful, Athens might need to identify and anticipate these tendencies in her opponent.

I	II
430–428. Plague at Athens.[79]	430. Spartan expedition against Zakynthos;[80] 429, Spartan-led campaign against Akarnania.[81]
428–7. Revolt of Lesbos.[82]	427. Spartan-led fleet sent to E. Aegean to help Lesbos.[83]
427. Revolution at Kerkyra.[84]	427. Sparta sent fleet to Kerkyra.[85]
427/6–426/5. Recurrence of plague at Athens[86] (special vulnerability of Naupaktos).[87]	426. Sparta sent force against Naupaktos;[88] battle of Olpai (426/5).[89]
425/4. Allies and former allies of Athens appealed for Spartan aid to Thraceward region.[90]	424. Expedition under Brasidas sent to Thraceward region.[91]
413–412. Aftermath of Sicilian disaster; revolts (proposed or consummated) of Khios, Erythrai, Lesbos, Euboia, Knidos, Rhodes.[92]	412. Sparta assembled large fleet in E. Aegean; aided revolts of Khios, Erythrai, Lesbos, Knidos, Rhodes.[93]
412–411. Athenian siege of Khios;[94] 411, spring, rule of the Four Hundred at Athens imminent or actual.[95]	411, spring. First Spartan intrusion into Hellespontine area.[96]
411. Rule of the Four Hundred; opposition from Athenian fleet at Samos; Byzantion offered to revolt;[97] secession of Thasos.[98]	411. Peloponnesian ships promoted revolts of Byzantion[99] and Euboia;[100] Peloponnesians overran Aigina.[101]
405. Athenian disaster at Aigospotamoi.	405–404. First Peloponnesian naval blockade of Athens.[102]

Athenian strategy, at least in the earliest years of the war, was largely that of Perikles. We recall that, in Thucydides' view, Athens "was becoming while in name a *dēmokratia* in reality the rule of the first man" — Perikles.[103] The latter, as general or perhaps even in an informal capacity, during the first Peloponnesian invasion of 431 had the power to prevent a meeting of the assembly, normally Athens' sovereign executive body.[104] Thucydides has much to say about Perikles' strategy.[105] He reports his stress on the importance of finance, reserves of money being, in Perikles' view, usually a main cause of military success.[106] Perikles is shown telling the Athenians in 431 that they had an income from the Empire of about 600 talents a year and a reserve in coin and treasure well over 6,500 talents in value.[107] Elsewhere Thucydides notes that Perikles sought to regulate the moods of the Athenian people, sobering or encouraging them when he perceived them to be unreasonably confident or scared.[108] The speech reviewing finance was made at a worrying time, with the Peloponnesians on the point of invading Attikē; Perikles was concerned to raise spirits. On a different occasion he might have put his figures into perspective by recalling the cost of regaining control over Samos a few years earlier (some 1,276 talents[109]);the siege of Poteidaia, already in progress, was eventually to cost some 2,000.[110] In urging the importance of financial reserves, Perikles had in mind the military opportunism which both sides would seek to practise; the Spartans, he observed on an earlier occasion, would be impeded by their own lack of reserves — "The opportunities of war will not wait".[111] Athens set up a reserve fund of 1,000 talents, for defensive use if the enemy should attack the city by sea;[112] it was eventually used after the loss of the great fleet at Syracuse. This was the city's provision for a rainy day. But Perikles, with thinking that a modern financier would recognise, evidently believed also in having funds available to exploit a sunny one.

To preserve Athens' finances it was necessary, as Perikles argued, to keep firm control of the Empire, the source of tribute and other revenue.[113] To do that, the fleet must be kept in readiness.[114] Athens should not tackle the main Peloponnesian army in the field; victory would be inconclusive, whereas defeat would precipitate revolts by Athens' subjects looking to exploit her resulting weakness.[115] Perikles compared Athens to an island, to which the citizens should withdraw, and from which fleets could be sent to police the Empire and strike against the

Peloponnese. The Empire would provide them with other lands than Attikē.[116] But Athens should not seek to conquer new territory while the war lasted, for fear of making blunders which the enemy could exploit.[117]

Noting that Perikles urged his countrymen to show restraint, to care for the navy, not to add to the Empire in wartime and not to endanger the city, Thucydides writes that the Athenians (after Perikles' death) "did the opposite of all these things".[118] Several modern scholars have disagreed.[119] In Thucydides' defence it should be noted that he need not have meant that the Athenians, after Perikles' death, consistently rejected the policies mentioned in every respect; all that his words *need* mean is that each policy was breached at least once.[120] But Thucydides' criticism of the Athenians for "doing the opposite" is at least misleading, since there is no qualifying statement here, to make clear that in many ways the Athenians did follow Perikles' strategic ideas after his death. Thus the main Athenian hoplite force never tackled the Peloponnesian army in pitched battle, and Athens was treated as an island even when the Spartans had a permanent base in Attikē, from 413. Strenuous measures were taken to keep the Empire under control, as, for example, by besieging Mytilēnē in 428–427 and by intervention at Khios in 425–424 to prevent secession.[121] The Sicilian expedition, like the earlier attempts to conquer Boiotia (in 424) and to use Sparta's former allies to overthrow her by battle in the Peloponnese (in 418), could plausibly be represented as departures from Perikles' policies. But, as will shortly be argued, the invasion of Sicily was not quite so remote from Periklean principles as has often been thought. A suggestion will be made presently as to why Thucydides may have overemphasised the difference between Perikles and his successors in the matter of strategy.

How wise was Perikles? The Ten Years War, in which his policies were largely followed by Athens, ended in frustration for the Spartans, predictably. Periklean strategy, by excluding a decisive land battle, forced on Sparta either an acceptance of the *status quo* or an attempt to destroy Athens' far-flung Empire.[122] As we have seen, Athenian naval power and Sparta's domestic circumstances combined to make the latter course an unpromising one. And if forced to admit stalemate, Sparta would lose face. It was clear to all that she had begun the war with a far greater prize in view. Sparta's rhetoric about liberating the Greeks would add to the humiliation of a settlement which left Athens in control of the Empire. Perikles may have foreseen the embarrassment of Sparta. The words with which Thucydides reports the strategic aim of Perikles do not suggest that he envisaged triumph; but rather "winning through" — qualified success by virtue of surviving unconquered.[123] The humbling of Sparta, in consequence of a stalemate with Athens, might be expected to cause unrest among Sparta's own allies, as indeed occurred.[124] But the Spartans had overcome much trouble of that kind earlier in the century; the collapse of the Peloponnesian league was not predictable.

There is, in short, no indication that Perikles thought his policies could bring Athens decisive victory. This has important consequences for our view of the wisdom of his position. In a passage which has often been overlooked, Thucydides reports Perikles as attempting to restore Athenian morale in 430, and as using in the process some remarkably ambitious words:

> You [Athenians] think that your empire extends only to the allies, but I make clear to you now that you are supreme masters of ... the whole [of the sea], both to the extent that you now administer it and to any further point that you may desire. There is no one, neither the King of Persia nor any other people in the world as it now is, able to stop you sailing with your fleet prepared as it is at present.[125]

Elsewhere Thucydides refers (with disapproval, it has often seemed) to the Athenians' desire for greater gains,[126] at later stages of the war. A misleadingly polarised picture has formed; Perikles, cautious and restraining, is contrasted with irresponsible and greedy demagogues who came after. But Perikles, as portrayed by Thucydides, offered a boundless vision of naval expansion; his words, if remembered in more promising circumstances than those of 430, could scarcely have been more inflammatory. Perikles makes a qualification, which Thucydides mentions twice, in respect of expanding the Empire: it should not be attempted in wartime.[127] But unless Sparta had been decisively crushed, for the present purpose it might have made little difference whether or not Athens and Sparta were formally at war. As we have seen, Perikles appears to have shown some awareness of Sparta's wish to seize opportunities in wartime. The Spartans' record might also have suggested to him, and certainly should with hindsight to us, that once Athenian forces were distracted by an expansionary scheme in some far-away region, Sparta would be very likely to break any peace and to attack. Perikles, it may seem, was inciting the Athenians to expand their Empire without providing any way of attaining the security at home which he himself regarded as essential for such expansion.

In other respects, however, Perikles' acumen is undeniable. In 431, as Peloponnesian troops ravaged in Attikē, much livestock was already beyond their reach, having been transported to Euboia and other neighbouring islands where, in accordance with Perikles' policy, it could be defended by Athens' sea power.[128] Thucydides suggests that Perikles owed his influence in part to his being obviously and strongly resistant to bribery[129] — an interesting reflection on the reputation of other politicians.[130] In 431 he told the Athenians that if the enemy in their ravaging spared his own estate in Attikē, whether because King Arkhidamos had been friendly with him in the past or as a way of embarrassing him, he would donate the property to the city.[131] Farmers whose property was being damaged were among the most enthusiastic of those Athenians pressing for a full-scale battle against the Peloponnesians.[132] Determined to resist this pressure, Perikles by his promise guarded astutely against the argument, 'Our estates are suffering as a result of his policies, but *his* isn't', which would have been very similar in form and force to one argument against a corrupt politician: 'He is profiting from his policies in a way that we aren't.'

In 431 Athens sent out a fleet of 100 ships, the first of many which during the war were to ravage coastal districts of the Peloponnese.[133] This initial venture may have been timed to exploit the absence from home of the main Peloponnesian forces, which were still in Attikē.[134] What was it meant to achieve? In a speech on the eve of war, Perikles had reportedly said that Athens might occupy a fortified base (or bases) in the Peloponnese.[135] The expedition of 431 did indeed try (without success, due to the intervention of the Spartan Brasidas) to capture a walled position in Messenia, named Methōnē,[136] though Thucydides does not say to what end. In 425, some four years after Perikles' death, the course of the war was changed in Athens' favour through the occupation of Pylos, a headland in Messenia. It may be tempting, particularly if we enjoy the idea of Perikles as a strategic genius, to assume that he foresaw the full benefits which resulted from this policy. But, as will be argued later, the Pylos campaign succeeded more through an uncharacteristic and therefore unpredictable Spartan blunder than through Athenian acumen. When Perikles mentioned the possibility of occupying fortifications in enemy territory, it was with the idea of taking reprisal if the Peloponnesians should first do as much in Attikē.[137] But during the Ten Years War they did not do so: that is, the condition for Perikles' proposal was not fulfilled.

The raids on the Peloponnese, and the conditional plan to occupy a base or bases there, fit into a pattern of Periklean thinking, whereby Athens' moves were almost to parallel those of Sparta. In the diplomatic exchanges with the Spartans just before the war, Perikles persuaded the Athenians to tell Sparta that they would cease excluding the Megarians when Sparta ceased her exclusion of Athenians and subjects of Athens; that they would give their subjects autonomy if Sparta gave full autonomy to the cities under her influence; that they would not start war but would fight back if attacked by Sparta.[138] Also, when Sparta in her pre-war propaganda had sought to exploit a supposed religious curse upon Athens, the Athenians under Perikles' leadership had found similar curses to use against her.[139] It was seemingly Perikles' policy against Sparta to take counter-measures which would be seen as balancing, and no more; an eye for an eye, rather than two eyes (or a leg) for an eye. This is unlikely to have resulted from lack of imagination in the Athenian leader. Rather, he probably meant to signal with this conspicuous symmetry that Athens' purpose was not aggressive, and that Sparta's influential fear of her was misplaced. Such a policy would cohere with Perikles' (apparent) belief that it was impractical for Athens to aim for the military conquest of Sparta.

If this theory is correct, Athens attacked the Peloponnese to do damage and go away, to match what Sparta achieved in the case of Attikē.[140] A similar intention probably lay behind the invasion of the Megarid in 431, with Perikles in person leading the citizen army of Athens in full force. Thucydides writes:

> This was definitely the greatest army of Athenians ever brought together, their city being still at its zenith and not yet affected by the plague. For there were not fewer than 10,000 hoplites present who were Athenian citizens (apart from them, those at Poteidaia numbered 3,000); not less than 3,000 metics also took part in the invasion as hoplites; in addition there was a large mass of light-armed troops. After ravaging most of the land [of Megara] they went home.[141]

Now, ravaging could be done with the aim of bringing a state permanently under the control of the ravagers; Athens was later to damage the territory of Melos with that purpose.[142] But Perikles' policy was not to conquer fresh territory during the war; consistently with that he turned for home without making any obvious attempt to subdue the state of Megara. Invasion of the Megarid became regular for Athens, answering Sparta's incursions into Attikē. The policy must have served also the important purpose of venting the frustrations of Athenian men, who had been forced to look on as the Peloponnesians destroyed their property. It was an acknowledged ideal of Greek manhood to damage one's enemies as well as to help one's friends.[143] (In modern times the Christian doctrine of turning the other cheek has perhaps done much to prevent this ideal from being expressed, but not so much to stop its being acted on.) Given the impact of the Peloponnesians on Attikē, it was a political necessity for Perikles to release Athenian aggression, just as it would have been unthinkable for the British government to refrain from bombing Germany after the Blitz, however unpromising such piecemeal destroying was in strategic terms. Vengeance on Megara would be the sweeter because of the role of Megarian complaints in Sparta's diplomatic offensive before the war. In 431 Athens made her control of Aigina absolute by evicting the local people and replacing them with Athenian settlers. Vengeance again was involved, the Athenians blaming Aigina for inciting Sparta to make war in the first place.[144] Also, Perikles could show the Athenians by this action how his policy of rigour towards the Empire might compensate them for losses in Attikē.

Pericles' Funeral Speech

In the winter of 431/0 Perikles was chosen, as a man of outstanding intellect and reputation, to make a public speech in honour of those Athenians who had recently died in the war.[145] Thucydides represents his speech at length; nowadays it is commonly referred to as The Funeral Speech, though the historian makes it clear that public speeches with a similar purpose were made at Athens throughout the war.[146] This first occasion was evidently meant by Thucydides to stand as a model of what followed, rather as the disturbances on Kerkyra in 427 were described at length as a guide to later *stasis* elsewhere.[147] Such a guide was necessarily imperfect, as Thucydides was aware,[148] due to the variation in cases. In the present case, Perikles' speech may reflect a certain insensitivity and aloofness in his character. (Contemporary comic poets referred to him as Olympian Zeus.[149]) He is shown advising those who had lost adult sons to bear up in the hope of having other children, while those now too old should console themselves with the thought that most of their lives had been fortunate and that they did not have long to go.[150] Again, parental ears might not be soothed by Perikles' argument that where the dead had been morally inferior the patriotic quality of their death outweighed their defects.[151] The standard psychology of bereavement is more closely reflected by the maxim *de mortuis nil nisi bonum* ('(Say) only good about the dead').

Much of Perikles' praise for the dead takes the form of praising the city of which they were part and for which they died, Athens. In modern times the speech has often been used as a quarry for fine expressions concerning the city. But the ideas in it are perhaps not representative of sophisticated Athenian thinking at every stage of the classical period. Rather, the speech seems especially concerned with those areas in which Athens could be contrasted with her arch-enemy of the day, Sparta. War and other inter-state rivalry still shape our self-images. In Britain, in the aftermath of the war against Nazi Germany, there was a proud and vigorous cliché, 'It's a free country'; along with memories of fascism, this has since faded. Similarly, much recent American rhetoric about the Land of the Free is shaped by the image of Russia. It is possible nowadays to read the Periklean funeral speech without much thought of the Spartans, who are named in it only once. But scholars have long identified additional, implied, comparisons and others may remain to be discovered.[152]

Perikles states that at Athens individuals contribute in their own way towards the common good, free from suspicious surveillance of their everyday lives by neighbours.[153] We should recall that at Sparta life was regimented, and checking one's neighbour's morality was an institution.[154] "We have provided the most extensive relaxations from toil (*ponoi*),"[155] says Perikles. In contrast, words from the root *pon-* were characteristic of descriptions of the regime at Sparta; that city was famous for its toil. Perikles cites Athens' finely-furnished homes;[156] at Sparta personal and civic luxury was frowned on. At II 39 1, with Sparta yet to be mentioned explicitly, the audience is expected to have taken the point already, for the speech continues, "In our military practices too we differ from the opposition"; note the 'too'. Athens, Perikles claims, is an open city which does not use *xenēlasiai* (regular expulsions of foreigners, a distinctively Spartan institution) to prevent the gathering of military intelligence.[157] A contrast is then drawn between the spontaneous courage of the Athenians and the rehearsed manoeuvres, deceits and toilsome (*epiponos*) educational system of the Spartans.

In modern times perhaps the best-known element of this funeral speech is the claim that Athens is an education to Greece.[158] For us, knowing the impact of Athenian writers and artists on other societies down the ages, it is natural to interpret this in terms of High Culture. But, in the Greek, Perikles' claim refers to "the whole of the city": far more seems to be meant than the activities of Athens' cultivated and creative elite. Did Athenian society in its totality serve as a lesson to the rest of Greece? In a formal and compulsory sense Athens did export *dēmokratia*, as we saw when dealing with the mechanisms of the Athenian Empire.[159] (Not long after Perikles' speech Athens refounded the city of Notion, a casualty of vicious *stasis*, on the lines of the Athenian constitution.[160]) We may never know how far the *dēmokratiai* which flourished under Athenian protection in the fifth century, and to some extent in the fourth, were products also of conscious enthusiastic imitation of Athens by local people.[161] On the other hand, our patchy information reveals copious reverence for, and imitation of, the Spartan way of life. We hear of laconisers, sporting cloaks in the Spartan manner and cauliflower ears which showed their owners' attachment to the Spartan institution of boxing.[162] Prominent men of Athenian origin, Kritias, Xenophon, Plato, showed in their different ways profound regard for the Spartan system.

It is true that Plato's academy at Athens attracted men, and perhaps women, from other Greek states; Athens was undoubtedly an education to Greece in intellectual matters, the philosophers Anaxagoras and Aristotle being among the most famous to be drawn there. But when the Athenian Plato drew up schemes for the ideal organisation of a complete community, it was to Spartan institutions more than to Athenian that he turned for inspiration.[163] The respect for Sparta reflected in the works of Xenophon and Plato will have owed much to the fact of Sparta's victory in the Peloponnesian War and her subsequent domination of Greece. But from closer to Perikles' time we have evidence of a

special regard for Spartan manhood, not least among ordinary
Athenians; Spartans, it was sometimes thought, would never
surrender, were too fearsome to be opposed, while the arrival of a
commander from Sparta was an inspiring event for her allies.[164]
The sentence which contains Perikles' claim about the whole of
Athens being an education to Greece continues with the suggestion that the individual Athenian was unmatched in his versatility.
In contrast, Spartans were esteemed for their systematic qualities.
But in praising Athens as the producer of superior men and as an
education to others Perikles may well have been consciously
laying claim to two forms of glory attained by Sparta. If so, he was
delivering to the enemy an indirect but profound compliment.

Plague at Athens

In the campaigning season of 430, the Spartans and their allies
again invaded Attikē, staying to ravage for about 40 days — the
longest such invasion, says Thucydides.[165] Far more seriously for
Athens, at the same period there broke out in the city the great
plague. At its height the pestilence lasted initially for two years,
and recurred for "not less than a year" from the winter of 427/6;
Thucydides' figures suggest that it killed about one-third of the
men in the wealthier sections of Athenian society.[166] Since
Thucydides suggests that mortality was especially high among
homeless refugees from the countryside,[167] we may guess that
among the poor the proportion of deaths was at least as high as
among the wealthy, since in general the conditions of the poor
would more closely resemble those of the refugees. The historian
himself suffered from the disease, but with his characteristic
restraint in matters of autobiography he mentions this only once
and briefly, to establish his claim to knowledge; he describes the
plague in great detail, as a lesson to posterity "if ever it should
recur".[168]

Modern medicine has not been able to establish a complete
identity between the symptoms described by Thucydides and
those of any ailment known from recent times; it has been
suggested that the disease as the Athenians knew it has since died
out.[169] But in its psychological details Thucydides' account tallies
impressively, as so often, with independent descriptions from
other times. He suggests that people's despair, on finding
themselves to have the disease, took away their power of

resistance.[170] Traditional morality lapsed:

> No fear of gods or law of men restrained them. On the one
> hand, because they saw that everyone was dying in the same
> way they judged piety to be no different from impiety for
> practical purposes.[171]

Burial rites were neglected, and those with corpses to burn stole
the funeral pyres of others.[172] Some, who recovered from the
plague, hoped in their elation that they would never die of any
other disease.[173] Thucydides shows that some Athenians believed
that the pestilence was the work of Apollo, traditionally
represented as a sender of disease, keeping in this case his
promise made through the Delphic oracle to help the Spartans in
the war. It was observed that the plague had broken out
immediately upon the Peloponnesians' invasion of Attikē, and
that, although it ravaged Athens, it scarcely touched the
Peloponnese.[174] There was dispute about an old prophecy; had it
said that a Dorian war, when it came, would be accompanied by
plague (*loimos*) or famine (*limos*)? Predictably, writes Thucydides,
the version involving plague won; "people shaped their memory
in accordance with their current suffering".[175]

Reports of reactions to bubonic plague in London during 1665–
6, when a similar proportion of the population died, make an
instructive comparison. On demoralisation aiding the disease:

> the very sinking fears they have of the plague, hath brought
> the plague and death upon many; some by the sight of a
> coffin in the streets, have fallen into a shivering, and
> immediately the disease hath assaulted them, and Serjeant
> Death hath arrested them.[176]

On the interest in whether piety was a defence:

> At the first so few of the religiouser sort were taken away
> that ... they began to be puffed up and boast of the great
> difference which God did make. But quickly after they all
> fell alike.[177]

Traditional burials were abandoned, individual graves being
replaced by pits for a great number of the dead. On a decline in
general morality, Pepys wrote of the plague "making us cruel as

doggs one to another".[178] The disease, and the Great Fire of September 1666, were compared with Christian prophecy, it being noticed that 666 was the number associated with Antichrist in the Revelation of St John. The Lord Chancellor, Clarendon, wrote of "the dismal year of 1666, in which many prodigies were expected, and so many really fell out".[179] (Perikles in Athens referred to the plague as a *daimonion*, a supernatural thing, according to Thucydides.[180])

Having the enemy without and the plague within, Athenians diverted their own energies and attentions with another mighty expedition against the Peloponnese. Under Perikles' leadership it ravaged both the territories of Epidauros and Troizen and also coastal Lakonia, where the little town of Prasiai was captured but sacked (rather than occupied).[181] Later, the force moved to the Thraceward area and supported the siege of Poteidaia, the defenders of which were still holding out after some two years.[182] (The place was surrendered in the following winter, the inmates having been reduced to cannibalism.[183]) Plague, however, travelled north with the Athenian expedition; of some 4,000 hoplites, around 1,050 died from the disease in little more than a month.[184]

After their various losses the Athenians offered peace terms to Sparta against Perikles' wishes, as we have seen.[185] When the terms were rejected, there was widespread anger against Perikles, who was fined (on a charge unspecified by Thucydides), and seemingly deposed from office. However, with a glancing criticism of *dēmokratia* Thucydides goes on: "Not long afterwards, as a crowd is apt to do, they elected him general again and entrusted all their affairs to him."[186] In the autumn of 429, Perikles died; Thucydides writes the emphatic, perhaps over-emphatic, tribute to his strategy that we have already noticed.[187]

Spartan campaigning and the capture of Plataia

In the first half of the Ten Years War, before she lost her fleet as a result of the Pylos episode,[188] Sparta was involved in some unsuccessful naval ventures. In 430, with the plague distracting Athens, the Spartans with 100 ships invaded the isle of Zakynthos, off the north-western Peloponnese, and tried by ravaging to induce the government of the place to give up its alliance with Athens.[189] Being at sea much the weaker of the great powers,

Sparta used early in the war the frequent recourse of the weak: terrorism. Merchant seamen from neutral states, as well as from cities allied with Athens, were killed when captured by the Spartans.[190] (When a similar policy was applied in the eastern Aegean in 427, by the unimpressive Spartan admiral Alkidas, it was vigorously opposed by local supporters of Sparta, who pointed out the contrast with Sparta's professed policy of freeing Greece.[191]) In 429 a fleet of Korinthian and other ships reacted to a numerically inferior Athenian fleet, near Rhion in the Korinthian Gulf, by forming a circle, to prevent the feared Athenian manoeuvre of *diekplous* (breaking through an enemy's line and attacking in the rear).[192] The Athenian admiral, Phormion, then had his ships sail round and round their opponents, causing the latter to contract their circle from fear of attack. He awaited his opportunity in the form of a predictable wind which, when it came, made the crowded enemy ships fall foul of each other. He then attacked, with triumphant results. Later that summer, in the same region, a reinforced Peloponnesian fleet under Spartan instruction tackled Phormion's ships with some success. But when one of the latter sank an unwary pursuer by nimbly doubling back under cover of an anchored merchant ship, the whole moral advantage shifted. The Peloponnesian fleet fell into confusion and itself fled. The fear created by Phormion's little fleet in both these episodes is a measure of Athens' naval reputation, and recalls the fright which Spartan land forces at other times engendered in Athenians and others. Similarly, there was a lack of conviction about Sparta's attempts to make a naval raid on Peiraieus, at a time when it was unguarded,[193] and to reinforce Mytilēnē in its revolt against Athens.[194] In both cases the Peloponnesian ships failed to get through, because of lack of daring in their Spartan commanders, which Thucydides evidently disapproved of.[195]

In 429, instead of invading Attikē (where plague still was), Sparta and allies moved against Athens' traditional ally, Plataia.[196] A siege developed, which was to last some two years, even though Plataia seemingly always had fewer than 500 defenders and was faced at first with the full might of the Peloponnesian league, an army likely to have been at least twenty times as numerous.[197] Athens valued her relations with Plataia; Plataian refugees were later given the rare honour of Athenian citizenship *en masse*.[198] But, even after Perikles' death, Athens stayed true to his policy of not challenging the main Peloponnesian army by land; no expedition was sent to relieve Plataia.[199]

Thucydides wrote that his work in general excluded story-telling.[200] He might have argued that colourful and morally satisfying elements in an account were all too likely to have been invented to entertain and edify. It is certainly a useful rule of thumb for the analyst of history (including gossip) that, other things being equal, of two rival versions the less entertaining or morally neat is the one to be preferred. But life does have its picturesque moments, and in connection with Plataia Thucydides recounts several which derive an added brightness from the sombre general setting of the historian's work. (The effect is rather similar to that created by the sparse elements of simple colour in the *Seven pillars of wisdom* of T. E. Lawrence.) Thucydides pictures the besieged Plataians using chains to suspend a beam outside their walls, then dropping it to snap off the heads of their enemies' battering rams.[201] He describes the defenders, anxious to estimate the height of a wall some way off which they had to climb, setting a large group of men individually to count its courses of bricks over and over again, then comparing the totals, to minimise error.[202] When a large section of the Plataians made their escape by night, a process Thucydides recounts with close and exciting detail, to throw pursuers off the scent they decided to take at first a road which led not to their obvious destination, Athens, but into enemy country. The historian then describes the Plataians observing in the darkness the blazing torches of their enemies as, duly misled, they went off in pursuit down the Athens road.[203] Thucydides had the eye of a good journalist; graphic narrative of this quality occurs elsewhere in his work, from time to time. But in his historiography as in his politics he was in strong reaction against vulgarity (rather as Lawrence was in concepts and style). We may wonder whether his desire not to resemble writers who told pretty stories led Thucydides to repress his graphic talent more than realism required.

When the remaining Plataians surrendered in 427, Sparta had all the men executed and the women enslaved. Their city was later demolished and its territory fell into the power of the old arch-enemy, Thebes.[204] Thucydides reports at length a speech made by the Plataian captives before their execution; it may be thought a magnificent exposition of the city's claim to mercy. Among other considerations, Plataia had fought loyally alongside Sparta in the Persian Wars. (The Spartans themselves seemingly made a similar point about Athens, when justifying their decision not to destroy that city in 404.[205]) For years Plataians had tended the graves of Spartans killed fighting Persia. Plataia had sent many of her citizens to help Sparta against the helot revolt in mid-century. She had entered the present war after an unprovoked attack on her by Thebes, and had committed no improper aggression against Sparta.[206] The last phrases attributed to the Plataians may suggest why Thucydides considered their speech worthy of such prominence in his history; these urge the Spartans "to be our saviours, and not, while liberating the rest of the Greeks, to destroy us". The historian may be commenting on the Spartans' pose as liberators.[207] When the Spartans did destroy the Plataians, he says in explanation that the Spartan attitude was adopted "almost entirely on account of the Thebans, whom the Spartans thought useful people for the war".[208] Later, in 416, speakers from the island community of Melos claimed to hope that the Spartans would be their saviours against Athenian aggression. Thucydides reports Athenian speakers on that occasion as replying that the Spartans, in their treatment of other peoples, "are distinguished above everyone else in our experience for thinking that what is pleasant is honourable, and what is profitable is just. Thinking of that kind does not conduce to the salvation you now unreasonably have in mind."[209] The Athenian prediction proved correct; Sparta did not attempt to save Melos. It may seem that the severe view of Spartan morality attributed to partisan Athenians opposing Melos is remarkably close to Thucydides' own view of Sparta's conduct in this Plataian episode to which he gives so much attention.

Athens and Mytilēnē

Shortly before recounting the end of Plataia, Thucydides describes in detail an episode suggestive of the morality of Athens. In 428 the city of Mytilēnē and most of the rest of Lesbos had revolted from the Athenian Empire.[210] Thucydides shows Mytilenean spokesmen urging the Peloponnesians to help them and to exploit the rare opportunity presented by Athens' distraction.[211] As we have seen, Sparta reacted with an attempt to mount a second invasion of Attikē in the one year (428), but was thwarted by her allies; she also sent out a naval force, the first from Sparta recorded as having operated in the eastern Aegean for half a century, but it failed to reach Lesbos. Mytilēnē was weakened by *stasis*; the oligarchs who organised the revolt evidently judged that they should not fully trust their own *dēmos* to resist the Athenians, and chose to employ mercenaries from elsewhere.[212] When, under severe pressure from the besieging Athenians, the authorities did at last distribute hoplite equipment to the *dēmos*, the latter promptly mutinied, threatening to hand the city over to Athens unless the ordinary citizens were given more food. At this, the oligarchs themselves surrendered the city to the Athenians.[213] How was Athens to treat captured Mytilēnē?

Thucydides gives much attention to differing opinions at Athens on what would be a suitable punishment. Death was the first decision, for all male citizens of Mytilēnē who were of military age, with enslavement for the women and children; a trireme was sent with instructions accordingly. Then came a change of heart; on the next day the Athenians reflected that their decision had been "cruel" — exceptionally good evidence, as we have seen, for the view that tender-hearted morality has some influence in inter-state politics.[214] In favour of the stern sentence was the orator Kleon, whom Thucydides here introduces (hostilely) as "in this, as in all things, the most violent of the citizens, and also by far the most persuasive to the *dēmos* at that time".[215] He argued for mass execution as an example to other subjects who might think of revolt, and reminded Athenians of the high cost of crushing defection.[216] (Shortly before, to pay for the siege of Mytilēnē Athens had imposed a wealth tax, *eisphora*, on her own citizens for the first time in the Peloponnesian War.[217]) Whether Kleon's drastic proposal fell within Perikles' scheme of "keeping a firm grip" on the Empire is unclear, given the vagueness of that expression.[218] Speaking against Kleon, Diodotos explicitly avoided the argument from pity; for him, the question whether there should be a general massacre at Mytilēnē was reducible to the question of what suited Athens.[219] This does not mean that he considered his audience uninterested in the subject of pity. He *may* have calculated that he could take for granted the support of many who objected to a massacre as cruel, and that he could best persuade the more hard-hearted by stressing that his own gentler policy in no way depended on subordinating Athens' interests to those of the Mytileneans. In any case, according to Thucydides, Diodotos argued that "as things are, the *dēmos* in every city is friendly towards you [Athenians]" and could, if properly treated, be kept alienated from the local oligarchs in a way which profited Athens. However, if Athens were to destroy the *dēmos* of Mytilēnē, in any other city that revolted the *dēmos* would have an interest in supporting the oligarchs who began the insurrection, through fear that all alike would be killed if the revolt were crushed.[220]

By a very narrow margin, the Athenian assembly voted for Diodotos' line. A second trireme was sent; fortified by food and promises from Mytilenean representatives in Athens, its crew raced towards Lesbos to forestall the wholesale massacre. Thucydides emphasises how near Athens came to destroying Mytilēnē. The first order had got through and was about to be executed when the second message arrived. And the crew of the second trireme was only able to make the speed it did through the chance fact that it met no unfavourable wind. In the event, the number of Mytileneans put to death was slightly over a thousand; in stressing that the killing might well have been greater, and that expediency played such a large part in Athenian thoughts, Thucydides may seem to be using the Mytilenean episode in a parallel with the Plataian, to pass a general comment on the morality of the two great powers. We shall discuss later the suggestion that Thucydides had a low opinion of the strategy of both Athens and Sparta. It may be that he also wished to communicate a severe judgement on their selfishness.[221]

Spartans at Kerkyra and in central Greece

In 427 the *stasis* in Kerkyra, an important ally of Athens, gave Sparta an opportunity; she duly sent a fleet.[222] Its commander, however, was Alkidas, whose great caution had recently caused Mytilēnē to be left almost unaided. He won a sea battle off Kerkyra, but there then seems to have developed a clash between two Spartan traditions. Thucydides, who elsewhere suggests that Sparta was in general defective in daring, observes now that the Spartan force after its victory "lacked the daring to move against the city" (of Kerkyra).[223] Alkidas may be seen as representing the Spartan tradition of caution.[224] Opposed to him in opinion now was Brasidas, who was evidently well in tune with the traditional opportunism of his people. He urged Alkidas to sail against the city, according to a report which Thucydides passes on; Kerkyra at the time was in a promising state of "much confusion and fear".[225] Spartan hierarchy decided the matter; Kerkyra was not

attacked; Alkidas outranked Brasidas.[226] The Spartans again sent
a fleet when, in 425, Kerkyra suffered from another exploitable
problem: hunger. Thucydides describes them as "thinking, with
a great famine present in the city, that they would easily gain
control".[227] Sparta, to re-apply a phrase of Richard Aldington,
"had a nose for carrion like a starving condor of the Andes". The
fleet of 425 was recalled without achieving its aim; the Athenians
had occupied Pylos.[228]

The Pylian episode of 425 will be considered shortly. In 426,
the year between her two descents on Kerkyra, Sparta turned
away from an invasion of Attikē; numerous earthquakes occurred,
which were taken as ominous.[229] Also, the plague was again
raging in Athens.[230] Accordingly the Spartans moved against
important Athenian interests elsewhere. Across the water from
Athens' precious refuge of Euboia, Sparta now established a
colony in which other Greeks were invited to participate:
Herakleia in Trakhis. The site appealed also as a station for
Peloponnesian troops on the road towards Thrace.[231] In the long
run Herakleia was not a success; it was worn down by attacks
from neighbours and was administered by Spartan officials in a
way which alienated their own allies.[232] But, when founded, it
must have seemed likely to achieve several purposes cheaply, in
keeping with Sparta's traditional economy of action. Not only did
it threaten two areas of the Athenian Empire, Euboia and the
Thraceward region, so as — at the very least — to put Athens to
the expense of counter-measures. It also would help Spartan
campaigns in central mainland Greece, as in 426, when an army
— partly from Herakleia — moved against Naupaktos, Athens'
base on the gulf of Korinth.[233] That army itself failed. Unsuccessful against Naupaktos, it moved northwest to Olpai, where it was
defeated by the Athenian general Demosthenes and politically
finessed. After the battle Demosthenes granted a truce whereby
the Spartan-led force deserted its local allies; he hoped thus to
undermine the credit of Sparta and her Peloponnesian allies in the
region.[234] Sparta was not the only Greek power to sow division
deliberately.

The Pylos episode

In 425 came Athens' most important success of the Ten Years
War. Men from an Athenian fleet, delayed by bad weather on its

way to Kerkyra and Sicily, fortified the headland of Pylos in Messenia, Sparta's territory of the south-western Peloponnese.[235] As we shall see, there were grave drawbacks to the plan of Demosthenes, who arranged this action at Pylos. But Sparta reacted with an uncharacteristic blunder. Next to Pylos was the isle of Sphakteria, lying across the mouth of a natural harbour. The Spartans planned to block with ships the entrances to the harbour, at each end of the island, and thus to deny a safe anchorage to Athenian vessels. To secure the island itself, a garrison was shipped in, comprising — in addition to helot attendants — 420 hoplites, of whom many were Spartiates.

Sparta's blunder lay in not foreseeing the chance that Athenian naval power would be sufficient to force the entries to the harbour and thus to cut off the men on the island. We may guess that Sphakteria, lying so close to the mainland, seemed virtually to be part of it and thus to fall within the sphere of Sparta's traditionally dominant land forces. In any case, Athenian ships did cut off and besiege the island garrison. Demosthenes and Kleon, with a special force sent from Athens, opposed the men on the island with overwhelming numbers. Light-armed troops wore down the slower-moving Spartan hoplites with missiles from a safe distance. (In normal conditions Peloponnesian cavalry would have kept the light-armed away; on the island Sparta had no cavalry.) After taking heavy losses, and having no prospect of being relieved, the Spartan force on the island surrendered.

Spartan troops were not expendable. Yet some 120 Spartiate hoplites were now carried off into captivity at Athens; others (probably forty or more) had been killed on the island.[236] To us, exposed to the statistics of world war, some 160 soldiers may seem trivial in strategic terms. But at Sparta, with its few thousand citizens and its communal style of life, everyone would have relatives or friends among the prisoners or the dead; Thucydides suggests that members of leading families were especially numerous among the captives.[237] Sparta seems to have been better equipped psychologically to deal with the death than with the surrender of her soldiers.[238] The shock of mass surrender must have been great. But the captives at Athens were not disowned. In effect they became hostages, to be killed if Sparta invaded Attikē.[239] The Athenian countryside thus went un-ravaged by a Peloponnesian army from the summer of 425 until 413 and the occupation of Dekeleia. Many Athenians must have blessed Demosthenes and Kleon. But how much of their success was due to wisdom rather than luck?

Demosthenes had permission from Athens to take action on the Peloponnesian coast. But, faced with the reality of Pylos, his colleagues scorned his plan to fortify the place.[240] A good recent study has stressed the unpromising aspects of Demosthenes' proposal to garrison Pylos, with Messenians from Naupaktos.[241] Although Pylos was served by a good harbour, Spartan land forces might easily come to control most of its shore. Sparta could even establish a fortified base of her own in the area, to check the raids by the Messenians which Demosthenes sought to procure. Water on Pylos was scarce, and supplies would have to be imported by sea — a great strain on Athens, and impossible in winter.[242] Sparta had the advantage of far shorter lines of communication. That she would give hostages, in the form of the men on Sphakteria, was not predictable.

With Kleon the case is complicated by the question of how far the account of Thucydides has been affected by the historian's emotion. During the Athenians' blockade of Sphakteria, tension grew in Athens at the thought that the approaching winter might interrupt the guard on the island and allow the Spartans to escape. Kleon was blamed for having rejected an offer of peace made by Sparta earlier in the episode. Thucydides' famous description of the ensuing debate in the assembly has coloured many hostile accounts of the Athenian *dēmokratia*. It is also now widely admitted to be infected with hostility towards Kleon. Kleon is shown, cornered in debate, seeking to deflect attention and responsibility onto his personal enemy, the general Nikias, by saying that, to preserve their opportunity, the Athenians should send a further force to Sphakteria, and that to capture the island was easy, if the generals were men. He himself would have done it, had he been in command. Nikias replied that, so far as the generals were concerned, Kleon could take any force he wanted and have a try. Kleon accepted this offer, thinking it mere words. However, on realising it to be seriously meant, he tried to withdraw, saying that Nikias, not he, was the general. The Athenians in the assembly reacted to his new reluctance by shouting at him to sail, "as a crowd tends to do".[243] Seeing no escape, Kleon agreed to go, specified a force of men from outside Athens to accompany him, and boasted that he would have the Spartans dead or alive within twenty days of his arrival at Pylos.

There was some laughter among the Athenians at his empty

boasting, but sensible people were gladdened by the thought that they would get one of two good things; either they would be rid of Kleon [if he failed], which they thought the likelier alternative, or, if they were wrong in that they would defeat the Spartans.[244]

Later, after describing the success of Demosthenes and Kleon on Sphakteria, Thucydides notes that Kleon's promise was fulfilled, "although it was mad".[245]

The main impression conveyed by this episode may be one of irresponsibility. The campaign at Sphakteria might well help to end the war, in Athens' favour, if it were well conducted. Yet control of it was apparently handed over without consideration to a commander who was himself both unprepared and reluctant, at the insistence of an assembly pursuing a petty advantage. Indeed, Thucydides' account suggests that there was a large element of pleasure, even of fun, in the proceedings. The assembly insisted, "as a crowd *philei*" ('tends' or 'likes' to do); there was laughter; the sensible ones were gladdened.

Is Thucydides' record of this occasion wholly correct? He was, or was about to become, an Athenian general himself. Whether he was present we do not know, but he would certainly be well informed. His account may well be right, as scholars have traditionally thought. However, in the light of Thucydides' unusual hostility towards Kleon, a different view may be put forward *as a possibility*. As usual we should distinguish between, on the one hand, words and actions perceptible to a contemporary witness and, on the other hand, motives which were at best only inferable. Reconstructing the psychology of one we detest or despise (as Thucydides did Kleon) is dangerous. To take, for clarity, the familiar case of a moral extreme from modern history: who now wants to gain insight into Hitler's anti-jewishness? Repulsion obstructs enquiry. How well has Thucydides reconstructed Kleon? Did the latter really stumble into the Sphakteria command? While we must preserve all the details which were directly perceptible by Thucydides or his informants, a different psychology may generate fewer problems than does the one suggested by Thucydides.

When given the command, Kleon specified — apparently on the spot — all the men he would need. This may suggest premeditation. Similarly the "mad" promise about twenty days. Kleon was no great strategist, as is shown by the circumstances of his death in 422 in a rout near Amphipolis. But as a politician who could master the assembly he was outstandingly effective, as Thucydides emphatically suggests.[246] Being thus a man of rare political intelligence, Kleon would probably have realised that to make a commitment, publicly and with little forethought, concerning the resources and the time he would need at Sphakteria might well create a noose for himself. More significantly still, in the circumstances as outlined by Thucydides to have made a commitment in that way would have been gratuitous.

Is it possible, instead, that Kleon had appraised the situation carefully in advance, judged (rightly or wrongly) that a military triumph on Sphakteria was within his grasp, and set out to engineer his own appointment to command? His striking claim, that if he had been in command he would have captured the island, could have been contrived to that end. There was obviously a good chance that it would evoke a challenge that he match his words with deeds. Whether Kleon could have predicted Nikias' offer to stand down is unclear. Nikias was to make an offer to resign on another, later, occasion, and his resignation in 425 was in keeping with the cavalier disregard for his responsibility for his own troops, as made clear by Thucydides in connection with later events in Sicily.[247] We cannot tell whether Athenians had access to relevant information on Nikias' character as early as 425. But Kleon was in a position to guess (or even to arrange) that someone in the assembly would respond to his proud claim by proposing him (Kleon) as commander. And he might also calculate that by seeming to back away he would intensify and cement a popular wish for him to command. His record as a demagogue suggests that he needed few practical lessons in what "a crowd likes to do", even from Thucydides.

What about the irresponsibility of others present on this occasion? How sensible it was to give Kleon command depends on what evidence the Athenians had for expecting strategic competence in him. On this we are in the dark; we cannot argue from Thucydides' silence that Kleon had given no such evidence. Also, Athenian culture involved less of a distinction than does our own between the roles of politician and general. The long career of Perikles had reinforced the idea that one man might be both successfully. Appointing Kleon, a successful orator, to a military command was, even if wrong, not an eccentric decision by Athenian norms. Finally, to come to the "sensible people" who were gladdened by the prospect of Kleon's (and thus their own city's) failure: even they cannot be dismissed as wholly irresponsible. In domestic politics it seems that Kleon posed as champion of the poor against the rich;[248] in the spirit of *stasis*, of putting class before city, it might well seem to some of the wealthy worth a defeat to be rid of an opponent whom the assembly had often found so persuasive. Did Thucydides indeed mean the wealthy and their supporters by his phrase "sensible people"? His word in Greek, *sōphrosi*, is cognate with *sōphrosynē*, which for him as for other partisan Greeks meant, in a constitutional context, oligarchy.[249]

Athens tries to exploit her advantage

The mass surrender at Sphakteria astounded Greece; Athens was rampant. Athenians no doubt meant to exploit the changed Hellenic opinion when, in late 425, they published demands for an increase in imperial tribute. Many individual cities were to pay far more than before, while others were held liable seemingly for the first time.[250] Sparta, with some 120 of her citizens effectively hostages at Athens, could no longer hope to invade Attikē as a means of winning the war.[251] Even before Sphakteria fell she offered peace, on terms which she was unwilling for her allies to learn and which therefore in all probability sacrificed their interests to those of Athens.[252] After Sphakteria Sparta tried again and again for peace, no doubt offering even larger concessions.[253] The Athenians kept refusing and sending the Spartan envoys away.

In recent times Athens has been much criticised for her refusal. But Sparta's record, of wanting peace when she had no opportunity to exploit and of breaking the peace when she had, may have suggested to Athenians that Athens' advantage should not be given away. As it was, in 421 when peace was made Athens gave back the prisoners but Sparta failed to deliver her own main hostage, Amphipolis. Even if Athenians in 425 had thought Sparta's fragile word to be worth having, as a few years later they did, they could sensibly have argued that first their victory at Sphakteria must be shown not to have been a freak. Otherwise Sparta might quickly come to resent a disadvantageous peace that was seen as having resulted from a single blunder. 'We were not really defeated' is a potent cry, which Kleon and his colleagues in the assembly were in a position to predict. For, on Kleon's advice, the *dēmos* had recently demanded back from Sparta the places ceded by Athens in her rare crisis of 446/5, places "which the [Spartans] did not capture in war, but by ... agreement of the Athenians at a time of disaster [for Athens], when they needed a peace treaty more [than they do now]".[254] Sparta might even, having got back her men, break the treaty under which she did so with a triumphant quotation of Athens' own words about "agreement ... at a time of disaster". Towards the end of the Second World War British propagandists proposed to weaken German resistance by issuing false news of surrender on radio frequencies normally used by German stations. The proposal was vetoed by the authorities, who knew how powerful had been the idea in Germany that Germans had not really lost the First World War, but had been "stabbed in the back". That idea had helped create the Second World War; there was proper concern to avoid generating another myth which would promote a Third.[255] Athenians likewise might argue that the coup at Sphakteria was not enough; before Sparta would make a worthwhile peace treaty she had to be convinced that she had been truly worsted.

In the aftermath of Sphakteria, Athens achieved much less than she attempted, but more than is sometimes suggested in modern accounts. In breach of Periklean policy she sought to add large areas to her dominions by conquering Megara and Boiotia. Respecters of Perikles might perhaps have argued that after Sphakteria Sparta was hamstrung in a way which Perikles could not have foreseen, and that in consequence expansionism was safer than he had envisaged. Superficially more similar to Perikles' policy, and much more successful, were the seaborne raids on the fringes of the Peloponnese. In 424 a force led by Nikias and others captured the large and important island of Kythera, to the south of Lakonia. Populated by *perioikoi* and with a garrison sent by the Spartans, the place fell more easily through the secret collaboration of a local faction with Nikias.[256] (Nikias may have remembered this success years later when, in very different circumstances, he clung to a hope that *stasis* would deliver Syracuse into his hands.[257]) Athens now had a staging post for voyages round the Peloponnese and a base for raids on Sparta's coasts. When raids came, Sparta could do little.[258] In a remarkable passage, often undervalued,[259] Thucydides makes it clear that the Spartans were close to despair, demoralised by the defeats on Sphakteria and Kythera and dreading internal revolution (presumably in the form of a helot revolt):

> the many pieces of ill fortune, coming together in a short
> time and contrary to reasonable expectation, had produced
> in them the greatest panic, and they feared a second
> disaster, like the one on the island [Sphakteria]. Conse-
> quently they became less bold still about facing battles and
> thought that whatever they set their hand to would fail,
> because they had lost confidence in their own judgement as
> a result of their previous inexperience of adversity.[260]

An element in this pessimism was religious, as Thucydides may
hint with his reference to the cluster of ill fortune.[261] Elsewhere
he shows that Spartans attributed their setbacks in the Ten Years
War to religious offences: the breach of a peace treaty by their ally
Thebes in 431;[262] their own refusal to accept arbitration under the
same treaty,[263] and the (alleged) bribery of a priestess at
Delphoi by the Spartan king, Pleistoanax.[264] Such religious
thinking might involve the dispiriting conviction that further
suffering, because divinely planned, was likely or unavoidable. If
Athens is to be blamed for missing an opportunity of making a
lasting and favourable peace with Sparta, criticism should
perhaps focus on 424 rather than the previous year.

It has been suggested, in good modern works, that Athens
could have won the war conclusively if she had done more to
incite a helot revolt.[265] There is perhaps a danger here of
underestimating the intelligence both of the Athenians and of the
Spartans. Athens had received a vivid lesson on the vulnerability
of Sparta in this area, having helped the Spartans to resist the
great revolt at Ithōmē in the late 460s. Since then she had no
doubt learnt from her dealings with the former helots whom she
installed at Naupaktos; members of that community helped
Athens in the Sphakteria campaign.[266] For Athens not to have
played the helot card might seem stupid. But in the 420s what
more could Athens have done to promote a general insurrection of
helots? She might perhaps have established small, permanent,
garrisons in other coastal regions of Lakonia and Messenia.
Against these the Spartans might be expected to establish
blockading garrisons of their own. Then would arise the task of
convincing helots that their chance had indeed come. How, if at
all, might that be done? Messenians from Naupaktos, still
speaking the dialect of the helots,[267] might penetrate and inform

the helot communities of Sparta's predicament. But would they carry sufficient credit to make the helots willing to risk the lethal counter-measures of the Spartans? We recall that the two great helot revolts of the classical period were in response to developments that the helots could directly perceive: the earthquake of the mid-460s and the Theban invasion after Leuktra. The Spartans were masters of the techniques of dividing, isolating and deceiving their opponents, with special methods of keeping the helots in the dark.[268] Only on the coasts might helots readily be convinced of Athens' strength, but we cannot assume that Sparta failed to act accordingly. Sparta's concern for defence of her coasts against pirates is made clear by Thucydides.[269]

In *stasis* at Megara in 424, leaders of the democratic faction tried to hand over their city to Athens,[270] but the Athenian troops who came to exploit their opportunity were thwarted by the appear-ance of an army led by the Spartan Brasidas.[271] Similar proposals were made to Athens by democratising factions in cities of Boiotia; simultaneous risings were planned, to be supported by Athenian intervention.[272] However, the latter in the event was mistimed, and the Boiotian authorities had warning from an informer.[273] At Delion, in eastern Boiotia, Athens lost a hoplite battle with heavy casualties (late in 424).[274] Sparta was not directly involved in the battle, but her strategic thinking was affected. When she was ready again for aggression against Attikē, she could think of leaving a permanent garrison on Athenian soil in the belief that Boiotian hoplites, their superiority over their Athenian counterparts now established, would be able to defend it.[275]

Brasidas' campaign in north-eastern Greece

The last great movement of the Ten Years War consisted of Brasidas' march to the Thraceward region and his winning over of important Athenian possessions there. As with every other Spartan venture into a new area during the Peloponnesian War, a special opportunity beckoned; allies and former allies of Athens had invited Sparta's assistance in support of revolts proposed or already existing.[276] In sending Brasidas' expedition the Spartans, as with the founding of Herakleia, were killing several birds with one stone. Dangerous helots were removed from Sparta, and recruited — exceptionally — into Brasidas' army.[277] Sparta might gain territory to be swapped for the prisoners from Sphakteria.

(Brasidas claimed that he had made the Spartan authorities swear solemnly to leave independent any allies he might acquire; this would exclude their use as bargaining counters with Athens,[278] but also proves that the idea was in the air, as we guess from the fact that it was put into action in 421 after Brasidas' death.[279]) Also, some Spartans might even be glad that Brasidas himself was being sent away. He had a very long road to travel, through districts accessible to Athenian seaborne troops, and with hoplites far below the Spartiate standard:[280] his chance of being killed was great. Envy was an important element in Spartan society,[281] and Brasidas already had an enviable reputation in the role most esteemed at Sparta, as a soldier.[282] If his claim about extracting an oath from the Spartan authorities was correct, he was willing to assert himself in Spartan politics in a way likely to be abrasive. Such was the feeling against him later, after his success in the north, that he was refused reinforcements by Sparta at one stage — through jealousy on the part of the leading men, as Thucydides says.[283] It may be that Brasidas and his army were seen as dispensable. With Attikē barred, the Spartan authorities must have been looking around anxiously for an area in which they could do something drastic. Yet their concern for their precious manpower would be intense after the losses at Sphakteria. Brasidas' cheap gamble suited admirably.

Once in the Thraceward region, Brasidas behaved with memorable tact and restraint — more acceptably, in short, than other Spartan commanders abroad. Selecting their evidence unconsciously, in accordance with wishful thinking,[284] Greeks who thought of collaborating with Sparta years later were to remember Brasidas, and not Alkidas; Brasidas "seemed to be a good man in every way, and left behind a firm hope that the others [Spartan commanders] were like him", says Thucydides — pointedly.[285] Arriving at Akanthos, a subject state of Athens in Khalkidikē, Brasidas was met by the classic split: a democratic faction, seemingly the majority, reluctant to revolt from Athens to Sparta, and others, not democrats, who sided with Sparta.[286] But Brasidas, and not Athens, had an army at the gates, and a hostage, the crops of the Akanthians almost ready for harvest, representing months of past work and future food.[287] Allowed into the city on his own to speak, Brasidas produced artful rhetoric; "He was an able speaker — for a Spartan", Thucydides notes.[288] He flattered the inhabitants of the obscure statelet, telling them that they were "people with a reputation for intelligence, forming an important city".[289] (Because it appeals to wishful thinking, flattery rarely fails completely.) He spoke deceptively about the circumstances of his success, and the Athenian failure, in the Megarid.[290] And, with consummately smooth impertinence, he affected a personal tone of wounded innocence about his reception at Akanthos: "I am surprised that you have shut the gates against me; I thought you would be glad to see me."[291] After receiving Brasidas' personal assurance about the oath at Sparta to leave independent any states he might bring over, Akanthos let his army in.[292] Stagiros, a nearby town with historic links with Akanthos, likewise accepted Brasidas and revolted from Athens, in the same summer (of 424).[293] Argilos followed.[294]

Near Argilos, and thus slightly to the east of the peninsula of Khalkidikē, lay Amphipolis, a city dear to the heart of Athens, which had founded it during 437/6. Amphipolis generated much revenue for the Athenians and also sent timber for their navy.[295] The River Strymon, which skirted the city and contributed to its defence, gave access to Athenian seaborne forces but also provided a defensible line against a land army of Athens' enemies marching eastwards towards the strategically vital Hellespont.[296] Yet most of the inhabitants of this jewel of cities were not of Athenian origin.[297] When Brasidas approached, capturing many unsuspecting citizens outside the walls and thus gaining hostages,[298] he induced in Amphipolis shock, fear for those captured, and a dread of *stasis*.[299] He offered moderate terms of surrender,[300] which were made more attractive by the belief that prompt help from Athens could not be depended on.[301] Amphipolis capitulated.[302]

Help did come from an Athenian force, in time to save from Brasidas the port of Eion, downstream of Amphipolis.[303] In command of this force, of seven ships, was Thucydides the historian.[304] After his failure to save Amphipolis he was exiled from Athens.[305] Yet in spite of this official judgement on his skill (or honesty) he makes no direct and elaborate essay in self-defence, as most authors would have done. The motive(s) for the historian's famous restraint may only be guessed at. He may have wished to avoid affecting the appearance of his work, the "possession for ever", with anything resembling a personal tract for the times. Even the identity of those who proposed his exile is not made clear; here we may perhaps see the desire of a superior man not to give such clues to his own psyche as would be given by the naming of his enemies. If the chief of these was Kleon (as many have suspected[306]), and if Thucydides consciously desired to damn his memory, as a connoisseur of source criticism he might have expected to do that more effectively by not making clear to later readers his personal grounds for resentment.

After the fall of Amphipolis the fears and hopes of Athens came into some sort of balance with those of Sparta. Sparta had earlier lost her confidence of winning the war by means of ravaging Attikē; now, with the setbacks in Boiotia and the north, Athens had lost the faith induced by Sphakteria.[307] Sparta feared opposition in the Peloponnese, and not only from helots; the expiry of a treaty would soon allow the old enemy, Argos, to join Athens against Sparta,[308] while other Peloponnesian states might go over to Argos, or Athens, or both.[309] Athens feared the spread of revolt in her own sphere.[310] Further, she yearned for the restoration of Amphipolis, rather as Sparta did for her men captured on Sphakteria. In the spring of 423 Athens and Sparta made a truce for one year.[311] Hostilities continued in the Thraceward region, where Brasidas did not share the enthusiasm of his home government for peace. Contrary to the terms of the truce, he accepted into alliance two states which revolted from the Athenian Empire, Skiōnē and Mendē.[312] Mendē was regained soon afterwards by an Athenian expedition under Nikias and a colleague, with the aid of a democratic faction within the town.[313] (Skionē fell in 421, deserted by Sparta; its citizens were variously massacred and enslaved by Athens.[314]) Nikias's rival, Kleon, himself recaptured a town, Torōnē, which had gone over to Brasidas.[315] But when Kleon moved against Amphipolis, he allowed his force to be caught out of position by Brasidas, who seized his opportunity albeit with a force inferior in quality to that of Kleon.[316] There resulted a triumph of Spartan economy; some 600 were killed on the Athenian side including Kleon, against seven in the army of Brasidas.[317] Another fact characteristic of Sparta was the courage of her commander; among the seven dead was Brasidas himself.[318] He was buried at Amphipolis with lavish honours.[319]

The Peace of Nikias, and its aftermath

Thucydides notes that with the deaths of Brasidas and Kleon there were removed two strong opponents of peace.[320] (The comedian Aristophanes referred to the pair as "the twin pestles of war",[321] Greece, in his metaphor, being the substance ground down by their pressure.) Thucydides says that Brasidas, his own former opponent whom he respected,[322] opposed peace because of the good fortune and prestige which he derived from war.[323] Kleon, according to Thucydides, "thought that if there were a rest from hostilities his own evil-doing would be more obvious and his slanders less credited".[324] We should like to know how Thucydides came to think this. It is unlikely that Kleon, whose position in a *dēmokratia* always depended on public support, ever made an accessible confession of a personal interest in maintaining war, and still less likely that he spoke of himself as evil-doing and slanderous. Thucydides attributes unavowed motives with less apparent caution than we should like.[325] Two other leading Greeks, Pleistoanax and Nikias, are treated similarly in connection with the moves for peace after the battle of Amphipolis. Pleistoanax, a king at Sparta, is said by Thucydides to have been eager to end the war with Athens, to free himself of harmful accusations within his city, to the effect that Sparta's setbacks in war were divine punishment for his improper return from exile.[326] At Athens, Nikias is given a similarly personal motive by Thucydides; he had had a good war and wished to quit while ahead.[327]

In the spring of 421 Athens and Sparta made a treaty of peace, supposedly for fifty years;[328] it came to be known as the Peace of Nikias. Both sides were to give up their gains, with some exceptions. Sparta secured protection for some of the states in the Thraceward region which had come over to her, but Athens was given a free hand with the luckless natives of Skiōnē. Each side was to release its prisoners. Lottery determined which side began the process of surrendering its gains; it fell to Sparta to free her captives, which she did, and to send orders to the north east for the implementation of the treaty there. Klearidas, the Spartan official ordered to hand over Amphipolis, refused to do so, for the sake of the people of the region.[329] In the event the city was relinquished by Sparta, but remained independent of Athens for the rest of its history. Athens retaliated by not handing back Pylos and Sphakteria; she did, however, release the prisoners from the island.[330]

The return of the precious Spartiates occurred soon after Athens and Sparta had sworn a further treaty, this time one of mutual defence.[331] Athens, in a remarkable clause, was required to help Sparta in the event of a helot revolt.[332] The Spartans, as we might infer from this, faced severe problems close to home, in addition to those recurrently posed by the hostility of the helots and of Argos. In 423/2 there had been a bloody battle between Mantineia and Tegea, with their respective alliances,[333] a clear sign of Sparta's diminished control over the vital central Peloponnese.[334] Korinth rejected Spartan authority by refusing to accept the Peace of Nikias; under its terms Athens was not obliged to return Sollion and Anaktorion, two Korinthian colonies won during the Ten Years War.[335] Elis would not swear to the peace;[336] nor would Megara which had lost Nisaia.[337] Boiotia likewise abstained, because of a clause requiring that she lose the border fort of Panakton to Athens.[338] In short, Sparta's alliance seemed to be crumbling; her reputation had been much reduced by the affair of Sphakteria and by the contrast between her grand professions about liberation and the actual outcome of the Ten Years War.[339]

The diplomatic manoeuvres, in many cases sterile, by which Peloponnesian states sought to protect themselves in the aftermath of the Peace, cannot be treated in detail here.[340] But the temporary severance of Sparta from some of her most important allies must be seen as a success for Athens. We recall that, with her small population, Sparta depended on the hoplite armies of her allies for her existence as a great power. In his account of the year 420 Thucydides introduces the Athenian Alkibiades, "a man still young by the standards of any other city, but revered for the reputation of his ancestors".[341] We see that even in the *dēmokratia* of Athens egalitarianism had its limits; Alkibiades' uncle was Perikles. To break with Sparta and to ally with Argos was the policy favoured by Alkibiades. Recording this, Thucydides immediately gives a selfish motive for it; Alkibiades had been affronted by the fact that the Spartans had negotiated their agreements with Athens through other men and not through him. They had ignored him on account of his youth,[342] in spite of the role of his ancestors as representatives, *proxenoi*, of Sparta at Athens, a role which he had tried to resume by acting considerately towards the prisoners from Sphakteria.[343]

Of the Greek leaders whom Thucydides portrays as subordinating *polis* to self, Alkibiades constitutes the most florid case. Later in his career, when in exile from Athens and under a sentence of death passed there, he was to give astute and seemingly influential advice first to Sparta and then to Persia on how to damage his native city. In 420, wishing to discredit a Spartan embassy to Athens, he successfully played on the Spartans' habit of deceit. He persuaded the envoys, who had stated in the Athenian council that they had come with full powers to negotiate, to deny this when they appeared at the assembly.[344] Alkibiades was then able to denounce the Spartans as never telling a consistent story. In doing this he was also playing skilfully on Athenian public opinion. For, a few years earlier, the Athenians had intercepted a memorable message in which the Persian authorities accused Sparta in almost exactly the same terms.[345]

Not long afterwards, as urged by Alkibiades, the Athenian assembly made a treaty of mutual defence with Argos, Elis and Mantineia.[346] This was, of course, a move against Sparta, although Athens' treaties of peace and alliance with the Spartans were not formally revoked.[347] At the Olympic games of 420, Sparta suffered the humiliation of being excluded by the host state, Elis.[348] (It was probably in the Olympic contest of 416 that Alkibiades triumphed with the chariot teams of which he was patron. In a speech which Thucydides records, Alkibiades echoes Perikles,[349] and justifies his sporting expenses in terms of inter-state politics, claiming that the other states of Greece

> have come to believe that [Athens] is even more powerful than in reality she is, because of my brilliant show at the Olympic festival, as a result of my having entered seven chariots, a number never before entered by a private individual, and come first and second and fourth.[350]

Modern analysts, seeking to explain the importance attached by the great powers to the Olympics of recent times, talk vaguely of a concern for "national prestige". Alkibiades' speech is more precise and profound. For politicians the main point of athletic success was (as perhaps it still is) to suggest military strength.

Alkibiades' policy of alliance with Peloponnesian states against Sparta led, in 418, to the full-scale hoplite battle of Mantineia. On the one side were the Spartans, with the Tegeates and other allies; on the other were Argos and Mantineia, with contingents from Athens and elsewhere.[351] The Spartan commander, King Agis, was under unusual pressure from home to distinguish himself, after missing a rare opportunity of damaging Argos, shortly before.[352] Whether Athens was wise to bring matters to the point of battle is doubtful. She was predictably about to play to Sparta's strength, which lay in hoplite fighting, and would give her enemy a chance to recover from the humiliation of Sphakteria. On the other hand, Alkibiades and his supporters might argue that Athens was going for a great prize, the crippling of Sparta, with fairly small risk to herself; the Athenian element in the allied army came to some 1,300,[353] and the bulk of the fighting would fall on better-reputed Dorian hoplites of the Peloponnese. In the event the battle went Sparta's way, after some initial success for troops from Mantineia and Argos.[354] Many ran away before engaging, for fear of the Spartans.[355] By her victory, Sparta regained her reputation among the Greeks generally; ill fortune, it now seemed, had made her fail in the Ten Years War, but the mentality of her men was the same as before. They had not gone soft.[356] Sparta now set about intervening in other states of the Peloponnese, to restore her dominance.[357]

Athens and Melos

In 416 Athens sent a force to subdue the Aegean island of Melos, where the inhabitants claimed descent from a Spartan colony of much earlier times and had given help to Sparta against Athens in recent years.[358] Athenian spokesmen in 416 evidently asked to address the *dēmos* of Melos, but were allowed only to speak to the oligarchs.[359] The latter perhaps feared that local democrats might do a deal with the Athenians in the democratic interest; there was to be some secret dealing later.[360] Thucydides records a debate between the oligarchs of Melos and the spokesmen of Athens: the status of this, "the Melian Dialogue", has been much disputed.[361] The Athenians are portrayed as refusing to argue from certain normal moral premises, as suggesting that it was unrealistic to expect a strong state to respect the sovereignty of a weaker, and as rejecting a commonplace view of the gods as defenders of the weak against the strong.[362] Some have suspected that official spokesmen of Athens could never have argued thus, and that Thucydides has put words into their mouths, to illustrate what he saw as the real, cynical, motivation behind conventional hypocrisies.[363] It has also been suggested that Thucydides wished to point a moral about arrogance preceding a fall, in the manner of contemporary tragedy;[364] the historian's account of the debate, and of the siege and massacre which followed, immediately precede his record of the expedition to Sicily, where Athens herself came to grief.

The latter point may be dealt with first. In no other context does Thucydides give any indication of believing in divine punishment, and he is dismissive to the point of unfairness when dealing with the divination of his contemporaries.[365] The idea of Thucydides as a tragedian in prose is no more than a pretty suggestion, lacking any proper support. What should we make of the idea that the arguments given to the Athenian spokesmen are out of keeping with such speakers or with the occasion? Is this correct?

Thucydides described his work as one meant to be a possession for ever, but he assumed that his readers would for ever have a good understanding of the constitutional background to Athenian and Spartan procedure. What would readers possessing that mental background most easily make of the Melian Dialogue? Perhaps the most striking feature of the debate for such a reader would be its consisting of short exchanges, rather than of long speeches. Explanatory remarks about this unusual structure are made prominently at the start of the debate. The Athenians emphasise the fact that they are not being brought to speak to the *dēmos*:

> Since the arguments are not to be put to the great body (*plēthos*) of the citizens, presumably (*dē*) so that the many may not be deceived when they hear for the one time our seductive and untested claims in a continuous speech — for we realise that this is the meaning of bringing us in front of the oligarchs — you sitting in your council should use an even safer procedure. Not using a single speech, but point by point....[366]

Would an informed reader take this as sincere? In an age of *stasis*, do envoys from the greatest of democratic states admit without protest that the characteristic procedure of their own state, the long speech to a mass audience, could profitably be dismissed; in short, that in this matter gloriously successful Athens was wrong, and obscure, oligarchic, Melos was right? Surely the utterance quoted would be taken by Thucydides' original readers as ironic. Various details point that way. The word *plēthos* had a strongly pro-democratic overtone;[367] in using it, the Athenians are indeed making a glancing protest against their inability to address the mass of citizens. The word *dē*, as often, expresses disapproval or disbelief. The reference to an *even* safer procedure also contains a sneer, since according to oligarchic theory the alternative method, the long speech to a mass audience, was not safe at all. The ironic tone was seemingly meant to extend to other sections of the debate; the Athenians later refer to a long speech they might have delivered as "a disbelieved abundance of words",[368] and slyly urge the Melian oligarchs (the *oligoi* — 'the few'), "Don't allow yourselves to become like the many."[369]

There is, then, a clear suggestion that the Athenian speakers resented the oligarchic circumstances of the Melian Dialogue. In the late fifth and early fourth centuries there seems to have been a fashion in anti-democratic circles for political analysis which rejected idealistic motives and spoke with harsh openness about selfish reality.[370] The "Old Oligarch" wrote in this vein about the constitution of Athens; other examples occur in the dialogues of Plato.[371] When the Athenian speakers on Melos found themselves among oligarchs, did they employ the mental agility of which Perikles had boasted,[372] and aggressively adopt an ironic version of the oligarchic style of argument? The implied reasoning might then have been rather as follows: "You are too sophisticated to be taken in by idealistic and seductive arguments? Very well, we will give you none, but rather the hard truth for men of experience, superior to the many." We observe that when the Athenians reject certain of the claims of justice, they stress that "both we and you [Melians] know" such to be unrealistic.[373] The oligarchs, perhaps, had brought this brutal style of argument on themselves, in the Athenian view. If this interpretation is possible, we may be freed from the suspicion that Thucydides has seriously misrepresented the tone of the occasion. He may have known that the Athenian speakers argued as he shows, from irritation; his original readers may have understood that when those speakers rejected idealism they did so in irony.

We may thus be moved one step away from the view that Thucydides meant the Melian Dialogue as a condemnatory picture of crude, mighty Athens crushing pitiable little Melos. We may move further if we observe, with de Ste. Croix,[374] how imprudent Thucydides must have thought the Melian oligarchs. The latter are shown relying on the prospect of help from Sparta.[375] The Athenians, however, suggest that for Sparta to send help to Melos would require great boldness, given that Athens ruled the waves, whereas the Spartans in reality were

abnormally cautious.[376] We have already noticed Thucydides'
own, emphatically expressed, view that Sparta lacked boldness.[377] The Melians argue that a sense of honour will make the
Spartans help them.[378] The Athenians reply that, while the
Spartans behave virtuously to each other, they are conspicuous in
treating non-Spartans in a way which confuses virtue with their
own self-interest.[379] Again, this closely resembles Thucydides'
own view, as we saw it expressed in the case of the Spartans at
Plataia.[380] The Melians speak of their trust in divinely-sent good
fortune.[381] The Athenians condemn reliance on divination in a
crisis, using forthright language which recalls Thucydides' own
on the subject.[382] The last word in the debate falls to the
Athenians, who accuse the Melians of wishful thinking:

> you judge the future to be more certain than the present
> which you actually see, and in your eagerness you regard the
> unseen future as already taking place. In trusting the
> Spartans and good fortune and your hopes you have taken
> an enormous risk, in which your failure will be correspond-
> ingly great.[383]

With this should be compared Thucydides' own words, noticed
earlier,[384] about the mistaken tendency of people to employ
"unexamined hope" and "obscure wishful thinking". We may
now see more clearly part of Thucydides' reason for giving so
much attention to the Melian Dialogue. If, as we suspect, the
Athenians did take the line in argument which he records, they
very likely forced the Melians to make explicit the reasons why
they believed in the value of resistance rather than merely to
concentrate in the conventional way on their moral justification.
And their reasons for resistance touched on a number of errors in
which Thucydides took a strong interest, as witness his remarks
elsewhere. He goes on to recount, comparatively briefly, the
subsequent fate of Melos. Conquered by Athens, the captured
men of military age were killed, the children and women
enslaved.[385]

Thucydides might have given the Melian oligarchs a more
reasonable case had he included the consideration that Athens
had invaded Melos ten years earlier in the hope of conquest, but
had gone away unsuccessful.[386] The memory of this would surely
influence the Melians. We recall that, on Thucydides' showing,
the Spartan invasion of Attikē in 431 was attended by a belief that

history might repeat itself. The playing down by Thucydides of reputable reasoning, and the heavy emphasis on mistakes, are features which the Melian episode seems to share with the next part of the historian's work, the account of Athens' invasion of Sicily. That case will be examined in a moment. First, it may be important to remember that Thucydides both intended his work as a possession for ever, and also believed that human nature might long remain constant.[387] He may perhaps have had a didactic concern to warn against error, which has shaped his selection of material. Another, less rational, motive which might lead the same way is suggested at the end of the present chapter.

Athens' expedition to Sicily

Thucydides begins his account of the expedition to Sicily by recording that the Athenians (in the winter of 416/5) desired to send a force in the hope of conquering the island.[388] In the same prominently-placed sentence there is a glancing reference to Athenian naval forces which had intervened in Sicily in the 420s,[389] but also the more striking statement that the mass of Athenians did not know how big the island was, or how numerous were its inhabitants; nor did they realise that the war they were undertaking was not much inferior in scale to the war against the Peloponnesians. This latter theme is then amplified and emphasised by a long excursus in which Thucydides reviews the history and peoples of Sicily.[390] The Athenians' decision to send the great expedition of 415 might have been made to seem less rash if Thucydides had here laid similar emphasis on the fact that the smaller forces of the 420s had come home without serious loss, if with little immediate profit. The experience of the 420s corresponds interestingly with the suggestion made by Thucydides later in Book VI: that there was at Athens rather more confidence in the safety of the great expedition than in its prospect of conquest.[391] Athenian rationale might also have been made clearer had Thucydides recalled the point made in an earlier book, that a purpose of intervention in the 420s had been to explore Sicily with a view to its possible conquest.[392] Knowledge gained in that period places a limit on the Athenian ignorance. But much ignorance there must have been, on Thucydides' showing. And that ignorance helps to explain another important element in the decision to send the great expedition: divination.

When, in 413/2, the Athenians at home learnt of the catastrophe in which the Sicilian venture had ended, they were angry with (among others) "the oracle-mongers and prophets and whoever by using divination in any way at that time had made them hope to capture Sicily".[393] The role of religious prophecy in the Sicilian expedition is complex and important; it is discussed in Chapter 9. But divination can be seen in general to have been most influential when secular evidence seemed weak, as many Athenians surely sensed it to be on the question whether they could conquer Sicily.

A further element in the decision was, no doubt, wishful thinking. Thucydides describes the Athenians generally as gripped by "a passion" for the expedition. The old men thought that they would either conquer or, at any event, suffer no serious loss with such a large force; the younger ones were confident of their own safety and yearned for sightseeing in foreign parts (a motive appealed to in recent years by advertisers recruiting for the British armed forces). The masses and the troops hoped to earn wages in the short term and to acquire a resource — Sicily — which would supply earnings for ever.[394] The great champion of the scheme, Alkibiades, is assigned motives of his own. According to Thucydides, he acted out of rivalry towards Nikias and especially from a love of military command, which he hoped would lead to the conquest by himself of Sicily and Carthage, and to his own enrichment and glory.[395] Thucydides implies that, to live up to his reputation in Athens, Alkibiades wished to spend such sums on racehorses and other things as were beyond his existing means.[396] These the inhabitants of Sicily might be made to supply.

As so often with events in need of explanation, it is helpful to ask about the Sicilian expedition 'Why *now*?'. In 415 Athenians might think along the lines prescribed by Perikles, about the prospects for naval expansion in remote waters when there was peace at home. Nikias, seeking to quell the enthusiasm of his fellow Athenians for the sending of the Sicilian expedition, seems to reveal their thinking. He states (in Thucydides' account) that the Athenians desire Sicily because of contempt for the power of Sparta and her allies.[397] In reality, Nikias claims, this is not a *kairos*; Athens has her timing wrong, and the Spartans are looking eagerly for an Athenian failure which would allow them to attack and to restore their reputation.[398] In reply, Alkibiades argues that a rare opportunity exists; "the Peloponnesians have never been more pessimistic about their chances against us than they are now".[399] It was several years since a Spartan army had ventured beyond the Peloponnese in an attack on Athenian interests. Thucydides suggests that the Spartans were fearful of incurring divine punishment by making war in breach of the oaths of 421.[400] While encouragement was given by Sparta to those who might wish to plunder Athenian possessions, the Spartans as a community held back, perhaps in the traditional Greek belief that an expedition abroad was especially vulnerable to the intervention of heaven.[401] As we have seen, Perikles' strategy had not promised to crush Sparta. Those Athenians who thought as he had, might well believe that the Spartans' present timid quiescence was the most favourable condition they could hope for, as a setting for their own expansion overseas. Also, in 416/5 the small state of Egesta in western Sicily urgently requested Athenian aid for her war against neighbouring Selinous. Selinous was backed by Syracuse, and Egesta could argue that a victorious Syracuse might one day intervene in mainland Greece against Athens herself.[402] Egesta claimed to have great supplies of treasure for the support of an Athenian expeditionary force; Thucydides tells of envoys from Athens, who were sent to check on the treasure and deceived by a ruse.[403] Alliance with Egesta could be expected to provide both a physical base, and the show of a moral basis, for the intervention of Athens in Sicily.

The three generals appointed to command the great expedition, Alkibiades, Lamakhos and Nikias, were given by the assembly a set of instructions which may seem strange. They were to aid Egesta, to recreate — if possible — the city of Leontinoi (which Syracuse had helped to break up some years before[404]), and to transact all other business in Sicily as they thought best for Athens.[405] Knowing as we do that the war with Syracuse was to preoccupy, and eventually to overwhelm, the Athenian expedition, we may find it incongruous that there is no explicit mention of Syracuse in these instructions. In explanation, Dover suggests that many Athenians hoped to subdue Syracuse by diplomacy and accordingly did not wish to publish their purpose.[406] The size of the expeditionary force was increased as a result of an argument from Nikias who, according to Thucydides' reading of his motives, had hoped rather that the Athenians would be put off the project entirely by the scale of the armament which he claimed was necessary.[407] The fleet which sailed for Sicily included 134 triremes, 100 of them Athenian.[408] (The reinforcing fleet of 413 comprised another 73 vessels, approximately.[409]) The eventual catastrophe was to engulf more than half of the warships which Athens had controlled.[410]

Before the expedition of 415 sailed for Sicily, there occurred the worrying incident of the mutilation of the Hermai. (On this see Chapter 9.) Hermes was the god of travellers; the defacing of his statues was taken as a bad omen for the voyage and also as the work of plotters against the *dēmokratia*.[411] Divination on this occasion did not prove decisive. The expeditionary force set sail, but not before enemies of Alkibiades had made an accusation against him of involvement in the sacrilege. In a famous sunlit passage, Thucydides describes the exuberant departure from Peiraieus; drink offerings to the gods were poured from precious vessels, and the sailors then raced each other as far as Aigina.[412] It is hard at this point not to think (as perhaps Thucydides meant his readers to do) of the gloom and degradation in which the campaign was to end.

When the fleet arrived in Sicilian waters, the Athenians received a double disappointment. Rhēgion, formerly an ally,[413] would not help,[414] and the truth was discovered about the small resources of Egesta.[415] Nikias, always unenthusiastic about the expedition, seized the opportunity to argue that, after helping Egesta against Selinous, the Athenians should merely parade their strength in the sight of other cities and then go home — unless they met an unexpected chance to win over a city.[416] Alkibiades wanted a diplomatic campaign to precede possible warfare against Syracuse and Selinous.[417] Lamakhos argued for a prompt attack on Syracuse, to exploit the unpreparedness and shock of the inhabitants in the face of Athens' armada, before familiarity did its usual work.[418] Thucydides himself seems to have sympathised with Lamakhos; later, in language which echoes that of the general, he records that the eventual delay in attacking Syracuse did cause the Syracusans to gain confidence in themselves and contempt for the Athenian force.[419] The historian also accepts that Athenian delay made possible the arrival at Syracuse of the (crucial) aid from the Greek mainland, under the Spartan Gylippos.[420]

The military aspects of the Sicilian expedition are recounted by Thucydides at great length, and cannot be treated here with a corresponding degree of detail. The profound influence of religion, at the beginning and at the end of the campaign, is dealt with in Chapter 9 below. Religious argument played a part in the unhappy selection of Nikias as commander and in the removal of Alkibiades from command. The latter was recalled to face a charge of sacrilege at Athens, but fled to Sparta, where his advice seems to have done the Athenian cause great damage. Lamakhos, having failed to secure the adoption of his scheme for an early attack on Syracuse, was killed fighting there in the summer of 414.[421] Sole command thus devolved on Nikias.[422] Besieging Syracuse, he failed to evaluate or intercept the assistance which Sparta was sending to the city in the shape of Gylippos' force.[423] However, so as not to dwell unduly through hindsight on unpromising aspects of the Athenian campaign, we should stress — with Thucydides — the desperation at Syracuse which preceded Gylippos' arrival. By the period of Lamakhos' death the Athenians had established a superiority on land as well as at sea; the Syracusans had given up hope of preventing them from sealing off the city with siege walls, and other Sicilian communities, which had previously been neutral, were now sending help to the Athenian side, no doubt because it seemed likely to win.[424] In Syracuse the pessimism had religious overtones and there was mutual suspicion within the citizen body: an assembly was planned, to discuss capitulation, when news came of the approach of Gylippos. In Thucydides' words, "to such a point of danger had Syracuse come".[425] Syracuse was the chief city of Sicily; had it fallen, the way was open to a great Athenian expansion in the area. Although detailed speculation on the subject is pointless, the idea that Athens might have come to dominate the entire Mediterranean should not be dismissed merely with the objection that she was still a city state. Rome later had imperial provinces from Spain to Asia Minor before she conferred her citizenship on most of Italy.

Although the force of Gylippos which entered Syracuse was not large,[426] the morale of the Syracusans was fortified,[427] not only by the access of fresh troops but by the consideration that Sparta had not despaired of their city, and that a Spartan general was now in control.[428] Syracuse seized, and kept, the initiative. In good Spartan style, Gylippos led a raid on a weak section of the Athenian siege wall, by night.[429] Shortly afterwards, having won a land battle, the Syracusans (again by night) built a wall of their own which crossed the line of the Athenian fortification and permanently prevented it from cutting off their city.[430] The Athenian force, rather than Syracuse, became the besieged. In the summer of the following year (413) Gylippos captured the headland of Plēmmyrion, on the far side of the Great Harbour from Syracuse,[431] threatening the importation by sea of supplies to the Athenians and causing gloom in their ranks. Camped along an unhealthy coastal strip within the harbour, unable to dry or repair their ships properly, the Athenians had the depressing sight of their opponents gaining mastery of the element on which they themselves had traditionally dominated, the sea.[432]

Later in the same summer Demosthenes arrived with a fleet to reinforce the Athenians. The Syracusans were temporarily dismayed at the scale of their enemies' resources; Thucydides writes with approval of Demosthenes' decision to make a prompt attack which would exploit the mood in Syracuse.[433] His aim was to regain control of the heights of Epipolai where the Syracusans had their counter-wall, and thus to reinstate the siege of the city. But his daring night attack on the heights ended in confusion and defeat. He then suggested that the whole Athenian force should leave Syracuse quickly, a proposal which, if acted upon, would probably have extended the life of the Athenian Empire by many years. But Nikias would not go.[434] He had private information from a faction within Syracuse, knew of financial distress in the city and hoped for its betrayal. He also claimed to prefer the prospect of an honourable death for himself at the hands of the Syracusans to that of a dishonourable one at the hands of his own people in Athens, where tolerance for unsuccessful generals was known to be small.[435] Nikias appears in this to have used the device of the false alternative, one of the most effective tricks of rhetoric down the ages. He had in reality another option: voluntary exile. (We may think of Churchill who, when accused in parliament of surrounding himself with yes-men, enquired whether his opponents would prefer him to surround himself with no-men.) Dover writes:

> Nikias' pride and consequent cowardice in the face of personal disgrace lead him to put forward as disgraceful a proposition as any general in history: rather than risk execution, he will throw away the fleet and many thousands of other people's lives, and put his country in mortal peril.[436]

Comparable is Julius Caesar's self-centred excuse for starting a civil war: that his personal status was dearer to him than life itself.[437] Interestingly, Thucydides was very far from being appalled by Nikias' conduct. Recording his execution by the

Syracusans after the Athenian surrender, Thucydides writes that "he, least of all my Greek contemporaries, deserved such a fate".[438] (The word 'least' is emphasised in the Greek.) The historian's judgement, which goes on to refer to Nikias' practice of virtue, seems inescapably to elevate Nikias above his contemporaries, and thus implicitly to make light of his demerits.[439] Even if we allow for some degree of the enthusiasm familiar in obituary, Thucydides' words reflect strikingly on his own values. The passage seems to accord with our evidence for Thucydides' being far more concerned about Athenian grandees than about the masses. It is not impossible that the two men, generals at the same period, were friends; in any case, there were grounds for fellow-feeling not only in their social and economic positions but also in the pressure applied to each, as general, by a critical *dēmos*.[440]

Worsening circumstances eventually persuaded even Nikias to relax his resistance to the idea of leaving.[441] But, when the Athenians were ready to sail, there came the lunar eclipse which modern astronomy has dated to 27 August 413. This was taken as an omen forbidding prompt departure, not only by Nikias but even by the majority of his men, who previously had been yearning to leave. The consequent delay gave the Syracusans time to prepare for the naval fighting by which they sought to prevent the Athenians from escaping their weak position.[442] Thucydides describes graphically the reactions of the onlookers on the Athenian side, when the final sea battle came; some were swaying in suspense.[443] The Syracusans won. It is a measure of the demoralisation among the sailors in the Athenian fleet, and of the state of their equipment, that when their generals required them to man the remaining ships next day for a further attempt to break out of the Great Harbour, the men refused, in spite of their still having a numerical superiority in ships over the enemy.[444]

Abandoning their fleet and (amid distressing scenes) their disabled men, the Athenian forces set off on a retreat by land; within a few days they had become separated into two sections, and each of these was compelled to surrender to the pursuing Syracusans.[445] The annihilation of so large a force was exceedingly rare; perhaps the fate of Athens' Egyptian venture in the mid-450s presents a single parallel from the classical period. The disaster in Sicily cannot be ascribed simply to numerical inferiority. Indeed, it is not certain that the numbers on the Athenian side *were* inferior to those of the opposing forces.[446] At the start of their retreat the Athenians had a host of not less than 40,000, according to Thucydides,[447] although many of these would be sailors, ineffective as infantry. During their time in Sicily the Athenians had sustained many casualties, but also (like the Syracusans) had acquired many allies. The number 40,000 happens to be similar to the approximate figure we may reach by multiplying the number of the triremes in the two fleets sent by Athens (134 + *c*.73) by the number of the men normally forming the crew of a trireme (*c*.200).[448] In aggregate, then, the Athenian numbers had very likely grown since the expedition's first days in Sicily. And yet in 415 the Athenian army brought by the first fleet had been able to drive off the field the full hoplite levy of Syracuse.[449] Two recurrent themes in Thucydides' account of the last days help to explain the collapse of this once potent army; a sense of guilt and of imminent divine punishment, and an extreme shortage of supplies.[450] In the last moments of the retreat, men within range of enemy spears fought each other for water from a bloody stream.[451]

The Ionian War and the fall of Athens

When news reached mainland Greece and the Aegean that the Sicilian expedition and thus most of Athens' naval forces had ceased to exist, there was great activity among the enemies of the Athenians. A rare opportunity had obviously arrived. There is only space here to deal in outline with the policies of Athens, her dissident allies, Sparta and Persia during the last decade of hostilities (413–404) — often called the Ionian War, because of the concentration of warfare in that district. Study of the period should reinforce a principle of analysis useful in our scholastic as in our private lives: never to assume uncritically that a group which presents itself as solid actually is so. Athens split; in 411 there was revolution in the city with an oligarchic group, the Four Hundred, taking control, while the Athenian fleet stationed in Ionia (at Samos) remained democratic. There were severe strains on the Spartan side with ill will and conflict of policy between commanders;[452] at one point Lysandros apparently gave back to his Persian paymaster funds needed for Sparta's impoverished fleet, rather than see them go to his official successor, Kallikratidas.[453] Persia, which no doubt looked to wear down the Greeks generally as well as to eradicate the Athenian Empire in its time of weakness, suffered from division between her satraps. Pharnabazos, governor of the province of Phrygia in north-western Asia Minor, and Tissaphernes, his counterpart to the south, did not harmonise their necessarily delicate relations with the two Greek powers but on occasion were in open competition.[454] And among the more important of Athens' allies and former allies, such as Samos and Khios, there was *stasis*, with oligarchic factions being more in favour of collaboration with Sparta than were their democratic rivals.[455]

While the Sicilian expedition was still in existence, in 413, Sparta set up a permanent fortress in Attikē — at Dekeleia, which was about half way between the city of Athens and the frontier of Boiotia, whence aid might come to the fortress.[456] Sparta had threatened to create some such fortified base in 421;[457] her action now may have been prompted by the arguments of Alkibiades.[458] Thucydides describes with emphasis the severe harm sustained by Athens as a result of the occupation of Dekeleia.[459] The enemy now dominated her countryside all the year round, damaging livestock, agriculture and operations at the silver mines of Laureion.[460] Athens' slaves were encouraged to run away to Dekeleia; according to Thucydides, more than 20,000 did so, most of them skilled workers. Some idea of the economic significance of this number may be got from our knowledge of Athens' circumstances in 406, when the city could not find enough free men, citizens or others, to crew a fleet of some 110 triremes.[461] Such a fleet required approximately 22,000 sailors. Although some men were already abroad on war service, and others would need to be retained to garrison Athens against forces from Dekeleia, it is impressive that the number of able-bodied citizens available to man the city's main battle fleet can scarcely have exceeded and may very well have fallen short of the number of slaves who had escaped. Dekeleia created additional problems in that supplies from Euboia could no longer be brought across northern Attikē, but now had to come instead on a long voyage round Cape Sounion. Also there was the strain of being in constant readiness to repel an attack on the city of Athens. To meet their new expenses, the Athenians now tried to increase revenue by substituting for the imperial tribute a tax of 5 per cent upon the seaborne trade of their subjects.[462]

After Athens had lost two fleets in Sicily, Sparta made her first determined attempt of the war to win naval control of the Aegean, assembling a large fleet of her own. Perikles, long before, had foreseen the severe difficulty the Spartans would have in providing money to pay ships' crews.[463] (Sailors, unlike hoplites, could hardly live off the land, and Sparta did not have tributary allies to help her build up large reserves of capital.) Perikles' contemporary, King Arkhidamos, had apparently envisaged the Persians' supplying funds for Sparta's war against Athens,[464] remembering perhaps how Persia had spent money at Sparta in the 450s with an anti-Athenian purpose.[465] But the Spartans for long hesitated over collaborating with such partners; we recall the Persian complaint of the mid-420s that no two Spartan envoys said the same thing.[466] No doubt what restrained Sparta was the price which Persia would attach to her help. Sparta would be asked to concede that the Greeks of Asia Minor belonged to the Great King, a concession which would negate her claim to be fighting Athens for the liberation of Hellas. If Sparta agreed to the Persian demand, Athens would be presented with a magnificent theme for propaganda; she could represent her own Empire as the only guarantee of Hellenic rule in the cities of Greece, and could triumphantly recall Sparta's suggestion, made in the aftermath of Mykalē, that Ionia be abandoned (in effect, to the Persians). However, in 412 Spartan officials made a treaty of alliance which conceded to the Persians all territory which had ever been possessed by the Great King's ancestors.[467] As D. M. Lewis puts it, the phrasing of this treaty "sent more experienced diplomats through the roof when they saw it".[468] One of the Great King's predecessors, Xerxes, had possessed Greek territory as far as Boiotia and Athens. Before long Sparta substituted more modest and vague verbal concessions to Persia,[469] but the first, extravagant, treaty deserves a brief explanation. That the Spartans who made it were simply lying about their willingness to see the King extend his rule to mainland Greece is not an attractive hypothesis, in view of Sparta's religiosity as evidenced on other occasions; the treaty with Persia would involve formal oaths. More likely the Spartans believed that Persian control over areas of mainland Greece was not enforceable, because the Mede after decades of quiescence in the west would be unwilling to risk a repetition of Xerxes' experience. But the cost of this treaty to Sparta's immediate reputation would be considerable; in particular, how would the valued ally Boiotia react to being pronounced the property of Persia? Behind Sparta's sacrifice we may detect an unusually urgent working of her traditional sense of opportunity, which the Persians perhaps identified and exploited in their demands. It may have seemed vital to Sparta to get the resources for a fleet quickly, while the Athenian navy and its reputation were still afflicted by the catastrophe at Syracuse.

Within a few months of the news from Sicily important subject states of Athens were in revolt, relying on assistance from Sparta. Mytilēnē was quickly regained by Athens, and Khios was put under a blockade which for a time seemed promising, though in the event Khios was not recaptured.[470] More than domestic failures, disasters in foreign policy tend to bring down governments.[471] In part this may be because all classes feel the humiliation of a failure abroad, whereas in domestic affairs one person's loss is usually another's gain. Also, disasters abroad, such as the rout of an army or the loss of territory, are usually well defined and are often abrupt — and therefore obvious to all. On learning of the defeat in Sicily, the Athenians at home decided to modify their democratic constitution by creating a board of elders to examine proposals.[472] In 411, after further setbacks in the form of the Spartan challenge at sea and the revolts of former subjects, the *dēmokratia* of Athens fell, and was replaced by the oligarchy of the Four Hundred. Thucydides observes that it was "a difficult thing to end the freedom of the Athenian *dēmos*, which had been established for about a century".[473] Among the additional explanatory facts which he records are the hope (encouraged from a distance by Alkibiades, now with Tissaphernes) that the change of regime would clear the way for Athens to receive money from Persia,[474] and the fear for their lives of democrats who might otherwise have sought to resist the change.[475] A campaign of murder was carried out by the oligarchic revolutionaries;[476] the prominence of one victim, Androkles, a democrat and opponent of Alkibiades, served to advertise the campaign and to intimidate.[477] Also, many democrats did not know whom to trust in opposing the oligarchs, since some whom no one would have thought capable of turning to oligarchy were now seen to be among the revolutionaries.[478] But the Four Hundred suffered from disasters of their own in foreign affairs, most notably the loss of Euboia, which revolted and joined Sparta, causing at Athens panic and dire economic loss.[479] Byzantion was also lost,[480] as were states (including Thasos) in which the Four Hundred had set up governments of brother-oligarchs.[481]

The Athenian fleet at Samos remained democratic through the influence of the poor who traditionally manned it — the "naval crowd".[482] There was a widespread desire among the Athenians at Samos to sail home and tackle the oligarchs, a move which in Thucydides' view would have caused Ionia and the Hellespont to fall immediately into enemy hands. He gives credit for having prevented this to Alkibiades, who was now with the fleet and acceptable to many fellow-citizens after his flight from the Spartans and ambivalent career with Tissaphernes.[483] In Athens the Four Hundred were faced with hostility on land from Sparta and at sea from the navy of their own city. Many of the oligarchic leaders sought an agreement with Sparta, being prepared if necessary to surrender the city and to see it lose its Empire, fleet and walls, provided that they themselves were physically safe.[484] Among those willing for this sacrifice of city to self was, almost certainly, Antiphon.[485] A focus of opposition to the oligarchy was provided by the construction of a fortification at Ēetioneia, part of Peiraieus; many suspected, correctly, that it was intended to let in the enemy.[486] Agitation was consummated when news came of the loss of Euboia. The Four Hundred were ejected in favour of a broader oligarchy, made up of the owners of hoplite equipment, the Five Thousand.[487] Of this short-lived constitution, which at least purported to exclude the poor, Thucydides writes favourably, stating that it formed a moderate blend of the interests of the few and the many.[488]

Xenophon depicts King Agis of Sparta as observing from Dekeleia numerous grain ships bringing Athens her vital food from the area near the Black Sea,[489] and as drawing the correct strategic conclusion. The narrows at the Hellespont and the Bosphorus were the areas in which to locate and challenge this traffic. A Spartan fleet first entered the Hellespont in 411, when Athens had many distractions, including revolutionary conflict and the siege of Khios;[490] the fleet helped to bring about the revolt from Athens of Byzantion. (The Athenians were to recapture Byzantion in 408.[491] It is some indication of the intensity of conflict in this region that, even from the imperfect surviving evidence, we can trace Kyzikos in the Propontis as having passed out of or into Athenian control on no fewer than five occasions in the last seven years of the Peloponnesian War.[492]) At Kynossēma in the Hellespont during 411, and off Kyzikos in the following year, Athens won great victories over Spartan naval forces.[493] The latter battle generated the famous laconic despatch from the Spartan survivors, which fell into Athenian hands: "The good times are over. Mindaros [the admiral] is dead. The men are starving. We don't know what to do."[494]

195

After Kyzikos, Sparta made Athens an offer of peace, suggesting that the two powers exchange prisoners, withdraw their respective garrisons (from Dekeleia and Pylos), but otherwise hold what they had.[495] For refusing this offer Athens has been criticised with varying degrees of severity. But the Athenians had to reckon with the stability of Spartan opportunism. Why should they make peace now, when events were going their way, knowing that Sparta was very likely to resume war when Athens next faced a crisis? Athenians had to confront the argument that Persian financial aid for Sparta might be inexhaustible. Athens might succeed in destroying a succession of Spartan fleets, only to find each one replaced from Persia's vast resources, whereas a single naval defeat for Athens might fatally cut her supply of food.[496] But Athens could reasonably hope, against this, that Sparta's new alliance with Persia would prove fragile, coming as it did after so many years of suspicious diplomacy. And, even if Persia did supply the ships, could the Peloponnesians find seamen for a long run of defeats? Athenians might recall that their own defeated sailors in 413 had simply refused to man the still-substantial fleet against Syracuse. Additionally, there was a prospect of Spartiate prisoners becoming so numerous at Athens, as a result of Athenian naval victories, that Spartan action might eventually be restricted rather as it had been after Sphakteria.[497]

The history of Thucydides breaks off near the end of summer 411. Thereafter source-criticism is far less fruitful. Xenophon, whose *Hellenika* begins near the point where Thucydides' account ends, had a good knowledge both of Sparta and of his native Athens,[498] but provides a narrative which is sparse in most respects. A disproportionate amount of the space which he gives to the period from late 411 to 404 is taken up with a slanted account of the harsh treatment given by Athens to the victorious generals of Arginousai (406 BC). The account of the period given by Diodorus may be above his usual standard, because of its use of material from the fourth-century writer now known as the Oxyrhynchus Historian,[499] but, as so often with Diodorus, there are grave problems of chronology. It is symptomatic of the state of our information that, with Thucydides no longer available, there are rival systems of dating within the period 410–406.[500] During that time Athens gained strength, and Alkibiades won credit for his part in the process, until the failure of a deputy caused him to be disgraced and removed (permanently). Persian subsidies had allowed Sparta to rebuild her navy, which in 406 was heavily defeated by Athens at Arginousai (near Lesbos). After the battle, Athens put her generals on trial in irregular and prejudicial circumstances, for failing to rescue shipwrecked sailors (or, according to Diodorus, their corpses[501]). The generals were judged and executed as a group, scandalising Xenophon and many modern critics of the *dēmokratia*. Few would now try to justify the treatment of these commanders. But in a little-noticed passage Diodorus records (under the year 377/6) a later Athenian admiral who abstained from the pursuit of a beaten enemy and chose instead to rescue survivors and corpses from his own side, "for he recalled the battle of Arginousai" and the fate of the generals.[502] Executing a victorious commander for fatal negligence towards his own men is foreign to most modern thinking. But the high value placed by the *dēmokratia* on the life of the common man, and the suspicion towards powerful officials, are not self-evidently stupid and (as Diodorus suggests) may in their own way have saved lives on occasion.

After the defeat at Arginousai, Sparta once more rebuilt her fleet with the aid of Persian money.[503] Kyros, son of the Great King, gave lavishly to the vigorous Spartan commander, Lysandros. In 405 the latter challenged Athenian control of the Hellespont, capturing the town of Lampsakos; the Athenian fleet which arrived to give battle took up station across the strait at Aigospotamoi, where there was no harbour.[504] Alkibiades, now a private citizen, appeared and urged that the ships be taken to a defensible harbour nearby, in order to fight only at a time of the Athenians' own choosing; his advice was rudely rejected. Or so Xenophon writes. We recall, however, his intense interest in demonstrating that Athens was harsh and foolish in its treatment of commanders.[505] (He himself was an officer exiled by his fellow Athenians.) For several successive days the Athenian fleet sailed across to challenge the Spartans to battle. As the latter repeatedly refused to come out of their harbour and fight, Athens' sailors on returning to shore left their ships as if Lysandros intended not to engage. Seeing the chance offered by the Athenians' pattern of action, Lysandros brought his fleet across to catch the opposing ships almost entirely unmanned. Without a proper battle and with scarcely any casualties on his side, the Spartan commander was able to capture almost 170 of Athens' fleet of 180. The corn supply of the Athenians was now cut, and the military side of the Peloponnesian War was almost at an end. To intensify the ensuing famine at Athens, Lysandros sent back to the city Athenians whom he found in various parts of the Aegean. The howl which ran from Peiraieus to Athens, accompanying the news of Aigospotamoi, was the death knell of the Athenian Empire. After the surrender of the city in 404, Athens lost her Long Walls and all but a few of her remaining warships. But Sparta resisted the demands of Korinth and Thebes for the city itself to be destroyed. She had won the war with a stroke of characteristic opportunism, economy and military deception. She now set about dominating the peace with another favoured technique, creating rivalries to keep central Greece divided and ruled. For this, the survival of Athens was necessary.

Thucydides' estimate of the conduct of the war

This final episode of Spartan acumen leads to a last question about Thucydides: why does he seem to have so low an opinion of the conduct of the war by both of the great powers? His emphasis on error was noted above in the case of the Sicilian expedition; so were his severe comments on Perikles' successors in general and on Kleon in particular. Several points may be briefly added. Thucydides' comment on the failure of Athenians at home to make proper arrangements for the Sicilian expedition after its departure has seemed an unfair slight, in view of the help which he elsewhere records as sent under Demosthenes.[506] His critical references to the Athenian *dēmos*, and to *dēmoi* in general,[507] sit oddly with his suggestion elsewhere that the (democratic) Syracusans were the people who fought most effectively against Athens, because they most resembled the Athenians in character.[508]

Thucydides shows some respect for Sparta's domestic achievement,[509] and of Spartan individuals active in the war, Brasidas is complimented.[510] But he seemed to Thucydides to be untypical of his city. The historian makes several pointed references to lack of daring on Sparta's part, as well as the remarkable claim that in many matters the Spartans proved to be the most convenient enemies in the world from Athens' point of view,[511] a claim which is hard to reconcile with the astute and consistent military opportunism of Sparta attested by Thucydides' own narrative. This low estimation of Sparta's performance seems to cohere with the similar judgement applied to Athens; in Thucydides' view the great power of Athens was brought down not by Spartan genius but by Athenian mistakes.[512]

Why has Thucydides apparently underestimated both Athens and Sparta? There exists a common form of inverted loyalty whereby a disappointed partisan ascribes failure to defects of his own side rather than to the real merits of the opposition.[513] There is reason to suspect that this attitude was particularly common among Athenians after the surrender of 404 when some, at least, of Thucydides' work was written.[514] Speculation about the psychology of one so profound and reserved as Thucydides is perilous,[515] but we may wonder whether he evolved his own sophisticated version of distorted loyalty to his city, Athens, and blamed her too much. Alternatively (or in addition) one may apply a valuable commonplace of psychology, that people tend to perceive in others the motives and methods to which they themselves are most given. (The idea is reflected in the English sayings 'the pure see only the pure' and 'set a thief to catch a thief'; compare the development of the Greek word *euēthēs*, which originally meant 'of good character' but came to mean 'naive', 'incapable of perceiving the bad in others'[516].) Among Thucydides' many striking observations on the misguided psychology of others is the statement that, at the start of the war, there was a general feeling among Sparta's eager partisans that things were held up wherever they themselves could not be present.[517] Did Thucydides' personal situation from 424 give rise to a similar feeling in himself? Exile had abruptly eliminated his influence at Athens, and a characteristic emotion of the distinguished person in exile is frustration. Frustration in Thucydides' case might flow from the memory of his previous position of influence as general, and also from a lively sense of what his powerful intellect might have achieved in practical politics. The statement that his history was meant as a possession for ever is not the utterance of a modest man. It may be fair to ask whether it was personal experience which gave Thucydides insight into the delusion of frustrated partisans, that without their help nothing progressed satisfactorily. Was it exile which caused his account of the intelligent calculations of both sides to give way occasionally to erratic generalisations about their incompetence?

Notes

Except where otherwise indicated, references are to Thucydides.

1. V 26 2. Cf. references at de Ste. Croix, *Origins*, 295.
2. IV 104 4 etc.
3. V 26 5.
4. IV 28 3.
5. V 103 2.
6. IV 108 4.
7. On divination, see Chapter 9. With Thucydides on wishful thinking compare the works of Karl Marx, which contain a massive analysis of the operation and failings of capitalism ('sovereign reason') and brief, flimsy treatment ('careless hope') of the prophesied socialist alternative. The promised land has no sociology.
8. I 93 2 with Gomme, *HCT*, ad loc.
9. Thucydides on eclipses: I 23 3, II 28, IV 52 1, VII 50 4. For modern astronomical findings, F. K. Ginzel, *Spezieller Kanon der Sonnen- und Mondfinsternisse*, 58f., 413. All six solar eclipses occurred in the period covered by Thucydides' surviving text.
10. Plut. *Life of Perikles* 35 2.
11. III 87 3.
12. VIII 72 2.
13. Cf. II 31 2 and Gomme, *HCT*, II, 388 and *The population of Athens in the fifth and fourth centuries BC.*, 12, n. 2.
14. VII 86 5.
15. III 98 4. 'The war' seems to mean at least the Ten Years' War, if not the whole Peloponnesian War.
16. VI 60 2.
17. VI 53 2.
18. Exceptional are Thucydides' comments on the suffering of the obscure little town of Mykalēssos; VII 29 5, 30 3.
19. IV 80 3f. and Chapter 6.
20. Chapter 3.
21. II 65 12, VIII 96 5. While stressing the power and daring of Athens, VII 28 also refers disapprovingly (s.3) to *philonikia* (over-competitiveness).
22. I 22 1.
23. On one experiment involving memories of twentieth-century political history, E. K. Warrington and H. I. Sanders, *Quarterly Journal of Experimental Psychology*, 23 (1971), 432–42. See also ch. 12 ('Down Memory Lane') of T. Harrisson's *Living through the Blitz*.
24. I 22 1; de Ste. Croix, *Origins*, 7ff. for a good introductory discussion.
25. G. Cawkwell, *Yale Classical Studies*, XXIV (1975), 66 on Thuc. I 121 – 122 1, 141–3. On the origins of Thucydides' style, J. H. Finley, *Harvard Studies in Classical Philology*, 50 (1939), 35–84.
26. See Chapter 9.
27. VI 16–18 with Chapter 3 above; VI 89 6.

28. IV 108 5.
29. See Chapter 6.
30. For Sparta, see Chapter 6; for Athens, Chapter 7.
31. Gomme-Andrewes-Dover, *HCT*, IV, 229.
32. Cf. III 13 4 with 16 2.
33. In commenting on Brasidas' falsehoods, Thucydides records that they were influential; thus, not to have included them would itself have been misleading.
34. IV 92 5.
35. V 56 5.
36. V 75 4.
37. Arist. *Pol.* 1269a 38f.
38. See Chapter 9.
39. IV 65 4.
40. VII 28 3 with n. 21 above.
41. Xen. *Hell.* V 2 25.
42. I 81 3.
43. See Chapter 3.
44. III 70.
45. Cf. the awkwardness of Arkhidamos' apology for the proposal to collaborate with Persia against Athens; I 82 1.
46. VIII 21, 73 2. One thinks of *Animal Farm*.
47. VIII 91 3.
48. VIII 68 1 and below.
49. VIII 92 1 and below.
50. II 2 2.
51. II 2 3.
52. VII 18 2.
53. II 4 2, 4.
54. II 3 2.
55. Chapter 3, n.188.
56. II 6 2.
57. E.g. V 25 1. The war was not of Arkhidamos' making, and he died in the middle of it (427/6); de Ste. Croix, *Origins*, 295.
58. II 16 1.
59. II 21 2 – 22 1, q.v. (with II 20 4) for the special sufferings now of Athenians from the rural district of Akharnai. Also, Aristophanes' *Akharnians*, *passim*. On the extent of damage done by the invasions of Attikē, P. A. Brunt, *Phoenix*, 19 (1965), 265f., V. D. Hanson, *Warfare and agriculture in classical Greece*, Ch. 8.
60. II 20 1, 4.
61. I 127 2 and Chapter 4. It has been suggested that one reason why German bombing in 1941 concentrated on the East End of London was a hope that the poor there would resent the relative safety of wealthier Londoners further west.
62. II 14 2, 16 1.
63. II 16 2 – 17 3, 52 1–3.
64. II 59 1–2.
65. V 14 3, VII 28 3, though contrast I 81 6.
66. Esp. I 81 6.

67. II 18 5.
68. II 21 1.
69. The longest of the invasions, that of 430, lasted only for 40 days or thereabouts; II 57 2.
70. I 19.
71. III 89 1. On fear of plague cf. II 57 1.
72. See below.
73. III 15 1f., 16 2.
74. III 15 2.
75. II 7 2, with the argument of Gomme (*HCT*, ad loc.) that the figure of 500 is impossible. Numbers were particularly exposed to misrepresentation when a manuscript was copied.
76. II 13 8.
77. VIII 26 1, 35 1.
78. Definition of a new area is bound to be somewhat arbitrary, in respect of both space and time. 'New' here is applied to areas in which Sparta had not had armed forces during the previous three years.
79. II 47 3.
80. II 66.
81. II 80 1ff.
82. III 2 1.
83. III 16 3; 26 1.
84. III 69 2; 70 1ff.
85. III 69 2; 76; cf. IV 2 3.
86. III 87 1.
87. III 102 3f., referring to the reluctance now of the Akarnanians in defending Naupaktos. Cf. III 98 for the previous Athenian defeat by the Aitolians, with the consequent loss of prestige in the area.
88. III 100ff.
89. III 106ff.
90. IV 79 2. Cf. IV 108 3ff.; 108 6, with IV 132 2f.; V 12f.
91. IV 70 1; 78.
92. VIII 5 4 (Khios and Erythrai); 5 1 (Euboia); 5 2 (Lesbos); 35 1 (Knidos); 44 (Rhodes).
93. VIII 12 3; 23 1, 5; 26 1; 35 1; 39 1 (assembly of large fleet); VIII 14; 22–23 4; 24 6; 35 1f.; 44 1f. (aid to revolts).
94. VIII 24.
95. VIII 63 3.
96. VIII 62 1.
97. VIII 80 2.
98. VIII 64 3f.; cf. 64 5 for other allied secessions at this time.
99. VIII 80 3.
100. VIII 95.
101. VIII 92 3.
102. Xen. *Hell.* II 2 9.
103. II 65 9.
104. II 22 1.
105. I 143 3 – 144 1; II 13 2–9, 65 7.
106. II 13 2.
107. II 13 3–5 with Gomme, *HCT*, ad loc. on the problem presented

by the figure 600.

108. II 65 9.

109. See Gomme, *HCT*, I, 355f.

110. II 70 2.

111. I 142 1.

112. II 24 1 with VIII 15 1.

113. II 13 2.

114. II 13 2; 65 7.

115. I 143 5.

116. I 143 4–5.

117. I 144 1; II 65 7.

118. II 65 7.

119. E.g. Gomme, *HCT*, ad loc. and *JHS*, LXXI (1951) 70–80; P. Cartledge, *Sparta and Lakonia*, 239.

120. II 65 11. Thucydides elaborates here by mentioning what he saw as the selfish and dangerous schemes of individuals, which Athens adopted in spite of their irrelevance to the war. These he does not identify, though shortly afterwards he mentions the Sicilian expedition, in a slightly different connection.

121. On Mytilēnē, see below. On Khios, IV 51. Raids against Megara and naval action against the Peloponnese, both begun under Perikles, were continued after his death.

122. G. Cawkwell, *Yale Classical Studies*, XXIV (1975), 53ff.

123. P. A. Brunt, *Phoenix*, 19 (1965), 259; de Ste. Croix, *Origins*, 208.

124. Cf. Brunt, 255ff.

125. II 62 2.

126. IV 21 2; 41 4, cf. VI 13 1.

127. I 144 1; II 65 7.

128. II 14 1. On the importance of Euboia to Athens, VIII 95 2; 96 1f.; Brunt, op. cit., 265.

129. II 65 8, cf. 60 5.

130. On bribery at Athens see Chapter 7.

131. II 13 1.

132. II 21 2f.

133. II 23 2, 25.

134. II 23 2, cf. 56 1.

135. I 142 4.

136. II 25 1f.

137. I 142 4.

138. I 144 2, 145.

139. I 127 1 – 128 2.

140. De Ste. Croix, *Origins*, 209; H. D. Westlake, *Essays on the Greek historians and Greek history* 84–100, for debate on Perikles' attitude to fortifications in the Peloponnese.

141. II 31 2. On this conspicuous occasion Thucydides could surely have given a better estimate of numbers, had he been more interested in the history of the poor.

142. II 66 2, III 91 2f. A similar ploy was used in the protection rackets of the early twentieth century and before. The technique of Al Capone and Bugs Moran is foreshadowed with elegant irony by the

nineteenth-century historian Thomas Macaulay, describing the boyhood of Robert Clive, the future conqueror of India: "Some lineaments of the character of the man were early discerned in the child ... he formed all the idle lads of the town into a kind of predatory army, and compelled the shopkeepers to submit to a tribute of apples and half-pence, in consideration of which he guaranteed the security of their windows." (*Essay on Lord Clive*).

143. E.g. Eur. *Androm.* 438, Lysias IX 20.

144. II 27 1; cf. I 67 2; 139 1; 140 3.

145. II 34.

146. II 34 7.

147. Esp. III 82.

148. III 82 2.

149. Aristoph. *Akharnians* 530; Kratinos fragments 71, 111, 240, 241 (Kock).

150. II 44 3f.

151. II 42 3.

152. Gomme, *HCT*, II, 107 seems to underestimate the frequency and importance of the implicit references to Sparta.

153. II 37 2.

154. For what follows on Sparta, see Chapter 6.

155. II 38 1.

156. Ibid.

157. II 39 1.

158. II 41 1.

159. Above, Chapter 3.

160. III 34.

161. On the fourth century, see now the references at G. E. M. de Ste. Croix, *The class struggle in the ancient Greek world*, 296, n. 48.

162. Plat. *Protag.* 342 b-c; cf. Aristoph. *Birds* 1280ff., Dem. LIV 34.

163. Chapter 6, n. 48.

164. See below on reactions after Sphakteria and during the battle of Mantineia (IV 34 1; 40 1; V 72 4); cf. the extraordinary celebration of Brasidas in the Thraceward region (IV 121 1; V 11 1) and the impact of Gylippos on Syracuse (esp. VII 1f.). Also III 37 3–5; V 105 4.

165. II 57 2.

166. III 87 1–3 with Gomme, *HCT*, ad loc.; cf. II 13 6, 8.

167. II 52 1f.

168. II 48 3.

169. Cf. Gomme, *HCT*, II, 150–3; A. J. Holladay and J. Poole, *CQ*, 29 (1979), 282–300. Holladay and Poole point out (pp. 295ff.) that Thucydides' account contains the concepts of contagion (II 51 4, 58 2) and of acquired immunity to a particular disease (II 51 6), concepts otherwise rare or unknown until relatively modern times.

170. II 51 4.

171. II 53 4, on which see Chapter 9.

172. II 52 4.

173. II 51 6.

174. II 54 4f. with Chapter 9.

175. II 54 2f.

176. T. Vincent, quoted in L. W. Cowie, *Plague and fire, London 1665–6*, 31.
177. R. Baxter, in Cowie, op. cit., 41.
178. Ibid., 48.
179. Ibid., 59.
180. II 64 2.
181. II 56.
182. II 58.
183. II 70.
184. II 58 2f.
185. II 59 1f; 60ff.; IV 21 1. For a possible religious element in Athenian motivation now, see Chapter 9.
186. II 65 2–4.
187. II 65 6ff.
188. IV 16, 23 1.
189. II 66.
190. II 67 4.
191. III 32.
192. On this episode, see II 83–92 and Gomme, *HCT*, ad loc.
193. II 93 (winter 429/8).
194. On which see below.
195. II 93 4, 94 1 (Peiraieus, involving the normally bold Brasidas); III 27 1, 29 1, 31 (Mytilēnē). On Spartan caution, S. Hodkinson, *Chiron*, 13 (1983), 239–81.
196. II 71ff.
197. On the Plataians' numbers, II 78 3, III 68 2 with Gomme, *HCT*, ad loc.
198. III 55 3 with Gomme, *HCT*, ad loc.
199. Cf. III 20 1.
200. I 22 4, cf. 21 1.
201. II 76 4.
202. III 20 3.
203. For the story of the escape, III 20–4.
204. III 68 1–3.
205. Xen. *Hell*. II 2 20.
206. III 53–9.
207. E.g. II 8 4, IV 85 1.
208. III 68 4.
209. V 105 4.
210. III 2 1ff.
211. III 13 3f., cf. III 39 3.
212. III 18 1, and cf. 18 2.
213. III 27 8.
214. III 36 4. Also, the Athenian naval crew were in no hurry to deliver the "alien" death sentence; III 49 4.
215. III 36 6.
216. Esp. III 39 8, 40 7.
217. III 19 1 with Gomme, *HCT*, ad. loc. on the scarcity of our information about the history of this tax.
218. II 13 2. Interestingly, though, Kleon is shown as echoing the

language of Perikles, according to whom the Empire was "like a tyranny" (II 63 2); for Kleon it was simply "a tyranny"(III 37 2).

219. III 44 1, 48 1. But at III 47 3, where the Mytilenean *dēmos* are described as benefactors of Athens whom it would be unjust to kill, Diodotos may have forgotten himself.

220. III 47 2ff.

221. For the narrative facts in the above paragraph, III 49 – 50 1.

222. III 69 2, 76ff.

223. III 79 2.

224. Though see Chapter 6 on the extreme risks taken by Spartan commanders with their own lives.

225. III 79 3.

226. Ibid.

227. IV 2 3.

228. IV 8 2.

229. III 89 1.

230. III 87 1f.

231. III 92 4.

232. III 93, V 12 1, 52 1, Xen. *Hell.* I 2 18.

233. III 100 2.

234. III 109.

235. The episode of Pylos and Sphakteria forms the bulk of IV 3–41.

236. Of the 420 soldiers under Spartan command at the start of the Athenian attack, 292 were captured alive; that is, 128 — between a quarter and a third — were killed. Spartan courage on other occasions makes us suspect that the death rate of Spartiates now was not less than that of their non-Spartiate colleagues, in which case the initial number of Spartiates was rather greater than 160.

237. V 15 1.

238. See Chapter 6.

239. IV 41 1.

240. IV 2 4, 3 2ff.

241. A. J. Holladay, *Historia*, 27 (1978), 399–427, and esp. 414–16. The Messenians, as descendants of helots from the Ithōmē campaign, would be reliably anti-Spartan, and their dialect would equip them for infiltration into Spartan territory; IV 3 3.

242. IV 26 2, 27 1.

243. IV 28 3.

244. IV 28 5.

245. IV 39 3.

246. III 36 6, IV 21 3.

247. VII 48 4 with K. J. Dover in *HCT*, ad loc. See VI 23 3 for another offer by Nikias to resign a command.

248. Esp. [Arist.] *Ath. Pol.* 28 3.

249. See VIII 64 5, cf. 24 4 and above, Chapter 3. A valuable account of the Sphakteria debate will be found in G. Grote, *History of Greece*, vol. VI, Ch. 52.

250. Thucydides notoriously omits these developments. For a review of the (mainly inscriptional) evidence, Meiggs, *AE*, ch. 18. Meiggs explores the possibility that there was a stepped increase in tribute in the

years up to and including 425, and considers the evidence for a general
rise in prices against which the increase of 425 may need to be judged.
251. Cf. IV 41 1.
252. E.g. IV 19 1, 20 4, 22.
253. IV 41 3f.
254. IV 21 3. Compare Nikias 10 years later; VI 10 2.
255. Sefton Delmer, *Black boomerang*, 199.
256. IV 53f.
257. VII 48 2f., 49 1.
258. IV 55f.
259. Though cf. D. M. Lewis, *Sparta and Persia*, 28, n. 10.
260. IV 55 3f. The Spartans had previously relied on their judgement
to produce constant success, or at least safety from failure.
261. On a run of ill fortune as the work of the gods, see Chapter 9.
262. VII 18 2.
263. Ibid.
264. V 16 – 17 1.
265. Lewis, loc. cit.; Cartledge, *Sparta and Lakonia*, 266; S.
Hornblower, *The Greek world*, 133.
266. Esp. IV 36.
267. IV 3 3.
268. See Chapter 6.
269. IV 53 3.
270. IV 66 3.
271. IV 70ff.
272. IV 76.
273. IV 89.
274. IV 90ff. For the casualties, IV 101 2.
275. P. A. Brunt, *Phoenix*, 19 (1965), 268–70.
276. IV 79 2, 80 1.
277. IV 80 2, 5.
278. IV 86 1, 88 1.
279. IV 81 2 and below.
280. V 8 2 and Brunt, op. cit., 274.
281. See Chapter 4.
282. II 25 2, IV 11 4 – 12 1.
283. IV 108 7.
284. Cf. IV 108 4.
285. IV 81 3.
286. IV 84.
287. Ibid.; IV 87 2, 88 1.
288. IV 84 2.
289. IV 85 6, cf. 87 6.
290. IV 85 7 with 108 5.
291. IV 85 3.
292. IV 88 1.
293. IV 88 2. Both Stagiros and Akanthos, like Argilos (IV 103 3),
were colonies of Andros; IV 84 1; 88 2 and Meiggs, *AE*, 335.
294. IV 103 3f. Thucydides (ibid.) stresses the sense of *kairos* of the
Argilians, long hostile to Athens.

295. IV 108 1.
296. Ibid. Amphipolis also helped to protect the goldmines exploited by the historian Thucydides (IV 105 1), though how much this concerned his fellow citizens is unclear.
297. IV 106 1.
298. IV 104 1, 106 1.
299. IV 104 1, 4, 106 1.
300. IV 105 2 – 106 1.
301. IV 106 1.
302. IV 106 2.
303. IV 106 3 – 107 2.
304. IV 104 4 – 105 1, 106 3f.
305. V 26 5.
306. Cf. G. Grote, *History of Greece*, VI, 414 (Everyman edition).
307. V 14.
308. V 14 4.
309. Ibid. and V 22 2.
310. V 14 2.
311. IV 117–19.
312. Esp. IV 122 6, 123 1.
313. IV 129f.
314. V 32 1.
315. V 2f. (summer 422). Torōnē had joined Brasidas in 424/3 (IV 110ff.). For the suggestion that Kleon now achieved more than Thucydides makes clear, B. D. Meritt and A. B. West, *American Journal of Archaeology*, 29 (1925) 56–69 with Meiggs, *AE*, 338, n.4.
316. V 6–11; for the conscious opportunism, V 9 4–6, 10 5; for the inferiority of Brasidas' troops, V 8 2.
317. V 11 2.
318. V 10 8, 11. On the high proportion of Spartan commanders who died in battle see Chapter 6.
319. V 11 1; cf. his reception earlier at Skiōnē; IV 121 1.
320. V 16 1.
321. Aristoph. *Peace* 236–84.
322. II 25 2, IV 81, 84 2.
323. V 16 1.
324. Ibid.
325. Cf. Brunt, op. cit., 277, n. 78.
326. V 16 1 – 17 1.
327. V 16 1, where a less selfish motive is also mentioned, briefly.
328. V 17 2 – 20 1.
329. V 21, cf. V 35 3.
330. V 24 2.
331. V 22 2 – 24 2.
332. V 23 3.
333. IV 134.
334. On Sparta's problems in the Peloponnese at this period, Brunt, *Phoenix*, 19 (1965), 255–60; Cartledge, *Sparta and Lakonia*, 245ff. On the importance to Sparta of Tegea, Chapter 4.
335. II 30 1, IV 49. On Korinth's rejection of the peace, e.g. V 17 2,

30 2 with Gomme-Andrewes-Dover, *HCT*, IV, ad loc.

336. V 17 2.

337. Ibid.

338. Ibid., V 18 7.

339. V 28 2.

340. On this subject see now R. J. Seager, *CQ*, 26 (1976), 249–69.

341. V 43 2. See Andrewes in Gomme-Andrewes-Dover *HCT*, IV, 48f. for the calculation that Alkibiades was "32 or a little more".

342. The hierarchy of age was exceptionally important to Spartans; see Chapter 6.

343. V 43 2.

344. V 45. Alternatively, Thucydides' Greek may just mean not that the Spartans denied this, but that they refused this time to state it when questioned. See Gomme-Andrewes-Dover, *HCT*, IV, 51–3 for problems presented by Thucydides' account here.

345. IV 50 2.

346. V 46 5–47.

347. V 48 1.

348. V 49f.

349. See Chapter 3.

350. VI 16 2.

351. V 64ff.

352. V 63.

353. V 61 1; VI 16 6 with Gomme-Andrewes-Dover, *HCT*, IV, ad loc.

354. V 72 3.

355. V 72 4.

356. V 75 3.

357. V 76 1, 81, 82 1, 83 1f; Cartledge, *Sparta and Lakonia*, 257f.

358. V 84 1ff. Meiggs-Lewis, no. 67 for Melos' contribution to the Spartan side in the war.

359. V 84 3, 85.

360. V 116 3.

361. For recent discussions, Gomme-Andrewes-Dover, *HCT*, IV, ad loc.; de Ste. Croix, *Origins*, 13ff. (with an introduction to the large bibliography on the subject).

362. V 89, 104 – 105 3.

363. Cf. Andrewes in Gomme-Andrewes-Dover, *HCT*, IV, 161.

364. Grote, *History of Greece*, VII, 163f. (Everyman edition); F. M. Cornford, *Thucydides Mythistoricus*, Ch. 10.

365. See Chapter 9.

366. V 85.

367. Above, Chapter 3.

368. V 89.

369. V 103 2.

370. Cf. Meiggs, *AE*, 390f. on Old Oligarch I 14.

371. See the arguments of Kallikles in the *Gorgias* and of Thrasymakhos in *Republic* I.

372. II 41 1.

373. V 89.

374. De Ste. Croix, *Origins*, 14.

375. V 104, 106, 108, 110.

376. V 109.

377. For references, see below, n. 511.

378. V 104.

379. V 105 4.

380. III 68 4, cf. I 132 5, where Thucydides in his own person suggests a similar distinction concerning the behaviour of the Spartans towards each other and towards outsiders.

381. V 104.

382. V 103 2, cf. V 26 3, VII 50 4 and below, Chapter 9.

383. V 113.

384. IV 108 4, cf. III 3 1.

385. V 116 3f.

386. III 91 1-3; for the circumstances see Meiggs, *AE*, 328.

387. I 22 4, III 82 2.

388. VI 1 1.

389. E.g. III 86 1ff., 115 2ff., IV 2 2; Meiggs, *AE*, 320f., 345f.; J. K. Davies, *Democracy and classical Greece*, 104ff.

390. VI 2 1 – 6 1.

391. VI 24 3.

392. III 86 4.

393. VIII 1 1.

394. VI 24 3.

395. VI 15 2. On Carthage, VI 34 2, 90 2f.; Aristoph. *Knights* 1302ff.; M. Treu, *Historia*, III (1954/5), 41-57 (in German).

396. VI 15 3.

397. VI 11 5.

398. VI 9 3; 10 2, 4; 11 4, 6.

399. VI 17 8. Alkibiades also argues, earlier in the same chapter, for the exploitation of *stasis* and other divisions in Sicily.

400. VII 18 2.

401. V 115 2; for the traditional Greek belief, Hesiod, *Works and days* 238-47. For Spartan superstition about ventures abroad, V 54 2, 116 1, cf. VI 95 1, VIII 6 5; R. C. T. Parker in A. Powell (ed.), *Classical Sparta*.

402. VI 6 2f.

403. VI 6 2, 8 1f., 46.

404. V 4 2f.

405. VI 8 2.

406. Gomme-Andrewes-Dover, *HCT*, IV, 228, citing V 17 4; V 48.

407. VI 24 1ff., 26 1.

408. VI 43 (with Gomme-Andrewes-Dover, *HCT*, IV, ad loc.), cf. 31 3.

409. VII 42 1.

410. II 65 12.

411. VI 27.

412. VI 32 1f.

413. Meiggs-Lewis, no. 63.

414. VI 44 3.

415. VI 46 1.

416. VI 47.

417. VI 48.
418. VI 49.
419. VI 63 2, cf. VII 42 3.
420. VII 42 3.
421. VI 101 6.
422. VI 103 3.
423. VI 104 3, cf. VII 1 2 for an attempt at interception. The expedition of Gylippos seems to have flowed from the advice to Sparta of Alkibiades; VI 90 – 93 3.
424. VI 102 4-103.
425. VI 103 4, VII 2.
426. VII 1 5.
427. VII 2 2.
428. Cf. Gomme, *HCT*, II, 287.
429. VII 4 2.
430. VII 6 4.
431. VII 23f.
432. VII 12 3f.; 47 2; 50 3.
433. VII 42, cf. VI 63 2.
434. VII 48 – 49 1.
435. VII 48 4; cf. the action earlier of Demosthenes himself; III 98 5.
436. Gomme-Andrewes-Dover, *HCT*, IV, 426.
437. Caesar, *Civil war* I 9 2.
438. VII 86 5.
439. Commenting on this passage, Dover gives a useful review of the virtues and faults revealed by Nikias in his career, but seems not to confront the emphatic phrase 'least of all my Greek contemporaries', with its implications for Thucydides' own moral position.
440. Like Thucydides, Nikias was rich (VII 86 4) and drew much of his wealth from the mining of precious metal (Xen. *Poroi* IV 14). For popular censure of Nikias in 420, V 46 4f. Another thing which Nikias may well have shared with Thucydides is the enmity of Kleon.
441. VII 50 1-3.
442. VII 51.
443. VII 71 3.
444. VII 72 3f.
445. VII 75ff.
446. Statistics for the Syracusan side are more seriously incomplete than those for the Athenian forces. I have tried to collect the relevant passages of Thucydides at *Historia*, XXVIII (1979) 29 and nn. Nikias was apparently able to claim that the Athenians still had some superiority in infantry shortly before the retreat from the Great Harbour; VII 63 2.
447. VII 75 5.
448. Hdt. VII 184 1, VIII 17, cf. Thuc. VI 8 1 with Gomme-Andrewes-Dover, *HCT*, ad loc.
449. VI 67 2; 70. No allowance has been made in the above for the effect on Athenian numbers of special troop-carrying ships which might transport more than 200 men each; VI 43 with Gomme-Andrewes-Dover, *HCT*, IV, 308ff., 452. On the other hand, much space in the two expeditionary fleets would be taken by non-combatant slaves. Since

many of them had run away by the last days of the campaign (VII 75 5), the final host of 40,000 (+) may well have contained a lower proportion of non-combatants than did the two fleets.

450. VII 60 2, 75 5, 80 1, 83 4, cf. 84 4f.

451. VII 84 5.

452. On disagreements of Astyokhos and Pedaritos, (e.g.) VIII 32 3, 38 4.

453. Xen. *Hell*. I 6 9f.

454. VIII 6 1-3. On this subject in general see now D. M. Lewis, *Sparta and Persia*.

455. References at de Ste. Croix, *Historia*, III (1954-5), 6ff.

456. VII 19 1f.

457. V 17 2.

458. VI 91 6f., 93 1f.

459. VII 27 3 – 28 4.

460. Brunt, *Phoenix*, 19 (1965), 267, n. 47 for references to damage to silver mining. V. D. Hanson, *Warfare and agriculture in classical Greece*, 127ff.

461. Xen. *Hell*. I 6 24, Diod. XIII 97.

462. VII 28 4. On the question how long this tax existed, Meiggs, *AE*, 369.

463. I 141 2ff., cf. 142 1.

464. I 82 1.

465. I 109 2f.

466. IV 50 2.

467. VIII 18.

468. Lewis, op. cit., 90, citing VIII 43 3.

469. See, in addition to Lewis (op. cit.), de Ste. Croix, *Origins*, 155, 313f.

470. VIII 23 2f. On the blockade of Khios, (e.g.) VIII 24 2ff., 55 2 – 56 1.

471. With what follows compare the fall of Kimon after the expedition to Ithōmē. In modern history, those British Prime Ministers of the twentieth century who were forced out of office by their own party, Asquith, Chamberlain, Eden, fell because of failure in foreign policy. Cf. the American Presidents Johnson and Carter.

472. VIII 1 3; cf. P. J. Rhodes, *The Athenian boule*, 216.

473. VIII 68 4.

474. VIII 47 2, 53 1 – 54 2.

475. VIII 66.

476. VIII 65 2, 66 2, 70 2.

477. VIII 65 2.

478. VIII 66 5.

479. VIII 95 1 – 96 2.

480. VIII 80 3 (Byzantion); cf. 92 3 (Aigina).

481. VIII 64 3ff.

482. For the phrase, VIII 72 2, cf. 86 5.

483. VIII 86 4f. Alkibiades had seemingly advised Tissaphernes to limit his help to Sparta, to prevent her from crushing Athens outright; VIII 45f. For a view of Alkibiades' wisdom in 411 which differs sharply

from that of Thucydides, G. Grote, *History of Greece*, VIII, 49 (Everyman edition).

484. VIII 91 3.

485. Cf. esp. VIII 90 1f. According to Thucydides, Antiphon in *aretē* (VIII 68 1) was second to none of his Athenian contemporaries.

486. VIII 90ff.

487. VIII 97 1f.

488. VIII 97 2 with Andrewes, *HCT*, ad loc.; de Ste Croix, *Historia*, V (1956), 1-23.

489. Xen. *Hell.* I 1 35.

490. VIII 80 2f., cf. 62 1.

491. Xen. *Hell.* I 3 15-21.

492. Diod. XIII 40 6; Thuc. VIII 107 1; Diod. XIII 49 4; Xen. *Hell.* I 1 19. In addition, Athens must finally have lost Kyzikos soon after Aigospotamoi, if not earlier. See Lewis, op. cit., 128.

493. VIII 104 1 – 106 5; Xen. *Hell.* I 1 16-18.

494. Xen. *Hell.* I 1 23 and Chapter 6.

495. Diod. XIII 52.

496. For a collection of ancient references to the provision of resources to Sparta by Persia in the Ionian War, see W. K. Pritchett, *The Greek state at war*, I, 47; also de Ste. Croix, *Origins*, 155f.

497. Lewis, op. cit., 126, citing Diod. XIII 52 3 and Androtion, *FGH* 324, F44.

498. See Chapter 6.

499. See I. A. F. Bruce, *Historical commentary on the Hellenica Oxyrhynchia*.

500. W. S. Ferguson, *CAH*, V, 483-5; N. Robertson, *Historia*, XXIX (1980), 282-301.

501. Diod. XIII 101 1; contrast Xen. *Hell.* I 7 4ff. and esp. 11. See A. Andrewes, *Phoenix*, 28 (1974), 112-22.

502. Diod. XV 35 1.

503. Xen. *Hell.* II 1 10-12, cf. Thuc. II 65 12.

504. Xen. *Hell.* II 1 17-32, Diod. XIII 105.

505. Diodorus' version is less favourable to Alkibiades; XIII 105.

506. II 65 11 with Gomme, *HCT*, II, 196.

507. See Chapter 3 above.

508. VIII 96 5, cf. VII 55 2 with Gomme-Andrewes-Dover, *HCT*, ad loc.

509. VIII 24 4.

510. See above on Brasidas' rhetorical competence and moderate conduct towards Sparta's allies.

511. VIII 96 5; IV 55 4; cf. III 29 1, 31 2, 33 1, IV 55 2, VI 93 1.

512. Cf. II 65 7ff.

513. See further Chapter 6.

514. See Chapter 7, on the treatment of "sycophants" at the end of the Peloponnesian War.

515. See Chapter 3.

516. Compare Dem. LIV 38.

517. II 8 4.

6

Life within Sparta

Spartan secrecy and deceptiveness

What went on inside Sparta was a question which intrigued many
Greeks of other cities. In the fourth century, during or soon after
the period of Sparta's empire, several studies of the subject were
published.[1] Xenophon, the author of one of them, began his work
by observing that the Spartans had the greatest power of any
Greek community but also one of the smallest populations.[2] This
paradox was no doubt widely felt; Sparta's extraordinary
dominance called for an explanation. For this, Thucydides,[3]
Xenophon and others looked to the political and social arrangements within Sparta. Yet Sparta was secretive, as we have seen,[4]
and has left us no literary record of her own from the classical
period. Reconstructing the internal arrangements of Sparta is
more difficult than tracing her external military ventures, which
happened before a crowd of witnesses. Non-Spartans admitted
into Spartan territory were subject to periodic expulsion, the
xenēlasia ('driving out of foreigners'), which some contemporaries
believed to be a device for preserving Spartan secrets.[5] Those who
visited Sparta, or disseminated information about her, were often
(though not always) Lakonisers, Sparta's partisans. Such were the
Athenians Kritias and Xenophon. Our problem with Sparta's
internal history is rather similar to that faced by dispassionate
Western students of modern China, where the movements of
foreigners are restricted, communication with outsiders is
guarded, while much that is reported derives from the uncheck-
able accounts of enthusiasts.

Caution is made still more important by a fact which shrewd
contemporary observers of Sparta came to understand very well:

214

the Spartans were masters of deception. Modern works have tended to overlook this. Thus the author of one valuable recent book refers to the devious commander Derkylidas as "ostentatiously unSpartan in his Sisyphos-like cunning".[6] The idea that the Spartans were honest and decent may have its roots in the record of Thucydides, that Greeks at the start of the Peloponnesian War favoured the Spartans as potential liberators and that the general Brasidas behaved with encouraging rectitude.[7] Faith in Spartan honour may even have come on occasion from the assimilation of Sparta to the English boarding school, with its professed virtues of "owning up" to the truth and "playing the game".[8] To have left this image of virtue may be one of the greatest attainments of deceptive Spartan propaganda.

From contemporary Greek sources we hear of deception worked by Spartan officials on their own citizen soldiers, on Sparta's subject population, the helots, and on enemy states. Xenophon records two cases in which a Spartan general, on learning of a defeat for Spartan forces elsewhere, announced it to his troops as a victory, to sustain morale.[9] Thucydides writes of the helots' being deceived with attractive promises by the Spartan authorities, as a preliminary to massacre.[10] The seditious Kinadon was removed from Sparta by means of a lie, according to Xenophon.[11] In these cases we are not dealing with some untruth uttered briefly by a cornered politician, such as might be found in any society. Rather, each deception was supported by careful arrangements and appears to have been successfully maintained for as long as necessary.

Life at Sparta in several ways resembled that of a military camp — a point familiar in antiquity.[12] Spartan deceit may be best understood in this light. To mislead an enemy was widely regarded as quite proper, if not commendable.[13] (The attitude is common today; if we wish to refer without disapproval to a deceptive arrangement, as of household furniture or shop goods, we may talk of things being "*strategically* placed".) Xenophon writes of the Spartan king, Agesilaos:

> In a further respect he appeared to have achieved something characteristic of a proper general (*stratēgikon*): when war was declared and deception as a result became religiously permissible and just, he completely outclassed Tissaphernes [his Persian enemy] in deceit.[14]

Xenophon may also cast light here on the religiosity, in other circumstances, for which the Spartans were noted.[15] He describes how Agesilaos, in a previous period of truce, had steadfastly and ostentatiously refused to break his oath while knowing that the other party, Tissaphernes, was breaking his.[16] There is little doubt that religious rectitude appealed to Spartans partly for its own sake.[17] But religiosity had a further attraction: it might entice opponents into failing to guard against the deception which Sparta had in store for them, following the moral alchemy of a declaration of war. In addition, in war and peace alike there were many opportunities to deceive without oath-breaking or even uttering a direct lie. And the moral distinction between war and peace might be overlooked at times because of the permanent militarism and permanent military threat under which the Spartans lived. Sparta would always be aware that the image she transmitted was an important instrument of war.

Cases of Spartan commanders seeking to deceive a foe are numerous. Lysandros' triumphant outwitting of the Athenians at Aigospotamoi may be the most important.[18] In 392 the Spartan Pasimakhos lured men of Argos into battle by equipping warriors of Sparta with shields bearing a sigma, the distinctive blazon of the far less formidable state of Sikyon. According to contemporary report, he went into battle saying "by the twin gods, these sigmas will deceive you, Argives, into coming to fight us".[19] Spartan boys of the classical period learnt to steal as part of their education.[20] Thucydides reports Brasidas as seeking to persuade his soldiers of the virtue of a surprise attack, aimed at exploiting an enemy's mistake: "These stealthy actions involve the greatest glory when they most deceive the enemy and most benefit one's friends."[21] The word here translated as 'stealthy actions', *klemmata*, is cognate with the regular word for 'to steal', *kleptein*, and — if it was not Brasidas' own — was perhaps chosen by Thucydides as illustrating a connection between the two Spartan institutions of juvenile theft and adult military deceit.[22] At least in later antiquity, a legend existed of a Spartan boy who, after stealing a pet fox cub, bravely chose to endure in silence while the animal inflicted a fatal wound under his cloak, rather than to cry out and be detected.[23] The tale has traditionally been told as reflecting courage. But it also should be seen as glamorising deception. We are far from the values implied in the tale of young George Washington; the Spartan boy is noted not because he could not tell a lie, but because he would not tell the truth.

In classical Athens there was a different connection made between the Spartans and foxes, animals proverbial for deceit. A character in comedy was made to allude to the Spartans as "little foxes ... with treacherous souls, treacherous minds".[24] The point could be applied in action. Alkibiades, by duplicity of his own, succeeded in discrediting Spartan envoys by persuading them to seek to mislead the Athenian assembly.[25] Iphikrates, an Athenian general of the fourth century, heard at one point that the Spartan commander of an opposing force, Mnasippos, was dead. He reacted by remaining ready for battle. "For", in Xenophon's words, "he had not heard the news about Mnasippos from any eye-witness, but was on his guard, suspecting that the statement had been issued to deceive".[26] For an Athenian commander, careful source-criticism in Spartan matters was not an academic luxury; it was a means of staying alive.

Central to the Spartans' image was the idea that the political and social arrangements of their city were largely static and of very ancient origin.[27] Thucydides, who could state with impressive rigour that events much earlier than the Peloponnesian War were too remote in time to be strictly knowable,[28] was persuaded that by 404 BC the Spartans had been enjoying the same political system "for slightly more than four centuries".[29] That system was said by Spartans and others (though not by Thucydides) to be the creation of one Lykourgos.[30] The historicity of Lykourgos will not be dealt with here. Even Plutarch, a writer not noted for attending closely to defects in his sources, observed that ancient traditions concerning Lykourgos were profoundly contradictory.[31] Modern attempts to date the reforms which produced Sparta's famed way of life have created a further museum of contradiction.[32] For our purposes, statements about what Lykourgos ordered or banned are important in that they may reveal Spartan ideals and practices of the classical period. Historical fiction is fact about the society which produces it. Changes within the "Lykourgan" system were no doubt themselves attributed before long to Lykourgos.[33] (We may think of the Russian fondness of ascribing current arrangements to Lenin.)

Sparta's willingness to falsify the past may be seen with unusual clarity where the past in question was that of other Greek cities. Soon after the end of the Peloponnesian War the Spartan ephors decided to establish "ancestral constitutions" in the cities of Greece.[34] How were they to determine what for each state was an ancestral constitution? We are hardly to imagine Sparta sending out its most literate men, to imitate in every city Thucydides' technique of examining informants and inspecting old inscriptions. Rather, the Spartans were almost certainly doing what Thucydides has described them as doing in allied states in the fifth century: "taking care that they were governed by oligarchy in a way that favoured Sparta".[35] The form of oligarchy used would be given the label 'ancestral constitution' irrespective of historical precision, to meet the accusation that these new governments were alien implants imposed by Sparta, and to exploit the folk memory that *dēmokratia*, recently swept aside by the Spartans, was only a few generations old and far less old than oligarchy. Spartan traditions about their own history were probably shaped to meet current political needs. King Arkhidamos of Sparta boasted, according to Thucydides, that Spartan education effectively suppressed criticism of political arrangements at home.[36] This was deliberate; Sparta excelled at avoiding internal revolution and, as we shall see, many aspects of Spartan life were ingeniously contrived to promote harmony. One way of containing dissent was to convince potential revolutionaries that the system had succeeded in resisting change for centuries. We recall that Spartan officials at times practised deception upon their own citizens, and not only upon helots and outsiders.

The literary sources for Spartan life

A more promising field for investigation is the daily life, social and political, of the Spartans. This was observable by a succession of visitors who were not Lakonisers, politicians who came on diplomatic missions; Themistokles is the most famous example. Diplomacy, then as now, was inevitably combined with spying. (In seventeenth-century England, envoys of a hostile state were customarily blindfolded.[37]) Adverse criticisms of Sparta made by writers who generally admired her are also of much value, because of the argument from bias. And certain conspicuous facts about Spartans abroad, such as the names and the death-rate of commanders, can be exploited by us as reflections of life within Sparta. Before surveying the problems presented by individual sources, it should be noted — on the positive side — that not only do our sources cohere encouragingly on particular features of

Spartan society, but those features themselves form coherent patterns. To create and impose falsely such a consistent picture, in a sphere which was checkable by an intelligent few among her opponents, may seem a task beyond the mendacity even of Sparta.

Modern reconstructions of Sparta's internal history have tended to draw heavily on Plutarch's *Life of Lykourgos*. This is the source of various colourful claims which have become familiar; for example, that Spartan babies were inspected by elders, who ordered weaklings to be cast out; that mothers washed babies in wine to test and toughen them; that boys in winter tried to keep warm with vegetation for bedding.[38] In other spheres, scholars are very wary of trusting Plutarch for details of what occurred many centuries before his own time. It may perhaps be argued that the exceptional conservatism of Sparta gives unusual value to a late source. But we cannot yet be sure how successfully conservative Sparta was. Conspicuous institutions such as the dual kingship, the ephorate and helotage did indeed persist throughout the classical period. But while forms, especially such noted ones, might be preserved to give an image of stability, practical realities could change.[39] Xenophon, as we shall see, believed that possession of an empire — from 404 BC — made the Spartans disobedient to "the laws of Lykourgos".[40]

Although Plutarch cannot be ignored,[41] we should try to reconstruct our history mainly from writers of the fifth and fourth centuries, to reduce the risk of distortion. Even with these earlier writers considerable problems arise. When dealing with Sparta, Thucydides appears to depart twice from his normal, rigorous, procedures of criticism: on the age of the constitution and on the details of Pausanias' downfall.[42] On both subjects his account seems to coincide with the interests of the Spartan authorities. In a general preface to his work the historian tells of the difficulties he regularly faced from informants who told divergent stories.[43] But in a way the very diversity of those accounts might be of value, in that it obviously called for criticism and a suspension of belief. We may suspect, though only suspect, that Thucydides — through being used to the famous variety and freedom of speech at Athens — was at times taken off guard by a unanimity on the part of informants from Sparta, a state so disciplined as to produce almost a 'party line'. In communicating with Thucydides, in particular, Spartans may have been encouraged to adhere to official history by the knowledge that they were addressing someone who, although now an exile, had formerly campaigned against Sparta as a general of the great enemy state, Athens, and would still have influential friends there.

Xenophon, less intelligent than Thucydides in most respects, warmly admired many aspects of Sparta and must be treated as a partisan source. Exiled from Athens, probably for aligning himself with Sparta,[44] he was made welcome by eminent Spartans and given an estate in the north-western Peloponnese.[45] His sons may even have been admitted to the Spartan process of education.[46] However, his *Hellenika* (a history which begins at 411, near the point where Thucydides' account breaks off), his laudatory *Agesilaos* (on the Spartan king of that name), and the *Constitution of the Spartans* are, when used carefully, sources of great importance. Although Xenophon omits certain failings of the Spartans,[47] he is candid enough to include much to Sparta's discredit.

Plato and Aristotle, while more profound than Xenophon, resemble him somewhat in their analyses of Sparta. Both philosophers were intrigued by Spartan political arrangements, which each treated with a mixture of severe criticism and deep respect.[48] The rapid decline undergone by Sparta in the decades after 404, first in her reputation abroad, then in her military power, may have caused these and other analysts to exaggerate Spartan defects to some extent. As a study of modern journalism should reveal, changes of fortune — and trends generally — receive disproportionate attention as compared with static reality. Also, the special Greek fascination with the downfall of the mighty, reflected in the literary genre of tragedy, might be exercised by the case of Sparta, causing some to look for a religious explanation. Numerous faults in the Spartans were identified, which were — or could have been — used to account for their fall. The laws of Lykourgos were no longer obeyed;[49] Spartans were indulging in forbidden luxury at home;[50] the women were out of control and had taken over aspects of administration;[51] Spartan education did not fit men for peace;[52] there was a severe shortage of population;[53] Spartan wickedness had provoked the gods.[54]

These claims (except for the last one) probably reflect important realities, and will be examined below. But some exaggeration has very likely occurred in the *degree* of importance ascribed to particular faults, as a result of two common processes of error. One, already noted elsewhere,[55] is the tendency of disappointed partisans to dwell on the failings of their favoured party to the exclusion of merits possessed by opponents.[56] Since Xenophon, Plato and Aristotle, who report the faults of Sparta, were in different degrees sympathetic with her, it may be that they made too much of Spartan defects, and too little of the merits of Sparta's conqueror, Thebes. Second, there is the common fallacious tendency of reductionism; reducing to a single cause an explanation which should be complex. We hear this working daily. ("The trouble with you is...") Popular Marxism is a form of it. ("It's all economics ... ") Traditional Christianity has used the Devil, Anti-Communism the Reds, and so on. These two processes of error have been instructively combined in our own day, in British attempts to explain the loss of the British Empire; the explanation has been seen as lying within Britain, rather than within (e.g.) the USA and USSR, and has been widely agreed to be a single "deep-seated malaise". But on what that malaise might be, there is no consensus. After Athens lost the Peloponnesian War, there was a general feeling in the city that the Athenian side was responsible, and one element of it in particular — the "sykophants"[57] — was hated and persecuted for having caused the loss of empire. In the case of Sparta and her fall, we shall see special reason to suspect Aristotle of a form of reductionism, albeit less crude, involving the Spartans themselves.

Pressure for homogeneity: the dining group, marriage, homosexuality

Thucydides may have been at fault to claim that Sparta's internal good order was over 400 years old by 404 BC. However, his belief that effective order existed during his own period of political maturity, down to 404, cannot be set aside. He was surely right in stating that Sparta's ability to dominate other *poleis* derived from the stability of her own domestic arrangements.[58] (He might have said the same of Athens. Conversely, two large Greek states which seem to achieve very little in external affairs in relation to their size, Argos and Kerkyra, are recorded as the scene of ferocious civil strife.[59]) The immediate and irresistible pressure upon Sparta to avoid discord among her citizens came, as we have seen,[60] from the desire to keep the huge population of helots at work and away from their masters' throats. In a famous passage, of which the exact meaning is disputed,[61] Thucydides states either that "most of the relations between the Spartans and the helots were of an eminently precautionary character"[62] or that "Spartan policy is always mainly governed by the necessity of taking precautions against the helots".[63] In any case, since both helots and Spartans had an acute sense of military opportunity,[64] we should expect strenuous attempts to prevent dissension among the Spartans which the helots might exploit. Much of this chapter will be about the mechanisms whereby the unity and discipline of the Spartans were maintained.[65]

Adult male Spartans were obliged to belong to a particular dining group,[66] which met at night.[67] Inability to share the expenses of this institution disqualified a man from citizenship, at least in Aristotle's day.[68] So, presumably, did unwillingness to participate; Xenophon writes that Lykourgos excluded from the citizen body anyone who shrank from the rigorous customs of Spartan life.[69] Nightly dining together was undoubtedly meant to consolidate Spartan society and preserve its traditions.[70] The citizens of Sparta were known as the *homoioi* ('the equals' or 'those who are similar'),[71] and the *homoioi* had to be homogenised. Xenophon observed that in the other cities of Greece social gatherings usually consisted of men of a particular age, whereas at Sparta old and young met together, in an atmosphere consequently more restrained and conducive to the transmission of the older men's wisdom.[72] Cultural differences and disruptive friction between generations might thus be minimised. (Athens certainly had such friction; at one point, Thucydides shows an Athenian orator appealing for the assembly not to split politically on age lines).[73] According to Herodotos, Sparta was the only Greek state in which the young made way in the street, and gave up their seats, for their elders.[74] Spartan veneration of the old is reflected also in the institution of the *gerousia*, a court of elders with power over important cases.[75] It is probable that the influence of the elderly, as in other societies, tended — and was expected to tend – towards conservatism in politics. Plato suggests that at Sparta only the old were allowed to criticise the local practices;[76] such change as there might be had seemingly to be filtered through the society's most conservative age-group.

The dining group might also be expected to unify the fighting men and their seniors by diverting attention and affection from the family. Family life, in modern societies at least, appears to be responsible for much of the difference between the characters of individuals; political reformers seeking to generate new, standardised, personalities have sought to reduce the influence of parents upon children.[77] Family life may cause people to put the interests of relatives before those of the state; accordingly, reformers ancient and modern have tried to replace family loyalty with something wider. Plato's Republic, in many ways an idealised version of Sparta,[78] involved citizens not knowing their own close kin but instead treating as relatives all their fellow citizens.[79] Thus, it was hoped, affection might be transferred to the wider community. Aristotle wrote of Greek cities with an extreme form of *dēmokratia*, in which the state accepted from women charges of political disloyalty against their own male relatives.[80] In National Socialist Germany children informed similarly against their parents;[81] a recent Head of State of West Germany[82] was no doubt reacting consciously against that system when he said "I do not love the State; I love my wife."

At Sparta, Xenophon informs us, a husband in the early stages of marriage was discouraged from being seen entering or leaving his wife's presence.[83] The reason, he suggests, was a theory that stronger children would be born to couples who yearned lustily for each other rather than being almost sated with sexual activity.[84] Perhaps such a theory was influential at Sparta. But we have seen elsewhere that our sources are more likely to be right when they report directly observable facts (such as, in this case, signs of disapproval directed against an indiscreet husband) than when they seek to reconstruct the psychology behind those facts. Young Spartans were trained in stealth, as has been observed. They were also taught to travel at night.[85] It should be doubted whether the taboo which Xenophon mentions would have been expected to reduce by very much the sexual activity of young husbands with their wives. To do so might seem to risk reducing the number of conceptions, and among precisely those people, the youngest and strongest, who could be expected to have the fittest children. In other ways the Spartans took drastic measures to keep up the citizen population.[86] An alternative explanation of the taboo may be preferable.[87] Rather than being expected to have much effect on the amount of marital sex, the restriction might be meant to limit the time young couples spent together. As a proportion of that time, hours spent in sexual activity would increase, to the exclusion of activities productive of wider forms of mutual influence. The first years of marriage at Sparta may have been meant to teach wives and husbands to see each other mainly as sexual partners, and to produce, in George Eliot's phrase, "a merely canine affection". Xenophon tells strikingly and repeatedly of how news of military defeat was greeted by Spartans. Those whose relatives had died (bravely, as was presumed) appeared most gratified, whereas close kin of the (possibly ignoble) survivors seemed ashamed.[88] It seems that model Spartans did not love their families; they loved the State.

Aspects of Spartan society conduced less to heterosexuality than to homosexuality.[89] In his *Laws* Plato wrote that homosexuality resulted from the (male) dining groups and from male nudity in gymnasia.[90] Records of Sparta from the classical period seem to refer to homosexual boyfriends at least as often as to wives. Particularly revealing are some assertions by Xenophon on this subject. According to him, Lykourgos encouraged association between man and boy, where it was the boy's character that was admired, but decreed that obvious lust for a boy's body should be rejected utterly.[91] Xenophon suggests that the lawgiver was successful in this respect. "However," he adds guilelessly, "I am not surprised that some people do not believe this." Among those people was Xenophon himself at other times, when the need to praise Sparta was less prominent in his mind.[92] The claim that Sparta avoided homosexuality should be compared with the assertion recorded later by Plutarch, that there was no adultery at Sparta,[93] and with the statement made to foreigners during the Cultural Revolution of the 1960s, that there was no adultery in China.

Aristotle writes that soldierly and warlike peoples appear to be profoundly influenced either by heterosexual or by homosexual attachments.[94] It seems to have been his view that Spartans were devoted to the heterosexual kind,[95] which would give strong support to Xenophon's general claim. However, Aristotle proceeds to use the idea of the Spartans' eager sexuality to explain his own (indignant) observation that, during the period of Sparta's empire, much was administered by women. If Aristotle's opinion on heterosexuality was evolved as an explanation of the prominence of Spartan women, it may seem to be feebly based. That prominence can be accounted for easily without assuming that male Spartans were unusually attached to their women. From a very small citizen population Sparta had to supply soldiers and administrators to control a large empire, after 404. In the resulting shortage of trustworthy men to control things at Sparta, citizen women might well prove indispensable, particularly since they had more knowledge of the men's world than (for example)

224

their cloistered Athenian sisters.[96]

On the subject of Spartan sexuality we are faced with conflicting generalisations from Plato, on the one hand, and Xenophon with Aristotle, on the other. Detail is a proper test of the general statement, and references to particular homosexual attachments of Spartans are conspicuous even by Greek standards.[97] The regent Pausanias was betrayed to the ephors, according to Thucydides, by a former boyfriend (*paidika*).[98] Xenophon's hero, King Agesilaos, whose own relations with attractive boys forced themselves on the writer's attention, had a son, Arkhidamos, whom Xenophon describes as in love with a handsome Spartan youth named Kleonymos.[99] Alketas, a Spartan commander, is recorded by Xenophon as having lost control of the Euboian town of Oreos as a result of paying attentions to a local boy.[100] Homosexuality may have been seen as making a positive contribution to the solidarity of the *homoioi*. Partners, or former partners, acted in battle and elsewhere under each other's gaze or even by each other's side. Thus each might have a special motive for not bringing discredit — or danger — on himself or his mate.[101] According to Xenophon, Kleonymos gave Arkhidamos his word — after receiving some vital help from Arkhidamos' father — that he would try to take care that Arkhidamos would never be ashamed of his friendship.[102]

> He did not lie; during his lifetime at Sparta he performed every action that is esteemed there, and at Leuktra was the first Spartan to die, fighting ... in the midst of the enemy. His death pained Arkhidamos to the limit, but, as he had promised, he brought him credit and not disgrace.

If Xenophon is right, the nature of Arkhidamos' affection for the other man was not discreditable. Nor was his eventual grief, which contrasts interestingly with the fortitude displayed by, and thought creditable in, relatives of those who died in the same battle. We read elsewhere in Xenophon's *Hellenika* of a Spartan commander, Anaxibios, who found himself in a hopeless military position and chose, with fellow officers, to stand his ground and die. The rest of the force fled, save for Anaxibios' *paidika*, who stayed by his side, evidently until death.[103] Xenophon's point in referring to this devoted individual by his sexual status, and not by his name, is probably that the sexuality produced the exceptional loyalty. In spite of himself, Xenophon allows us to see why in a warrior society homosexual affections may have been privileged.

In their dining groups Spartans — rich and poor together — ate the same food,[104] the plainness of which became famous.[105] Thus were neatly removed two potential sources of friction between different sections of the citizen group. Rich men of other Greek cities were sometimes referred to as 'the stout'. Plato, who stated that an oligarchically-controlled *polis* was in reality two cities, of rich and poor, alluded — with his fat rich man and his thin pauper — to conspicuous differences in diet which might encourage division and revolution.[106] Not only did the system of dining groups meet that problem; it also seems to have excluded the *symposion*, the private drinking party at which wealthy men of like mind might reinforce their social distinctness and perhaps plot revolution.[107] (The phenomenon of Dutch Courage was familiar to Greeks and Romans; Julius Caesar was to be described as the only man to undertake revolution while sober.[108]) Megillos, the Spartan character in Plato's *Laws*, boasts that in the cities controlled by Sparta there are no *symposia* and no one gets away with drunkenness.[109] Other contemporaries with an admiration for Sparta praise the city for her sobriety. Xenophon commends King Agesilaos for regarding drunkenness as madness,[110] as indeed it would have been, given the sense of military opportunity which the helots shared with the Spartans. Predictable mass intoxication at a festival of citizens would have presented rebellious subjects with a wonderful chance; Kritias wrote in the late fifth century that the Spartans had no day set aside for excessive drinking.[111] But apart from its military aspect, drunkenness might amount to a display of luxury, irritating to the poor onlooker;[112] that, too, helps to explain the sobriety of Sparta.

In addition to the schooling together of the children of rich and poor, further devices for promoting social harmony included the wearing by the rich of clothes "of a sort that even any poor man could get"[113] (compare modern remarks on "classless" denim). Thucydides comments on the Spartans' moderation in dress, and on the unusual lengths to which better-off Spartans went in assimilating their style of life to that of ordinary citizens.[114] There was also a limited sharing of wealth outside the dining groups.[115] (Athens for her own reasons of social harmony had laws to restrain the spending of the wealthy on *symposia*[116] and other forms of display.[117]) But, given the existence of rich men, to deny any outlet for showing off wealth might itself be provocative — to the wealthy themselves. And the discontented rich are usually in a better position to make a revolution than the discontented poor. In Athens a permitted form of display involved expensive horses, which could serve the common good as cavalry mounts in wartime. Rich Athenians often chose for their children names with the element *-hipp-*, 'horse'.[118] Similarly at Sparta. In a single source, Xenophon's *Hellenika*, we meet Alexippidas, Euarkhippos, Herippidas, Hippokrates, Kratesippidas, Lysippos, Mnasippos, Orsippos, Pasippidas and Zeuxippos, all prominent Spartans and therefore likelier than not to be from the wealthier section of society.[119] It is also made clear by Xenophon that horses used in battle by Spartan cavalry were reared by "the richest men" of Sparta.[120]

The enthusiasm of many Spartans for patronising chariot-racing teams is well documented.[121] In the early fourth century, as wealth poured in from Sparta's new overseas empire, this lavish competition seems to have caused a certain tension. Xenophon records King Agesilaos as having tried to demonstrate that the production of fine chariot-horses was not a mark of manly virtue but rather of wealth, by persuading his sister, Kyniska, to rear a victorious team.[122] We do not know whether Agesilaos succeeded in reducing the eagerness of rich men for this sport. (Its aura may be better appreciated if we recall the vicarious virility now associated with motor racing.) There is, however, some evidence that Kyniska's victory had the effect of inducing other rich women to patronise chariot teams.[123] Ironically, by advertising his point that it was wealth rather than manliness which counted in this sphere, Agesilaos may have intensified the competition by bringing in a new group of enthusiasts. The participation of women would seem to confirm that one motive of patrons had no reference to gender, but was the display of the very wealth which Agesilaos hoped to belittle.

Military training and the schooling of the young

In his *Constitution of the Spartans* Xenophon writes that Lykourgos arranged for the Spartans to dine communally, where they could be observed easily, because he knew that when people are at home they behave in their most relaxed manner.[124] Since the standards of public morality at Sparta were strenuous, we might anyway have expected to find an unusually large proportion of life being spent under public supervision.[125] Another, more strenuous, activity, which again must have involved lengthy exposure to public view, was military training. The Periklean funeral speech, likely of course to reflect some Athenian bias against Sparta, suggests that Spartan soldiers depended more on preparation and deceit than on spontaneous courage.[126] Xenophon states that the Spartan hoplite formation is not, "as most people think", exceedingly complex.[127] But even he admits that Spartan soldiers perform with great ease manoeuvres which others think very difficult,[128] and that fighting in an improvised position, amid confusion, "is not ... easily learnt except by those schooled under the laws of Lykourgos".[129] It hardly needs saying that the apparent simplicity in the movements of any superior athlete or trained human formation is likely to be the product of laborious practice. Xenophon's willingness to concede the importance to the Spartans of training, and his reluctance to admit the existence of complexity in their manoeuvres, together fit very well with a theme of Spartan propaganda which we identified in an earlier chapter.[130] Sparta wished to discourage the idea that there was anything clever about her military actions, which an intelligent opponent might learn to counter at little cost. Instead, emphasis was laid on the hardness of Spartan hoplites and of their training, which enemies from more comfortable cities might despair of matching. If, distrustful of this Spartan theme, we assumed that Xenophon's "most people" were right, and that there was much complexity in the manoeuvres taught at Sparta, we should be able to account — in agreement with the Periklean funeral speech[131] — for the periodic expulsions of foreigners from Sparta.[132] These could have been the occasions for practising the more complicated, or the deceptive, moves. Manoeuvres involving all or most of the army would have needed concealment additionally so as to protect a secret of great significance — the size of Sparta's fighting population.

Xenophon, who cannot with consistency argue that the expulsions were meant to hide complex manoeuvres, suggests instead that their purpose was to remove foreign influences.[133] This may be part of the explanation. But it raises a less familiar question, which Xenophon does not tackle: why did Sparta not exclude foreigners all the year round? Diplomacy might be conducted a few miles from the city,[134] and trade carried on at some remote frontier or coast. Given the generally coherent pattern of Sparta's political arrangements, and her policy of promoting ignorance and error in her enemies, the admission of Greeks from other states (including, it seems, the astute and menacing Perikles[135]) is unlikely to have resulted from oversight. Some positive benefit was probably expected. It will be argued below that the Spartans were skilled in visual propaganda. Their practice of this in many other contexts may suggest that they allowed limited access to their city precisely in order that visitors would take away impressive images. The idea of such motivation was certainly known to the Greeks; it is involved in Herodotos' story about Greek spies, captured by the Persians on the eve of Xerxes' invasion, and deliberately set free to report the daunting facts about the scale of the Great King's forces.[136]

Aristotle, who has words of strong disapproval for the Spartan system of educating the young,[137] concedes that "one might praise" the Spartans for the great care they took in having that system run communally by the state.[138] What Xenophon says of other Spartans was no doubt true also of children: that any who evaded the burdensome processes imposed by the state were excluded by the rules of Lykourgos from the privileges of citizenship.[139] By educating the children of rich and poor together, Sparta eliminated much friction which might otherwise have arisen in adult life, among those of diverse upbringing. Perikles (as reported by Thucydides), Xenophon and Aristotle concur in describing Spartan education with words from the Greek root *pon-*, which connotes toil or suffering. Perikles speaks of the practice in suffering undergone by young Spartans, as their education prepared them to show manly courage (*to andreion*).[140] Aristotle states that the Spartans made their children bestial through *ponoi*, with the aim of producing manly courage (*andreia*).[141] He goes on to blame Sparta for concentrating on this quality to the exclusion of others. In this context Aristotle is interested in explaining the military downfall of Sparta. He seems to have meant that Sparta fell because other states had come to match her training while having additional attainments which Sparta lacked. Here he perhaps exaggerates the narrowness of Sparta's educational ideals and attainment. Elsewhere in the same work he has a different explanation of the city's downfall which he does not mention here, that Sparta perished through shortage of population.[142] In this second context there is in turn no reference to the explanation involving narrowness of character. It may be that the two explanations were intended as complementary.[143] On the other hand, there may be at work in both passages the tendency to inflate a single factor into *the* deep-seated malaise. (In passing, it is interesting that Aristotle, even while blaming Sparta for narrowness and bestiality, seems to have accepted the Spartans' own propaganda point,[144] that their sheer toughness had brought them to power.)

When Xenophon describes Spartan education, he has a very different angle from Aristotle. He writes earlier in the fourth century, to explain the success, at the time, of his friends the Spartans. In spite of his plain bias, he is more plausible than Aristotle when he asserts that Spartan education produced useful qualities besides crude animal courage. Xenophon stresses the instilling of obedience and *aidōs* — willingness to defer to the moral opinions of others.[145] Both qualities have their dangers; as Euripides hinted,[146] *aidōs* might be good or bad, depending on the nature of the moral opinions deferred to. But in a state outnumbered and hemmed in by potential enemies, as Sparta was, the cohesion promoted by these two qualities would in general be of the greatest importance. The willingness of Spartans to die on the battlefield, which will be examined below, was not a result merely of bestial courage, whatever that might be. It derived in part from a sophisticated and perhaps peculiarly human consideration, that death was preferable to life with dishonour of the hurtfulness which Sparta contrived for cowards. Not only was that dishonour imposed with unusual vigour;[147] Spartan *aidōs* would involve an unusual sensitivity to the community's disapproval.

A detailed and believable account of the rigours of Spartan upbringing is given by Xenophon in his *Constitution*. Boys were supervised by an adult of high standing, in contrast, as Xenophon notes, to the child-minders of other Greek cities, who were slaves.[148] This reflects not only the importance attached to education at Sparta, but also the difficulty of keeping children and youths to so strict a discipline. Slacking must have been a familiar and threatening event,[149] and was heavily punished by the adult supervisor.[150] Young men with whips also punished delinquents.[151] (This is one of several references to the role of the whip in Spartan education;[152] Plato observes that Spartans were educated "not by persuasion but by violence".[153]) Children were made to go barefoot and to wear only a single cloak whatever the season.[154] They were also kept hungry, and were permitted to steal food.[155] Boys caught doing so were severely whipped, but only as an incentive to steal more discreetly.[156]

Theft offended against two ideals of Spartan society: obedience and respect for elders. So assuming, by rule of thumb, rationality in this successful society, we should look for some considerable benefit, one sufficient to outweigh that disadvantage. The military usefulness of a training in deceit has already been stressed, and Xenophon states that boys stole in order to become better warriors.[157] But we are left vague as to the military context in which a soldier might need to live off the land. In another passage, Xenophon writes that Spartans on expedition were discouraged from going far from camp, at least in some circumstances.[158] The aftermath of defeat might require irregular foraging, but the Spartan system did not countenance the survival of defeat. The education in theft may need a different explanation. The helot revolts which we hear of were mostly large affairs, which Sparta could not keep secret, if only because she needed outside help to deal with them. How common were small-scale revolt and brigandage? That we hear little of them is hardly surprising. Masters of deceit, secrecy and military opportunism, the Spartans were not going to advertise gratuitously their own distractions. In connection with the Athenian seizure of Pylos in Messenia, Thucydides states that the Spartans had previously been inexperienced in regard to brigandage and the kind of fighting which went with it.[159] His opinion cannot be dismissed, though we may wonder how he arrived at it. He is in effect putting forward a very large and vulnerable generalisation — that in a long preceding period the Spartans had always or almost always been uninvolved with brigandage — about a state whose desire to obscure its own circumstances he notes in this very passage. Also, he himself records that, at the start of the Pylos episode, the Athenians got help from Messenian brigands "who happened to be present".[160] We may suspect that irregular fighting in Spartan territory had a longer history than Thucydides' Peloponnesian informants could or would make clear. Since Tegea over the northern border would not harbour runaway helots, taking to the hills or the coasts and living by plunder off the rich lands of Lakonia and Messenia may have been the resort of numerous small groups of helots who had lost patience with their masters. Guerrilla notoriously imposes its own tactics on the opposition. That, perhaps, was why young Spartans were taught to live off the land, deprived of food and normal clothing.

Jealousy, competitiveness and attitudes to death

Oligarchies in general were known for their internal jealousies.[161] At Sparta concern with social and political precedence seems to have been intense.[162] It was fostered — deliberately or not — in childhood, a stage which is in any society particularly exposed to hierarchic thought, through the fact that among children age, strength and sophistication roughly correspond.[163] We hear of a large range of names applied to different age-groups of children at Sparta,[164] which may reflect the nurturing of an unusually lively sense of status based on age, a sense meant in later life to contribute to the Spartan reverence for seniority.[165] Certainly the *mastigophoroi*, the young men with the whips, must have formed an unforgettable pinnacle of juvenile society. Xenophon writes that young adult men competed for selection as members of an elite group. The reasons for the inclusion or rejection of each individual were made very clear, he states. If this is correct, it would be hard to resist Xenophon's own conclusion, that competitiveness and thus a sense of hierarchy were being bred deliberately.[166] Rivals would "box out of rivalry wherever they met".[167] If this was a way for a young man to restore his esteem, considerable value must have been attached to the physical powers needed for a successful beating-up.

Other Greeks were convinced of the exceptional bravery of Spartans. According to Thucydides, the decision of about 120 Spartans to surrender when trapped on Sphakteria, rather than to die fighting, was for Greeks generally the most surprising event of the Peloponnesian War.[168] There is little doubt that the educational system of Sparta succeeded in producing the desired *andreia*, in most cases. Of this courage one indicator, not easily affected by Spartan propaganda, is the number of commanders who died in battle abroad. An elite bodyguard was provided for kings in combat,[169] so that we should expect them to be killed only in an overwhelming defeat, as was Leonidas at Thermopylai and Kleombrotos at Leuktra. But the death-rate of other commanders is indeed impressive. Brasidas and Lysandros, perhaps Sparta's best generals in our period, both perished in battle; so did the admirals at Kyzikos (Mindaros), Arginousai (Kallikratidas) and Knidos (Peisandros). The defeat which carried off Anaxibios and his boyfriend involved the deaths of some twelve Spartan harmosts (imperial governors), according to Xenophon.[170] Pasimakhos died fighting "with few against many".[171] Mnasippos was killed while in a small detachment.[172] Of particular interest is the death of another Spartan commander, Phoibidas, who went down fighting with no more than "two or three others" of his army.[173] In another connection, Xenophon described him as "far more in love with the idea of doing something outstanding than of staying alive".[174]

There was at Sparta a profound reverence for death in battle. The poet Tyrtaios, whose works were long revered among Spartans, referred to a soldierly death in terms which recall to us the interesting slogan of Nationalist troops in the Spanish Civil War:- 'Viva la Muerte' ('Long live Death').[175] After a heavy defeat at Lekhaion, during the Korinthian War, there was much grief in the Spartan army, according to Xenophon, "except for those whose sons or fathers or brothers had died there. They went about radiant as if they had won a victory, rejoicing in what had happened to their families".[176] Again, after the catastrophe of Leuktra, there was a remarkable exhibition when the bad news reached Sparta. Xenophon concedes that the ephors felt some grief at the report, "as was inevitable, I suppose", and felt obliged to instruct the women not to cry out. However, "on the following day those who had lost relatives were to be seen going about in the open, radiant and well turned-out, whereas few were in evidence of those whose relatives had been reported to have survived, and they went about humbled and gloomy".[177] Xenophon seems to have approved of this display of soldierly values, and may have exaggerated somewhat. He may have intended a contrast with the way in which Athens reacted to *its* worst catastrophe, the battle of Aigospotamoi, news of which (according to Xenophon) approached Athens from Peiraieus to the accompaniment of a travelling howl.[178] However, Xenophon's account of Spartan reactions to the deaths of relatives cannot be wholly rejected. It is part of a coherent picture, emerging from other sources as well as from different sections of Xenophon's own writings, of Spartan reverence for death in battle. It seems that such a death was — for men — a condition of being named on a gravestone.[179] A brave death established an unanswerable claim to merit. Even at Athens, where civilian attainments were valued far more than at Sparta, Perikles could state that a patriotic death wiped out any blemishes on a citizen's previous record.[180]

Any Spartan who refused to be brave in the field faced the prospect of thorough, energetic, contempt at home. Herodotos tells of two soldiers from Leonidas' doomed army of Thermopylai, who missed the general slaughter. One, named Pantites, was said to have been degraded on his return to Sparta, and to have hanged himself. The other, Aristodamos, was similarly humiliated; he was nicknamed 'the trembler' and no Spartan would talk to him. As a result, at the subsequent battle of Plataia he "obviously wanted to die" according to other Spartans present, and fulfilled his desire spectacularly.[181] We recall the idea ascribed by Thucydides to Brasidas, that fear of disgrace was one of the main elements of soldiering.[182] Xenophon has much detail on the disgrace contrived at Sparta for cowards; they cannot find wives, he writes, nor will men marry their female relatives; they are not allowed to look happy, on pain of being beaten; they have to give up their seats to younger men.[183] This last requirement might not seem particularly hurtful, if we applied our modern adult values, that is. Its punitive power may be better understood by recalling the values of our childhood; an eleven-year-old, in England at least, may be mortified at being demoted in favour of someone a year or two younger. A similarly childlike quality is suggested by a further detail of Xenophon's; an adult coward was punished by not being chosen when teams were picked for ball games. Sparta preserved into adult life the acute dependence of the child on the approval of peers .[184] In our own society, where personal rejection exists of a kind which even an adult finds intolerable, a common recourse is to change job or to move house, to escape bad opinions. But for a Spartan there was no escape. The whole male community of Sparta by the early fourth century was smaller than many modern secondary schools. A Spartan soldier would be aware that, if he was once stigmatised for cowardice, rightly or wrongly, there would be no hope of a bearable future. Everybody would know him.

Laconic speech and the rejection of books

We have seen that Spartans of the classical period have left us no books.[185] So little is heard of reading or writing by the Spartans that serious scholarly attention has been paid to the question whether they were illiterate.[186] However, a few inscriptions do survive from archaic and classical Sparta,[187] along with some references in literature to the use of written messages by Spartan military commanders and the home authorities. Thucydides' story of the fall of Pausanias contains mention of several such messages.[188]

Xenophon states that, after defeating the admiral Mindaros (in 410), the Athenians intercepted a Spartan despatch intended for the government at home: "The good times are over. Mindaros is dead. The men are starving. We do not know what to do."[189]

In Xenophon's account the intercepted message is in Laconian dialect, as well as laconic style. Spartans appear to have prided themselves on avoiding, even on inability to understand, lengthy and complex argument,[190] and this they could hardly have done had they exposed themselves to a literature very like that of Athens. In the Funeral Speech, where Perikles is shown contrasting Athens with Sparta in numerous ways, the Athenians are praised as "not thinking that words [or "theory"] damage action".[191] At Sparta, the case perhaps was otherwise. Again, "we [Athenians] enjoy theorising, without being soft".[192] In Spartan eyes, it may be that theorists were softies. Thucydides portrays Brasidas, "an able speaker — for a Spartan",[193] as defending himself before a battle with the boast, "I shall show that I am not someone better at advising the next man than at going into action himself."[194] A Spartan who dealt with words had to meet the suspicion of softness with eloquent deeds. Brasidas' courage on this occasion was to get him killed. In Spartan theory, a man did not multiply words: he acted.[195] A book, in contrast, was a veritable heap of words.

The idea that manliness involves few words has flourished in many cultures, including our own. Successful embodiments of modern popular ideals, such as Simon Templar ("The Saint"), James Bond, Batman and the heroes of Hollywood westerns, make few and terse speeches. When they do speak, they are unanswerable. This may be from force of manly will ("But, Simon..." "No 'buts', Penelope!") or through generalising truism — which may achieve unanswerability at the cost of becoming tautologous, as in the apocryphal line from a western, 'A man's gotta do what a man's gotta do.' In classical Greece rhetoric was notoriously slick and effective. The Spartans, in spite of their apparent disdain for words, were noted for a form of word-play of their own: laconic speech.[196] Numerous alleged examples circulated in later antiquity.[197] But one case recorded by the contemporary Thucydides may show with unusual clarity the value of such speech to the Spartans. One of the men from the Spartan force which had surrendered on the isle of Sphakteria was met at Athens with the insulting suggestion that the only brave men to go to the island had died there. His reply, which

Thucydides claims to report in the original Laconian dialect, was as follows: "An arrow would be *very* valuable if it picked out the brave."[198] Being true, general, terse, relevant and clever, this defence achieved vast circulation among Thucydides' later readership if not among contemporaries. Laconic rhetoric at its best could abort the rhetoric of others. One-line wit tends to lack logical completeness, and much Greek literature reflects a taste for the logically thorough. To overcome this, Spartan one-liners might need to be very shrewd. But with brevity went the positive quality of memorability. By evolving the laconic style, the Spartans found an ingenious way of making their mark in contemporary debates without sacrificing their warlike image through wordy and bookish eloquence.

The claim of King Arkhidamos, that Spartans were not so educated as to be able to criticise their own constitution, is evidence both of restriction in the use of books and of a motive for that restriction. Reading might promote political disunity. For one thing, books from outside Sparta would bring in alien ideals.[199] Also, private reading of diverse material away from the pressures of the dining group, or even private reflection on common texts, would encourage diversity of opinion. Oral culture, shared by the dining group,[200] was far likelier to produce the homogeneity of character which embattled Sparta required. We recall that the Catholic church, in its dread of political and doctrinal schism at the Reformation, energetically opposed the circulation of the Bible in contemporary translations. The church's belief, that individuals would draw contradictory conclusions from their own study of the text, was reasonable. A doctrine transmitted orally to congregations by a centrally controlled clergy offered a far greater chance of cohesion. Catholic writers pointed, after the Reformation, to the innumerable and mutually contradictory forms of Protestantism;[201] in this they are comparable with the Greek political theorists of the classical period who objected to the diversity of character, action and constitutional detail under *dēmokratia*.[202] The tragedian Sophokles, in the *Ajax*, makes the Spartan character Menelaos preach the virtue of *aidōs*, deference to the will of the group, and decry repeatedly the freedom of the individual to do whatever he likes.[203] Athens, the city most blamed for that freedom, was also the headquarters of literacy. From their own viewpoint, the Spartans acted sensibly in seeking to preserve limitations on action by imposing limitations on thought.

Mechanisms of justice and subordination

A deliberate refusal to use written texts appears also in the administration of Spartan justice. Aristotle suggests disapprovingly that the ephors, "sovereign over important legal cases", reached judgements independently of written documents and the laws, relying instead on their own discretion.[204] He, like Xenophon and Plato, likens the ephors to tyrants,[205] rulers traditionally represented as having transcended law, written and unwritten.[206] Spartan arrangements contrast strongly with those of democratic Athens, where an enormous body of law was inscribed on stone and papyrus to be inspected by "anyone who wanted" (in the telling Athenian formula), as a protection for the individual against arbitrary, or at least unexpected, legal sanctions. But in drafting laws it is notoriously difficult to arrive at formulae which encompass all offensive acts, while excluding all which are inoffensive. For one thing, circumstances and the ingenuity of offenders are not wholly predictable. Sparta evidently cut the knot. Because of the exceptional danger in which the tiny Spartan community always was, it may well have seemed that there was little or no place for law, with its inevitable loopholes, whereby a subversive act might go unpunished.

Writing of the regent Pausanias, Thucydides refers to "the way in which the Spartans traditionally treat their own people, being not quick to consider any irremediable step in the case of a Spartan citizen without unchallengeable proof".[207] Death sentences, then, were not imposed as readily as elsewhere. So we should expect. A small beleaguered community might be rather foolish to whittle down its own numbers[208] or to risk the bitter dissension consequent on a judicial killing of doubtful justice. But the qualifications made in Thucydides' statement are also important. He emphasises, by repetition, that the judicial caution is applied to "their own people", "in the case of a Spartan citizen". Others, such as helots, might be treated very differently, as we shall see.[209] And even in the case of citizens it is only "irremediable" sanctions which are described by Thucydides as the objects of great caution.

An episode from the Peloponnesian War may help to illustrate the latter distinction implied by Thucydides. The Spartans who had surrendered on Sphakteria, and who were released by Athens in 421, were degraded *en masse* from full citizenship shortly after their return home. The authorities who decided this were very far from acting on the basis of incontestable proof of wrongdoing; they moved from *fear* that the returned men would prove subversive.[210] At some later point the men were reinstated, which confirms that their harsh treatment had been merely precautionary. Such official action may seem remote from modern practice. But Sparta could regard herself as permanently under severe threat, and we should recall the restrictions on freedom which normally occur in our own times in the event of a profoundly menacing war. To take one relevant example, in Britain during the Second World War British nationals were imprisoned not for breach of any law but on suspicion of willingness to work for Hitler. The episode of the returned prisoners casts an interesting light both on Sparta and on Thucydides' attitude towards her. In praising Spartan government of this and earlier periods he uses the verb *eunomeisthai*,[211] a word which might be mechanically translated as 'to have a good system of laws'. But what Sparta had was not so much law as *order*. And Thucydides knew that when he praised her.

Spartan order involved a degree of obedience to the authorities which impressed both Xenophon and Plato.[212] According to Xenophon, at Sparta influential men took pride in their eager obedience towards officials, whereas in all other cities such men thought it beneath their dignity to seem to have any fear of those in office.[213] Xenophon's "influential men" were presumably on the whole the wealthy, yet the ephors, to whose near-tyrannic power they deferred, were often poor, as Aristotle makes clear, at least at the time of their election.[214] The philosopher claims plausibly that it was their participation in the ephorate which made the mass of ordinary Spartiates, those who were not rich, happy with the constitution.[215]

It may well be that most citizens of Sparta, those who were neither aristocrats nor in office, lacked the power to initiate business in the general assembly.[216] But the power of their representatives, the ephors, was enormous. Thucydides' account of the debate in 432, about whether to make war against Athens, shows the ephor Sthenelaïdas first making a partisan speech in the assembly and then managing the crucial vote in a way which suited his cause.[217] In measuring the vote of the assembly numeracy was not employed; in Thucydides' words, "they [i.e. the Spartans] decide by shout and not by ballot".[218] Aristotle describes as "excessively childish" the method by which ephors were elected,[219] which may have involved a similar measurement of shouts.[220] Recently de Ste. Croix has characterised the shouting as a "primitive method of decision", and written of the Spartans as having "failed to develop" a proper voting procedure.[221] Yet he also refers to the shouting as "deliberately preserved".[222] Spartans would be aware of the greater precision available in the Athenian method of counting ballots. Apart from the considerable pleasure of preserving a local tradition, what could Sparta rationally have hoped to derive from continuing to elect by shout?

Where the volume of rival shouts was similar, and was judged by a high official such as an ephor, that person was effectively given a casting vote.[223] Obedient Spartans might have thought it entirely proper for their authorities to have such power. Less obviously, the Spartan system possessed one refinement not found in the superficially more sophisticated method of counting ballots. As often, it may help us to understand ancient history if we try to apply the psychological refinement required in our daily lives. We are commonly faced with a group whose members have conflicting wishes about the use of some indivisible resource. Three people may wish to use the family television to watch a mildly appealing old film; the other two may desire intensely to watch the climax of some sporting contest on another channel. In such a situation, if we are concerned to preserve long-term harmony, we give greater weight to the wishes of greater intensity. This, imperfectly, the Spartan system might do; those with most intense wishes would no doubt tend to shout loudest. Sparta's unusual need to preserve the harmony of her citizens has already been noted, and many of her social arrangements are explicable in the light of that. It is, of course, far from certain that the system of shouting was maintained for the reason we have outlined. But unless we can show that it was not, we have no right to dismiss that system as inept. It would be dangerous, even on the authority of Aristotle, to assert that a people as successful as the Spartans did not know their own business.[224]

Sparta's use of the visual

Another Spartan skill which is insufficiently appreciated may be the creation of visual propaganda. Indeed, once we have recognised Sparta's small use of words and great interest in deception, we might almost predict a sophistication in the use of visual images. In an earlier chapter it was noted that the (official?) stories of the downfall of three members of Spartan royalty involved memorable details appealing to the visual imagination; Kleomenes madly slashing his own flesh, Leotykhidas sitting on a glove full of ill-gotten silver, Pausanias talking treasonably in the presence of concealed ephors.[225] Spartan use of the memorable image often went beyond mere imagination. When an army of the Peloponnesian league contained Spartan hoplites, it might be important to draw attention to them, to let Sparta's reputation do its work on enemy minds.[226] The red cloaks worn by Spartan troops proved distinctive and memorable,[227] as they were surely intended to be. (Aristotle suggested that they were meant to be the colour of blood.[228]) The famous long hair of Sparta's soldiers was meant to be conspicuous and intimidating; according to Xenophon, "Lykourgos ... allowed the hair to be grown long, thinking that in this way [Spartans] would appear as larger and be more frightening."[229] With the leonine Spartans we may compare the French grenadiers and British guardsmen of the nineteenth century, with their large hats.

Records of visual propaganda cluster around Agesilaos, one of the most closely observed of Sparta's commanders. According to his admirer Xenophon, he accoutred his army in such a way that "it gave the impression of consisting entirely of bronze and scarlet".[230] Believing that contempt for the enemy fortified men for battle, he ordered that enemy prisoners be sold naked. The spectacle of the latter, fat, white and not hardened by toil (*ponos*), convinced Agesilaos' soldiers, according to Xenophon, that the war would be virtually the same as fighting against women.[231] (Centuries later, Plutarch wrote of a Spartan tradition of forcing helots to get drunk, to provide an educational spectacle for young citizens.[232]) Xenophon praises the impression created by the sight of Agesilaos' physical arrangements at Ephesos:

> you could see the gymnasia full of men exercising, the hippodrome full of horsemen riding, the javelin-throwers and the archers at target practice ... The market-place was full of armaments and horses for sale, while the bronze-smiths and carpenters, ironworkers, leatherworkers and painters were all preparing military equipment. As a result you would truly have thought the city a workshop of war. One would also have been fortified to see first Agesilaos then the other soldiers wearing garlands ... which they offered up

to the goddess Artemis. For wherever men revere the gods, train for war and practise to obey the authorities there it can be expected that everything will radiate optimism.[233]

There can be little doubt as to where Agesilaos learnt to project the image of a city as a workshop of war — at Sparta itself.

On a less happy occasion, Agesilaos led home through the Peloponnese a Spartan force which had been badly defeated. He did so in a way calculated to conceal the fewness of the survivors. Their arrival at Peloponnesian towns was arranged for a late hour, and their departure for dawn.[234] A British scholar has suggested recently that "the Spartans' practice of starting at night on expeditions out of Lakonia" was due to the high incidence of sunshine in that part of the Peloponnese.[235] We have already seen, in the case of Meiggs and Ionia, an English historian invoking the weather to account for an event better explained by differences within a society.[236] In the present case, if Spartan armies did generally set out from home by night,[237] the analogy of Agesilaos' furtive march should suggest that the purpose was to deceive. And the obvious targets of the deception are the helots, who were to be kept in the dark as to how many of their masters were going away. We shall see below independent grounds for suspecting that helots in any case were kept under curfew at night. Spartan numbers were a well-guarded secret, as Thucydides found.[238] Kinadon, a would-be revolutionary at Sparta, is reported to have tried to win support for his scheme by demonstrating just how few the Spartans at home actually were.[239] Was it partly to obscure this matter that the Spartans continued to live dispersed in villages, as Thucydides remarks,[240] rather than in a centralised *polis*, where their numbers would be more readily observed?

We have seen that one Athenian general of the fourth century, Iphikrates, had learnt to guard against Spartan military deception. The reported action of Theban commanders, after their brilliant and decisive defeat of the Spartans at Leuktra, suggests that they may have learnt even more. They apparently caused the corpses of Spartiates to be displayed on the battlefield separately from the others. Some 400 were seen to have died; other Greeks might remember the profound setback caused to Sparta 50 years before by the temporary loss of 120. Thebes countered Spartan secrecy with a flash of publicity, using Sparta's own technique of the memorable visual image. When the Thebans invaded Lakonia in the aftermath of the battle, the Spartans were forced to make an even clearer demonstration of their fewness. Using their utmost numbers to defend their home villages the Spartans, in Xenophon's significant phrase, "both *were* very few and were *seen* to be".[241] By publicising Spartan numbers and Spartan losses Thebes perhaps did as much to undermine the power of her enemy as she did by winning at Leuktra and by freeing the Messenian helots. The illusion of Spartan strength, for long sustained with systematic ingenuity, was now at an end.

Population size and distribution of wealth

The size of the Spartan citizen population at different times forms an obscure subject, as the secrecy of Sparta might lead us to expect. However, it is widely accepted by scholars that citizen numbers declined markedly in the period 479–371.[242] Aristotle, writing some years after the end of that period, referred to the Spartans as unable to field even 1,000 citizen soldiers, although possessing territory capable of supporting 30,000 hoplites and cavalrymen besides.[243] According to Aristotle, some Spartans were exceedingly rich, while others had very little; the land was owned by a wealthy few.[244] Since to be a citizen of Sparta a man needed a certain income from land, the poverty of many might cause citizen numbers to drop. Aristotle seems to attribute the concentration of Spartan wealth, and the shrinking of citizen numbers, to local rules which allowed an estate to be transferred from one family to another as gift, bequest or sole-heiress's inheritance. This evidently contrasted with Athens, where a wealthy heiress, for example, normally married within the wider family. Under Spartan rules, it seems, money tended to marry money, leaving bride, groom and descendants enormously rich, while other blood relatives of the bride were impoverished.

We should like to know the effect on the distribution of wealth, and so on the number of citizens, of the treasure which poured into Sparta as she assumed control of the former Athenian Empire.[245] In a comparable case from the Roman Empire, an effect of Augustus' bringing to Rome vast treasure from conquered Egypt was to drive up prices of Italian land.[246] The question whether there may have been acute inflation at Sparta is complicated by our ignorance of how far the Spartans used coinage, on which there seems to have been a formal ban.[247] Did

242

moderately-off Spartans sell land during the empire, tempted by inflated prices, and thus contribute to their own, or their descendants', eventual impoverishment? According to Aristotle, Spartan rules sought to discourage the sale of land.[248] But a voluntary, illegal, economic transaction is — in the language of sociologists — a "crime without a victim". Since the parties principally concerned would share an interest in deceiving the authorities, the threat of detection may have been so small as not to deter many. Land might change hands as "gift" or even as "dowry" which secretly was being paid for. Private dwellings at Sparta are the likeliest place for illicit money and treasure to have been stored.[249] In this one respect the "Lykourgan" system might have achieved its aim better if private residence had been entirely abolished in favour of life in barracks.

Female citizens

The citizen women of Sparta were believed to lead unusual lives by Greek standards.[250] In trying to reconstruct certain aspects of their existence we have to beware not only of ancient theorists looking for an explanation of Sparta's rapid decline but also, possibly, of our own enthusiasms over a community of women with exceptional access to information and influence.

Discrimination against girls and female babies may well have been less at Sparta than in other parts of Greece. In an incomplete passage of his *Constitution of the Spartans*, Xenophon implies a contrast: whereas other states, he observes, feed girls on a meagre diet.[251] He then passes on to a different point of contrast between the Spartans and other Greeks in respect of the status of females, and fails to make explicit what he evidently understood: that Spartan girls got more nourishment.

Other Greeks, Xenophon continues, require girls to sit quietly and work wool, whereas at Sparta physical training is arranged for females no less than for males; contests of running and of strength exist for each sex.[252] (Elsewhere in Greece the report of such public displays by Spartan girls aroused much disapproving or prurient interest.[253]) We may perhaps think of modern ideals of sexual equality. However, the motive ascribed by our Greek sources to the physical training of girls is far from feminist. Xenophon suggests that the exercise was meant to produce strong mothers, with a view to the production of strong offspring.[254]

Kritias writes similarly.[255]

But we have learnt to distinguish in point of reliability between ancient reports of *what* happened in antiquity and those stating *why* things happened. Is it possible that Xenophon and Kritias have misleadingly assimilated Spartan motives to those of their own society, whether through the common process of misperceiving as familiar what in reality is different, or as a means of commending to non-Spartans an unsympathetic Spartan practice?

In having citizen girls train and reveal their bodies in view of men, Sparta differed greatly from Athens and other Greek cities with their ideals of sexual segregation and feminine modesty. Other Spartan practices, differing even more markedly, are recorded by Xenophon. An elderly husband with a young wife was encouraged to use another man, whose physique and character he admired, to impregnate his wife. And a man wishing not to cohabit with a wife, but desiring fine children, could breed with "any distinguished woman with fine offspring ... once he had persuaded her husband".[256] Sparta breached monogamy, obviously for the sake of producing more and superior children.[257] This gives considerable support to the claim that a eugenic motive lay also behind the physical training of females. Aristotle confirms that Sparta took unusual measures to promote child-rearing, giving exemption from military service and taxation respectively to those who fathered three or four sons.[258] In view of Sparta's attachment to the persuasive use of the visual image, we may even take seriously Plutarch's suggestion, that "the processions of the maidens, their removal of clothes and their contests where young men could see" were intended to incite men to marry.[259] Xenophon, in a different — Athenian — context, describes light-heartedly an erotic tableau involving an athletic slave woman which caused those male onlookers who had not married to swear that they would.[260]

If the physical training of girls at Sparta had arisen from a belief that they should on principle share in honoured activity equally with males, we might expect to find some involvement of females in military drill. But we learn nothing of the kind. The argument from silence here is of unusual force, because there was at Athens (as elsewhere) almost an obsession among men with the idea of warrior women. Herodotos records that the Athenians offered a huge reward, of 10,000 *drakhmai*, for the capture alive of Artemisia, a captain in Xerxes' navy of 480; "for they considered it terrible that a woman should be fighting against Athens".[261]

Athenian vase-painters and sculptors made innumerable representations of the legendary female warriors, the Amazons.[262] The Athenians, who made such play with the partial nudity of Spartan girls at their exercise, would surely have toyed unforgettably with the idea of female Spartan warriors, had there been such.

In the aftermath of Leuktra the army of Thebes approached the villages where the Spartans lived; the behaviour of the Spartan women on this occasion confirms their lack of military training. According to Xenophon, "they could not stand even the sight of the smoke [raised as the Thebans ravaged] because they had never before seen enemies."[263] Aristotle goes further: "they did not make themselves useful, as women do in other cities [during an invasion], but they created more of a confused din than the enemy".[264] While there may be some exaggeration here, caused by theorising about the responsibility of women for Sparta's decline, the two passages together do suggest that the military contribution of female Spartiates on this rare occasion of trial was not praiseworthy. If Sparta had intended its training of girls to produce warlike women, the eminent local knowledge of military drill would have ensured success. The hypothesis of training for motherhood seems confirmed. A possibility remains, however, that the exercising of Spartan women was adopted or retained at least in part because of an eagerness of women themselves to share, within supposed feminine limits, in the prestige of local athleticism. The political influence of women within Sparta seems to have been unusually great by Greek standards. Was it that which produced also the apparent parallelism in Spartan funerary practice, whereby the inscription of a name on a gravestone was allowed only for a man killed in battle or a woman killed by childbirth?[265] In any case, this practice is further evidence of the value placed on motherhood.

About the circumstances in which Spartan girls or women were given in marriage we have little information. There is some suggestion that a female Spartiate married on average a few years later than her Athenian counterpart.[266] It has been argued that Spartan women owned their own dowries, which again would involve a difference from Athens.[267] Aristotle, censuring Sparta for her economic arrangements, states that "nearly two-fifths of the whole country belongs to women, because there are many sole heiresses and also because [Spartans] give large dowries."[268] A sole heiress, as we have seen, may often have married a man

outside her own wider family. She might thus be less constrained
by her family from threatening or going through with divorce, as
compared with an Athenian heiress married to one of her own
kin. The threat of divorce, when seen as realistic, gave power to a
woman who had brought her husband great wealth;[269] other
things being equal, the greater the wealth, the greater the power
would be. It should be stressed that we do not know whether
Spartan women had the power to effect divorce purely through
their own will. But if, like Athenian women, they had, then that
fact — when combined with the large number of sole heiresses
and of other women with large dowries — may be sufficient to
explain Aristotle's indignant remark about female ownership of
much Spartan land. No formal ownership of great wealth by
women need perhaps be posited.

Aristotle complained about the freedom enjoyed by Spartan
women. He reported a saying that Lykourgos had tried to subject
the women to his rules, but had given up on meeting feminine
resistance.[270] This, of course, may tell us more about the classical
period than about the mythical lawgiver. Like Plato, Aristotle
considered it a serious fault in Sparta that only the male part of
the population had — in his opinion — been regulated, and used
a word from the root *tryph-*, connoting luxurious living, to
describe the extravagance and indiscipline of the Spartan
women.[271] However, it seems that the only satisfying detail which
we possess on this subject is that concerning expenditure by
women on horse-racing.

We have already encountered three facts which may have
caused Spartan women to be more assertive outside the home
than those of other cities: their financial position, their outdoor
training and the absence abroad of many men in the period of
Sparta's empire. Among his disapproving comments, Aristotle
writes: "during the period of their [the Spartans'] empire, many
things were administered by the women. Yet what is the difference between having rulers who are ruled by women and an actual
government of women?"[272] The premiss that female government
would be absurd is considered by Aristotle to be so obvious and
cogent that he does not trouble even to make it explicit; we recall
his remark in another context on the inherent inferiority of
women's intelligence.[273] Sadly, this statement about the Spartan
empire also lacks any detailed illustration; we shall probably
never know which decisions during Sparta's ascendancy Aristotle
would have attributed to *gynaikokratia*,[274] government by women.

Perioikoi

Little is known, either, of the *perioikoi*, free people but not citizens of Sparta, who lived in Spartan territory. Their name means literally 'those who live around'; they seem, that is, to be defined in terms of the Spartiates, whom they may well have outnumbered. Herodotos records that 5,000 *perioikoi* went as hoplites to the battle of Plataia in 479, the same number as he gives for the Spartiate force there.[275] But whereas most of the male Spartiate population of fighting age would be in the latter force, we cannot assume that the hoplite *perioikoi* made a majority of *their* able-bodied male population. Elsewhere in Greece it was normal for hoplites to be outnumbered by a mass of the poor. Evidently some *perioikoi* were wealthy; Xenophon writes of a Spartan expedition in the early fourth century which attracted many perioikic volunteers who were *kaloi kagathoi* — a regular expression for aristocrats or stylish gentry.[276] Since the late fifth century the *perioikoi* may well have formed a majority of those armies which our Greek sources describe simply as *hoi Lakedaimonioi* ('the Spartans').[277] If the *perioikoi* were indeed integrated into Sparta's hoplite formation, that would say much both about their loyalty and about the amount of time they spent in military training. A phalanx which lost its coherence was, in Aristotle's word, "useless",[278] and the Spartiates could not risk their difficult manoeuvres ending in disarray through the presence of *perioikoi* who were uncooperative or untrained.

A *perioikos* named Phrynis was, in 413/2, trusted by the Spartan authorities to assess the military situation on the isle of Khios; on the strength of his report Sparta was willing to risk a fleet.[279] Another *perioikos*, one Deiniadas, commanded a fleet for Sparta at the same period.[280] Sections of the *perioikoi* did rebel against Sparta on occasion.[281] But even during the Theban invasion of 370–369, the best opportunity for revolt in almost a century, many — probably a majority — stayed loyal.[282] The fidelity, military skill and numbers of the *perioikoi* were very likely crucial for the Spartiates in their efforts, before the Theban invasion, to keep the helots in check. In explaining the loyalty of the *perioikoi* we should note the prosperity which allowed them to be hoplites or even gentry, and also the sense of social superiority to the helots, which might compensate for feelings of resentment towards the ultimate masters, the Spartiates.[283] Also, *perioikoi* were scattered in many communities, describable in the post-

miniature *poleis*.[284] We have seen that elsewhere in the Peloponnese Sparta insisted on allies — who were potential enemies — living dispersed rather than in a centralised community.[285] Evidently that policy of divide and rule might have its uses nearer home. It would impede cooperation between the *perioikoi* and would make it at least as hard for the helots to assess the numbers of *perioikoi* as it was to count the Spartiates.

The helots

There is little doubt that both these groups were far outnumbered by the helots. Xenophon has the rebellious non-Spartiate Kinadon point, in a very Spartan use of the visual, to the spectacle of Spartiates in their market-place massively out-numbered by social inferiors;[286] of these, helots probably formed the great majority. Herodotos, it will be recalled, wrote of seven helots present for every Spartiate at the battle of Plataia, where Sparta's citizen army must have approached full strength.[287] The labour of helot women freed female Spartiates from much domestic work; when Xenophon mentions the physical training and athletics on which Spartiate women spent time, he says in explanation that "Lykourgos believed that female slaves would suffice for producing clothes."[288] (On helots described as slaves, see below.) As we saw in an earlier chapter, the militarised way of life of Spartiate men was made both possible and necessary by the mass of helots.[289] The helots worked the fields for the Spartans, as Aristotle makes clear.[290] The extreme distaste of the Spartans for manual crafts (other than military), which Herodotos records,[291] no doubt reflected the concentration of such work in helot hands. These, then, were the people who fed and clothed the Spartiates. Yet our ignorance about them is exemplified by the fact that we do not know, from our literary sources at least,[292] the name of a single individual helot from the classical period. Occasionally an individual may be traceable, such as the woman of Aulon who (according to Xenophon) "was said to be the most beautiful in the place, and was apparently seducing Spartans old and young who went there".[293] But even in this case we cannot be sure that the (unnamed) woman was a helot rather than one of the *perioikoi*.

Some fundamental aspects of helot status are revealed clearly, if obliquely, by Thucydides. In the 420s, as an exceptional measure, some 700 helots had been given arms and sent to campaign under the command of Brasidas.[294] They were rewarded thus: "The Spartans voted that the helots who had fought with Brasidas should be free and should live wherever they wanted."[295] From which we infer that other helots were not free and did not have a free choice of domicile. Two of the commonest Greek words for a chattel slave are *doulos* and *oiketēs*; Thucydides strongly suggests that each of them could be applied to a helot.[296] However, in later antiquity it was believed that the helots had a rather different status from the slaves of other Greek cities, perhaps because Sparta regarded them as the property of the state rather than of individual citizens.[297]

On the conditions in which helots worked, on the land or in houses, we have virtually no detailed information. The poet Tyrtaios, composing perhaps in the late seventh century, referred to helots as burdened like donkeys and as having to hand over to their masters half of what they produced on the land.[298] This proportion is so large that some have thought it the result of an unusual emergency rather than the regular rate of impost. Part of the role of helot women was probably the bearing, and perhaps the rearing, of illegitimate children sired by Spartiates. Xenophon writes pointedly of the numerous "bastards of the Spartiates, fine looking men with some share in the noble aspects of the city's way of life", who took part in a Spartan military expedition of the early fourth century.[299] If these men had been descended on both sides from Spartiate parents, mating perhaps according to the unusual arrangements described in the *Constitution of the Spartans*, Xenophon might scarcely have felt a need to assert that they had a fine bodily appearance. More likely their mothers were helots, who may perhaps have raised their own status a little in cases where a father felt some pride in a son.[300]

The treatment of the helots by their masters was regarded as harsh by Plato and Aristotle.[301] The typical Spartiate was described by the former as gentle to free men but "savage to slaves *(douloi)*, not considering them beneath his dignity as a properly educated man does". Aristotle referred to the helots as having lives full of suffering, plotting against and hating the Spartiates. Citing sections of Aristotle's work, of which the originals are now lost, Plutarch states that the ephors, on entering office (each year), declared war on the helots, so that killing them would be religiously permissible. He also describes the practice known as the *krypteia* ('secret').[302] According to Plutarch (and, it may well be, according to Aristotle) this involved young men, chosen by the Spartan authorities for their brains, going into the countryside equipped only with food and daggers. They killed any helot they caught on the roads at night, and often went into the fields and killed the strongest helots there.[303] Killing the strongest suggests a considered system; a policy of terrorising helots into political abjectness by removing potential leaders. The principle of cowing one's subjects by murdering the most eminent may have been familiar in Greece; Herodotos significantly refers to it as a device for maintaining tyranny.[304] We shall consider in a moment an episode described by Thucydides which reflects a rather similar policy. But what was the point of killing any helot caught on the roads at night? Sheer intimidation, perhaps. But it would make more sense to assume that the helots were under curfew, as a means of checking brigandage and seditious movements. Any helot travelling at night would then have invaded the sphere of the lords of darkness.

In 424, with Athenians at the coastal base of Pylos in Messenia encouraging helots to defect,[305] Sparta was under unusual pressure. In this connection Thucydides makes his general remark about the precautionary nature of Spartan arrangements *vis-à-vis* the helots,[306] and goes on to record an incident which arose (apparently at this time or a little before) from Sparta's fear of "the intractability and the sheer number" of the helots. The Spartans made a proclamation to the latter, calling on them

> to select whoever of them claimed to have proved outstand-ing in Sparta's interest in war, as they [the Spartans] were going to free them. They [the Spartans] did this as a test, thinking that the men with the spirit to think themselves worthy of being freed first were the ones likeliest to attack them. Having made the selection to the number of 2,000 or thereabouts, the helots for their part put on celebratory garlands and went round the temples, as men who had gained their freedom; but the Spartans not long afterwards did away with them, leaving it mysterious how each of them was killed.[307]

If we react to this episode with revulsion, we may be tempted to compare it with the best-known episode of twentieth-century depravity. That, however, would distort the picture of Sparta. There was no question of a Final Solution for helots, because the Spartan economy palpably depended on them. (The episode gives a further check on helot numbers, in relation to those of the Spartiates. The latter may have numbered fewer than 3,000 — males of fighting age — by this period, yet they evidently reckoned that they could kill 2,000 of the most impressive helots, and emancipate hundreds more after service with Brasidas, without spoiling their own economy.) While not preventing the occasional massacre, Sparta's economic dependence would restrict the frequency of such killing. In Thucydides' episode, the Spartans outraged the feeling of just claim which their freely given promise must have engendered, and rewarded conspicuous service with murder. One cannot do such things very often without dissolving a society. To be restrained from desperate attempts to "eat the Spartans raw" (in a phrase reported by Xenophon[308]), helots had to be convinced that probably neither they nor their close relatives would be slaughtered. The organisation and secrecy, with which the Spartans were able to kill something approaching their own number of vigorous men, are noteworthy in themselves. However, although they succeeded in denying their intended victims enough warning to take evasive action, the facts in outline of course emerged with time. Relations with the helots thereafter would need a long convalescence.[309]

In some respects, as we have seen,[310] helots had more in common with the poor citizens of other Greek states than they did with the slaves there. Helots were Greek, they greatly outnumbered their rulers, and the Messenians at least among them had corporate and traditional aspirations to freedom. In describing the conflict within Greek cities, between the impoverished majority of citizens and the wealthy few, Thucydides says — in a famous passage — "social conflict involved numerous harsh developments for the cities, such as happen and will always happen, so long as human nature remains the same."[311] Thucydides' prescience may be appreciated if we compare his and other testimony on social conflict in Greece with aspects of the warfare between rich and poor in modern Latin America, where the wealthy few are often referred to by a revived Greek word, *oligarquía*. The verb Thucydides uses for the Spartan treatment of the 2,000, *aphanizo* ('make to disappear'), has a striking parallel in contemporary Spanish. The 'disappeared ones', *desaparecidōs*, are a conversational commonplace in Latin America. The following is from a modern partisan source on El Salvador:

One technician of the government's Institute for Agricultural Transformation tells the following story: 'The troops came and told the workers the land was theirs now. They could elect their own leaders and run the co-ops. The peasants couldn't believe their ears but they held elections that very night. The next morning the troops came back and I watched as they shot every one of the elected leaders.'[312]

This may be mere folklore, though Thucydides' precedent should make us pause. In any case, with their visual propaganda and their state secrecy, their efficient deceits and mass killings, there is without doubt something very modern about the Spartans.[313]

Notes

1. Arist. *Pol*. 1333b. Kritias' work on Sparta (see below) dates from the late fifth century.
2. Xen. *Const. Spart*. I.
3. Thuc. I 18 1.
4. Above, Chapter 4.
5. Thuc. II 39 1. On the *xenēlasia*, see below.
6. P. Cartledge, *Sparta and Lakonia*, 275f.
7. Thuc. II 8 4, IV 81 2f., cf. 111 57 1.
8. Cf. T. Rutherford Harley, 'The public school of Sparta' in *Greece and Rome*, III (1934) 129ff. The comparison, though not well made by Harley, does have some value.
9. Xen. *Hell*. I 6 36f.; IV 3 13f.
10. Thuc. IV 80 3f., on which see below.
11. Xen. *Hell*. III 3 8ff.
12. Isok. VI 81; Plat. *Laws* 666e; Plut. *Life of Lykourgos* XXIV 1; cf. Arist. *Pol*. 1324b.
13. Cf. Virgil, *Aeneid* II 390.
14. Xen. *Ages*. I 17.
15. See, e.g., above, Chapter 4, nn. 122f.
16. Xen. *Ages*. I 10ff.
17. See esp. Thuc. VII 18 2.
18. Xen. *Hell*.II 1 22–8. Compare King Kleomenes at Sepeia; Hdt. VI 77f.
19. Xen. *Hell*. IV 4 10; Arist. *Nik. Eth*. 1117a.
20. See below.
21. Thuc. V 9 5.
22. It will be argued below that juvenile theft was itself seen by Spartans as a training for guerrilla.
23. Plut. *Life of Lykourgos*. XVIII 1.
24. Aristoph. *Peace* 1067f.
25. Thuc. V 45.
26. Xen. *Hell*. VI 2 31. Further on Sparta's reputation for deceit: Hdt. IX 54; Thuc. II 39 1; Eur. *Andromakhē* 446ff.
27. E.g. Hdt. I 65 2ff.; Xen. *Const. Spart*. I 2 and *passim*, *Ages*. I 4. Contrast Arist. *Pol*. 1313a on the establishment of the ephorate.

28. Thuc. I 1 3, discussed above, Chapter 1.

29. Thuc. I 18 1.

30. Above, n. 27.

31. *Life of Lykourgos* I 1. The element 'Lyk-' in the name meant 'wolf'. It may be significant that two other militaristic peoples, the Romans and the Turks, have given a prominent role to a wolf in their respective foundation myths.

32. For references, P. Oliva, *Sparta and her social problems*, 63–70. Sensibly sceptical remarks on Sparta's early history have been made recently by M. I. Finley, *The use and abuse of history* 161f., C. G. Starr, *Historia*, XIV (1965), 257–72.

33. Compare the suggestion of Xen. *Const. Spart.* VII that Lykourgos knew about coinage and took measures against it. Coinage in Greece appears not to antedate the late seventh century, whereas many of those who take Lykourgos seriously date him considerably earlier.

34. Xen. *Hell*. III 4 2, cf. II 3 2, V 2 7.

35. Thuc. I 19.

36. Thuc. I 84 3, cf. Plat. *Laws* 634d–e. Plato suggests (*Hippias Major* 285d) that the Spartans liked stories involving genealogy, a genre notoriously contrived to evoke awe for contemporary arrangements by stressing the antiquity and nobility of their roots. Officially, Spartan kings were descended from Herakles (e.g. Hdt. VIII 131; Xen. *Ages*. I 2). However, some reforms were remembered as post-Lykourgan; Hdt. V 75 2; Xen. *Const. Spart.* XII 3f; cf. Arist. *Pol.* 1313a.

37. Samuel Pepys, *Diary*, entry for 3 April 1667.

38. Plut. *Life of Lykourgos* XVI.

39. Spartan practices are sometimes compared closely with those of supposedly primitive peoples in recent times; see, e.g., H. Jeanmaire, *REG*, XXVI (1913), 121–50. It is, however, a highly subjective and dangerous procedure to identify particular Spartan customs as primitive and therefore as already of great antiquity by the start of the classical period. Finley rightly suggests that a traditional practice which survived into classical times is likely to have retained some social value (op. cit., 164). To which we might add that if the social value could cause the retention of something 'primitive' in the fifth or fourth century, it might perhaps cause the *invention* then of some such thing. But the category 'primitive' is probably best abandoned, as too vague.

40. Xen. *Const. Spart.* XIV.

41. On Plutarch as a source for Spartan history, E. N. Tigerstedt, *The legend of Sparta in classical antiquity*, II, 226–64.

42. See above, Chapter 4.

43. Thuc. I 22 3.

44. J. K. Anderson, *Xenophon* 147–9.

45. Ibid., 165.

46. Diogenes Laertius II 54.

47. Most notably, their failure to prevent the secession, in 370 or 369, of Messenia.

48. Cf. E. Rawson, *The Spartan tradition in European thought*, 64: "it is possible crudely to equate the Gerousia to [Plato's] guardians, the *homoioi* to [his] auxiliaries and the *perioeci* and helots to Plato's artisans".

To which may be added (e.g.) Plato's ideas on literary censorship and salutary deceit. On Aristotle, ibid., 72.

49. Xen. *Const. Spart.* XIV.
50. Plat. *Rep.* 548a–b.
51. See below.
52. Arist. *Pol.* 1271b, 1338b.
53. Ibid., 1270a.
54. Xen. *Hell.* V 4 1.
55. Above, Chapter 5.
56. Like much else in the psychology of partisanship, this may be clearly seen nowadays at a football match. Disappointed supporters more readily jeer their own side than applaud the opposition; afterwards, 'We were awful' is far commoner than 'They were good'.
57. See below, chapter 7.
58. Thuc. I 18 1.
59. On Argos, see especially Diod. XV 57 3 — 58 4; on Kerkyra, Thuc. III 70–81, IV 46ff.
60. Chapter 4.
61. Thuc. IV 80 3.
62. Cf. Gomme, *HCT*, III, 547f.
63. G. E. M. de Ste. Croix, *Origins*, 92.
64. On the Spartans, see above, Chapter 4; on the helots, Arist. *Pol.* 1269a.
65. For a subtle and wide-ranging review of internal tensions which Sparta had to overcome, S. Hodkinson, *Chiron*, 13 (1983) 239–81.
66. E.g. Hdt. I 65 5; Xen. *Const. Spart.* V 2–7; cf. Alkman quoted at Strabo X 482.
67. Xen. op. cit. V 7.
68. Arist. *Pol.* 1271a, which refers to the arrangement as "ancestral". However, cf. Xen. *Const. Spart.* X 7 (a vaguer, idealising, passage).
69. Xen. *Const. Spart.* X 7.
70. Cf. Xen. *Const. Spart.* V 2. A similar rationale has been put forward in our own day for preserving communal dining among members of Cambridge colleges and trainee barristers at the Inns of Court.
71. E.g. Xen. *Hell.* III 3 5, *Const. Spart.* X 7, XIII 1.
72. Xen. *Const. Spart.* V 5.
73. Thuc. VI 18 6; cf. Xen. *Mem.* III 5 15; W. G. Forrest, *Yale Classical Studies*, XXIV (1975), 37–52.
74. Hdt. II 80 1.
75. Xen. *Const. Spart.* X 2 (the old more respected than those physically in their prime); Arist. *Pol.* 1270b (senility and the *gerousia*); cf. Xen. *Hell.* V 3 20, *Const. Spart.* XIII 7; Plat. *Laws* 634d–e. See de Ste. Croix, *Origins*, (index, under *Sparta; Gerousia*).
76. Plat. *Laws* 634d–e.
77. As, e.g., in Communist Russia and National Socialist Germany.
78. See above, n.48.
79. Plat. *Rep.* 463c ff.
80. Arist. *Pol.* 1313b.
81. R. Grunberger, *Social history of the Third Reich*, 151f.

82. Gustav Heinemann.

83. Xen. *Const. Spart.* I 5.

84. Cf. the idea expressed in *King Lear* (Act I, scene 2), that bastards get from the circumstances of their conception a superior vigour as compared with the legitimate, "got [conceived] 'tween asleep and wake".

85. Xen. *Const. Spart.* V 7; Plat. *Laws* 633c; cf. Thuc. IV 103 1, 110 1, 135 1, V 58 2, VII 4 2; Diod. XIII 72 3.

86. See below.

87. According to one modern suggestion, by effectively not recognising a marriage in its early stages the Spartans sought to facilitate divorce in cases of infertility; W. K. Lacey, *The family in classical Greece*, 198.

88. Below, and nn. 176f.

89. P. A. Cartledge, *Proceedings of the Cambridge Philological Society*, 27 (1981), 17–36.

90. Plat. *Laws* 636a–c.

91. Xen. *Const. Spart.* II 13.

92. At *Hell.* V 3 20 the word *paidikōn* may refer to homosexual boyfriends (as de Ste. Croix suggests, *Origins*, 140) or, as often, merely to things of childhood.

93. Plut. *Life of Lykourgos* XV 10.

94. Arist. *Pol.* 1269b.

95. Ibid.

96. Further on Spartan women, see below.

97. In general on the openness of homosexuality in archaic and classical Greece see K. J. Dover, *Greek homosexuality, passim* and especially the evidence cited there from vase-painting.

· 98. Thuc. I 132 5. The person in question was not a Spartiate.

99. *Hell.* V 4 25. Xenophon evidently felt some awkwardness over Agesilaos' own relations with the ardent Persian boy Megabates; *Ages.* V 4–7 (cf. esp. 6 with *Const. Spart.* II 14); cf. *Hell.* IV 1 39f. (Agesilaos' regard for another youth, "still at the desirable age").

100. Xen. *Hell.* V 4 57.

101. Cf. Xen. *Symposion* VIII 34f.

102. Xen. *Hell.* V 4 33.

103. Xen. *Hell.* IV 8 38f.

104. Xen. *Const. Spart.* V 3; Arist. *Pol.* 1294b. On the kings' double rations, Xen., op. cit. XV 4.

105. E.g. Hdt. IX 82. Tales proliferated, as of the visitor from luxurious Sybaris, who felt he had at last understood the Spartans' willingness to die in battle when he had experienced one of the meals on which they had to live; Athenaeus 518e.

106. Plat. *Rep.* 551d, 556d; cf. 422e–423a.

107. Aristophanes' *Wasps* gives a lively comic sketch of a vehement democrat converted into an arrogant oligarch by attending a symposion; esp. 1326–449; cf. N. R. E. Fisher in Powell (ed.), *Classical Sparta*.

108. Suetonius *Life of the Divine Julius* 53. Cf. Arist. *Nik. Eth.* 1117a.

109. Plat. *Laws* 637a–b.

110. 'Xen. *Ages.* V 1; cf. *Const. Spart.* V 4.

111. In H. Diels — W. Kranz, *Die Fragmente der Vorsokratiker*, 88, no.

6; translated by K. Freeman, *Ancilla to the pre-Socratic philosophers*, 154f. Cf. Plat. *Laws* 637b for communal drunkenness at Sparta's colony Taras (later Tarentum), at a festival; Sparta herself is contrasted.

112. Pittakos, the anti-aristocratic ruler of Mytilēnē, made famously severe regulations against drunkenness; Arist. *Pol.* 1274b, *Rhet.* 1402b.

113. Arist. *Pol.* 1294b.

114. Thuc. I 6 4.

115. Xen. *Const. Spart.* VI 3; Arist. *Pol.* 1263a.

116. [Arist.] *Ath. Pol.* 50 2.

117. S. C. Humphreys, *JHS*, 100 (1980), 96–126.

118. See esp. Aristoph. *Clouds* 63ff.

119. Xen. *Hell.* II 3 10; III 4 6; I 1 23; I 1 32; III 2 29; VI 2 4; IV 2 8 etc. See now S. Hodkinson in Powell (ed.), *Classical Sparta*.

120. Xen. *Hell.* VI 4 10f., cf. *Ages.* IX 6. The mobility given by the horse might allow Spartiates to combine supervision of their large estates with the necessary attendance at Sparta itself. Also, mounted Spartans would present an intimidating spectacle to helots.

121. E.g. de Ste. Croix, *Origins*, 355; Cartledge, *Sparta and Lakonia* (n. 6), 233.

122. Xen. *Ages.* IX 6.

123. Pausan. III 8 1, 15 1, 17 6, V 12 5.

124. Xen. *Const. Spart.* V 2.

125. Sparta is very likely the target of the remarks in the Periklean funeral speech (Thuc. II 37 2) about suspicion and disapproval directed against fellow citizens who sometimes allow themselves to relax; cf. Xen. *Const. Spart.* IV 4.

126. Thuc. II 39 1.

127. Xen. *Const. Spart.* XI 5.

128. Ibid., 8.

129. Ibid., 7.

130. Chapter 4.

131. Thuc. II 39 1: "we [Athenians] never use exclusion of foreigners (*xenēlasiai*) to prevent anyone from learning or seeing something which, being revealed, it would profit an enemy to see; we rely not for the most part on preparation and deceit but rather on spontaneous courage".

132. See the references collected by H. Schaefer in Pauly-Wissowa-Kroll, *RE* (article under *xenēlasia*).

133. Xen. *Const. Spart.* XIV 4.

134. Cf. Xen. *Hell.* II 2 13, 19, on the use of Sellasia.

135. Thuc. II 13 1 makes it clear that King Arkhidamos of Sparta was *xenos* of Perikles. The institution of *xenia* involved the exchange of hospitality.

136. Hdt. VII 146f.

137. See below.

138. Arist. *Pol.* 1337a.

139. Xen. *Const. Spart.* III 3, cf. X 7.

140. Thuc. II 39 1, cf. 4 and I 84 3, where King Arkhidamos is reported as speaking of the severity (*khalepotēs*) of the Spartan upbringing.

141. Arist. *Pol.* 1338b.

142. Ibid., 1270a.

143. Aristotle might perhaps have argued that the narrowness of the Spartan education blinded the community to the danger of the declining population.

144. Cf. Thuc. I 84 4.

145. Xen. *Const. Spart.* II 2; cf. Thuc. I 84 3. *Aidōs* was recognised as a divinity at Sparta; Xen. *Symp.* VIII 35.

146. Eur. *Hipp.* 385–7. At the Nuremberg trials after the Second World War, obedience to orders was ruled unacceptable as a defence to charges of war crimes. In other words, international law — as defined by the presiding powers — required (on pair of death) that certain orders be disobeyed or evaded.

147. See below.

148. Xen. *Const. Spart.* II 2.

149. Xenophon has a word for it, used several times — *rhadiourgein* (*Const. Spart.* II 2, IV 4, V 2, XIV 4).

150. Ibid. II 2.

151. Ibid.

152. Xen. *Const. Spart.* II 9, *Anab.* IV 6 15; Plat. *Laws* 633b.

153. Plat. *Rep.* 548b.

154. Xen. *Const. Spart.* II 3f.

155. Ibid., 5–7; *Anab.* IV 6 14f.

156. Xen. *Const. Spart.* II 8.

157. Ibid., 7.

158. Ibid., XII 4.

159. Thuc. IV 41 3.

160. Thuc. IV 9 1, cf. 53 3.

161. Plat. *Rep.* 550e, cf. Thuc. VIII 89 3.

162. Above, Chapter 4.

163. A personal reminiscence. A nephew, when aged about nine, told me that God would do such-and-such. I said that I wasn't sure there was a god. He replied, "But Mummy says there's a God. (*pause*) And she's older than you!" Adult Spartans would have understood; see, e.g., Plat. *Laws* 634d–e.

164. C. M. Tazelaar, *Mnemosyne*, 20 (1967), 127–53.

165. See above, nn. 74f.

166. Xen. *Const. Spart.* IV 2ff.

167. Ibid., 6.

168. Thuc. IV 40 1.

169. Hdt. VIII 124 3; Thuc. V 72 4; Xen. *Const. Spart.* IV 3.

170. Xen. *Hell.* IV 8 39.

171. Xen. *Hell.* IV 4 10; cf. the case of Khalkideus, Thuc. VIII 24 1.

172. Xen. *Hell.* VI 2 22.

173. Ibid., V 4 45.

174. Ibid., V 2 28.

175. Tyrtaios in *Elegy and iambus*, ed. J. M. Edmonds, I, 68–73. On '*Viva la Muerte*' and a famous reaction to it, H. Thomas, *The Spanish civil war*, Ch. 29.

176. Xen. *Hell.* IV 5 10.

177. Ibid. VI 4 16.

178. Ibid. II 2 3.
179. Below, n. 265.
180. Thuc. II 42 2f.
181. Hdt. VII 231f., IX 71.
182. Thuc. V 9 9.
183. Xen. *Const. Spart.* IX 5.
184. For ancient comparisons of the Spartans with children, Plat. *Rep.* 548b; Arist. *Pol.* 1270b (on which see below).
185. We hear of a work by King Pausanias, from the early fourth century. But that, significantly, was produced in exile; Strabo 366.
186. See now P. A. Cartledge, *JHS*, XCVIII (1978), 25–37.
187. For references, Cartledge, loc. cit.
188. Thuc. I 128 6f., 131 1, 132 5–133. Implausible though parts of this story may be, Thucydides' belief in the possibility of written messages is important.
189. Xen. *Hell.* I 1 23. An alternative reading of the first phrase gives 'The ships are lost.'
190. Chapter 4, n.13.
191. Thuc. II 40 2.
192. Ibid. 40 1.
193. Thuc. IV 84 2.
194. Thuc. V 9 10.
195. Thuc. V 69 2. In Sophokles' *Ajax* the Spartan character Menelaos is made to say that it would be disgraceful for him to be thought to use words when he could use force instead; 1159f. Cf. 1142–9 with the words attributed by Thucydides to Brasidas (V 9 10).
196. Cf. Hdt. III 46; Ion of Khios frag. 107 (ed. A. von Blumenthal); Plat. *Protag.* 342e.
197. See, e.g., Plutarch's *Apophthegms of Spartans* (*Moralia* 208b–236e) and *Apophthegms of Spartan women* (*Moralia* 240c–242d); E. N. Tigerstedt, *The legend of Sparta in classical antiquity*, II, 16–30.
198. Thuc. IV 40 2. The word used here for 'arrow' also meant 'spindle'.
199. In Nazi Germany Dr P. J. Goebbels, Minister of Propaganda and Public Enlightenment, organised a well-publicised bonfire of socialist and "Jewish" literature.
200. Cf. A. Gide, *The immoralist*, pt. 2, ch. 2: "one always has to be alone to invent anything".
201. E.g. J.-B. Bossuet, *Histoire des variations des églises protestantes*. The Catholic poet G. K. Chesterton, in *Lepanto*, contrasted Protestant northern Europe, "full of tangled things and texts and aching eyes" with the martial simplicity of a hero from the Catholic south, Don John of Austria, "riding to the sea ... calling through the blast ... crying with the trumpet".
202. Plat. *Rep.* 557c–d; compare Aristotle's disapproval of "everyone living as he likes" under *dēmokratia* (*Pol.* 1319b).
203. Soph. *Ajax* 1073–87.
204. Arist. *Pol.* 1270b; cf. Plut. *Life of Lykourgos* 13 1ff.
205. Arist., ibid.; Xen. *Const. Spart.* VIII 4; Plat. *Laws* 712d.
206. Whence the conscious paradox of Thucydides' remark that the

tyrants of Athens showed respect for the city's laws; VI 54 6, cf. [Arist.] *Ath. Pol.* XVI.

207. Thuc. I 132 5.
208. Cf. Xen. *Hell.* V 4 32.
209. Cf. V 105 4. Plato makes a similar distinction concerning Sparta, explicitly; *Rep.* 549a.
210. Thuc. V 34 2. The thing which, it was feared, might make the former prisoners-of-war subversive was their own fear of being degraded. The Spartans in this way made a problem for themselves; their constitution simply was not equipped for mass surrendering.
211. Thuc. I 18 1.
212. Plat. *Rep.* 549a.
213. Xen. *Const. Spart.* VIII 2.
214. Arist. *Pol.* 1270b; on the bribery of ephors, Arist., ibid. and 1272a–b.
215. Arist. *Pol.* 1270b.
216. Ibid., 1272a; de Ste. Croix, *Origins*, 128–30.
217. Thuc. I 85 3 – 87 3; see above, Chapter 4.
218. Thuc. I 87 2.
219. Arist. *Pol.* 1270b.
220. See Plut. *Life of Lykourgos* XXVI (on election to the gerousia).
221. De Ste. Croix, *Origins*, 130, 349.
222. Ibid., 130.
223. Plutarch's account of the way in which volume of shouts was assessed, unlike Thucydides' record of the vote involving Sthenelaïdas, seems to reflect a (post-classical?) attempt to have the assessors judge without prejudice.
224. For a different defence of the shouting, D. M. Lewis, *Sparta and Persia*, 41f.
225. Chapter 4.
226. Cf. Thuc. IV 34 1, V 72 4.
227. Aristoph. *Lysistratē* 1138–41; Xen. *Const. Spart.* XI 3 etc.
228. Arist. fragment 86 at C. Mueller, *Fragmenta historicorum Graecorum*, II, p.130.
229. Xen. *Const. Spart.* XI 3, but cf. Arist. *Rhet.* 1367a.
230. Xen. *Ages.* II 7.
231. Ibid., I 28; *Hell.* III 4 19 is almost identical.
232. Plut. *Life of Lykourgos* XXVIII.
233. Xen *Ages.* I 26f; *Hell.* III 4 16–18 is almost identical; cf *Const. Spart.* XIII 5.
234. Xen. *Hell.* IV 5 18.
235. G. Huxley, *Hermathena*, 128 (1980), 41.
236. Above, Chapter 1.
237. Cf. Hdt. IX 10.
238. Thuc. V 68 2.
239. Xen. *Hell.* III 3 5.
240. Thuc. I 10 2.
241. Xen. *Hell.* VI 5 28. On the Thebans at Leuktra, Plut. *Mor.* 193b, Pausan. IX 13.
242. For initial bibliography on the question of Spartiate numbers see

above, Chapter 4, nn. 15–16.

243. Arist. *Pol.* 1270a.

244. Ibid.

245. E.g. Xen. *Ages.* I 17ff., 34; *Hell.* II 3 8; for circumstances pregnant with bribery: *Hell.* III 1 5, V 3 14, cf. Arist. *Pol.* 1272a–b.

246. Suetonius, *Life of the Divine Augustus* 41.

247. Our sources are confusing. Xenophon (*Const. Spart.* VII 5f.) writes of a ban on the private ownership of gold and silver, and of the use instead of currency which was cumbersome and hard to conceal. Yet the huge fine imposed by the state on King Agis in 418 is expressed by Thucydides in monetary terms (V 63 2, with Gomme-Andrewes-Dover, *HCT*, ad loc.). The state evidently had access to easily portable currency in precious metal; Xen. *Hell.* I 6 9. With an imperial power it could hardly be otherwise. Disobedient individuals no doubt had their own caches; Xen. *Const. Spart.* XIV 3, Plat. *Rep.* 548a–b.

248. Arist. *Pol.* 1270a.

249. See above, n. 247.

250. On Spartan women, P. Cartledge, *CQ*, 31 (1981), 84–105.

251. Xen. *Const. Spart.* I 3.

252. Ibid., 3f.

253. See, for example, the poetical quotations at Plut. *Comparison of Lykourgos and Numa* III 3f.

254. Xen. *Const. Spart.* I 4.

255. Frag. 32 in the editions of Diels-Kranz and Freeman (above, n. 111).

256. Xen. *Const. Spart.* I 8f., cf. Polybius XII 6b 8.

257. Xenophon (loc. cit.) suggests, without being specific, that there were further forms of permitted non-monogamous activity.

258. Arist. *Pol.* 1270b.

259. Plut. *Life of Lykourgos* XV 1.

260. Xen. *Symposion* IX 7.

261. Hdt. VIII 93.

262. Perhaps the best known is Exekias' vase-painting of Penthesileia being killed by Akhilles; British Museum *Catalogue of Greek and Etruscan vases*, II, B210.

263. Xen. *Hell.* VI 5 28.

264. Arist. *Pol.* 1269b. Aristotle's Greek is sometimes taken to mean that women in other cities were themselves useless at such times. For a syntactical parallel relevant to the translation given here, see the last sentence of *Pol.* 1272a (with 1270b). For historical support, Thuc. II 4 2, III 74 1 on the participation of women elsewhere in street fighting.

265. Plut. *Life of Lykourgos* XXVII (emending the text to *lekhous*, in the light of IG V 1 713–14).

266. Plut. *Lyk.* XV 3, cf. Xen. *Const. Spart.* I 6.

267. G. E. M. de Ste. Croix, *Classical Review*, 20 (1970), 277f., cf. 389; D. M. Schaps, *Economic rights of women in ancient Greece*, 43f., 88; cf. P. Cartledge, *CQ*, 31 (1981), 97ff.

268. Arist. *Pol.* 1270a with S. Hodkinson, *CQ*, 36 (1986), 394–404.

269. See Chapter 8.

270. Arist. *Pol.* 1270a.

271. Arist. *Pol.* 1269b; Plat. *Laws* 806c.

272. Arist. *Pol.* 1269b.

273. See Chapter 8.

274. The passive participle *gynaikokratoumenoi* is used at 1269b in connection with the Spartans.

275. Hdt. IX 10f.

276. Xen. *Hell.* V 3 9.

277. Hdt. VII 234; Thuc. IV 54 3; A. Toynbee, *Some problems of Greek history* 365ff.

278. Arist. *Pol.* 1297b.

279. Thuc. VIII 6 4f.

280. Thuc. VIII 22 1.

281. Thuc. I 101 2, cf. IV 54 3; Xen. *Hell.* VI 5 25, 32, VII 2 2, cf. III 3 6.

282. Even when exaggerating Sparta's problems at this stage, Xenophon does not claim that the proportion of *perioikoi* in revolt was a majority (*Hell.* VII 2 2, with the lucid exposition of G. Grote, *History of Greece*, X, Ch. LXXVIII).

283. Aldous Huxley in *Brave new world* gives a useful caricature of social under-classes despising or resenting each other, in a way contrived to perpetuate their subjection.

284. Hdt. VII 234; Strabo VIII 362.

285. Above, Chapter 4. Further on the *perioikoi* see now P. Cartledge, *Sparta and Lakonia*, Ch. X. R. T. Ridley, *Mnemosyne*, XXVII (1974), 281–92 points out the slenderness of our evidence for the economic role of the *perioikoi*.

286. Xen. *Hell.* III 3 5.

287. Hdt. IX 10; cf. Xen. *Hell.* V 5 28f.

288. Xen. *Const. Spart.* I 4.

289. Chapter 4.

290. Arist. *Pol.* 1272a, cf. Plat. *Rep.* 547d.

291. Hdt. II 167, cf. Plat. loc. cit., Arist. *Rhet.* 1367a.

292. For inscriptions identified as relating to manumissions, *IG*, V, 1, nos. 1228–32, with P. Cartledge, *Sparta and Lakonia*, 179–80.

293. Xen. *Hell.* III 3 8.

294. Thuc. IV 80 5, cf. VII 19 3, IV 80 3. Normally the Spartans, like other slave owners, tried to keep their human property away from weapons; Kritias frag. 37 (Diels, Freeman), Xen. *Const. Spart.* XII 4.

295. Th. V 34 1. Not long afterwards the Spartans stationed these former helots on the frontier with Elis, seemingly as a garrison (Thuc., loc. cit.). This does not mean that the men were not fully emancipated. As the experience of nineteenth-century America should remind us, a freed slave has to make a living and for that reason may accept land or employment even from a former master. Political and economic freedom are not the same thing.

296. Thuc. V 23 3 (*doulos*), VIII 40 2 (*oiketēs*); cf. Xen. *Const. Spart.* VI 3, XII 4.

297. Strabo VIII 365; Pausan. III 20 6; cf. Plat. *Alkib.* I 122d.

298. Quoted at Pausan. IV 14 5.

299. Xen. *Hell.* V 3 9.

300. For a treatment of the question whether the obscure group known as *mothakes* were bastards of Spartiate fathers, P. Oliva, *Sparta and her social problems*, 174ff. See the same author (ibid., 166ff.) for references to the similarly obscure *neodamōdeis*, for whom there is evidence from the late fifth and early fourth centuries.

301. Plat. *Rep.* 549a; Arist. *Pol.* 1269b; cf. Kritias frag. 37 (Diels, Freeman).

302. Cf. Plat. *Laws* 633b–c.

303. Plut. *Life of Lykourgos*, XXVIII. In the same chapter Plutarch tries to dissociate Lykourgos from the savagery of the *krypteia*, arguing from the "gentleness" (*praotēs*) of other Lykourgan arrangements. This is the same concept which distorted Plutarch's account of Kimon (see Chapter 1). Perhaps the priest Plutarch was himself a gentle character and, like other biographers down the ages, has falsely imputed his own ideals to his subject.

304. Hdt. V 92.

305. Thuc. IV 41 2f., cf. 3 3, 80 1.

306. Thuc. IV 80 3.

307. Thuc. IV 80 3f.

308. Xen. *Hell.* III 3 6.

309. Cf. Cartledge, *Sparta and Lakonia*, 247.

310. Chapter 4.

311. Thuc. III 82 2.

312. *Socialist Worker* (London) 11 April 1981, 4.

313. There is an interesting collection of parallels to be drawn between the Spartans and the German National Socialists as represented by Hermann Goering, a war hero given to laconic, generalising, pronouncements. Spartans would have applauded Goering's statement that "personal heroism must always count for more than technical novelties" (R. J. Overy, *Goering, the Iron Man*, 13). With the Spartan soldier who, after being defeated by missiles, decried arrows as "spindles" (Thuc. IV 40 2, with Gomme, *HCT*, ad loc.), compare Goering and his pronouncement that radar was "simply a box with wires" (Overy, 199). Spartans professed to prefer deeds to words; Goering stated, "I don't just say I'm going to do something, I actually do it" (Overy, 13). Compare the Nazi idea that to emphasise action was fascist, to emphasise reason bourgeois (ibid.). Spartans boasted of their ignorance; Goering claimed "I am proud of not knowing what justice is" (ibid.). With Sparta's attitude towards Athens, compare Goering's statement that Nazis "were, are and will always be foes to the death against the principle of democracy" (Overy, 23). Sparta was, and is, famous for the extent to which the interests of the community took precedence over those of the individual; Goering stated, "I will be resolved to ignore the fate of individuals if the well-being of the community demands it" (Overy, 51). We have observed certain childlike qualities in the Spartans. Goering was described by a fellow Nazi (Goebbels) as an "upright soldier with the heart of a child" (Overy, 14). A feature of childhood is obedience to authority and the underdevelopment of conscience. The Spartan killers of the 2,000 helots evidently did as they were told. Compare Goering: "I have no conscience. My conscience is Adolf Hitler" (Overy, 231).

7
Athenian *Dēmokratia*

That we study Athens and Sparta is a result in part of the internal stability which each achieved. In a Greek world where civil strife tended to direct energy inwards, Sparta's unique form of oligarchy succeeded in avoiding violent overthrow in Lakonia for centuries, while the Athenian constitution in the classical period was subject only briefly to interruption — by the oligarchic regimes of 411–410 and 404–403. Both states were thus free for much of the time to export their energies, with political consequences which we know. Also, in the case of Athens, there resulted sufficient wealth and leisure to produce the literature and art which give classical Greece much of its lasting interest. But in the methods by which they achieved internal stability, Sparta and Athens differed profoundly. In his *Politics*, Aristotle observes, "When a city contains many men who are excluded from political life and are poor, inevitably that city is full of enemies."[1] Clear-sightedly acknowledging an idea of this kind, Sparta officially recognised as enemies her own excluded and poor Greek population, the helots; a formal declaration of war against them was made each year by the Spartan government.[2] In contrast, Athens dealt with the threat of internal enmity by including the poor in political life. There resulted a constitution noted for "habitual gentleness".[3]

To most observers, ancient and modern, gentleness and political tolerance have seemingly been of less interest than conflict and intolerance. Our source material concentrates largely on discord. Modern taste for conflict (as reflected, for example, in our press) may compound the cognitive bias of the ancient sources, and deflect attention from such peaceable aspects of Athenian life as are recorded. Thus, for example, it has traditionally been found interesting that the Athenians put to death Sokrates.[4] Less attention is given to the tolerance shown by Athens towards Plato, a disciple of Sokrates, a relative of Kritias (the execrated oligarch of 404–403)[5] and the author of sophisti- cated anti-democratic theory.

Athens' achievement of social peace may be played down for a further reason. The internal conflict which most threatened Greek communities was one between rich and poor, and many scholars of recent times have found analysis in those terms uncongenial, probably because it recalls modern social tensions. Of those who do confront the subject, the most important — de Ste. Croix — gives relatively little space to Athens, precisely because of the Athenians' success in mitigating conflict. In his words, "[in Athens] the class struggle on the political plane was probably much milder than in any other Greek city".[6] Yet that mildness was attained by methods which reflect ingenuity on the Athenians' part and deserve study in their own right. Such is the volume of material on Athenian political life, and the range of sources in which it is contained, that the present chapter is inevitably more summary than others in this book. Our interest here is not only in the reconstruction of Athenian procedures but also in relating those procedures to the problems which they were meant to address.[7]

`Athenians called their system *dēmokratia*,[8] which is only crudely translatable as 'democracy'. On the meaning of the ancient term Aristotle makes some helpful comments. He reports that *dēmokratia* was commonly taken to mean rule by the majority (of male citizens, that is), and also personal freedom.[9] The word for freedom in this connection — *eleutheria* — is the one commonly used as the negation of chattel slavery; even the oligarch Kritias is reported as having used it in referring to *dēmokratia*,[10] and thus as apparently having accepted, with the democrats, that the position of the poorer citizens under an oligarchy was comparable with that of slaves.[11] Aristotle, like Plato, noted and deplored the personal diversity which resulted from the freedom of individuals under *dēmokratia* to live as they pleased;[12] the stereotyping achieved by Spartan education made an obvious contrast.[13] Democrats in their rhetoric emphasised the role of the "great mass" (*plēthos*) of citizens under *dēmokratia*,[14] exploiting the fact that the name of the rival system, *oligarkhia*, meant· literally the rule of a few. But in Aristotle's view the application of the terms *dēmokratia* and *oligarkhia* did not depend

Athenian Dēmokratia

simply on whether a *polis* was ruled by a majority or by a minority
of citizens; if a ruling majority were to be rich, that would not
constitute *dēmokratia*, and if a ruling minority were to be poor,
that would not make *oligarkhia*. Instead, the decisive fact was
whether the ruling class of the *polis* was rich or poor; the rule of
the rich (whatever their numbers) was *oligarkhia*, the rule of the
poor (however few) was *dēmokratia*. It happened, however, that
everywhere the rich were few and the poor were many.[15]

Aristotle's words should raise the question how, if *dēmokratia*
was indeed the rule of the poor, under that system the poor could
allow the rich to continue in existence. Why did the poor not seize
their wealth in every case? Aristotle was aware that on occasion
such expropriation did happen.[16] Yet he also writes of the rich
continuing to exist under *dēmokratia*,[17] and indeed of their being
necessary for its survival. At Athens, even after the expulsion of
the oligarchs of 404–403, the democrats behaved with restraint
towards the rich. Remarking on this, Aristotle (or a pupil)
suggests that in any other city democrats in such circumstances
would have undertaken a widespread redistribution of land.[18]
When the Athenians heard of a massacre of the rich carried out by
democrats at Argos in 370, far from celebrating they reportedly
ordered a religious sacrifice to purge Athens of the effects of the
evil report.[19] Although the rich at Athens did come under
pressure at times (as we shall see), the ideal of the integrity of
private property was (at least in the latter part of the fourth
century) expressed in an oath sworn regularly by officials of the
dēmokratia.[20]

The rich in reality had great power in Athens. When
Thucydides describes the damage sustained by rural properties in
Attikē at the start of the Peloponnesian War, he refers to the
dēmos (i.e. the poor) as losing what little it had, while the rich who
lost much are described calmly as *hoi dynatoi* — the powerful
ones.[21] Virtually the same language is used by an anonymous
oligarchic writer in distinguishing between the poor and the rich
(*dynatōtatoi*). He admits, against his bias, that at Athens the latter
were given the highest military offices.[22] In short, *dēmokratia* in
an Athenian context involved a compromise of interests between
different classes. Why the mass of citizens, whose votes were
sovereign, settled for that arrangement, how it worked in practice
and varied from time to time, will be considered below.

We noted in earlier chapters some of the ways in which poorer
citizens of Athens profited from decisions of the assembly;

265

especially in the fifth century, many received land-holdings abroad, pay for military service, and benefits — financial and aesthetic — from a large programme of public works. The democratic constitution will be shown below to have offered further important rewards to the ordinary Athenian, in the form of pay for service in the courts, in allotted office, and (in the fourth century) in the assembly. All this helps to explain the acquiescence of the poor in a *dēmokratia* where the rich retained much influence. Perhaps no less important for social tranquillity was the enhanced social status of the Athenian poor, which we shall try to illustrate, and which some described simply as "freedom". Political aspirations, and the sense of the possible, would be greatly influenced (then as now) by information on what was happening in comparable, and especially neighbouring, states. Sadly little is now known about the constitutional arrangements of most mainland Greek *poleis* in the classical period. But, so far as can be determined, those states provided no relevant model of a secure, happy, *dēmokratia* in which private riches and their influence had been abolished. Reflection on politics beyond his borders is unlikely to have prompted the ordinary Athenian to think of consistent levelling. Instead, the generally prevailing and menacing reality of oligarchy would implant caution and perhaps a complacent thankfulness for the gains which the poor of Athens *had* made.

Population and distribution of wealth

On the size of the adult male citizen population of Athens, and on the distribution of wealth within the citizen body, our information is imprecise and unsatisfactory, but it does in some respects give a roughly consistent picture.[23] Writing about an event of the early 490s BC, Herodotos describes a diplomat as able to prevail upon "30,000 Athenians".[24] The Greek phrase, literally 'three myriads', is obviously an approximation, but an approximation which referred to the whole adult male citizen body and not to the attendance at an assembly.[25] In a comedy of the early fourth century Aristophanes wrote of "more than thirty thousand citizens";[26] Plato used a similar phrase about the size of a dramatic audience in the Athens of the late fifth century.[27] Gomme described the figure of 30,000 for Athenian men as having become "so completely conventional that it is not worth discussion".[28] Conventional and inaccurate it certainly is. But the qualifying phrase 'more than', used by both Aristophanes and Plato, means that they are not merely giving an ossified version of the tradition used by Herodotos. Also, to be conventional, the figure of 30,000 — with or without the qualifying phrase — probably needed to be at least roughly consistent with contemporary Athenian information on the subject. Public opinion on this topic might well be worth something, because in a *polis* the size of the adult male citizen body was closely and obviously related to a political fact of the first importance — the size of its military forces. Admittedly Thucydides on occasion claims to be unable to give figures concerning the mass of poorer citizens;[29] this need not mean, however, that he had no idea on the subject. Rather, he may have been dissatisfied with the level of precision attainable.

It is Thucydides who gives the most reliable and important figures we do have, relating to those Athenians who had enough wealth to provide their own hoplite equipment in 431. He reports Perikles as informing the Athenians that they had at the time 13,000 hoplites, in addition to the 16,000 involved with guarding forts and the walls of Athens itself.[30] Of the 16,000, some were very old or very young citizens, while others were not citizens but metics, members of other states allowed to live at Athens.[31] The population of Athenian citizens had almost certainly grown since the beginning of the fifth century, the period to which Herodotos' figure referred. New wealth, generated by campaigns against Persia and deriving from allies and subjects of Athens around the Aegean, will have increased the number of children that Athenians felt they could afford to rear. We hear that in 451/0 Perikles successfully sponsored a restriction on eligibility for citizenship. In future only those of Athenian citizen parentage on both sides would qualify. (Previously the mother was not required to be a citizen of Athens.) The reason for this change, as given by our source, was "the great number of citizens".[32] However, early in the Peloponnesian War, and shortly after Perikles gave the figures for hoplites which we have noted, the plague killed perhaps a third of the citizen population.[33] Military defeats, as at Delion, Syracuse and Aigospotamoi, also reduced Athenian numbers importantly.

During the oligarchic revolution of 411 it was decided to restrict full rights of citizenship to those who could afford hoplite equipment.[34] Initially it was claimed that this would give a franchise of 5,000;[35] in the event — according to an orator writing a few years later — 9,000 were enrolled.[36] The figure of 9,000 recurs in connection with a later restriction of the franchise. In 322, under the anti-democratic influence of Macedon, full rights of Athenian citizenship were limited to men of a certain wealth; the minimum figure may have been 2,000 *drakhmai*.[37] (At that period an unskilled labourer in full employment might expect to earn some 450 *drakhmai* per annum, a skilled one some 750.[38]) Our sources, which are late, disagree as to the number of Athenians excluded by this arrangement; Diodorus says more than 22,000, Plutarch more than 12,000.[39] But Diodorus gives the number of remaining citizens as about 9,000.[40] The coincidence with the 9,000 recorded of the hoplite enrolment of the late fifth century is interesting; it has been suggested that the property qualification imposed in 322 was not arbitrary but was intended once again to produce a hoplite franchise.[41]

It may seem that the hoplite population of Athens amounted to a highly influential portion — perhaps not far from a third — of the adult male citizenry.[42] At the end of the fifth century, when the reputation of the *dēmokratia* was almost at its lowest, a proposal was made to exclude from citizenship all who owned no land in Attikē. There survives a fragment of a speech made against the proposal. It was probably in the interest of its author to exaggerate as far as he dared the number of citizens who would suffer exclusion; the number he gave was, it seems, 5,000.[43] It appears, then, that the great majority of Athenians owned land in Attikē, even though the amount owned was in many cases small.[44] Rules of inheritance required an estate to be divided equally among surviving sons,[45] a fact which contributed greatly to the wide spread of wealth.

Commentators ancient and modern have stressed the politically stabilising effect of a large landowning class of moderate means. Aristotle, who believed that virtue in general was an intermediate state,[46] argued that such a class could preserve a constitution by throwing its great weight (which, in the case of hoplites, involved effective privately-owned armament) against provocative measures, whether from the very poor or the very rich.[47] He probably had Athens in mind. In the same context he wrote that large cities suffered less than others from *stasis* through having a large intermediate class, and that *dēmokratiai* were more stable than oligarchies for a similar reason.[48] To Aristotle and his readers Athens was the most conspicuous instance both of a large state and of a *dēmokratia*; his generalisations about stability and a large intermediate class could scarcely conflict with the perceived situation of Athens.

The tragedian Euripides has the character Theseus condemn as subversive both the very rich and the very poor, the rich as useless and greedy for more, the poor as enviously provoking the rich.[49] According to Theseus, it is the class in between which preserves cities, guarding whatever form of order a state seeks to impose. Athenians in Euripides' audience sentimentalised over the remote and mythical figure of Theseus, as in some sense a founder of their city's constitution.[50] The ideas assigned to him here by Euripides were meant to be received sympathetically, and may be taken as evidence in themselves that a respect for moderation in wealth was common at Athens in the second half of the fifth century. Solon, a sixth-century politician regarded as another great contributor to the Athenian constitution, owed his excellence as a lawgiver, Aristotle suggests, to his being a member of the group with intermediate wealth.[51] On Solon and the ideal of moderation more will be said below.

Citizens of intermediate wealth, according to Aristotle, did not yearn to possess other people's property, in the way the poor did.[52] If that was true, why was it? On the face of things, those of moderate wealth might hope to profit from being more aggressive. An important recent study has shown that there were at Athens many men far richer than ordinary hoplites. It seems that for a long time the burden of liturgies — expensive personal contributions to such things as public military equipment and public entertainment — fell only on citizens whose private wealth exceeded three talents, that is nine times the amount needed to qualify for citizenship under the oligarchic arrangements of 322.[53] To explain why the hoplites, in spite of such disparities, might be trusted to oppose the expropriation of the very rich, it is not quite sufficient to note that they themselves were not poor. By today's standards many hoplites no doubt lived in wretched conditions. But for determining their social status and outlook, what mattered was their wealth relative to the rest of their own society; a hoplite had the satisfaction of reflecting that most of his fellow citizens had less than he did. He had a privileged position to lose, and in politics the fear of loss is usually more potent than the hope of gain.[54] These two elements, status and the fear of loss, are alluded to by Aristotle in explaining passivity among even the poor: "the poor and those excluded from political office are willing to keep quiet provided that no one treats them with *hybris* (degrading arrogance) or takes away any of their property".[55]

Sources

Before looking in detail at the working of the Athenian system, we need at least a brief review of our source material and of the main historical developments (so far as they are known) within and just before the classical period. Two short ancient works survive under the title *Constitution of Athens*. One, by an unknown author whose work was once attributed to Xenophon, seems to belong to the late fifth century — perhaps the 420s — and makes much reference to the Athenian Empire. Its strong apparent bias has caused its author to become known as the Old Oligarch. His repeated reference to the poor as rogues and to the rich as "the good" will not seriously mislead the critical reader. More deceptive is the work's binary presentation of Athenian politics; as we have already seen, there are important distinctions to be made in addition to that between rich and poor. But on occasion the Old Oligarch has astute things to say. His awareness of the divergent interests of different Athenian groups is one which not all the authors of modern treatises have matched, and he has the virtue, rare in the writer of a political tract, of allowing an important element of rationality in a system which he deplores.[56] Indeed, the work concedes so much to the internal logic of the *dēmokratia* that one should at least raise the question whether its author was himself a democrat, playing devil's advocate. However, a feature which does suggest the work of a genuinely passionate oligarch is the distinction drawn, in point of demerit, between the poor democrat and the rich one. The poor democrat, the author states, is pardonable, because every man can be forgiven for promoting his own interest, "but the man who is not poor and yet prefers to live in a *dēmokratia* rather than in an oligarchy is a man ready to do wrong."[57] It is a commonplace of modern political experience that zealots, and especially frustrated ones, tend to express more rancour against deviants and backsliders from their own group than against the acknowledged enemy.[58]

The *Constitution of Athens* (abbreviated as *Ath. Pol.*), written in the second half of the fourth century by Aristotle, or by a pupil familiar with his style and ideas,[59] makes a less partisan and somewhat more systematic attempt to describe Athenian institutions. We have already noted the probably approving comment of its author on "habitual gentleness". The work, however, is patchy. Much, for example, is said about the empanelling of the courts, whereas there is no direct treatment of the most important · of democratic institutions, the assembly. Democratic politicians are divided, again somewhat schematically, into leaders of the rich and poor respectively, and the list of their names stops near the end of the fifth century rather than continuing to Aristotle's own time.[60] In connection with the fifth century the author is capable of serious error;[61] in contrast, the account of Athenian procedures of his own day — given towards the end of the work — contains much trustworthy detail.

No surviving ancient work gives a thorough and competent account of what the main elements of Athenian *dēmokratia* were meant to achieve. We are left to surmise from scattered hints why Athens rejected the traditional systems of government, oligarchy and tyranny, and preferred cumbersome structures employing citizens *en masse*. While approval of the Athenian constitution is rare in ancient writings, eloquent hostility is common. The concern of Thucydides and of other writers to illustrate failings of *dēmokratia* has contributed to one of the most regrettable defects in the surviving picture of Athens: the lack of proper record of ordinary meetings of the general assembly.[62] The few meetings on which we have much information are exceptional in that the participants would have seen them as of critical importance; also, in most cases they seem to have been selected for description because they were thought to be unusually disreputable. We have suggested elsewhere that Thucydides' account of the Athenian debate on how to treat Mytilenean captives in 427 was meant to illustrate lamentable morality.[63] His record of the debate about Sphakteria in 425 was intended to convey the "madness" of the orator Kleon, and the irresponsibility of the assembly in acting "as a crowd tends to do".[64] The account of the preliminaries to the Sicilian expedition again seems to emphasise the discreditable.[65] Thucydides does, on one occasion, show Perikles making an obviously intelligent speech to the assembly, which accepts his arguments;[66] but the historian weakens any wish in his readers to set this to the credit of *dēmokratia* by observing later that, while in name a *dēmokratia*, Athens under Perikles was becoming in reality the rule of the first man.[67] The meetings of the assembly which Xenophon recounts at great length in his *Hellenika* produced the harshly prejudicial trial of generals who had presided over the naval victory of Arginousai.[68] On Xenophon's own showing the trial was in breach of normal Athenian procedure, and the consequent execution of the generals was later regretted.[69] Demosthenes, an Athenian orator who flourished in the mid-. fourth century, has left a graphic and memorable account of an assembly which met in the crisis of 339/8, when Philip of Macedon invaded central Greece. He emphasises that, when the herald invited speakers to come forward to advise the assembly, no one did.[70]

To come to more recent treatments of ancient Athens: scholarly judgements during the last two centuries have often involved a remarkable compartmentalisation. There has been general and enthusiastic recognition of the intelligence of Athenian drama (and indeed of Athens' surviving literature generally). Athenian strategy during the Persian Wars, and Perikles' military planning later, have likewise been respected. Yet to presume a fundamental intelligence in the workings of Athenian politics and administration has been almost an eccentric act. Grote, who did presume as much, was virtually mocked. (B. B. Rogers, the translator of Aristophanes, coined the word 'grote-esque'.) And, as we have seen, an eminent scholar could write in the *Cambridge Ancient History* that Athens' government of her Empire provided a "warning which gives some slight value to even the worst of failures".[71] There is a paradox here. The audiences which the great dramatists rightly expected to please were mass audiences; indeed, it has been calculated that the Theatre of Dionysos held far more people than could be contained in the assembly.[72] The strategists whose acumen can be demonstrated most satisfactorily, Themistokles and Perikles, were politicians of the assembly, where their intelligence had to be assessed before power was given to them. To assume that surviving ancient accounts have done justice to the governing of Athens would lead to impasse. We might well wonder how a mass audience which sustained such playwrights and politicians could regularly allow unprepossessing scenes such as its ancient critics report in the assembly.

One topic may illustrate the prevailing tone of our source material. Ancient critics converge in accusing the Athenian *dēmokratia* of inconsistency. Early in the Peloponnesian War, Perikles was fined and seemingly deposed from office; Thucydides writes of the Athenians, "not long afterwards, as a crowd is apt to do, they elected him general again and entrusted all their affairs to him".[73] He reports the successful orator Kleon as lecturing the assembly on the dangers of inconsistency.[74] When they learnt the fate of their great Sicilian expedition, the Athenians were angry with the orators who had shared the enthusiasm for sending it, "as if they themselves had not voted for it".[75] The Old Oligarch complains similarly that the *dēmos* can renounce its own earlier decisions and blame the individuals who proposed them, its members claiming that they were not present when a decision was taken and that they do not approve of it.[76] The comedian Aristophanes, a persistent mocker of the radical *dēmokratia*,[77] composes a like charge of inconsistency in connection with the making of Athenian foreign policy in the early fourth century.[78] Antiphon, an orator who became one of the oligarchs of 411, writes that the Athenians had repented of certain executions.[79] Xenophon makes a similar point about the execution of the generals after Arginousai, as we have seen. Plato writes drily of *dēmokratia* allowing men, who had been sentenced at one time to exile or death, to remain in the city, circulating in public as if invisible.[80] His lesser-known namesake, Plato the comic poet, writes — of changes in the law of Athens — "go away for three months and it is no longer the same city".[81]

Some praise of Athens does survive. The freedom of speech enjoyed there is mentioned with notable frequency.[82] But much of the extant praise has a lyric vagueness or the careful dutifulness characteristic of formal public occasions.[83] There is little of the warmth and detail possessed by the many surviving negative criticisms. Yet it would be profoundly wrong to conclude from this that the *dēmokratia* had few positive qualities to offer its citizens. Experience of our own press should perhaps suggest that scandal in general gets fuller coverage than virtue. And indignation may do more than contentment for the production of eloquent political works. In politics as in love,[84] when affection for the familiar is goaded into song, the cause is often insecurity. It is interesting that some of the more memorable praise of Athenian *dēmokratia*, by Perikles and Euripides, came at a time of unusual fear for the city, the early Peloponnesian War.[85] One may compare the quantity of patriotic literature which appeared in Britain during the second World War.[86] In normal times the higher enthusiasms of modern writers, when positive, tend to be reserved for social arrangements remote in space or time. Orwell in the 1930s damned England in *The road to Wigan Pier*, and wrote his *Homage to Catalonia* with (detailed) lyricism on anarchist

Spain. Shaw idealised Stalin's Russia. Henry Williamson wrote of "the Great Man across the Rhine". Similarly, perhaps, ancient critics of the Athenian constitution cried up contemporary Sparta (Xenophon), or a hypothetical version of Sparta (Plato), or the Good Old Days of Athens (Aristophanes). For it is of great importance to bear in mind that the severe ancient critics of *dēmokratia*, whose judgements we must assess, were all Athenians, or men who spent much of their lives at Athens.[87] The negative comments of these insiders must be taken seriously, and the more so when there is a consensus, as there is on the point of democratic inconsistency. But to expect our sources to reveal with corresponding warmth the virtues of *dēmokratia* might be as naïve as looking to the higher literature of pre-war England for a fair review of that country's merits. With familiarity, English freedoms had grown — as T. E. Lawrence put it — like water in the mouth. Plato's tribute in the *Republic* to the tolerance and diversity within Athens is a sneer. Yet those qualities made possible the production of his work. One measure of a society's sophistication is the calibre of its internal critics.

The history of Athenian *dēmokratia*

When analysing the internal workings of Athens, it is worth bearing in mind the principle we have applied to Sparta: given the positive achievements of the society in question, the more weaknesses we perceive in it, the more confidently should we posit countervailing strengths which made the achievements possible. In what follows, the Athenian system will be analysed mainly by topics rather than chronologically. But a brief chronological framework is needed, concentrating on events affecting our main theme — the Athenian attainment of tolerance between those of greatly differing wealth.

In the early sixth century there was at Athens a social problem more inflammatory than any recorded there of the classical period. Our best evidence for the problem is a series of utterances in verse by the man called upon to solve it, Solon.[88] (Seemingly he held the office of *arkhōn* in 594/3.[89]) Because Solon came to be revered as a founder of Athens' constitution, men in the classical period were probably eager to ascribe to him valued aspects of contemporary arrangements. It follows that the laws and achievements of Solon, as represented in the fifth and fourth centuries,

need to be treated cautiously in the light of possible anachronism.[90] Solon's poetry is a better guide, if only because the stylistic
requirements of verse — and especially metre — make it a far
more tenacious medium than prose. The poetry makes it clear
that the poor of Athens complained of people being enslaved for
defaulting on legal obligations; also, land was being pledged in a
way that was somehow resented.[91] Solon was pressed by the poor
to cancel obligations and redistribute land. He himself seems to
have believed that rich men had acquired excess and should
accept moderation;[92] "for we shall not obey you", he writes,
apparently aligning himself with the poorer citizens. He wrote of
arrogance accompanying love of money,[93] and, in a traditional
complaint against the rich, deplored "bent" judgements in the
courts.[94]

There is a strong argument from silence that the reforms of
Solon did not involve any, or much, bloodletting. In addition,
Solon wrote of himself as avoiding violent reform.[95] He claims to
have freed the land of markers (which recorded mortgage or some
other obligation),[96] and to have restored many Athenians who had
been sold abroad as slaves.[97] Solon strikingly anticipates the
classical *dēmokratia* in his preoccupation with social harmony. He
writes of himself as having thrown a "strong shield" around each
of two groups; the *dēmos* and, on the other hand, the possessors of
power and wealth.[98] He boasts of having resisted pressure to give
"the bad" (i.e. the poor) equal shares in the land with "the good"
(i.e. the rich);[99] we recall the arkhons' oath to respect private
property, as sworn in the classical period. Solon is concerned to
minimise *hybris*, socially disruptive arrogance which (as we shall
see) the *dēmokratia* was to outlaw.[100] His opposition to corrupt
judgements in the courts anticipates the elaborate precautions
which were to be taken in the next two centuries. He apparently
intended that the poor should follow the rich as their leaders;[101]
such was to be normal practice in the classical period, to some
extent avowed even in theory.[102] In commending political
gentleness, Solon uses a word cognate with that used some two
and a half centuries later in the Aristotelian *Ath. Pol.*, to praise
the *dēmokratia*.[103] Whether, as Solon claimed, a different leader
would not have "restrained the *dēmos*" but would have "snatched
the cream from the milk" (i.e. expropriated the rich) is
uncertain.[104] Perhaps he was exaggerating, to persuade the rich to
accept such losses as his arrangements entailed for them. But
Solon does seem to have been concerned to answer critics who

believed he had not taken enough from the rich.[105] To explain why an arbitrator, such as himself, was initially acceptable to both sides, it may help to assume a pre-existing spirit of moderation. But even if Solon did not create such a spirit, his restrained. reforms are likely to have provided an important defence against violent *stasis*.

Some political animosity remained. After several attempts, Peisistratos was able (in 546 or thereabouts) to establish a tyranny. In other cities a tyrant led an assault on the aristocracy.[106] But there are several indications that the Athenian tyranny was, for the most part, mild — which suggests in turn that the opposition to it was usually tepid. The tyranny ended in blood and was remembered with widespread disapproval;[107] after an attempt on his life, Hippias, the son of Peisistratos, "killed. many of the citizens"[108] and was ejected. His attempt to have himself reinstated by a foreign enemy, the invading Persians of 490, ensured that a bad reputation became permanent. However, Thucydides stresses that the tyrants of Athens behaved with a great degree of virtue and intelligence.[109] Relations with the aristocrats were not always hostile. Herodotos records that Peisistratos was for a time in alliance with Megakles, head of a leading aristocratic family, the Alkmeonids.[110] The alliance was to break; the Alkmeonids eventually helped prominently in the expulsion of Hippias (510 or thereabouts), and not long afterwards (508/7) one of their number, Kleisthenes, made important moves towards the establishment of *dēmokratia*.

Surviving details of the Kleisthenic revolution are sadly few.[111] Kleisthenes was remembered as the creator of the ten tribes, on which the democratic structures of the classical period were largely based. Each tribe, composed of numerous units called demes, was to supply (for example) one of the annually elected panel of ten generals, and fifty members for the deliberative and executive council known as the *boulē*. The tribes were artificial entities, transcending — no doubt deliberately — divisions between town and country and between different areas of Attikē where large landowners might hold sway.

Herodotos' account of the war against King Xerxes of Persia suggests that the *dēmos* was sovereign in Athens by 480.[112] Later, in Aristotle's time, it was believed that the Council of the Areiopagos, a conservative body consisting of ex-arkhons, had played· a prominent role in the resistance to Persia, and had in consequence great influence in Athenian domestic affairs for almost two decades afterwards.[113] It is far from certain that this belief was correct; the role of the Areiopagos may have been improperly magnified in retrospect by conservative theorists. Unfortunately the *Ath. Pol.*, which is our main source for this doubtful account, is also the earliest surviving source for many details of a supposedly related process in which we should like to be able to believe: the radicalisation of the *dēmokratia* in the mid-fifth century.[114] According to the *Ath. Pol.* the wealthy in the aftermath of the Persian invasion had been led by Kimon, while the opposing faction, described as the *dēmos*, was headed by Ephialtes.[115] That Kimon and policies associated with him were discredited in the late 460s, as a result of the débâcle at Mount Ithōmē, we can infer from the account of Thucydides.[116] The *Ath. Pol.* represents Ephialtes as leading a successful attack on the powers of the Areiopagos, at a time which (we can see) coincides plausibly with the period of Kimon's discredit. Another fourth-century source records Ephialtes as having transferred the text of Solon's laws from the Akropolis to the market-place and the meeting-place of the *boulē*;[117] that the law should be knowable by all, and not kept under the control of a few, became a fundamental tenet of the *dēmokratia*. We are also told that Ephialtes was murdered, which is consistent with the idea that he was perceived by some as an important political threat.[118] The *Ath. Pol.* records that five years after Ephialtes' death the right to enter the lottery for appointment as *arkhōn* was extended to the *zeugitai*, the next-to-lowest of the four property classes.[119]

Kimon is recorded as having used his great personal wealth for patronage at Athens — a procedure which has traditionally won political support for aristocrats.[120] From the mid-century, public funds were used for building projects and other community purposes, on a scale which greatly reduced the power of aristocratic spending to impress.[121] The *Ath. Pol.* describes Perikles as having introduced pay for Athenian jurors, "to counter Kimon's wealth with a demagogic device of his own".[122] But we have learnt to distinguish in point of reliability between descriptions of public events and of private motives. Payment for public service was necessary to ensure that ordinary, poor, Athenians could afford to serve. Lottery was another characteristic device of the *dēmokratia*; in selecting officials it discriminated in favour of ordinary citizens, whereas election favoured the big names. The use of lottery to choose members of the *boulē* is first recorded of Athens by Thucydides in connection with the year 411.[123] But it had probably come into use there by the mid-fifth century, since Athens insisted on its use for the *boulē* at Erythrai when imposing a pro-Athenian *dēmokratia* on that town, most likely in the late 450s.[124]

In the fifth century much use was made of ostrakism,[125] a process whereby eminent politicians were, by a mass vote of the citizen body, exiled for ten years (without loss of property). Ostrakism was apparently not used in the fourth century, a period in which aristocrats had less prominence in Athenian politics. Themistokles certainly fell victim to it;[126] so, probably, did Kimon in the late 460s and Thucydides son of Melesias some twenty years later.[127] As a device for reducing instability in policy, ostrakism was gentler than assassination or indefinite exile, and thus reduced the risk of feud. Its existence reveals that the Athenians saw great importance in the leadership of a few individuals. For, had political decisions not been seen as controllable in large measure by a few durable champions, there would have seemed little point in the prolonged removal of a very few men. Following the removal of Thucydides son of Melesias came the period of Perikles' ascendancy, the incipient "rule of the first man". A person of great and lasting eminence was likely to be of wealthy family; Perikles was, on his mother's side, of Alkmeonid descent.[128]

After the death of Perikles in 429 the leaders of Athens in the Peloponnesian War were, according to Thucydides, "more the equals of each other"; "as each one aimed at becoming the first man", affairs were conducted more in accordance with the humours of the *dēmos*.[129] Thucydides may well have written with some passion on this subject, as a result of his views on Kleon, the most influential of Perikles' immediate successors. It is doubtful whether the change in leadership after Perikles' death was quite as marked as Thucydides suggests.[130] Of the men who competed for primacy during the war, some were very rich; Nikias and Alkibiades (the latter of Alkmeonid descent) lavished their personal wealth in promoting their careers.[131] There is, however, some evidence of a move away from aristocratic manners and, as the cost of the war grew, many rich men came under severe pressure. The comedian Aristophanes refers to popular leaders now as "sellers" of this or that commodity;[132] Kleon, for example, is portrayed as a leather-seller.[133] As historical evidence, jibes on this theme have a twofold significance. Aristophanes who, to judge by his victories in the dramatic contest, knew his audience, evidently thought that among his many hearers there was a powerful dislike of vulgar manners in high places, and that jokes against such manners would evoke more sympathy than hostility or, at the very least, would be tolerated. (The Athenians at some stage felt it necessary to pass a law to protect tradespeople from derision.[134]) On the other hand, Aristophanes' jokes suggest that politicians with non-aristocratic mannerisms now had enough support to bring them to prominence. He teases Kleon persistently for his harsh voice.[135] Later the *Ath. Pol.*, drawing on a tradition hostile to Kleon, says that he was the first speaker to shout and use abuse from the platform in the assembly.[136] Traditional privilege was eroded also by irregular but heavy taxes on wealth, *eisphorai*, during the war.[137] In addition many wealthy individuals faced a threat of court action which might lead to heavy loss of property; as we shall see, at the end of the war a violent and widespread reaction occurred against the "sykophants", men thought to have profited improperly from prosecuting, or threatening to prosecute, the rich.

As democrats lost confidence following the catastrophic defeat in Sicily (413), oligarchs at Athens saw a chance. The revolution of the Four Hundred (in 411) began with a campaign of terror and assassination against democratic leaders. But foreign policy failures of their own caused the Four Hundred to be replaced by the so-called constitution of the Five Thousand, under which full political rights were restricted to those able to afford their own hoplite equipment.[138] The restored *dēmokratia* of 410 BC judicially executed two leaders of the Four Hundred, Antiphon and Arkheptolemos;[139] others fled. This in turn no doubt contributed somewhat to the violence of the Thirty, the oligarchy which Sparta installed after the surrender of Athens in 404. The killing carried out by the Thirty, not only for political reasons but apparently for the sake of personal profit,[140] damned their memory at Athens, save perhaps in one significant respect. Their persecution of supposed malefactors, and especially of "sykophants" — provokers of the rich — was remembered with approval.[141] After the Thirty had been ejected by an army of Athenian democrats, in 403, the restored *dēmokratia* broke the cycle of violence by an act of restraint remarkable when one considers the inflammatory record of the late oligarchy. It was decided to forbid informal and protracted persecution of the supporters of the Thirty, and even surviving members of the Thirty themselves were not to be attacked informally if they offered to give formal account of their actions.[142] Xenophon and the *Ath. Pol.* give credit to the *dēmokratia* for this lenience, which they show to have been long-lasting.[143] The motive for it was not, therefore, mere dread of further Spartan intervention; had that been the case, persecution could have been carried out from 395, when Athens again challenged Sparta in war. It is evidence of the success of the democrats' restraint that, in more than 80 years which intervened between the removal of the Thirty and the suppression of *dēmokratia* by the Macedonians (in 322), there was at Athens no revolutionary interruption.

For most of the first half of the fourth century our knowledge of Athenian history is no more than an outline; rather more information survives from the subsequent period of struggle with Macedon. Although the *Ath. Pol.* ceases to name political leaders of the rich and poor after the end of the fifth century, divisions on those lines remained important. A fragment from an anonymous fourth-century writer (the "Oxyrhynchus Historian") and some lines of Aristophanes show that in the early fourth century the rich were markedly less eager for war than were the poor.[144] The position of the poor was consolidated soon after 400 by the introduction of pay for attending the assembly; that the level of pay was within a short time twice increased may reflect sustained pressure from needy citizens.[145] In the courts, prejudice might sometimes be aroused against riches and the arrogance which they were believed to generate,[146] but poverty also could bring a man into suspicion. Even when the *Ath. Pol.* was written, in the second half of the fourth century, a formal check was still made, when an Athenian entered office, as to which of the four categories of wealth applied to him. We are told that, when the question about wealth was put, no one would ever admit to being one of the *thētes*, the largest and poorest group.[147] From which we conclude that false answers were given and were probably well known to be given. But the fact that the formal requirement was not revoked suggests that *dēmokratia* was not securely recognised as rule by the poor. The idea of the virtuous middle was still influential.

The assembly

The great policy-making body of the *dēmokratia*, in both domestic and external affairs, was the general assembly, the *ekklēsia*. When

Thucydides wishes to make clear the process whereby Athens took decisions of the greatest importance, such as how to react to Spartan threats of war (in the late 430s) and whether to invade Sicily (in 415), it is to the assembly that he directs attention. To. some degree the problems and the positive capacities of such a body are foreign to us. Familiarity with a modern governmental assembly, such as the British parliament or the American congress, is helpful to the understanding. But there are great differences between modern systems and the Athenian. For example, the modern assembly is supported by a bureaucracy far larger than the assembly itself and is informed in addition by a professional press. Ordinary citizens are excluded from participation; the active members are professional politicians, assembling day after day and organised in formal parties. None of this was true of the *ekklēsia*, even though some politicians consistently enjoyed large support and were thought to represent a particular section of society. With its informality the Athenian assembly in some ways more resembles a general meeting of students on a modern university campus, with orators avoiding partisan labels addressing a similarly undefined majority, among which small organised factions lurk rather than advertise their exact identity; wit is enjoyed; the discomfiture of almost any speaker relished. However, student meetings have very little power, and their membership changes completely every few years. In contrast, the *ekklēsia* ran a large city and — for half a century — an empire besides; its members could participate for life, and thus were better placed to apply corporate experience — to form, in short, a mature institution. In a (respectful) book about the *dēmokratia*, A. H. M. Jones referred to Athenian policy-making methods as "anarchic".[148] For the modern critic, brought up in a centralised state, the study of near-anarchy should involve a certain caution.

How often the *ekklēsia* met was politically an important question; the frequency of meetings determined which groups within the population could afford to play a full part. The *Ath. Pol.* records the holding of four meetings in every prytany, that is, four in every 36 days.[149] Of these, one was required to take a vote of confidence on the officials then serving, to deal with the corn supply and the defence of the country, to hear the laying of certain important accusations[150] and announcements about certain property which had become subject to transfer. At another meeting of the assembly formal petitioners could address the people on any subject. The other two sessions were for all other

business, and were bound by law to consider religious matters
and affairs relating to heralds and ambassadors (respectively
messengers and negotiators between states).[151] In a valuable study
of the *ekklēsia* M. H. Hansen has argued that during the period
referred to by the *Ath. Pol.* (roughly, the third quarter of the
fourth century) four meetings was the maximum in a prytany.[152]
In support of the idea of some such limit are the words of the orator
Demosthenes, concerning the year 347/6: "since there was no
assembly remaining, due to [the assemblies] having been used up
beforehand ... the *dēmos* [i.e. the assembly] having put the *boulē*
in charge ..."[153]

There is an obvious objection to the theory that the number of
ekklēsiai per prytany was strictly limited. If it was, the Athenians
could have expected at times to find themselves with sudden and
important decisions to make near the end of a prytany but unable
to call an assembly. However, Hansen cites epigraphic evidence
suggesting that a disproportionately large number of assembly
meetings occurred near the end of a prytany.[154] It may be, then,
that the Athenians were aware of the problem outlined above, and
countered it by holding back meetings against some emergency
late in the 36–day period. Since the disadvantage of a limit on
meetings is obvious, we should look for a countervailing
advantage to explain why the Athenians tolerated it, if indeed
thèy did. If an indefinite number of assemblies had been allowed,
in addition to those required by law, a fear might have arisen that
the *ekklēsia* would develop into a daily institution. As we shall see,
it was often impossible to attract sufficiently large numbers to the
assembly; the more frequent the meetings became, the more
serious that problem was likely to grow. Athenians who lived in
the country, as most did before the Peloponnesian War, would in
most cases be hard pressed to attend very frequently. And those
who could attend day after day were likely to represent special
interests, financially speaking. The very rich, with no need to
attend to work elsewhere, would be well placed to attend in force.
In the fourth century, when attendance was paid, the very poor
might also be present in disproportionate strength. Such developments, promoting the influence of the extremes in society, would
conflict with the powerful ideology of the middle. Moreover, if
the frequency of meetings caused the numbers at each to dwindle,
it would be easier to bribe an influential proportion of those
attending. The fear of bribery, that is especially of illicit influence
for the rich, haunted the *dēmokratia*; part of the theory behind the

mass jury in the law courts was that it was difficult to bribe.[155] A limit on the number of assemblies may, then, have been well suited to Athenian ideals.

In what numbers did the Athenians attend the assembly? In the revolutionary period of 411, emissaries of Athens' new oligarchy, the Four Hundred, sought to reassure the great Athenian force at Samos, in which democrats predominated. The oligarchs claimed that the oligarchy was not a narrow one, but had in reality 5,000 members, whereas because of military expeditions and commitments abroad Athenians had never yet met to discuss anything, however important, in numbers as great as 5,000.[156] It is not clear, and quite likely was not meant to be clear, how long a period had seen attendances of the assembly consistently lower than 5,000. It was in the oligarchs' interest to play down the numbers as far as possible and to exploit memories of the recent past, in which war and plague had shrunk the total of citizens active in politics at Athens. But the speakers' scope for distortion was small; they were addressing an audience intensely interested, suspicious, and in possession of much first-hand experience of the assembly. The reference to military expeditions may suggest that the oligarchs conceded that in peacetime numbers in the *ekklēsia* had risen over 5,000. But the check on inaccuracy provided by their audience means that, as an approximate maximum, the figure of 5,000 must be taken seriously as applying to the very recent past.

The assembly usually met on the lower slopes of the small hill known as the Pnyx, close to the Agora and the Akropolis. Recent excavations of the area, combined with estimates of the space needed to seat each person, have suggested that in the fifth century the maximum to be accommodated was some 6,000, whereas early in the fourth century the area was expanded to hold some 6,500 or possibly 8,000 — depending on how the speakers' platform, the *bēma*, was placed.[157] The slight increase may reflect the introduction, in the early fourth century, of pay for attendance. Aristotle contrasts negative and positive devices for procuring participation in government. (Compare the stick and carrot of modern administrative cliché.) The negative kind consists of fines for those who do not take part, the positive of pay for those who do.[158] One memorable Athenian technique of a negative kind has sometimes been misunderstood. In a comedy produced early in the Peloponnesian War, the *Akharnians* of 425, Aristophanes makes a character complain that, with an assembly due, "the Pnyx here is deserted, while the people are chatting in the Agora, twisting and turning to avoid the painted rope. Even the Prytaneis[159] ... will arrive late."[160] Now, the detail about the Pnyx being deserted is very likely the comic exaggeration of a poet critical of the contemporary *dēmokratia*, but the audience is expected to understand the glancing reference to the painted rope. An ancient commentator on this passage states:

> they used to spread out ... the wattle screens and block the roads which led elsewhere than to the assembly and remove the goods for sale in the markets, to prevent people spending time on them. Throwing around the people a painted rope, they drove them together into the assembly. This they did to prevent delay; anyone who got smeared with the paint paid a fine.[161]

Scholia are often made valueless by gross error, or through the possibility that their information has been constructed simply by inference from the passage under consideration. But here no such error is evident, and there is plausible additional information (on the screens and the saleable goods) seemingly from an independent source. The motive imputed for the use of the rope, a wish to avoid delay, is easily derivable directly from Aristophanes' text. On the other hand, it makes good sense. Anyone familiar with modern business meetings should know the tendency for the start of formal proceedings to be delayed by informal conversation, especially when the participants know each other well but have not met for some time previously.[162] Sessions of the *ekklēsia* were probably so spaced that material would accrue in between for much conversation, especially between men who normally lived some distance apart. The use of the painted rope should not, then, be taken as evidence in itself of Athenian concern over low attendance of the assembly.[163]

At the beginning of the fourth century low attendance of the *ekklēsia* was almost certainly recognised as a problem. The introduction then of payment for attending is plausibly explained by the *Ath. Pol.* as an attempt to end absenteeism and ensure that "the *plēthos*" came — so that valid decisions could be taken.[164] One obol per session was the original fee; this was quickly raised to two then three obols (half a *drakhmē*).[165] These payments, large in aggregate, were thought necessary even at a time when public resources had been depleted by the loss of income from the

Empire. It may be that defeat in the Peloponnesian War had
caused disenchantment with the *dēmokratia*, and a widespread
reluctance to participate in its governing body. Also, the severe
damage done to personal finances by the war and its aftermath
had probably made many (and not just the very poor) feel they
could not afford time for an unpaid meeting when their personal
affairs needed to be restored.[166] Later in the fourth century, when
prosperity had to some degree returned, attendance at the
assembly seems to have risen. Hansen points out that some 60
men are known to have been made citizens by decree in the period
from 368 to 322, and in each case a vote was required in which
more than 6,000 Athenians took part.[167] By the time that the *Ath.
Pol.* was written, payment for most meetings of the assembly had
been increased to one *drakhmē* and for the "sovereign" meeting
(which volume of business might cause to last longer than the
others) to one and a half.[168] This increase was part of a general
rise in the cost of labour.[169] The fact that payment was
maintained at all should not be taken to imply that Athenians
continued to fear a crisis in attendance if it were to be removed.
Income once established is quickly seen as a moral right by its
recipients; politicians threaten it at their peril.

Who spoke in the assembly? Meetings were too few for most
Athenians to be able to speak regularly. In formal terms, every
adult male Athenian, irrespective of social class, had the right to
speak — save for those personally deprived of civic rights for
some offence or failure.[170] Meetings were addressed with the
simple question, 'Who wishes to speak to the assembly?'.[171] The
invitation had once, it seems, been qualified; Aiskhines cites as
obsolete a question of the form, 'Who of those over fifty wishes to
address the assembly?'.[172] Only when the older men had spoken
were their juniors invited. Some informal discrimination against
the young speaker may well have existed in the classical period.[173]
In settled societies age normally dominates. Fear that the young
would prove revolutionary was reinforced at Athens by the fact
that a regular element in Greek expressions for revolution, *neōter-*,
was conspicuously present in a common word meaning 'younger
men' (*neōteroi*).

Plato puts the following into the mouth of his revered Sokrates:

> I think the Athenians are astute … I observe, whenever we
> gather for an assembly, when the city needs to do something
> involving building, builders are summoned to advise on the

subject; when ship-construction is in question, shipwrights, and so on with every subject that they think can be taught and learned. And if someone else tries to give them advice, whom they do not think to be a specialist craftsman, even if he is very handsome, and rich and one of the nobility, none the less they will not have it, but they jeer at him and make a row until the would-be speaker either is defeated by the row and stands down or ... [is removed by officials].[174]

The belief that experts should rule was of great importance in Plato's philosophy. (Probably its best-known expression is in the *Republic*, with the doctrine of philosopher-rulers.) Didactic enthusiasm may just have caused Plato to exaggerate the deference shown to experts at Athens. But normally he was strongly biased against the *dēmokratia*, which for one thing gave formal power to a mass of uneducated laymen. His concession against bias, in the matter of the attention paid to specialists by the lay assemblymen, probably reflects real behaviour of that kind on the Athenians' part. The wry comment on the rejection of inexpert advice even from handsome rich noblemen suggests that on other, supposedly non-technical, matters such men were heard with unusual respect. We shall see much evidence from elsewhere that they were.

Noisy and derisive reactions were common at Athenian public meetings.[175] It is impossible to know to what extent potential speakers were intimidated by the prospect of such. Cross-cultural assumptions are dangerous here; there is, for example, at present a great difference between ordinary British and ordinary American people in respect of willingness to speak to a large audience.[176] The fact that Athenian outspokenness (*parrhēsia*) was famous may suggest a certain boldness, by Greek standards.[177] But as to what those standards were outside Athens we have little evidence, save in the case of Sparta, a state exceptional in many ways and hardly supplying a basis for generalisation. As we have seen, (p.279 and n. 134), the Athenians judged it necessary to use legislation to protect tradespeople from insult referring to their status; poverty in itself might make a man suspect. Accordingly, humility or a fear of contempt can be assumed to have prevented some men of low status from speaking. Education at Athens varied greatly in accordance with family' wealth; unlike Sparta, the city had no homogenising system of communal education for all young citizens. In Athenian education, rhetoric was a main element;[178] a man of wealthy background often had, along with political advantages such as inherited confidence in himself and inherited deference in his audience, a formal training in techniques of public speaking. He also, in his mature years, might have the leisure to inform himself thoroughly of political developments and to make personal alliances. Extreme wealth, like extreme poverty, incurred prejudice at Athens but the very rich man had far more resources than the very poor for countering it.

The recorded speeches of influential Athenians, both from the assembly and the law courts, are in many cases very long by modern standards. It hardly needs saying that to assemble and control material of such length would require, or at least be much facilitated by, formal training. A speech written by Lysias refers to "men incapable of speaking" — in the sophisticated style required in court, that is.[179] The successful orator Demosthenes could tell an Athenian audience that Solon "saw that most of you, while you have the right to speak in the assembly, in fact do not".[180] In a different context he gives poverty and "incapacity to speak" among reasons why some do not defend their own interests in court.[181] In the Funeral Speech Perikles is reported as commending political activism,[182] but even in this idealising context he implies that some were more active than others: "Some men are concerned with both their private affairs and affairs of the city; the others, while their work is their main concern, manage to have a fair grasp of the city's affairs."[183] In the fourth century "the orators" were frequently referred to as a distinct group, and may even have had a special legal status.[184] In connection with the democratic council, the *boulē*, Demosthenes distinguishes between "the speakers" and the lay members, the majority, some of whom may have been absent for most of the time.[185]

The question of who had influence in the assembly is closely related. *Rhetores*, like 'politicians' today, could be a word of contempt; thus for comic effect Aristophanes includes it in a list of rogues, along with 'temple-robbers' and 'sykophants'.[186] But to have the ear of the *dēmos* repeatedly was obviously to be in an influential position; the ambivalence of the orator's situation is nicely captured by the words of a speaker who describes himself as "neither one of the men who regularly bother you [with speeches] nor one of the politicians you trust".[187] The best-established case of such trust concerns the orator and general

Perikles. Thucydides' comment, that (under Perikles' influence) Athens was becoming a state under the rule of the first man, while in theory a *dēmokratia*,[188] suggests that the ascendancy of Perikles, because to some extent informal, might be fragile. As well as having sufficient authority to prevent a meeting of the assembly during a crisis,[189] Perikles was able to guide Athens' reaction to Spartan diplomacy on the eve of the Peloponnesian War. The Athenians, in Thucydides' phrase, "voted as he urged and replied to the Spartans in accordance with his advice, both on particular points and in general".[190] Even after Perikles' death (in 429) Athens continued to follow in several respects the military policies he had laid down.[191] But the control which the *dēmos* continued to hold over him in his lifetime is shown by an episode in 430, when his policy in the matter of seeking peace with Sparta was overridden and he himself was subjected to a fine.[192] However, "not long afterwards ... they [the Athenians] elected him general again and entrusted all their affairs to him".[193]

One important reason for Perikles' influence over the *dēmos* was, in Thucydides' judgement, that "he was clearly most averse from the receipt of gifts".[194] From this passage alone we could infer that Athenians of the period expected much bribery of their politicians. Informal accusations of bribery and of other financial misbehaviour were commonplace.[195] Orators in numbers were said to enrich themselves at the public expense, not only by an Aristophanic character in raillery[196] but also by perhaps the most eminent orator of the fourth century, Demosthenes[197] — a man whose own career gave rise to some interesting accusations in this sphere.[198] The question of how frequent and important was actual bribery will be considered briefly below.[199] But there is significance in the mere fact that orators were widely viewed as likely to be bribed, for that suggests that they were thought to have power to deliver what the bribers wanted. Particularly noteworthy (if it is not a result of gross comic exaggeration) is a remark in Aristophanes' *Ploutos* implying that bribery of the orators could ensure that scandal or prosecution was avoided.[200] It would have constituted an important restriction on the power of the *dēmos* if, in a city the size of Athens, information could be controlled by a group small enough to be effectively bribed by men of wealth.

What problems are characteristic of government by general assembly, and how far did Athens tackle and surmount them? The *ekklēsia*'s sense of drama and fun, and sheer enjoyment of its own power, might cause a certain irresponsibility, as we have seen in connection with the debate about Sphakteria. But moments of entertainment have a benign side — and not only in mass democracy. They may aid concentration, and help to create healthy attendance at meetings. (In the British House of Commons important business is frequently discussed with fewer than twenty members present in the chamber, whereas predictably entertaining sessions, as for example when a weakened minister comes under personal attack, are preceded by a happy buzz of a packed house.)

The charge of inconsistency against the Athenian *dēmos* may be more serious. In assessing it, one should first notice a possible bias in theorisers, modern and ancient. Such people tenaciously demand logical consistency of a treatise — rightly in those cases (a big majority) where the author is in a position to review the whole treatise in a very short period before communicating it. But in the case of political or other decisions taken over a much longer period, consistency may be unreasonable to demand and damaging to impose. A theorist might be satirically defined as one who, on grounds of consistency, rejects half a loaf in favour of no bread. A certain inconsistency was virtually built into the Athenian assembly through the variation in attendance from one meeting to another. Without anyone's mind having changed, a majority in favour of some general policy could disappear as past voters absented themselves and men previously absent attended. In addition, minds might be changed in a way not wholly sensible as a result of an Athenian method of voting. How voting was done, in different circumstances and at different times, is imperfectly known.[201] But show of hands was a familiar method. Aristophanes humorously raises a question of how imaginary women who invade the assembly will know to raise their hands when they are used to raising their legs.[202] More seriously, Xenophon records an episode in 406 when business of the assembly was postponed "because it was then late, and it was not possible to see the hands clearly".[203] Modern experience suggests that, when a decision is being made, those deciding are in many cases influenced to conform by knowledge of how their peers have decided. In politics this is notorious as the "bandwaggon" effect. But it has also been identified and measured in the results of expert academic assessment.[204] If, as is probable, voting by show of hands had this effect at Athens, the instability produced by variation in attendance may have been compounded.

For all we know, Athenians may have been aware of this disadvantage in the system of voting by show of hands. For such voting also had — in another respect — an important advantage which could have seemed to justify it against the alternative· method, voting by secret ballot (which the Athenians used in their lawcourts). Direct democracy is expensive in time. To have used secret ballot for all votes of the assembly would have caused very much of the citizens' time to be taken waiting to vote and waiting for votes to be counted. Show of hands was cruder but far quicker, allowing much more business to be done in the few days a month when assemblies met. To have extended the time given to assemblies, in order to accommodate innumerable ballots, would have introduced a distortion of its own by tending to exclude from regular participation certain groups of citizens for whom attendance was difficult.

A device which might restrain instability was ostrakism. When a minority of citizens was sufficiently large or organised to dominate the assembly from time to time and thus to threaten an oscillation in the policy of the state, ostrakism weakened the minority with minimal harm to its members' rights, by removing their leader.[205] There was also some legal restraint on those who would reopen in the assembly a question already decided there. Thucydides represents Nikias as trying to do such a thing, while significantly attempting to convince the president of the assembly (an ordinary citizen, chosen by lot to serve for one day) that under the circumstances doing so would not cause the president to be successfully prosecuted.[206] In the case of the Mytileneans in 427 the assembly of Athens did reopen a decided matter and reverse its decision.[207] The second, less severe, decision — taken partly for moral˙reasons — recalls the inconsistency which Plato derided, whereby men sentenced to death at Athens were eventually allowed to live and circulate freely there.(p.273 and n.80).

In his *Constitution of Athens* the Old Oligarch describes oligarchies as obliged to adhere to their alliances and oaths, because the authorities are personally identified with them. He contrasts a *dēmos*, which can renege on an agreement, blaming whoever proposed it and put it to the vote; in a *dēmokratia*, he claims, individuals can say of what an assembly decided "I wasn't there and I don't approve."[208] Whether contemporary oligarchies in general really did show more respect than Athens for agreements we cannot tell. The oligarchy of Sparta was not above blame in this respect. Spartans themselves were eventually satisfied that they had been chiefly to blame for breaking the Thirty Years Peace;[209] the ephors who had agreed to the Peace of Nikias in 421 were succeeded by others who opposed it,[210] and in · general Sparta's relations with Athens in the sixty years from 465 suggest that consistency in aggressive opportunism took priority over consistent adhesion to treaty.[211] For all we know, oligarchies which did not (unlike Sparta) change leading officials annually may have kept to their agreements more often. In any case the Old Oligarch's point, about collective decisions in a *dēmokratia* being disowned eventually as the work of misguided speakers, is echoed by Thucydides, in his reporting of the *dēmos'* reaction to news of the catastrophe in Sicily.[212] But at times such fluidity might be a strength; the anonymity of voters in the assembly allowed the *dēmos* to alter its policy in the light of new information without the acute fear of loss of face which characterises a leader whose policy has failed. The practical ambivalence of consistency is illustrated by the last stages of the Sicilian expedition. Confronted with clear evidence of failure, ordinary Athenians, once so keen on the venture, clamoured to abandon it[213] — a superficially inconsistent move, but one which might have saved the Athenian Empire. However, the commander Nikias feared, or claimed to fear, that most of these men who pressed to leave would, on reaching Athens, change their tune and accuse their generals of having left improperly.[214] That Nikias chose to stay, with disastrous results, may have been caused in part by fear of democratic inconsistency; but he was almost certainly influenced by a desire not to admit personal failure, a desire which produces excessive consistency especially in oligarchs and other leaders.

The Sicilian expedition illustrates a further point about *dēmokratia*, one so simple as often to be overlooked. Military campaigns of the Athenians were conducted under a form of limited autocracy or oligarchy — that is, under the rule of a general or generals who, although answerable to the *dēmos* at Athens, governed their men in the field or at sea without reference to any regular democratic organisation there. This concentration of power made it possible for Nikias to state, and act on, his self-interested preference for staying in Sicily (thus risking, though he did not say so, the lives of tens of thousands of his men).[215] A general assembly could mistake its own interest, but was unlikely ever to subordinate so clearly the interest of its own masses to that of one man.

Anyone familiar with large public meetings today will know of certain problems which the Athenian assembly needed to avoid or to tackle, such as irrelevance from speakers, foolish motions and the introduction to meetings of seemingly important but not immediately verifiable news. The passage from Plato's *Protagoras* quoted above reveals two mechanisms whereby the *ekklēsia* might assert its sense of relevance — the barracking and the physical removal of offending speakers. Irrelevance may even have been a crime at law.[216] Drunkenness might occur (as it has in the British House of Commons[217]); there is a comic reference to a drunkard being removed by the (Skythian) archers — state slaves, who enforced order at the assembly.[218] To deceive the assembly was an offence in law, at least in some circumstances.[219] But the possibility of punishment would not always deter naïve men from making genuinely mistaken claims. The processing of news, and the preparation of sensible motions, were made functions of an ancillary body, the *boulē*, to which we now turn.

The *boulē*

Before a motion could be voted upon by the *ekklēsia*, it had first to be approved for the *ekklēsia's* consideration by the *boulē*.[220] Only occasionally, so far as we know, was the *boulē* under instructions from the *ekklēsia* as to what business should be laid before the latter.[221] Demosthenes, contrasting the capacity of the Athenians to react to news with that of autocratic and oligarchic states, wrote:

> ... under constitutions of those kinds everything is done swiftly at a command. In contrast you [Athenians] must first have the *boulē* hear everything and propose motions, and not at any time either, but at the prescribed occasions for heralds and embassies. Then you must hold an *ekklēsia*, at a time in accordance with the law.[222]

This is the work of an orator; we should suspect some overdrawing. That the *boulē* could on occasion react speedily to important news by calling an *ekklēsia* is suggested by the same orator elsewhere, when describing the arrival at Athens of the shocking report that Philip had penetrated central Greece and taken the strategic position of Elateia (in 339/8):

It was evening when someone came to report to the presiding group [of the *boulē*]²²³ that Elateia was captured. Some of the presidents immediately got up, in the middle of dinner, removed the occupants of booths in the agora ... others sent for the generals and called for the trumpeter. The city was in uproar. The next morning, at daybreak, the presidents called a meeting of the *boulē*, and you [Athenians] went to the assembly; and before the *boulē* had carried out its business and proposed a motion for the assembly, the whole *dēmos* had taken its seats. The *boulē* came; the presidents delivered the information which had been reported to them and introduced the man who had come to report it; he spoke, then the herald asked, 'Who wishes to address the assembly?'²²⁴

Limits to any rhetorical distortion in the latter passage were set by the fact that Demosthenes was giving this description of impressive events to men who had participated in them, after an interval of only eight years. In the passage previously quoted, on relative slowness of official Athenian reactions, the extent of overdrawing would be controlled by the knowledge of democratic procedure ingrained by repetition in an Athenian audience. The predigestion of material by the *boulē*, and a slight delay (in normal times) before the *ekklēsia* dealt with the resulting motion, helped to prevent the assembly from being coerced ("bounced", in today's civil service slang) by an unrepresentative group putting an unexpected motion. Some period of notice would normally be of use in allowing interested citizens (and especially those in the country) to arrange to attend the *ekklēsia*.²²⁵ And the *boulē* itself was constituted, as we shall see, so as to be broadly representative of the citizen body. A man who happened not to be serving on the *boulē* at a particular time could request permission to propose a subject for the *boulē's* consideration, with a view to its eventual referral to the *ekklēsia*.²²⁶ Such a proposal to the *boulē* had to be in writing, perhaps because the mere effort of formulating matter in writing often filters out the more casual intervention and imposes more careful consideration than does an oral suggestion. That the *boulē* frequently succeeded in matching or influencing the views of the wider public in the *ekklēsia* is made clear by inscriptions in which the assembly is recorded as decreeing that details are to be arranged "as the *boulē* has recommended".²²⁷

As well as preparing business for the assembly, the *boulē*

executed many of the assembly's decisions, supervised officials and oversaw much day-to-day administration. A decree of the assembly concerning a colony on the Adriatic laid down that "if this decree is found to need addition ... the *boulē* is empowered to make it by [its own] vote, provided that it [the *boulē*] does not undo any of the arrangements voted by the *dēmos* [i.e. the assembly]"[228] (The last clause suggests that the *boulē* may at times have exceeded its agreed role; elsewhere we seem to read of the *boulē* doing just that, in putting to death without trial a man who threatened to revive *stasis* by undoing the amnesty granted to supporters of the Thirty.[229]) The Aristotelian *Ath. Pol.* states that "the *boulē* tries most [accused] officials, and particularly those who handle money. Its judgement is not final, but appeal against it can be made to a regular court."[230] The important role of the *boulē* in financial and other daily administration is witnessed by the Old Oligarch, writing perhaps a century earlier: "the *boulē* has to consider ... many matters connected with revenue ... many other matters arising constantly concerning the city ...; it has to receive the [imperial] tribute, and to take care of the docks and holy places."[231] On naval matters, compare a surviving decree of 325/4, which records that the *boulē* had to meet daily by the harbour to supervise the departure of a fleet.[232] That the *boulē* supervised collection of tribute is confirmed by a decree of the mid-fifth century.[233]

The role and composition of the *boulē* reflected a compromise between two ideals: that Athens should have a day-to-day civil government, and that the mass of Athenians should govern the city. There is little doubt that the great majority of Athenians could not think of participating daily in government without pay, and that to provide pay for a daily mass meeting was beyond the city's means. The compromise lay in creating in the form of the *boulē* a body which met every day (except on state holidays), which was small enough to pay (its formal membership was 500) and to which appointment was by lot,[234] from those over thirty years old.[235] Membership rotated; no man could serve for more than two years of his life.[236] Each year was divided into ten periods of approximately 36 days, the prytanies; the 500 members were correspondingly divided into ten equal groups. Each group of 50 took its turn to preside in the *boulē* for 36 days.[237] Rotation of membership impeded one common route to corruption; a transient councillor makes a much less attractive target for dishonest approaches than one likely to have power for years.

(Modern experience of local government, in the USA and Britain, has suggested that corruption is especially likely where one party rules uninterruptedly for many years.[238]) Rotation also reduced the chance that members of the *boulē* would develop attitudes and interests distinct from those of the general population. (It is a commonplace of analysis that in modern legislative assemblies even opposing members have far more in common with each other than they do with their fellow partisans outside. In the reaction of youth around 1970, informal student administrations were set up which closely — and almost certainly unconsciously — resembled Athenian arrangements, in having a lesser body with rotating membership serving an assembly to which all might belong and which was sovereign.[239] A reason often given for this was fear of unrepresentative representatives.)

In practice the Athenian *boulē* may have been somewhat biased towards the wealthy. As we have seen, quite late in the fourth century a rule excluding from allotted office those who belonged to the very large, and poorest, class — the *thētes* — had still not been repealed. The *Ath. Pol.* suggests that it was evaded: "even now, when people about to enter the lottery for office are asked to which class they belong, no one would say 'the thetic' ".[240] But this implies in turn that an honest answer might still cause a *thēs* to be excluded. Did formal rule (or informal attitudes) discourage many *thētes* from participating in the *boulē*, or from making themselves conspicuous there if they did serve? A surviving list of members of the *boulē* (in 336/5) seems to show that wealthy families were, statistically speaking, somewhat over-represented.[241] The low level of pay for members may have encouraged a tendency in this direction; the five obols per day payable in the 320s was much lower even than an unskilled labourer's wage.[242] Some bribery seems to have occurred. Aristophanes' lines about the *prytanis* with his "hollow" hand outstretched for money are in keeping with the comedian's personal hostility to the radical democracy.[243] But a reform of the early fourth century seems to reflect a general belief in the likelihood of corruption. Until then, each meeting of the assembly was chaired by a person chosen by lot from among the 50 *prytaneis* then presiding over the *boulē*. But under the new system one of the presiding *prytaneis*, chosen by lot, conducted a second lottery among the nine groups other than his own to select a chairman of the assembly for one day.[244] This arrangement might inhibit corruption in two ways; it made the panel from which chairmen would emerge far wider and thus harder to suborn, and it restricted collusion affecting the chair between men who had come to know each other through serving in the same prytany.

Officials

The use of lottery to choose officials was seen as characteristic of *dēmokratia*. Election, in contrast, could be seen as an oligarchic device;[245] it favoured the aristocrat in a society (such as Athens) which normally treated aristocrats with respect. Lottery favoured the obscure, ordinary, citizen. The *Ath. Pol.* attempts to summarise:

> They [the Athenians] choose by lot all the officials concerned with day-to-day administration, except the treasurer of the military fund, the people in charge of the theoric fund[246] and the superintendent of wells. These they appoint by election ... They also elect all military officials.[247]

This refers to a time in the second half of the fourth century; we read in the same source that under the Empire the Athenians had provided pay for some 700 civilian officials at home over and above the many jurors and *boulē* members.[248] Such widespread distribution by lot of authority and wealth must have spread in the Athenian masses a feeling that the state was *theirs*; the value of such an attitude in promoting stability needs little stressing. No one could hold an allotted civilian office more than once, save for the post of *boulē* member.[249]

The election of individuals to administer large funds at Athens seems to have been a fourth-century development.[250] One man, Euboulos, was prominent at mid-century in administering the theoric fund, with power comparable with that of a modern minister of state.[251] In part this may have resulted from the complete failure of democratic Athens in a conflict with former allies, the "Social War" of the mid-350s, and from the financial straits which followed.[252] We recall the shift away from democratic procedure which occurred following the Sicilian catastrophe of 413;[253] military defeat often undermines a regime. In contrast, an elective institution which was prominent throughout the classical period was the panel of ten generals, to which reappointment was allowed.

Modern critics have often called attention to the severe treatment which the *dēmos* of Athens could impose on generals, even those with some record of success, such as Miltiades and the commanders at Arginousai.[254] This treatment is found remarkable because of its dissimilarity to the rather gentle handling of strikingly unsuccessful generals in many modern societies. The points of similarity between the position of a modern general and that of his Athenian counterpart are easier to overlook. Yet these too are noteworthy, because they represent a sharp contrast with the democratic procedures normal in most areas of Athenian life. The power of an Athenian general on campaign was great, and not very different in degree from that of modern commanders. The primitive forms of communication constraining Athens meant that citizens at home were always out of date in their knowledge of remote campaigns in progress; it was inevitable that much power should be delegated to people in the field. But on the face of it there seems no reason why some form of democratic assembly or council should not have existed in the field, at least as a check on a commander. Yet, as we have seen, there was none.[255] Nor do we often hear of informal *dēmokratia*, in the form of mutiny.[256] The soldier Xenophon reports some disobedience as a familiar occurrence among Athenian cavalry and hoplites on campaign, but evidently accepts that the (more numerous) sailors of Athens were notably well disciplined, and obedient towards their officers.[257] These opinions (conveyed through characters in a dialogue) should be taken all the more seriously because they run counter to the normal bias of Xenophon (and probably of his readers) in favour of the wealthy and against the poor. Notoriously the Athenian fleet was crewed by the poor, the "naval mob".

Xenophon's distinction between the poor and the better-off in respect of discipline is valuable for a further reason; it concerns an activity, military campaigning, in which Athenians could be observed functioning *en masse* in groups defined largely by social class. In contrast, when the social classes mixed, as in the streets, the *agora*, the *ekklēsia* and the *boulē*, the fact of mixing might bring a certain tendency towards uniformity in behaviour and in many cases it might be impossible to tell from appearance to which · class an individual belonged. Campaigns, then, might intensify and clarify social differences. Xenophon's words suggest that in the main the poor of Athens asserted themselves, trusted their own judgement, much less than did the hoplite class and the rich.

Since the Athenians were very often at war, and in large measure obeyed their generals on campaign, the personality of those generals would be seen as controlling the chances of survival and prosperity. The choice of generals is perhaps the clearest reflection of where the Athenian people believed that competence and incorruptibility lay. In a remark which again is important because counter to a powerful bias of its author, the Old Oligarch states that the *dēmos* (that is, the un-rich mass) "recognises that it does better by not holding [the generalship and other top military posts] itself, but by allowing the most powerful [that is, the rich] to hold them".[258] This was probably written early in the Peloponnesian War. The prominence of rich and aristocratic generals in the fifth century is well known; Kimon, Perikles, Nikias and Alkibiades were all of wealthy and (save perhaps for Nikias) of noble background. In the fourth century aristocratic generals are less in evidence, but a recent study has suggested that in that period Athenians continued for the most part to appoint as generals men of wealthy ancestry.[259]

At the end of the classical period Theophrastos saw it as characteristic of the smarmy man or the petty snob to want to sit next to the generals in the theatre.[260] Aiskhines found it conceivable that the descendants of generals should be privileged in speaking in the assembly, even though (formally) they were not.[261] Earlier a play of Euripides contained a vigorous complaint about the standing of generals. The latter gain sole credit, it is alleged, for victories which are in fact the work of many thousands of warriors. "Sitting arrogant in their authority ... they think they know better than the *dēmos* ... whereas the *dēmos* has ten thousand times their wisdom, if only it could add the daring and the will."[262] These levelling sentiments, especially the interesting reference to the *dēmos* and its lack of self-confidence, seem out of place in the mouth of Euripides' character, Peleus (father of Akhilles), a mythical chieftain in an aristocratic setting. The incongruity points rather to a contemporary significance for the poet's audience. In short, the generalship was the most consistently prestigious and important of Athenian offices; the choice of wealthy and aristocratic men as generals reflects the limits of the *dēmos*' faith in itself, and helps to explain why the rich of Athens normally accepted the *dēmokratia*.

The courts and Athenian law

The courts of Athens, with their mass juries, were prominent in the making, as well as the enforcement, of law. Modern scholars have done much careful work in classifying their procedures.[263] However, rather less has been done to explain those procedures by reference to the political ideals of the period. Partly as a result, disparaging and patronising modern remarks are commonplace, not least from British scholars. Thus A. R. W. Harrison writes critically of "the general looseness of Athenian juridical concepts".[264] Behind much of the criticism lies a picture, accurate or not, of English justice: "the Athenians were much looser than we should be";[265] "Demosthenes introduces much irrelevant matter ... a fault countenanced by the general laxity of practice in the Athenian law courts, and perhaps due to the size of the Athenian jury, and the absence of any effective control over the proceedings such as is exercised by an English judge"; "the invective is more furious than would be allowed in an English court".[266]

In a noted recent study of Greek ideas (*Merit and responsibility* by A. W. H. Adkins) the author writes thus:

It is impossible to read a Greek [i.e. Athenian] forensic speech without being struck by the curious practices which are permitted, and the curious pleas which are considered relevant. One may reflect briefly that this is a natural result of the popular nature of these courts, and pass on; and there is some truth in this....[267]

If, in reading a Greek forensic speech, one has in mind the practice of a modern court of law, the most prominent oddity in Greek practice is the never-failing mention, where such have been performed, of the speaker's services to the state, not as a mitigating circumstance when he has been found guilty, but as a plea intended to justify his acquittal.[268]

... it is unreasonable to expect a popular assembly at any period, least of all one in which political theory is in its infancy, and in fact understood by none...[269]

... such thought may well be beyond the capabilities of a popular court.[270]

... questions of responsibility are hopelessly confused in the Athenian popular courts.[271]

We have already noticed the difficulty involved in the view that the mass audiences of Athenian drama could appreciate work of the highest quality while the mass audiences of political proceedings were lamentably unintelligent. It is a contention of this book. that the Greeks in general were not fools, and that to approach any culture in a patronising or condemnatory spirit is likely to blunt the understanding. Simply to counter the idea of the Athenians as failed Englishmen, it should be observed that there are aspects of English legal practice which might be effortlessly dismissed by someone with the values of an Athenian democrat. In contrast to Athenian openness, the selection of members of the public in England for the initial call to jury service is performed secretly by the executive, in accordance with criteria which are not published:[272] in the case of certain political trials by "vetted" jury, the selection of jurors is informed by communications from a secret police force. In Athens sentence was normally decided by a jury of the accused's peers; in England sentence is passed by a judge who is in no case elected to judicial position and who (in a crown court) is usually a person of very wealthy family. In Athens it was left open to the public to decide when and whom to prosecute; in England the matter is effectively controlled by the government and its executive (with results widely interpreted as partisan in inspiration[273]). Yet it would be profoundly mistaken to proceed from such (substantial) criticism to a general condemnation of English law, as being no more than a conspiracy of a wealthy establishment.[274] In the study of Athenian as of English law, any sense of superiority is profitably suspended in the search for ingenuity.

That courts could be an instrument for the oppression of the poor by the wealthy was a Greek belief of long standing, reflected in the work of Hesiod and Solon. An Athenian device which offered a high degree of protection against such abuse was the mass jury. About the precise numbers of jurors on particular occasions our information is disappointing. The *Ath. Pol.* gives as 6,000 the number paid (per year) at some stage of the Athenian Empire.[275] Even though not all may have been sitting at any one time, this number would make (by modern standards and probably by ancient)[276] a large proportion of a community to be involved in legal business.

The author of the *Ath. Pol.* records that in his own day disputes about large sums of money (i.e. over 1,000 *drakhmai*) were heard by 401 jurors, those about smaller sums by 201.[277] (The number of jurors was probably made odd to avoid a tie; Athenian courts decided by simple majority.[278]) We hear of several juries of 2,000 or more[279], including one of 6,000.[280] Significantly, this jury of 6,000 is recorded in a case involving the *graphē paranomōn*, the indictment of a man for proposing unconstitutional legislation[281] This process could be used even against a bill already passed by the assembly. But if the assembly was to be overruled, it could hardly be by an unrepresentative body. The number 6,000 corresponds with modern estimates of the maximum attendance of the assembly in the fifth century. It may well be that in creating a jury of that size the Athenians were consciously forming almost a second assembly, one which would in size be equal to, if not larger than, the first and which would be superior in its mode of composition, in that it could not be so easily packed by those with a special interest.[282] The atmosphere of a trial under the *graphē paranomōn* seems often to have been one of legislative debate rather than criminal prosecution. Aiskhines states that formerly friends brought actions against each other under this procedure, and that one man could boast publicly of having been indicted under it 75 times.[283] Since a court under the *graphē paranomōn* was effectively part of the legislature,[284] for the same reason that no minority, however specialised, could be given *formal* control over the assembly, no body of specialist lawyers could be allowed formally to govern the court.

The mass jury also guarded against improper influence of the rich exerted by means of bribery. It was well understood that a large group was much harder to bribe effectively than a small one.[285] Since participants in bribery usually shared an interest in secrecy, the extent of the practice cannot be determined. But the sheer volume of references to bribery[286] on its own suggests two things. First — if we believe that the Athenians had in general a fair idea of their own business — that some bribery went on. Second, that since bribery was believed to be common, men would be encouraged to practise it by the dilution of the sense of guilt and of vulnerability which generally occurs when it is believed of an offence that "everybody's doing it".[287] Even large juries were thought to have included at times a significant proportion of bribed men.[288] The *Ath. Pol.* has much detail on a system of empanelling jurors which had obviously been devised to reduce bribery.[289]

The threat of violence from powerful individuals (and others) provided a further motive for the use of very large juries. In his work *Against Meidias*, designed to incite resentment in poor Athenians against rich, Demosthenes suggests that potential prosecutors have been deterred from acting against the wealthy Meidias by fear of the man and of his companions.[290] Elsewhere a speaker includes among the standard reasons for murder a fear in the intending murderer that the person to be murdered is about to prosecute him.[291] The use of violence or intimidation against jurors might well be feared, if juries were small. Where juries are small in a modern legal system, that fear has proved important. The need to reduce influential intimidation and bribery of jurors was cited to justify two recent changes in English criminal law: the moving of jurors to a position in court where they could not be seen and identified from the public gallery, and the acceptance of majority (rather than unanimous) verdicts.[292]

How well represented on Athenian juries were different social groups is an important question, not satisfactorily answerable. The *Ath. Pol.* reports a complaint that ordinary Athenians were (in some sense) over-represented, as a result of their making more effort than did "the respectable" (i.e. those of long-established wealth) to take part in the lottery by which jurors were selected.[293] But quite who made the complaint, and what was their idea of the point at which ordinary jurors became too numerous, is unknown. Jury pay, raised from two to three obols per day in the 420s,[294] seemingly remained at the latter level down to the time of the *Ath. Pol.*[295] In the late fifth century three obols represented half what a skilled labourer might be paid on a building project; a century later the proportion had shrunk to about a fifth.[296] Often, then, a labourer might judge that he could not afford to serve as a juror. However, it has recently been argued that three obols were sufficient to support a small family in the fourth century as well as the late fifth;[297] many poor men, unable to find more lucrative work, must have welcomed the income, particularly since it was combined with a certain power and with the entertainment provided by the conflict of litigants.

The cross-questioning of witnesses, a central element in modern court cases, had no such place in Athenian courts. For much of the fourth century, witnesses had to give their evidence by written deposition before the hearing began;[298] during the hearing they could not alter or add to the evidence, but merely had to attest to it.[299] It may be (as is sometimes suggested) that the lack of prominence of witnesses resulted in part from the structure of Athenian courts, where the panels of jurors (or, strictly, of jurors-cum-judges) were too large for each member to have time for systematic questioning. But in the assembly the Athenians evidently accepted that some should be allowed to make long speeches to the obvious exclusion in practice of others'. ability to be heard. Why, likewise, should not some jurors have put questions to a witness? The litigant himself seems to have been exposed to challenges, in the form of questions or disbelieving noises, coming informally from the jury in the course of his speech.[300] Some further explanation is needed as to why witnesses were not examined on their testimony before the courts.

It was probably common opinion in Athens that a witness might well be connected corruptly with one side in court.[301] In Demosthenes' attack on Meidias the point is made clearly that a rich man could procure a dishonest witness with particular ease.[302] The device of the long speech directed attention not to the dubious words of a corruptible few (witnesses), but to public argument from probabilities; as the author of a standard treatise on Greek rhetoric puts it, "probabilities could not be bought".[303] However, a plausible argument could scarcely be constructed from general principles alone. It would need to include particular details about one or both parties to the litigation. And if the words of witnesses were not wholly to be trusted concerning such details, a question arises as to how details were established. We shall see that litigants in their speeches emphasised their own and their ancestors' public actions, which often included financial generosity towards the *dēmos* of which there was lasting record. Probabilities could not simply be bought, but in some cases money might be necessary for their procurement.

Since they had *some* role in the legal process, witnesses to the facts of a case were probably able to confer a certain advantage on the wealthy litigant. Similarly with the *synēgoroi*, who spoke up for litigants on their general character; they too, according to Demosthenes, were easy for the rich to procure.[304] It was thought necessary to illegalise the receipt of money for such advocacy.[305] The rich at times came under great pressure in the courts, as will shortly be seen. We should note now the capacity of the rich for organising in their own defence, and especially Thucydides' reference to the sworn societies (*xynōmosiai*, the regular word for conspiracies) which pre-existed the oligarchic revolution of 411 and which were intended to promote their members' interests in legal cases.[306] The oligarch Peisandros is recorded as having approached all of these societies in seeking help for the projected overthrow of the *dēmokratia*.[307] Evidently they existed mainly if not entirely to help the wealthy.[308] Also helpful to the rich was the practice of having one's lawcourt speech written by a skilled legal writer, a *logographos*. (Many such speeches survive, composed for clients or friends by Lysias, Isaios, Demosthenes and others.) Although to receive money as a *logographos* might be illegal,[309] a voluntary transaction of this kind would be hard to prevent and evidently could be lucrative;[310] high fees, of course, would discriminate against the poor.[311]

In Athenian law prosecutions of men accused of actions against the public interest were regularly brought by private citizens, by "anyone who wanted",[312] using the process called *graphē*.[313] This freedom of access is remote from normal modern practice of criminal law, and is often described — with reference to modern law — in negative terms. Thus one scholar writes, "there was no public prosecutor at Athens".[314] More accurately it might be said that there was no *state* prosecutor, since members of the public themselves were free to prosecute. The assumption behind the modern phrase 'public prosecutor', that officials of the state can be relied upon properly to represent the public, would almost certainly have been rejected by Athenian democrats. Indeed, free access to prosecution was seen as central to democratic theory; in the *Ath. Pol.* that access is described as one of the elements of Solon's constitution which seemed most favourable to the *dēmos*.[315] For one thing, it maximised the chance that a wronged person would find someone to vindicate him in court.[316]

Critics have often pointed to certain disadvantages of allowing lay people to prosecute. Two in particular will be touched on below: the risk of widespread blackmail ("I shall prosecute you unless you give me..."), and the probability that inexperienced prosecutors addressing courts controlled by laymen would — like inexperienced essay-writers today — tend to irrelevance and moralising. Blackmail and forensic irrelevance were familiar and problematic topics to Athenians.[317] Why, then, did the resourcefulness of Athens not give rise to a state prosecution system? Athenians would fear that a small group of officials might often be prevented from prosecuting by bribery. By making the number of potential prosecutors almost as great as the entire adult male citizen population, the *dēmokratia* reduced the chance that money would protect the authors of widely-known offences. The Athenian system also guarded against a subtler form of corruption: failure to prosecute because of political or social links between an offender and officials in control of the process of prosecution. Corruption of this sort causes recurrent scandal in modern states. Athenians would surely have predicted such trouble, from a centralised system of prosecution. We have only. to recall Aiskhines' statement that, in a bygone period, "not only rival politicians but even friends used to prosecute each other" under the *graphē paranomōn*.[318] The orator expects his audience to find remarkable such breaches of solidarity, even when the "friends" were comrades in military and political action rather than men personally fond of each other.[319]

To act as prosecutor took time, was stressful and could create (or intensify) enmities. To encourage the lay prosecutor there was no fixed payment, such as an official prosecutor today receives. Instead, in many cases a successful prosecutor was rewarded with a substantial proportion of the fine levied on the convicted defendant.[320] (Compare the arrangement in Victorian England whereby a gamekeeper could receive half of the fine paid by a poacher convicted on his evidence.)[321] The Athenian prosecutor's reward may seem arbitrary; why should a prosecutor receive much more if his opponent was rich, and thus paid a large fine, than if he was poor? But the question is answered if one reflects on the special resources, legal and illegal, which a rich man could deploy in his own defence and which otherwise might deter a would-be prosecutor. A potential prosecutor of humble attainments and means but with a fairly good case would reflect on the possibility of being routed in court by a rich defendant with superior rhetorical training, help from a top speech-writer and eminent *synēgoroi*. And a routed prosecutor usually ran the risk of being caught by the mechanism which the Athenians used to restrain unrealistic indictments. In most cases the prosecutor who received less than one-fifth of the votes of the jury was liable to a heavy fine, of 1,000 *drakhmai*.[322] Prosecutors whose motives appeared ugly might also face disgrace or punishment as "sykophants", a politically important label, to which we now turn.

The term 'sykophant' is prominent in Athenian legal and political writing.[323] Yet in the extant literature the word is nowhere satisfactorily defined; nor do we possess a detailed and reliable account of any individual who was, by general consent, a sykophant. When the *Ath. Pol.* was written there was a law or laws against sykophancy, which suggests that there was some agreement on the meaning — or perhaps *a* meaning — of the word.[324] But the frequency of the term in invective suggests that it was a potent political cry, and that in turn suggests that its meaning was stretched by partisans eager to apply it to opponents. Aiskhines confirms the latter point when he writes of. "the name given to rogues in general — 'sykophant' ".[325] However, many usages of the word reflect an idea of misusing prosecution, or the threat of it, for personal profit. (Allowable motives in a prosecutor were impartial concern for justice and personal enmity against the defendant. But to live by prosecution was widely viewed as despicable.[326]) The writers who use the term most often or most memorably are Aristophanes and Isokrates, both sympathisers with the rich against the radical *dēmokratia*. Thus, for example, the plot of Aristophanes' *Birds* (of 414) involves two conservative Athenians fleeing from their litigious city, and being pestered by a sykophant.[327] The politicians most noted for their opposition to sykophants were the Thirty, virulent anti-democrats. Rich men, and oligarchs who claimed to speak for them, would inevitably resent a prosecutor who might use a court to seize for himself much of another man's fortune. Theophrastos saw it as characteristic of an oligarchic man to complain that "the sykophants make life in the city intolerable" and that there were "terrible things which we have to put up with in the courts".[328]

After Athens' final defeat in the Peloponnesian War, indignation in the city against "sykophants" appears to have been strong. Xenophon records that, when in the aftermath of the war the Thirty put anti-aristocratic sykophants to death, some Athenians happily co-operated while the rest (apart from those who had themselves been involved in sykophancy) had no objection.[329] Xenophon's evidence has, as usual, to be examined for conservative bias, but here is almost certainly correct. For Lysias, whose family suffered severely from the Thirty,[330] wrote for a democratic jury after the fall and disgrace of the Thirty that if the latter had restricted themselves to acting against sykophants and other rogues the democrats would have thought them good men.[331] The *Ath. Pol.* describes Athens as rejoicing at the killing of the sykophants.[332] Probably because defects in one's own side make a satisfying explanation for defeat, sykophants were widely identified as a main cause of Athens' defeat at the hands of Sparta. It was alleged that pressure from travelling Athenian sykophants had driven the rich among Athens' allies into their damaging oligarchic revolts.[333] Hostility towards sykophants survived for most, at least, of the fourth century; one litigant even felt it

necessary to begin a speech with the words 'That I am not acting
as a sykophant...'.[334] At least after 404, fear of the damning label
no doubt did something to restrain potential prosecutors of the
rich.

In what sense, if any, was there at Athens a rule of law? The
Old Oligarch states that the *dēmos* "*is* the law at Athens".[335]
Xenophon, reporting the scandalous debate on how to deal with
the generals of Arginousai in 406, writes that when a procedure
proposed in the assembly was challenged as unconstitutional,
"the great mass (*plēthos*) shouted that it would be terrible if one
were not to allow the *dēmos* to do whatever it wanted".[336] These
reports should not, however, suggest that the *dēmos* ruled quite
capriciously. The Old Oligarch's words are qualified in Greek
with the particle *dē*, which may suggest that they were expected to
be found surprising. Xenophon records the Athenians as having
eventually repented of their treatment of the generals.[337]

A more promising statement, part of a work less obviously
biased against the *dēmokratia*, is made in the *Ath. Pol.*; there the
dēmos is described as having "made itself sovereign over
everything"; "all things are administered by decrees (*psēphismata*)
and by courts in which the *dēmos* rules".[338] However, a recent
survey of fourth-century procedure has suggested that the
assembly, when acting on its own, confined itself to regulating the
particular case and did not make legislation of general applica-
bility — except at moments of crisis.[339] (The late-fifth-century
breach of procedure, after Arginousai, itself occurred at a
moment of rare emotion.) At normal times in the fourth century
the assembly seemingly respected the right of a standing
committee, the *nomothetai*, to validate laws in conjunction with
the assembly — which perhaps reflects an awareness of the need
for proposed legislation to be considered for rather more time
than the meetings of the assembly could afford.[340] Our information on the laws (*nomoi*) valid in the fourth century is hardly
sufficient to allow calculations of how often decrees of the
assembly contradicted some aspect of a law.[341] But where such a
thing was thought to have happened, the mechanism of the *graphē
paranomōn* existed to give a carefully constituted body the chance
to review the allegedly offending decree.[342]

That the laws and decrees of Athens should be available for
consultation in permanent form was of great importance to the
dēmos, to judge by the extraordinary expense incurred in
inscribing legislation on stone during the era of *dēmokratia*. In a

play of Euripides we meet the view that laws, when in writing, gave to the poor man rights equal to those of the rich.[343] A contrast may be understood with courts under an oligarchic constitution; the judges of a bygone age, who were remembered as having favoured the rich, were probably also remembered as having stated the law arbitrarily to justify their decisions, at a time when the litigant was unable to check and cite a written text.

For part of the classical period it may have been left to the litigant to quote the text of any law he thought relevant. But a law threatening with the death penalty those who cited non-existent laws suggests that this practice created serious problems.[344] A less heavy-handed attempt to prevent abuses is reflected in a rule of the early fourth century, that laws quoted must be set down in writing and read out by a court official.[345] In the constitutionally turbulent period at the end of the fifth century, rival litigants may have produced contradictory statements of the law in court.[346] In reaction to the turbulence, the *nomothetai* were established to systematise the law and (probably in the early fourth century) a record office was set up, in a building called the *Mētrōon*, where laws and decrees could be inspected by the public.[347]

Writing in 330, Aiskhines complains that "nowadays" at the start of a case under the *graphē paranomōn* the jurors are inattentive during the reading of the charge and of the law which the defendant has allegedly contravened.[348] His audience for this complaint was an Athenian jury in such a case: he could hardly have hoped to deceive.[349] However, such was the frequency of cases under the *graphē paranomōn* in the fourth century that jurors at times may have expected to be familiar, from repeated quotation, with the law or laws supposedly contravened, while the decree under scrutiny might be well known from recent publicity. Also, the notion of illegality may on occasion have been viewed as a convenient fiction, with the real purpose of the court being to review a proposed decree on its general merits, almost as a second *ekklēsia*.

A more general reflection on the quality of Athenian legalism is contained in a passage of Aristotle's *Rhetoric*. Describing rhetorical techniques to be used in court, Aristotle gives two opposed approaches. If a written law tells against one's case, one should invoke the clause in the juror's oath about using one's "best discretion", and claim that this means the written laws should not always be applied rigorously. One should argue that fairness is a constant thing, whereas written laws often change; that a particular law is not valid because it is not just, as a law must be. One should also "fight in this way against the law", by arguing (where appropriate) that the circumstances for which it was framed no longer exist. If, on the other hand, the written law supports one's case, one should say that the clause about using "best discretion" does not exist to allow verdicts which run counter to law but to permit a verdict to be made in good faith where the law is obscure to the juror. One should say that a law, if not applied, might as well not exist; that while the law, like a doctor, sometimes does err, it is a sound general principle to act on the assumption that the law, like the doctor, is correct, since that principle causes less harm in aggregate than does the general habit of disobedience.[350] Aristotle in this context certainly has Athens in mind; and the clause which he quotes about "best discretion" was part of the Athenian juror's oath.[351] Modern states are familiar with particular laws under which the authorities will not prosecute or juries not convict. But Aristotle's remarks appear to be so wide in their application as to suggest that the litigant at Athens was in general less sure of his ground than his counterpart in a modern state. In particular, the doubt as to the meaning of the juror's oath concerns a matter so elementary and obvious (after Athens had had at least a century's experience of intensive litigation), as to suggest either that there was a certain mass blindness or (much better) that different elements within the city could not agree on the relation between the laws and the courts.[352] The picture of uncertainty which Aristotle implies is borne out by passages of surviving speeches in which litigants plead with the jurors to enforce the law.[353]

An Athenian speech-writer might also take diverse positions, according to the needs of the moment, on the subject of admissible evidence. In one passage Lysias writes disparagingly of a practice by defendants "which is customary in this city", namely:

> making no defence to the [formal] accusations made, but saying other things about themselves, sometimes to deceptive effect, demonstrating to you that they are good soldiers, or that they captured many enemy ships when they served as trierarchs or that they brought over enemy cities to our side.[354]

On another occasion he writes for delivery by a client:

> I did these things [acts of military bravery] ... so that if I were ever wrongly put in jeopardy [in court] I should get full justice because of the improved standing they gave me in your eyes.[355]

Again,

> I have served as trierarch five times, and fought in four sea battles and paid many special taxes [*eisphorai*] in wartime; also I have been second to none in the way I performed my other liturgies. ...the reason that I went to greater expense than the city ordered was this — that you would think better of me and that if some great misfortune [prosecution on a serious charge] were to befall me I should be in a better position to make contest.[356]

There is much evidence to suggest that success in court was made likelier by a record of good service to the community.[357] The liturgy, a form of service often invoked and more easily demonstrable than many, was only performed by the wealthy. It has been objected that the value placed by juries upon such service gave an improper advantage to wealthy litigants.[358] It might be difficult to find any legal system, ancient or modern, which has not given an important degree of privilege to wealth, if only in the form of superior access to the most respected lawyers. Modern systems differ from the Athenian in not (openly) admitting evidence of public service to bear on the verdict; in that respect wealthy people who may have used their wealth and position benificently cannot so easily profit from the fact. But at the stage of sentencing, considerations of a convicted person's social usefulness are prominent. It is not immediately clear that there is much practical difference between the modern custom of rewarding a previously good or eminent character with a nominal punishment, and the acquittal by an Athenian court of a man with such a character but clearly guilty as charged. Acquittal *might* of course be misinterpreted as a sign that the court was indifferent to the offence. But so might a nominal punishment issued by a modern court. The significance of the acquittal by an Athenian court of a clearly guilty man depended on whether it was understood by contemporaries that his past service rather than innocence as charged had won him the acquittal. If that was understood, other offenders and potential offenders could still expect to be punished on the same charge. And that the importance of character evidence was widely understood is made certain by the sheer volume of it in extant speeches from the Athenian courts.

The idealist Cato the Younger was once accused by an astute fellow Roman of talking as if he were in the Republic of Plato rather than among the dregs of Romulus.[359] We too should beware of judging the Athenian treatment of the rich without allowing for certain harsh realities of the time. These included a widespread and powerful pressure from rich men to be above the law. Xenophon's report on the military indiscipline of wealthy Athenians has already been noted. Xenophon also says that in the cities of Greece (other than Sparta) men of influence — by which he almost certainly means men of wealth — were unwilling to seem to have any fear of the authorities, thinking it beneath their dignity.[360] Such insubordination at Athens would recall the threat, at different times remote or pressing, with which the *dēmokratia* always lived — of oligarchic revolution. Athenian court procedure offered to the menacing rich a form of reward and social insurance. They could hope (though not assume) that they would have an honoured and privileged status in court, on condition that they used their wealth to perform important services for the community. Along with this near-promise, as stick with carrot, went a threat, that not to spend generously would be taken as evidence of an anti-democratic attitude and would leave a man exposed to attack in court.[361] Particularly at times of public shortage, the cash to be got for the community by condemning a rich defendant could tempt an Athenian jury.[362]

The latitude given to character evidence helped to guard against another form of political disruption. It is usually possible to stay within a set of explicit rules of behaviour while being so offensive as to be (intentionally or not) subversive.[363] Aristotle's comment on the power of rich men's arrogance to cause political upheaval has already been noted.[364] But at Athens a rich man may not have been able to protect his wealth from legal seizure merely by keeping the law and performing liturgies.[365] He probably also had to behave civilly. Otherwise evidence of his offensive demeanour might one day prejudice a court against him. In his (undelivered) speech against Meidias, Demosthenes seeks to influence his audience by describing Meidias' snobbish and abrasive behaviour in boasting audibly in public about his precious vases.[366] Effectively to punish such behaviour may seem severe. But if haughtiness and gloating, widely practised, could inflame the poor against the rich and contribute to *stasis*, it may well have been sensible to exercise clear and drastic sanction against such conduct.

The liturgies which rich men performed, whether at state behest or as volunteers, included most famously the trierarchy and the *khorēgia*. The former involved the maintenance for a year of a large warship and its equipment, while a *khorēgos* met the cost of preparing a chorus for an occasion such as a dramatic contest at the festival of Dionysos. At times the liturgy system came under strain. The Old Oligarch seems to record legal action against trierarchs for not repairing their ships.[367] Aristophanes in comedy suggests that the trierarchy might be shirked and that the task of maintaining a decrepit trireme was dreaded.[368] In the mid-fourth century defects in the system provoked a general overhaul.[369] But there was also much zeal shown by trierarchs at times. Thucydides describes lavish spending on the Sicilian expedition:

> the trierarchs made payments over and above the wages provided by the state...; they also used expensive equipment ... with each trierarch going to extreme lengths in his eagerness to ensure that his own ship most excelled in its appearance and its speed.[370]

In the performance of liturgies, the element of competition was important.[371] Even in a military context competition might be formal, and indeed a matter of bitter dispute. A speech survives which formally disputes the crown awarded to the first trierarch to have his ship ready.[372] (Dilatory trierarchs, on the other hand, were on occasion liable to be imprisoned;[373] we see again the combination of promise and threat.) Isokrates refers to an attempt by a *khorēgos* to rig the voting in a dramatic contest.[374] (Demosthenes' complaint against Meidias involved an allegation that Meidias had tried to prevent a *khorēgos*, Demosthenes himself, from winning the prize.[375]) The intense and dogged pursuit of prizes suggests that the motive of the liturgy-performer was not simply philanthropy or obedience to the law. Much personal pride was evidently involved. Many may also have been eager for general recognition of their spending. The most effective recognition of this was reserved for the winner; only he could record his performance permanently and conspicuously, by displaying the crown he received or by setting up a bronze tripod.

Such a monument gave enduring claim to political support.
(Compare the argument of Alkibiades that his great expenditure
justified his eminent position in the state.[376]) It was also a form of
legal insurance which might last a family for generations;[377] Isaios.
has a litigant cite his ancestors' tripods.[378] In contrast a
competitor in a liturgical contest who came last was exposed to
the taunts of an opponent in court.[379] In view of the forensic and
political importance of a man's liturgical record, it was rather
misleading of one modern scholar to write, "The choregia seems
to have been, at least in the fourth century, one of the great
occasions at Athens for 'conspicuous waste' ".[380] One defendant,
who cites his expenditure as a *khorēgos* and a victory by himself at
the Dionysia (recorded with a tripod),[381] states:

> I was thinking that this [my inherited wealth] caused me to
> be wickedly set upon by my enemies acting as sykophants,
> but that I was deservedly protected by you [Athenians] as a
> result of [my expenditure upon you].

It may now appear that two of the most despised of Athenian
institutions, the power of "sykophants" and the latitude given to
evidence in court, were intimately connected with one of the most
revered Athenian attainments, drama.

To survey the contents of Athenian drama is beyond the scope
of this book. However some brief (and tentative) comment may
be made, in connection with our theme of collaboration between
the social classes. Aristophanes, one of the most successful of
comic dramatists, was derisive about the contemporary
dēmokratia, as we have seen. His creation of a comic character
named Demos (in the *Knights* of 424) and his satire on the courts
(in the *Wasps* of 422) reflect a degree of tolerance in his audience;
indeed, the *Knights* won first prize. But a general characteristic of
comedy was its mockery of eminent contemporaries, which in
most cases meant rich contemporaries. The Old Oligarch reports
the Athenians as being well aware that

> the individual who is the target of comedy is usually not one
> of the democratic group or one of the mass, but is either rich
> or noble or powerful, whereas some few of the poor and the
> democrats are targets but only then because of their
> activism and their seeking to have more than the *dēmos*
> does.[382]

Now it may seem unimportant that the targets of comedy tended to be rich. After all, for comedy to appeal to a very large audience individuals satirised must be widely known. And the widely known, perhaps in every society, tend to be wealthy. But in most. societies, ancient and modern, the mere fact that the widely known have also tended to be the powerful and the rich has prevented their being satirised with the combination of trenchantness and openness permitted at the Athenian Dionysia. Comedy reflected the power of the *dēmos*, and released some popular resentment of grandees.

In tragedy eminent characters, mainly aristocratic and from a mythic period, provided a satisfying spectacle by their sufferings. According to Aristotle, tragedy characteristically afforded pity and terror.[383] The first emotion might give the poor *dēmos* the luxury of patronising the eminent; the second (like the first) might reassure the poor that the rich were not after all to be greatly envied. The central figures of tragedy are not simple villains;[384] in the matter of moral complexity we are closer to George Eliot than to Dickens. Nor was tragedy tragic in the modern sense; the downfall of a thoroughly good man, as Aristotle notes,[385] would not be pitiful or frightening but revolting. A few tragedies referred to contemporary subjects; these may prove unusually revealing, since we know much more about Athenian attitudes to contemporary circumstances than to the heroes of myth. Aiskhylos's *Persai*, on the downfall of an arrogant enemy of Athens, proved acceptable and (with its three companion plays) won first prize. On the other hand, a tragedy by Phrynikhos on the fall of Miletos (recently an ally of Athens) not only failed but caused its author to be heavily fined.[386] Tragic drama, in its complexity, may have regularly evoked not only pity and terror but also an element of resentment or distaste towards the main character. Certain tragedies of Euripides (*Iphigeneia among the Taurians* and *Helen*), in which the central figures do not fall but are rescued from adversity, have raised problems of definition for the genre. But in spite of their happy endings it is with sufferings of the eminent that they mainly deal. The more important that theme was felt to be for the definition of tragedy, the less of a problem there is in explaining how the Euripidean plays just mentioned were seen as belonging to the genre.

Where, as in most tragedies, the central figure does fall, the fall is not ·brought about by some proto-democratic leveller, on the lines of Homer's Thersites, but is often encompassed by a divinity. However, as has frequently been observed, the gods of tragedy have themselves been to an extent democratised. They are not so much the self-interested cheats and philanderers of earlier myth. Rather they enforce a certain order, justice. And justice is a cry by which the weak traditionally defend themselves against the strong. (One of the first sentences learnt by a modern child, for use against adults, is 'That's not fair'.) One breach of justice which exercises the gods of tragedy is *hybris* of eminent mortals against other mortals.[387] And *hybris* of grandees against itself was a preoccupation of the Athenian *dēmos*. It may well have given a certain satisfaction to democrats to see at the Dionysia wealthy men funding a spectacle in which mythological analogues of themselves, often displaying the supposed special vice of their class, received severe punishment from the highest moral authority.

Democratic Athens in the classical period remained the home of tragedy.[388] For much of that period the theoric fund existed, to ensure that the poor could afford to attend. Athens was noted for the large number of its religious festivals; Perikles boasted of it in the Funeral Speech.[389] The Old Oligarch writes, with obvious schematisation, that the Athenians held "twice as many festivals as other people".[390] He connects religious practice with the fact of *dēmokratia*:

> the *dēmos*, recognising that it is beyond the resources of poor individuals to sacrifice and feast...has devised this means whereby they may. The city sacrifices many victims at public expense. But it is the *dēmos* [i.e. the poor] which feasts and draws lots for the victims.[391]

(He also comments in this connection on the provision of fine buildings for the use of the poor at Athens.[392]) Details of Athenian cult cannot be explored here, but that there was a genuinely religious element in the celebrations may be inferred from the evidence we collect elsewhere on the standing of divination.[393] The rich had a prominent role in religious festivals, and not only in the production of drama. The Panathenaic procession to the Akropolis (portrayed in the Parthenon frieze)[394] gave a chance to display personal finery and, above all, that symbol of Greek wealth — the horse. When an Athenian mother is shown in comedy as having grand ambitions for her son, it is in such a scene that she imagines him, driving his horse-drawn chariot.[395]

Our information on the informal relations in public of rich and poor is often colourful, but largely reflects attitudes of the wealthy. The Old Oligarch, stating that at Athens slaves and metics enjoy the greatest excess of freedom, reports that it is not possible to hit such people, "nor will a slave make way for you". He explains that if the law had allowed a slave or metic or ex-slave to be hit, Athenian citizens would often have been struck by mistake. For the *dēmos* of Athens dressed no better, and had physiques no better, than slaves and metics.[396] Plato writes rather similarly about manners in the street in a *dēmokratia*; no doubt he had in mind his own city, Athens.

> Without personal experience of it, no one would believe how much more freedom domestic animals have [in a democratic as compared with a non-democratic city]. The proverb says that dogs get just like their mistresses; so do horses and donkeys, habitually walking along like free men giving themselves airs, bumping into anyone who meets them in the road, unless he gets out of the way[397]

Plato's main point here is, of course, about the human residents of the democratic city with their contagious liberty. He exaggerates; in this context male and female slaves are described as having no less freedom than their owners.[398] But if, as we may suspect, personal violence and the sense of degradation were less common at Athens than elsewhere, it may well be that fewer men than elsewhere took out anger and frustration upon animals, leaving the latter less inhibited.[399]

A speaker in Xenophon's *Symposion*, who represents himself as having ceased to be rich, boasts of no longer having to fear sykophants. Also, "rich men now get up to offer me their seats, and make way for me in the street".[400] There is exaggeration again ("Now I am like a tyrant, whereas before I was definitely a slave."). But, for all the overstatements, the three authors quoted above combine to suggest that in Athens rich men were not always deferred to in public as they would have liked. (That there was some deference to the wealthy is certain,[401] but our sources with their anti-popular bias would find that less worthy of remark.) Allied to the lack of extreme physical deference was a certain freedom of ordinary Athenians to speak against their social superiors; Plato has Sokrates say that, of Greek cities, Athens has most freedom of speech.[402]

Behind the public demeanour of the rich there lay, as Xenophon suggests, the fear of the courts, where the difference between popularity and unpopularity might mean the difference between safety and financial ruin. In particular the poor were protected by the law of *hybris*. This forbade gratuitously insulting behaviour even towards a slave, evidently so as to discourage a practice which might one day be applied to a citizen.[403] A passage of Aristophanes' *Wasps* may illustrate — when allowance is made for comic distortion — the kind of behaviour the Athenians feared, and in consequence how fearsome was the law of *hybris*.[404] A non-aristocratic Athenian has been to a *symposion*, the characteristic social occasion of the rich and fashionable. In his boorishness he inadvertently produces a parody of upper-class behaviour. He becomes noisily drunk,[405] and makes insulting remarks about the Athenian courts (of which he had previously been an enthusiastic supporter). On his way home, with a flute girl, he damages the wares of a female bread-seller, a poor citizen, whom he proceeds to patronise with a line of elegant — and insultingly irrelevant — chat, after the manner of a grandee.[406] A man then appears who has been hit by the reveller, and threatens the latter with a charge of *hybris*. This terrifies the reveller's sober son: "A charge of *hybris*? For god's sake don't bring that, please." And he offers immediately to pay whatever compensation the reveller's victim names.

Metics and slaves

The metics, whom we saw to have been protected from *hybris*, were a large and economically important group in classical Athens.[407] Thucydides records them as having contributed "not less than 3,000 hoplites" to Athens' full levy in 431, when the city's armed might was at its greatest.[408] If we could assume that the metics, like many other immigrant groups in history, tended to perform the less desired economic roles, it would follow that a higher proportion of their number probably fell below the hoplite level of wealth than was the case with the body of Athenian citizens. In that case, the 3,000 or more metic hoplites of the year 431 would suggest a total metic population at that time considerably greater than the 10,000 recorded of a point in the late fourth century.[409] Metics provided revenue in the form of direct taxation.[410] Some were extremely wealthy. Polemarkhos, brother of Lysias the future speech-writer, had 120 slaves working in his shield factory; the family property seems to have raised the enormous sum of 70 talents when it was sold by the Thirty — at a time of financial shortage in Athens.[411] The family could boast of having been invited to Athens by Perikles,[412] and their home provides the setting for Plato's dialogue, the *Republic*.[413] The social contacts and the wealth of these exceptional metics may, in normal times, have acted as an informal defence for the far more numerous poor of metic status, who would also commend themselves by their economic and military usefulness. Metics had no right to own land in Attikē, nor could they form part of the assembly or of a jury. These restrictions no doubt served to reduce any disruptive sense in ordinary Athenian citizens that metics presented a threat. To represent the interests of metics was part of the duty of the *polemarch*, an Athenian official appointed by lot.

In the informal status of slaves at Athens there was much variety, depending in part on the area of the economy in which they were engaged and on how visible they were.[414] Although slaves at Athens did not outnumber their masters to the extent that the helots at Sparta outnumbered the Spartiates, their economic position was still of great importance. Our best figure comes from Thucydides; he writes of more than 20,000 slaves, in large measure skilled men, escaping to the Peloponnesians after Sparta (in 413) established a base in Attike at Dekeleia.[415] A total of more than 150,000 for the male slaves at Athens in 330, quoted from the orator Hypereides, has generally been mistrusted, as seeming too high.[416] Many slaves were engaged in agriculture, probably the main area of the Athenian economy. (Compare Thucydides' statement that most Athenian citizens lived in the country — before the forced migration of 431[417].) The silver mines at Laureion, which helped to pay for the large amounts of grain imported by Athens, used many slaves. Xenophon, writing in the mid-fourth century but looking back to an earlier time, recalls that Nikias alone had 1,000 slaves of his own in these mines, while two other men had 600 and 300 respectively.[418] Xenophon seeks to persuade the Athenians that the mines could employ 10,000 state slaves or more, in addition to the privately owned workers.[419] Groups of slaves were also used in workshops and small factories, Polemarkhos's 120 being the largest recorded.[420] Female slaves were often occupied in "workshops" of a different kind.[421] Only exceptionally were slaves employed as fighters on campaign,[422] since an armed slave was dangerous to his master's side unless promised his freedom. But, as attendants to fighting men, slaves frequently served; Thucydides suggests that each of the hoplites in the large force used against Poteidaia was accompanied by a slave.[423] At home, the household slave was such a familiar figure that the word for one, *oiketēs*, became virtually a general term for 'slave'.

Who owned slaves? The case of the hoplites at Poteidaia suggests that ownership was widespread. A speech of Lysias states that everyone at Athens was a slave-owner,[424] while a speech of the mid-fourth century urges the members of an Athenian jury to think of the *oiketēs* whom each of them has at home.[425] But we may recall the successful barrister who, in 1960, asked an English jury whether a certain novel of D. H. Lawrence was something they would like their servants to read. An orator may know that a suggestion does not apply to many in the audience, while calculating that such people will be flattered to be treated as if it did. Plato writes that the largest element in a *dēmokratia* consists of citizens who do not own very much, and who support themselves with their own labour[426] — which is compatible with the ownership of a few slaves, or of course none. Aristotle observes that lack of slaves forces poor men to use wives and children instead.[427] The sum of 72 *drakhmai* is recorded as the price of one small child at Athens in the late fifth century, whereas the range 100–300 *drakhmai* may have encompassed most adult slaves at the time.[428] The cost of a single, ordinary slave may, then, have been close to an average year's income for an Athenian labourer. An extraordinary slave could be worth far more. The courtesan Neaira is said to have been valued at 3,000 *drakhmai* in fourth-century Korinth;[429] Nikias reportedly paid twice that sum for a mine overseer.[430]

The question whether Athens could have run a participatory democracy without slavery is too large, and perhaps too nebulous, to be treated here.[431] If we are to imagine slavery as abolished in favour of a wages system, we should need to know of what kind that system would be, since some forms extract far more value from employees than others, and some forms produce more wealth than others. Obviously the leisure provided by slaves was of great importance for many of the grandees who tended to lead the *dēmokratia* and for some of the hoplites who contributed to its stability. But it is conceivable that a system of wages would have yielded a similar amount of leisure to such men, as employers rather than slave-owners. Slavery could be wasteful; Plato comments on the cost (rather than the profit) involved in keeping slaves.[432] Some of the leisure gained by incurring that cost would be used in a way which helped the *dēmokratia*, but much would not. The *Odyssey* contains the interesting comment that Zeus takes away half a man's worth on the day he becomes a slave.[433] This seems to anticipate the modern commonplace, that people work better when working for themselves.

Nowhere in our sources do we seem to have any reference to a serious fear of an uprising (as distinct from peaceful flight) by Athens' slaves. This may suggest that in the main the slaves of Athenians were treated relatively gently. For one thing, slaves made collectively desperate by ill-treatment were likely, sooner or later, to pose a threat. Also, in commenting on the huge number of slaves at Khios, Thucydides remarks that punishment of offending slaves was the harsher because of the size of the slave population, which was greater than that of any other state save Sparta.[434] He seems to have meant that the harshness flowed from fear of revolt, and thus that where there was no such fear treatment might be milder. At Athens to kill a slave was illegal.[435] The protection given to slaves from other forms of violence and from extortion made sense, according to the Old Oligarch, as a means of safeguarding the sums of money which some slaves at Athens were allowed to own.[436] Without protection, such slaves would be easy targets. For the wage-earning slave the highest incentive was the prospect of being allowed by the master to purchase freedom. In a famous (and exceptional) case a slave named Pasion made much money as a banker, and acquired not only freedom but Athenian citizenship.[437] We have already noted complaints from conservative sources about liberties enjoyed by slaves at Athens. The democratic orator Demosthenes expected his Athenian audience to accept that the freedom of speech allowed to many slaves in the city was greater than that possessed by citizens in some other states.[438] Aristotle records the view of some that slavery was unjust, because based on violence.[439] The liberation of the slaves who fought at Arginousai, and the support for later, similar, moves,[440] show that there was no overwhelmingly dominant idea at Athens that slaves were by nature unfit for freedom. Indeed, it would be very surprising if there had been, since alongside the mass of slaves of non-Greek origin there were many formerly citizen Greeks, whom the Athenians had enslaved in the course of their imperialism.[441]

Evidence also exists of bad relations between slave and Athenian master. A speech of Lysias refers to slaves as naturally hating their masters;[442] reflecting on their lost freedom, many first-generation slaves surely would. The great number of. escapers to Dekeleia is eloquent. They had probably been promised freedom. But they could expect severe punishment if caught and returned to their owners. And, even if they succeeded in reaching Dekeleia, they were putting themselves at the mercy of men who were noted for treating severely, and making false promises to, their own unfree population.[443] Flogging of slaves may have been frequent at Athens; Aristophanes has a grim joke about a slave's being unaware of the beating he is getting.[444] (Compare the princess and the pea.) Slaves were tortured to extract evidence for use in lawcourts.[445] Yet there is a suggestion that to make a threat of torture against a slave in public counted as bad behaviour.[446] It may just be that in the treatment of slaves a distinction applied rather like the one which now affects behaviour towards domestic animals — gentleness being the required form in public and in the case of known individuals, whereas out of sight and towards a mass different standards apply. A slave who was one of hundreds belonging to the same master, away from the general view in the silver mines or on a large farm, could perhaps expect usage profoundly unlike that of the *paidagōgos* who taught a child of wealthy family or of the young slave who was a rich man's sexual pet. We recall that the remark about freedom of speech for slaves applied to "many" rather than to all of their number. In the unlevelled *dēmokratia* of Athens, slaves too may have had their hierarchy.

Notes

1. Arist. *Pol.* 1281b, cf. 1274a.
2. Aristotle, cited by Plutarch, *Life of Lykourgos* 28 7.
3. [Arist.] *Ath. Pol.* 22 4 — written near the end of the classical period.
4. For introductory references to the voluminous modern literature on this topic, see the bibliography in G. Vlastos (ed.), *The philosophy of Socrates*. Still of great value is the account of G. Grote, *History of Greece*, vol. IX, ch. 68. This sets Sokrates in his political context, and avoids the common fault of adopting exclusively his viewpoint. While two versions survive of Sokrates' defence (*Apology*), written by Xenophon and Plato, the prosecution case is not extant, and we are thus unable to apply the traditional legal principle, *audi alteram partem* ('Hear the other side').

The reaction against Sokrates in 399 was inspired in part by hatred of the oligarchy of the Thirty, only recently deposed; Sokrates was remembered as the educator of its leader, Kritias (Aiskhines I 173). Sokrates' proposal, on being found guilty, that his sentence should be to dine at the Prytaneion (in fact a high honour), must have seemed to many to reflect the contempt for the democratic courts for which oligarchs of the time were noted; Plato, *Apology* 36d-e. Even Xenophon, an admirer of Sokrates, attributed the latter's fate in part to his offensively grand style of speech at the trial; *Apology* I 1 with *Memorabilia* IV 4 4.

5. Plato's mother was Kritias' first cousin.

6. G. E. M. de Ste. Croix,*The class struggle in the ancient Greek world*, 296, cf. 290.

7. Accessible modern accounts of Athenian constitutional procedure and law include: C. Hignett, *A history of the Athenian constitution to the end of the fifth century BC*; A. R. W. Harrison, *The law of Athens*; A. H. M. Jones, *Athenian democracy*; D. M. MacDowell, *The law in classical Athens*. See also the various works of M. H. Hansen cited below.

8. E.g. Perikles, quoted in Thuc. II 37 1.

9. Arist. *Pol.* 1294a, 1310a, 1317a-b, 1318a; cf. below n.438.

10. Xen. *Hell.* II 3 24; for the view of democrats that not living as one liked was the mark of a slave, Arist. *Pol.* 1317b.

11. Cf. Arist. *Pol.* 1274a.

12. Arist. *Pol.* 1310a; Plat. *Rep.* 557b-c. Plato writes that a city under *dēmokratia* becomes "stuffed" with freedom and equality of speech.

13. See Chapter 6 on the Spartan *homoioi* ('similars').

14. See p.47.

15. Arist. *Pol.* 1279b–1280a.

16. Ibid., 1281a, 1318a, cf. 1305a, 1309a.

17. Ibid., 1309b–1310a.

18. [Arist.] *Ath. Pol.* 40 3.

19. Diod. XV 57 3 – 58 4; Plut. *Moralia* 814b.

20. [Arist.] *Ath. Pol.* 56 2.

21. Thuc. II 65 2.

22. Old Oligarch, I 3.

23. A. W. Gomme's *The population of Athens in the fifth and fourth centuries BC* still forms a useful introduction to this subject, though compare now the critical references in P. D. A. Garnsey, *'Grain for Athens'* in *Crux: Essays presented to G. E. M. de Ste. Croix*, ed. P. A. Cartledge and F. D. Harvey, 62–75. Also important is M. H. Hansen, *Demography and democracy*.

24. Hdt. V 97.

25. The site of the assembly was far too small for such a number — see below.

26. Aristoph. *Ekkl.* 1132f.

27. Plat. *Symposion* 175e.

28. Gomme, op. cit. 3.

29. Thuc. III 87 3, cf. II 31 2.

30. II 13 6–9 with Gomme, *HCT*, ad loc. In addition, Perikles spoke of 1,200 cavalry and 1,600 archers.

31. On metics see below. Thucydides (II 31 2) records that "not less than 3,000" metics campaigned as hoplites with an Athenian force in 431.

32. [Arist.] *Ath. Pol.* 26 4 with P. J. Rhodes, *A Commentary on the Aristotelian Athenaion Politeia*, 331f.; cf. Plut. *Life of Perikles* 37 3.

33. See p.157.

34. Thuc. VIII 97 1.

35. Ibid.

36. Lysias XX 13.

37. Diod. XVIII 18 4f., cf. Plut. *Life of Phokion* 28.

38. A useful survey of our scanty evidence for wages and prices in classical Athens is given by M. M. Markle in *Crux* (above, n. 23), 293–7.

39. Diod. XVIII 18 5; Plut. *Life of Phokion* 28.

40. Diod., ibid.

41. A. H. M. Jones, *Athenian democracy* 81.

42. On attempts to calculate the total population (slave and free) of Athens on the basis of ancient information on the amount of grain imported; see now Garnsey, op. cit.

43. Lysias XXXIV with the brief summary by Dionysios of Halikarnassos.

44. Cf. Plat. *Rep.* 565a.

45. E.g. Isaios VI 25 and cf. Dem. 43 19, J. K. Davies, *Wealth and the power of wealth in classical Athens* 75.

46. See, e.g., the *Nikomakhean Ethics, passim.*

47. Arist. *Pol.* 1295b.

48. Ibid., 1296a.

49. Eur. *Supplices* 238–45.

50. See (even) Thuc. II 15 1f.

51. Arist. *Pol.* 1296a; cf. *Ath. Pol.* V 3.

52. Arist. *Pol.* 1295b.

53. J. K. Davies, op. cit., 28 and chart facing p.36; *Athenian propertied families* XXIII–XXIV.

54. Cf. Thuc. II 44 2.

55. Arist. *Pol.* 1297b. On the dangerous elasticity of Greek terms meaning 'poor', Davies, op. cit. (n. 45), 10,13.

56. E.g. I 1 and III 1. On the Old Oligarch see further G. W. Bowersock, *Harvard studies in classical philology*, 71 (1966), 33ff., A. W. Gomme, *More essays in Greek history and literature*, 38–69.

57. Old Oligarch II 20.

58. The point is well made in the film *The Life of Brian*; as satire against the modern British left, a zealot of ancient Palestine, belonging to the Popular Front for the Liberation of Judaea, is shown as having to be reminded that the enemy is the occupying power, Rome, and not the Judaean People's Liberation Front.

59. For a brief introductory treatment (with some bibliography) of the question of authorship, see P. J. Rhodes, op. cit., 61–3.

60. Ch. 28.

61. See below, n. 113.

62. On Thucydides' attitude towards the *dēmokratia*, see Chapters 3 and 5.

63. p. 164.
64. pp. 167f.
65. p. 184.
66. Thuc. I 145 and preceding chapters.
67. Thuc. II 65 9.
68. p. 197.
69. Xen. *Hell.* I 7 12ff., 34.
70. Dem. XVIII 169f.
71. H. Last in *CAH*, XI, 435.
72. A. W. Pickard-Cambridge, *The theatre of Dionysus in Athens*, 141.
73. Thuc. II 65 2–4.
74. Thuc. III 37 3.
75. Thuc. VIII 1 1.
76. Old Oligarch II 17.
77. On Aristophanes' general political bias, de Ste. Croix, *Origins* 355–76.
78. Aristoph. *Ekkl.* 193ff.
79. Antiphon *Murder of Herodes* 91; cf. Isok. XV 19, *Ath. Pol.* 28 3.
80. Plat. *Rep.* 558a.
81. Gomme's translation (*HCT*, II, 300) of Plato the Comedian frag. 220 (in the edition of T. Kock).
82. See below, and also G. T. Griffith, 'Isegoria [lit. 'equality of speech'] in the Assembly at Athens' in E. Badian (ed.), *Ancient Society and Institutions (Studies Presented to Victor Ehrenberg)*, 115–38.
83. See, e.g., the Periklean funeral speech in Thuc. II; Lysias II.
84. Cf. Oscar Wilde's saying, 'The very essence of romance is uncertainty.'
85. Eur. *Supplices* 399–455 with (on the date of the play) G. Zuntz, *The political plays of Euripides*, 56ff.
86. E.g., F. Thompson's *Over to Candleford* (1941) and A. L. Rowse's *The spirit of English history* (1943).
87. With the possible exception of the Old Oligarch.
88. For an accessible text and translation of Solon's poetry, J. M. Edmonds, *Elegy and Iambus* (Loeb), I, 114ff.
89. On the chronology see the introductory bibliography at Rhodes, op. cit. (above, n.32), 120–2.
90. C.Hignett, *A history of the Athenian constitution to the end of the fifth century* BC, 18f.
91. On Solon in general, A. Andrewes, *The Greek tyrants* 84–91.
92. Solon cited in [Arist.] *Ath. Pol.* 5 3.
93. Ibid.
94. Line 39 of the verse quoted at Dem. XIX 255.
95. [Arist.] *Ath. Pol.* 12 3.
96. Ibid., 12 4.
97. Ibid.; cf. lines 25–7 of the verse quoted at Dem. XIX 255.
98. [Arist.] *Ath. Pol.* 12 1, cf. 12 5.
99. Ibid., 12 3, though contrast the lines quoted at Plut. *Life of Solon* 3 3, where Solon states that "many bad men are rich, many good men poor".
100. [Arist.] *Ath. Pol.* 12 2.

101. Ibid.

102. Alkibiades quoted at Thuc. VI 16 1–5; cf. Perikles at Thuc. II 40 2.

103. *praünei*, at lines 39f. of the verse at Dem. XIX 255; cf. *praotēs* at [Arist.] *Ath. Pol.* 22 4.

104. [Arist.] *Ath. Pol.* 12 4f.

105. E.g. *Ath. Pol.* 12 3–5.

106. Andrewes, op. cit., *passim*.

107. E.g. Thuc. VI 60 1 and the references collected in Gomme-Andrewes-Dover, *HCT*, IV, 323.

108. Thuc. VI 59.

109. Thuc. VI 54 5, cf. 54 6.

110. Hdt. I 60 2 — 61 2.

111. For an introduction to the very large modern bibliography on the subject, Rhodes, op. cit. (above n.32), 240ff.

112. Hdt. VII 142, cf. V 78, VI 131 1, Thuc. VIII 68 4.

113. Arist. *Pol.* 1304a, [Arist.] *Ath. Pol.* 23 1f., 25–26 1. On the severe problems presented by the cited passages of the *Ath. Pol.*, see Rhodes's commentary, (above, n. 32), esp. pp. 283–6, 319f.; also the same author's *The Athenian boule*, 201–7. In particular, the role attributed to Themistokles appears to be gravely anachronistic.

114. For a fuller and easily accessible modern treatment of this topic, see J. K. Davies, *Democracy and classical Greece*, ch. 4.

115. [Arist.] *Ath. Pol.* 28 2. Kimon's enthusiasm for Sparta, patron of oligarchic states, gives some support for this view; see pp. 21, 23.

116. See pp. 21f.

117. Anaximenes *Philippika*, in F. Jacoby, *Die Fragmente der Griechischen Historiker*, 72, F13; cf. Rhodes, *The Athenian boule*, 201ff.

118. [Arist.] *Ath. Pol.* 25 4.

119. *Ath. Pol.* 26 2. The four classes were, in descending order of wealth, the *pentakosiomedimnoi, hippeis, zeugitai* and *thētes*; C. Hignett, *History of the Athenian constitution*, 99ff., 142f., 174, 224ff.

120. [Arist.] *Ath. Pol.* 27 3, cf. Plut. *Life of Kimon* 10.

121. See pp. 59–65 on the building of the Parthenon, and J. K. Davies, *Wealth and the power of wealth in classical Athens*, 91.

122. [Arist.] *Ath. Pol.* 27 3.

123. Thuc. VIII 66 1, 69 4.

124. Meiggs-Lewis, no. 40, lines 8f., and see above, p. 47. Pay was provided for the *boulē* by 411: Thuc. VIII 69 4.

125. On the origins and mechanics of ostracism, A. R. Hands, *JHS*, LXXIX (1959), 69ff., G. R. Stanton, *JHS*, XC (1970), 180–3 and Rhodes's commentary (above, n. 32) on the *Ath. Pol.* 267–71.

126. Thuc. I 135 3.

127. On Kimon see Chapter 1; on Thucydides son of Melesias, Plut. *Life of Perikles* XVI 3.

128. Hdt. VI 131 2.

129. Thuc. II 65 10.

130. See p. 150.

131. On Nikias, see p. 396; on Alkibiades pp. 62f.

132. See esp. lines 129ff. of the *Knights* (produced in 424) with de Ste.

Croix, *Origins*, 234, 359–62, *The class struggle in the ancient Greek world*, 290.

133. *Knights* 136. In reality Kleon perhaps owned slaves who worked leather. In Britain during the mid-1960s, after the leadership of the Conservative Party had passed from the 14th Earl of Home to Mr ' Edward Heath, the latter was frequently satirised as "The Grocer".

134. Dem. LVII 30.

135. *Knights* 137 etc. (See A. H. Sommerstein's edition of the play, p. 151.)

136. [Arist.] *Ath. Pol.* 28 3.

137. Thuc. III 19 1 with Gomme, *HCT*, ad loc.

138. See pp. 194f.

139. Lysias XII 67; cf. Thuc. VIII 68 2.

140. See esp. the speech no. 12 of Lysias, who lost a brother in the persecution; also [Arist.] *Ath. Pol.* 35 4. For the charge that the Thirty, in their rapacity, were comparable with the sykophants they attacked, Xen. *Hell.* II 3 22, cf. Lys. XII 6.

141. Lys. XXV 19, *Ath. Pol.* 35 3, cf. Xen. *Hell.* II 3 12.

142. Andokides I 90, Xen. *Hell.* II 4 43, *Ath. Pol.* 40.

143. Xen. *Hell.* II 4 43, *Ath. Pol.* 40 2f.

144. *Hell. Oxy.* 1 2f., Aristoph. *Ekkl.* 197f.

145. Below, nn. 164–5.

146. As in the speech Demosthenes wrote against Meidias (= Dem. XXI).

147. [Arist.] *Ath. Pol.* 7 4.

148. A. H. M. Jones, *Athenian democracy*, 124.

149. [Arist.] *Ath. Pol.*. 43 3f., 6.

150. *Eisangelia* on which see now M. H. Hansen, *Eisangelia: the sovereignty of the people's court in Athens in the fourth century* BC.

151. [Arist.] *Ath. Pol.* 43 3f., 6; cf. Aiskhines I 23.

152. M. H. Hansen, *The Athenian ecclesia*, 35–72, esp. 59.

153. Dem. XIX 154. Demosthenes could hardly be mistaken, or hope to deceive his Athenian audience, on the question of whether assemblies were limited in number, rather than being callable at will. Athenian practice in that matter would frequently be of conspicuous importance. The inference from Demosthenes' text, that the number of meetings was limited, is worth much more than Hansen's calculation of the number of meetings in one particular prytany on which we have information, the eighth of 347/6. That calculation depends unhealthily on the supposed ability of Athenians in 343 to remember with confidence much exact chronology of the earlier year. Unless that ability existed, the orators Aiskhines and Demosthenes, on whom Hansen depends, could have safely misled.

154. Hansen, *The Athenian ecclesia*, 43f.

155. Dem. XXIV 37; cf. *Ath. Pol.* 41 2.

156. Thuc. VIII 72 1.

157. Hansen, op. cit., 16ff.

158. Arist. *Pol.* 1297a.

159. Those members of the *boulē* responsible for convening the *ekklēsia* in a particular prytany.

160. Lines 19–24.
161. The Greek text of the scholion is in F. Dübner, *Scholia Graeca in Aristophanem*, 3.
162. Seminars at the London Institute of Classical Studies often start late because scholars, assembled from various colleges, are slow to leave their chat in the tea-room next door.
163. Contrast Hansen, *The Athenian ecclesia*, 10.
164. [Arist.] *Ath. Pol.* 41 3.
165. *Ath. Pol.* 41 3; Aristoph. *Ekkl.* 292, 392. Half a *drakhmē* per day was at the time a living wage; see Markle (above, n. 38), 276ff.
166. On the poverty at this period see p. 344.
167. *The Athenian ecclesia* 10–16; cf. Andok. I 87, Dem. 24 59, Dem. 59 89.
168. [Arist.] *Ath. Pol.* 62 2.
169. See Markle (above, n. 38), 293ff.
170. E.g. Aiskh. I 27ff. G. T. Griffith (above n. 82) argues tentatively that *isēgoria* — equal speech for (almost) all — was introduced into the assembly shortly before the middle of the fifth century.
171. Aiskh. I 27, Dem. XVIII 170; cf. (from the late fifth century) Aristoph. *Akh.* 45 and (from the early fourth) Aristoph. *Ekkl.* 130.
172. Aiskh. III 4, cf. I 23f., III 2 and Griffith (above n. 82), 119f.
173. Lys. XVI 20.
174. Plat. *Protag.* 319b-c cf. *Gorg.* 455b-c with the comments of T. Irwin in his *Plato: Gorgias*, 119.
175. On din in the courts, and its effects, V. Bers in *Crux* (above, n. 23) 1–15; for laughter in the assembly, see e.g. Thuc. IV 28 5, Aiskh. I 83f.
176. The Americans in general speak far more readily.
177. See, e.g., Plato's complaint about *parrhēsia* in the democratic city; *Rep.* 557b.
178. W. Jaeger, *Paideia*, I, 290f., 293, 315.
179. Lys. XXX 24.
180. Dem. XXII 30, cf.XXIII 5.
181. Dem. XXI 141.
182. Thuc. II 40 2. This public statement of an ideal should be compared with Perikles' preventing an assembly from meeting during a crisis in 431; Thuc. II 22 1.
183. Following Crawley's translation. This passage, however, presents textual problems; see Gomme, *HCT*, ad loc.
184. Aiskh. I 28–30, 186; Hypereides IV 8; Deinarkhos *Against Demosthenes* 71; A. R. W. Harrison, *The law of Athens*, II 204f; S. Perlman, *Athenaeum*, XLI (1963), 327–55, esp. 353f.
185. Dem. XXII 36f.
186. Aristoph. *Ploutos* 30f.; cf. Dem. XXI 189f.
187. Dem. XXIII 4.
188. Thuc. II 65 9.
189. See above, n. 182.
190. Thuc. I 145.
191. See chapter 5, and contrast Thuc. II 65 7.
192. See p. 159.

193. Thuc. II 65 4. The earlier debate about policy towards Kerkyra may also have involved an important degree of popular resistance to the advice of Perikles: Thuc. I 44 1.

194. Thuc. II 65 8.

195. E.g. Kleon, as reported by Thucydides, III 40 1; cf. III 38 2, 42 3, 43 1, Aiskh. III 103–5.

196. Aristoph. *Ploutos* 567ff.

197. Dem. XXI 189, XXIV 142.

198. E.g. Aiskh. III 103–5, and (on Demosthenes' involvement with Harpalos) E. Badian, *JHS*, LXXXI (1961), 16–43 esp. 31–6; R. Lane Fox, *Alexander the Great* 541–3.

199. For a clear and helpful treatment of the subject see F. D. Harvey in *Crux* (above, n. 23) 76–117.

200. Lines 377–9.

201. A. L. Boegehold, *Hesperia*, XXXII (1963) 366–74, E. S. Staveley, *Greek and Roman voting and elections*, 83–7, M. H. Hansen, *The Athenian Ecclesia* 103–21, cf. P. J. Rhodes, *The Athenian boule*, 39.

202. Aristoph. *Ekkl.* 263–5.

203. Xen. *Hell.* I 7 2.

204. An experiment with the double marking of undergraduates' exam scripts at a British university revealed that the average extent of deviance between different academic markers was more than four times greater in cases where the second examiner marked in ignorance of the first examiner's verdict than where the second examiner knew the earlier mark. P. J. McVey, *University of Surrey Dept. of Electronic and Electrical Engineering Report TR24*, pt. 2 sec. 7.

205. Cf. Plut. *Life of Perikles* XI on the pernicious balance of power between Perikles and Thucydides son of Melesias, before the ostrakism of the latter. The circumstances of Hyperbolos' ostrakism may also suggest that his rivals were close to balancing each other in power; Plut. *Life of Alkibiades* XIII 4f., *Life of Nikias* XI.

206. Thuc. VI 14 with Gomme-Andrewes-Dover, *HCT*, ad loc.

207. See pp. 163f.

208. Old Oligarch II 17.

209. Thuc. VII 18 2.

210. Thuc. V 36 1.

211. See chapters 4 and 5.

212. Thuc. VIII 1 1.

213. Thuc. VII 47 1, 48 4.

214. Thuc. VII 48 4.

215. Ibid.

216. Aiskh. I 35.

217. E.g. Samuel Pepys, *Diary*, entry for 19th December 1666. In the 1790s the Prime Minister, William Pitt the Younger, entered the Commons drunk on one occasion, with Henry ('Hal') Dundas. A contemporary classical scholar (Porson) wrote in satire:
Pitt: I can't discern the Speaker, Hal; can you?
Dundas: Not see the Speaker! Damn me, I see two.

218. Aristoph. *Ekkl.* 143.

219. Hdt. VI 136, Dem. XX 100, 135, XLIX 67, Hypereides IV 1 and

esp. 8.

220. [Arist.] *Ath. Pol.* 45 4. The standard work is P. J. Rhodes, *The Athenian boulē;* for bouleutic motions amended in the assembly, ibid., 71f., 278f.

221. See Rhodes, op. cit., 56, 65, 68.

222. Dem. XIX 185 (of 343).

223. The *prytaneis*.

224. Dem. XVIII 169f.

225. There is late evidence from lexica that for normal meetings of the *ekklēsia* the *boulē* had to give five days' notice of time and place, and perhaps also of agenda; Rhodes, op. cit., 20.

226. Dem. XXIV 48.

227. Meiggs-Lewis, no. 37, lines 15f.; no. 69, line 51; no. 94, line 32. For a systematic study of the *boulē's* influence on the assembly's decisions, Rhodes, *The Athenian boulē*, 52–81.

228. M. N. Tod, *A selection of Greek historical inscriptions* II, no. 200, lines 264–9.

229. [Arist.] *Ath. Pol.* 40 2 with Rhodes' commentary (above n. 32) on the passage; cf. 45 1.

230. [Arist.] *Ath. Pol.* 45 2, but see Rhodes, ad loc. on problems affecting the translation of the last sentence.

231. [Arist.] *Ath. Pol.* III 2.

232. Tod, op. cit., no.200, lines 242–51; Rhodes, op. cit., 119f.

233. Meiggs-Lewis, no. 46 lines 5f. and *passim*; cf. no. 69 (from the mid–420s).

234. Thuc. VIII 69 4, [Arist.] *Ath. Pol.* 43 2, [Dem.] LIX 3.

235. E.g. Xen. *Mem.* I 2 35.

236. [Arist.] *Ath. Pol.* 62 3.

237. Rhodes, op. cit., 16ff.

238. Examples cited (rightly or wrongly) in recent years include the Borough of Queens in New York and (in the UK) certain districts of Tyne and Wear.

239. On the Sorbonne in 1968, P. Seale and M. McConville, *French Revolution 1968*, ch. 6. Some four years later students of the North West London Polytechnic also had a structure of this kind. (Author's own information.)

240. [Arist.] *Ath. Pol.* 7 4, cf. Old Oligarch I 2.

241. Rhodes, op. cit., 5f.

242. [Arist.] *Ath. Pol.* 62 2 (the five obols). For the fact (though not the level) of pay in the late fifth century, Thuc. VIII 69 4.

243. Aristoph. *Thesm.* 936–8; cf. Old Oligarch III 3.

244. [Arist.] *Ath. Pol.* 44 2f.; Rhodes, op. cit., 23–6.

245. Arist. *Pol.* 1294b, though cf. 1317b. J. W. Headlam's *Election by lot at Athens* is still a useful treatment of the subject.

246. The theoric fund distributed money to the mass of the population, nominally to facilitate the purchase of theatre tickets; for an introductory discussion and bibliography, P. J. Rhodes, *A commentary on the Aristotelian Athenaion Politeia*, 514f. The fund itself may well have been a fourth-century invention; Rhodes, loc. cit.

247. [Arist.] *Ath. Pol.* 43 1. See also 54 3, 5 and Dem. XXI 171.

248. [Arist.] *Ath. Pol.* 24 3.

249. [Arist.] *Ath. Pol.* 62 3, referring to the author's own day.

250. Rhodes, op. cit., 513–5.

251. G. L. Cawkwell, *JHS*, LXXXIII (1963), 47–67.

252. Cf. Cawkwell, *JHS*, CI (1981), 54f.

253. Thuc. VIII 1 3.

254. For details of the frequent use against generals of the process of impeachment, M. H. Hansen, *Eisangelia, passim.*

255. Contrast the Spartan arrangement whereby two ephors accompanied a king on campaign; Xen. *Const. Spart.* 13 5.

256. Sailors in an Athenian force successfully opposed their generals' wish to put to sea after a defeat by Syracuse in 413 (Thuc. VII 72 3f.), though probably only a minority among them were Athenians; Thuc. VII 63 3f. with Gomme-Andrewes-Dover, *HCT*, ad loc.

257. Xen. *Mem.* III 5 18f.

258. Old Oligarch I 3.

259. J.K. Davies, *Wealth and the power of wealth in classical Athens*, 122–30.

260. Theophrastos *Characters* 5 or 21 (depending on the placing of the passage in question).

261. Aiskh. I 27.

262. Eur. *Andromakhē* 693–702.

263. As (in English) R. J. Bonner and G. Smith, *The administration of justice from Homer to Aristotle*; A. R. W. Harrison, *The law of Athens*; D. M. MacDowell, *The law in classical Athens* and M. H. Hansen (titles at nn. 254 and 281).

264. Harrison, op. cit., II, 34, cf. 17, 53 on further Athenian "failure" and looseness in legal practice.

265. Ibid., II, 53.

266. J. R. King, *Demosthenes: Speech against Meidias*, XIII.

267. A. W. H. Adkins, *Merit and responsibility*, 201.

268. Ibid.

269. Ibid., 207.

270. Ibid., 206.

271. Ibid., 208. Further modern criticism is quoted in ch. XI ('Estimates of Athenian justice') of Bonner and Smith, op. cit., vol. II.

272. A recent study of practice in Manchester discovered that students were being systematically excluded from the call to jury service.

273. As with the decisions in the mid-1980s to prosecute the civil servants Sarah Tisdall and Clive Ponting for communicating information against the government's interest, but not to prosecute civil servants in the Westland affair who divulged classified information in the government's interest.

274. One crude measure of the achievement of the English law is the extent to which its principles, and sometimes its trappings, have been imitated in countries as diverse as the United States and Nigeria, which emerged from colonial status with no general love of British constitutional forms.

275. `[Arist.] *Ath. Pol.* 24 3, cf. Aristoph. *Wasps* 662.

276. In a comedy of Aristophanes (*Clouds*, 206–8) a character denies

that a spot indicated on a map can be Athens, because he can see no
jurors sitting. Cf., on the prominence of the courts in Athenian life,
Aristoph. *Knights* 1316f., *Birds* 40f., 108f.

277. [Arist.] *Ath. Pol.* 53 3.
278. Cf. Rhodes' commentary (above, n. 246) on the *Ath. Pol.*, p.
729.
279. Lys. XIII 35 (2,000); Deinarkhos *Against Demosthenes* 52
(2,500).
280. Andok. I 17.
281. On the *graphē paranomōn* see now M. H. Hansen, *The sovereignty
of the people's court in Athens in the fourth century* BC *and the public action
against unconstitutional proposals.*
282. [Arist.] *Ath. Pol.* 63–5, with Rhodes' commentary (above, n.
246) on the system of lottery used to empanel courts in Aristotle's day.
283. Aiskh. III 194f.
284. Cf. Lys. frag. 87 (Teubner edn); Hansen, op. cit., esp. pp. 62–5.
285. Dem. XXIV 37, Arist. *Pol.* 1286a, [Arist.] *Ath. Pol.* 41 2, cf.
Old Oligarch III 7 (reading *syndekasai*).
286. For a selection of the most important, see F. D. Harvey in *Crux*
(above, n. 23), 76–117.
287. Cf. Arist. *Nik. Eth.* 1110a, 1118b, 1152a.
288. [Arist.] *Ath. Pol.* 27 5.
289. See above, n. 282.
290. Dem. XXI 20.
291. Lys. I 44, cf. Antiphon II a 5f.
292. The minimum majority acceptable now in England and Wales is
of 10:2. This may help us to understand why in Athens, where bribery
was more feared than it is in Britain today, a bare majority of jurors' votes
was sufficient to determine a verdict.
293. [Arist.] *Ath. Pol.* 27 4; on the lottery, see above, n. 282.
294. Aristoph. *Knights* 51, 797–800; scholia on *Wasps* 300 and *Birds*
1541.
295. [Arist.] *Ath. Pol.* 62 2.
296. On jury pay see now M. M. Markle in *Crux* (above, n. 23), 265–
97.
297. Markle, loc. cit. On arguments, largely inconclusive, which
purport to gauge the social composition of juries from the tone of
references in lawcourt speeches towards wealth and poverty, Markle
282ff.
298. Lykourgos *Against Leokrates* 19.
299. Dem. 45 44. On witnesses in general, Bonner and Smith, op.
cit., II, ch. 6.
300. E.g. Lys. XIII 76 and the references at Bers, *Crux* (above, n. 23),
9. On the general subject of informal noise from jurors, Bers, 1–15.
301. Dem. XIX 216, XXI 139, XXIX 28.
302. Dem. XXI 112, cf. Plat. *Gorg.* 523c.
303. G. Kennedy, *The art of persuasion in Greece*, 32.
304. Dem. XXI 112, cf. [Andok.] IV 15, Dem. 44 3, Lyk. *Against
Leokrates* 138. On *synēgoroi* see Harrison, *The law of Athens* II, 158f.
305. [Dem.] 46 26.

306. Thuc. VIII 54 4.

307. Ibid.

308. Cf. Thuc. VIII 68 1 on the great forensic skill which the oligarchic Antiphon put at the disposal of others (especially, no doubt, of those who shared his ideals).

309. Antiphon frag. B I (in *Minor Attic orators* (Loeb edition), I.

310. Cf. Aristoph. *Clouds* 466ff., Isok. XV 38.

311. Compare Lord Justice Sir James Mathew: "In England, Justice is open to all, like the Ritz hotel"; R. E. Megarry, *Miscellany-at-Law*, 254.

312. [Arist.] *Ath. Pol.* 9 1, cf. Aristoph. *Plout.* 917f.

313. On the distinction between *graphē* and *dikē* see Harrison, *The Law of Athens*, II, 74ff. The distinction has been likened to that between criminal and civil proceedings in modern law, but the comparison may mislead. Homicide, for example, was the subject of *dikē*, not of *graphē*.

314. Harrison, op. cit., II, 6. Harrison here notices certain exceptional circumstances in which the initiative in bringing a matter to court had to be taken by a magistrate and not by a private citizen.

315. [Arist.] *Ath. Pol.* 9 1, cf. Lyk. *Against Leok.* 3f.

316. Cf. Plut. *Life of Solon* 18.

317. See below, and Aiskh. I 178f.

318. [Arist.] *Ath. Pol.* III 194.

319. He cites (s. 195) a single case in support of his statement, making no clear mention of personal friendship between the two men involved, but rather of military and political companionship.

320. MacDowell, *The law in classical Athens*, 62.

321. H. Hopkins, *The long affray*, 225.

322. Bonner and Smith, op. cit., II, 56f.; Harrison, op. cit., II, 83. For exceptional cases, where there was no risk to the prosecutor, Isaios III 46f.

323. For an attempt to treat this large, shapeless, topic systematically, J. O. Lofberg, *Sycophancy in Athens*.

324. [Arist.] *Ath. Pol.* 43 5. For one view of this reported law, and bibliography, see L. W. A. Crawley in *Auckland classical essays, presented to E. M. Blaiklock*, ed. B. F. Harris, 77–94.

325. Aiskh. II 99; cf. Isokrates' frequent use of the word, as e.g. at XV 312ff.

326. E.g. Andok. I 99, [Dem.] XXV 50–3. On prosecution as a duty, cf. Dem. XXIV 173f.

327. E.g. lines 44, 1410ff. On Isokrates, above, n. 325.

328. Theophrastos *Characters* 26.

329. Xen. *Hell.* II 3 12.

330. Lys. XII *passim*. Lysias' brother, Polemarkhos, was killed by the Thirty; s. 17.

331. Lys. XXV 19.

332. [Arist.] *Ath. Pol.* 35 3.

333. Lys. XXV 19, Isok. XV 316–8; cf. Old Oligarch I 14, Aristoph. *Peace* 632ff., *Birds* 1422ff., Antiphon *Murder of Herodes* 78.

334. [Dem.] LIII 1.

335. Old Oligarch I 18.

336. Xen. *Hell*. I 7 12.

337. Ibid., I 7 34.

338. [Arist.] *Ath. Pol.* 41 2.

339. M. H. Hansen, *The Athenian ecclesia*, 183–91.

340. Hansen, loc. cit. with 190f. On *nomothetai* see further MacDowell, *The law in classical Athens* 48f. and *JHS*, XCV (1975), 62–74; Harrison, *JHS*, LXXV (1955), 26–35.

341. Hansen (op. cit., 191) gives the number of *nomoi* cited by the orators as over 100, but only six are preserved on stone (which constitutes the best title to authenticity). For the fifth century profound difficulties are created by the linguistic usage of our sources; the same rule can be described, according to occasion, either as a *nomos* or a *psēphisma*; K. J. Dover, *JHS* LXXV (1955), 17f., F. Quass, *Nomos und Psephisma*, esp. s. III.

342. For the rule that a law could not be overruled by a decree, Andok. I 87. The frequent use of the *graphē paranomōn* need not imply a correspondingly frequent belief that a decree had offended against a law. For all we know, this *graphē* may often have been used merely to secure a second general examination of proposed legislation. See below on jurors' inattentiveness, at trials involving the *graphē paranomōn*, when the precise nature of the alleged illegality was announced.

343. Eur. *Supplices* 433ff.

344. [Dem.] XXVI 24.

345. Harrison, op. cit., II, 135.

346. Lys. XXX 3, cf. G. M. Calhoun, *Classical Philology*, 9 (1914), 140ff.

347. Dem. XIX 129; MacDowell, *The law in classical Athens*, 48.

348. Aiskh. III 192.

349. More dubious is the orator's claim that juries of an earlier generation paid far more attention at that stage of a case; here his scope for error or mendacity was far greater.

350. Arist. *Rhet.* 1375a-b.

351. Dem. XXIV 149–51; Bonner and Smith, *The administration of justice from Homer to Aristotle*, II, 152–5; J. F. Cronin, *The Athenian juror and his oath*; MacDowell, op. cit., 43f.

352. Comparable, though of much shorter duration, was the uncertainty produced in English case law when, recently, a senior judge of appeal, Lord Denning, was observed to go against precedent.

353. E.g. Dem. XXI 177, XXII 46.

354. Lys. XII 38, cf. XXI 19.

355. Lys. XVI 17.

356. Lys. XXV 12f.

357. In addition to the passages quoted above, see e.g. Lys. XXX 26f., Isaios V 45, Dem. XXI 225.

358. Cf. Adkins, *Merit and responsibility* 202; Davies, *Wealth and the power of wealth in classical Athens* 95.

359. Cicero, *Letters to Atticus* II 1 8.

360. Xen. *Const. Spart.* 8 2. On the identification of men of influence (*dynatōteroi*) with men of wealth, see above, p. 265.

361. Cf. Lys. XXVI 4 on liturgies causing a rich man's political

loyalty to be trusted.

362. Lys. XXVII 1; cf. Aristoph. *Knights* 1358–60.

363. Recognition of this fact is reflected in British army regulations, which include a catch-all section for acts subversive of discipline.

364. Above, n. 55.

365. Cf. Dem. XXI 169f.

366. Dem. XXI 158.

367. Old Oligarch III 4.

368. Aristoph. *Frogs* 1065f., *Knights* 912–8.

369. B. Jordan, *The Athenian navy in the classical period*, esp. 73ff.

370. Thuc. VI 31 3.

371. Cf. Isok. VII 53f. on competition between *khorēgoi*.

372. Dem. LI 1 and *passim*.

373. Ibid., 4.

374. Isok. XVII 33f. That lottery was used to choose the judges may reflect a widespread fear of bribery.

375. E.g. Dem. XXI 13–18.

376. Thuc. VI 16 1ff., cf. Arist. *Pol.* 1321a.

377. Cf. Lys. XIV 24, XXVI 4; Plat. *Gorg.* 472a–b. With the reference in the last passage to Nikias and his family tripods, cf. Plutarch's circumstantial account of Nikias' attempts to avoid attack by "sykophants"; *Life of Nikias* 5.

378. Isai. V 41.

379. Isai. V 36.

380. E. R. Dodds, in his edition of Plato's *Gorgias*, p. 245.

381. Lys. XXI 1f., 17.

382. Old Oligarch, II 18.

383. Arist. *Poetics* VI 2, XIII 2, XIV 1 etc.

384. *Ibid.*, XIII 4.

385. *Ibid.*, XIII 2.

386. Hdt. VI 21.

387. See the important remarks of N. Fisher, *Greece and Rome*, 26 (1979), 32ff.

388. Cf. Plat. *Lakhes* 183b.

389. Thuc. II 38 1, cf. Aristoph. *Clouds* 309f., Plat. *Alkibiades* ii 148e, Isok. IV 43–6. For an attempt to estimate the number of festival days, J. D. Mikalson, *The sacred and civil calendar of the Athenian year*, 201. Mikalson stresses, however, that some labourers worked through festivals, even the Panathenaia (*IG*, II^2, no. 1672, lines 32f.).

390. Old Oligarch III 8.

391. Ibid., II 9.

392. Ibid., II 9f.

393. Chapter 9.

394. p. 66.

395. Aristoph. *Clouds* 63–70. There was display of jewellery at festivals by women of wealthy family, to the gratification no doubt of their men.

396. Old Oligarch I 10.

397. Plat. *Rep.* 563c.

398. Ibid., 563b.

399. Cf. also the way in which agitation in the 1960s and '70s in defence of weaker sections of humanity led in the 1980s to action on behalf of captive animals.

400. Xen. *Symp.* IV 30–2.

401. Compare the obedience shown by the poor on military campaigns, and Plat. *Rep.* 465c.

402. Plat. *Gorg.* 461e, cf. Eur. *Hippolytos* 421–3, *Ion* 670–2.

403. Aiskh. I 15, 17; Dem. XXI 45–9. In general on this topic, N. R. E. Fisher, *Hybris*.

404. Lines 1326–449.

405. On the connection perceived by Greeks between drunkenness and the rich, see p. 226 and Eur. *Antiopē*, frag. 184 (Teubner edition).

406. Lines 1256–61.

407. On this topic in general, see now D. Whitehead, *The ideology of the Athenian metic*.

408. Thuc. II 31 1f., cf. I 143 1, III 16 1.

409. Cf. Whitehead, op. cit., 97f. Metic numbers no doubt shrank in the late fourth century, after the conquest of Athens by Macedon.

410. Whitehead, op. cit., esp. 75ff.

411. Lys. XII with *P. Oxy.* XIII 1606, lines 30, 153–5. The unpleasant circumstances of the confiscation and the uncertainty of the political outlook affecting such property would combine with the general shortage of cash at the end of the Peloponnesian War to make the 70 talents a low price.

412. Lys. XII 4.

413. Plat. *Rep.* 328b.

414. A useful collection of source material in translation is T. Wiedemann, *Greek and Roman slavery*.

415. Thuc. VII 27 5.

416. Hyp. frag. B 18 in *Minor Attic orators*, II (Loeb edition).

417. Thuc. II 14 2. On slaves in Athenian agriculture, see the references provided by G. E. M. de Ste. Croix, *The class struggle in the ancient Greek world*, 505f., and M. H. Jameson, 'Agriculture and slavery in classical Athens' in *Classical Journal*, 73 (1977–8), 122–45. E. M. Wood, *American Journal of Ancient History*, 8 (1983), 1–47.

418. Xen. *Poroi* I 14f.

419. Ibid., 22–6.

420. References to industrial slavery are collected by Davies, *Wealth and the power of wealth in classical Athens* 41ff.

421. See pp. 366f.

422. As, e.g., at Arginousai in the crisis of 406; Aristoph. *Frogs* 693f., Xen. *Hell.* I 6 24.

423. Thuc. III 17 4 with Gomme's commentary, *HCT*, II, 275f.

424. Lys. V. 5.

425. Dem. XLV 86.

426. Plat. *Rep.* 565a. Xenophon's figures for slaves in the silver mines (*Poroi* IV 14f.) suggest that in the late fifth century an owner would commonly expect to make no more than one obol per day in profit even from an able-bodied male slave. A man could not support a family, at least in any comfort, on such a sum.

427. Arist. *Pol.* 1323a; cf. 1252b on the use of an ox as substitute for a slave.

428. See the list of prices at J. K. Davies, *Democracy and classical Greece* 100f. In wartime one Persian magnate bought slaves wholesale at 20 *drakhmai* each; Thuc. VIII 28 4 with Xen. *Anab.* I 7 18.

429. [Dem.] LIX 30.

430. Xen. *Mem.* II 5 2.

431. A. H. M. Jones, *Past and Present*, I (1952), 13-31; M. I. Finley, *Historia*, 8 (1959), 145-64.

432. Plat. *Rep.* 465c.

433. Hom. *Od.* XVII 322f.

434. Thuc. VIII 40 2.

435. [Arist.] *Ath. Pol.* 57 3; Lykourgos *Against Leokrates* 65; D. M. MacDowell, *Athenian homicide law in the age of the orators* 20ff., etc.

436. Old Oligarch, I 11; cf. Andokides I 38. For the wage-earning slave, see e.g. Isai. VIII 35.

437. E.g. Isok. XVII, Dem. XXXVI, [Dem.] XLVI; cf. Dem. XLV 71f. for another slave banker who gained his freedom.

438. Dem. IX 3.

439. Arist. *Pol.* 1253b. For references to Greek theoretical opposition to slavery, W. K. C. Guthrie, *History of Greek philosophy*, III, 155-60.

440. [Arist.] *Ath. Pol.* 40 2, [Plut.] *Moralia* 849a.

441. As at Skyros (Thuc. I 98 2), Skiōnē (V 32 1), Melos (V 116 4). The non-Greek origin of a large proportion of the slaves at Athens is well illustrated in the list cited at n. 428 above. De Ste. Croix suggests plausibly that the diverse origins of slaves at Athens and in many other Greek cities contributed to the slaves' lack of rebelliousness. He contrasts the helots; *Origins*, 90 and cf. Arist. *Pol.* 1330a.

442. Lys. VII 35.

443. This raises the question of how much Athenian slaves had heard about Sparta before they fled. It was surely in the interest of Athenian masters to inform their slaves about the condition of the helots.

444. Aristoph. *Frogs* 654ff.

445. MacDowell, *The law in classical Athens* 245–7.

446. Aristoph. *Ploutos* 874–9.

8

Citizen Women of Athens

Revealing remarks from Antiquity about the activities and circumstances of Athenian women are more numerous than might be supposed. The modern analysis of this evidence is still at an early stage of development: the scope for students to offer improvements to existing theory is unusually obvious.[1] As with other areas of Greek social history, the source material for a study of Athenian women is scattered through a very large number of ancient texts. The labour involved in assembling and evaluating this material partly explains why social history has been much less studied than political, for which a large proportion of the evidence is conveniently contained in the works of two writers, Herodotos and Thucydides. Yet the frequent adjustment needed when reconstructing ancient social history, to allow for the varied characteristics of numerous sources, closely resembles the process by which we adjust to innumerable sources in evaluating everyday information of our own time. In the assessment of ancient (and modern) statements, judgement must often be suspended where little is known about context and the author's purpose. For the study of Athenian women a special caution is made necessary by the fact that almost all relevant statements from Antiquity originated with, or have at least been mediated by, men. One consequence of this fact is that our information, and the reconstruction we base upon it, tend to concern the relations between women and men. And yet, in a society largely segregated by gender, as was Athens, relations within the female group must have been, for many women and in many ways, far more important.

There are many surviving statements of ideal relating to Greek women. These are often of great interest, but their value as evidence needs cautious assessment. A statement of ideal *may*, depending on the circumstances in which it was uttered, reflect the wishes only of its author. In other respects its value as evidence may be the exact reverse of what first appears. A female, non-Athenian, writer stated that women should not wear gold, emeralds or make-up.[2] Whether the writer's views were widely shared in her community, and so formed an important influence on women's behaviour, we cannot tell. It is, however, almost certain that some women had worn, and were thought likely to go on wearing, gold and the rest: people do not normally trouble to forbid or advise against behaviour of a kind which they have neither experienced nor heard of. Much social history can be reconstructed on the principle that stated ideals tend to be a negation of what is, at least to some extent, actually happening.[3]

A better-known profession of an ideal concerning women is that ascribed by Thucydides to Perikles, as part of a speech of 431/0. Perikles is reported as attributing great glory to those women who were least spoken of among men, whether for praise or blame.[4] Perikles here speaks as the representative of the Athenian community on a solemn occasion, the funeral of warriors killed fighting for Athens in the first year of the Peloponnesian War. The nature of the occasion indicates that the ideals expressed were likely to be shared, or at least not opposed, by Perikles' fellow citizens, his audience.[5] We should notice, in addition, that the ideal of female segregation was judged to be in need of reinforcement by Perikles' statement. Women in some numbers were, it seems, being spoken of among men. A similar argument applies to the idea, commonly expressed at Athens,[6] that citizen women should stay at home, going no further than the outer door of their home. The frequency with which we meet this idea reflects a body of opinion probably sufficient to constrain female behaviour to some extent. But that same frequency should suggest that the ideal asserted was continuing to be breached.

The behaviour of women was commonly appraised with words from the root *kosm-*, which often implied the orderly separation of things.[7] As we shall see, not only activity in public but also the living quarters of some private houses were segregated on sexual lines. Statements of ideal also occur in the form of complaints and jokes, to the effect that women went to excess in eating,[8] drinking,[9] talking[10] and sexual activity (or the desire for it).[11] Great caution is needed if we seek to use such references as evidence for women's behaviour, since they typically involve no precise indication of what was the desirable or acceptable standard which women allegedly exceeded.

Among the most valuable general remarks, for our purposes, are those made by Aristotle, particularly in his *Politics*. Two sections of Aristotle's work are relevant immediately. He writes that having a *gynaikonomos*, an official to control the movements of women,[12] would not be compatible with *dēmokratia*, 'for,' he asks rhetorically, 'how is it possible to prevent the wives of the poor from going out?' Aristotle spent much of his life, in the mid-fourth century, at Athens under the *dēmokratia*: if the wives of the Athenian poor had been prevented from going out at that period, he would hardly write as he does. The inference made above, that numerous women did not stay at home, seems to be confirmed.[13] Also, Aristotle illustrates the need for caution in interpreting ancient claims that women transgressed certain ideals. Greek remarks about talkative or complaining women may suggest the modern stereotype of women as gossips. Aristotle, however, notes that "a woman would seem to be a chatterbox if she were as restrained (*kosmia*) as a good man".[14] When it came to conversation, that is, what was thought proper for a man was judged excessive in a woman. We shall see evidence of a similar disparity of standards as regards eating and sexual activity.

Athenian lawcourt speeches, with their frequent references to women, date mainly from the fourth century. The clients who commissioned them, and delivered the versions heard in court,[15] would in most cases be known to be prosperous.[16] The speeches survive because esteemed in Antiquity for their elegant Greek. Their authors, who tended to be famous in their own time, were no doubt expensive to hire. The speeches frequently contain lies, or at least statements made in careless disregard of the truth. Paradoxically, this may even enhance the value for us of their statements on domestic life. If these works had been written with a thorough and energetic love of truth, what they told us of this or that person's marital history might reflect no more than the peculiarities of a family. However, since the orators were concerned to be plausible rather than accurate, their statements reflect the jurors' ideas of what might *generally* be expected in the behaviour of prosperous Athenians. It is obviously valuable to identify such expectations, although we should be aware that Athenian men would not be perfectly informed about the cloistered world in which many women lived, a world carefully constructed so as to be inaccessible to men outside the immediate family.[17] We hear of men boasting to each other about their wives,[18] which suggests not only that they presented a biased set of information but also that the wives in question could not be talked to or seen; for then boasting might have been unnecessary or impossible. The idea enunciated by Perikles is also of importance here, that women gained great glory by being very rarely spoken of among men. This notion is not self-contradictory;[19] the word for 'men' reported by Thucydides means 'males', not 'people'. The passage seems to mean that a woman might have a great reputation among women while, for closely related reasons, being seldom referred to by men; if so, that would imply an impressive degree of insulation between the worlds of women and men.

To judge by the volume of published material, Greek women have been studied far more intensively in the years since 1970 than at earlier periods; the revival of feminism has prompted much sympathetic, and perhaps some unsympathetic, interest.[20] When we deal with a subject with lively implications for modern politics, there is an obvious danger that we may — depending on our temperament — either exaggerate or play down certain features, to yield a convenient picture of thorough infamy, or of general decency. In the present case, features likely to be distorted include the limitations on movement, conversation and sexual contact which applied to many women and girls, at least in the prosperous sections of Athenian society. To modern tastes, there may seem to have been more satisfaction in the lives of *hetairai*, courtesans often attached to particular men and employed for their sexual and conversational abilities, especially at drinking parties, from which citizen wives were excluded.[21] However, as S. B. Pomeroy makes clear, it would be seriously wrong to assume that Athenian citizen women generally envied the *hetairai* their way of life.[22] The latter were normally slaves, or citizen women whose poverty left them few choices. Plato, who was most unusual in advocating a common way of life for women and men,[23] conceded that women would passionately and powerfully resist his scheme for them to attend communal meals because they were used, as he put it, to a life in the shadows.[24] The point is echoed in an undervalued and psychologically sensitive collection of historical sketches, the *Dialogues of the hetairai*, by the post-classical Greek writer Lucian. An impoverished Athenian widow plans to make her naïve young daughter into a *hetaira*, and tempts her with the prospect of riches, "from being with very young men, drinking with them and sleeping with them in exchange for money". "Just like Lyra, Daphnis' daughter?" asks the girl. "Yes." "But *she*'s a *hetaira*."[25] By force of poverty, the wives of some citizens worked outdoors, particularly in retail trades:[26] they again may seem to us to have lived more rewarding, because more colourful and varied, lives than their wealthier counterparts. But this activity, too, was commonly looked down on as fit only for slaves. In contrast, the cloistered existence was a badge of high status, and was almost certainly valued as such by many women.

Education and the circumstances of marriage

In the sections of Athenian society of which we hear most, the prosperous classes, the main purposes of a citizen woman's existence were seen as domestic: looking after husband, family, managing the house and bringing up children. Such education as a citizen girl received was likely to be a preparation for this role. In an early fourth-century dialogue on estate management, the *Oikonomikos*, Xenophon represents the wives of two of his genteel characters as having had a very sheltered upbringing. Kritoboulos had married "a young child, who had seen and heard as little as possible";[27] Iskhomakhos' wife had been brought up "with great care that she should see, hear and say as little as possible".[28] The purpose of Xenophon's treatise was didactic, to improve household management by both women and men. He evidently needed to establish the point that women, or rather girls, required more effective education in this area than they sometimes received. His literary purpose may perhaps have caused him to exaggerate slightly, but his female characters, and especially Iskhomakhos' wife who is shown receiving a detailed domestic training from her husband, had to be recognisable types for the author's message to be plausible. We can believe that some parents strove to keep their daughters innocent by sheltering them from information, and that as a result girls could enter marriage knowing very little. However, Xenophon significantly admits that a girl before marriage might learn to make wool into a garment, to distribute wool-working to slave women and to regulate her diet.[29] Literacy had obvious uses for domestic management, facilitating the keeping of records. Xenophon refers to Iskhomakhos and his wife as using a written list when dealing with a female steward.[30] How common were literate women?

A fragmentary quotation attributed to Theophrastos, a fourth-century writer, teacher, and associate of Aristotle, includes these words: "in the case of women education in literacy seems to be most essential, to the extent that it is useful for household management".[31] If this were all that survived of the fragment, Theophrastos' words might seem to represent no more than a philosopher's ideal, as unpopular and unrealistic in its own day as Plato's scheme for educating men and women together. However, the fragment goes on: "Further refinement [i.e. in literacy] makes women too idle in all other spheres, turning them into chatter-boxes and busybodies." This seems to be written as a comment on a real rather than merely hypothetical development. So does a fragment of the fourth-century comic poet Menandros: "Teach a woman letters? A serious mistake! — like giving extra venom to a terrifying snake."[32]

Plato refers to the pleasure derived from tragic drama by "those women who are educated":[33] this raises the difficult question whether women attended dramatic performances:[34] if they did not, reading may be meant here.[35] In any case, Plato seems to mean that the education of some women went beyond simple domestic activity. In Greek tragedy which, in spite of normally being set in a remote and mythic past, often reflects the attitudes and behaviour of classical Athens,[36] some eminent women are shown as literate, others as illiterate.[37] The decision of a playwright in a particular case as to whether to portray a female character as literate may have depended on the needs of the plot; it seems that an Athenian audience was expected to see nothing strange in either state.[38]

A legal speech, probably from the end of the fifth century, depicts a woman as addressing a gathering of men on a distressing family matter. But, it is stated, before she did so she claimed to be unused to speaking among males.[39] The fact that the speech-writer troubled to report (or invent) this claim suggests that it was meant to help his client's appeal to the jury. The picture of a modest woman, forced by ill-treatment to overcome her reticence, was no doubt expected to be poignant and to tell against the litigant's adversary who had allegedly been responsible for her troubles.[40] The idea that women should talk little, and especially to men, is so widely attested that it probably did restrict conversation to some extent. Aristotle's remark, that a woman who was as voluble as a restrained man would be thought a chatterbox, suggests that many — if not most — women talked less, at least to men. The restraint thought proper for women in conversation can be economically explained in parallel with the restraint on female literacy, as advocated in the words attributed to Theophrastos. The wish to prevent women becoming busybodies can be expressed, in less loaded language, as a wish to restrict intervention by women in what were seen as male spheres of activity. Also, conversation with men might of course be suspect because of intimacy that might result.

Plato believed women to be less intelligent than men, actually and potentially.[41] Aristotle had a similar belief in the inferiority of women's intellects.[42] Unlike many corresponding remarks from various epochs, the comments of the two philosophers cannot simply be dismissed as the predictable ideology of a ruling group. In Plato's case, his belief about female intelligence was seriously inconvenient for an argument which was of great importance to him, that women and men should be educated, and should rule, together.[43] That he made this awkward concession may be taken as evidence of an impressive gulf, in his day, between the relative attainments of the sexes. Indeed, since men had far greater freedom of movement, and so enjoyed better access to formal and informal education, it would be surprising had there not been some intellectual disparity between the sexes. We may believe, with hindsight, that the philosophers' estimate of potential female intelligence was mistaken, and that their mistake lay in not discounting sufficiently the impact of cultural differences on men and women. When writing about a different aspect of women, Aristotle made a further error which is interestingly similar in form. He suggested that women were naturally pale, as a result of loss of blood through menstruation.[44] The pallor of Athenian women, an interesting fact in its own right,[45] resulted rather from a housebound existence, enveloping clothes and, perhaps, certain deficiencies of diet.[46] In this case, we accept Aristotle's direct observation, but, in the light of our knowledge of different cultures, diverge from him in the explanation of it. His, and Plato's, perception of a difference between men's and women's intelligences is obviously of a more complex and fallible kind than an observation about complexions. But here, too, the perception itself must be given some weight in an account of what was actually happening.[47]

There is a considerable economic cost in keeping women at home, sheltered from the world of men. The use of slaves, to do work that might have been done more cheaply by the wives and daughters of citizens, may have been most common among Athenians in the fifth century, when imperial conquests supplied much captive labour.[48] But there is evidence that, towards the end of the century, there was a sharp increase in the pressure on citizen women to work, both at home and outside. A substantial part of the male citizen population was killed in the Peloponnesian War. And, after the Spartan establishment of a fortified base near Athens in 413, over 20,000 slaves ran away.[49] A speaker in the mid-fourth century reports a tradition that many citizen women had worked as wet-nurses, wool-workers and fruit-pickers at the period of catastrophe for Athens — by which is meant the years around 404.[50] Xenophon portrays a previously-wealthy citizen, Aristarkhos, as claiming that he was unable to support the sisters, nieces and female cousins who had taken refuge with him in the poverty and turbulence following Athens' final defeat in the Peloponnesian War.[51] Aristarkhos explains that, being free women and relatives of his, they cannot be made to earn their keep, as slaves would be. He is advised, however, that their status should not cause them "to do nothing other than eat and sleep". They should indeed be put to work. Aristarkhos accepts the advice, buys wool for the women to work and, in Xenophon's didactic tale, a picture of contented female industry follows. However, the very stress that is laid on this contentment may suggest that Xenophon's readers expected a rather different reaction from the women.

A similar adjustment to Athens' reduced circumstances after the loss of her empire may be reflected in a famous exchange of conversation in Xenophon's *Oikonomikos*. The gentlemanly Kritoboulos is asked:

> "Is there anyone to whom you trust more important things than you entrust to your wife?" "No." "And is there anyone with whom you have less conversation?" "Certainly not many people." "And you married her when she was just a young child, who had seen and heard as little as possible?" "Correct." "So, when it comes to something that needs saying or doing, it would be much more surprising if she got it right than wrong."[52]

Xenophon then proceeds with his argument for an improved training of wives as domestic managers, adding, in a rather different connection, a sharp reference to "women who spend their time sitting around grandly".[53] The early fourth century saw the publication by both Xenophon and Plato of arguments for more education, and more strenuous work, for women. Aristophanes, as we shall see, produced in the 390s a dramatic fantasy about women taking over the government of Athens. It may be that these ideas arose from the increase in work done by citizen women in the years around 400. That increase had seemingly been eroded by the mid-fourth century; we have seen that a speaker then looked back on the activity of women at the end of the Peloponnesian War as the bygone result of an unusual crisis. Wet-nursing and the rest were, he implies, normally tasks for slaves.[54] The period around 400 allows us to see how the levels of education and work thought proper for women were affected by the overall supply of labour at Athens. The ideal of the uneducated bride, of leisured female relatives and of wives who could "spend their time sitting around grandly" was a vulnerable product of prosperity and slave labour.

One bride mentioned in the *Oikonomikos* was, as has been noted, "a very young child": another was "not yet 15".[55] Largely on the strength of this latter case, the age of 14 is sometimes represented by scholars as the norm for an Athenian girl at marriage. Such precision is not justified.[56] But marriage at some stage in the early or mid teens does seem to have been normal for Athenian girls. A passage of Xenophon may mean that in Athens girls married earlier than in Sparta.[57] Aristotle recommended some delay; women should be married at about 18.[58] A legal speech of the mid-fourth century tells of a man who married at about 18, but this man states that his daughter, because of her age, was later capable of being mistaken for his sister.[59] The gap in ages between a father and his child was, it seems, usually of much more than 18 years. Since, for reasons which we shall see, it was very common for children to be born within a year or two of a marriage, we should conclude that at the period of the speech Athenian bridegrooms were normally much older than 19 and thus were also much older than their wives.[60] (It should be recalled that the speech on which this conclusion partly depends was designed to convince an audience of Athenian jurors, who would certainly be well informed on such an everyday matter.) The gap which would be usual between husband and wife in the matter of experience will help to explain the great concern shown by Athenian men for the sexual fidelity of their wives; competition from much younger men was evidently a problem.[61] It also helps to explain the scarcity of conversation between spouses, and the near-insulation of their respective worlds. A woman, then, might know very little at marriage; she might be prevented, by her own choice or others', from meeting many men; she might also talk very little to the one man with whom regular conversation was permitted. The mental separation of women from men may indeed have been impressive.

Whatever her age, a female citizen was legally under the control of a man, her *kyrios*.[62] This person was, in most cases, a close relative: father, brother or uncle. Among prosperous Athenians the choice of a husband seems generally to have been made by this *kyrios*.[63] However, Xenophon suggests that a girl's mother might have some say in the matter.[64] When a widow remarried, it was sometimes to a man nominated in her late husband's will, which would also provide for her dowry.[65] This reflects the fact that legal control over a married woman and her property was shared between her husband and the *kyrios* who would normally be her blood relative.[66] A girl who had been brought up in the sheltered way commended by many Athenians would no doubt be considered to lack the experience needed for choosing a husband. (A speaker in a legal case of the early fourth century boasts that his sister and nieces "have lived so properly (*kosmiōs*) that they are embarrassed to be seen even by their male relatives".[67]) However, such ideals may on occasion have distorted the record of what actually occurred. If a girl of wealthy family had influenced the choice of her husband, her family might be loth to admit it, at least in a lawcourt speech, for fear of making her seem to know too much about men — or to be vulgar.

In the choice of a spouse, the experience of rich and poor may have differed importantly. The young daughter of a poor citizen was likely to come out of doors, on various errands, more often than her wealthy counterpart. (Aristotle notes that the poor, lacking slaves, use their wives and children as labour instead.[68]) She might thus see rather more of men and youths; personal attraction on both sides would be more likely to occur than in the case of a girl from a wealthy family. Marriage for love is scarcely mentioned in Athenian legal speeches.[69] However, in the New Comedy of the fourth century and later there are many plots connecting marriage with erotic love. Comedy tended to deal with characters who were socially far less elevated than the people mentioned in the surviving legal speeches.[70] It may be that the interest of New Comedy in marriage for love reflected a pattern of behaviour more familiar, or more readily admitted, among ordinary Athenians than among the wealthy.

Among prosperous Athenians it was the rule that a bride's family should provide a dowry.[71] The size of the dowry varied, both in absolute terms and as a proportion of the wealth of the giver. Lawcourt speeches mention dowries ranging from under 5 per cent of the giver's resources to nearly 20 per cent.[72] (As D. M. Schaps has observed, in his important work on the economic position of Greek women, the large dowries mentioned in the fiction of New Comedy reflect much exaggeration.[73] We may compare the tendency of modern film-makers to seek to interest their audiences by describing the pursuit of a million dollars, or multiples thereof.) The larger a dowry was, the likelier it was, perhaps, to supply a dominant motive for the groom's interest in the bride. During the marriage, the dowry was administered by the husband, often to his own advantage.[74] However, in case of divorce, the dowry could be reclaimed by the woman's *kyrios*.[75] If her husband died, a woman might leave his household, taking her dowry with her.[76] If she chose to stay, and had sons who were legally of age, it became their duty, as it had been their father's, to support her out of the wealth she had brought to the marriage.[77] If a husband was seen to waste his wife's dowry, she or her *kyrios* might decide on divorce, to rescue what remained of it.[78] But, as we shall see, divorce may have had disadvantages for a woman such that the threat of it often failed to give protection.

A girl without a dowry was quite likely not to get a husband, or a husband from the wealthier classes, at least. A speaker in a legal case asks rhetorically "Who would ever have married the dowerless daughter of a man without wealth and in debt to the state?".[79] To allow a girl to remain unmarried was thought to be seriously wrong.[80] There was, accordingly, both moral and legal pressure on men to provide dowries for their female relatives, except perhaps where the men belonged to the poorest group of Athenians, the *thētes*.[81] (*Thētes* formed a large section of the citizen population at Athens, although their social history is poorly documented compared with that of their more prosperous fellow-citizens.) The reluctance of numerous men to take a bride without a dowry may seem to reflect an unpleasantly mercenary attitude. As usual, however, it is more fruitful to seek to understand than to condemn. Mercenary motives there undoubtedly were, and in brides as well as grooms. But other motives must be considered. As we have seen, husband and wife might well share the idea that certain economic functions should not be performed by the wife: this might help to make marriage seem an expensive business for which a dowry could reasonably be·demanded. Also, a man who took a wife without a dowry, as some did,[82] would expect that if he and his wife had a daughter he would notwithstanding be obliged to provide a dowry for her, perhaps within 15 years of his own marriage. A system of rotating property, once established, is not easily interrupted, by the individual or the group. One should also recall that the personal connections between men and women, which in modern Western societies tend to make financial considerations subordinate at the time of marriage, seem to have been carefully prevented from forming among the marriageable young of prosperous Athenian families.

Xenophon, intending to present a commendable picture of upper-class marriage, portrays his character Iskhomakhos as arguing to his wife that, just as she is not improved by make-up, so he would not be made more attractive to her by exaggerating his own wealth.[83] Seemingly it is legitimate for her to be attracted by his real wealth.[84] In lawcourt speeches which, we should recall, tend to reflect widespread ideas of what was normal among prosperous Athenians, motives for arranged marriages are said to involve the wealth[85] and high status[86] of the marriage partner or their family, the character of the groom,[87] and friendship[88] or blood relationship between the families of bride and groom. Isaios, in a speech of the mid-fourth century, gives as proof that an uncle and nephew had become enemies the fact that, while the uncle had two daughters and knew that the nephew had money, neither daughter married the nephew.[89] This strongly implies that marriage between such relatives was very common.[90] Where there was a blood relationship, or friendship, between the families of the spouses, that might be seen as giving a certain protection to the wife.[91] Not only would the bride's *kyrios* know something beforehand of the character of the groom, but the wish to retain the goodwill of the woman's immediate relatives might well affect the man she married in his treatment of her.

A class of bride receiving an unusual amount of attention from ancient and modern writers is the heiress, the *epiklēros*, especially when she inherited a large estate.[92] In law Athenian women were forbidden to make transactions involving more than the value of a *medimnos* of barley.[93] (Even in times of scarcity this would be

equal to no more than a few days' wages for a skilled labourer.[94])
When a girl or woman became sole heiress to an estate, through
the death of father or brother, there was no question of leaving
her legally in charge of the wealth. She became assignable in
marriage to one of her own relatives, who would then have a
certain control over the wealth until a son of the marriage came of
age.[95] The order in which male relatives qualified to marry an
epiklēros was fixed by law, and seems to have been similar to that
which governed the inheritance of property where no *epiklēros*
existed.[96] Indeed, the word *epiklēros* meant literally 'she who goes
with the estate'.[97] Where such a woman was already married,
divorce might be insisted on, to make way for the new marriage;[98]
in some cases the groom of the *epiklēros* had himself divorced a
wife to become eligible.[99] Disadvantages of an arrangement which
offered for marriage a girl or woman who might be attached to a
large amount of wealth and could be claimed by an elderly relative
were no doubt obvious to the Athenians. A law seems to have
required that the husband of an *epiklēros* should have sex with her
on (at least) three occasions a month.[100] This appears to
acknowledge the danger that an heiress would be married, for her
wealth, by a relative who would not or could not have children by
her. In view of the ways in which it might be abused, why did the
arrangement for *epiklēroi* exist?

It is sometimes suggested, as by A. R. W. Harrison[101] and W.
K. Lacey,[102] that the marriage of an *epiklēros* to a close relative
was intended to preserve the *oikos* (household) of her dead father.
Certainly there is evidence that Athenians found the extinction of
an *oikos* poignant and wretched.[103] However, Schaps points out
that the arrangement for marrying *epiklēroi* did not prevent *oikoi*
from perishing.[104] In the narrow sense of *oikos*, a man, his
children, and their descendants in the male line, the entity would
not be preserved by the deceased's daughter marrying, say, her
father's brother or nephew. Any resulting sons would not be part
of the deceased's *oikos*, unless as a result of formal adoption. And
adoption was not a part of the arrangements for marrying an
epiklēros to a relative.[105] In wider senses of *oikos*, descendants of
the deceased's father or grandfather, the failure of the deceased to
be survived by a son would not create any presumption that the
oikos was in danger of extinction, since the deceased might be
survived by brothers, uncles, and their sons.

The assignment of an *epiklēros* was treated as a matter of public
importance, with an announcement in the assembly making clear

her identity and status, followed by a prompt official hearing to decide between claimants.[106] Schaps sensibly suggests that a purpose of these urgent arrangements was to protect the *epiklēros*.[107] He notes that without some special arrangement for such an heiress, there would have been a danger that an unscrupulous *kyrios* would keep her unmarried while he himself exploited her wealth. The Athenian system would in most cases find her a husband promptly, by obliging the nearest male relative to decide rapidly whether to marry her himself, and undertake sexual relations, or to see her assigned to another who would do so. But since in some cases the *epiklēros* already had a husband whom she was now required to divorce even against her wishes, we should admit that the system was rather obviously a compromise between the interests of the woman and those of certain male relatives. Schaps notes that the Athenian treatment of heiresses was different from that prescribed in the laws of Gortyn, a Cretan state about which a moderate amount is known.[108] In deciding who could claim an heiress, the Gortynians departed radically from the order of precedence they normally followed in the inheritance of property; the hand of the heiress could not be claimed by any male in the female line.[109] But since the complex arrangements for heiresses at Athens and at Gortyn are in other respects strikingly similar, Schaps may go too far when he distinguishes sharply between their relative purposes. The Gortynian code compromised the normal order of property rights in the interests of the heiress, allowing her in some cases a choice as to whom to marry.[110] The Athenian system also made a compromise, by refusing to allow any relative, whatever his precedence in other matters, to be *kyrios* of an *epiklēros* unless he married and tried to impregnate her. In the case of both states, the compromise gave protection to some heiresses. The arrangements at Gortyn may give more support to Schaps' interpretation of the Athenian system than he himself allows.

Married life

Xenophon's character Iskhomakhos, intended to be a plausible paragon,[111] is shown explaining to his young wife "why I married you, and why your parents[112] gave you to me".[113] He mentions a concern on both sides that the husband and wife respectively should have the best available partner to share household and children. He also refers to the joint interest of the spouses in bringing up children to be the best possible allies and providers for the parents' old age.[114] The frequent lawsuits between citizens, and perhaps also the violence in the streets, help to explain the reference to allies for the married couple.[115] And, since there was no state pension for the elderly, the needs of a parent in old age would ideally have a son or sons to supply them.[116] Adult sons were required by law to support elderly parents; daughters, however, were not.[117] (Women, it will be recalled, were forbidden to take part in any but minor financial dealing.) A daughter, indeed, might well need a dowry, and thus be a cause of financial loss rather than of gain to her parents' household. An Athenian man who married in his thirties or later might see the appearance of an heir as immediately important, if not urgent. The moral pressure on a young wife to produce a son (which might of course involve multiple child-bearing) was, predictably, great; it included the prospect of enhanced status if a son were born, and the unwelcome possibility of divorce if the marriage were not fertile.

The carvings on Athenian funerary monuments from the fourth century often show a deceased wife accompanied by a child. In many cases the wife will have died in childbirth. It has been calculated on the evidence of Greek skeletons from the classical period that the average longevity of adult women was of about 36 years — some nine years less than that of men;[118] child-bearing will be at least part of the reason for the disparity. The children shown in the idealised stock scenes on funerary stones are obviously intended to reflect credit on women who had succeeded in child-bearing, whatever the circumstances of their deaths. Athenian men commonly appear in funerary art as armed warriors. At Athens, as at Sparta, a comparison was made between the role of men as soldiers and that of women as bearers of children,[119] both roles being stressful, dangerous and vital for the community. In Euripides' *Medeia*, during a famous lament over the condition of women, the heroine states that she would rather fight in three battles than give birth to one child.[120]

The improvement in status offered to a woman who bore a child is illustrated in the speech on the killing of Eratosthenes, written by Lysias some time around 400. The speaker, Euphiletos, is concerned to prove that he killed Eratosthenes in accordance with the law on adultery, having, in his own house, caught Eratosthenes in bed with his (Euphiletos') wife. He describes the early part of his marriage and the beginning of his wife's affair. His account of his private life would scarcely be verifiable in court: much of it may be fictitious. But the behaviour described was calculated to be found plausible and reasonable by a jury of Athenians:

> When I decided to marry and brought a wife into my house, at first my practice was not to bother her overmuch but also not to give her too much freedom. I kept an eye on her, as far as was possible, and gave her my attention, as one would expect. But when a child was born, then I began to trust her and I put her in charge of all my things, believing that the closest of connections had now been formed. And at first she was the best wife in the world; she was a clever domestic manager, thrifty and controlled everything meticulously. But when my mother died ...[121]

The speaker goes on to explain that when his wife was outdoors for the funeral she was spotted by Eratosthenes, which led to the affair. The passage is interesting in several ways. To modern minds the speaker's references to his wife, and his control over her, seem paternalistic. However, we should note that, even by contemporary Athenian standards, Euphiletos had an unusual need to assert that he had been a protective husband. He had to show that he had not by negligence contributed to his wife's infidelity. (Compare Euripides' *Andromakhē* 590ff., where a character blames Menelaos for the elopement of his wife Helen, whom he had neglected to guard with bolts and slaves. As often, Euripidean comment on the position of women, though set in a remote and mythic past, closely reflects what we know or might infer to have been the case in his own time, the late fifth century.) The detail about the mother's funeral serves the same purpose; the speaker uses it to suggest that when the wife was first seen by Eratosthenes, she was outdoors on a legitimate mission, not because she had been given an improper freedom of movement. For our main purpose at present, what matters most is that the jury might expect the production of a child to lead to a great increase in the status and power given to a wife.

A woman whose marriage was infertile might be divorced by a husband anxious to try elsewhere for children. Aristotle states that childless couples split up more readily than others (although he does not give desire for children as the explanation).[122] Two Euripidean tragedies contain remarks which seem likely to reflect contemporary Athenian attitudes. Medeia states that if her husband had had no children, his desire for another woman would have been forgivable.[123] In the *Andromakhē*, a wife is described as "childless and hated by her husband".[124] Infertility in marriage was not always seen as the fault of the wife. A speech of Isaios tells of an ageing husband who offered to divorce his wife to let her have children elsewhere; the families of the two parties stayed on very good terms after the divorce.[125] In many cases divorce was not thought to leave a stain on the character of those involved; this is surmised partly from the fact that speakers in legal cases appear not to use divorce as evidence of bad character in their opponents.[126] The formal process of divorce seemingly was straightforward, either party being able to register the divorce as a fact with a particular official.[127] However, Lacey and Pomeroy may mislead slightly when they, respectively, state that "for most married couples divorce was easy"[128] and "Divorce was easily attainable...and there was no stigma attached."[129] The formal simplicity of divorce may have been combined with great informal disadvantages for women, and we hear of very few divorces which proceeded from the wife's side.[130] Medeia is made to say that divorce is not creditable for women.[131] The speech in which she does so contrasts the position of men and women in several respects, and a contrast is probably intended here too. A wife who took the initiative in divorce might be suspected of lacking the docility thought proper in women.[132] (In a speech of the mid-fourth century we read of a woman divorced partly because she was not *kosmia* and "would not listen to" her husband.[133]) Such a woman, unless she had a large dowry, might find it hard to attract another husband; it might be harder still if the previous marriage left her fertility in grave doubt. (It should be recalled that in the amicable divorce described by Isaios the husband effectively announced that the infertility was on his side.) A comment in Euripides' *Andromakhē* is again a probable reflection of the author's own society. A character imagines the embarrassment of a father whose childless daughter has been divorced after a violent clash of wills with her husband. The father is addressed thus:

When you try to give her in marriage, what will you say to some other man? That your daughter is a properly restrained woman, running away from a bad husband? That will not be true. Who will marry her? Or will you keep her at home without a man, a sort of grey-haired widow?[134]

Where a husband was obviously causing a marriage to be infertile, a wife might perhaps undertake divorce with a sense of relief. But, in an age which scarcely offered women the chance of an interesting and respected career away from the home,[135] divorce without subsequent remarriage might hold the frightening prospect of loneliness, loss of status and of a social role, and eventually of an impoverished old age.[136] It is hardly surprising that we hear of unmarried women seeking to assess their chances of matrimony by the use of divination,[137] a frequent recourse of the insecure.[138]

There exists colourful evidence that some Athenian women smuggled other women's babies and sought to pass them off as their own. This evidence deserves rather fuller examination than it seems previously to have received. There would be great risks to be faced by a wife who sought to smuggle a baby. If many did so, or even were seriously thought to do so, we should conclude that the status given to a mother was enormously more welcome to women than that of a childless wife or divorcee. What is the evidence?

Athenian comic drama, and especially the New Comedy, was much concerned with the humour of situation. We hear of five comedies entitled *Hypobolimaios*, the technical term for a person smuggled in infancy and falsely claimed by a woman as her own child.[139] The dramatic potential of such smuggling may of course have spread the idea of it out of all proportion to its actual frequency, if any. Tragedy, too, exploited the theme. The orator Demosthenes, when uttering abuse of a political opponent, Meidias, says

> Who of you does not know the secret of his birth, like something from a tragedy? ... His true mother, the one who bore him, had the greatest good sense possible: his apparent mother, the one who had him smuggled in, was the most stupid woman in the world. You can tell that from the fact that the real mother sold him as soon as he was born, while the other woman bought him when she could have purchased a better one for the same price.[140]

Is it suggested here that baby-smuggling happened mainly in drama? When someone today describes a real event with the phrase 'just like on television', we may suspect that the event is of

354

a kind not common in the untelevised world. In Demosthenes' case, however, the reference to tragedy may mean something very different. Tragedy was mainly concerned with myths about aristocratic families. Demosthenes' point may be that Meidias was of humble birth, but later declared to be, as we know,[141] the child of a distinguished family; a smuggled baby in a tragedy was likely to be similar.[142] Also, since the act of importing a baby would be of its nature secretive, if ever tragedy showed or (more likely) described it, that might give a fuller and more memorable picture than any available to most Athenians from their ordinary lives, even if some smuggling of babies was going on.

In his play *Thesmophoriazousai* ('Women Celebrating the Thesmophoria'), Aristophanes has a graphic fantasy about a woman who falsely claims to her husband that she is about to give birth, and keeps up the pretence of labour pains for ten days until she manages, through an assistant, to buy a baby.[143] The baby is then smuggled into the house, its mouth plugged with bees' wax to prevent it crying. The point about purchase, found also in Demosthenes, is interesting; in Aristophanes it seems to have no dramatic purpose, except perhaps to satisfy an audience familiar with the practical details of such tales.[144] Also, the poet thought that his audience needed no explanation of the woman's motive: this too was no doubt familiar. Deceit of the husband would be thought a regular part of baby-smuggling; if husband and wife agreed on the need to obtain an heir from outside the family, legal adoption was available without the risks of smuggling.[145]

If baby-smuggling was widely thought to occur at Athens, we should expect there to have been a law penalising it. Entitlement to the status of citizen was jealously limited; a law of the mid-fifth century, attributed to Perikles, insisted that citizens in future be of citizen parentage on both sides, and not merely — as before — on the father's.[146] Also, since a woman who falsely claimed to be in labour would probably need an accomplice to bring her an infant, if baby-smuggling actually went on, we might expect to hear something of blackmail against such mothers or against people claiming descent from them. Centuries after the classical period, the author of a glossary of Attic phrases included the following attempt at definition:

What is the *hypobolēs graphē*? It is a form of accusation. When someone accused someone else of having been a smuggled baby, the latter was charged in connection with such smuggling (*hypobolē*) and if convicted had to be sold as a slave.[147]

In his history of Athenian law, L. Beauchet objected to this record, arguing that the law of Athens, gentle and relatively humane, would only have punished the authors of a crime, and would not have deprived a free child of its liberty merely because of an act committed by others.[148] This objection seems unsound. The fate of a person proved to have been smuggled as a baby need not have been seen as a punishment, but as a reversion to that person's original status. If baby-smuggling was thought to go on, it may well have been assumed that most of the babies involved were of slave parentage. A male infant of citizen parentage was, as we have seen, of great social value,[149] and with the prevailing standards of medicine and hygiene it may generally have seemed sensible to rear several sons to ensure the survival of one. Such infants were, perhaps, not often disposed of. Male slave babies, on the other hand, were often unwelcome. Xenophon refers to the need to use bolts to keep slaves in a house from meeting and breeding.[150] Hesiod, centuries earlier, had suggested that a female slave with a baby might be discriminated against in the labour market.[151] Aristophanes, in a further comic reference to baby-smuggling, writes of a wife who gives birth to a girl, then swaps her for the male baby of a slave.[152] And in Euripides' *Alkestis* a character of noble birth who, in rhetorical exaggeration, questions his own parentage, suggests to his father that he was in origin a slave baby but had been "smuggled in and put to your wife's breast".[153] It may seem that one cannot dismiss the evidence of the glossary that there was a formal Athenian process to deal with baby-smuggling, though — given its lateness — that evidence can hardly be treated as decisive. On the further point of blackmail, we do indeed hear — though again from comedy[154] — of an Athenian paying to prevent an accusation that he had been a smuggled baby.

Perhaps the most important single reference to this subject is by Plato who, in a glancing comparison, writes

Everything that produces offspring has suitable nourishment for that offspring, which is why also one can easily tell a woman who has genuinely given birth from one who has not, but who is trying to pass off someone else's baby as her own — if she does not have the source of nourishment for the child.[155]

356

This matter-of-fact and apparently serious reference to baby-smuggling seems to be aimed at a readership which believed that such things happened. For the reason Plato refers to, the lack of mother's milk in a woman who has not at some stage been pregnant, the opportunity of smuggling a baby may have seemed limited for the most part to those women who had access to a wet-nurse. Since any such importing of a baby was meant to be inconspicuous, often involving the women's rooms which no outsider might enter, Athenians themselves would lack accurate information on the extent, if any, of this activity. However, it is virtually certain that baby-smuggling was widely believed to occur. The reality of this practice was something that most Athenians may have been in no position to verify. However, they must have known of the existence of social pressure which seemed capable of driving women to this, in spite of the risks of discovery, divorce and lasting disgrace.[156]

The great economic and social importance of being able to establish the parenthood of an Athenian was probably a main reason for the tendency in prosperous circles for women to be confined to the home, where opportunities for illicit sex, or damaging rumours of it, were restricted. Once it was established that a wife had had sex with a man other than her husband, her future offspring could not be accepted as citizens.[157] The concern with sexual propriety is clearly illustrated in a statement about women's movements attributed to the fourth-century orator, Hypereides: "a woman who goes out of the home should be of an age at which the people who meet her ask, not whose wife she is, but whose mother she is".[158] The home was viewed almost as a sacrosanct retreat; in legal rhetoric, horror is expressed at invasion of the home by outsiders.[159] Typically, the house of a wealthy family had only one door to the outside: the women's quarters lay furthest from it, with the men's in between.[160]

When using the evidence of comedy to reconstruct history, one has to recall that the style of humour varies. A joke in the Old Comedy of Aristophanes may be funny because it exaggerates reality: Athens in the late fifth century produced non-aristocratic politicians, so Aristophanes showed one as a vulgar sausage-seller.[161] A joke may invert normal reality, as when a humble old man tries to behave like an aristocrat.[162] Or the humour of a passage may be surrealistic, as when a character in Aristophanes' *Peace* flies to heaven on a dung-beetle. The humour of Aristophanes' *Ekklēsiazousai* ('Assembly Women') may have depended on an ingenious combination of exaggeration and inversion; the idea of women taking over the government of Athens represented an inversion of the rule that women did not attend, or have votes in, the sovereign assembly, but it also involved an extension of a process which, around 400 BC, had actually been happening — the emergence from home of large numbers of women to take part in economic activity. In the same play a wife's unexplained absence from home immediately raises a question, among men, as to her sexual morality.[163] When she returns, Blepyros, her husband, asks

> "Where have you been, Praxagora?" "What's that to you, dear?" "What's that to me? How charmingly naïve!" "At least you won't say I've been out with my lover." "Not *one* lover perhaps; it could be several." "There is actually a test you could use for that." "What?" "See whether my head smells of perfume." "What: don't women get screwed without perfume?" "This one doesn't, unfortunately." [164]

Since there is evidence from more serious sources that male concern over possible sexual delinquency by women was thought quite commendable, Blepyros' interest in the subject was probably not meant to be amusing in itself. Rather, Aristophanes' intention seems to have been to use a familiar and serious kind of questioning to lead up to the unexpected joke about the effect of perfume.[165]

When a writer makes a statement, his or her motive obviously tends to be a fear that otherwise some may deny or overlook the truth it refers to. On the other hand, what is obvious and indisputable may not be stated. The Athenian taste for thorough logic has a benign effect in this area. Yet we should still be watchful for the unspoken assumption, in the lawcourt speeches, in comedy and elsewhere; a belief so widely accepted that an author can take it for granted is likely to have been of some importance. In Aristophanes' *Ekklēsiazousai* while the women are out governing Athens the men stay at home. After describing how this comes about, Aristophanes proceeds without explanation to recount the abolition, in this women's state, of private property. Scholars have sensibly suggested that the author is here satirising contemporary communistic theories, forerunners of Plato's scheme in the *Republic*. But that does not explain why Aristophanes did not trouble to account dramatically for the development of communism out of government by women. The reason for this omission is perhaps as follows. It could have been assumed by Aristophanes' audience that women, if given power and freed from the control of men, would engage in widespread sexual activity outside marriage — as men themselves in fact did.[166] If that happened, the paternity of children would become hopelessly confused. But the transmission of private property depended on the establishment of paternity. The emancipation of women might thus make the system of private property unworkable, by a process too obvious, perhaps, for Aristophanes to have to spell out.

The theory that a man's proper sphere of activity was outside the house, while a woman's was inside, is stated explicitly in Xenophon's *Oikonomikos*, a work written perhaps at a time in the early fourth century when the segregation of the sexes was seen to have been somewhat eroded. Nature, says Xenophon, has fitted the sexes for their separate roles, in accordance with the will of god.[167] Aristotle expresses disapproval of the rule established by some wives, who were *epiklēroi*, over their husbands; for either spouse to have complete control over the other is usurpation, comparable with oligarchy in a state.[168] Presumably Aristotle understood the home as the area in which wives should be sovereign. Work done away from the home by poorer women will be discussed shortly. For young women of prosperous family, the occasions on which an outing was permitted were well defined:[169] festivals (some of which were exclusively for women);[170] funerals;[171] childbirth involving a relative or neighbour.[172] We also hear of women going out to do laundry or to borrow things from neighbours.[173] These occasions would give important chances of conversation with other women.[174] Conversation with men was discouraged; there may have been a special term of disapproval for a woman who talked much with men: *androlalos*, 'man chatting'.[175] Women could also be censured for answering the door, which might involve willingness to deal with men.[176] Women's interest in activity outside the house led typically to "peeping out" (*parakyptein*).[177]

How women felt about the limitation of their movements is not recorded. If we were right to suggest that those limitations varied over the years, becoming stricter as slave labour became more plentiful in the mid-fifth century, more relaxed around the turn of the century and stricter again later, some irritation — and perhaps some relief — may have resulted as standards changed, depending on the temperaments of individuals. Euripides may not be simply projecting male feelings when he makes Andromakhe describe her frustration:

> Whatever chaste activities have been devised for women, I toiled at and performed in Hektor's house. In the first place, a woman who does not stay in is ill reputed through the very fact, whether she's doing wrong or not: I put aside my longing to go out, and stayed at home.[178]

We have seen, however, that Athenian society probably so shaped the values and tastes of women that in many cases they would have clung with determination to a cloistered life, partly as a reflection of high status. The orator Demosthenes expected an Athenian audience in the 340s to pity the sufferings of a certain free woman who had been forced to take part in the sexual rough-house of a drinking party:[179] such involvement degraded a citizen, by assimilating her to *hetairai* and whores.[180] From Greece, as from classical Islam, we hear of hysterical illness in a woman being cured by the threat of being undressed in the sight of men;[181] without necessarily being true, such accounts may reflect a real and profound aversion of women from the eyes of male strangers. Athenian vase-painting shows women escorting each other outdoors, using a shared veil to ward off glances:[182] again the analogy with Islam is obvious.

Accidental attributes of aristocrats and the rich often become the objects of widespread imitation, because of their association with such people. It was no doubt because women of high status were sheltered, and happened to become pale from their time indoors, that pallor in women was valued. A tanned face would suggest that a woman worked outdoors; as we shall see, such activity went with poverty and low status, and could be derided.[183] When, in the *Ekklēsiazousai*, Praxagora's revolutionary colleagues put on oil and sunbathe, their purpose is not to make themselves attractive, it is to be mistaken for men.[184] On Athenian black-figure vases males are shown with dark flesh, but females with light. References to men's appreciation of pallor in women are frequent, and come from many periods of Greek history.[185] In the Homeric poems Nausikaa and Andromakhe are "white-armed".[186] Aristophanes imagines a woman being alluringly advertised as "both very beautiful and very pale".[187] White lead was used by women of various classes, to achieve pallor instantly.[188] Greek values and behaviour in this sphere have been echoed elsewhere in later times; a French writer of the sixteenth century, praising the English, stated that their men were "handsome and ruddy", their women "fair as alabaster".[189]. The value now placed upon a suntan (of certain kinds) lacks the sexual differentiation, but otherwise corresponds closely to Greek attitudes. What suggests wealth remains fashionable. But the industrial revolution took the mass of ordinary workers from the fields into factories, shops and offices: pallor became common-place and a suntan came to reflect leisure and wealth. In women's cosmetics the road from white lead to brown liquid is surprisingly direct.

Work (other than child-bearing)

We have already seen much evidence of the valued role of wives as domestic managers. The need for efficiency in this sphere was seen as another reason for requiring sexual fidelity of the wife. Lysias, commenting on the Athenian rule that a lover should be more severely punished than a rapist, suggested that the lover (unlike the rapist) corrupted the wife's spirit, confused the paternity of the children and got the whole house under his control — an interesting testimony to the wife's power.[190] In the oration against Neaira, a courtesan who at one stage ran away with some property belonging to her man,[191] a speaker of the mid-fourth century contrasts the roles of *hetairai*, concubines and wives. Women in the first two categories are kept, he states, to provide respectively for pleasure and for the daily needs of the body. Wives, on the other hand, had the role of producing legitimate children and of being "faithful guardians of the things in the house".[192] This description of the role of wife was meant to be plausible to an Athenian jury, although it was shaped as an attack on Neaira who, as the speaker stresses, was unable by virtue of her status to produce legitimate children and did not prove a faithful guardian of her man's property. It was no doubt understood that *hetairai* could not be employed as faithful guardians because of the possibly conflicting interests of the various men whom they knew.

The model wife in Xenophon's *Oikonomikos* is advised to do work which involves some physical exercise, such as kneading dough, shaking and folding cloaks and bedclothes, and walking around to supervise the slaves.[193] The exercise, it is said, would give her a better appetite, make her healthier and help her appearance to be more alluring to her husband than that of the slave women. In less wealthy households there might be more pressing reasons for a wife to do physical work. The *Ekklēsiazousai* has a comic list of women's domestic functions:

> They all dip wool in warm water, in the old-fashioned way...
> They sit down and do the cooking, as women did before.
> They carry things upon their heads, as women did before.
> They run the Thesmophoria, as women did before.
> They do the baking of flat cakes, as women did before.
> They wear their husbands down, as women did before.
> They have their lovers in the house, as women did before.
> They get some fancy extra food, as women did before.
> They have a taste for unmixed wine, as women did before.
> They love it when they're being shagged, as women did before.[194]

The comments in the latter part of this list, about adultery, gluttony, heavy drinking and great sexual appetite, are of a kind frequently made concerning women in Athenian comedy.[195] If the severe sanctions against adultery by a wife were normally employed when the act was proved, it may seem unlikely that jokes about wifely infidelity reflected commonplace behaviour. The activities and tastes mentioned in the latter part of the list may be unrepresentative of the majority of women. If so, how should that affect our view of the practices mentioned in the earlier part? As usual, a careful look is needed at how the comic poet is getting his effect.

Ancient and modern comedians are fond of a technique whereby material of a particular tone puts the audience in a certain frame of mind, which is then triumphantly jolted by a remark of very different tone. The technical term for such humour in ancient comedy is *para prosdokian*, 'contrary to expectation'.[196] Using this style Hermippos, a comedian contemporary with Aristophanes, composed a long, sober-looking list of Athens' imports: "From Cyrene silphium stems and ox hides, from the Hellespont mackerel ..." and so on, until mention is made of the commodity supplied by King Perdikkas of Macedon: "lies by the shipload".[197] In the passage quoted above from the *Ekklēsiazousai*, this again seems to be the technique in use. The remarks about misbehaviour by women would have gained a certain comic force from following a list of wifely activities which the audience knew to be realistic.

Even a sheltered girl might know about wool-working, as we have seen from Xenophon's *Oikonomikos*. Another section of the *Ekklēsiazousai* shows a woman in more humble circumstances working wool because, as she is made to say, "my small children have no clothes".[198] That women carried things such as pitchers of water on their heads is shown by Athenian vase-paintings. Herodotos also makes this clear, in a passage which was meant to inform his Greek readers about the Egyptians but which may now be even more useful for the light it throws on the Greeks themselves. He writes about ways in which the Egyptians differed from "the rest of mankind". Among the Egyptians, "men carry burdens on their heads, whereas women do so on their shoulders". The Greeks, it is understood, did things the other way round: such an idea, imputed by a Greek to a Greek audience, obviously has considerable authority. Similarly when Herodotos states in this context that in Egypt women frequent the market, while men stay home and weave, we are being given information, indirectly but reliably, about Greek norms.

Some Athenian women took paid employment outside the home, as we have seen. The comedies of Aristophanes make repeated references to tradeswomen, one of whom is shown boldly challenging a man for interfering with her goods and threatening him with legal action.[199] The law which forbade women to perform large financial transactions left scope for petty trade, and may sometimes have been broken with impunity. A woman named Artemis is recorded on an inscription as having sold reeds (for building) to the value of 70 *drakhmai*, a sum far beyond the price of a *medimnos* of barley.[200] Athenian notions of the rule of law were very different from those general in the West today (see Chapter 7. For the present we may note that speakers in Athenian legal cases feel obliged at times to argue not only that an accused has broken a law but that, this being so, some punishment is required.) Market traders, male and female, had low status. At some stage the Athenians passed a law against those who taunted such traders with their profession.[201] To provoke legislation, these taunts must have been frequent and wounding. Whether the law was enforced is unclear, but the attitudes which provoked it seem to have been widespread in Aristophanes' time. The comic poet in several plays teases the tragedian Euripides with the idea that the latter's mother was a greengrocer.[202] To judge by his marked bias in the selection of targets for satire, Aristophanes had values which were more aristocratic than those of most Athenians.[203] But his inclusion of the joke about Euripides' mother in at least four plays suggests that his audience was not strongly averse to jokes against tradespeople. It was suggested above that more women went out to work in the difficult years around 400 BC than at other stages in Athenian history. Aristophanes' plays belong of course to that period; the prominence in them of references to tradeswomen may reflect the novelty to his audience of having so many women at work in public.

Relations with the husband

Those Athenians with the education and leisure to read Xenophon's *Oikonomikos* were expected to recognise that husband and wife might have very few conversations.[204] There was much that tended to prevent spouses from sharing interests. The large gap which normally existed between the ages of husband and wife would mean, as Lacey points out,[205] that friends might seldom be shared. A source of much conversation between the spouses might thus be lost. The differences in experience and outlook which arose from disparity in ages would be combined with effects of segregation within the house and of dissimilarity in the type of work done by each partner.

There were, however, some areas of contact. Husband and wife would share pleasures and problems in connection with their children. Aristotle stresses the bond between the marriage partners which children created.[206] We have seen that the choice of Iskhomakhos as husband is represented as having been made by "the parents" of his wife. An Athenian vase of the classical period shows a father looking on while his young wife encourages their baby son to crawl.[207] A well-known passage of the speech against Neaira predicts an exchange of conversation between the jurymen, after they have returned home, and their female relatives:

When you get home, what would each of you say to your wife or daughter or mother when she asks "Where have you been?" When you reply "Judging a case", she will immediately ask, "Who was on trial?"[208]

The case in question, in which Neaira was accused of usurping citizen status, would be of special concern to Athenian women. But we should notice that the questions 'Where have you been?' and 'Who was on trial?' were assumed to be predictable before the subject of Neaira was raised. Athenian jurors were, in most cases, of lower social status than Xenophon's intended readership.[209] It may be that among ordinary Athenians shortage of space in the home, and shortage of slaves,[210] brought wife and husband together and into conversation more often than in wealthy circles.

The availability of slaves may similarly have affected sexual relations between husband and wife, as will be argued below. Difference in ages between spouses would also have been important in this area, causing parity of sexual desire to be achieved less often. Aristotle gives the opinion that girls who had sex very young became too lustful;[211] in another context he cites "the pleasure of young people" as an example of intensity.[212] Suspicion and jealousy on the part of middle-aged husbands towards wives in their teens may have contributed to the restrictions on women's movements.

In defining the term *akratēs* ('lacking in self-control'), Aristotle states that no one would apply it to a woman:[213] the context shows that he had sexual activity in mind. He was of course aware that some women had illicit affairs of their own will, and that adverse criticism of women for this was commonplace. He may perhaps have meant that, although women were open to blame for such activity, the word *akratēs* did not occur in the course of that blame. As an explanation of why this word was not applied to women, Aristotle writes that women took a passive role in the sexual act. But since a married woman who had an affair would normally have to collaborate actively with the lover, this can hardly be the whole explanation of why the term was never applied to such a woman — if Aristotle indeed meant that. If Aristotle on the other hand had in mind not the whole range of female sexual activity but normal intercourse between husband and wife, this difficulty would disappear. In that case he would have to mean that no one would blame a wife for having excessive sex with her husband *because she did not have any control over its frequency*, and that no one would even wrongly believe that she did. This would not only suggest that wives did not take the initiative in this sphere. It would also imply that they were not able to limit their husbands' sexual access to them. For, if a wife had been able to do so, but had nevertheless agreed to a husband's

365

excessive advances, she might herself have qualified as lacking in self-control.

Medeia is made to state that a woman's husband is "master of her body", and that his advances cannot be refused.[214] In the *Ekklēsiazousai*, after the women have taken control of the city, two men are shown predicting the impact of this on themselves:

> "My wife will go for court service and not me?" "And you won't be supporting your household any more, your wife will." "No more having to groan at dawn when it's time to get up?" "No, that's women's affair now ..." "There's something I'm really afraid of for men of our age — that women, now they control the city, will use force to ... make us screw them." "And what if we don't manage to?" "They won't give us breakfast ... Enforced sex would be terrible." "But if it helps the city, every man should do it."[215]

Given Aristotle's comments, the humour here is easily understood. And, in keeping with the general humour of inversion, the last sentence quoted would have point if normally it was women who were supposed to consider the needs of the city and submit to their spouses' demands.[216] In Aristophanes' *Lysistratē*, which portrays women of Greece as having withdrawn their sexual favours from men, the heroine gives instructions on how to touch certain male ambassadors who approach the women: "Don't handle them harshly or roughly, or in the ignorant way that men used to handle us, but touch them as you'd expect a woman to — intimately."[217] Remarks on the roughness and ignorance of male caresses are commonplace today in feminist writings. It is interesting that, in an age when feminist theory was scarcely prominent in men's culture, a similar comment should have penetrated into a work written by a man for a theatre audience consisting wholly or mainly of men. One may suspect that lack of sexual adjustment must have been quite marked for that to happen. One possible source of male indelicacy should now be examined.

The impact of prostitution and slavery on marital relations

Xenophon represents Sokrates as saying bluntly, "you surely do not suppose that it is sexual lust which makes people have children; the streets and brothels are full of people who will satisfy that".[218] The speech against Neaira reminds an Athenian audience why "we have" *hetairai* and concubines.[219] That speech also refers calmly to a brothel as a "workshop" and to prostitution as "working with the body".[220] Athens publicly recognised prostitution by taxing it.[221] What effect did this widespread practice have on relations between wives and husbands?

Many wealthy Athenians would be customers of prostitutes, as we shall see. But there was some social pressure against a husband taking a prostitute home,[222] or spending large sums on prostitution after receiving a big dowry from his wife.[223] Perhaps the most frequent clients of the women obliged to carry on this trade were young men before the time of marriage. A speech of Demosthenes suggests that it may have been seen as characteristic of young men to be in love with *hetairai* and to get into fights over them.[224] Isokrates refers to young men frequenting the schools at which courtesans were taught to play the flute.[225] The speech against Neaira, which gives a revealing and unintentionally poignant account of her childhood and youth, tells of two men at Korinth who bought her, for their joint sexual use, as a young woman.[226] But when about to take wives, they sold Neaira her own freedom, with the stipulation that they did not want to see her, their former *hetaira*, plying her trade in Korinth[227] where, presumably, they intended to live with their wives. In the *Ekklēsiazousai* the leader of the revolutionary women informs her husband,

> "I want to put an end to all prostitution of females." "Why?" "That's obvious. So that these women [the citizens] can have the young men at their peak. There's no reason why dolled-up slaves should steal the sex which belongs to free women."[228]

In view of the preceding evidence, the humour here may seem to involve a fairly straightforward reflection of Athenian life.

Because of its scale and circumstances, the prostitution within Athens may be profitably compared with that of Victorian London. There, out of a total population of some 3 million, about 80,000 females were active in the trade, according to a nineteenth-century calculation adopted by a Bishop of Exeter.[229] In both cultures prostitution flourished alongside, and perhaps partly because of, an intense emphasis in the prosperous classes on the chastity of women. One benefit of an analogy between cultures may be that, once certain points of resemblance have been established between the two terms, the second term may be seen to present additional features which can then usefully be tested for in the first. In the case of Victorian London, there were serious complaints that prostitution was undermining the institution of marriage. One group of prosperous mothers stated publicly that their numerous eligible daughters had between them received scarcely any serious offers of marriage, a fact which the daughters attributed to the counter-attractions of pretty *demimondaines* in Hyde Park. It seems worth asking whether something similar was true in Athens.

One obvious case of prostitution seeming to impinge upon marriage is that of Hipparetē, who is recorded as having set off to perform the formalities of divorce when her husband, Alkibiades, brought prostitutes home.[230] Less obvious is the question whether in Athens, as perhaps in London, attachment to prostitutes of various kinds caused many men to postpone marriage. One may guess that Lucian was being realistic in imagining a mother remonstrating with her son: "that Kharmides, he's the same age as you ... he's getting married now and settling down: how much longer are *you* going to be with a *hetaira*?".[231] In another of his *Dialogues of the hetairai* Lucian describes the fury of parents against a son who refuses to marry a girl with a huge dowry, 5 talents, because of his fondness for a courtesan.[232] This last instance, although fictional, is plausible in so far as it involves a courtesan having influence over a young man who moves in wealthy circles. Buying the time of an attractive woman was likely to be very costly; sour remarks about the expense of hiring prostitutes are numerous in Greek writings.[233] A character in Aristophanes' *Wealth* states, graphically,

> ... and they say that the *hetairai* of Korinth pay no attention when a poor man happens to make a pass at them, but if a rich man does they turn their bottoms towards him straightaway.[234]

We have seen that Aristotle describes poor men as using their wives and children to perform domestic tasks, because they lacked·slaves. In a similar way, poverty may have caused many Athenians to direct a higher proportion of their sexual attentions towards their wives than was normal among the wealthy.[235]

The violence connected with prostitution may also have had some effect on marital relations. A woman who wished to receive no callers, perhaps because she was already with a man, would bar her door. This led to furious and frequent scenes of door battering in the streets of Athens as frustrated clients, ardent after a night's drinking, sought admission.[236] An Athenian vase shows one returning reveller hammering in similar style at the door of a woman who, to judge by the cut of her hair, is not a slave but his wife.[237] When a prostitute had her door battered thus, a man who was inside with her might emerge and fight with the new-comer.[238] We have already met the idea, reported by Demosthenes, that fighting over *hetairai* was characteristic of young men. Vase painting also shows drunken brawls over women, although often in a mythic setting.[239] Lucian suggests the possibility of another, and more sinister, form of violence. He depicts a young courtesan as explaining to her mother that she must remain faithful to her one male patron, stingy though he is, because he has threatened to kill her if she has another man. To this the mother replies, "How many other men make threats like that!"[240] We have seen reason for thinking that young men of some wealth were especially likely to spend time with prostitutes and *hetairai*. In many cases it would be these men who later married the young and sheltered daughters of the wealthy. Yet in such cases sexual disharmony between husband and wife is likely to have been frequent. The sensibility needed in relations with a girl bride, who has been brought up to "see and hear as little as possible", may not easily result from a previous ten or fifteen years spent with boisterous and drunken whoring.

Less spectacular than prostitution, but perhaps even more pervasive and influential for marital relations, was the sexual activity of men with their domestic slaves.[241] We have seen that Euphiletos, who defends himself for the killing of Eratosthenes, was concerned to represent his own behaviour as having been reasonable and, in particular, as not having contributed to his wife's infidelity. Yet he represents his wife as accusing him of having made a sexual attempt on the slave girl: "You tried to drag her around before, when you were drunk."[242] The accusation is not denied. Here our knowledge of the speaker's bias enhances for us the significance of what he says. The fact that he is strongly inclined not to make damaging confessions suggests that sexual activity with the slave girl was expected not to be found shameful by the jury, and not to seem sufficient to provoke a reasonable wife to infidelity. Xenophon's character Iskhomakhos suggests that his wife should try to enhance her appearance, to compete with any slave woman for (it is understood) his attentions.[243]. Iskhomakhos who gives this self-revealing advice is represented as a model character: Xenophon's readership was evidently expected to see no paradox. In the same work, Iskhomakhos is made to suggest that, if his wife proves to be a very good one, she will not need to fear that as she grows older she will lose respect in the home. He goes on to hint that it is the future fading of her looks that he has in mind.[244] This, of course, implies that some wives might reasonably have such a fear. The frequent accessibility, to many wealthy husbands, of young slave women in the house may well be connected with this fear. Much sexual activity with them on the husband's part would tend to depress the emotional and sexual importance of the wife to the husband, and to be a source of bitterness, presenting as it did the prospect of increasing neglect of the wife.[245] It seems that, in the case of his infidelity with domestic slave women, there was little or no restraint on the husband in the form of disapproval from his male peers in general. It remains to be seen what pressure a wife might apply.

The defences and influence of women

The treatment received by Athenian women would depend, as with other social groups, on how far they could reward, punish or escape from those who behaved acceptably or unacceptably towards them. The ability to do such things must, of course, have varied greatly between individual women according to their intelligence,[246] energy, self-confidence and sexual desirability.[247] Other important variables may, however, be perceived. Divorce, the ultimate legal sanction against an unsatisfactory marriage, was easily achieved in its formal aspects, but, as we have seen, it was probably repellent to the majority of women, in part because of expected difficulties in finding another husband. There is also reason to think that women with very large dowries might cause intense competition among suitors. We might, then, predict that divorce would in general be less unattractive to such women than to others and that the threat of it would give them more influence. Because well-dowered women might expect relatively little difficulty in achieving remarriage, their husbands, who could reckon similarly, would have more reason to take seriously a threat of divorce. Also, to repay a large dowry at short notice, or to pay the required 18 per cent per annum interest in the event of non-repayment,[248] might well cause a husband an unacceptable drop in his standard of living. A wife with a big dowry might be able, to some extent and in some cases, to restrict the freedom of a rich husband to do as he fancied with slave women; she might also be able to secure careful treatment of herself in other respects. A dowry, in short, provided a wife with a hostage:[249] this may have been part of the reason why a prosperous Athenian *kyrios* was required to give her one.

There are many comments by Greek writers on the influence given to a wife by a large dowry. These tend to be complaints that the influence is excessive. This should not, however, be assumed to mean that men generally disapproved of influence arising from a dowry; in many periods of history adverse comment and bad news can be observed to create more interest and attain wider circulation than complaisant remarks and good news. Among the adverse criticism in the present case was a statement by Plato that dowries could cause slavish behaviour in husbands,[250] a remark in a fragment of Euripides' *Phaethon* about a free man who has become a "slave of his marriage-bed, having sold his body for a dowry",[251] and Aristotle's comments on *epiklēroi* who dominated their husbands.[252] In the *Andromakhē* of Euripides the character Hermione, daughter of Menelaos, implies that the wealth she brought to her marriage contributes to her freedom of speech,[253] a freedom which another (and by intention more sympathetic) Euripidean princess denies herself.[254] An Athenian funerary inscription praises a dead woman for having combined in the same person nobility of descent and good conduct: perhaps these two attributes were thought normally not to go together. In the exceptional record of citizen women in amorous pursuit of a man (the charismatic grandee Alkibiades), we note that the women are described as *semnai* ('superior', 'haughty').[255]

Legal arrangements also existed whereby the *arkhōn epōnymos* was empowered to deal with complaints of mistreatment of *epiklēroi*.[256] Parents were protected by law against abuse by their sons,[257] and we hear of a restriction on the rights of speech of any man who failed to provide food and shelter for his father and mother.[258] It may, however, have been difficult to find prosecutors to protect the rights of *epiklēroi* and parents. The male relatives who might normally be expected to provide legal representation were, in case of neglect or abuse, precisely the people against whom an action would need to be brought. Prosecutors who acted in the interests of parents and heiresses were given unusual immunity,[259] which suggests that some difficulty had indeed been experienced in obtaining volunteers for this role.

Euripides makes a character say that the power of a woman wronged by her husband lies in her parents and friends;[260] in other cases of trouble, the husband himself would of course be expected to help.[261] It is evident why special legal arrangements were needed to protect an elderly woman, whose parents and husband would probably be dead and whose surviving friends might be few. Two important (and somewhat neglected) passages of Aristotle and Plato illustrate different ways in which a woman's influence might be exerted within her family. Aristotle writes that for a tyranny to be stable the women in the tyrant's circle must not behave with degrading arrogance towards other women, "since the arrogance of women as well [as that of men] has caused the downfall of many tyrannies".[262] It is implied that the male relatives of women treated with arrogance have found it necessary to avenge the insults by plotting against the tyrannies in question.[263] Plato writes that a woman might resent the fact that her husband was not one of the ruling group in his city, and that as a result she was treated as an inferior among other women. She might see that the husband was not standing up for his rights politically or in court, and complain to her son that his father was "too relaxed in his attitude" and "not a man", and use "all the other various accusations with which wives drone on repetitively about such things".[264] Plato sees a woman of this kind as capable by her criticism of shaping the character of her son. We may imagine that if a woman did have recourse to complaining to her son in such matters, she very probably had been frustrated in arguing directly to the husband. In the case of Neaira it was made clear that wives, daughters and mothers might apply formidable pressure to their menfolk concerning the conduct of public affairs. But, since in most circumstances women lacked the right to present evidence to a court without permission from the *kyrios*,[265] and they could not appear in the assembly, informal pressure would often fail. When that happened, there is likely to have been bitterness and insecurity. The ultimate sanction which might be available to a woman with a large dowry has already

Citizen Women of Athens
been considered. A poorer wife would be able to withdraw her goodwill, or part of her labour. But within a family the results of withdrawing goodwill are usually somewhat unsatisfactory for all. And the poverty which could make a husband depend on his wife's labour would mean that the wife herself, if she chose to work with reduced effect, would be exposed to drab consequences.

Notes

1. Valuable modern studies include: K. J. Dover, 'Classical Greek attitudes to sexual behaviour' in *Arethusa*, 6 (1973), 59–73; A. W. Gomme, 'The position of women in Athens in the fifth and fourth centuries BC', in his *Essays in Greek history and literature*, 89–115; J. P. Gould, 'Law, custom and myth: aspects of the social position of women in classical Athens' in *JHS*, 100 (1980), 38–59; P. Herfst, *Le Travail de la femme dans la Grèce ancienne*; W. K. Lacey, *The family in classical Greece*; S. B. Pomeroy, *Goddesses, whores, wives and slaves*; D. C. Richter, 'Women in classical Athens' in *Classical Journal* 67 (1971), 1–8 (with useful insights, but to be read with great caution); G. E. M. de Ste. Croix, 'Some observations on the property rights of Athenian women' in *Classical Review*, n.s., 20 (1970), 273–8; D. M. Schaps, *Economic rights of women in ancient Greece*; H. J. Wolff, in *RE*, vol. 23A, 133–70 (on dowries; in German); M. R. Lefkowitz and M. B. Fant, *Women's life in Greece and Rome* is an important collection of source material in translation.
2. Phintys. The Greek text is in H. Thesleff, *The Pythagorean texts of the Hellenistic period*, 153.
3. Thus in recent times there have been more arguments in the West for clean air than for clean water. This is not because clean air is more widely valued, but because the reverse is true.
4. Thuc. II 45 2.
5. Though see W. K. Lacey in *Proceedings of the Cambridge Philological Society*, n.s., 10 (1964), 47–9.
6. See below.
7. See, e.g., G. S. Kirk and J. E. Raven, *The presocratic philosophers*, 228–9.
8. E.g., Aristoph. *Thesm.* 418ff., *Ekkl.* 226; cf. Hesiod, *Works and days* 703–4.
9. E.g., Aristoph. *Clouds* 555f., *Lysist.* 114, *Thesm.* 347ff., 630ff., 733ff., *Ekkl.* 43ff., 132ff., 227 and especially the anthology at Athenaeus, 440e–442a. A work in terracotta from Olynthos shows a female figure tightly holding a container of wine; *Excavations at Olynthos*, vol. 4, 83. A pre-classical vase shows a woman siphoning wine into her mouth; photograph at C. Seltman, *Wine in the ancient world*, pl. VIIIa (following p. 80). On wine-siphoning cf. Aristoph. *Thesm.* 556f.
10. E.g., Aristoph. *Ekkl.* 120; Theophrastos *Characters* 28; cf. Soph. *Ajax* 293 with Arist. *Pol.* 1260a; Eur. *Troi.* 651–2.

11. Aristoph. *Ekkl.* 228 (though contrast *Lysist.* 165f.); on adultery by women, *Thesm.* 340ff., 477ff.

12. On historic *gynaikonomoi*, C. Wehrli, *Museum Helveticum*, 19 (1962), 33–8.

13. Arist, *Pol.* 1300a; cf. 1323a.

14. Arist. *Pol.* 1277b. However, the text is uncertain at this point; instead of *lalos* ('chatterbox'), Aristotle may have written *alalos* ('taciturn'). This would reverse his meaning, but the point about separate standards would remain.

15. The surviving text of a speech may contain alterations made with a view to its circulation in written form.

16. Compare the very large dowries mentioned in lawcourt speeches; Schaps, op. cit. 99.

17. Lacey, op. cit. (above, n. 1) 168 notes that the most elementary facts about the identity of certain women became questionable in the courts; Isaios III 30–4, VI 13ff., VIII 9f.; Dem. XLIII 29ff., cf. LIX 119ff. But similar questions could arise about a man; Isaios IV 2f.

18. Theophrastos *Characters* III; cf. Semonides frag. 7 lines 112f. (in M. L. West (ed.), *Iambi et elegi Graeci*).

19. Contrast Gomme, op. cit., 101.

20. See, e.g., the two issues of *Arethusa* devoted to the subject of women in antiquity; 6 (1973) and 11 (1978). Perhaps rather different in inspiration is H. Lloyd-Jones's edition of Semonides, *Female of the species: Semonides on women* (1975).

21. The painter Apelles was reportedly mocked for bringing to a drinking party a young woman who was a virgin, not a *hetaira*; Athenaeus 588d.

22. Pomeroy, op. cit. (n. 1), 92. On Aspasia, the famous courtesan and consort of Perikles, see Xenophon, *Memorabilia* II 6 36, *Oikonomikos* III 14; Plat. *Menexenos* 235e ff.; Plut. *Life of Perikles* 24f., 30, 32.

23. Plat. *Rep.* 451c–7c; *Laws* 794c–d, 804d–6c, 813e–4c. For public hostility to such ideas, *Laws*, 781b–c.

24. Plat. *Laws* 781c.

25. *D.H.* 6. Lucian, who spent some time at Athens, was writing in the second century AD. His work cannot be used as direct evidence for the classical period, but it contains much that may cast light on it, as here.

26. See below and Herfst, op. cit., 34–51.

27. Xen. *Oik.* III 13.

28. Ibid., VII 5.

29. Ibid., VII 6.

30. Ibid., IX 10.

31. In Stobaeus, *Eclogae* IV, p. 193, no. 31.

32. Frag. no. 702 in T. Kock, *Comicorum Atticorum Fragmenta*.

33. Plat. *Laws* 658d. We hear of a few women, from the Peloponnese, who received teaching at Plato's Academy; Diogenes Laertius III 46 and W. D. Ross (ed.), *Aristotelis Fragmenta Selecta*, 23–4.

34. See especially Plato, *Gorgias* 502b–d; V. Ehrenberg, *The people of Aristophanes*, 27f.; A. Pickard-Cambridge, *The dramatic festivals of Athens*, ch. 6.

35. There may also have been informal recitations of tragedies, or

parts of tragedies; Plut. *Life of Lysandros* 15 and *Life of Nikias* 29.

36. Several instances, from the work of Euripides, will be given below.

37. Illiterate or partly so: Eur. *Iphigenia among the Taurians* 584f. and cf. Soph. *Trakhiniai* 155ff. Literate: Eur. *Hippolytos* 856ff., *Iphigenia at Aulis* 111ff., 891ff. On the general subject of literacy at Athens, F. D. Harvey, *REG*, 79 (1966), 585–635.

38. The woman represented as arguing from written documents at Lysias XXXII 14 may have been understood as knowing their contents from her own reading or from taking advice.

39. Lysias XXXII 11.

40. Compare the pathos extracted by Lykourgos (*Against Leokrates* 40) from the fact that Athenian citizen women in a crisis of the 330s felt obliged to come to their doors and beg for information.

41. Plat. *Rep.* 455c–e, though he states that many women are better than many men at many things. Compare *Laws* 658d and *Seventh Letter* 355c.

42. Arist. *Pol.* 1254b, *Poetics* 1454a.

43. See above, n. 23.

44. Arist. *Generation of animals* 727a, 728a.

45. See below.

46. Xen. *Const. Spart.* I 3 and compare n. 8 above.

47. The presumption that women in general were politically less well informed than men may lie behind the story that women were used as spies at Syracuse; for an analogous story from classical Islam, P. K. Hitti, *History of the Arabs*[8], 325.

48. See, e.g., Thuc. I 98 1–2, V 32 1, V 116 4 and below.

49. Thuc. VII 27 5.

50. Dem. LVII 35, 45; for the date see sections 18, 42.

51. Xen. *Mem.* II 7.

52. Xen. *Oik.* III 12f.

53. Ibid., X 13.

54. Dem. LVII 45.

55. Xen. *Oik.* VII 5.

56. The reading 'fourteen years old' in [Arist.] *Ath. Pol.* LVI 7 is conjectural.

57. Xen. *Const. Spart.* I 6. Compare Dover, art. cit. (n. 1), 61.

58. Arist. *Pol.* 1335a; cf. Isaios VI 14, Aristoph. *Lysist.* 591–7.

59. [Dem.] XL 12, 56.

60. As Plato recommends; *Rep.* 460e, *Laws* 721a–b, 785b, 772d.

61. Euphiletos, the speaker of Lysias I, refers to his wife's lover, whom he admits to having killed, as *neaniskos*, 'a very young man'; s. 37 and cf. s. 20.

62. For references, see Gould, art.cit. (above, n. 1), 43.

63. See especially Isaios III 64. Compare Dem. XLI 4 for a father breaking up an existing marriage to place his daughter with another man. A groom might also depend on the initiative of his father in matchmaking; Isaios II 18.

64. Xen. *Oik.* VII 10.

65. Dem. XXVII 4f: XXIX 43; XXXVI 8; XLV 28, 35.

66. Gould, loc. cit.
67. Lys. III 6.
68. Arist. *Pol*. 1323a.
69. [Dem.] XL 27 for sexual attraction within a somewhat unusual liaison; compare Isaios III 28.
70. For example, peasants, small traders and slaves. See V. Ehrenberg, *The people of Aristophanes*, esp. chs 5 and 7.
71. Schaps, op. cit. (above, n. 1) 74–88. [Dem.] XL 25 conveniently attests both that a groom of eminent family would expect a dowry and that a wealthy *kyrios* would provide one.
72. Schaps, op. cit., 78.
73. Schaps, op. cit., 99.
74. Dem. XLVII 56ff. with Schaps, op. cit., 142, n. 18; Menandros, *Epitrepontes* 1064–7 (in F. H. Sandbach (ed.), *Menandri reliquiae selectae*); cf. Aiskhines I 95, where the wife in question is an *epiklēros*. (On *epiklēroi* see below.)
75. Except perhaps where the wife had been divorced for sexual infidelity; Schaps, op. cit., 83. For the normal rule see, e.g., Isaios III 35f.
76. [Dem]. XL 6.
77. [Dem]. XLII 27; XLVI 20.
78. Menandros, loc. cit.
79. [Dem.] L!X 8, 112f.
80. [Dem.] XL 4; LIX 113; Dem. XLV 74; Lysias XII 21.
81. [Dem.] XLIII 54, though cf. LIX 113.
82. Lys. XIX 14f.; Isaios II 5 which shows that there was a special term for the dowerless bride, *aproikos*.
83. Xen. *Oik*. X 3ff.
84. Ibid. X 5f., cf. Isok. XVI 31.
85. Compare Andok. I 117ff. and the accusation rebutted at Lys. XIX 13ff. Also, Isaios VII 11f.
86. Lys., ibid.; cf. Plat. *Politikos* 310b.
87. Lys. XIX 15.
88. Andok. I 117ff.; Isok. XIX 46; Isaios II 4f., VII 11f.
89. Isaios VII 11f.
90. See W. E. Thompson, *Phoenix*, 21 (1967), 273–82, *California Studies in Classical Antiquity*, 5 (1972), 211, n. 2.
91. [Dem.] LIX 22.
92. See now Schaps, op. cit., 25–47.
93. Isaios X 10; compare the comic inversion at Aristoph. *Ekkl*. 1024f. and the less pleasant humour at Aiskh. I 110f.
94. [Dem.] XLII 20, 31 for barley at 18 and 6 *drakhmai* per *medimnos* at different times; *IG*, II ^{2}, no. 1672, lines 282f. for a price of three *drakhmai* at a period when a skilled labourer might receive 2½ *drakhmai* per day (ibid., lines 26–8, 31f.).
95. [Arist.] *Ath. Pol*. LVI 6f. for the role of the *arkhōn epōnymos* in protecting *epiklēroi* from abuses; cf. Lys. XV 3; Isaios III 46; Dem. XXXV 48; [Dem.] XXXVII 33, XLIII 74.
96. For the normal order of precedence in inheritance of property, [Dem.] XLIII 51; Isaios XI 1f. For the order of claimants to the hand of

an *epiklēros*, e.g. Isaios III 64, 74. For the claim of a great-uncle to marry an *epiklēros*, Isaios III 63. See also Schaps, op. cit., 33 with references there given.

97. Compare Isaios III 74.
98. Isaios III 64.
99. Dem. LVII 41 and Hypothesis to Dem. XXX.
100. Plut. *Life of Solon* XX.
101. *The law of Athens*, I, 136, n. 2.
102. Lacey, op. cit. (above, n. 1), 141.
103. [Dem.] XLIII 11f; cf. Lacey, op. cit., chs 1 and 4.
104. Schaps, op. cit. (above, n. 1), 32.
105. Schaps, ibid., and [Dem.] XLIII 12–15.
106. [Arist.] *Ath. Pol.* XLIII 4 with P.J. Rhodes, *A commentary on the Aristotelian Athenaion Politeia*, 526.
107. Schaps, op. cit., 40f. In some cases the *epiklēros* would be poor and in need of help from, rather than protection against, relatives.
108. See especially R. F. Willetts, *The law code of Gortyn* (*Kadmos*, Supplement I, 1967).
109. Willetts, columns VII and VIII; compare column V for the rights of relatives in the female line in other matters of inheritance.
110. Ibid., column VIII.
111. Contrast Andok. I 124–7 with F. D. Harvey, *Classical views*, XXVIII (1984), 68–70.
112. Not 'father', NB.
113. Xen. *Oik*. VII 10.
114. Ibid., 11f.
115. Cf. Lacey, op. cit. (above, n. 1), 156.
116. In Euripides' play, Medeia taunts Jason after killing his sons; "Your troubles haven't started. Wait until you are old"; line 1396, cf. 1032–7.
117. See below, n. 258.
118. Pomeroy, op. cit. (above, n. 1), 68.
119. On Sparta, see Chapter 6.
120. Lines 250f.
121. Lys. I 6f.
122. Arist. *Nik. Eth.* 1162a. One anxious Greek husband put the following question to the oracle of Zeus and Diōnē at Dōdōnē: "Herakleidas ... asks ... concerning offspring, whether there will be any from his wife, Aiglē, whom he has at present" (H. W. Parke, *The oracles of Zeus*, 265).
123. Lines 489–91.
124. Line 33, cf. 904f.
125. Isaios II 7–12.
126. W. E. Thompson, *California Studies in Classical Antiquity*, 5 (1972), 221.
127. Isaios III 8, 35, 78; Dem. XXX 17, 26. [Andokides] IV 14.
128. Lacey, op. cit. (above, n. 1), 108.
129. Pomeroy, op. cit. (above, n. 1), 64.
130. As Pomeroy indeed notes; ibid.
131. Lines 236f. The writer who recounts Hipparetē's attempt to

divorce Alkibiades feels it necessary to stress that she was a woman of good character; [Andok.] IV 14; cf. Plut. *Life of Alkibiades* VIII.

132. A fragment from the fourth-century comedian Anaxandrides refers to the difficulty of divorce for a woman who is *kosmia*; T. Kock, op. cit. (above n. 32), no.56.

133. [Dem.] LIX 51.

134. Lines 344–8.

135. Medeia is made to state that when relationships at home go wrong a man can get solace outside the home, whereas a woman is utterly dependent on one person — the husband; lines 244–7. A few women could live honoured lives outside the home as priestesses: Pomeroy, op. cit. (n. 1), 75–8.

136. Cf. Dem. XXIX 26, XLV 74.

137. Aristoph. *Lysist.* 591–7; cf. Theokritos, Idyll II (= Lefkowitz and Fant, op. cit. (above n. 1), 130).

138. Thuc. V 103 2 and below, Chapter 9.

139. The comedies are by Alexis, Kratinos the Younger, Eudoxos, Menandros and Philemon. The verbal root is *hypoball-*, 'throw (or put) underneath' — in this case putting to the breast may be understood: Eur. *Alkestis* 639.

140. Dem. XXI 149; cf. Isaios VI 22f.

141. J. K. Davies, *Athenian propertied families*, 385–7.

142. See below, n. 153 and cf. the infant Oidipous; Eur. *Phoinissai* 28–31.

143. Lines 502–18.

144. If babies had to be bought, that might suggest that the exposure of (male) infants was uncommon; on this form of infanticide see G. E. M. de Ste. Croix, *The class struggle in the ancient Greek world*, 103; Lacey, op. cit. (above, n. 1), 164f.; Pomeroy, op. cit. (above, n. 1), 69f.

145. Schaps, op. cit. (above, n. 1), 32. If a wife could reasonably be expected to deceive her husband with a pretended pregnancy, one might infer that there was a taboo on sexual relations in the later months of pregnancy; cf. Aristoph. *Thesm.* 508f; Theophrastos *Characters* XVI.

146. [Arist.] *Ath. Pol.* XXVI 4; cf. Dem. LVII 30 for a relaxation later in the fifth century, followed by renewed restriction. See also Lacey, op. cit. (n. 1), 102f.; Rhodes, op. cit. (above, n. 106), 331–4.

147. I. Bekker, *Anecdota Graeca*, I, 311f.

148. L. Beauchet, *Histoire du droit privé de la république athénienne*, II, 418.

149. Compare Aristoph. *Ekkl.* 549, though contrast Hesiod, *Works and days* 376f., and the references collected ad loc. in M. L. West's edition.

150. Xen. *Oik.* IX 5.

151. Hesiod, op. cit., 602f.

152. Aristoph. *Thesm.* 564f.

153. Lines 636–9.

154. Telekleides frag. 41 (in T. Kock, op. cit.).

155. *Menexenos* 237e.

156. Herodotos (V 41) reports suspicion at Sparta that the wife of a king planned to smuggle a baby; officials checked by attending her lying-

in. So, for similar reasons, numerous persons of state attended the confinement, in 1688, of Mary of Modena, the wife of King James II of England.

157. [Dem.] LIX 86f.
158. Hypereides (ed. F. Blass), frag. 205.
159. Dem. XXI 79; [Dem.] XLVII 53, 56.
160. Gould, art. cit. (n. 1), 48.
161. In the *Knights*. On the interpretation of Aristophanic humour see especially G.E.M. de Ste. Croix, *Origins*, Appendix XXIX.
162. Aristoph. *Wasps* 1326–448.
163. Line 350.
164. Lines 520–6.
165. On the humour of surprise, see below.
166. See below.
167. Xen. *Oik*. VII 30.
168. Arist. *Nik. Eth*. 1160b–1161a.
169. Slaves were used as escorts; e.g. Theophrastos *Characters* 22 and cf. Eur. *Androm*. 590ff.
170. See, e.g., Isaios VIII 19 on women running the Thesmophoria and Aristophanes' play on that theme, the *Thesmophoriazousai*.
171. Lys. I 8; Plut. *Life of Solon* 21; D. C. Kurtz and J. M. Boardman, *Greek burial customs*, ch. VII; S. C. Humphreys in *JHS*, C (1980), 99f.
172. Aristoph. *Ekkl*. 528ff., 549.
173. Eur. *Helen* 179ff., *Hippolytos* 121ff. (superior, purple-dyed, garments are involved in both cases); Aristoph. *Ekkl*. 446–9; Theophrastos *Characters* 10.
174. So Eur. *Hippolytos* 121ff.
175. Theophrastos, op. cit., 28; there is, however, some doubt about the Greek text here.
176. Ibid.
177. E.g., Aristoph. *Peace* 979–85, *Thesm*. 797, *Ekkl*. 884; Lucian *D. H*. 2.
178. Eur. *Troiades* 645–50.
179. Dem. XIX 196–8.
180. [Dem.] LIX 24, 48.
181. Plutarch, *Moralia* 249c; P. K. Hitti, *History of the Arabs*, 309.
182. Cf. Aristoph. *Lysist*. 531–3.
183. The Roman poet Ovid mentions sunburn as the attribute of an inept peasant woman; *Art of love* III 303–5.
184. Lines 62–5.
185. E. Irwin, *Colour terms in Greek poetry*, 116ff.; T. Breitenstein, *Recherches sur le poème Mégara*, 40.
186. E.g. Hom. *Iliad* VI 377; *Odyssey* VI 101. Cf. Eur. *Medeia* 1148.
187. Aristoph. *Ekkl*. 699.
188. Ibid. 878; Xen. *Oik*. X 2.
189. *Antiquarian Repertory*, IV (1809), 510f.
190. Lys. I 33.
191. [Dem.] LIX 35.
192. Ibid., 122. Lacey (op. cit. (above, n. 1), 113) states that the

wording of this passage does not exclude care of the (husband's) body and the provision of his pleasure from the desired role of a wife. Our knowledge of Greek social life may make us expect such a meaning, but the Greek is not naturally so interpreted. The expressions about *hetairai*, concubines and wives are parallel in form: if we interpret the first two as 'meaning 'we have *hetairai* mainly or entirely for pleasure, and concubines mainly or entirely for the daily needs of the body', we should perhaps take the third expression also to mean 'we have wives mainly or entirely to produce legitimate children and to be faithful guardians, etc.'

193. Xen. *Oik.* 10–12.

194. Lines 215–17, 221–8.

195. See above, nn. 8, 9, 11.

196. Arist. *Rhet.* 1412a; Demetrios of Phaleron 152.

197. Quoted by Athenaeus, 27e–28a.

198. Line 92.

199. Aristoph. *Wasps* 1388–1408.

200. *IG* II^2 1672, line 64. However, Artemis may not have been an Athenian citizen; Schaps, op. cit. (above, n. 1), 63. Further on women in trade, ibid., 61f.

201. Dem. LVII 30f. Notice the apologetic manner in which the speaker here admits to selling ribbons.

202. Aristoph. *Akharnians* 478, *Knights* 19, *Thesmophoriazousai* 387, *Frogs* 840.

203. De Ste. Croix, *Origins*, Appendix XXIX.

204. See above, n. 52.

205. Lacey, op. cit. (above, n. 1), 163. Compare Eur. *Medeia* 1153 for advice to a wife to let her husband choose her friends.

206. See above, n. 122.

207. *Catalogue of the Greek and Etruscan vases in the British Museum*, III, 252 (= E 396).

208. [Dem.] LIX 110, though contrast Aristoph. *Lysist.* 512–16.

209. Cf. Dem. LVII 31 and above, Chapter 7.

210. Arist. *Pol.* 1323a.

211. Ibid., 1335a; *Historia Animalium* 581b.

212. Arist. *Nik. Eth.* 1148a.

213. Arist. *Nik. Eth.* 1148b.

214. Eur. *Medeia* 233, 237 with D. L. Page's edition, ad loc. Contrast Hypereides I 7 with I 3.

215. Lines 460–72.

216. Genteel Englishwomen have (allegedy) been advised to "close their eyes and think of England".

217. Lines 1116–18.

218. Xen. *Mem.* II 2 4.

219. [Dem.] LIX 122.

220. E.g. ss. 30, 67, 108; cf. Hdt. II 135, Aiskh. I 119. Plato expected that a law requiring men to confine their sexual activities to their wives would meet great resistance; *Laws* 838e–841e; cf. Menandros (ed. A. Koerte) frag. 198.

221. Aiskh. I 119f.; Philonides (ed. Kock) frag. 5 with de Ste. Croix, *Origins*, 398; Pollux VII 202.

222. Cf. [Dem.] LIX 22.
223. Dem. XXXVI 45.
224. Dem. LIV 14; cf. Antiphanes, frag. 239 (Kock).
225. Isok. IV 287.
226. [Dem.] LIX 29–30.
227. Ibid., 30.
228. Lines 718–22.
229. On the subject in general, J. R. Walkowitz, *Prostitution and Victorian society*.
230. [Andokides] IV 14; Plut. *Life of Alkibiades* VIII.
231. Lucian *D.H.* II.
232. Ibid., IV.
233. Arkhilokhos, frag. 142 (Bergk); Hdt. II 135; cf. Aristoph. *Thesm.* 345f., *Wealth* 242–4; Isaios X 25; [Dem.] LIX 29.
234. Lines 149–52. On the significance of this, see Dover, art. cit. (n. 1), 66.
235. This would explain why the Xenophontic Sokrates thought it necessary to rebut the idea that child-bearing resulted from lust.
236. Aristoph. *Wasps* 1253f., *Ekkl.* 947f., 960–77; cf. Lysias III 6; Antiphanes, frag. 239 (Kock).
237. The woman's hair, unlike a slave's, is not cropped; cf. Pomeroy, op. cit. (above, n. 1), 83.
238. Theophrastos *Characters* 27; Lucian *D.H.* IX, XV.
239. E.g., Lacey, op.cit. (above, n. 1), pl. 19.
240. Lucian *D.H.* VII, cf. XV.
241. Aristoph. *Peace* 1138; Theophrastos, op. cit. 4.
242. Lys. I 12.
243. Xen. *Oik.* X 11–12.
244. Ibid., VII 42–3.
245. Isaios VI 18–21, for the extreme case in which an old man allegedly left his wife and went to live with a former prostitute whom he had owned.
246. Eur. *Supplices*, 40–1.
247. Cf. Xen. *Oik.* VII 42–3. Athenian law invalidated wills proved to have been made by men acting (by contemporary standards) unreasonably through the influence of women; Dem. XLVI 14, 16, XLVIII 56.
248. [Dem.] LIX 52.
249. Isaios III 28, 35–6, for the dowry as protection against divorce.
250. Plat. *Laws* 774c.
251. Euripides frag. 775 in A. Nauck, *Tragicorum Graecorum Fragmenta*[2] = lines 158–9 in J. Diggle's edition of the *Phaethon*.
252. Arist. *Nik. Eth.* 1161a.
253. Lines 151–3.
254. Eur. *Troiades* 646–50.
255. Xen. *Mem.* I 2 24.
256. Isaios III 46; [Dem.] XLIII 75; [Arist.] *Ath. Pol.* LVI 6.
257. [Arist.] *Ath. Pol.*, ibid.
258. Aiskh. I 28; cf. Xen. *Mem.* II 2 13, Isaios VIII 32, Dem. XXIV 105, 107, Theophrastos, op. cit., 6, Diog. Laert. I 55.
259. [Arist.] *Ath. Pol.* LVI 6; Dem. XXXVII 46.

260. Eur. *Androm.* 676, cf. *Medeia* 945; Hypereides, II 6.
261. [Dem.] LIX 12.
262. Arist. *Pol.* 1314b.
263. Ibid., 1315a; compare the avenging at Athens of the tyrannic insult against the sister of Harmodios, Thuc. VI 56f.
264. Plat. *Rep.* 549d–e.
265. A. R. W. Harrison, *The law of Athens*, II, 136f., 145 (citing Dem. LVII 67); D. M. MacDowell, *Athenian homicide law in the age of the orators*, 102ff. At *Politics* 1313b, another important and neglected passage, Aristotle describes a development of the final form of *dēmokratia*, namely *gynaikokratia*, 'rule of women' (in the home), "so that they may carry reports outside against the men". For the acceptance at Athens of a woman's evidence, in what was seen as a crisis for *dēmokratia*, Andokides I 16.

9

Religious Prophecy at Athens

Our ancient sources suggest that in all social classes the lives of
Athenians were profoundly affected by religious prophecy. Signs
from gods were sought and interpreted in the regulation of private
affairs. Divination also influenced decisions on strategy, at one
stage possibly preserving, but ultimately helping to shatter, the
naval power of Athens. Herodotos, Thucydides and Aristotle give
considerable detail on the impact of faith in religious prophecy.
Comic sources imply that divination was one of the most familiar
aspects of Athenian life.[1] We can occasionally detect traces of
ancient controversy as to whether divination deserved to be
influential,[2] but there seems to have been no dispute that it
actually was so. Thucydides records "the majority" of men in one
large Athenian force as having based a crucial decision on a
religious prophecy.[3] In another connection he represents an
Athenian speaker as stating that most people depend on divination in crises.[4] Yet the influence of religious prophecy on the
Greeks forms a subject which has been neglected by most modern
scholars.[5] As a result there is scope for much reconstruction. In
addition, the unusual resistance of scholars to ancient evidence on
this topic may, paradoxically, make the subject an unusually
helpful one in illustrating the nature of modern historical method.

Greek religion lacked the widespread and tenacious organisation, regulating matters of cult and doctrine, which has
characterised Christian churches. What one Greek interpreted as
an omen of divine purpose might be disregarded by another
theist. The prophecy issued by one shrine might be at odds with
that from another.[6] Even the priestess of Apollo at Delphoi, the
most widely revered source of oracles in Greece, was sometimes
suspected of having prophesied from corrupt motives.[7] Patterns

of belief can, however, be identified.

Some Greek prophecy concerned personal existence after death. Rewards and sufferings in an afterlife were predicted in doctrines associated with the mysteries of Demeter and Persephone, which were celebrated in Attikē at Eleusis, and with the cult of Orpheus.[8] Plato worked similar ideas into a philosophic scheme in the *Phaidōn*, where he offered a speculative account of a heaven which philosophers could expect. But doctrines of an afterlife cannot be shown to have had great influence at Athens, in spite of the popularity of the Eleusinian mysteries. On public occasions references to the subject were commonly guarded or agnostic, stating what might happen *if* the dead had any consciousness.[9] In the 340s the orator Aiskhines expected an Athenian audience to assume that a dead person was not aware of funerary cult performed in his honour.[10] Diotima, a priestess, is represented by Plato as stating that the only possible immortality for human beings lay in the possession of offspring.[11]

More influential, it seems, were those prophecies which concerned events in the lifetime of the subject. A standing and widespread belief was that certain kinds of behaviour would be divinely requited during the agent's life by prosperity and good fortune, or the reverse. Thucydides describes a collapse of normal morality at Athens during the great plague, early in the Peloponnesian War:

> No fear of gods or law of men restrained them. On the one hand, because they saw that everyone was dying in the same way, they judged piety to be no different from impiety for practical purposes. On the other hand, no one expected to live long enough to pay a legal penalty for wrongdoing[12]

Thucydides here explains an unusual development in morality by reference to what was presumably an unusual lack of fear of the gods. The clear implication is, that in normal times expectation of divine punishment or protection was influential over behaviour.[13] When describing the "cruel" civil strife which broke out during the Peloponnesian War, Thucydides similarly suggests that concern about divine intervention had lost its usual force;

> As a means of guaranteeing the undertakings which they [the partisans] gave to each other, shared acts of lawbreaking were at least as common as references to divine law.[14]

...on neither side did the leading partisans act with religious scruples; instead they got a better reputation by using high-sounding language when they performed some heinous action.[15]

...for bringing about a reconciliation no assurance had the necessary credibility nor any oath the power to intimidate.[16]

If these remarks came from a believer in prophecy, regretting an alleged decline in piety since a remote and perhaps idealised period,[17] we might be justified in distrusting them. However, Thucydides in the above passages seems to be recording changes in religiosity within his own time. Also, there is no indication that he was a theist: rather, sections of his work suggest that he rejected the principle of religious prophecy. He states with emphasis and apparent exaggeration that all but one of the oracles trusted in the Peloponnesian War had failed to be reliably fulfilled;[18] elsewhere he seems to blame the general Nikias for his attachment to "divination and the like".[19] In recording effects of religious beliefs which he apparently did not share, Thucydides seems to have made a distinction which is not always applied by modern critics: that propositions may be untrue while also being influential. The point was made elegantly in the early seventeenth century by Francis Bacon, in an essay on prophecies:

My judgement is that they ought all to be despised, and ought to serve but for winter talk by the fireside. Though when I say despised, I mean it as for belief: for otherwise the spreading or publishing of them is in no sort to be despised. For they have done much mischief.[20]

In examining the possible impact of divination on the Athenians we should not be inhibited by a feeling that we are committing ourselves thereby to a belief in the Olympian divinities.

The idea that, through divine arrangement, the good would prosper and the bad would not, is expressed on innumerable occasions in the classical period, especially in tragedy, but also in more worldly contexts.[21] In an exceptional fragment of tragedy, written by the oligarchic Athenian politician Kritias, the divine requital of human behaviour is described as the fiction of a clever man, intended to enforce morality. According to this account, the idea that divinities knew everything was contrived to deter secret evil-doing, and frightening natural events such as thunder and lightning were cunningly appropriated as signs of divine anger.[22] An effect of this high-minded fraud was to "quench lawlessness with the laws". We should not of course assume that a view expressed in a fragment of drama is the author's own.[23] It is interesting, however, that this rejection of religious grounds for morality should have been composed by a politician who, as a social warrior of the late fifth century,[24] may well have belonged to the class of partisans described by Thucydides as impious.

Also in the late fifth century, in his speech on the Murder of Herodes the orator Antiphon arranged for his client to argue that he could not be guilty of murder as charged, because after the alleged crime he and some fellow travellers had enjoyed a smooth sea voyage and had sacrificed without eliciting bad omens.[25] In this argument from religious orthodoxy, designed to appeal to an Athenian jury, two elements are of particular interest. First, the idea that divine punishment of a great crime is not occasional or belated, but prompt and reliable — at least when the guilty person goes on a voyage. Without such an assumption the argument from lack of disaster on a particular voyage would have had little force. Second, the notion that the divine punishment of a guilty person might fall also on those around him, even when the latter were innocent of his offence.[26] A belief that mere contact with the guilty could cause religious pollution was embodied in Athenian law; in some circumstances a man accused of murder had to plead his case offshore in a boat, to a jury on land, to avoid contaminating Attikē.[27] This belief may have developed from one which still seems reasonable: that a community which knowingly or negligently sheltered a guilty person was culpably promoting evil.[28] Even the irrational element, that the innocent might be contaminated by the guilty, does not seem entirely alien to modern processes of thought. If the innocent children of the far-from-innocent Dr Goebbels had survived the Second World War, how widely would they have been accepted as uncontaminated by association? In any case, the Greek view that innocent people might be caught up in the divine punishment of the guilty represented an attempt to explain the world as it was. In that world, as today, malefactors through *natural* processes undeniably tended to cause special suffering for innocent people close to them.

In the *Politics* Aristotle argues that an autocratic ruler, to protect his position, needs to exploit the belief in divine favour for the pious:

he [the autocrat] must be seen always to be exceptionally concerned with religion. For people are less afraid that someone of that sort will do anything illegal or abnormal to them — if they think that the ruler is in awe of the supernatural and concerned about the gods. And they plot against him less, because thinking that he has the gods among his allies.[29]

Fear of gods acted as a social cement particularly in respect of oaths. In modern Western societies the ultimate guarantee is the personal signature, breach of a signed undertaking being punishable at law, or at least by loss of standing and credibility. It is, however, misleading to refer to the Greeks as "signing" treaties or other agreements. Rather, the guarantee of an undertaking between states or individuals was normally the religious oath, which depended for its force not only on the threat of disgrace and discredit but also on a self-invoked religious curse, as, for example, that children of the oath-breaker should not resemble him but should be monsters.[30] The gods invoked in such oaths, because thought to value their own credit as moral enforcers, were expected to act upon the curse where an oath was violated. When, in 421, Athens agreed first to peace then to alliance with Sparta, among the eminent men who took the oaths on behalf of the city was the soothsayer Lampon. Thucydides identifies the men of Athens who swore to each agreement: in both lists the name of Lampon comes first. That this reflects some practical priority is suggested by a corresponding list of Sparta's oath-takers: in this, the first to be named are the two kings.[31] Lampon was chosen for this role no doubt because he represented conspicuously the Athenian belief that oaths were divinely enforced.[32]

The will of the gods could be altered, or ascertained, by sacrifice; the state of a victim's entrails was thought to reflect the divine attitude.[33] Conveniently, where the meat of a victim was eaten at a sacrifice, the gods were assumed to enjoy those parts which men did not consume: fat and bones.[34] At the beginning of a hazardous venture, such as a military expedition or a long voyage, correct religious observance was thought especially important. Scenes of departing soldiers who pour sacrifices of wine ("libations") onto the ground survive in Athenian vase-painting. Thucydides gives a graphic account of the prayer and libations at the departure from Athens of the Sicilian expedition.[35]

In sacrifice, prayer and divination the commonest subjects of concern appear to have been survival, wealth and health. Aristophanes, in his *Wealth* (*Ploutos*) of 388 BC, jokingly suggests that without the wish to acquire riches there would be no sacrifice.[36] A particularly revealing collection of enquiries put to an oracular shrine survives from Dōdōnē in north-western Greece, where Zeus and his consort Diōnē were believed to inspire answers. The concern of many of the enquirers with their own prosperity corresponds with the Aristophanic remark about Athens. The questions extant from Dōdōnē were inscribed on small tablets of lead; their subject-matter and occasionally their spelling and syntax indicate that the authors were humble — that is, perhaps, typical — Greeks of the area:

> "Kleotas asks Zeus and Diōnē whether it is better and profitable for him to keep sheep.";
> "Shall I be a fisherman?";
> "Did Dorkilos steal the cloth?";
> "Thrasyboulos asks by sacrificing and appeasing which god will he have healthier eyes.";
> "Gerioton asks Zeus whether he should marry.";
> "Herakleidas asks Zeus and Diōnē for good fortune and asks the god about offspring, whether there will be any from his wife Aiglē whom he now has.";
> "Lysanias asks Zeus and Diōnē whether the child with which Annyla is pregnant is his."

The last question suggests with unusual clarity the difficulty facing those who produced verbal oracular responses, and helps to explain the carefully contrived imprecision for which such responses are famous.[37]

Divination in politics: the early and mid-fifth century

Athenian faith in divination during the mid-fifth century may well have been influenced by an episode which occurred just before that period, when the great Persian invasion of Attikē was imminent. In 480 (or perhaps 481[38]) the Athenians sought strategic advice from Delphoi, where Apollo was believed to inspire prophecies concerning the will of his father, Zeus. According to the account of Herodotos, by far our most important source for the events of the Persian Wars, the envoys of Athens received the following message from the priestess:

> O miserable men, why sit there idly? Flee, abandon the furthest dwellings of the land and the high heads of a wheel-shaped city.[39] For the head does not remain fast, nor the body, nor the feet below nor the hands, nor is anything of the middle left, but all is in sorry plight. Fire and keen Ares,[40] driving a Syrian-born chariot, throws it down. Many other towered cities will he destroy, not yours alone. Many temples of the immortals he will give to raging fire; they now stand flowing with sweat, trembling with fear, while from their rooftops black blood is poured, foreseeing the necessary evil. But go from the shrine, apply your mind to woes.[41]

The envoys refused to return to Athens with only this prophecy, no doubt fearing that their own reputations would be infected by the nature of the bad news.[42] They demanded to receive some better forecast, threatening otherwise to stay in the shrine until they died. The Delphic authorities, for their part, must have wished to avoid both the religious pollution caused by death within the sacred precinct [43] and the durable resentment which would ensue if the envoys died as a result of Delphic defeatism. A further prophecy was issued:

> Pallas Athena cannot placate Olympian Zeus, though she prays with many words and intense cunning. But this further word I will say to you, having made it firm as steel. When all else is captured that lies within the frontier of Kekrops and the shelter of holy Kithairon,[44] far-seeing Zeus grants to the Tritoborn Athena a wooden wall that alone shall be unravaged, helping you and your children. Do not stay still, awaiting cavalry or host of foot coming from the mainland, but turn your back, withdraw; a time for you to stand to face them will also come one day. O divine Salamis, you will be death to children of women when Demeter [i.e. corn] is scattered or gathered together.[45]

The envoys returned with this prophecy to Athens, where its significance became the subject of much dispute.[46]

When scholars assess the status of a recorded prophecy, a question usually — and sensibly — asked is, 'Does the prophecy correspond so closely with what actually happened as to suggest fraudulent composition *ex eventu* [i.e. with retrospective knowl-·edge of how things turned out]?' However, we should also allow that a genuine prophecy may to some extent match the outcome of events because people deliberately followed the prophecy. In a secular sphere, medicine with its use of placebos has for centuries exploited the fact that a forecast can be self-fulfilling.[47] As the seventeenth-century philosopher Thomas Hobbes wrote (in connection with political divination in the English Civil Wars), prophecy has been "many times the principal cause of the event foretold".[48] In the present case, it has often been noted that the complete pessimism of the first oracle and the almost unrelieved defeatism of the second seem to rule out much falsification *ex eventu*. A pious fraud would surely have hinted clearly at triumph over Persia. There is in addition a degree of correspondence with events which may reflect the influence of a genuine prophecy. The main Athenian force did withdraw from the city, as the prophecy advised, without resisting the enemy's cavalry or infantry in Attikē — an interesting move, as we shall see. But the second prophecy, as preserved, says nothing about withdrawal from the Persian fleet; in the event, that was the only arm of the Persian force which the Athenians in large numbers did resist locally, at Salamis. Debate at Athens on how to react to the coming invasion is represented by Herodotos as having taken the form of argument about the meaning of the second oracle, with its references to a "wooden wall" and to deaths at Salamis.[49] He suggests that the favoured interpretation was the one proposed by Themistokles: that the safe "wooden wall" meant Athens' fleet, and that Salamis would prove deadly for the enemy, not for Athenians. It was decided that the full forces of Athens should be used to resist the invader by means of the fleet, "in obedience to the god".[50]

Most Athenians, then, decided to abandon homes and estates to destruction, to evacuate non-combatants and to fight a naval battle off the coast of Attikē, by Salamis.[51] Would these decisions have been taken without the influence of divination? We cannot be sure; it is seldom that we can study the resistance of a Greek state to a force both so vast and so superior numerically as was the Persian armament now. However, at the approach of a superior force it was common for a Greek community to stand siege behind city walls. The Athenians in 480 probably had a city wall surviving from the sixth century; if not, they would have had time to create one since learning in 481 of the Persians' plan to invade.[52] Withdrawal behind the city wall offered the prospect of saving far more property than would survive an evacuation, and would also have had obvious sentimental attractions.[53] When the might of the Peloponnesian alliance descended in 429 on the little town of Plataia, the Plataians chose and adhered to a strategy of this kind — until dissuaded, Thucydides notes,[54] by a general and a soothsayer.

When the Delphic prophecies arrived at Athens is unclear.[55] Herodotos implies that they came at a very early stage, and that subsequently Athenians planned to take part in a defence by land of the pass at Tempē, in north-eastern Greece.[56] If so, it would seem that the Delphic advice to flee from Persian cavalry and foot was not accepted immediately and consistently. However, an inscription, the "Themistokles Decree", may suggest that the Athenians had decided on evacuation before they contributed their naval contingent to the next stage of resistance, to the north of Euboia, near Artemision.[57] As the Persian forces drew nearer, the Delphic prophecies of horror may have contributed greatly to the pessimism implied by the decision to abandon Athens. Herodotos describes the execution of that decision after the defence at Artemision and Thermopylai had failed. His account is something which scholars have rarely been willing to confront:

> They made haste with the evacuation of these [children and slaves], both from desire to obey the oracle and above all for the following reason: Athenians say that a large snake lives in the shrine, a guardian of the Akropolis; they say this, and they put out offerings to it every new moon on the assumption that it exists. The monthly offerings consist of honey cake. This honey cake, which previously used always to be consumed, now was untouched. When the priestess of Athena had communicated this, the Athenians abandoned the city in greater numbers and with more eagerness, on the grounds that the goddess had abandoned the Akropolis.[58]

Such an omen would have reinforced the Delphic warning about the fate of Athens' "high heads" (*akra karēna*), which clearly referred to the Akropolis. But has Herodotos exaggerated the importance of divination for Athenian strategy?

The text of Herodotos' history contains at one point an emphatic defence of oracles — a defence which, incidentally, suggests that some contemporaries did deny the validity of such divination.[59] It may perhaps be suspected that Herodotos, as a convinced theist, has made too much of the influence of prophecy in 480, from a desire to present an improving picture of religious faith rewarded; the Athenian strategy of that year had been, as his readers knew, broadly successful. However, Herodotos was probably writing near the middle of the fifth century: some check on his accuracy would be provided by the memories of eye-witnesses. The events immediately preceding the Persian invasion would be intensely experienced, and so perhaps were unusually well remembered by some.[60] Also, we should notice Herodotos' guarded language about the sacred snake. By repeating that "the Athenians say" the snake exists, and by stating that they sacrifice to it "because they assume that it exists", he seemingly refuses to commit himself to accepting the Athenians' religious argument. And yet he also suggests that the reasoning about the snake was more influential than the Delphic oracle in hastening the evacuation. This hardly seems to be the position of one who sought to commend Athenian religious faith as a model.[61] When next we have detail of debate at Athens on how to react to an invasion of Attikē, there is the testimony of Thucydides for the prominent role of divination.[62] There seems no good reason for scholars who generally take Herodotos as a useful guide for the events of the Persian Wars to discount his version of the evacuation of Athens in 480.

At the mid-fifth century, when Athens controlled Boiotia and dominated central Greece, Sparta sent a military force to restore the Delphic shrine to the control of native Delphians.[63] The Athenians, it seems, had used their power in the area to put the shrine under the management of neighbouring Phokis. After the Spartans had left, an Athenian force arrived, removed the Delphians from control once more and handed over to Phokis.[64] In this episode, which probably belongs between 450 and 447, both Athenians and Spartans were no doubt concerned to advertise their secular power. But Sparta's campaign at least was referred to, Thucydides shows, as a sacred war:[65] Spartans and Athenians alike may have had a combination of religious and profane motives for removing opponents from control of the oracle.[66] Each side perhaps wanted *promanteia*, the right to have its enquiries answered before those of others.[67] According to

Plutarch, both sides now inscribed a claim to *promanteia* on the bronze statue of a wolf at Delphoi.[68] Plutarch was priest of the shrine in the early second century AD:[69] this detail may derive from a surviving local monument and tradition.

Athenian influence over Delphoi would be lost or greatly reduced as a result of the battle of Koroneia (447 or 446).[70] An inscription from the mid-fifth century, now thought to refer to this battle,[71] has been found at Athens. It alludes to the supposed intervention of a demigod who, it is stated, "made sure that all mortals from now on could reflect on the fulfilment of prophecies as reliable".[72] This may suggest that prophecy had been appealed to before the battle, and had been overridden, but then apparently justified by the disastrous outcome. Plutarch suggests that there was some dispute at Athens on whether to send the force which, in the event, went to Koroneia.[73] Whether divination was involved, we can only guess. There may have been some further allusion to the subject in a pair of statues which a later Greek traveller, Pausanias, reported as standing together at Athens; one showed Tolmides, who was the commander at Koroneia, while the other showed a soothsayer who served him.[74] In any case, from this thinly documented period of Athenian history we seem to have traces, in the form of the inscription and the record of the statues, of two official references to prominent divination.

A further Athenian inscription, of 446–445, records arrangements made for Euboia after the crushing of the revolt there.[75] A certain Hierokles is to perform sacrifice "in accordance with the oracles".[76] At this period the population of the Euboian town of Hestiaia was forced to leave, and was replaced by settlers from Athens: their community came to be known as Oreos.[77] Some 25 years later an Athenian comedy, satirising Hierokles as a charlatan, referred to him as "the oraclemonger from Oreos".[78] There is no evidence that Hierokles had settled at Oreos; rather, there is a comic reference to his being honoured at Athens with dining at the public expense in the late 420s.[79] The soothsayer Lampon was long remembered in connection with the colonising of Thouria in 444/3.[80] (That area was no doubt thought to need especially careful religious treatment, being associated, as Aristotle states, with religious pollution arising from the failure of an earlier colony.[81]) Aristophanes' *Clouds* (of 423) probably refers to Lampon with its expression *Thouriomanteis* ('soothsayers of Thouria') yet, as we have seen, Lampon at this period was prominent in the politics of Athens rather than of Thouria.[82]

Lampon certainly and Hierokles probably were remembered over decades for their roles in organising colonial settlement, which suggests once more the importance attached to religion at the start of great and risky enterprises.

Prophecy in the Peloponnesian war

At the outbreak of the Peloponnesian War divination flourished.[83] Thucydides shows that in 431 oraclemongers were chanting many prophecies, both in city-states about to be involved in the war and in others.[84] Later in that year, when the Athenians faced the decision whether to tackle the invading Peloponnesian army or to shelter behind their city walls, oraclemongers chanted "all kinds of oracles".[85] Thucydides suggests that prejudice dictated which each person listened to,[86] although in another connection he shows that divination had the power to reverse the strongly held views of a mass of Athenians.[87] The historian gives few details of the prophecies which he repeatedly indicates were of importance. Even the divination which he describes as having "made the Athenians hope to capture Sicily", before the disastrous expedition to that island, is passed over briefly.[88] However, some reconstruction seems possible.

From the beginning of the war until its end, Thucydides notes, it was prophesied that hostilities would last for "thrice nine years".[89] The origin of the prophecy is not stated. We look, then, for help from possible analogues, and find that in 413 it was prophesied that Athenian forces should not move, for fear of disaster, until "thrice nine days" had elapsed.[90] The latter prophecy was a result of a lunar eclipse, as Thucydides makes clear, and thrice nine days — when added to the day of the eclipse — would equal a lunar month.[91] The withdrawal of the moon's light was seen as divinely ordained, and no doubt as symbolising the withdrawal of divine protection for the lunar period. Now, in 431 — on 3 August, by our calendar — there was an almost total eclipse of the sun,[92] an event which even at the time Athenians had some reason to connect with the action of the moon.[93] Thucydides does not specify Athenian reaction to this, though he does record the interest of Greeks at the start of the war in a supposedly prophetic earthquake and in "every other event of that kind".[94] We may suspect that the prophecy about thrice nine years of war derived from the solar eclipse, which occurred very close to the opening of hostilities. This impressive event might plausibly have been claimed to represent the start of a long period of profound misfortune, such as the war then beginning. The predicted length of that period could have resulted from a calculation which combined the solar unit, the year, with the lunar number, 'thrice nine'. If so, the prophecy may have reduced pressure for a quick and peaceful resolution of hostilities; prophecy derived from the lunar eclipse of 413 was to be highly persuasive, as we shall see. That there was pressure at Athens for a prompt peace will appear shortly: it too had the support of divination.

Before the Peloponnesian War began, the Delphic oracle, it was believed, had issued a prophecy that the Spartans would win, if they fought according to their ability, and that Apollo would help them, when invited and when not.[95] At first, Athenians who heard of this prophecy may have suspected it; the restored Delphic authorities had strong secular motives for desiring a Spartan victory. But in 430 came a great plague, killing a large proportion of the population of Athens[96] and demoralising survivors. Apollo was traditionally represented as a sender of plague,[97] and Thucydides states that Athenians now assimilated events to the prophecy: the disease had broken out in Athens coincidentally with the arrival of a Peloponnesian force of invasion, it affected Athens more than any other place and hardly touched the Peloponnese.[98] Perikles is represented by Thucydides as suggesting that the plague was *daimonion*, of supernatural origin.[99] With part of Apollo's prophecy now vindicated, the other part which conditionally prophesied Spartan victory must have caused much alarm. In 430, after the outbreak of the plague, Athens sought — against Perikles' advice — to make peace with Sparta: Thucydides does not say so, but it may be that the prophecy was part of the reason.

After the death of Perikles in 429, the politician Kleon appears to have grown in influence at Athens.[100] In his *Wasps* of 422 Aristophanes pointedly shows a supporter of Kleon's as more respectful towards divination than is an opponent.[101] In the *Knights* (of 424) another opponent is made to say that Kleon "chants oracles" to the *dēmos*.[102] In evaluating this remark, we look, as usual with comedy, for evidence of the type of humour being used in the particular context. We find that other remarks made here about Kleon combine moderate exaggeration of his historical characteristics with realistic comment upon them. Thus Kleon here is "most wicked and slanderous", a claim very similar to one made in all seriousness by Thucydides,[103] while his domination of the *dēmos*, suggested by Aristophanes, also corresponds with Thucydides' picture.[104] The linking of Kleon with divination, done in several passages by Aristophanes, seems to reflect a real tendency of the politician. In another section of the *Knights* Kleon is shown competing with a fictional rival for popular favour. The medium of competition is divination about Athenian politics; Kleon produces a succession of prophecies, and his opponent beats him by deploying an even more impressive set.[105] The historical Kleon was, according to Thucydides, at times "most persuasive to the mass"[106] and "by far the most persuasive person to the *dēmos*".[107] Given his evident grasp of popular psychology, Kleon's apparent attachment to religious prophecy reflects interestingly upon Athenian values.

A great rival of Kleon's was Nikias: he too was conspicuously involved with prophecy. When Thucydides explains a decision of Nikias in 413 with the words "for he was somewhat excessively given to divination and that kind of thing", he is of course making a general comment about Nikias' behaviour.[108] Much of what Plutarch has to say on this subject we cannot check. He states that Nikias gave the credit for his military successes to divine intervention, and that when he had succeeded in making the "Peace of Nikias" with Sparta in 421, the Athenians "kept talking about Nikias, saying that he was a man beloved of the gods and that, because of his piety, he had been divinely allowed to give his name to the greatest and finest of good things [i.e. peace]".[109] But archaeology has provided remarkable confirmation of one element in Plutarch's account of Nikias' pious career. Plutarch records lavish patronage by Nikias of Apollo's shrine on Delos, which included the setting up of a bronze model of a palm tree.[110] (Leto, the divine mother of Apollo and Artemis, had given birth to them on Delos while leaning on a palm tree.) Inscriptions on Delos record gifts made to the temple by "Nikias the Athenian".[111] Also found on the island was a circularly shaped stone, cut at the top in a way appropriate for the support of a column, and inscribed NIKIAS: it may once have borne the palm tree.[112]

Plutarch describes Nikias as presiding over an occasion of pageantry and religious reform on Delos: this should probably be identified with the Athenians' purification of Delos and reorganisation of its festival, ascribed by Thucydides to the winter of 426/5.[113] Thucydides notes that an oracle was taken as the justification of these proceedings. It should also be observed that the plague had recurred in the previous year, which probably persuaded some to look for a way of appeasing Apollo.[114] Conveniently, his birthplace lay — unlike Delphoi — firmly within Athenian control. Delos was a shrine traditionally used by Ionians; reconstructing its festival under Athenian management would also be useful in a secular way, advertising Athens' concern for the heritage she shared with the numerous Ionians under her rule. But there is a distinctively religious character to the Athenians' actions in expelling the Delians from their island in 422, as suffering from some ancient impurity, and then reinstating them in the following year.[115] On the latter occasion the Athenians had at heart, according to Thucydides, their defeats in battle (in which the work of Apollo was evidently suspected) and a prophecy from the god at Delphoi. This hasty reinstatement, of people whose hatred they had incurred, no doubt involved much loss of face for the Athenians: for that reason it would in any case be hard to explain as mere secular propaganda.

The annihilation in 413 of Athens' great armada against Syracuse converted her position in Greece with almost theatrical speed and thoroughness. For years before 413 the Athenian fleet had been unchallenged in its domination of the Aegean and seas beyond. After the defeat in Sicily, the most important of Athens' subjects revolted, and Sparta with Persian help first countered then destroyed her remaining naval power. In a series of brief references, Thucydides records divination as prominent and influential at many stages of the Sicilian expedition. On the basis of this account we may well see this use of religion as one of the main elements in Athens' imperial decline.

When news was brought to Athens, in 413/2, of the disaster in Sicily, the Athenians were angry both with the orators who had shared their enthusiasm for sending the expedition and also with "the oraclemongers and prophets and whoever by using divination in any way at that time had made them hope to capture Sicily".[116] This passage of Thucydides is a remarkable testimony to the power of divination. It has, however, traditionally received little attention from scholars, partly, no doubt, because Thucydides does not elaborate on the forms of prophecy involved.[117] We have already seen evidence from several other sources, and from Thucydides himself, of the role played by divination when difficult decisions were imminent, concerning military and other ventures. A decision with few or no apparent precedents might be particularly difficult, and divination — like other forms of argument — would tend to be most influential when alternative grounds of prediction were least helpful. Thucydides shows that the size and population of Sicily were seriously underestimated at Athens;[118] most Athenians lacked experience of the area[119] and some surely realised the significance of their own ignorance. The shortage of secular evidence may have created a vacuum for the diviners to fill.

One optimistic religious argument of the time has been traced. Alkibiades, perhaps the most influential proponent of the plan to invade Sicily, is shown as suggesting that the expedition, if sent, would exploit the good fortune (*eutykhia*) of Nikias, one of its commanders.[120] As Dover observes, "Alkibiades' argument only makes sense if *eutykhia* is treated as an abiding characteristic, and that is logically irreconcilable with its treatment as pure chance."[121] Rather, this good fortune seemed a mark of divine favour: compare the phrase 'divinely sent fortune' (*tei .. tykhei ek tou theiou*) used by another speaker in Thucydides.[122] Nikias himself is represented as arguing to his men in 413 that his past life of piety and justice enhanced the prospect of good luck for himself, and so for them.[123] As a commander of the expedition, Nikias was not perhaps an obvious choice. He had objected to the venture in principle, and could be expected to quarrel with his fellow general (and arch-rival) Alkibiades.[124] In the event, his management of the campaign proved disastrous. If, as seems possible, Nikias owed his appointment in part to religious prophecy, that in itself would be an important element in the decline of Athens.

Shortly before the Sicilian expedition was due to leave Athens, a frightening sacrilege was performed. Athenian statues of the god Hermes were systematically damaged, their faces and genitals being mutilated.[125] Thucydides records that the Athenians took this event seriously because it seemed to be an omen for the expedition and part of a revolutionary plot.[126] Hermes was the god of travellers; his disposition might well seem important on the eve of a very long voyage. His statues were no doubt assaulted for that reason, with the hope that the expedition would be cancelled from fear of divine revenge. This seeming omen, unlike the lunar eclipse two years later, did not seriously obstruct the movement of the expeditionary force. Lacking help from Thucydides, we cannot be sure why. It may have been argued that the mutilators, none of whom seemed to have been publicly identified before the fleet sailed, were unlikely to take part in the expedition which they evidently opposed[127]. That might seem to reduce the danger of divine action against the fleet. Also, anyone who argued for cancellation or postponement of the voyage might meet the objection that this was precisely what the mutilators had wanted. Nikias, the general-elect with a conspicuous record of religious observance, would surely be consulted as an authority on the significance of the sacrilege. Yet we do not hear that he used the mutilation as an argument for delay. With hindsight, we may suspect that his position was deeply embarrassing. Eukrates, his brother, was shortly to be accused of having mutilated the statues of Hermes;[128] Diognetos, very probably another brother, was also to be accused — of the supposedly related crime of profaning the mysteries of Eleusis.[129] Both accusations, when first made, were found plausible.[130] If Nikias had reason to think they would be made, or would be plausible if made, he may have been anxious to avoid seeming to exploit the mutilation in a way which might harmonise suspiciously with his original opposition to the venture. If Nikias did discount the omen, that would make an important difference from the circumstances of 413, when the religious argument for a delayed departure was to have his strong support.

Alkibiades, probably the most talented general with the Sicilian expedition, lost his command at an early stage when recalled to Athens to face a religious charge, that of profaning the mysteries.[131] His enemies carefully exploited the accusation, for reasons which were at least in part secular.[132] It was argued with some persuasiveness that offences against Demeter and Hermes were parts of a single plot against the *dēmokratia*.[133] But the cult of Demeter, allegedly profaned by Alkibiades, was cherished by Athenians and may have been the source of much prestige for their city.[134] The religious charge would be important also for its own sake, as Alkibiades' later behaviour suggests; after his restoration to Athens in 407, he made a show of leading a military escort for the procession to Demeter's shrine at Eleusis,[135] no doubt partly to restore his reputation for religious propriety.

In the late summer of 413 came an episode which was to provide the most famous case of Greek divination. Having despaired of their long efforts to capture Syracuse, the Athenians were ready to sail out of the Great Harbour and to safety. Then, on 27· August, a lunar eclipse occurred and the move was postponed — with fatal results, since the Syracusans were thus given time to trap and destroy the Athenian fleet. Rarely in Greek history do we have such good evidence for the power of a single motive. Shortly before the eclipse the Athenian troops, faced with continued suffering from disease and from the newly reinforced Syracusan army,[136] were anxious to leave. Nikias is shown as implying that most of them were clamouring to go.[137] Thucydides in his own person refers to the Athenian soldiers as resentful of the delay in departing.[138] Yet when the eclipse occurred, on the eve of departure,

> the majority of the Athenians, taking it to heart, urged the generals to wait. And Nikias — for he was somewhat excessively given to divination and that kind of thing — said that he would not even discuss again the question of departure until there had been a wait of thrice nine days, in accordance with the soothsayers' interpretation. That was how the Athenians' delay came about.[139]

Nikias' calculations were probably a mixture of the religious and the secular. Thucydides shows him as fearing that his return to Athens after an unsuccessful campaign would bring his own execution.[140] But pure faith in divination must be seen as a major reason for the shift in the wishes of his men. They were aware that to linger near Syracuse was a danger to all and was likely to be fatal for some: that awareness was based on recent and direct experience, and simple inference. To remove the resulting strong wish to leave quickly would require faith of a most potent kind.

After the fleet had been lost, the Athenian force in Sicily began its last journey by land. In explaining the low morale of the troops, Thucydides contrasts the prayer and hymns which had accompanied their original departure from the Peiraieus and the words of ill omen attending this move from the Great Harbour of Syracuse.[141] Mention was no doubt being made of death and disaster, by those departing and by the disabled left behind to their fate.[142] It was commonly believed by Greeks, as by others today, that a reference to evil might bring on the evil.[143] In addition, the disabled begged not to be abandoned and made appeals in the names of the gods.[144] These their distressed comrades were unable to answer.

The belief that good and evil were requited by gods caused Greeks, when much ill luck had occurred, to look for some past offence for which the ill fortune might be a punishment. (Compare the question, not always rhetorical, which nowadays is asked in adversity: 'What have I done to deserve this?') In this way the Spartans certainly, and the Athenians possibly, explained setbacks to themselves in the early Peloponnesian War.[145] Athenians were evidently thinking along these lines during the last days of the Sicilian expedition. That they hit on a plausible sin, their own scarcely-provoked attack on Syracuse, must have worsened their morale, by confirming an expectation of divine — that is, perhaps unavoidable — punishment. Thucydides reports much self-recrimination among the Athenian force before the retreat from Syracuse,[146] and shows Nikias trying to convince his men that their aggression against Syracuse would not elicit a crushing divine punishment, that their misfortunes had not been deserved.[147] Nikias was unsuccessful; three days later a thunderstorm occurred, and "the Athenians became even more depressed as a result, thinking that all this too was happening in order to destroy them".[148] The expression here translated as 'in order to' implies purpose, and the purpose presumed to lie behind a thunderstorm must be supernatural.

Many secular pressures contributed to the weakening and final collapse of the retreating army. Thucydides emphasises the hunger and thirst of the troops, their lack of supplies and the obvious difficulty of escaping from Sicily after the loss of the fleet.[149] He states that there were not less than 40,000 in the host which retreated from the Great Harbour.[150] Many of these were non-combatants or sailors hardly equipped for fighting on land, but what we know of the strength of their Syracusan opponents might still cause us not to expect the débâcle which occurred, unless allowance is made for a wretched state of morale.[151] A speaker elsewhere in Thucydides is made to suggest that it was normal for people in desperate circumstances to be sustained in their morale by divination.[152] With the Athenians now, the opposite occurred. Having "made them hope to capture Sicily", then having shaped the expedition in several ways, religious prophecy recurred powerfully at its end, preparing the Athenians psychologically for defeat.

Prophecy and cross-cultural method

The political history of classical Greece has in many respects been intensively studied over the previous century and a half: for this reason it is remarkable that so few attempts have been made to reconstruct the political role of divination.[153] Even the plainest statements of Herodotos and Thucydides on the subject have often been neglected, which is again intriguing, given the degree of respect normally shown to those authors. No scholar has sought in print to justify this eclectic method. Explanation of it must therefore be tentative, but may help to identify a characteristic of historical technique which goes far beyond the treatment of divination, and which may profitably be modified.

The revered anthropologist E. E. Evans-Pritchard, after studying the methods and importance of divination among the Azande people of the Nile-Congo divide, noted the reaction to his findings: "I have described to many people in England the facts, and they have been in the main incredulous or contemptuous".[154] One may well suspect that incredulity or contempt has also been the normal attitude of historians to evidence of divination in the ancient world. Compare the brief dismissal by one scholar of evidence concerning Roman prophecy derived from birds: "In any case it is just not credible that Romans of any century allowed birds to choose military leaders..."[155] This instance of incredulity is, as usual, unexplained. However, the widespread reluctance to accept evidence on the influence of divination may seem to arise from the view that such influence is alien to patterns of thought in modern Western societies. When Herodotos and Thucydides tell us of secular patterns of thought in the Greeks, these seem in the main to make sense according to Western standards. Thucydides, indeed, is often praised because psychological observations of his apply closely to modern human nature. Where our ancient sources present a recognisable picture of human nature, they are in general believed. But with divination the case is different: the evidence concerns unfamiliar behaviour, and tends to be set aside. The unusual neglect of this subject may, that is, reveal an influential feature of normal historical method: a tendency, when assessing evidence, to use one's own culture as a touchstone. This approach, known to anthropologists as 'ethnocentric', has obvious dangers, which may explain why historians have been reluctant to appeal to it frankly when rejecting testimony concerning divination. Cultures vary; rather than depend on the one which we may happen to know, as many as practicable should be used to check and cast light on the evidence from the ancient world. Also, if one is tempted to argue, "Such-and-such cannot

have happened in Greek society because it does not in our own",
some care should be taken to establish that one does indeed know
what happens in our own.

The medieval and modern history of Europe and Africa
contains much which impressively resembles Greek evidence on
the role of prophecy. There are also, of course, important
divergences. But when scholars intuitively reject Greek testimony
in this area it is perhaps not merely with the thought that "this
particular form of divination cannot really have been so influential", but on the vaguely formulated grounds that "no divination
so far-fetched can have had such effect". A brief survey of
findings from other cultures may weaken that general negative.

In recent African history we read of prophecy by lot, by people
"possessed" by supernatural power, and by other individuals
claiming to have had inspired visions: all three kinds of prophecy
are recorded also from classical Greece.[156] A study of oracular
shrines in the Gold Coast (Ghana) connected their growth with
insecurity caused by the cocoa industry;[157] again, we have seen
evidence that Greeks used divination in pursuit of prosperity, and
turned to prophecy especially at times of secular insecurity. In the
1850s the Xhosa people of southern Africa, when facing severe
pressure from expanding white communities, were crushed as a
result of faith in prophetic vision:

> In times of stress the Bantu peoples were too readily led
> astray by prophets. After the expulsion from the Zuurveld it
> was Makana ... The mantle later descended upon ...
> Nonquase and her uncle Umhlakaze ... Inspired by these
> two national enthusiasts ... the leading tribes in the course
> of 1856 prepared themselves, killing their cattle freely and
> squandering their stores of grain; they were to eat and make
> themselves strong against a day in February 1857 — a Great
> Day of the Lord when grain was to sprout, cattle were to
> spring out of the ground, warriors to come back from the
> dead and, with the help of a 'great hurricane', sweep the
> white man into the sea. The Day came and the sun went
> down as usual; but 'when the chiefs called upon their
> warriors, they were answered by the wail of a starving
> people'. The Ama-Xhosa were now broken indeed.
> Immense numbers died of starvation.[158]

Evans-Pritchard records that among the Nuer people of north-eastern Africa prophets report divine directions in war, and sacrifice for the success of military ventures.[159] That their activity is highly valued is made probable by the large herds of cattle given to them after successful raids. We recall the role of Athenian diviners in wartime, and the reward received by Hierokles.

To move to medieval Europe: it has recently been shown that much of the enthusiasm of the poor for the crusades arose from prophecies about a struggle with Antichrist and the arrival of the Millennium; crusaders were to be rewarded by a mass apotheosis at Jerusalem.[160] In the Middle Ages and later, the political prophecy had such influence in England and Wales as to provoke repeated attempts to control it by law,[161] and to draw much acid comment from other countries. In the 1530s the Spanish Ambassador to England stated that the English were peculiarly credulous and easily persuaded by prophecies to revolt;[162] in the civil wars of the mid-seventeenth century much influence was ascribed to the astrologer William Lilly, who was employed officially by Parliament.[163]

Various commentators on the cultures mentioned above have noted the special influence achieved by prophecy at times of insecurity.[164] In 1976 an uneasy awareness in South Australia of the proximity of a geological fault contributed to a widespread panic, which was precipitated by a forecast from a previously obscure clairvoyant; Adelaide was to be divinely punished on a specified date, by an earthquake and tidal waves. The Premier of South Australia commented on the worrying number of those who had sold their houses before fleeing. He himself judged it necessary to demonstrate his disbelief by appearing in public at the time and place appointed for the disaster. Australian newspapers observed:

> The amazing, discomforting thing is how many of Adelaide's 800,000... people actually do take it [i.e. the prophecy] seriously. Even those who laugh it off don't seem to have entirely convinced themselves.[165]

> It was a sobering experience ... to see the extent to which public anxiety could be built up by absurd scare-mongering in a supposedly educated modern community.[166]

The flight from Athens in 480 comes to mind. However, in that case superimposed on the rational grounds for fear was a prophecy not from a previously unknown individual but from the most revered shrine in Greece.

In rare crises, even normally despised forms of prophecy may be appealed to. During the Second World War, in his attempts to locate the captured Mussolini, the German SS chief, Himmler, used several soothsayers. The latter had first to be extracted from prison, where they had been sent accused of causing the flight to Britain of Hitler's deputy, Rudolf Hess.[167] In 1982, during attempts to find the kidnapped General Dozier, the US Defense Department is reported to have used clairvoyants.[168]

During the Second World War a systematic study was made of attitudes towards astrology among the population of Britain. The results cast an interesting light on Thucydides:

> In 1941 somewhere around 40–50 per cent said they had some belief in it [i.e. astrology]; in the first half of 1942 it was about 30–35 per cent; later in that year it was in the 20's; and since then it has been in the teens. The pattern is fairly clear. Till the entry of Russia into the war, the future was a matter for faith ... Since then it has become increasingly probable that the future will work out all right without astral intervention ... turning events away from the logical, reasonable looking sequence.[169]

The study also concluded that:

> Under physical and mental stress, about one in four of those who question or reject the existence of God admit that they pray to Him for help out of difficulty or danger.[170]

These findings correspond remarkably with words attributed by Thucydides to an Athenian speaker in 416:

> You are weak and your fortunes are on a knife-edge: do not do what most men do who still have some human means of saving themselves but who under pressure lose sight of their obvious grounds for hope and turn to invisible help, to soothsaying and oracles and everything of the kind which destroy people with the hopes they create.[171]

It may be inevitable that we judge the credibility of ancient writers by reference to an idea of human nature which is drawn

largely from our own world. That idea will, however, be
impoverished and unnecessarily misleading if it is formed only by
an unsystematic survey of those sections of modern society which
we find it most congenial to contemplate. For one thing, those
sections are likely to be the ones which most resemble our own
circle; and thus we may in effect be reconstructing the past in our
own image. That, perhaps, was the approach which led numerous
scholars to find negligible or intractable the remarks of
Thucydides and others on the impact of prophecy. A careful look
even at the modern culture of European countries has the effect of
releasing much ancient testimony from limbo. In the present case
it reveals Thucydides as a precise judge of human nature in an
unexpected area. The philosopher Descartes once described the
dangers of a narrow study of the ancient world:

> to live in the company of men of other times is almost the
> same thing as to travel. It is good to know something about
> the manners and customs of other nations so that we may
> judge more sanely of our own, and may not think that
> whatever is contrary to our own mode of life is both
> ridiculous and unreasonable, as is usually the case with
> those who have seen nothing. But a man who has spent too
> much time in travelling becomes in the end a stranger in his
> own country; and a man who has too much curiosity about
> what happened in past centuries usually shows a great
> ignorance of what is happening in this one.[172]

However it is not only the case that attention to the past may
damage one's grasp of the present; ignorance of our own era may
also subvert our understanding of the past.

Notes

1. In addition to Aristophanes (on whom see below), seven comic
poets of the late fifth century mention one or more of the leading diviners
by name; Athenaeus 344e; scholia on Aristophanes *Birds* 988, *Peace*
1031, 1046; I. Bekker, *Anecdota Graeca* 96, 1.18. Theophrastos
Characters gives a sketch of the superstitious man.
2. Hdt. VIII 77 (whether or not this chapter was written by
Herodotos himself); see also below.
3. Thuc. VII 50 4.
4. Thuc. V 103 2.

5. Important exceptions to this tendency are G. Grote, *A history of Greece*, esp. vol. VII, ch. 58–60; M. P. Nilsson, *Cults, myths, oracles and politics in Ancient Greece*; H. W. Parke and D. E. W. Wormell, *The Delphic oracle*; H. W. Parke, *The oracles of Zeus*; Gomme-Andrewes-Dover, *HCT*, IV, *passim*. E. R. Dodds' valuable work *The Greeks and the irrational* should be read with caution. It tends to reinforce the familiar and misleading distinction between superstitious masses and rationalist elite in fifth-century Athens. On the faith of Herodotos, Sokrates and Xenophon see respectively Hdt. VIII 20, 96 (and cf. 77); Plato, *Apology* 31c–d, Xen. *Mem.* I 1; Xen. *Anabasis* III 1, 5ff., VI 1 22ff.

6. Compare Xen. *Hell.* IV 7 2.

7. Hdt. V 63 1, VI 66; Thuc. V 16 2.

8. W. K. C. Guthrie, *The Greeks and their gods*, ch. 10; K. J. Dover, *Greek popular morality*, 261–8.

9. Dover, op. cit., 243ff.

10. Aiskh. I 14. Rather, Aiskhines states, it is custom and religion which are honoured by such cult. However, contrast Lysias XII 100.

11. Plat. *Symposion* 207d–208b.

12. Thuc. II 53 4.

13. This is not to say that ideas of divine behaviour were always the source of morality. Often the opposite was true, with at least the more original thinkers projecting onto divinity their various notions of correct behaviour. Xenophanes complained that people depicted gods in their own image (frag. 14–16 in the collection of Diels-Kranz). Similarly the aristocratic Homeric poems had shown divinities behaving like human aristocrats (see, for example, Hera's dressing to seduce Zeus in *Iliad* XIV), whereas Hesiod with his sense of personal grievance had put more emphasis on Zeus' defence of the oppressed. Aristophanes refers to his enemy Kleon as "hated by the gods" (*Clouds* 581); compare from later times Cicero's description of Pompeius Strabo as "detested by the gods and the aristocracy" (*pro Cornelio*, quoted by Asconius p. 79C), and Florence Nightingale's note to herself, "I MUST remember God is not my private secretary" (C. Woodham-Smith, *Florence Nightingale*, 529). The wishful thinking of each individual was not, however, omnipotent in matters of theology. The wider culture enforced some lessons; many Greeks accepted that they themselves, as well as others, might be punished by the gods.

14. Thuc. III 82 6.

15. Thuc. III 82 8.

16. Thuc. III 83 2.

17. Compare, e.g., Aristoph. *Clouds* 961ff., Lysias XXX 18ff.

18. Thuc. V 26 3; compare II 17 2. On the general subject of Thucydides and divination see C. A. Powell, *Bulletin of the Institute of Classical Studies*, 26 (1979), 45–50.

19. Thuc. VII 50 4.

20. Bacon, *Essay on prophecies* (1629 edn).

21. See below.

22. The Greek text is in *Tragicorum Graecorum fragmenta*, ed. A. Nauck, 598f.

23. In this case the fragment is ascribed to a play entitled *Sisyphos*.

Religious Prophecy at Athens

Sisyphos was notorious for the punishment divinely imposed on him. It may be that Kritias' play involved the triumphant falsification of the rationalist view noted above; compare the *Oidipous Tyrannos* of Sophokles, in which the principle of divination is rejected but then vindicated (esp.lines 707ff.).

24. Kritias was prominent in the oligarchy of the Thirty (the "Thirty Tyrants").

25. Antiphon. *Her.* V 81ff.

26. Hesiod, *Works and days* 238–47; Sophokles, *Oidipous Tyrannos* 95ff.; Antiphon, *Tetralogy* I 1 10; Xen. *Hierōn* IV 4. Compare Dodds, op. cit., ch. 6.

27. D. M. MacDowell, *Athenian homicide law in the age of the orators*, ch. 14. On religious pollution in general, R. Parker, *Miasma*.

28. Cf. Antiphon *Tetralogy* I 1 3; [Dem]. LIX 109.

29. Arist. *Pol.* 1314b–1315a; Aristotle suggests that religiosity could, however, be taken to excess. For a list of supposedly extravagant religious practices, such as sacrificing at every wayside shrine and refusing to approach a woman in childbed, Theophrastos *Characters* XVI.

30. See, e.g., the oath in M. N. Tod, *A selection of Greek historical inscriptions*, II, no. 204; cf. Dem. LIV 40f. For the fear of perjury, [Dem]. LIX 60.

31. Thuc. V 19 2, 24 1.

32. Further on the prominence of Lampon, see below and Meiggs-Lewis, no. 73 with P. Foucart, *BCH*, IV (1880), 241ff.

33. As, e.g., in the successful sacrifices cited by the defendant in connection with the murder of Herodes; above.

34. Hesiod, *Theogony* 556f.; Menandros cited by Athenaeus 146e.

35. Thuc. VI 32 1f.

36. Lines 133ff., cf. 1171–84, *Ekkl.* 781 and (on Rome) Juvenal, *Satire* X 23–5.

37. On these and other enquiries at Dōdōnē, H. W. Parke, *The oracles of Zeus*, 259–73. The philosopher Herakleitos observed, "The lord whose oracle is in Delphoi neither speaks out nor conceals, but gives a sign." (frag. 93, Diels-Kranz).

38. On the chronology see below and n. 55.

39. On other possible meanings of the phrase here translated as 'the furthest dwellings of the land', J. Labarbe, *La Loi navale de Thémistocle* 119, n.1 .

40. The god of war.

41. Hdt. VII 140.

42. For this psychology, blaming the messenger for the message, Hdt. VI 21, Dem. III 32.

43. Cf. Thuc. III 104 2.

44. I.e. within Attikē.

45. I.e. at springtime or harvest.

46. Hdt. VII 142f.

47. Thus Isaac Judaeus, a physician of the late ninth and early tenth centuries AD: "Comfort the sufferer by the promise of healing, even when you are not confident, for thus you may assist his natural powers." — in

T. W. Arnold and A. Guillaume (eds), *The legacy of Islam,* 325. In eighteenth-century London it was observed that the success of quack physicians "is rather founded on the faith of the patient, than any real merit in the doctor or his prescriptions"; *A narrative of the life of Mrs. Charlotte Charke* (1929 edn), 37.

48. T. Hobbes, *English works* (ed. W. Molesworth), VI, 399.

49. Hdt. VII 142ff.

50. Hdt. VII 144.

51. The few who preferred to stay, and to defend the Akropolis, could point to a different interpretation of the phrase 'wooden wall'; Hdt. VII 142, VIII 51 2.

52. Thuc. VI 57 1–3 (the sixth-century wall); I 89 3 — 91 4 (rapid rebuilding of a city wall after the Persians' withdrawal); Xen. *Hell.* III 2 10.

53. Great loss, however, was inevitable; most Athenians of the time had their homes in the country; Thuc. II 16 1.

54. Thuc. III 20 1f., 22 1. Compare Diod. XIV 54 5f. on the role of an "old oracle" early in the fourth century, when the city of Messana was faced with invasion.

55. Chronology, as has been noted (above, Chapter 1), is an unusually vulnerable aspect of memories: Herodotos' history depended mainly on old memories and oral tradition. In the present case, scholars have reasonably doubted whether Delphoi would have been so firmly pessimistic before the Persian forces had moved from Asia Minor, as Herodotos suggests. However, the oracle's reference to Salamis need not mean that the prophecy should be dated shortly before the battle. The Salamis strait could have been considered long in advance as a place for naval resistance. Did the Athenians ask at Delphoi both for general advice on resistance and for guidance about Salamis in particular? Compare the double request to the divinities of Dōdōnē made by Herakleidas (quoted above, p. 388).

56. Hdt. VII 173.

57. For the Greek text of, and an introductory bibliography concerning, this problematic document, Meiggs-Lewis, pp. 48–52.

58. Hdt. VIII 41.

59. Hdt. VIII 77, cf. VIII 53 1.

60. On the special case of chronology, above n. 55. A more general caution about wartime memories is advised by T. Harrisson, *Living through the Blitz,* ch. 12.

61. Herodotos also notes that divination encouraged some Athenians to make their disastrous attempt to defend the Akropolis; VIII 51.

62. On 431; see below, p. 394.

63. Thuc. I 112 5.

64. Ibid.

65. Ibid.

66. The case for Phokian control of the shrine had some historical support; Hom. *Iliad* II 517–19, Diod. XVI 23 5f.

67. See H. W. Parke, *CQ,* XXXVII (1943), 19–22, on the restrictions as to when the oracle could be consulted.

68. Plut. *Life of Perikles* 21.

69. Plut. *Moralia* 792f; *SIG³*, 829A and cf. C. P. Jones, *JRS*, LVI (1966), 66ff.

70. Thuc. I 113. See above, Chapter 4.

71. The text, with restorations, may most conveniently be found in *CQ*, XXXII (1938), 80–8. For other bibliography see Gomme, *HCT*, I, 339, with D. W. Bradeen, *Hesperia*, XXXIII (1964), 25ff.

72. Lines 7–8.

73. Plut. *Life of Perikles* 18.

74. Pausan. I 27 5.

75. Meiggs-Lewis no. 52.

76. Lines 64–7.

77. Thuc. I 114 3; above, p. 72.

78. Aristoph. *Peace* 1045ff.

79. Ibid., 1084.

80. Aristoph. *Clouds* 332 with scholion; Diod. XII 10 4; Plut. *Moralia* 812d; Photios' Lexicon, entry under *Thouriomanteis*.

81. Arist. *Pol.* 1303a.

82. See above, nn. 31–2, 80.

83. On the religious element in the pre-war quarrel between Athens and Megara, G.E.M. de Ste. Croix, *Origins* 254ff., 279ff.

84. Thuc. II 8 2.

85. Thuc. II 21 3.

86. Prejudice, of course, is commonplace in the reception of almost all political evidence; compare the way in which modern newspapers select and slant news to accord with the opinions of their readers.

87. In 413: see below.

88. Thuc. VIII 1 1 and below.

89. Thuc. V 26 3f.

90. Thuc. VII 50 4.

91. Cf. Plut. *Life of Nikias* 23 9.

92. Thuc. II 28, with Gomme, *HCT*, ad loc.

93. See Thuc. II 28 and Plut., op. cit., 23 2 with Powell, art. cit. (above, n. 18), 47f.

94. Thuc. II 8 3.

95. Thuc. I 118 3, 123 1f., II 54 4f.

96. Thuc. II 47 3 — 54 5, and above, Chapter 5.

97. Hom. *Iliad* I 43ff.; cf. Pausan. I 3 3.

98. Thuc. II 54 5.

99. Thuc. II 64 2.

100. Above, Chapter 5.

101. Lines 158–61, cf. 799ff.

102. Line 61.

103. Aristoph. *Knights* 45; cf. Thuc. V 16 1.

104. Aristoph. *Knights* 58–70; cf. Thuc. III 36 6, IV 21 3. Other points of correspondence between the Aristophanic and the historical Kleon: Kleon is a shouter (*Wasps* 596; cf. [Arist.] *Ath. Pol.* 28 3); the comic character Philokleon is a forceful champion of imperialism (*Wasps* 620; cf. Kleon himself at Thuc. III 37ff.), and violently anti-Spartan (*Wasps*·1159ff.; cf. Thuc. IV 22 2).

105. Lines 999–1095. Other sustained references to political divi-

nation; *Peace* 1043–126, *Birds* 959–91.
106. Thuc. IV 21 3.
107. Thuc. II 36 6.
108. Thuc. VII 50 4.
109. Plut. *Life of Nikias* IX 8.
110. Ibid., III.
111. *BCH*, X (1886), 465, lines 113f.
112. *BCH*, XXXIV (1910), 389ff.
113. Plut. *Life of Nikias* 3 5ff.; Thuc. III 104. Compare F. Courby, *Explorations archéologiques de Délos*, XII, 221–4, though his chronological reconstruction should be treated with caution.
114. Diod. XII 58 6; on the return of the plague, Thuc. III 87 1–3.
115. Thuc. V 1, 32 1.
116. Thuc. VIII 1 1. Translations of this passage, such as those of R. Crawley (Everyman edn) and R. Warner (Penguin edn), tend to mislead by making it unclear whether the diviners were successful in creating the hope. Thucydides with his word *epēlpisan* states that they were, as scholia on this passage make clear; cf. K. J. Dover, *Greek popular morality*, 135. Further on the translation of this crucial term, C. A. Powell, 'Religion and the Sicilian expedition', *Historia*, XXVIII (1979), 15f.
117. For later stories, Plut. *Life of Nikias* 13 2ff., 14 7; Pausan. VIII 11 12; Dio Chrysostom XVII 17 with Parke, *The oracles of Zeus*, 136f., Powell, art. cit., 17ff.
118. Thuc. VI 1.
119. Ibid. with Gomme-Andrewes-Dover, *HCT*, IV, 197. See, however, p. 184 above.
120. Thuc. VI 17 1.
121. In *HCT*, IV, 249.
122. Thuc. V 104. See also Lysias XXX 18ff. on *tykhē* arising from sacrifice.
123. Thuc. VII 77 2f.
124. Cf. Thuc. VI 8 4 — 24 1.
125. Thuc. VI 27 with *HCT*, ad loc., Aristoph. *Lysist.* 1093f. On the whole topic see now D. MacDowell, *Andokides on the Mysteries, passim*.
126. Thuc. VI 27 3.
127. Though cf. Thuc. VI 53 1.
128. Andokides I 43ff., 47.
129. Lysias XVIII 9f. with Andokides I 15 and MacDowell, ad loc.
130. Diognetos went into exile. On Eukrates, Andokides I 43ff.
131. Thuc. VI 61, cf. 53 1.
132. Thuc. VI 28 2, 29 3.
133. Thuc. VI 28 2. We know of four men who were eventually convicted of involvement in both acts of sacrilege: see Powell, art. cit., 25.
134. Above, p. 384 and Isokrates IV 28ff.
135. Xen. *Hell.* I 4 20; Plut. *Life of Alkibiades* 34.
136. Thuc. VII 47 2, 50 1ff.; cf. 60 2.
137. Thuc. VII 48 4.
138. Thuc. VII 47 1.
139. Thuc. VII 50 4. The syntax of the Greek, which refers to the

wishes of the Athenian majority in parallel with those of Nikias in a single sentence, suggests that both are designated as causes of the delay.

140. Thuc. VII 48 4.

141. Thuc. VII 75 7.

142. Thuc. VII 75: s.3 refers to the dead being left unburied — which was a breach of religious custom.

143. Various menacing things were euphemistically named, to avoid the need for clear mention of the undesirable; night was *euphronē* ('kindly time'), the Furies were *Eumenides* ('Gracious Ones'), the left (sinister) side was *euōnymos* ('with a good name'). A similar idea is still with us. If we mention that a friend has recently lost a lot of weight, and someone suggests "Perhaps (s)he's got cancer", the reaction 'Shh!' seems to be not merely an appeal for good taste but an attempt to prevent utterance of the hated word from causing the evil. Greeks of the classical period often responded to pessimistic speech by urging *euphēmei*: 'Don't use words of ill omen.' The origin of this process of thought may be a common confusion known to logicians as the fallacy of the undistributed middle: 'All *a*'s are *x*'s, therefore all *x*'s are *a*'s.' 'Times of disaster are times when regrettable things are mentioned, therefore times when regrettable things are mentioned are times of disaster.'

144. Thuc. VII 75 4.

145. Thuc. VII 18 2, cf. V 16 1 — 17 1 (Sparta); V 32 1 (Athens).

146. Thuc. VII 75 5, cf. 77 1.

147. Thuc. VII 77 1–4.

148. Thuc. VII 79 3, cf. Hdt. VII 10e.

149. Thuc. VII 60 2, 71 7, 75 5, 80 1, 83 4, cf. 84 4f.

150. Thuc. VII 75 5.

151. See especially Thuc. VII 63 2 with 53 2f. and K. J. Dover in *HCT*, IV, 442. On Syracusan numbers, Powell, art. cit. (above, n. 116), 29.

152. Thuc. V 103 2.

153. However, a valuable introduction to some aspects of prophecy is provided by R. C. T. Parker in P. A. Cartledge and F. D. Harvey (eds), *Crux: Essays presented to G. E. M. de Ste. Croix*, 298–326. See also P. E. Easterling and J. V. Muir (eds), *Greek religion and society*.

154. E. E. Evans-Pritchard, *Witchcraft, oracles and magic among the Azande*, 313.

155. H. D. Jocelyn, *Proceedings of the Cambridge Philological Society*, 17 (1971), 56 n. For near disbelief, H. R. Trevor-Roper, *The last days of Hitler*[3], 113: "We read with incredulity ... of the astrological assurances of Goebbels and Himmler." With which compare now *The Goebbels diaries: the last days* (ed. H. R. Trevor-Roper), entry under 29 March 1945.

156. C. R. Whittaker, *Harvard Theological Review*, 58 (1965), 21ff.; M. J. Field, *Search for security* 87ff. Compare (on Greece) H. W. Parke and D. E. W. Wormell, *The Delphic oracle*; Parke, *The oracles of Zeus*, *passim*. On inspired visions, Hypereides IV 14.

157. Field, op. cit., 87.

158. W. M. MacMillan, *Bantu, Boer and Briton*, 341. The chief source for this episode is the work of Charles Brownlee who, as Gaika

Commissioner, witnessed much of it; his *Reminiscences of Kaffir life and history* includes two official communications written while the events were in progress (op. cit., 138ff., 395ff.) See also *The Oxford History of South Africa* (ed. M. Wilson and L. Thompson), I, 256ff.

159. E. E. Evans-Pritchard, *Nuer Religion*, 308.

160. N. Cohn, *The pursuit of the millennium, passim.*

161. R. Taylor, *The political prophecy in England*; B. Capp, *Astrology and the popular press: English almanacs 1500–1800*; K. Thomas, *Religion and the decline of magic*. For references to Tudor laws against divination, H. Rusche, *English Historical Review*, 84 (1969), 753, n. 2.

162. Thomas, op. cit., 472.

163. Ibid., 321, cf. 298, 342f., 371ff.

164. On the Xhosa and people of the Gold Coast see above; on the Nuer, Evans-Pritchard, *Nuer religion* 308f.; on medieval Europe, Cohn, op. cit., Taylor, op. cit., 87; on post-Renaissance England, Thomas, op. cit.

165. *The Australian*, 19 January 1976.

166. *The Canberra Times*, 20 January 1976.

167. W. S. Schellenberg, *The Schellenberg memoirs* (trans. L. Hagen) 199, 386. An account of Himmler's last hours of freedom, spent with an astrologer within sound of advancing enemy guns, recalls Plutarch's description of Nikias' last days with his diviners outside Syracuse; W. T. Wulff, *Tierkreis und Hakenkreuz*, 225f., Plut. *Life of Nikias* 24 1. On the general subject of astrology in Weimar and Nazi Germany, E. Howe, *Urania's children*.

168. *The Standard* (London), 2 February 1982, quoting ABC News. James Watt, US Secretary of the Interior in the Reagan administration, informed a committee of Congress, "I do not know how many future generations we can count on before the Lord returns" (*Sunday Times*, London, 5 December 1982). On modern Japan we read, "The year 1966 saw a birth-rate nearly 30 per cent lower than 1965 or 1967. This remarkable event is widely attributed to the fact that 1966 was the year of 'fire and horse' in the Japanese zodiac, regarded as unfavourable for the birth of female children" (R. H. Cassen, *India*, 45).

169. Mass Observation, *Puzzled people*, 60.

170. Ibid., 55f. Compare the words of a modern wartime song: 'There ain't no atheists in a foxhole'.

171. Thuc. V 103 2. The generalisation gains important support from the implication of Thucydides' contemporary Antiphon, that trust in "signs from the gods" was particularly marked at times of public danger; Antiphon V 81.

172. R. Descartes, *Discourse on method* (trans. A. Wollaston), 40.

Index

Greek spelling has been followed wherever possible. Thus, for example,
Aigina not Aegina
Aiskhylos not Aeschylus
Boiotia not Boeotia
Euboia not Euboea
Kerkyra not Corcyra
Korinth not Corinth
Lysandros not Lysander
ostrakism not ostracism
Phokaia not Phocaea,
but Plutarch (not Ploutarkhos), Thucydides (not Thoukydides).

We have not normally included in the index those references in footnotes which can easily be found from the main text.

Index

Artemisia: 244
Asia Minor: 10, 13
Aspasia: 374 n.22
Asquith, H. H.: 212 n.471
assembly: see under 'Athens'
astrology: 405
Astyokhos: 212 n.452
Athena: 13, 59, 66–7
Athenian Empire: Ch. 3, *passim*
  costs, benefits and popularity of:
    75–86
  income to Athens from: 48, 149
  modern partisanship concerning:
    19, 76–8
  number and size of states in: 47
  and poor of Athens: 65, 69
  See also 'Delian League'
Athens: population of: 192, 266–8
  distribution of wealth at: 267–70
  control over Delian League and
    subsequent Empire: Chs 1–3,
    passim
  navy of: 10, 17, 25–6, 53, 108, 147,
    149–50, 186–7, 190–1, 194, 197
  strategy in Peloponnesian War:
    143–5, 149–51, 160–1
  contrasted with Sparta in Perikles'
    funeral speech: 154–7
  dēmokratia of: Ch. 7 *passim*
  hostility of ancient sources to
    dēmokratia of: 272–4
  history of constitution: 274–80
  rule of law at? : 307
  theory of the virtuous middle:
    268–9, 280
  assembly (*ekklēsia*) of: 167–70,
    271–2, 280–93
  council (*boulē*) of: 276–8, 287,
    292–6
  courts of: 275, 299–313
  lottery at: 277–8, 294–6
  payment for office–holders and
    assemblymen: 277, 280, 284–5,
    295, 300, 302
  generals of: 276, 297–8
  orators of: 287–8
  hostility of modern scholars to
    legal system of: 299–300
  alleged inconsistency of: 272–3,
    289–91
  voting at: 289–90
Ath(enaiōn) Pol(iteia) of ? Aristotle:
    270–1
Attikē, invasion of: 64–5, 72, 81,
    112, 114, 116, 118–20, 122–3,

136, 143, 145–7, 152, 157, 166,
    170, 388–92, 395, cf.173
Augustus: 242
Aulon: 248
Azande, of Nile–Congo divide: 402

Bacon, Francis: 385
Batman: 235
Black Sea: 1, 13, 76, 195; see also
    under 'grain'
Blitz, the: 154
Boges: 16
Boiotia: 44, 56 n.55, 68, 72, 106,
    112, 142, 145, 171, 173, 178,
    193
Bond, James: 235
Bosphorus: 195
Bottiaians: 120, 124
boulē: see under 'Athens'
Boutheia: 46
Brasidas: 81, 84, 86, 96, 102, 121,
    152, 164–5, 173, 177, 198, 216,
    232, 235, 258 n.195
  campaign of in n.e. Greece: 173–6
Brea: 69
bribery: 72, 101, 103, 112, 152, 282–
    3, 288, 294–5, 301, 303, 334
    n.374
Britain, Great: 7, 129 n.43, 146, 154–5,
    171, 212 n.471, 238, 240, 390
  army of: 132 n.120, 185, 333 n.363
  and divination: 159, 404–5
  legal system of: 299–300, 302, 305,
    331 n.292
Brownlee, Charles: 412 n.158
Byzantion: 1, 76, 120, 148, 194–5

Cambridge: 254 n.70
Capone, Al: 203 n.142
Carter, Jimmy: 212 n.471
Carthage: 185
Cato the Younger: 311
Catulus: 130 n.63
causation: 126–7
Chamberlain, Neville: 212 n.471
Chesterton, G. K.: 258 n.201
China: 214, 224
chronology, insecurity of: 12, 107,
    196
Churchill, Winston: 189
Cicero: 407 n.13
Cilicians: 26–7
Clarendon, Earl of: 159
Classical Studies, Institute of
    (London): 326 n.162

Index

Index

Index

and marriage: 345–50
and childbearing: 345, 351–3, 359
work (other than childbearing):
  361–4
dowries: 347–8, 351, 370–1
relations with the husband: 364–6,
  369–70 and Ch.8 *passim*
sexual activity: 345–6, 349, 365–6,
  378 n.144
and baby–smuggling: 354–7
divorce: 347, 349, 352–4, 370–1
restrictions on financial dealing:
  348–9, 363
defences and influence of: 370–3
pallor of: 343, 360–1

citizens of Sparta: see under
  'Sparta: women'
World War, First: 7

Xanthippos: 1
xenēlasia: 156, 214, 228
Xenophanes: 407 n.13
Xenophon: 196–7, 220–1, 230, 407
  n.5
Xerxes: 1, 10, 24, 36, 104
Xhosas, the: 403

Zakynthos: 148, 159
zeugitai: 277, 325 n.119
Zeus: 320, 388, 407 n.13